THE OFFICIAL
1987 PRICE GUIDE TO
FOOTBALL CARDS

BY
DR. JAMES BECKETT

SIXTH EDITION

THE HOUSE OF COLLECTIBLES
NEW YORK, NEW YORK 10022

© 1986 Dr. James Beckett
All rights reserved under International and Pan-American Copyright Conventions.

Published by: The House of Collectibles
201 East 50th Street
New York, New York 10022

Distributed by Ballantine Books, a division of Random House, Inc., New York and simultaneously in Canada by Random House of Canada Limited, Toronto.

Manufactured in the United States of America

Library of Congress Catalog Card Number: 81-86222

ISBN: 0-87637-520-4

10 9 8 7 6 5 4 3 2 1

TABLE OF CONTENTS

ABOUT THE AUTHOR

Jim Beckett, the leading authority on sport card values in the United States, maintains a wide range of activities in the world of sports. He possesses one of the finest collections of sports cards and autographs in the world, has made numerous appearances on radio and television, and has been cited frequently in many national publications. Dr. Beckett was the recipient of the first Special Achievement Award for Contribution to the Hobby from the National Sports Collectors Convention in 1980 and the Jock–Jasperson Award for Hobby Dedication in 1983. He is the author of *The Sport Americana Football, Hockey, Basketball and Boxing Price Guide*, *The Official Price Guide to Football Cards*, *The Sport Americana Baseball Card Price Guide*, *The Official Price Guide to Baseball Cards*, *The Sport Americana Baseball Memorabilia and Autograph Price Guide*, and *The Sport Americana Alphabetical Baseball Card Checklist*. In addition, he is the founder, author, and editor of *Beckett Baseball Card Monthly*, a magazine dedicated to the card-collecting hobby.

Jim Beckett received his Ph.D. in statistics from Southern Methodist University in 1975. He resides in Dallas with his wife Patti, and his daughters Christina and Rebecca, while actively pursuing his writing and consultancy services.

ACKNOWLEDGMENTS

This edition of the *Price Guide* contains new sets and, of course, completely revised prices on all of the cards. A great deal of hard work went into this volume, and it could not have been done without a considerable amount of help from many people. Our thanks are extended to each and every one of you.

First, we owe a special acknowledgment to Dennis W. Eckes, Mr. Sport Americana, who had the vision to see where the hobby was going and the perseverance and drive to help it get there. The success of the Beckett price guides has been the result of a team effort. Although Denny has chosen no longer to be a co-author on price guides—in order to devote more time to his business, Den's Collector's Den—he is still on board as a special consultant.

Those who have worked closely with us on this and many other books have again proved themselves invaluable in every aspect of producing this book: *Baseball Hobby News* (Frank and Vivian Barning), John Bradley (JOGO), Cartophilium (Andrew Pywowarczuk), Mike Cramer (Pacific Trading Cards), Bill and Diane Dodge, Gervise Ford, Larry Fritsch, Mike Gallella, Mike and Howie Gordon, Wayne Grove, Danny Hitt, Alan Kaye *(Baseball Card News)*, Lew Lipset, Pat Quinn (Sports Collectors Store), Dick Reuss, Gavin Riley, John Spalding, *Sports Collector's Digest* (Bob Lemke), and Murvin Sterling.

Special thanks are extended to the Topps Chewing Gum Company for providing checklists and visual materials in order that this price guide could be complete.

Many other individuals have provided price input, illustrative material, checklist verifications, errata, and/or background information. At the risk of inadvertently overlooking or omitting some of these many contributors, we should like to personally thank ADC Sports, Big Andy's, Bay State Cards (Lenny DeAngelico), Beulah Sports, Bill Bossert (Mid-Atlantic Coin Exchange), Richard Boyle, Larry Calder, Dwight Chapin, Chriss Christiansen, Ralph Ciarlo, Collection de Sport AZ, Bob Elliott, Doak Ewing, Andy Friedman of Sports Cards for Collectors, M. M. Gibson, Dick Goddard, Ron Gold, Jeff Goldstein, Grand Slam Sports Collectibles, Julie Grove, Dave Grutz, Clayton Gum, David Hadeler, Ernie Hammond, James Holloway, Andy Holms, Dan Jaskula, Dave and Rosie Jones, Stewart Jones, Dave Jurgensmeier, Jim Kelley, Jim Kiecker, Jim Knowler, Thomas Kunnecke, Dan Lavin, Howie Levy of Blue Chip, Jim Macie, Rick Malone, Paul Marchant, Mike McDonald (Sports Page), Mark McDowell, Joe Michalowicz, Dick Millerd, Dick

Mueller, Ray Murphy, Max Nanney, Don Nichols, Don Niemi, Ralph Nozaki, Mike O'Brien, Nick Papp, Clay Pasternack, Nancy Paterson, Country Peddler, Tom Pfirrmann, John J. Pluta, Bill Reed, Reflections (Thomas Hamm), Tom Reid, Owen Ricker, Dave Ring, Jim and Ev Roberts, Mark Rose, Alan Rosen (Mr. Mint), George Rusnak, Jennifer Salems, Don Schlaff, Gerry Shebib, Jim Shoop, Art Smith, Rose Steckling, Don Steinbach, Lowell Storer, Jack Stowe, Del Stracke, Strikeout Sports Cards, Richard Strobino, Ian Taylor, Lee Temanson, Jim Thayer, 20th Century Sports (Gordon Reid), Rich Unruh, John Vanden Beek, Wally's Coins, Bill Wesslund, Richard West, Bill Wester, Mike Wheat, Bob Wilke (The Shoe Box), World Series Cards, Kit Young, Bill Zimpleman.

Finally, writing this book would have been a very unpleasant experience without the understanding and cooperation of my wife, Patti, and daughters, Christina and Rebecca. I thank them and promise them that I will pay them back for all those hours. While we're on the subject of family, my sister, Claire Beckett, who is my full-time assistant on *Beckett Monthly*, put in extensive overtime, carrying the administrative load on the magazine singlehandedly during the time that I was working on this book; those of you who subscribe to the *Monthly* already know what a super job Claire is doing. Thank you, everyone.

ADDITIONAL ACKNOWLEDGMENTS

We have appreciated all of the help we have received over the years from collectors across the country and indeed throughout the world. Because we made active solicitations to individuals and groups for input to this year's edition, we are particularly appreciative of help provided for this volume. While we receive many inquiries, comments, and questions regarding material within this book—and, in fact, each and every one is read and digested—time constraints prevent us from replying to all but a few such letters. We hope that the letters will continue, and that even though no reply is received, you will feel that you are making significant contributions, with your interest and comments, to the hobby.

ERRATA

There are thousands of names, tens of thousands of prices, and untold other words in this book. There may be a few typographical errors, a few misspellings, and possibly a number or two out of order. If you catch a blooper, drop me a note directly or in care of the publisher, and we will fix it up in the next year's issue. Thanks.

INTRODUCTION

Isn't it great? Every year this book gets bigger and bigger with all the new sets coming out. But even more exciting is that every year there are more collectors, more shows, more stores, and more interest in the cards we love so much. This edition has been enhanced and expanded from the previous edition. The cards you collect—who they are, what they look like, where they are from, and (most important to many of you) what their current values are—are enumerated within. Many of the features contained in the other Beckett price guides have been incorporated into this volume since condition grading, nomenclature, and many other aspects of collecting are common to card collecting in general. We hope you find the book both interesting and useful in your collecting pursuits.

While football cards (and other sports cards) were once considered way behind baseball cards in the eyes of sports card collectors, the fantastic growth of the sports memorabilia collecting hobby over the past few years has given rise to an ever increasing number of collectors, who are giving these minor sports (from the standpoint of collecting) another look. The emergence of football cards, in particular, is due in large part to the continuing and increasing popularity of the sport itself. This increased popularity has made the stars and superstars of the sport well known to millions of fans, who have watched them during the fall and winter and read about them year round. Not only have the standout quarterbacks and running backs become household names, but the wide receivers, defensive linesmen, defensive backs, head coaches, and even the kickers are justifiably receiving a good share of media coverage. Finally, the comparatively high cost of premium baseball cards has turned many card collectors to football card collecting as a more affordable means of hobby pursuit. Nevertheless, as you can see from this price guide, football cards are valuable—and they are perceived by their collectors as being a good value for their hobby dollars.

The Beckett guide has been successful where other attempts have failed because it is complete, current, and valid. This price guide contains not just one but three prices, by condition, for all of the football cards in the issues listed, which account for almost all of the football cards in existence. The prices were added to the card lists just prior to printing and reflect not the author's opinions or desires but the going retail prices for each card, based on the marketplace (sports memorabilia conventions and shows, hobby papers, current mail order catalogs, local club meetings, auction results, and other firsthand reportings of actual realized prices.)

To facilitate your use of this book, read the complete introductory section in the pages following before going to the pricing pages. Every collectible field has its own terminology; we've tried to capture most of these terms and definitions in our glossary. Please read carefully the section on grading and the condition of your cards, as you will not be able to determine which price column is appropriate for a given card without first knowing its condition.

Welcome to the world of football cards.

Sincerely, Dr. James Beckett

HISTORY AND BACKGROUND

Unlike baseball cards, which have their roots firmly placed in the tobacco issues of the late 19th century, non-baseball cards are relative newcomers on the scene. The first bubble gum issue dedicated entirely to football players did not appear until the National Chicle issue of 1935. Before this, athletes from several sports were pictured in the multisport Goudey Sport Kings issue of 1933. In that set, football was represented by three legends whose fame has not diminished through the years: Red Grange, Knute Rockne, and Jim Thorpe. But it was not until 1948 and the postwar bubble gum boom that the next football issues appeared. Bowman and Leaf Gum companies both issued football card sets in 1948. From that point on, football cards have been issued annually by one company or another up to the present time, with Topps Gum Company being the major company producing cards.

Football cards depicting players from the Canadian Football League (CFL) did not appear until Parkhurst issued a 100-card set in 1952. Parkhurst issued another CFL set of 50 small cards in 1956. Topps began issuing CFL sets in 1958 and continued annually until 1965, although from 1961 to 1965 the cards were printed in Canada by O-Pee-Chee. Post Cereal issued two CFL sets in 1962 and 1963; these cards formed the backs of boxes of Post cereals distributed in Canada. The O-Pee-Chee Company, which has maintained a working relationship with the Topps Gum Company, issued four CFL sets in the years 1968, 1970, 1971, and 1972.

Returning to American football issues, Bowman resumed issuing football cards (now with full-color fronts) from 1950 to 1955 (Bowman did not produce football cards in 1949), changing the size of the card twice during that period and in each case increasing the size of the card. Bowman was unopposed during the early fifties as the producer of football cards featuring pro football players. Topps Gum

Company (of Brooklyn) purchased the Bowman Company (of Philadelphia) in January, 1956.

Topps issued its first football card set in 1950 with a group of very small felt-back cards. In 1951 Topps issued what is referred to as the Magic Football card set; this set of 75 has a scratch-off section on the back that answers a football quiz. Topps did not issue another football set until 1955, when its All-American Football set paid tribute to past college football greats. After Topps purchased Bowman, Topps issued sets of National Football League (NFL) players until 1963. The 1961 Topps football set also included American Football League (AFL) players in the high series (133–198). Topps sets from 1964 to 1967 contained AFL players only. From 1968 to the present, Topps has issued a major set of football cards each year.

When the AFL was founded in 1960, Fleer issued a 132-card set of AFL players. In 1961 Fleer issued a 220-card set (even larger than the Topps issue of that year) featuring players from both the NFL and AFL. Apparently for that one year Topps and Fleer tested a reciprocal arrangement, trading the card-printing rights to each other's contracted players. The 1962 Fleer issue featured only players from the AFL, as did their 1963 issue, both sets being relatively short at 88 cards. Post Cereal issued a 200-card set of American football players in 1962 that contains numerous scarcities, namely, those players appearing on unpopular varieties of Post cereals. From 1964 to 1967 the Philadelphia Gum Company issued four 198-card NFL player card sets.

The above has been a thumbnail sketch of football card collecting from its inception to the present. It is difficult to tell the whole story in just a few paragraphs; there are several other good sources of information. Serious collectors should subscribe to at least one of the excellent hobby magazines or papers. We also suggest that you try to attend a sports collectibles convention in your area if possible. Card collecting is still a young and informal hobby; the chances are good that you will run into one or more of the "experts" in the field, who are usually more than happy to share their knowledge with you.

HOW TO COLLECT

There are no set rules on how to collect cards. Card collecting is a hobby, a leisure pastime. What you collect, how much you collect, and how much time and money you spend collecting are entirely up to you; the funds you have available for collecting and your own personal taste should determine how you collect. The information and ideas presented here are intended to help you get the most enjoyment from this hobby.

It is impossible to collect every card ever produced. Therefore, beginners as well as intermediate and advanced collectors usually specialize their collecting in some way. One of the reasons this hobby is popular is that individual collectors can define and tailor their collecting methods to match their own tastes. To give you some idea of the various approaches to collecting, we will list some of the more popular areas of specialization.

Many collectors select complete sets from particular years. For example, they may concentrate on assembling complete sets from all of the years since their birth or since they became avid sports fans. They may try to collect a card for every player during that specified period of time.

Many collectors wish to acquire only certain players. Usually the players are the superstars of the sport, but occasionally a collector will specialize in all of the cards of players who attended a certain college or came from a certain town. Some collectors are interested only in the first card, or rookie card, of a certain player.

Another fun way to collect cards is by the team. Most fans have a favorite team, and it is natural for that loyalty to be translated into a desire for cards of the players on that favorite team. For most of the recent years, team sets (all of the cards from a given team for that year) are readily available at a reasonable price.

COLLECTING/INVESTING

Collecting individual players and collecting complete sets are both popular vehicles for investment and speculation. Most investors and speculators stock up on complete sets or on quantities of players they think have good investment potential. There is obviously no guarantee in this book, or anywhere else for that matter, that cards will outperform the stock market in the future. After all, there are no quarterly dividends with baseball or football cards. Nevertheless, investors have noticed a favorable trend in the past performance of baseball, football, and other sports collectibles, and certain cards and sets have outperformed just about any other investment in some years. Some of the obvious questions are which cards, when to buy, and when to sell. The best investment you can make is in your education. The more you know about your collection and the hobby, the better the decisions you will be able to make. We're not selling investment tips. We're selling information about the current value of football cards. It's up to you to use the information contained herein to your best advantage.

OBTAINING CARDS

Several avenues are open to card collectors. Cards can be purchased in the traditional way at the local candy, grocery, or drug store, with the bubble gum or other products included. It is also possible to purchase complete sets of football cards through mail order advertisers found in sports media publications such as *The Sporting News, Baseball Digest,* Street & Smith's Yearbooks, and others. Many collectors will begin by subscribing to at least one of the monthly hobby publications, all with good up-to-date information; in fact, subscription offers can be found in the advertising section of this book. Most serious card collectors obtain old (and new) cards from one or more of the following three sources: (1) trading or buying from other collectors or dealers, (2) responding to sale or auction ads in the monthly hobby papers, and/or (3) attending sports collectibles shows or conventions. We advise that you try all three methods as each has its own distinct advantages: (1) trading is a great way to make some new friends; (2) monthly hobby papers help you keep up with what's going on in the hobby (and tell you when and where the conventions are happening); and (3) shows provide enjoyment and the opportunity to see millions of collectibles under one roof, along with hundreds or even thousands of other collectors attending who all share a common interest.

DETERMINING VALUE

Why are some cards more valuable than others? Obviously, the economic law of supply and demand is applicable to card collecting just as it is to any other field where a commodity is bought, sold, or traded.

Supply—the number of cards available on the market—is less than the total number of cards produced because a certain percentage of the cards are typically thrown away, destroyed, or otherwise lost. This percentage is smaller today than it has been in the past since more and more people have become increasingly aware of the value of their cards. For those who collect only "mint" condition cards, the supply of older cards can be quite scarce indeed. Until recently, collectors were not conscious of the need to preserve the condition of their cards. For this reason, it is difficult to know exactly how many 1956 Topps are currently available, mint or otherwise. It is generally accepted that there are fewer 1956 Topps in circulation than 1966, 1976, or 1986 Topps cards. If demand were equal for each of these sets, the law of supply and demand would raise the price for the least available set. Demand, however, is not equal for all sets, and this complicates matters further.

The demand for a card is influenced by many factors, among them: (1) the age of the card; (2) the number of cards printed; (3) the player(s) portrayed on the card; (4) the attractiveness and popularity of the set; and perhaps most important, (5) the physical condition of the card.

In general, the older the card, the lower the quantity of the card printed, the more famous the player, the more attractive and popular the set, or the better the condition of the card—the higher the value of the card. There are exceptions to all but one of these factors: the condition of the card. Given two cards similar in all respects except condition, the one in the better condition will always be valued higher.

While there are certain guidelines that help to establish the value of a card, the exceptions and peculiarities make any simple mathematical formula to determine value impossible.

REGIONAL VARIATION

Although prices may vary from the East to the West, or from the Southwest to the Midwest, the prices in this guide are nonetheless presented as a consensus of all sections of this large and diverse country. Likewise, the prices for a particular player's cards may well show a higher price in his home team's area. Sometimes even common player cards command a higher price with hometown collectors than in other parts of the country.

Two types of price variations exist among the sections of the country where a card is bought or sold. The first is the general price variation on all cards bought and sold in one geographical area as compared to another. Card prices are slightly higher on the East and West coasts and slightly lower in the middle of the country. The second is the specific price variation for a player card found in a certain geographical area and not found in another. For example, a Roger Staubach card would be valued higher in Dallas than in Miami because Staubach played in Dallas; therefore, the demand for Roger Staubach cards is higher in Dallas than it is in Miami. On the other hand, a Bob Griese card would be priced higher in Miami than in Dallas for similar reasons.

SET PRICES

A somewhat paradoxical situation exists in the price of a complete set versus the combined cost of the individual cards in the set, especially prevalent in the cards of the past few years. In nearly every case, the sum of the prices for the individual cards is higher than the cost for the complete set. The reasons behind this apparent anomaly lie in the habits of collectors and in the carrying costs of dealers. Each card in a set is normally produced in the same quantity as all others in its set (scarcities and rare series notwithstanding). However, many collectors pick up only stars, superstars, and particular teams. As a result, the dealer is left with a shortage of certain player cards and an abundance of others; therefore, he incurs an expense in simply carrying these cards. On the other hand, if he sells a complete set, he gets rid of a large number of cards at one time. For this reason, he is often willing to receive less money for a complete set. By doing this, he recovers all of his costs and also receives some profit.

SCARCE SERIES

The term *scarce series* is derived from the fact that cards issued before 1973 were typically made available to the public in more than one series, each of a finite number of cards, rather than all cards of the set being available for purchase at one time. At some point during the year, usually near the end of the football season, interest in football cards of that year wanes; consequently, the manufacturers produce a smaller number of these later series of cards. Many of the national football card issues prior to 1973 can be recognized in series. For example, Bowman used 36 cards on its standard printed sheets. (While the number of cards on printed sheets is usually the same as the number of cards in a particular series, such is not always the case.) Topps series have been composed of many different numbers of cards, including 55, 66, 80, 88, and others. Recently Topps has settled on what is now their standard sheet size of 132 cards.

PRESERVING YOUR CARDS

Cards are fragile. They must be handled properly in order to retain their value. Careless handling can easily result in a creased or bent card. It is, however, not recommended that tweezers or tongs be used to pick up your cards as they might mar or indent the surface, which would reduce a mint card to excellent condition. In general, your cards should be directly handled as little as possible (easy to say but harder to do). A collection stored in plastic pages in a three-ring album allows you to view your collection at any time without the need to touch the card itself. Plastic sheets are the preferred method of storing cards, although there are still many who use custom boxes, storage trays, or even shoe boxes. For a large collection, some collectors may use a combination of the above methods. When purchasing plastic sheets for your cards, be sure that you find the pocket size that fits your cards snugly; don't put your 1951 Bowmans in a sheet designed to fit 1981 Topps. Most hobby and collectible shops and virtually all collectors' conventions will have these plastic pages available in quantity for the various sizes available.

Damp, sunny, and/or hot—this is not a weather forecast; these are three factors to avoid in extremes if you are interested in preserving your collection. Too much (or too little) humidity can cause gradual deterioration in the condition of a card. Direct, bright sun (or fluorescent light) over time will bleach out the color of a card. Extreme heat accelerates the decomposition of the paper the card is printed on. On the other hand, cards have lasted over the past 50 years without much scientific intervention. The above factors typically present a problem only when carried to an extreme—but it never hurts to be cautious.

SELLING YOUR CARDS

Just about every collector sells cards or will sell cards one day. You may be interested in selling your duplicates or maybe your whole collection. You may sell to other collectors, friends, or dealers. You may even sell cards you purchased from a certain dealer back to that same dealer. In any event, it helps to know some of the mechanics of the typical transaction between buyer and seller.

Dealers will buy cards in order to resell them to other collectors who might be interested in the cards. Dealers will always pay a higher percentage for items that (in the dealer's opinion) can be resold quickly, and a much lower percentage for those items that are perceived as having a low demand and are slow moving. In either case, dealers must buy at a price that allows for the expense of doing business and a fair margin of profit. Virtually all dealers are interested in older complete sets and superstar cards in excellent condition. If you have cards for sale, the best advice we can give is that you get three offers for your cards and take the best offer, all things considered. Note that the best offer may not be the one with the highest amount. And remember, if a dealer really wants your cards, he won't let you get away without making his best competitive offer. Another alternative is to take your cards to the next convention nearby and either auction them off in the show auction or offer them for sale to some of the dealers present.

Many people think nothing of going into a department store and paying $15 for an item of clothing for which the store paid $5. But if you were selling your $15 card to a dealer, and he offered you only $5 for it, you might think his markup unreasonable. To complete the analogy: most department stores (and card dealers) that pay $10 for $15 items eventually go out of business. An exception to this is when the dealer knows that a willing buyer for the merchandise you are attempting to sell is only a phone call away. Then an offer of two-thirds or maybe 70% of the book value will still allow the dealer a reasonable profit due to the short time he will need to hold the card. Nevertheless, most cards and collections will bring offers in the 25% to 50% range. Material from the past five to ten years or so is very plentiful. Don't be surprised if your best offer is only 20% of the book value for these recent years.

NOMENCLATURE

Each hobby has its own nomenclature to describe the collectibles of that particular hobby. The nomenclature traditionally used for trading cards is derived from the *American Card Catalog* (ACC), published in 1960 by Nostalgia Press. This catalog, written by Jefferson Burdick (who is called the Father of Card Collecting for his pioneering work), uses letter and number descriptions for each separate set of cards.

The letter used in the ACC number refers to the generic type of card. While both sport and non-sport issues are classified in the ACC, we shall confine ourselves in this description to the sport issues. The following list defines the letters and their meanings as used by the ACC.

(none) or N—19th Century U.S. Tobacco
B—Blankets
D—Bakery Inserts Including Bread
E—Early Candy and Gum
F—Food Inserts
H—Advertising
M—Periodicals
PC—Postcards
R—Candy and Gum Cards 1930 to Present
T—20th Century U.S. Tobacco
UO—Gas and Oil Inserts
V—Canadian Candy
W—Exhibits, Strip Cards, Team Issues

Following the letter designation and an optional hyphen are one-, two-, or three-digit numerical descriptors that typically represent the company or entity issuing the cards, i.e., numbers 1 to 999. In several cases, the ACC number is further extended by an additional hyphen and an additional one- or two-digit numerical descriptor. For example, the 1957 Topps regular-series football card issue carries an ACC designation of R415-5. The *R* indicates a candy or gum card produced after 1929. The *415* is the ACC designation for Topps Chewing Gum football card issues. And, the 5 is the ACC designation for the 1957 regular issue (Topps fifth football set).

Like other traditional methods of identification, this system provides order to the process of cataloging cards; however, most serious collectors learn the ACC designation of the popular sets by repetitive use and familiarity, rather than by attempting to figure out what they might or should be.

From 1948 forward, all sets are normally referred to by their year, maker, type of issue, or any other distinguishing characteristic. An example of such a characteristic could be an unusual issue or one of several regular issues put out by a specific maker in a single year. Regional issues are usually referred to by year, maker, and sometimes by title or theme of the set.

GLOSSARY/LEGEND

Our glossary defines common terms frequently used in the card-collecting hobby. Many of the terms are also common to other types of sports memorabilia collecting. There are exceptions to some of the definitions presented; however, listing all of the exceptions would confuse the reader and detract from the usefulness of the glossary.

ACC—American Card Catalog.

AD CARD—See Display Card.

AFC—American Football Conference.

AFL—American Football League.

ALL-STAR CARD—A card portraying an All-Star player of the previous year that says "All Star" on its face.

ALPH—Alphabetical.

AS—All-Star (card).

ATG—All Time Great card.

AUTOGRAPHED CARD—A card that has been signed (usually on the front of the card) by the player portrayed on the card, with a fountain pen, felt tip, Magic Marker, or ball-point pen. This term does not include stamped or facsimile autographed cards.

BLANKET—A felt square (normally 5 to 6 inches) portraying a baseball player.

BOX—Card issued on a box or a card depicting a boxer.

BRICK—A group of cards, usually 50 or more and having some common characteristics, that is intended to be bought, sold, or traded as a unit.

CABINETS—Very popular and highly valuable cards on thick card stock produced in the 19th and early 20th centuries.

CHECKLIST—A list of the cards contained in a particular set. The list is always in numerical order if the cards are numbered. Some unnumbered sets are artificially numbered in alphabetical order, or by team and alphabetical within the team, for convenience.

CHECKLIST CARD—A card that lists in order the cards and players in the set or series. Older checklist cards in mint condition that have not been checked off are very desirable.

CL—Checklist.

COA—Coach.

COIN—A small disc of metal or plastic portraying a player in its center.

COLLECTOR—A person who engages in the hobby of collecting cards primarily for his own enjoyment, with any profit motive being secondary.

COLLECTOR ISSUE—A set produced for the sake of the card itself, with no product or service sponsor. It derives its name from the fact that most such sets are produced by collector/dealers.

COMBINATION CARD—A single card depicting two or more players (but not a team card).

COMMON CARD—The typical card of any set; it has no premium value accruing from subject matter, numerical scarcity, popular demand, or anomaly.

COMP—Card issued by the Post Cereal Company through their mail-in offer.

CONVENTION—A large weekend gathering at one location of dealers and collectors for the purposes of buying, selling, and sometimes trading of sports memorabilia items. Conventions are open to the public and sometimes feature celebrities, door prizes, films, contests, etc.

CONVENTION ISSUE—A set produced in conjunction with a sports collectibles convention to commemorate or promote the show.

COR—Correct or corrected card.

COUPON—See Tab.

CREASE—A wrinkle on the card, usually caused by bending the card. Creases are a common defect in cards, usually caused by careless collectors.

DEALER—A person who engages in buying, selling, and trading sports collectibles or supplies. A dealer may also be a collector, but as a dealer he anticipates a profit.

DIE-CUT—A card of which the stock is partially cut, allowing one or more parts to be folded or removed. After removal or appropriate folding, the remaining part of the card can frequently be made to stand up.

DISC—A circular card.

DISPLAY CARD—A sheet, usually containing three to nine cards, that is printed and used by the manufacturer to advertise and/or display the packages containing his products and cards. The backs of display cards are blank or contain advertisements.

DP—Double print (a card that was printed in double the quantity compared to the other cards in the same series).

E CARD—A candy or gum card produced and issued prior to 1930.

ERR—Error card (see also COR).

ERROR CARD—A card with erroneous information, spelling, or depiction on either side of the card. Note that not all errors are corrected by the producing card company.

EXHIBIT—The generic name given to thick-stock, postcard-size cards with single-color obverse pictures. The name is derived from the Exhibit Supply Company of Chicago, the principal manufacturer of this type of card. These are also known as Arcade cards, as they were found in many arcades.

FULL SHEET—A complete sheet of cards that has not been cut up into individual cards by the manufacturer (also called an uncut sheet).

HALL OF FAMER (HOF'er)—A card that portrays a player who has been inducted into the Hall of Fame.

HIGH NUMBER—The cards in the last series of numbers in a year in which these higher-numbered cards were printed or distributed in significantly lesser amounts than the lower-numbered cards. The high-number designation refers to a scarcity of the high-numbered cards. Not all years have high numbers in terms of this definition.

HL—Highlight card.

HOC—House of Collectibles.

HOF—Hall of Fame.

HOR—Horizontal pose on card as opposed to the more standard vertical orientation found on most cards.

IA—In action (type of card).

INSERT—A card of a different type, e.g., a poster, or any other sports collectible contained and sold in the same package along with a card or cards of a major set.

ISSUE—Synonymous with set but usually used in conjunction with a manufacturer, e.g., a Topps issue.

KP—Kid Picture (a subseries issued in the Topps football set of 1973).

LAYERING—The separation or peeling of one or more layers of the card stock, usually at the corner of the card.

LEGITIMATE ISSUE—A set produced to promote or boost sales of a product or service, e.g., bubble gum, cereal, cigarettes, etc. Most collector issues are not legitimate issues in this sense.

LID—A circular card (possibly with tab) that forms the top of the container for the product being promoted.

MAJOR SET—A set produced by a national manufacturer of cards containing a large number of cards. Usually 100 or more different cards are in the set.

MGR—Manager.

MINI—A small card; specifically, a Topps baseball card of identical design but smaller dimensions than the regular Topps issue of 1975.

MISCUT—A card that has been cut particularly unevenly at the manufacturer's cutting stage.

ML—Major League.

MVP—Most Valuable Player.

N CARD—A tobacco card produced and issued during the 19th century.

NFC—National Football Conference.

NFL—National Football League.

NON-SPORT CARD—A card from a set whose major theme is a subject other than a sports subject. A card of a sports figure or event that is part of a non-sport set is still a non-sport card; e.g., while the Look 'N' See non-sport card set contains a card of Babe Ruth, a sports figure, the card is a non-sport card.

NOTCHING—The grooving of the edge of a card, usually caused by the fingernail, rubber bands, or bumping the edge against another object.

NY—New York.

OBVERSE—The front, face, or picture side of the card.

OPT—Option.

P1—First printing.

P2—Second printing.

P3—Third printing.

PANEL—An extended card that is composed of two or more individual cards. Often the panel forms the back part of the container for the product being promoted, e.g., a Hostess panel, a Bazooka panel, an Esskay Meat panel.

PG—Price guide.

PLASTIC SHEET—A clear vinyl plastic page punched for insertion into a binder with standard three-ring spacing and containing pockets for insertion of cards. Many different styles of sheets exist with pockets of varying sizes to hold the many different sizes of cards.

PREMIUM—A card, sometimes on photographic stock, that is purchased or obtained in conjunction with or redemption for another card or product. The premium is not packaged in the same unit as the primary item.

PUZZLE CARD—A card whose back contains a part of a picture that, when joined correctly with other puzzle cards, forms the complete picture.

PUZZLE PIECE—A die-cut piece designed to interlock with similar pieces.

R CARD—A candy or gum card produced and issued after 1930.

RARE—A card or series of cards of very limited availability. Unfortunately, *rare* is a subjective term sometimes used indiscriminately. Rare cards are harder to obtain than scarce cards.

RB—Record Breaker card.

REGIONAL—A card issued and distributed only in a limited area of the country. The producer is not a major, national producer of trading cards.

REPRINT—A reproduction of an original card, usually produced by a maker other than the original manufacturer from a source other than the original artwork or negative.

REVERSE—The back or narrative side of the card.

ROOKIE CARD—The first regular card of a particular player or a card that portrays one or more players with the notation on the card that these players are rookies.

SA—Super Action or Sport Americana.

SASE—Self-addressed, stamped envelope.

SCARCE—A card or series of cards of limited availability. This subjective term is sometimes used indiscriminately to promote or hype value. Scarce cards are not as difficult to obtain as rare cards.

SEMI-HIGH—A card from the next to last series of a sequentially issued set. It has more value than an average card and generally has less value than a high number. A card is not called a semi-high unless the next to last series in which it exists has an additional premium attached to it.

SERIES—The entire set of cards issued by a particular producer in a particular year, e.g., the 1971 Topps series. Also, within a particular set, *series* can refer to a group of consecutively numbered cards printed at the same time, e.g., the first series of the 1957 Topps issue (numbers 1 through 88).

SET—One each of the entire run of cards of the same type produced by a particular manufacturer during a single year. In other words, if you have a complete set of 1976 Topps football cards, then you have every card from number 1 through number 528, i.e., all of the different cards that were produced.

SF—San Francisco.

SKIP-NUMBERED—A set that has many card numbers not issued between the lowest number in the set and the highest number in the set; e.g., the 1949 Leaf football set contains 49 cards skip-numbered from 1 to 144. A major set in which a few numbers were not printed is not considered to be skip-numbered.

SP—Single or short print (a card that was printed in lesser quantity compared to the other cards in the same series; see also DP and TP).

SPECIAL CARD—A card that portrays something other than a single player or team, for example, a card that portrays the previous year's statistical leaders or the results from the previous year's postseason action.

STAMP—Adhesive-backed papers depicting a player. The stamp may be individual or in a sheet of many stamps. Moisture must be applied to the adhesive for the stamp to be attached to another surface.

STAR CARD—A card that portrays a player of some repute, usually determined by his ability but sometimes referring to sheer popularity.

STICKER—A card with a removable layer that can be adhered to (stuck onto) another surface.

STOCK—The cardboard or paper on which the card is printed.

STRIP CARDS—A sheet or strip of cards, particularly popular in the 1920s and 1930s, with the individual cards usually separated by a broken or dotted line.

SUPERSTAR CARD—A card that portrays a superstar, e.g., a Hall of Fame member or a certain future Hall of Fame member.

T CARD—A tobacco card produced and issued during the 20th century.

TAB—A part of a card set off from the rest of the card, usually with perforations, that may be removed without damaging the central character or event depicted by the card.

TBC—Turn Back the Clock cards.

TEAM CARD—A card that depicts an entire team.

TEST SET—A set, usually containing a small number of cards, issued by a national card producer and distributed in a limited section or sections of the country. Presumably, the purpose of a test set is to test market appeal for this particular type of card.

TL—Team Leader card.

TP—Triple print (a card that was printed in triple the quantity compared to the other cards in the same series).

TR—Trade or traded.

TRIMMED—A card cut down from its original size. Trimmed cards are undesirable to most collectors.

VARIATION—One of two or more cards from the same series with the same number (or player with identical pose if the series is unnumbered) differing from one another by some aspect, the different feature stemming from the printing or stock of the card, not from an alteration. This can be caused when the manufacturer of the cards notices an error in one (or more) of the cards, makes the changes, and then resumes the print run. In this case there will be two versions or variations of the same card. Sometimes one of the variations is relatively scarce.

VERT—Vertical pose on card.

W CARD—A card grouped within a general miscellaneous category by the ACC. Included in this category are exhibits, strip cards, team issues, and those issues that do not conveniently fall into other established categories.

ADDITIONAL READING

Other literature on the collecting hobby can be divided into two categories: books and periodicals. We have furnished a listing for both books and periodicals that we feel would further your knowledge and enjoyment.

BOOKS AVAILABLE

The Encyclopedia of Baseball Cards, Volume I: 19th Century Cards by Lew Lipset (published by author, 1983). Everything you ever wanted to know about 19th-century cards.

The Encyclopedia of Baseball Cards, Volume II: Early Gum and Candy Cards by Lew Lipset (published by author, 1984). Everything you ever wanted to know about early candy and gum cards.

Hockey Card Checklist and Price Guide by Cartophilium (Andrew Pywowarczuk) (published by author, 5th edition). The most complete list of hockey card checklists ever assembled, including a listing of Bee Hive photos.

The Official Price Guide to Baseball Cards by Dr. James Beckett (House of Collectibles, 6th edition, 1986; $4.95). An abridgment of the *Sport Americana Price Guide* (see below) in a convenient and economical pocket-size format, providing Dr. Beckett's pricing of the major baseball sets since 1948.

The Sport Americana Alphabetical Baseball Card Checklist by Dr. James Beckett and Dennis W. Eckes (co-published by Den's Collector's Den and Edgewater Book Company, 2nd edition). An illustrated, alphabetical listing, by the last name of the player portrayed on the card, of virtually all baseball cards produced up to 1983.

The Sport Americana Baseball Address List by Jack Smalling and Dennis W. Eckes (co-published by Den's Collector's Den and Edgewater Book Company, 3rd edition, 1984). The definitive guide for autograph hunters giving addresses and deceased information for virtually all major league baseball players past and present.

The Sport Americana Baseball Card Price Guide by Dr. James Beckett (Edgewater Book Company, 8th edition, 1986; $11.95). The most comprehensive price guide/checklist ever issued on baseball cards. No serious hobbyist should be without it.

The Sport Americana Baseball Card Team Checklist by Jeff Fritsch and Dennis W. Eckes (co-published by Den's Collector's Den and Edgewater Book Company). Includes all Topps, Bowman, Fleer, Play Ball, Goudey, and Donruss cards, with the players portrayed on the cards listed with the teams for whom they played. The book is invaluable to the collector who specializes in an individual team as it is the most complete baseball card team checklist available.

The Sport Americana Baseball Memorabilia and Autograph Price Guide by Dr. James Beckett and Dennis W. Eckes (co-published by Den's Collector's Den and Edgewater Book Company, 1st edition). The most definitive book ever produced on baseball memorabilia other than baseball cards. More than one year in preparation, this book attempts to present in an illustrated, logical fashion information on baseball memorabilia and autographs that heretofore had not been available to the collector.

The Sport Americana Football, Hockey, Basketball and Boxing Card Price Guide by Dr. James Beckett (Edgewater Book Company, 4th edition, 1985; $11.95). The most comprehensive price guide/checklist ever issued on football, hockey, basketball, boxing, golf, and wrestling cards. No serious hobbyist should be without it.

The Sport Americana Price Guide to the Non-Sports Cards by Christopher Benjamin and Dennis W. Eckes (co-published by Den's Collector's Den and Edgewater Book Company, 2nd edition, 1983). The definitive guide on all popular non-sports American tobacco and bubble gum cards. Illustrations and prices for wrappers are also included.

PERIODICALS AVAILABLE

There are several magazines and periodicals about the card-collecting hobby that are published monthly, bi-weekly, quarterly, etc. One (or more) of those listed below should be just right for you.

Baseball Card News (Krause Publications). Monthly tabloid format with good mix of editorials, features, and ads.

Baseball Cards (Krause Publications). Sharp-looking quarterly magazine with interior color and mix of features and ads.

Baseball Hobby News (Frank and Vivian Barning, publishers). Monthly tabloid newspaper format with good mix of news, editorials, features, and ads.

Beckett Baseball Card Monthly (Dr. James Beckett, author and editor). The most extensive and accepted monthly price guide, with feature articles, who's hot and who's not section, convention calendar, numerous letters to and from the editor. It is the hobby's fastest-growing magazine.

Sports Collectors Digest (Krause Publications). Bi-weekly tabloid issues loaded with ads.

GRADING YOUR CARDS

Each hobby has its own grading terminology—stamps, coins, comic books, beer cans, right down the line. The collectors of sports cards are no exception. The one absolute criterion for determining the value of a card is its condition: the better the condition of the card, the more valuable it is. However, condition grading is very subjective. Individual card dealers and collectors differ in the strictness of their grading. The stated condition of a card should be determined without regard to whether it is being bought or sold.

The physical defects that lower the condition of a card are usually quite apparent, but each individual places his own value (negative value in this case) on the defects. We present the condition guide for use in determining values listed in this price guide.

The defects listed in the condition guide below are those placed in the card at the time of printing (uneven borders, focus), those that occur to a card under normal handling (corner sharpness, gloss, edge wear), or those due to environmental conditions (browning). Other defects found on cards are inflicted by human carelessness and in all cases should be noted separately and in addition to the condition grade. Among the more common alterations are tape, tape stains, rubber band marks, water damage, smoke damage, trimming, paste, tears, writing, pin or tack holes, any back damage, and missing parts (tabs, tops, coupons, backgrounds).

Rather than confuse the issue further, let us present the Condition Guide used for values in this price guide.

CONDITION GUIDE

MINT (M or MT)—A card with no defects. The card has sharp corners, even borders, original gloss or shine on the surface, sharp focus of the picture, smooth edges, no signs of wear, and white borders. There is no allowance made for the age of the card.

EXCELLENT (EX or E)—A card with very minor defects. Any of the following qualities would be sufficient to lower the grade of a card from Mint to Excellent: very slight rounding or layering at some of the corners, a very small amount of the original gloss lost, minor wear on the edges, slight unevenness of the borders, slight wear visible only on close inspection, slight off-whiteness of the borders.

VERY GOOD (VG)—A card that has been handled but not abused. Some rounding at all corners, slight layering or scuffing at one or two corners, slight notching on edges, gloss lost from the surface but not scuffed, borders somewhat uneven but some white visible on all borders, noticeable yellowing or browning of borders, pictures slightly off focus.

GOOD (G)—A well-handled card, rounding and some layering at the corners, scuffing at the corners and minor scuffing on the face, borders noticeably uneven and browning, loss of gloss on the face, notching on the edges.

FAIR (F)—Round and layering corners, brown and dirty borders, frayed edges, noticeable scuffing on the face, white not visible on one or more borders, cloudy focus.

POOR (P)—An abused card, the lowest grade of card. Frequently some major physical alteration has been performed on the card; collectible only as a fill-in until a better-condition replacement can be obtained.

Categories between these major condition grades are frequently used, such as Very Good to Excellent (VG–E), Fair to Good (F–G), etc. The grades indicate a card with all qualities at least in the lower of the two categories, but with several qualities in the higher of the two categories.

The most common physical defect in a trading card is the crease, or wrinkle. The crease may vary from a slight crease barely noticeable at one corner of the card to a major crease across the entire card. Therefore, the degree that a crease lowers the value of the card depends on the type and number of creases. On giving the condition of a card, creases should be noted separately. If the crease is noticeable only on close inspection under bright light, an otherwise Mint card could be called Excellent; whereas noticeable but light creases would lower most otherwise Mint cards to the VG category. A heavily creased card could be classified Fair at best.

PRICES IN THIS PRICE GUIDE

Prices found in this guide reflect current retail rates just prior to the printing of this book. They do not reflect the for sale prices of the author, the publisher, the distributors, the advertisers, or any card dealers associated with this guide. No one is in any way obligated to buy, sell, or trade his or her cards based on these prices. The price listings were compiled by the author from actual buy/sell transactions at sports conventions, buy/sell advertisements in the hobby papers, for sale prices from dealer catalogs and price lists, and discussions with leading hobbyists in the United States and Canada. All prices are U.S. prices in U.S. dollars.

INTERESTING NOTES

The numerical first card of an issue is the single card most likely to obtain excessive wear; consequently, you will typically find the price on the number 1 card somewhat higher than its inherent status would seem to justify. Similarly, but to a lesser extent, the numerical last card in an issue is also prone to abnormal wear because the first and last cards are exposed to the elements (human element included) more than any other cards. They are generally end cards in any brick formations, rubber bandings, stackings on wet surfaces, and the like.

Sports cards have no intrinsic value. The value of a card, like the value of other collectibles, can be assessed only by you and by your enjoyment in viewing and possessing these cardboard swatches.

Remember, you the buyer ultimately determine the price of each football card. You are the determining price factor in that you have ability to say no to the price of any card by not exchanging your hard-earned money for a given card. When the cost of a trading card exceeds the enjoyment or utility you will receive from it, your answer should be no. We assess and report the prices. You set them!

We are always interested in receiving price input from collectors and dealers from around the country; we happily credit major contributions. We welcome your opinions; your contributions assist us in ensuring a better guide each year. If you would like to join our survey list for the next edition of this book, and others authored by Dr. Beckett, please send your name and address to Dr. James Beckett, 3410 Midcourt, Suite 110, Carrollton, Texas 75006.

ADVERTISING

Within this price guide you will find advertisements for sports memorabilia material and mail order and retail sports collectibles establishments. All advertisements were accepted in good faith based on the reputation of the advertiser; however, neither the author, the publisher, the distributors, nor the other advertisers in the price guide accept any responsibility for any particular advertiser's not complying with the terms of his or her ad.

Should you come into contact with any of the advertisers in this guide as a result of their advertisement herein, please mention to them this source as your contact.

1950 BOWMAN

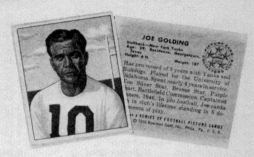

The 1950 Bowman set is Bowman's first color football set. The color quality on the cards is superior to previous Bowman sports' issues. The set is complete at 144 cards; the cards measure 2 1/16" by 2 1/2". The card backs feature black printing except for the player's name and the logo for the "5-Star Bowman Picture Card Collectors Club," which are in red.

			MINT	VG-E	F-G
	COMPLETE SET		525.00	240.00	50.00
	COMMON PLAYER (1-144)		2.75	1.25	.27
☐	1	Doak Walker, Detroit Lions	12.00	3.00	1.00
☐	2	John Greene, Detroit Lions	2.75	1.25	.27
☐	3	Bob Nowasky, Baltimore Colts	2.75	1.25	.27
☐	4	Jonathan Jenkins, Baltimore Colts	2.75	1.25	.27
☐	5	Y.A. Tittle, Baltimore Colts	20.00	9.00	2.00
☐	6	Lou Groza, Cleveland Browns	15.00	7.00	1.50
☐	7	Alex Agase, Cleveland Browns	3.25	1.50	.32
☐	8	Mac Speedie, Cleveland Browns	3.25	1.50	.32
☐	9	Tony Canadeo, Green Bay Packers	7.00	3.25	.70
☐	10	Larry Craig, Green Bay Packers	2.75	1.25	.27
☐	11	Ted Fritsch Sr., Green Bay Packers	2.75	1.25	.27
☐	12	Joe Goldring, New York Yanks	2.75	1.25	.27
☐	13	Martin Ruby, New York Yanks	2.75	1.25	.27
☐	14	George Taliaferro, New York Yanks	2.75	1.25	.27
☐	15	Tank Younger, Los Angeles Rams	5.00	2.35	.50
☐	16	Glenn Davis, Los Angeles Rams	12.00	5.50	1.20
☐	17	Bob Waterfield, Los Angeles Rams	12.00	5.50	1.20
☐	18	Val Jansante, Pittsburgh Steelers	2.75	1.25	.27

		MINT	VG-E	F-G
☐	19 Joe Geri, Pittsburgh Steelers	2.75	1.25	.27
☐	20 Jerry Nuzum, Pittsburgh Steelers	2.75	1.25	.27
☐	21 Elmer Angsman, Chicago Cardinals	2.75	1.25	.27
☐	22 Billy Dewell, Chicago Cardinals	2.75	1.25	.27
☐	23 Steve Van Buren, Philadelphia Eagles	10.00	4.75	1.00
☐	24 Cliff Patton, Philadelphia Eagles	2.75	1.25	.27
☐	25 Bosh Pritchard, Philadelphia Eagles	2.75	1.25	.27
☐	26 John Lujack, Chicago Bears	10.00	4.75	1.00
☐	27 Sid Luckman, Chicago Bears	14.00	6.50	1.40
☐	28 Bulldog Turner, Chicago Bears	9.00	4.25	.90
☐	29 Bill Dudley, Washington Redskins	7.00	3.25	.70
☐	30 Hugh Taylor, Washington Redskins	3.25	1.50	.32
☐	31 George Thomas, Washington Redskins	2.75	1.25	.27
☐	32 Ray Poole, New York Giants	2.75	1.25	.27
☐	33 Travis Tidwell, New York Giants	2.75	1.25	.27
☐	34 Gail Bruce, San Francisco 49ers	2.75	1.25	.27
☐	35 Joe Perry, San Francisco 49ers	14.00	6.50	1.40
☐	36 Frankie Albert, San Francisco 49ers	5.00	2.35	.50
☐	37 Bobby Layne, Detroit Lions	14.00	6.50	1.40
☐	38 Leon Hart, Detroit Lions	5.00	2.35	.50
☐	39 Bob Hoernschemeyer, Detroit Lions	2.75	1.25	.27
☐	40 Dick Barwegan, Baltimore Colts	2.75	1.25	.27
☐	41 Adrian Burk, Baltimore Colts	2.75	1.25	.27
☐	42 Barry French, Baltimore Colts	2.75	1.25	.27
☐	43 Marion Motley, Cleveland Browns	12.00	5.50	1.20
☐	44 Jim Martin, Cleveland Browns	2.75	1.25	.27
☐	45 Otto Graham, Cleveland Browns	25.00	11.00	2.50
☐	46 Al Baldwin, Green Bay Packers	2.75	1.25	.27
☐	47 Larry Coutre, Green Bay Packers	2.75	1.25	.27
☐	48 John Rauch, New York Yanks	2.75	1.25	.27
☐	49 Sam Tamburo, New York Yanks	2.75	1.25	.27
☐	50 Mike Swistowicz, New York Yanks	2.75	1.25	.27
☐	51 Tom Fears, Los Angeles Rams	10.00	4.75	1.00
☐	52 Elroy Hirsch, Los Angeles Rams	14.00	6.50	1.40
☐	53 Dick Huffman, Los Angeles Rams	2.75	1.25	.27
☐	54 Bob Gage, Pittsburgh Steelers	2.75	1.25	.27
☐	55 Bob Tinsley, Los Angeles Rams	2.75	1.25	.27
☐	56 Bill Blackburn, Chicago Cardinals	2.75	1.25	.27
☐	57 John Cochran, Chicago Cardinals	2.75	1.25	.27
☐	58 Bill Fischer, Chicago Cardinals	2.75	1.25	.27
☐	59 Whitey Wistert, Philadelphia Eagles	2.75	1.25	.27
☐	60 Clyde Scott, Philadelphia Eagles	2.75	1.25	.27
☐	61 Walter Barnes, Philadelphia Eagles	2.75	1.25	.27
☐	62 Bob Perina, Baltimore Colts	2.75	1.25	.27
☐	63 Bill Wightkin, Chicago Bears	2.75	1.25	.27
☐	64 Bob Goode, Washington Redskins	2.75	1.25	.27

		MINT	VG-E	F-G
☐ 65	Al Demao, Washington Redskins	2.75	1.25	.27
☐ 66	Harry Gilmer, Washington Redskins	3.25	1.50	.32
☐ 67	Bill Austin, New York Giants	2.75	1.25	.27
☐ 68	Joe Scott, New York Giants	2.75	1.25	.27
☐ 69	Tex Coulter, New York Giants	2.75	1.25	.27
☐ 70	Paul Salata, San Francisco 49ers	2.75	1.25	.27
☐ 71	Emil Sitko, San Francisco 49ers	2.75	1.25	.27
☐ 72	Bill Johnson, San Francisco 49ers	2.75	1.25	.27
☐ 73	Don Doll, Detroit Lions	2.75	1.25	.27
☐ 74	Dan Sandifer, Detroit Lions	2.75	1.25	.27
☐ 75	John Panelli, Detroit Lions	2.75	1.25	.27
☐ 76	Bill Leonard, Baltimore Colts	2.75	1.25	.27
☐ 77	Bob Kelly, Baltimore Colts	2.75	1.25	.27
☐ 78	Dante Lavelli, Cleveland Browns	8.00	3.75	.80
☐ 79	Tony Adamle, Cleveland Browns	3.25	1.50	.32
☐ 80	Dick Wildung, Green Bay Packers	2.75	1.25	.27
☐ 81	Tobin Rote, Green Bay Packers	4.00	1.85	.40
☐ 82	Paul Burris, Green Bay Packers	2.75	1.25	.27
☐ 83	Lowell Tew, New York Yanks	2.75	1.25	.27
☐ 84	Barney Poole, New York Yanks	2.75	1.25	.27
☐ 85	Fred Naumetz, Los Angeles Rams	2.75	1.25	.27
☐ 86	Dick Hoerner, Los Angeles Rams	2.75	1.25	.27
☐ 87	Bob Reinhard, Los Angeles Rams	2.75	1.25	.27
☐ 88	Howard Hartley, Pittsburgh Steelers	2.75	1.25	.27
☐ 89	Darrell Hogan, Pittsburgh Steelers	2.75	1.25	.27
☐ 90	Jerry Shipkey, Pittsburgh Steelers	2.75	1.25	.27
☐ 91	Frank Tripucka, Chicago Cardinals	3.25	1.50	.32
☐ 92	Garrard Ramsey, Chicago Cardinals	2.75	1.25	.27
☐ 93	Pat Harder, Chicago Cardinals	3.25	1.50	.32
☐ 94	Vic Sears, Philadelphia Eagles	2.75	1.25	.27
☐ 95	Tommy Thompson, Philadelphia Eagles	3.25	1.50	.32
☐ 96	Bucko Kilroy, Philadelphia Eagles	3.25	1.50	.32
☐ 97	George Connor, Chicago Bears	5.00	2.35	.50
☐ 98	Fred Morrison, Chicago Bears	2.75	1.25	.27
☐ 99	Jim Keane, Chicago Bears	2.75	1.25	.27
☐ 100	Sammy Baugh, Washington Redskins	22.00	10.00	2.20
☐ 101	Harry Ulinski, Washington Redskins	2.75	1.25	.27
☐ 102	Frank Spaniel, Baltimore Colts	2.75	1.25	.27
☐ 103	Charley Conerly, New York Giants	8.00	3.75	.80
☐ 104	Dick Hensley, New York Giants	2.75	1.25	.27
☐ 105	Eddie Price, New York Giants	3.25	1.50	.32
☐ 106	Ed Carr, San Francisco 49ers	2.75	1.25	.27
☐ 107	Leo Nomellini, San Francisco 49ers	7.00	3.25	.70
☐ 108	Verl Lillywhite, San Francisco 49ers	2.75	1.25	.27
☐ 109	Wallace Triplett, Detroit Lions	2.75	1.25	.27
☐ 110	Joe Watson, Detroit Lions	2.75	1.25	.27

		MINT	VG-E	F-G
☐ 111	**Cloyce Box,** Detroit Lions	2.75	1.25	.27
☐ 112	**Billy Stone,** Baltimore Colts	2.75	1.25	.27
☐ 113	**Earl Murray,** Baltimore Colts	2.75	1.25	.27
☐ 114	**Chet Mutryn,** Baltimore Colts	2.75	1.25	.27
☐ 115	**Ken Carpenter,** Cleveland Browns	2.75	1.25	.27
☐ 116	**Lou Rymkus,** Cleveland Browns	2.75	1.25	.27
☐ 117	**Dub Jones,** Cleveland Browns	4.00	1.85	.40
☐ 118	**Clayton Tonnemaker,** Green Bay Packers	2.75	1.25	.27
☐ 119	**Walt Schlinkman,** Green Bay Packers	2.75	1.25	.27
☐ 120	**Billy Grimes,** Green Bay Packers	2.75	1.25	.27
☐ 121	**George Ratterman,** New York Yanks	4.00	1.85	.40
☐ 122	**Bob Mann,** New York Yanks	2.75	1.25	.27
☐ 123	**Buddy Young,** New York Yanks	5.00	2.35	.50
☐ 124	**Jack Zilly,** Los Angeles Rams	2.75	1.25	.27
☐ 125	**Tom Kalmanir,** Los Angeles Rams	2.75	1.25	.27
☐ 126	**Frank Sinkovitz,** Pittsburgh Steelers	2.75	1.25	.27
☐ 127	**Elbert Nickel,** Pittsburgh Steelers	2.75	1.25	.27
☐ 128	**Jim Finks,** Pittsburgh Steelers	4.00	1.85	.40
☐ 129	**Charlie Trippi,** Chicago Cardinals	7.00	3.25	.70
☐ 130	**Tom Wham,** Chicago Cardinals	2.75	1.25	.27
☐ 131	**Ventan Yablonski,** Chicago Cardinals	2.75	1.25	.27
☐ 132	**Chuck Bednarik,** Philadelphia Eagles	11.00	5.25	1.10
☐ 133	**Joe Muha,** Philadelphia Eagles	2.75	1.25	.27
☐ 134	**Pete Pihos,** Philadelphia Eagles	7.00	3.25	.70
☐ 135	**Washington Serini,** Chicago Bears	2.75	1.25	.27
☐ 136	**George Gulyanics,** Chicago Bears	2.75	1.25	.27
☐ 137	**Ken Kavanaugh,** Chicago Bears	5.00	2.35	.50
☐ 138	**Howie Livingston,** Washington Redskins	2.75	1.25	.27
☐ 139	**Joe Tereshinski,** Washington Redskins	2.75	1.25	.27
☐ 140	**Jim White,** New York Giants	2.75	1.25	.27
☐ 141	**Gene Roberts,** New York Giants	2.75	1.25	.27
☐ 142	**William Swiacki,** New York Giants	2.75	1.25	.27
☐ 143	**Norm Standlee,** San Francisco 49ers	2.75	1.25	.27
☐ 144	**Knox Ramsey,** Chicago Cardinals	4.50	1.50	.30

1951 BOWMAN

The 1951 Bowman set of 144 witnessed an increase in card size from previous Bowman football sets. The cards were enlarged from the previous year to 2⅟₁₆" by 3⅛". The 144-card set is very similar in format to the baseball card set of that year. The card backs are printed in maroon and blue on gray card stock.

			MINT	VG-E	F-G
	COMPLETE SET		550.00	250.00	55.00
	COMMON PLAYER (1-144)		2.75	1.25	.27
☐	1	Weldon Humble, Cleveland Browns	5.00	1.50	.30
☐	2	Otto Graham, Cleveland Browns	20.00	9.00	2.00
☐	3	Mac Speedie, Cleveland Browns	3.25	1.50	.32
☐	4	Norm Van Brocklin, Los Angeles Rams	16.00	7.50	1.60
☐	5	Woodley Lewis, Los Angeles Rams	2.75	1.25	.27
☐	6	Tom Fears, Los Angeles Rams	9.00	4.25	.90
☐	7	George Musacco, New York Yanks	2.75	1.25	.27
☐	8	George Taliaferro, New York Yanks	2.75	1.25	.27
☐	9	Barney Poole, New York Yanks	2.75	1.25	.27
☐	10	Steve Van Buren, Philadelphia Eagles	9.00	4.25	.90
☐	11	Whitey Wistert, Philadelphia Eagles	2.75	1.25	.27
☐	12	Chuck Bednarik, Philadelphia Eagles	11.00	5.25	1.10
☐	13	Bulldog Turner, Chicago Bears	9.00	4.25	.90
☐	14	Bob Williams, Chicago Bears	2.75	1.25	.27
☐	15	John Lujack, Chicago Bears	9.00	4.25	.90
☐	16	Roy Rebel Steiner, Green Bay Packers	2.75	1.25	.27
☐	17	Earl Jug Girard, Green Bay Packers	2.75	1.25	.27
☐	18	Bill Neal, Green Bay Packers	2.75	1.25	.27
☐	19	Travis Tidwell, New York Giants	2.75	1.25	.27

		MINT	VG-E	F-G
☐ 20	**Tom Landry**, New York Giants	40.00	18.00	4.00
☐ 21	**Arnie Weinmeister**, New York Giants	6.00	2.80	.60
☐ 22	**Joe Geri**, Pittsburgh Steelers	2.75	1.25	.27
☐ 23	**Bill Walsh**, Pittsburgh Steelers	4.00	1.85	.40
☐ 24	**Fran Rogel**, Pittsburgh Steelers	2.75	1.25	.27
☐ 25	**Doak Walker**, Detroit Lions	10.00	4.75	1.00
☐ 26	**Leon Hart**, Detroit Lions	4.50	2.10	.45
☐ 27	**Thurman McGraw**, Detroit Lions	2.75	1.25	.27
☐ 28	**Buster Ramsey**, Chicago Cardinals	2.75	1.25	.27
☐ 29	**Frank Tripucka**, Chicago Cardinals	3.25	1.50	.32
☐ 30	**Don Paul**, Chicago Cardinals	2.75	1.25	.27
☐ 31	**Alex Loyd**, San Francisco 49ers	2.75	1.25	.27
☐ 32	**Y.A. Tittle**, San Francisco 49ers	14.00	6.50	1.40
☐ 33	**Verl Lillywhite**, San Francisco 49ers	2.75	1.25	.27
☐ 34	**Sammy Baugh**, Washington Redskins	22.00	10.00	2.20
☐ 35	**Chuck Drazenovich**, Washington Redskins	2.75	1.25	.27
☐ 36	**Bob Goode**, Washington Redskins	2.75	1.25	.27
☐ 37	**Horace Gillom**, Cleveland Browns	2.75	1.25	.27
☐ 38	**Lou Rymkus**, Cleveland Browns	2.75	1.25	.27
☐ 39	**Ken Carpenter**, Cleveland Browns	2.75	1.25	.27
☐ 40	**Bob Waterfield**, Los Angeles Rams	11.00	5.25	1.10
☐ 41	**Vitamin Smith**, Los Angeles Rams	2.75	1.25	.27
☐ 42	**Glenn Davis**, Los Angeles Rams	6.50	3.00	.65
☐ 43	**Dan Edwards**, New York Yanks	2.75	1.25	.27
☐ 44	**John Rauch**, New York Yanks	2.75	1.25	.27
☐ 45	**Zollie Toth**, New York Yanks	2.75	1.25	.27
☐ 46	**Pete Pihos**, Philadelphia Eagles	6.50	3.00	.65
☐ 47	**Russ Craft**, Philadelphia Eagles	2.75	1.25	.27
☐ 48	**Walter Barnes**, Philadelphia Eagles	2.75	1.25	.27
☐ 49	**Fred Morrison**, Chicago Bears	2.75	1.25	.27
☐ 50	**Ray Bray**, Chicago Bears	2.75	1.25	.27
☐ 51	**Ed Sprinkle**, Chicago Bears	2.75	1.25	.27
☐ 52	**Floyd Reid**, Green Bay Packers	2.75	1.25	.27
☐ 53	**Billy Grimes**, Green Bay Packers	2.75	1.25	.27
☐ 54	**Ted Fritsch Sr.**, Green Bay Packers	2.75	1.25	.27
☐ 55	**Al DeRogatis**, New York Giants	3.25	1.50	.32
☐ 56	**Charley Conerly**, New York Giants	7.50	3.50	.75
☐ 57	**Jon Baker**, New York Giants	2.75	1.25	.27
☐ 58	**Tom McWilliams**, Pittsburgh Steelers	2.75	1.25	.27
☐ 59	**Jerry Shipkey**, Pittsburgh Steelers	2.75	1.25	.27
☐ 60	**Lynn Chandnois**, Pittsburgh Steelers	2.75	1.25	.27
☐ 61	**Don Doll**, Detroit Lions	2.75	1.25	.27
☐ 62	**Lou Creekmur**, Detroit Lions	2.75	1.25	.27
☐ 63	**Bob Hoernschemeyer**, Detroit Lions	2.75	1.25	.27
☐ 64	**Tom Wham**, Chicago Cardinals	2.75	1.25	.27
☐ 65	**Bill Fischer**, Chicago Cardinals	2.75	1.25	.27

		MINT	VG-E	F-G
☐ 66	Robert Nussbaumer, Green Bay Packers	2.75	1.25	.27
☐ 67	Gordon Soltau, San Francisco 49ers	2.75	1.25	.27
☐ 68	Visco Grgich, San Francisco 49ers	2.75	1.25	.27
☐ 69	John Strzykalski, San Francisco 49ers	2.75	1.25	.27
☐ 70	Pete Stout, Washington Redskins	2.75	1.25	.27
☐ 71	Paul Lipscomb, Washington Redskins	2.75	1.25	.27
☐ 72	Harry Gilmer, Washington Redskins	3.25	1.50	.32
☐ 73	Dante Lavelli, Cleveland Browns	7.00	3.25	.70
☐ 74	Dub Jones, Cleveland Browns	4.00	1.85	.40
☐ 75	Lou Groza, Cleveland Browns	11.00	5.25	1.10
☐ 76	Elroy Hirsch, Los Angeles Rams	9.00	4.25	.90
☐ 77	Tom Kalmanir, Los Angeles Rams	2.75	1.25	.27
☐ 78	Jack Zilly, Los Angeles Rams	2.75	1.25	.27
☐ 79	Bruce Alford, New York Yanks	2.75	1.25	.27
☐ 80	Art Weiner, New York Yanks	2.75	1.25	.27
☐ 81	Brad Ecklund, New York Yanks	2.75	1.25	.27
☐ 82	Bosh Pritchard, Philadelphia Eagles	2.75	1.25	.27
☐ 83	John Green, Philadelphia Eagles	2.75	1.25	.27
☐ 84	H. Ebert Van Buren, Philadelphia Eagles	2.75	1.25	.27
☐ 85	Julie Rykovich, Chicago Bears	2.75	1.25	.27
☐ 86	Fred Davis, Chicago Bears	2.75	1.25	.27
☐ 87	John Hoffman, Chicago Bears	2.75	1.25	.27
☐ 88	Tobin Rote, Green Bay Packers	3.25	1.50	.32
☐ 89	Paul Burris, Green Bay Packers	2.75	1.25	.27
☐ 90	Tony Canadeo, Green Bay Packers	6.00	2.80	.60
☐ 91	Emlen Tunnell, New York Giants	10.00	4.75	1.00
☐ 92	Otto Schnellbacher, New York Giants	2.75	1.25	.27
☐ 93	Ray Poole, New York Giants	2.75	1.25	.27
☐ 94	Darrell Hogan, Pittsburgh Steelers	2.75	1.25	.27
☐ 95	Frank Sinkovitz, Pittsburgh Steelers	2.75	1.25	.27
☐ 96	Ernie Stautner, Pittsburgh Steelers	10.00	4.75	1.00
☐ 97	Elmer Angsman, Chicago Cardinals	2.75	1.25	.27
☐ 98	Jack Jennings, Chicago Cardinals	2.75	1.25	.27
☐ 99	Jerry Groom, Chicago Cardinals	2.75	1.25	.27
☐ 100	John Prchlik, Detroit Lions	2.75	1.25	.27
☐ 101	J. Robert Smith, Detroit Lions	2.75	1.25	.27
☐ 102	Bobby Layne, Detroit Lions	14.00	6.50	1.40
☐ 103	Frankie Albert, San Francisco 49ers	4.00	1.85	.40
☐ 104	Gail Bruce, San Francisco 49ers	2.75	1.25	.27
☐ 105	Joe Perry, San Francisco 49ers	9.00	4.25	.90
☐ 106	Leon Heath, Washington Redskins	2.75	1.25	.27
☐ 107	Ed Quirk, Washington Redskins	2.75	1.25	.27
☐ 108	Hugh Taylor, Washington Redskins	3.25	1.50	.32
☐ 109	Marion Motley, Cleveland Browns	7.00	3.25	.70
☐ 110	Tony Adamle, Cleveland Browns	3.25	1.50	.32
☐ 111	Alex Agase, Cleveland Browns	3.25	1.50	.32

		MINT	VG-E	F-G
☐ 112	Tank Younger, Los Angeles Rams	4.00	1.85	.40
☐ 113	Bob Boyd, Los Angeles Rams	2.75	1.25	.27
☐ 114	Jerry Williams, Los Angeles Rams	2.75	1.25	.27
☐ 115	Joe Goldring, New York Yanks	2.75	1.25	.27
☐ 116	Sherman Howard, New York Yanks	2.75	1.25	.27
☐ 117	John Wozniak, New York Yanks	2.75	1.25	.27
☐ 118	Frank Reagan, Philadelphia Eagles	2.75	1.25	.27
☐ 119	Vic Sears, Philadelphia Eagles	2.75	1.25	.27
☐ 120	Clyde Scott, Philadelphia Eagles	2.75	1.25	.27
☐ 121	George Gulyanics, Chicago Bears	2.75	1.25	.27
☐ 122	Bill Wightkin, Chicago Bears	2.75	1.25	.27
☐ 123	Chuck Hunsinger, Chicago Bears	2.75	1.25	.27
☐ 124	Jack Cloud, Green Bay Packers	2.75	1.25	.27
☐ 125	Abner Wimberly, Green Bay Packers	2.75	1.25	.27
☐ 126	Dick Wildung, Green Bay Packers	2.75	1.25	.27
☐ 127	Eddie Price, New York Giants	3.25	1.50	.32
☐ 128	Joe Scott, New York Giants	2.75	1.25	.27
☐ 129	Jerry Nuzum, Pittsburgh Steelers	2.75	1.25	.27
☐ 130	Jim Finks, Pittsburgh Steelers	4.00	1.85	.40
☐ 131	Bob Gage, Pittsburgh Steelers	2.75	1.25	.27
☐ 132	William Swiacki, Detroit Lions	2.75	1.25	.27
☐ 133	Joe Watson, Detroit Lions	2.75	1.25	.27
☐ 134	Ollie Cline, Detroit Lions	2.75	1.25	.27
☐ 135	Jack Lininger, Detroit Lions	2.75	1.25	.27
☐ 136	Fran Polsfoot, Chicago Cardinals	2.75	1.25	.27
☐ 137	Charlie Trippi, Chicago Cardinals	7.00	3.25	.70
☐ 138	Ventan Yablonski, Chicago Cardinals	2.75	1.25	.27
☐ 139	Emil Sitko, Chicago Cardinals	2.75	1.25	.27
☐ 140	Leo Nomellini, San Francisco 49ers	7.00	3.25	.70
☐ 141	Norm Standlee, San Francisco 49ers	2.75	1.25	.27
☐ 142	Eddie Saenz, Washington Redskins	2.75	1.25	.27
☐ 143	Al Demao, Washington Redskins	2.75	1.25	.27
☐ 144	Bill Dudley, Washington Redskins	8.00	2.50	.50

1952 BOWMAN SMALL

The 1952 Bowman set contains 144 cards, each of both a small and large size. The small cards measure 2¹/₁₆" by 3¹/₈", whereas the large cards measure 2½" by 3¾". The fronts and backs of both sets are identical except for size. The checklist below lists prices for the "small" set.

	MINT	VG-E	F-G
COMPLETE SET	700.00	320.00	70.00
COMMON PLAYER (1-72)	3.00	1.40	.30
COMMON PLAYER (73-144)	4.50	2.10	.45

		MINT	VG-E	F-G
☐	1 **Norm Van Brocklin**, Los Angeles Rams	20.00	7.00	1.50
☐	2 **Otto Graham**, Cleveland Browns	20.00	9.00	2.00
☐	3 **Doak Walker**, Detroit Lions	10.00	4.75	1.00
☐	4 **Steve Owen**, New York Giants	7.50	3.50	.75
☐	5 **Frankie Albert**, San Francisco 49ers	5.00	2.35	.50
☐	6 **Laurie Niemi**, Washington Redskins	3.00	1.40	.30
☐	7 **Chuck Hunsinger**, Chicago Bears	3.00	1.40	.30
☐	8 **Ed Modzelewski**, Pittsburgh Steelers	3.50	1.65	.35
☐	9 **Joe Spencer**, Green Bay Packers	3.00	1.40	.30
☐	10 **Chuck Bednarik**, Philadelphia Eagles	10.00	4.75	1.00
☐	11 **Barney Poole**, Dallas Texans	3.00	1.40	.30
☐	12 **Charlie Trippi**, Chicago Cardinals	7.50	3.50	.75
☐	13 **Tom Fears**, Los Angeles Rams	7.50	3.50	.75
☐	14 **Paul Brown**, Cleveland Browns	10.00	4.75	1.00
☐	15 **Leon Hart**, Detroit Lions	4.50	2.10	.45
☐	16 **Frank Gifford**, New York Giants	40.00	18.00	4.00
☐	17 **Y.A. Tittle**, San Francisco 49ers	12.00	5.50	1.20
☐	18 **Charlie Justice**, Washington Redskins	6.00	2.80	.60

			MINT	VG-E	F-G
☐	19	**George Connor**, Chicago Bears	6.00	2.80	.60
☐	20	**Lynn Chandnois**, Pittsburgh Steelers	3.00	1.40	.30
☐	21	**Bill Howton**, Green Bay Packers	3.50	1.65	.35
☐	22	**Kenneth Snyder**, Philadelphia Eagles	3.00	1.40	.30
☐	23	**Gino Marchetti**, Dallas Texans	10.00	4.75	1.00
☐	24	**John Karras**, Chicago Cardinals	3.00	1.40	.30
☐	25	**Tank Younger**, Los Angeles Rams	4.00	1.85	.40
☐	26	**Tommy Thompson**, Cleveland Browns	3.50	1.65	.35
☐	27	**Bob Miller**, Detroit Lions	3.00	1.40	.30
☐	28	**Kyle Rote**, New York Giants	9.00	4.25	.90
☐	29	**Hugh McElhenny**, San Francisco 49ers	10.00	4.75	1.00
☐	30	**Sammy Baugh**, Washington Redskins	25.00	11.00	2.50
☐	31	**Jim Dooley**, Chicago Bears	3.50	1.65	.35
☐	32	**Ray Mathews**, Pittsburgh Steelers	3.00	1.40	.30
☐	33	**Fred Cone**, Green Bay Packers	3.00	1.40	.30
☐	34	**Al Pollard**, Philadelphia Eagles	3.00	1.40	.30
☐	35	**Brad Ecklund**, Dallas Texans	3.00	1.40	.30
☐	36	**John Lee Hancock**, Chicago Cardinals	3.00	1.40	.30
☐	37	**Elroy Hirsch**, Los Angeles Rams	9.00	4.25	.90
☐	38	**Keever Jankovich**, Cleveland Browns	3.00	1.40	.30
☐	39	**Emlen Tunnell**, New York Giants	7.50	3.50	.75
☐	40	**Steve Dowden**, Green Bay Packers	3.00	1.40	.30
☐	41	**Claude Hipps**, Pittsburgh Steelers	3.00	1.40	.30
☐	42	**Norm Standlee**, San Francisco 49ers	3.00	1.40	.30
☐	43	**Dick Todd**, Washington Redskins	3.00	1.40	.30
☐	44	**Babe Parilli**, Green Bay Packers	5.00	2.35	.50
☐	45	**Steve Van Buren**, Philadelphia Eagles	10.00	4.75	1.00
☐	46	**Art Donovan**, Dallas Texans	8.00	3.75	.80
☐	47	**Bill Fischer**, Chicago Cardinals	3.00	1.40	.30
☐	48	**George Halas**, Chicago Bears	16.00	7.50	1.60
☐	49	**Jerrell Price**, Chicago Cardinals	3.00	1.40	.30
☐	50	**John Sandusky**, Cleveland Browns	3.00	1.40	.30
☐	51	**Ray Beck**, New York Giants	3.00	1.40	.30
☐	52	**Jim Martin**, Detroit Lions	3.00	1.40	.30
☐	53	**Joe Back**, Pittsburgh Steelers	3.00	1.40	.30
☐	54	**Glen Christian**, San Francisco 49ers	3.00	1.40	.30
☐	55	**Andy Davis**, Washington Redskins	3.00	1.40	.30
☐	56	**Tobin Rote**, Green Bay Packers	4.00	1.85	.40
☐	57	**Wayne Millner**, Philadelphia Eagles	5.50	2.60	.55
☐	58	**Zollie Toth**, Dallas Texans	3.00	1.40	.30
☐	59	**Jack Jennings**, Chicago Cardinals	3.00	1.40	.30
☐	60	**Bill McColl**, Chicago Bears	3.00	1.40	.30
☐	61	**Les Richter**, Los Angeles Rams	3.50	1.65	.35
☐	62	**Walt Michaels**, Cleveland Browns	5.00	2.35	.50
☐	63	**Charley Conerly**, New York Giants	9.00	4.25	.90
☐	64	**Howard Hartley**, Pittsburgh Steelers	3.00	1.40	.30

		MINT	VG-E	F-G
☐	65 Jerome Smith, San Francisco 49ers	3.00	1.40	.30
☐	66 James Clark, Washington Redskins	3.00	1.40	.30
☐	67 Dick Logan, Cleveland Browns	3.00	1.40	.30
☐	68 Wayne Robinson, Philadelphia Eagles	3.00	1.40	.30
☐	69 James Hammond, Dallas Texans	3.00	1.40	.30
☐	70 Gene Schroeder, Chicago Bears	3.00	1.40	.30
☐	71 Tex Coulter, New York Giants	3.00	1.40	.30
☐	72 John Schweder, Pittsburgh Steelers	3.00	1.40	.30
☐	73 Vitamin Smith, Los Angeles Rams	4.50	2.10	.45
☐	74 Joe Campanella, Cleveland Browns	4.50	2.10	.45
☐	75 Joe Kuharich, Chicago Cardinals	5.00	2.35	.50
☐	76 Herman Clark, Chicago Bears	4.50	2.10	.45
☐	77 Dan Edwards, Dallas Texans	4.50	2.10	.45
☐	78 Bobby Layne, Detroit Lions	16.00	7.50	1.60
☐	79 Bob Hoernschemeyer, Detroit Lions	4.50	2.10	.45
☐	80 John Carr Blount, Philadelphia Eagles	4.50	2.10	.45
☐	81 John Kastan, New York Giants	4.50	2.10	.45
☐	82 Harry Minarik, Pittsburgh Steelers	4.50	2.10	.45
☐	83 Joe Perry, San Francisco 49ers	10.00	4.75	1.00
☐	84 Ray Parker, Detroit Lions	5.00	2.35	.50
☐	85 Andy Robustelli, Los Angeles Rams	9.00	4.25	.90
☐	86 Dub Jones, Cleveland Browns	5.50	2.60	.55
☐	87 Mal Cook, Chicago Cardinals	4.50	2.10	.45
☐	88 Billy Stone, Chicago Bears	4.50	2.10	.45
☐	89 George Taliaferro, Dallas Texans	4.50	2.10	.45
☐	90 Thomas Johnson, Green Bay Packers	4.50	2.10	.45
☐	91 Leon Heath, Washington Redskins	4.50	2.10	.45
☐	92 Pete Pihos, Philadelphia Eagles	7.50	3.50	.75
☐	93 Fred Benners, New York Giants	4.50	2.10	.45
☐	94 George Tarasovic, Pittsburgh Steelers	4.50	2.10	.45
☐	95 Lawrence Shaw, San Francisco 49ers	4.50	2.10	.45
☐	96 Bill Wightkin, Chicago Bears	4.50	2.10	.45
☐	97 John Wozniak, Dallas Texans	4.50	2.10	.45
☐	98 Bobby Dillon, Green Bay Packers	5.00	2.35	.50
☐	99 Joe Stydahar, Los Angeles Rams	10.00	4.75	1.00
☐	100 Dick Alban, Washington Redskins	4.50	2.10	.45
☐	101 Arnie Weinmeister, New York Giants	7.50	3.50	.75
☐	102 Robert Joe Cross, Chicago Bears	4.50	2.10	.45
☐	103 Don Paul, Chicago Cardinals	4.50	2.10	.45
☐	104 Buddy Young, Dallas Texans	5.50	2.60	.55
☐	105 Lou Groza, Cleveland Browns	12.00	5.50	1.20
☐	106 Ray Pelfrey, Green Bay Packers	4.50	2.10	.45
☐	107 Maurice Nipp, Philadelphia Eagles	4.50	2.10	.45
☐	108 Hubert Johnston, Washington Redskins	4.50	2.10	.45
☐	109 Volney Quinlan, Los Angeles Rams	4.50	2.10	.45
☐	110 Jack Simmons, Chicago Cardinals	4.50	2.10	.45

	MINT	VG-E	F-G
☐ 111 **George Ratterman,** Cleveland Browns	5.00	2.35	.50
☐ 112 **John Badaczewski,** Washington Redskins	4.50	2.10	.45
☐ 113 **Bill Reichardt,** Green Bay Packers	4.50	2.10	.45
☐ 114 **Art Weiner,** Dallas Texans	4.50	2.10	.45
☐ 115 **Keith Flowers,** Detroit Lions	4.50	2.10	.45
☐ 116 **Russ Craft,** Philadelphia Eagles	4.50	2.10	.45
☐ 117 **Jim O'Donahue,** San Francisco 49ers	4.50	2.10	.45
☐ 118 **Darrell Hogan,** Pittsburgh Steelers	4.50	2.10	.45
☐ 119 **Frank Ziegler,** Philadelphia Eagles	4.50	2.10	.45
☐ 120 **Deacon Dan Towler,** Los Angeles Rams	5.00	2.35	.50
☐ 121 **Fred Williams,** Chicago Bears	4.50	2.10	.45
☐ 122 **Jimmy Phelan,** Dallas Texans	4.50	2.10	.45
☐ 123 **Eddie Price,** New York Giants	5.00	2.35	.50
☐ 124 **Chet Ostrowski,** Washington Redskins	4.50	2.10	.45
☐ 125 **Leo Nomellini,** San Francisco 49ers	7.50	3.50	.75
☐ 126 **Steve Romanik,** Chicago Bears	4.50	2.10	.45
☐ 127 **Ollie Matson,** Chicago Cardinals	12.00	5.50	1.20
☐ 128 **Dante Lavelli,** Cleveland Browns	7.50	3.50	.75
☐ 129 **Jack Christiansen,** Detroit Lions	9.00	4.25	.90
☐ 130 **Dom Moselle,** Green Bay Packers	4.50	2.10	.45
☐ 131 **John Rapacz,** New York Giants	4.50	2.10	.45
☐ 132 **Chuck Ortman,** Pittsburgh Steelers	4.50	2.10	.45
☐ 133 **Bob Williams,** Chicago Bears	4.50	2.10	.45
☐ 134 **Chuck Ulrich,** Chicago Cardinals	4.50	2.10	.45
☐ 135 **Gene Ronzani,** Green Bay Packers	4.50	2.10	.45
☐ 136 **Bert Rechichar,** Cleveland Browns	4.50	2.10	.45
☐ 137 **Bob Waterfield,** Los Angeles Rams	12.50	5.75	1.25
☐ 138 **Bobby Walston,** Philadelphia Eagles	4.50	2.10	.45
☐ 139 **Jerry Shipkey,** Pittsburgh Steelers	4.50	2.10	.45
☐ 140 **Yale Lary,** Detroit Lions	10.00	4.75	1.00
☐ 141 **Gordon Soltau,** San Francisco 49ers	4.50	2.10	.45
☐ 142 **Tom Landry,** New York Giants	45.00	20.00	4.50
☐ 143 **John Papit,** Washington Redskins	4.50	2.10	.45
☐ 144 **Buck Lansford,** Dallas Texans	10.00	3.00	.50

1952 BOWMAN LARGE

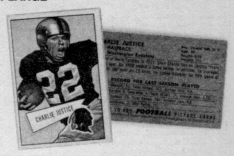

The 1952 Bowman set contains 144 cards, each of both a small and large size. The small cards measure 2¹⁄₁₆" by 3¹⁄₈", whereas the large cards measure 2½" by 3¾". The fronts and backs of both sets are identical except for size. The checklist below lists prices for the "large" set. In order to accommodate the enlarged art for the large set, certain numbers were systematically printed in lesser quantities due to the fact that Bowman apparently could not fit all the cards in the series on one sheet; the affected numbers are those which are divisible by nine and those which are "one more" than those divisible by nine. These shorter-printed (lesser quantity produced) cards are marked in the checklist below by SP.

		MINT	VG-E	F-G
	COMPLETE SET	2400.00	1000.00	300.00
	COMMON PLAYER (1-72)	4.50	2.10	.45
	COMMON PLAYER (73-144)	7.50	3.50	.75
☐ 1	**Norm Van Brocklin**, Los Angeles Rams	30.00	10.00	2.00
☐ 2	**Otto Graham**, Cleveland Browns	24.00	11.00	2.40
☐ 3	**Doak Walker**, Detroit Lions	12.00	5.50	1.20
☐ 4	**Steve Owen**, New York Giants	9.00	4.25	.90
☐ 5	**Frankie Albert**, San Francisco 49ers	6.00	2.80	.60
☐ 6	**Laurie Niemi**, Washington Redskins	4.50	2.10	.45
☐ 7	**Chuck Hunsinger**, Chicago Bears	4.50	2.10	.45
☐ 8	**Ed Modzelewski**, Pittsburgh Steelers	5.00	2.35	.50
☐ 9	**Joe Spencer SP**, Green Bay Packers	7.50	3.50	.75
☐ 10	**Chuck Bednarik SP**, Philadelphia Eagles	18.00	8.50	1.80
☐ 11	**Barney Poole**, Dallas Texans	4.50	2.10	.45
☐ 12	**Charlie Trippi**, Chicago Cardinals	9.00	4.25	.90
☐ 13	**Tom Fears**, Los Angeles Rams	9.00	4.25	.90

		MINT	VG-E	F-G
☐	14 **Paul Brown**, Cleveland Browns	18.00	8.50	1.80
☐	15 **Leon Hart**, Detroit Lions	6.00	2.80	.60
☐	16 **Frank Gifford**, New York Giants	50.00	22.00	5.00
☐	17 **Y.A. Tittle**, San Francisco 49ers	18.00	8.50	1.80
☐	18 **Charlie Justice SP**, Washington Redskins	15.00	7.00	1.50
☐	19 **George Connor SP**, Chicago Bears	10.00	4.75	1.00
☐	20 **Lynn Chandnois**, Pittsburgh Steelers	4.50	2.10	.45
☐	21 **Bill Howton**, Green Bay Packers	5.00	2.35	.50
☐	22 **Kenneth Snyder**, Philadelphia Eagles	4.50	2.10	.45
☐	23 **Gino Marchetti**, Dallas Texans	12.00	5.50	1.20
☐	24 **John Karras**, Chicago Cardinals	4.50	2.10	.45
☐	25 **Tank Younger**, Los Angeles Rams	6.00	2.80	.60
☐	26 **Tommy Thompson**, Cleveland Browns	5.00	2.35	.50
☐	27 **Bob Miller SP**, Detroit Lions	50.00	22.00	5.00
☐	28 **Kyle Rote SP**, New York Giants	15.00	7.00	1.50
☐	29 **Hugh McElhenny**, San Francisco 49ers	13.00	6.00	1.30
☐	30 **Sammy Baugh**, Washington Redskins	36.00	17.00	3.60
☐	31 **Jim Dooley**, Chicago Bears	5.00	2.35	.50
☐	32 **Ray Mathews**, Pittsburgh Steelers	4.50	2.10	.45
☐	33 **Fred Cone**, Green Bay Packers	4.50	2.10	.45
☐	34 **Al Pollard**, Philadelphia Eagles	4.50	2.10	.45
☐	35 **Brad Ecklund**, Dallas Texans	4.50	2.10	.45
☐	36 **John Lee Hancock SP**, Chicago Cardinals	60.00	27.00	6.00
☐	37 **Elroy Hirsch SP**, Los Angeles Rams	18.00	8.50	1.80
☐	38 **Keever Jankovich**, Cleveland Browns	4.50	2.10	.45
☐	39 **Emlen Tunnell**, New York Giants	9.00	4.25	.90
☐	40 **Steve Dowden**, Green Bay Packers	4.50	2.10	.45
☐	41 **Claude Hipps**, Pittsburgh Steelers	4.50	2.10	.45
☐	42 **Norm Standlee**, San Francisco 49ers	4.50	2.10	.45
☐	43 **Dick Todd**, Washington Redskins	4.50	2.10	.45
☐	44 **Babe Parilli**, Green Bay Packers	7.00	3.25	.70
☐	45 **Steve Van Buren SP**, Philadelphia Eagles	20.00	9.00	2.00
☐	46 **Art Donovan SP**, Dallas Texans	12.00	5.50	1.20
☐	47 **Bill Fischer**, Chicago Cardinals	4.50	2.10	.45
☐	48 **George Halas**, Chicago Bears	25.00	11.00	2.50
☐	49 **Jerrell Price**, Chicago Cardinals	4.50	2.10	.45
☐	50 **John Sandusky**, Cleveland Browns	4.50	2.10	.45
☐	51 **Ray Beck**, New York Giants	4.50	2.10	.45
☐	52 **Jim Martin**, Detroit Lions	4.50	2.10	.45
☐	53 **Joe Back**, Pittsburgh Steelers	4.50	2.10	.45
☐	54 **Glen Christian SP**, San Francisco 49ers	10.00	4.75	1.00
☐	55 **Andy Davis SP**, Washington Redskins	7.50	3.50	.75
☐	56 **Tobin Rote**, Green Bay Packers	6.00	2.80	.60
☐	57 **Wayne Millner**, Philadelphia Eagles	6.50	3.00	.65
☐	58 **Zollie Toth**, Dallas Texans	4.50	2.10	.45
☐	59 **Jack Jennings**, Chicago Cardinals	4.50	2.10	.45

		MINT	VG-E	F-G
☐ 60	Bill McColl, Chicago Bears	4.50	2.10	.45
☐ 61	Les Richter, Los Angeles Rams	5.00	2.35	.50
☐ 62	Walt Michaels, Cleveland Browns	6.50	3.00	.65
☐ 63	Charlie Conerly SP, New York Giants	50.00	22.00	5.00
☐ 64	Howard Hartley SP, Pittsburgh Steelers	7.50	3.50	.75
☐ 65	Jerome Smith, San Francisco 49ers	4.50	2.10	.45
☐ 66	James Clark, Washington Redskins	4.50	2.10	.45
☐ 67	Dick Logan, Cleveland Browns	4.50	2.10	.45
☐ 68	Wayne Robinson, Philadelphia Eagles	4.50	2.10	.45
☐ 69	James Hammond, Dallas Texans	4.50	2.10	.45
☐ 70	Gene Schroeder, Chicago Bears	4.50	2.10	.45
☐ 71	Tex Coulter, New York Giants	4.50	2.10	.45
☐ 72	John Schweder SP, Pittsburgh Steelers	60.00	27.00	6.00
☐ 73	Vitamin Smith SP, Los Angeles Rams	15.00	7.00	1.50
☐ 74	Joe Campanella, Cleveland Browns	7.50	3.50	.75
☐ 75	Joe Kuharich, Chicago Cardinals	7.50	3.50	.75
☐ 76	Herman Clark, Chicago Bears	7.50	3.50	.75
☐ 77	Dan Edwards, Dallas Texans	7.50	3.50	.75
☐ 78	Bobby Layne, Detroit Lions	22.00	10.00	2.20
☐ 79	Bob Hoernschemeyer, Detroit Lions	7.50	3.50	.75
☐ 80	John Carr Blount, Philadelphia Eagles	7.50	3.50	.75
☐ 81	John Kastan SP, New York Giants	18.00	8.50	1.80
☐ 82	Harry Minarik SP, Pittsburgh Steelers	30.00	14.00	3.00
☐ 83	Joe Perry, San Francisco 49ers	15.00	7.00	1.50
☐ 84	Ray Parker, Detroit Lions	8.50	4.00	.85
☐ 85	Andy Robustelli, Los Angeles Rams	13.00	6.00	1.30
☐ 86	Dub Jones, Cleveland Browns	9.00	4.25	.90
☐ 87	Mal Cook, Chicago Cardinals	7.50	3.50	.75
☐ 88	Billy Stone, Chicago Bears	7.50	3.50	.75
☐ 89	George Taliaferro, Dallas Texans	7.50	3.50	.75
☐ 90	Thomas Johnson SP, Green Bay Packers	20.00	9.00	2.00
☐ 91	Leon Heath SP, Washington Redskins	11.00	5.25	1.10
☐ 92	Pete Pihos, Philadelphia Eagles	11.00	5.25	1.10
☐ 93	Fred Benners, New York Giants	7.50	3.50	.75
☐ 94	George Tarasovic, Pittsburgh Steelers	7.50	3.50	.75
☐ 95	Lawrence Shaw, San Francisco 49ers	7.50	3.50	.75
☐ 96	Bill Wightkin, Chicago Bears	7.50	3.50	.75
☐ 97	John Wozniak, Dallas Texans	7.50	3.50	.75
☐ 98	Bobby Dillon, Green Bay Packers	8.50	4.00	.85
☐ 99	Joe Stydahar SP, Los Angeles Rams	90.00	42.00	9.00
☐ 100	Dick Alban SP, Washington Redskins	16.00	7.50	1.60
☐ 101	Arnie Weinmeister, New York Giants	11.00	5.25	1.10
☐ 102	Robert Joe Cross, Chicago Bears	7.50	3.50	.75
☐ 103	Don Paul, Chicago Cardinals	7.50	3.50	.75
☐ 104	Buddy Young, Dallas Texans	9.00	4.25	.90
☐ 105	Lou Groza, Cleveland Browns	18.00	8.50	1.80

		MINT	VG-E	F-G
☐ 106	Ray Pelfrey, Green Bay Packers	7.50	3.50	.75
☐ 107	Maurice Nipp, Philadelphia Eagles	7.50	3.50	.75
☐ 108	Hubert Johnston SP, Washington Redskins	75.00	35.00	7.50
☐ 109	Volney Quinlan SP, Los Angeles Rams	11.00	5.25	1.10
☐ 110	John Simmons, Chicago Cardinals	7.50	3.50	.75
☐ 111	George Ratterman, Cleveland Browns	9.00	4.25	.90
☐ 112	John Badaczewski, Washington Redskins	7.50	3.50	.75
☐ 113	Bill Reichardt, Green Bay Packers	7.50	3.50	.75
☐ 114	Art Weiner, Dallas Texans	7.50	3.50	.75
☐ 115	Keith Flowers, Detroit Lions	7.50	3.50	.75
☐ 116	Russ Craft, Philadelphia Eagles	7.50	3.50	.75
☐ 117	Jim O'Donahue SP, San Francisco 49ers	12.00	5.50	1.20
☐ 118	Darrell Hogan SP, Pittsburgh Steelers	10.00	4.75	1.00
☐ 119	Frank Ziegler, Philadelphia Eagles	7.50	3.50	.75
☐ 120	Deacon Dan Towler, Los Angeles Rams	8.50	4.00	.85
☐ 121	Fred Williams, Chicago Bears	7.50	3.50	.75
☐ 122	Jimmy Phelan, Dallas Texans	7.50	3.50	.75
☐ 123	Eddie Price, New York Giants	8.50	4.00	.85
☐ 124	Chet Ostrowski, Washington Redskins	7.50	3.50	.75
☐ 125	Leo Nomellini, San Francisco 49ers	11.00	5.25	1.10
☐ 126	Steve Romanik SP, Chicago Bears	50.00	22.00	5.00
☐ 127	Ollie Matson SP, Chicago Cardinals	25.00	11.00	2.50
☐ 128	Dante Lavelli, Cleveland Browns	11.00	5.25	1.10
☐ 129	Jack Christiansen, Detroit Lions	12.00	5.50	1.20
☐ 130	Dom Moselle, Green Bay Packers	7.50	3.50	.75
☐ 131	John Rapacz, New York Giants	7.50	3.50	.75
☐ 132	Chuck Ortman, Pittsburgh Steelers	7.50	3.50	.75
☐ 133	Bob Williams, Chicago Bears	7.50	3.50	.75
☐ 134	Chuck Ulrich, Chicago Cardinals	7.50	3.50	.75
☐ 135	Gene Ronzani SP, Green Bay Packers	75.00	35.00	7.50
☐ 136	Bert Rechichar SP, Cleveland Browns	11.00	5.25	1.10
☐ 137	Bob Waterfield, Los Angeles Rams	18.00	8.50	1.80
☐ 138	Bobby Walston, Philadelphia Eagles	7.50	3.50	.75
☐ 139	Jerry Shipkey, Pittsburgh Steelers	7.50	3.50	.75
☐ 140	Yale Lary, Detroit Lions	15.00	7.00	1.50
☐ 141	Gordon Soltau, San Francisco 49ers	7.50	3.50	.75
☐ 142	Tom Landry, New York Giants	90.00	42.00	9.00
☐ 143	John Papit, Washington Redskins	7.50	3.50	.75
☐ 144	Buck Lansford SP, Dallas Texans	300.00	60.00	12.00

1953 BOWMAN

The 1953 Bowman set of 96 cards continued the new larger card size. The cards measure 2½" by 3¾". The set is somewhat smaller in number than would be thought, since Bowman was the only major producer of football cards during this year.

	MINT	VG-E	F-G
COMPLETE SET	450.00	200.00	45.00
COMMON PLAYER (1-96)	3.00	1.40	.30
☐ 1 Eddie LeBaron, Washington Redskins	6.00	2.00	.50
☐ 2 John Dottley, Chicago Bears	3.00	1.40	.30
☐ 3 Babe Parilli, Green Bay Packers	4.50	2.10	.45
☐ 4 Bucko Kilroy, Philadelphia Eagles	3.50	1.65	.35
☐ 5 Joe Tereshinski, Washington Redskins	3.00	1.40	.30
☐ 6 Doak Walker, Detroit Lions	10.00	4.75	1.00
☐ 7 Fran Polsfoot, Chicago Cardinals	3.00	1.40	.30
☐ 8 Sisto Averno, Baltimore Colts	3.00	1.40	.30
☐ 9 Marion Motley, Cleveland Browns	7.50	3.50	.75
☐ 10 Pat Brady, Pittsburgh Steelers	3.00	1.40	.30
☐ 11 Norm Van Brocklin, Los Angeles Rams	12.50	5.75	1.25
☐ 12 Bill McColl, Chicago Bears	3.00	1.40	.30
☐ 13 Jerry Groom, Chicago Cardinals	3.00	1.40	.30
☐ 14 Al Pollard, Philadelphia Eagles	3.00	1.40	.30
☐ 15 Dante Lavelli, Cleveland Browns	7.00	3.25	.70
☐ 16 Eddie Price, New York Giants	3.50	1.65	.35
☐ 17 Charlie Trippi, Chicago Cardinals	7.00	3.25	.70
☐ 18 Elbert Nickle, Pittsburgh Steelers	3.00	1.40	.30
☐ 19 George Taliaferro, Baltimore Colts	3.00	1.40	.30

		MINT	VG-E	F-G
☐ 20	**Charley Conerly**, New York Giants	7.50	3.50	.75
☐ 21	**Bobby Layne**, Detroit Lions	14.00	6.50	1.40
☐ 22	**Elroy Hirsch**, Los Angeles Rams	10.00	4.75	1.00
☐ 23	**Jim Finks**, Pittsburgh Steelers	4.00	1.85	.40
☐ 24	**Chuck Bednarik**, Philadelphia Eagles	10.00	4.75	1.00
☐ 25	**Kyle Rote**, New York Giants	7.00	3.25	.70
☐ 26	**Otto Graham**, Cleveland Browns	16.00	7.50	1.60
☐ 27	**Harry Gilmer**, Washington Redskins	3.50	1.65	.35
☐ 28	**Tobin Rote**, Green Bay Packers	4.00	1.85	.40
☐ 29	**Billy Stone**, Chicago Bears	3.00	1.40	.30
☐ 30	**Buddy Young**, Baltimore Colts	4.50	2.10	.45
☐ 31	**Leon Hart**, Detroit Lions	4.50	2.10	.45
☐ 32	**Hugh McElhenny**, San Francisco 49ers	7.50	3.50	.75
☐ 33	**Dale Samuels**, Chicago Cardinals	3.00	1.40	.30
☐ 34	**Lou Creekmur**, Detroit Lions	3.00	1.40	.30
☐ 35	**Tom Catlin**, Cleveland Browns	3.00	1.40	.30
☐ 36	**Tom Fears**, Los Angeles Rams	7.00	3.25	.70
☐ 37	**George Connor**, Chicago Bears	7.00	3.25	.70
☐ 38	**Bill Walsh**, Pittsburgh Steelers	4.50	2.10	.45
☐ 39	**Leo Sanford**, Chicago Cardinals	3.00	1.40	.30
☐ 40	**Horace Gillom**, Cleveland Browns	3.00	1.40	.30
☐ 41	**John Schweder**, Pittsburgh Steelers	3.00	1.40	.30
☐ 42	**Tom O'Connell**, Chicago Bears	3.00	1.40	.30
☐ 43	**Frank Gifford**, New York Giants	25.00	11.00	2.50
☐ 44	**Frank Continetti**, Baltimore Colts	3.00	1.40	.30
☐ 45	**John Olszewski**, Chicago Cardinals	3.00	1.40	.30
☐ 46	**Dub Jones**, Cleveland Browns	4.50	2.10	.45
☐ 47	**Don Paul**, Los Angeles Rams	3.00	1.40	.30
☐ 48	**Gerald Weatherly**, Chicago Bears	3.00	1.40	.30
☐ 49	**Fred Bruney**, San Francisco 49ers	3.00	1.40	.30
☐ 50	**Jack Scarbath**, Washington Redskins	3.00	1.40	.30
☐ 51	**John Karras**, Chicago Cardinals	3.00	1.40	.30
☐ 52	**Al Conway**, Philadelphia Eagles	3.00	1.40	.30
☐ 53	**Emlen Tunnell**, New York Giants	7.00	3.25	.70
☐ 54	**Gern Nagler**, Baltimore Colts	3.00	1.40	.30
☐ 55	**Kenneth Snyder**, Philadelphia Eagles	3.00	1.40	.30
☐ 56	**Y.A. Tittle**, San Francisco 49ers	12.50	5.75	1.25
☐ 57	**John Rapacz**, New York Giants	3.00	1.40	.30
☐ 58	**Harley Sewell**, Detroit Lions	3.00	1.40	.30
☐ 59	**Don Bingham**, Chicago Bears	3.00	1.40	.30
☐ 60	**Darrell Hogan**, Pittsburgh Steelers	3.00	1.40	.30
☐ 61	**Tony Curcillo**, Chicago Cardinals	3.00	1.40	.30
☐ 62	**Ray Renfro**, Cleveland Browns	3.50	1.65	.35
☐ 63	**Leon Heath**, Washington Redskins	3.00	1.40	.30
☐ 64	**Tex Coulter**, New York Giants	3.00	1.40	.30
☐ 65	**Dewayne Douglas**, New York Giants	3.00	1.40	.30

	MINT	VG-E	F-G
☐ 66 **J. Robert Smith**, Detroit Lions	3.00	1.40	.30
☐ 67 **Bob McChesney**, New York Giants	3.00	1.40	.30
☐ 68 **Dick Alban**, Washington Redskins	3.00	1.40	.30
☐ 69 **Andy Kozar**, Chicago Bears	3.00	1.40	.30
☐ 70 **Merwin Hodel**, New York Giants	3.00	1.40	.30
☐ 71 **Thurman McGraw**, Detroit Lions	3.00	1.40	.30
☐ 72 **Cliff Anderson**, Chicago Cardinals	3.00	1.40	.30
☐ 73 **Pete Pihos**, Philadelphia Eagles	7.00	3.25	.70
☐ 74 **Julie Rykovich**, Washington Redskins	3.00	1.40	.30
☐ 75 **John Kreamcheck**, Chicago Bears	3.00	1.40	.30
☐ 76 **Lynn Chandnois**, Pittsburgh Steelers	3.00	1.40	.30
☐ 77 **Cloyce Box**, Detroit Lions	3.00	1.40	.30
☐ 78 **Ray Mathews**, Pittsburgh Steelers	3.00	1.40	.30
☐ 79 **Bobby Walston**, Philadelphia Eagles	3.00	1.40	.30
☐ 80 **Jim Dooley**, Chicago Bears	3.50	1.65	.35
☐ 81 **Pat Harder**, Detroit Lions	3.50	1.65	.35
☐ 82 **Jerry Shipkey**, Pittsburgh Steelers	3.00	1.40	.30
☐ 83 **Bobby Thomason**, Philadelphia Eagles	3.50	1.65	.35
☐ 84 **Hugh Taylor**, Washington Redskins	3.50	1.65	.35
☐ 85 **George Ratterman**, Cleveland Browns	3.50	1.65	.35
☐ 86 **Don Stonesifer**, Chicago Cardinals	3.00	1.40	.30
☐ 87 **John Williams**, Washington Redskins	3.00	1.40	.30
☐ 88 **Leo Nomellini**, San Francisco 49ers	7.00	3.25	.70
☐ 89 **Frank Ziegler**, Philadelphia Eagles	3.00	1.40	.30
☐ 90 **Don Paul**, Chicago Cardinals	3.00	1.40	.30
☐ 91 **Tom Dublinski**, Detroit Lions	3.00	1.40	.30
☐ 92 **Ken Carpenter**, Cleveland Browns	3.00	1.40	.30
☐ 93 **Ted Marchibroda**, Pittsburgh Steelers	3.50	1.65	.35
☐ 94 **Chuck Drazenovich**, Washington Redskins	3.00	1.40	.30
☐ 95 **Lou Groza**, Cleveland Browns	12.00	5.50	1.20
☐ 96 **William Cross**, Chicago Cardinals	6.00	1.50	.30

1954 BOWMAN

The 1954 Bowman set of 128 cards was produced in four series of 32, the third series (65-96) being somewhat more difficult to obtain. The cards measure 2½" by 3¾". The card backs feature the player's name in black print inside a red outline of a football. A "football quiz" question with upside-down answer is also given on the back. The player's statistical information from the previous season is summarized on the right-hand side of the back of the card.

		MINT	VG-E	F-G
	COMPLETE SET	275.00	120.00	27.00
	COMMON PLAYER (1-64)	1.00	.45	.10
	COMMON PLAYER (65-96)	3.50	1.65	.35
	COMMON PLAYER (97-128)	1.25	.60	.12
☐	1 Ray Mathews, Pittsburgh Steelers	3.00	.50	.10
☐	2 John Huzvar, Baltimore Colts	1.00	.45	.10
☐	3 Jack Scarbath, Washington Redskins	1.00	.45	.10
☐	4 Doug Atkins, Cleveland Browns	5.00	2.35	.50
☐	5 Bill Stits, Detroit Lions	1.00	.45	.10
☐	6 Joe Perry, San Francisco 49ers	6.50	3.00	.65
☐	7 Kyle Rote, New York Giants	5.00	2.35	.50
☐	8 Norm Van Brocklin, Los Angeles Rams	9.00	4.25	.90
☐	9 Pete Pihos, Philadelphia Eagles	5.00	2.35	.50
☐	10 Babe Parilli, Green Bay Packers	2.00	.90	.20
☐	11 Zeke Bratkowski, Chicago Bears	2.00	.90	.20
☐	12 Ollie Matson, Chicago Cardinals	5.00	2.35	.50
☐	13 Pat Brady, Pittsburgh Steelers	1.00	.45	.10
☐	14 Fred Enke, Baltimore Colts	1.00	.45	.10
☐	15 Harry Ulinski, Washington Redskins	1.00	.45	.10

		MINT	VG-E	F-G
☐ 16	**Bobby Garrett,** Cleveland Browns	1.00	.45	.10
☐ 17	**Bill Bowman,** Detroit Lions	1.00	.45	.10
☐ 18	**Leo Rucka,** San Francisco 49ers	1.00	.45	.10
☐ 19	**John Cannady,** New York Giants	1.00	.45	.10
☐ 20	**Tom Fears,** Los Angeles Rams	5.00	2.35	.50
☐ 21	**Norm Willey,** Philadelphia Eagles	1.00	.45	.10
☐ 22	**Floyd Reid,** Green Bay Packers	1.00	.45	.10
☐ 23	**George Blanda,** Chicago Bears	16.00	7.50	1.60
☐ 24	**Don Doheney,** Chicago Cardinals	1.00	.45	.10
☐ 25	**John Schweder,** Pittsburgh Steelers	1.00	.45	.10
☐ 26	**Bert Rechichar,** Baltimore Colts	1.00	.45	.10
☐ 27	**Harry Dowda,** Philadelphia Eagles	1.00	.45	.10
☐ 28	**John Sandusky,** Cleveland Browns	1.00	.45	.10
☐ 29	**Les Bingaman,** Detroit Lions	1.00	.45	.10
☐ 30	**Joe Arenas,** San Francisco 49ers	1.00	.45	.10
☐ 31	**Ray Wietecha,** New York Giants	1.00	.45	.10
☐ 32	**Elroy Hirsch,** Los Angeles Rams	6.00	2.80	.60
☐ 33	**Harold Giancanelli,** Philadelphia Eagles	1.00	.45	.10
☐ 34	**Bill Howton,** Green Bay Packers	1.25	.60	.12
☐ 35	**Fred Morrison,** Chicago Bears	1.00	.45	.10
☐ 36	**Bobby Cavazos,** Chicago Cardinals	1.00	.45	.10
☐ 37	**Darrell Hogan,** Pittsburgh Steelers	1.00	.45	.10
☐ 38	**Buddy Young,** Baltimore Colts	1.50	.70	.15
☐ 39	**Charlie Justice,** Washington Redskins	4.00	1.85	.40
☐ 40	**Otto Graham,** Cleveland Browns	12.50	5.75	1.25
☐ 41	**Doak Walker,** Detroit Lions	6.50	3.00	.65
☐ 42	**Y.A. Tittle,** San Francisco 49ers	9.00	4.25	.90
☐ 43	**Buford Long,** New York Giants	1.00	.45	.10
☐ 44	**Volney Quinlan,** Los Angeles Rams	1.00	.45	.10
☐ 45	**Bobby Thomason,** Philadelphia Eagles	1.50	.70	.15
☐ 46	**Fred Cone,** Green Bay Packers	1.00	.45	.10
☐ 47	**Gerald Weatherly,** Chicago Bears	1.00	.45	.10
☐ 48	**Don Stonesifer,** Chicago Cardinals	1.00	.45	.10
☐ 49	**Lynn Chandnois,** Pittsburgh Steelers	1.00	.45	.10
☐ 50	**George Taliaferro,** Baltimore Colts	1.00	.45	.10
☐ 51	**Dick Alban,** Washington Redskins	1.00	.45	.10
☐ 52	**Lou Groza,** Cleveland Browns	9.00	4.25	.90
☐ 53	**Bobby Layne,** Detroit Lions	11.00	5.25	1.10
☐ 54	**Hugh McElhenny,** San Francisco 49ers	5.00	2.35	.50
☐ 55	**Frank Gifford,** New York Giants	18.00	8.50	1.80
☐ 56	**Leon McLaughlin,** Los Angeles Rams	1.00	.45	.10
☐ 57	**Chuck Bednarik,** Philadelphia Eagles	6.50	3.00	.65
☐ 58	**Art Hunter,** Green Bay Packers	1.00	.45	.10
☐ 59	**Bill McColl,** Chicago Bears	1.00	.45	.10
☐ 60	**Charlie Trippi,** Chicago Cardinals	5.00	2.35	.50
☐ 61	**Jim Finks,** Pittsburgh Steelers	2.00	.90	.20

		MINT	VG-E	F-G
☐ 62	**Bill Lange**, Baltimore Colts	1.00	.45	.10
☐ 63	**Laurie Niemi**, Washington Redskins	1.00	.45	.10
☐ 64	**Ray Renfro**, Cleveland Browns	1.50	.70	.15
☐ 65	**Dick Chapman**, Detroit Lions	3.50	1.65	.35
☐ 66	**Bob Hantla**, San Francisco 49ers	3.50	1.65	.35
☐ 67	**Ralph Starkey**, New York Giants	3.50	1.65	.35
☐ 68	**Don Paul**, Los Angeles Rams	3.50	1.65	.35
☐ 69	**Kenneth Snyder**, Philadelphia Eagles	3.50	1.65	.35
☐ 70	**Tobin Rote**, Green Bay Packers	4.50	2.10	.45
☐ 71	**Arthur DeCarlo**, Pittsburgh Steelers	3.50	1.65	.35
☐ 72	**Tom Keane**, Baltimore Colts	3.50	1.65	.35
☐ 73	**Hugh Taylor**, Washington Redskins	4.00	1.85	.40
☐ 74	**Warren Lahr**, Cleveland Browns	3.50	1.65	.35
☐ 75	**Jim Neal**, Detroit Lions	3.50	1.65	.35
☐ 76	**Leo Nomellini**, San Francisco 49ers	11.00	5.25	1.10
☐ 77	**Dick Yelvington**, New York Giants	3.50	1.65	.35
☐ 78	**Les Richter**, Los Angeles Rams	4.00	1.85	.40
☐ 79	**Bucko Kilroy**, Philadelphia Eagles	4.00	1.85	.40
☐ 80	**John Martinkovic**, Green Bay Packers	3.50	1.65	.35
☐ 81	**Dale Dodrill**, Pittsburgh Steelers	3.50	1.65	.35
☐ 82	**Ken Jackson**, Baltimore Colts	3.50	1.65	.35
☐ 83	**Paul Lipscomb**, Washington Redskins	3.50	1.65	.35
☐ 84	**John Bauer**, Cleveland Browns	3.50	1.65	.35
☐ 85	**Lou Creekmur**, Detroit Lions	3.50	1.65	.35
☐ 86	**Eddie Price**, New York Giants	4.00	1.85	.40
☐ 87	**Kenneth Farragut**, Philadelphia Eagles	3.50	1.65	.35
☐ 88	**Dave Hanner**, Green Bay Packers	4.00	1.85	.40
☐ 89	**Don Boll**, Washington Redskins	3.50	1.65	.35
☐ 90	**Chet Hanulak**, Cleveland Browns	3.50	1.65	.35
☐ 91	**Thurman McGraw**, Detroit Lions	3.50	1.65	.35
☐ 92	**Don Heinrich**, New York Giants	4.50	2.10	.45
☐ 93	**Dan McKown**, Philadelphia Eagles	3.50	1.65	.35
☐ 94	**Bob Fleck**, Green Bay Packers	3.50	1.65	.35
☐ 95	**Jerry Hilgenberg**, Cleveland Browns	3.50	1.65	.35
☐ 96	**Bill Walsh**, Pittsburgh Steelers	4.50	2.10	.45
☐ 97	**Tom Finnan**, Baltimore Colts	1.25	.60	.12
☐ 98	**Paul Barry**, Washington Redskins	1.25	.60	.12
☐ 99	**Harry Jagade**, Cleveland Browns	1.25	.60	.12
☐ 100	**Jack Christiansen**, Detroit Lions	5.00	2.35	.50
☐ 101	**Gordon Soltau**, San Francisco 49ers	1.25	.60	.12
☐ 102	**Emlen Tunnell**, New York Giants	5.00	2.35	.50
☐ 103	**Stan West**, Los Angeles Rams	1.25	.60	.12
☐ 104	**Jerry Williams**, Philadelphia Eagles	1.25	.60	.12
☐ 105	**Veryl Switzer**, Green Bay Packers	1.25	.60	.12
☐ 106	**Billy Stone**, Chicago Bears	1.25	.60	.12
☐ 107	**Jerry Watford**, Chicago Cardinals	1.25	.60	.12

	MINT	VG-E	F-G
☐ 108 **Elbert Nickel**, Pittsburgh Steelers	1.25	.60	.12
☐ 109 **Ed Sharkey**, Baltimore Colts	1.25	.60	.12
☐ 110 **Steve Meilinger**, Washington Redskins	1.25	.60	.12
☐ 111 **Dante Lavelli**, Cleveland Browns	4.50	2.10	.45
☐ 112 **Leon Hart**, Detroit Lions	2.00	.90	.20
☐ 113 **Charley Conerly**, New York Giants	5.00	2.35	.50
☐ 114 **Richard Lemmon**, Philadelphia Eagles	1.25	.60	.12
☐ 115 **Al Carmichael**, Green Bay Packers	1.25	.60	.12
☐ 116 **George Connor**, Chicago Bears	4.50	2.10	.45
☐ 117 **John Olszewski**, Chicago Cardinals	1.25	.60	.12
☐ 118 **Ernie Stautner**, Pittsburgh Steelers	5.00	2.35	.50
☐ 119 **Ray Smith**, Chicago Bears	1.25	.60	.12
☐ 120 **Neil Worden**, Philadelphia Eagles	1.25	.60	.12
☐ 121 **Jim Dooley**, Chicago Bears	1.50	.70	.15
☐ 122 **Arnold Galiffa**, San Francisco 49ers	1.50	.70	.15
☐ 123 **Kline Gilbert**, Chicago Bears	1.25	.60	.12
☐ 124 **Bob Hoernschemeyer**, Detroit Lions	1.25	.60	.12
☐ 125 **Whizzer White**, Chicago Bears	2.50	1.15	.25
☐ 126 **Art Spinney**, Baltimore Colts	1.25	.60	.12
☐ 127 **Joe Koch**, Chicago Bears	1.25	.60	.12
☐ 128 **John Lattner**, Pittsburgh Steelers	5.00	1.25	.25

1955 BOWMAN

The 1955 Bowman set of 160 cards was Bowman's last sports issue before the company was purchased by Topps in January of 1956. Numbers above 64 are somewhat more difficult to obtain. The cards measure 2½" by 3¾". On the bottom of the card back is found a play diagram. Card backs are printed in red and blue on gray card stock.

		MINT	VG-E	F-G
	COMPLETE SET	215.00	90.00	20.00
	COMMON PLAYER (1-64)	.70	.32	.07
	COMMON PLAYER (65-160)	1.50	.70	.15
☐ 1	**Doak Walker**, Detroit Lions	9.00	2.50	.40
☐ 2	**Mike McCormack**, Cleveland Browns	3.50	1.65	.35
☐ 3	**John Olszewski**, Chicago Cardinals	.70	.32	.07
☐ 4	**Dorne Dibble**, Detroit Lions	.70	.32	.07
☐ 5	**Lindon Crow**, Chicago Cardinals	.70	.32	.07
☐ 6	**Hugh Taylor**, Washington Redskins	1.00	.45	.10
☐ 7	**Frank Gifford**, New York Giants	16.00	7.50	1.60
☐ 8	**Alan Ameche**, Baltimore Colts	3.00	1.40	.30
☐ 9	**Don Stonesifer**, Chicago Cardinals	.70	.32	.07
☐ 10	**Pete Pihos**, Philadelphia Eagles	3.50	1.65	.35
☐ 11	**Bill Austin**, New York Giants	.70	.32	.07
☐ 12	**Dick Alban**, Washington Redskins	.70	.32	.07
☐ 13	**Bobby Walston**, Philadelphia Eagles	.70	.32	.07
☐ 14	**Len Ford**, Cleveland Browns	3.50	1.65	.35
☐ 15	**Jug Girard**, Detroit Lions	.70	.32	.07
☐ 16	**Charley Conerly**, New York Giants	4.00	1.85	.40
☐ 17	**Volney Peters**, Washington Redskins	.70	.32	.07
☐ 18	**Max Boydston**, Chicago Cardinals	.70	.32	.07
☐ 19	**Leon Hart**, Detroit Lions	1.50	.70	.15
☐ 20	**Bert Rechichar**, Baltimore Colts	.70	.32	.07
☐ 21	**Lee Riley**, Detroit Lions	.70	.32	.07
☐ 22	**Johnny Carson**, Washington Redskins	.70	.32	.07
☐ 23	**Harry Thompson**, Los Angeles Rams	.70	.32	.07
☐ 24	**Ray Wietecha**, New York Giants	.70	.32	.07
☐ 25	**Ollie Matson**, Chicago Cardinals	4.00	1.85	.40
☐ 26	**Eddie LeBaron**, Washington Redskins	1.50	.70	.15
☐ 27	**Jack Simmons**, Chicago Cardinals	.70	.32	.07
☐ 28	**Jack Christiansen**, Detroit Lions	3.50	1.65	.35
☐ 29	**Bucko Kilroy**, Philadelphia Eagles	1.00	.45	.10
☐ 30	**Tom Keane**, Chicago Cardinals	.70	.32	.07
☐ 31	**Dave Leggett**, Chicago Cardinals	.70	.32	.07
☐ 32	**Norm Van Brocklin**, Los Angeles Rams	8.00	3.75	.80
☐ 33	**Harlon Hill**, Chicago Bears	1.50	.70	.15
☐ 34	**Robert Haner**, Green Bay Packers	.70	.32	.07
☐ 35	**Veryl Switzer**, Green Bay Packers	.70	.32	.07
☐ 36	**Dick Stanfel**, Detroit Lions	.70	.32	.07
☐ 37	**Lou Groza**, Cleveland Browns	6.00	2.80	.60
☐ 38	**Tank Younger**, Los Angeles Rams	1.25	.60	.12
☐ 39	**Dick Flanagan**, Pittsburgh Steelers	.70	.32	.07
☐ 40	**Jim Dooley**, Chicago Bears	1.25	.60	.12
☐ 41	**Ray Collins**, New York Giants	.70	.32	.07
☐ 42	**John Henry Johnson**, San Francisco 49ers ...	2.50	1.15	.25

			MINT	VG-E	F-G
☐	43	**Tom Fears**, Los Angeles Rams	4.00	1.85	.40
☐	44	**Joe Perry**, San Francisco 49ers	5.00	2.35	.50
☐	45	**Gene Brito**, Washington Redskins	.70	.32	.07
☐	46	**Bill Johnson**, San Francisco 49ers	.70	.32	.07
☐	47	**Deacon Dan Towler**, Los Angeles Rams	1.00	.45	.10
☐	48	**Dick Moegle**, San Francisco 49ers	.70	.32	.07
☐	49	**Kline Gilbert**, Chicago Bears	.70	.32	.07
☐	50	**Les Gobel**, Chicago Cardinals	.70	.32	.07
☐	51	**Ray Krouse**, New York Giants	.70	.32	.07
☐	52	**Pat Summerall**, Chicago Cardinals	5.00	2.35	.50
☐	53	**Ed Brown**, Chicago Bears	1.25	.60	.12
☐	54	**Lynn Chandnois**, Pittsburgh Steelers	.70	.32	.07
☐	55	**Joe Heap**, New York Giants	.70	.32	.07
☐	56	**John Hoffman**, Chicago Bears	.70	.32	.07
☐	57	**Howard Ferguson**, Green Bay Packers	.70	.32	.07
☐	58	**Bobby Watkins**, Chicago Bears	.70	.32	.07
☐	59	**Charlie Ane**, Detroit Lions	.70	.32	.07
☐	60	**Ken MacAfee**, New York Giants	1.00	.45	.10
☐	61	**Ralph Guglielmi**, Washington Redskins	1.00	.45	.10
☐	62	**George Blanda**, Chicago Bears	9.00	4.25	.90
☐	63	**Kenneth Snyder**, Philadelphia Eagles	.70	.32	.07
☐	64	**Chet Ostrowski**, Washington Redskins	.70	.32	.07
☐	65	**Buddy Young**, Baltimore Colts	2.50	1.15	.25
☐	66	**Gordon Soltau**, San Francisco 49ers	1.50	.70	.15
☐	67	**Eddie Bell**, Philadelphia Eagles	1.50	.70	.15
☐	68	**Ben Agajanian**, New York Giants	2.00	.90	.20
☐	69	**Tom Dahms**, Los Angeles Rams	1.50	.70	.15
☐	70	**Jim Ringo**, Green Bay Packers	6.00	2.80	.60
☐	71	**Bobby Layne**, Detroit Lions	9.00	4.25	.90
☐	72	**Y.A. Tittle**, San Francisco 49ers	9.00	4.25	.90
☐	73	**Bob Gaona**, Pittsburgh Steelers	1.50	.70	.15
☐	74	**Tobin Rote**, Green Bay Packers	2.00	.90	.20
☐	75	**Hugh McElhenny**, San Francisco 49ers	5.00	2.35	.50
☐	76	**John Kreamcheck**, Chicago Bears	1.50	.70	.15
☐	77	**Al Dorow**, Washington Redskins	1.50	.70	.15
☐	78	**Bill Wade**, Los Angeles Rams	2.00	.90	.20
☐	79	**Dale Dodrill**, Pittsburgh Steelers	1.50	.70	.15
☐	80	**Chuck Drazenovich**, Washington Redskins	1.50	.70	.15
☐	81	**Billy Wilson**, San Francisco 49ers	2.00	.90	.20
☐	82	**Les Richter**, Los Angeles Rams	2.00	.90	.20
☐	83	**Pat Brady**, Pittsburgh Steelers	1.50	.70	.15
☐	84	**Bob Hoernschemeyer**, Detroit Lions	1.50	.70	.15
☐	85	**Joe Arenas**, San Francisco 49ers	1.50	.70	.15
☐	86	**Len Szafaryn**, Green Bay Packers	1.50	.70	.15
☐	87	**Rick Casares**, Chicago Bears	2.50	1.15	.25
☐	88	**Leon McLaughlin**, Los Angeles Rams	1.50	.70	.15

			MINT	VG-E	F-G
☐	89	**Charley Toogood,** Los Angeles Rams	1.50	.70	.15
☐	90	**Tom Bettis,** Green Bay Packers	1.50	.70	.15
☐	91	**John Sandusky,** Cleveland Browns	1.50	.70	.15
☐	92	**Bill Wightkin,** Chicago Bears	1.50	.70	.15
☐	93	**Darrell Brewster,** Cleveland Browns	1.50	.70	.15
☐	94	**Marion Campbell,** San Francisco 49ers	2.50	1.15	.25
☐	95	**Floyd Reid,** Green Bay Packers	1.50	.70	.15
☐	96	**Harry Jagade,** Chicago Bears	1.50	.70	.15
☐	97	**George Taliaferro,** Philadelphia Eagles	1.50	.70	.15
☐	98	**Carleton Massey,** Cleveland Browns	1.50	.70	.15
☐	99	**Fran Rogel,** Pittsburgh Steelers	1.50	.70	.15
☐	100	**Alex Sandusky,** Baltimore Colts	1.50	.70	.15
☐	101	**Bob St. Clair,** San Francisco 49ers	1.50	.70	.15
☐	102	**Al Carmichael,** Green Bay Packers	1.50	.70	.15
☐	103	**Carl Taseff,** Baltimore Colts	1.50	.70	.15
☐	104	**Leo Nomellini,** San Francisco 49ers	5.00	2.35	.50
☐	105	**Tom Scott,** Philadelphia Eagles	1.50	.70	.15
☐	106	**Ted Marchibroda,** Pittsburgh Steelers	2.00	.90	.20
☐	107	**Art Spinney,** Baltimore Colts	1.50	.70	.15
☐	108	**Wayne Robinson,** Philadelphia Eagles	1.50	.70	.15
☐	109	**Jim Ricca,** Detroit Lions	1.50	.70	.15
☐	110	**Lou Ferry,** Pittsburgh Steelers	1.50	.70	.15
☐	111	**Roger Zatkoff,** Green Bay Packers	1.50	.70	.15
☐	112	**Lou Creekmur,** Detroit Lions	1.50	.70	.15
☐	113	**Kenny Konz,** Cleveland Browns	1.50	.70	.15
☐	114	**Doug Eggers,** Baltimore Colts	1.50	.70	.15
☐	115	**Bobby Thomason,** Philadelphia Eagles	2.00	.90	.20
☐	116	**Bill McPeak,** Pittsburgh Steelers	1.50	.70	.15
☐	117	**William Brown,** Green Bay Packers	1.50	.70	.15
☐	118	**Royce Womble,** Baltimore Colts	1.50	.70	.15
☐	119	**Frank Gatski,** Cleveland Browns	5.00	2.35	.50
☐	120	**Jim Finks,** Pittsburgh Steelers	2.00	.90	.20
☐	121	**Andy Robustelli,** Los Angeles Rams	4.50	2.10	.45
☐	122	**Bobby Dillon,** Green Bay Packers	2.00	.90	.20
☐	123	**Leo Sanford,** Chicago Cardinals	1.50	.70	.15
☐	124	**Elbert Nickel,** Pittsburgh Steelers	1.50	.70	.15
☐	125	**Wayne Hansen,** Chicago Bears	1.50	.70	.15
☐	126	**Buck Lansford,** Philadelphia Eagles	1.50	.70	.15
☐	127	**Gern Nagler,** Chicago Cardinals	1.50	.70	.15
☐	128	**Jim Salsbury,** Detroit Lions	1.50	.70	.15
☐	129	**Dale Atkeson,** Washington Redskins	1.50	.70	.15
☐	130	**John Schweder,** Pittsburgh Steelers	1.50	.70	.15
☐	131	**Dave Hanner,** Green Bay Packers	2.00	.90	.20
☐	132	**Eddie Price,** New York Giants	2.00	.90	.20
☐	133	**Vic Janowicz,** Washington Redskins	2.50	1.15	.25
☐	134	**Ernie Stautner,** Pittsburgh Steelers	5.00	2.35	.50

	MINT	VG-E	F-G
☐ 135 **James Parmer**, Philadelphia Eagles	1.50	.70	.15
☐ 136 **Emlen Tunnell**, New York Giants	5.00	2.35	.50
☐ 137 **Kyle Rote**, New York Giants	5.00	2.35	.50
☐ 138 **Norm Wiley**, Philadelphia Eagles	1.50	.70	.15
☐ 139 **Charlie Trippi**, Chicago Cardinals	5.00	2.35	.50
☐ 140 **Bill Howton**, Green Bay Packers	2.00	.90	.20
☐ 141 **Bobby Clatterbuck**, New York Giants	1.50	.70	.15
☐ 142 **Bob Boyd**, Los Angeles Rams	1.50	.70	.15
☐ 143 **Bob Toneff**, San Francisco 49ers	1.50	.70	.15
☐ 144 **Jerry Helluin**, Green Bay Packers	1.50	.70	.15
☐ 145 **Adrian Burk**, Philadelphia Eagles	1.50	.70	.15
☐ 146 **Walt Michaels**, Cleveland Browns	2.50	1.15	.25
☐ 147 **Zollie Toth**, Baltimore Colts	1.50	.70	.15
☐ 148 **Frank Varrichione**, Pittsburgh Steelers	1.50	.70	.15
☐ 149 **Dick Bielski**, Philadelphia Eagles	1.50	.70	.15
☐ 150 **George Ratterman**, Cleveland Browns	2.00	.90	.20
☐ 151 **Mike Jarmoluk**, Philadelphia Eagles	1.50	.70	.15
☐ 152 **Tom Landry**, New York Giants	30.00	14.00	3.00
☐ 153 **Ray Renfro**, Cleveland Browns	2.00	.90	.20
☐ 154 **Zeke Bratkowski**, Chicago Bears	2.50	1.15	.25
☐ 155 **Jerry Norton**, Philadelphia Eagles	1.50	.70	.15
☐ 156 **Maurice Bassett**, Cleveland Browns	1.50	.70	.15
☐ 157 **Volney Quinlan**, Los Angeles Rams	1.50	.70	.15
☐ 158 **Chuck Bednarik**, Philadelphia Eagles	6.50	3.00	.65
☐ 159 **Don Colo**, Cleveland Browns	1.50	.70	.15
☐ 160 **L.G. Dupre**, Baltimore Colts	3.00	.75	.15

1960 FLEER

The 1960 Fleer set of 132 cards was Fleer's first venture into football card production. The cards measure 2 ½" by 3 ½". American Football League players only are included in this set. This set was issued during the American Football League's first season. Several well-known coaches are featured in the set. The card backs are printed in red and black.

		MINT	VG-E	F-G
	COMPLETE SET	80.00	37.00	8.00
	COMMON PLAYER (1-132)	.45	.20	.04
☐	1 Harvey White, Boston Patriots	1.25	.25	.05
☐	2 Tom Corky Tharp, New York Titans	.45	.20	.04
☐	3 Dan McGrew, Buffalo Bills	.45	.20	.04
☐	4 Bob White, Houston Oilers	.60	.28	.06
☐	5 Dick Jamieson, New York Titans	.45	.20	.04
☐	6 Sam Salerno, Denver Broncos	.45	.20	.04
☐	7 Sid Gillman COACH, Los Angeles Chargers	3.00	1.40	.30
☐	8 Ben Preston, Los Angeles Chargers	.45	.20	.04
☐	9 George Blanch, Oakland Raiders	.45	.20	.04
☐	10 Bob Stransky, Denver Broncos	.45	.20	.04
☐	11 Fran Curci, Dallas Texans	.60	.28	.06
☐	12 George Shirkey, Houston Oilers	.45	.20	.04
☐	13 Paul Larson, Oakland Raiders	.45	.20	.04
☐	14 John Stolte, Los Angeles Chargers	.45	.20	.04
☐	15 Serafino Frazio, Boston Patriots	.45	.20	.04
☐	16 Tom Dimitroff, Boston Patriots	.45	.20	.04
☐	17 Elbert Dubenion, Buffalo Bills	1.00	.45	.10
☐	18 Hogan Wharton, Houston Oilers	.45	.20	.04
☐	19 Tom O'Connell, Buffalo Bills	.60	.28	.06

		MINT	VG-E	F-G
☐	20 **Sammy Baugh COACH**, New York Titans	9.00	4.25	.90
☐	21 **Tony Sardisco**, Boston Patriots	.45	.20	.04
☐	22 **Alan Cann**, Boston Patriots	.45	.20	.04
☐	23 **Mike Hudock**, New York Titans	.45	.20	.04
☐	24 **Bill Atkins**, Buffalo Bills	.45	.20	.04
☐	25 **Charlie Jackson**, Dallas Texans	.45	.20	.04
☐	26 **Frank Tripucka**, Denver Broncos	1.00	.45	.10
☐	27 **Tony Teresa**, Oakland Raiders	.45	.20	.04
☐	28 **Joe Amstutz**, Oakland Raiders	.45	.20	.04
☐	29 **Bob Fee**, Boston Patriots	.45	.20	.04
☐	30 **Jim Baldwin**, New York Titans	.45	.20	.04
☐	31 **Jim Yates**, Houston Oilers	.45	.20	.04
☐	32 **Don Flynn**, Dallas Texans	.45	.20	.04
☐	33 **Ken Adamson**, Denver Broncos	.45	.20	.04
☐	34 **Ron Drzewiecki**, Oakland Raiders	.45	.20	.04
☐	35 **J.W. Slack**, Los Angeles Chargers	.45	.20	.04
☐	36 **Bob Yates**, Boston Patriots	.45	.20	.04
☐	37 **Gary Cobb**, Buffalo Bills	.45	.20	.04
☐	38 **Jacky Lee**, Houston Oilers	.75	.35	.07
☐	39 **Jack Spikes**, Dallas Cowboys	.60	.28	.06
☐	40 **Jim Padgett**, Denver Broncos	.45	.20	.04
☐	41 **Jack Larsheid**, Oakland Raiders	.45	.20	.04
☐	42 **Bob Reifsnyder**, New York Titans	.45	.20	.04
☐	43 **Fran Rogel**, New York Titans	.45	.20	.04
☐	44 **Ray Moss**, Buffalo Bills	.45	.20	.04
☐	45 **Tony Banfield**, Houston Oilers	.60	.28	.06
☐	46 **George Herring**, Denver Broncos	.45	.20	.04
☐	47 **Willie Smith**, Denver Broncos	.45	.20	.04
☐	48 **Buddy Allen**, Oakland Raiders	.45	.20	.04
☐	49 **Bill Brown**, Boston Patriots	.45	.20	.04
☐	50 **Ken Ford**, New York Titans	.45	.20	.04
☐	51 **Billy Kinard**, Buffalo Bills	.45	.20	.04
☐	52 **Buddy Mayfield**, Houston Oilers	.45	.20	.04
☐	53 **Bill Krisher**, Dallas Texans	.60	.28	.06
☐	54 **Frank Bernardi**, Denver Broncos	.45	.20	.04
☐	55 **Lou Saban COACH**, Boston Patriots	1.00	.45	.10
☐	56 **Gene Cockrell**, New York Titans	.45	.20	.04
☐	57 **Sam Sanders**, Buffalo Bills	.45	.20	.04
☐	58 **George Blanda**, Houston Oilers	8.00	3.75	.80
☐	59 **Sherrill Headrick**, Dallas Texans	.60	.28	.06
☐	60 **Carl Larpenter**, Denver Broncos	.45	.20	.04
☐	61 **Gene Prebola**, Oakland Raiders	.45	.20	.04
☐	62 **Dick Chorovich**, Los Angeles Chargers	.45	.20	.04
☐	63 **Bob McNamara**, Denver Broncos	.45	.20	.04
☐	64 **Tom Saidock**, Dallas Texans	.45	.20	.04
☐	65 **Willie Evans**, Buffalo Bills	.45	.20	.04

		MINT	VG-E	F-G
☐	66 **Billy Cannon**, Houston Oilers	2.50	1.15	.25
☐	67 **Sam McCord**, Oakland Raiders	.45	.20	.04
☐	68 **Mike Simmons**, New York Titans	.45	.20	.04
☐	69 **Jim Swink**, Dallas Texans	.60	.28	.06
☐	70 **Don Hitt**, Houston Oilers	.45	.20	.04
☐	71 **Gerhard Schwedes**, Boston Patriots	.60	.28	.06
☐	72 **Thurlow Cooper**, New York Titans	.45	.20	.04
☐	73 **Abner Haynes**, Dallas Texans	2.00	.90	.20
☐	74 **Billy Shoemake**, Denver Broncos	.45	.20	.04
☐	75 **Marv Lasater**, Oakland Raiders	.45	.20	.04
☐	76 **Paul Lowe**, Los Angeles Chargers	2.00	.90	.20
☐	77 **Bruce Hartman**, Boston Patriots	.45	.20	.04
☐	78 **Blanche Martin**, New York Titans	.45	.20	.04
☐	79 **Gene Grabosky**, Buffalo Bills	.45	.20	.04
☐	80 **Lou Rymkus COACH**, Houston Oilers	.60	.28	.06
☐	81 **Chris Burford**, Dallas Texans	.60	.28	.06
☐	82 **Don Allen**, Denver Broncos	.45	.20	.04
☐	83 **Bob Nelson**, Oakland Raiders	.45	.20	.04
☐	84 **Jim Woodard**, Oakland Raiders	.45	.20	.04
☐	85 **Tom Rychlec**, Buffalo Bills	.45	.20	.04
☐	86 **Bob Cox**, Boston Patriots	.45	.20	.04
☐	87 **Jerry Cornelison**, Dallas Texans	.45	.20	.04
☐	88 **Jack Work**, Denver Broncos	.45	.20	.04
☐	89 **Sam DeLuca**, Boston Patriots	.45	.20	.04
☐	90 **Rommie Loudd**, Los Angeles Chargers	.45	.20	.04
☐	91 **Teddy Edmondson**, New York Titans	.45	.20	.04
☐	92 **Buster Ramsey COACH**, Buffalo Bills	.60	.28	.06
☐	93 **Doug Asad**, Oakland Raiders	.45	.20	.04
☐	94 **Jimmy Harris**, Dallas Texans	.45	.20	.04
☐	95 **Larry Cundiff**, Denver Broncos	.45	.20	.04
☐	96 **Richie Lucas**, Buffalo Bills	.75	.35	.07
☐	97 **Don Norwood**, Boston Patriots	.45	.20	.04
☐	98 **Larry Grantham**, New York Titans	.75	.35	.07
☐	99 **Bill Mathis**, New York Titans	.60	.28	.06
☐	100 **Mel Branch**, Dallas Texans	.60	.28	.06
☐	101 **Marvin Terrell**, Dallas Texans	.45	.20	.04
☐	102 **Charlie Flowers**, Los Angeles Chargers	.60	.28	.06
☐	103 **John McMullan**, New York Titans	.45	.20	.04
☐	104 **Charlie Kaaihue**, Oakland Raiders	.45	.20	.04
☐	105 **Joe Schaffer**, Buffalo Bills	.45	.20	.04
☐	106 **Al Day**, Denver Broncos	.45	.20	.04
☐	107 **Johnny Carson**, Houston Oilers	.45	.20	.04
☐	108 **Alan Goldstein**, Oakland Raiders	.45	.20	.04
☐	109 **Doug Cline**, Houston Oilers	.45	.20	.04
☐	110 **Al Carmichael**, Denver Broncos	.45	.20	.04
☐	111 **Bob Dee**, Boston Patriots	.45	.20	.04

		MINT	VG-E	F-G
☐ 112	**John Bredice**, New York Titans	.45	.20	.04
☐ 113	**Don Floyd**, Houston Oilers	.60	.28	.06
☐ 114	**Ronnie Cain**, Denver Broncos	.45	.20	.04
☐ 115	**Stan Flowers**, Los Angeles Chargers	.45	.20	.04
☐ 116	**Hank Stram COACH**, Dallas Texans	3.00	1.40	.30
☐ 117	**Bob Dougherty**, Oakland Raiders	.45	.20	.04
☐ 118	**Ron Mix**, Los Angeles Chargers	3.50	1.65	.35
☐ 119	**Roger Ellis**, New York Titans	.45	.20	.04
☐ 120	**Elvin Caldwell**, Boston Patriots	.45	.20	.04
☐ 121	**Bill Kimber**, Boston Patriots	.45	.20	.04
☐ 122	**Jim Matheny**, Houston Oilers	.45	.20	.04
☐ 123	**Curley Johnson**, Dallas Texans	.45	.20	.04
☐ 124	**Jack Kemp**, Los Angeles Chargers	22.00	10.00	2.20
☐ 125	**Ed Denk**, Boston Patriots	.45	.20	.04
☐ 126	**Jerry McFarland**, New York Titans	.45	.20	.04
☐ 127	**Dan Lanphear**, Houston Oilers	.45	.20	.04
☐ 128	**Paul Maguire**, Los Angeles Chargers	.90	.40	.09
☐ 129	**Ray Collins**, Dallas Texans	.45	.20	.04
☐ 130	**Ron Burton**, Boston Patriots	.60	.28	.06
☐ 131	**Eddie Erdelatz COACH**, Oakland Raiders	.60	.28	.06
☐ 132	**Ron Beagle**, Oakland Raiders	1.00	.25	.05

1961 FLEER

The 1961 Fleer set contains 220 cards. The cards measure 2½" by 3½". Most of the players are pictured in action with a background. The set contains NFL (1-132) and AFL (133-220) players. The cards are grouped alphabetically by teams. The backs are printed in black and lime green on a white card stock.

		MINT	VG-E	F-G
	COMPLETE SET	225.00	100.00	22.00
	COMMON PLAYER (1-132)	.50	.22	.05
	COMMON PLAYER (133-220)	.90	.40	.09
☐ 1	Ed Brown, Chicago Bears	1.00	.30	.05
☐ 2	Rick Casares, Chicago Bears	.80	.40	.08
☐ 3	Willie Galimore, Chicago Bears	.80	.40	.08
☐ 4	Jim Dooley, Chicago Bears	.70	.32	.07
☐ 5	Harlon Hill, Chicago Bears	.70	.32	.07
☐ 6	Stan Jones, Chicago Bears	.50	.22	.05
☐ 7	J.C. Caroline, Chicago Bears	.50	.22	.05
☐ 8	Joe Fortunato, Chicago Bears	.50	.22	.05
☐ 9	Doug Atkins, Chicago Bears	1.75	.85	.17
☐ 10	Milt Plum, Cleveland Browns	1.00	.45	.10
☐ 11	Jim Brown, Cleveland Browns	21.00	9.50	2.10
☐ 12	Bobby Mitchell, Cleveland Browns	2.50	1.15	.25
☐ 13	Ray Renfro, Cleveland Browns	.70	.32	.07
☐ 14	Gern Nagler, Cleveland Browns	.50	.22	.05
☐ 15	Jim Shofner, Cleveland Browns	.70	.32	.07
☐ 16	Vince Costello, Cleveland Browns	.50	.22	.05
☐ 17	Galen Fiss, Cleveland Browns	.50	.22	.05
☐ 18	Walt Michaels, Cleveland Browns	.80	.40	.08
☐ 19	Bob Gain, Cleveland Browns	.50	.22	.05
☐ 20	Hal Hammack, St. Louis Cardinals	.50	.22	.05
☐ 21	Frank Mestnick, St. Louis Cardinals	.50	.22	.05
☐ 22	Bobby Joe Conrad, St. Louis Cardinals	.70	.32	.07
☐ 23	John David Crow, St. Louis Cardinals	.80	.40	.08
☐ 24	Sonny Randle, St. Louis Cardinals	.70	.32	.07
☐ 25	Don Gillis, St. Louis Cardinals	.50	.22	.05
☐ 26	Jerry Norton, St. Louis Cardinals	.50	.22	.05
☐ 27	Bill Stacy, St. Louis Cardinals	.50	.22	.05
☐ 28	Leo Sugar, St. Louis Cardinals	.50	.22	.05
☐ 29	Frank Fuller, St. Louis Cardinals	.50	.22	.05
☐ 30	John Unitas, Baltimore Colts	9.00	4.25	.90
☐ 31	Alan Ameche, Baltimore Colts	1.00	.45	.10
☐ 32	Lenny Moore, Baltimore Colts	2.50	1.15	.25
☐ 33	Raymond Berry, Baltimore Colts	2.75	1.25	.27
☐ 34	Jim Mutscheller, Baltimore Colts	.50	.22	.05
☐ 35	Jim Parker, Baltimore Colts	1.75	.85	.17
☐ 36	Bill Pellington, Baltimore Colts	.50	.22	.05
☐ 37	Gino Marchetti, Baltimore Colts	2.25	1.00	.22
☐ 38	Gene Lipscomb, Baltimore Colts	1.00	.45	.10
☐ 39	Art Donovan, Baltimore Colts	1.75	.85	.17
☐ 40	Eddie LeBaron, Dallas Cowboys	1.00	.45	.10
☐ 41	Don Meredith, Dallas Cowboys	15.00	7.00	1.50
☐ 42	Don McIlhenny, Dallas Cowboys	.50	.22	.05

		MINT	VG-E	F-G
☐ 43	**L.G. Dupre**, Dallas Cowboys	.50	.22	.05
☐ 44	**Fred Dugan**, Dallas Cowboys	.50	.22	.05
☐ 45	**Bill Howton**, Dallas Cowboys	.70	.32	.07
☐ 46	**Duane Putnam**, Dallas Cowboys	.50	.22	.05
☐ 47	**Gene Cronin**, Dallas Cowboys	.50	.22	.05
☐ 48	**Jerry Tubbs**, Dallas Cowboys	.80	.40	.08
☐ 49	**Clarence Peaks**, Philadelphia Eagles	.50	.22	.05
☐ 50	**Ted Dean**, Philadelphia Eagles	.50	.22	.05
☐ 51	**Tommy McDonald**, Philadelphia Eagles	.80	.40	.08
☐ 52	**Bill Barnes**, Philadelphia Eagles	.50	.22	.05
☐ 53	**Pete Retzlaff**, Philadelphia Eagles	.70	.32	.07
☐ 54	**Bobby Walston**, Philadelphia Eagles	.50	.22	.05
☐ 55	**Chuck Bednarik**, Philadelphia Eagles	2.50	1.15	.25
☐ 56	**Maxie Baughan**, Philadelphia Eagles	.70	.32	.07
☐ 57	**Bob Pellegrini**, Philadelphia Eagles	.50	.22	.05
☐ 58	**Jesse Richardson**, Philadelphia Eagles	.50	.22	.05
☐ 59	**John Brodie**, San Francisco 49ers	4.50	2.10	.45
☐ 60	**J.D. Smith**, San Francisco 49ers	.50	.22	.05
☐ 61	**Ray Norton**, San Francisco 49ers	.50	.22	.05
☐ 62	**Monty Stickles**, San Francisco 49ers	.50	.22	.05
☐ 63	**Bob St. Clair**, San Francisco 49ers	.50	.22	.05
☐ 64	**Dave Baker**, San Francisco 49ers	.50	.22	.05
☐ 65	**Abe Woodson**, San Francisco 49ers	.50	.22	.05
☐ 66	**Matt Hazeltine**, San Francisco 49ers	.50	.22	.05
☐ 67	**Leo Nomellini**, San Francisco 49ers	1.75	.85	.17
☐ 68	**Charley Conerly**, New York Giants	2.50	1.15	.25
☐ 69	**Kyle Rote**, New York Giants	2.50	1.15	.25
☐ 70	**Jack Stroud**, New York Giants	.50	.22	.05
☐ 71	**Roosevelt Brown**, New York Giants	1.75	.85	.17
☐ 72	**Jim Patton**, New York Giants	.70	.32	.07
☐ 73	**Erich Barnes**, New York Giants	.50	.22	.05
☐ 74	**Sam Huff**, New York Giants	2.50	1.15	.25
☐ 75	**Andy Robustelli**, New York Giants	1.75	.85	.17
☐ 76	**Dick Modzelewski**, New York Giants	.50	.22	.05
☐ 77	**Roosevelt Grier**, New York Giants	1.75	.85	.17
☐ 78	**Earl Morrall**, Detroit Lions	1.50	.70	.15
☐ 79	**Jim Ninowski**, Detroit Lions	.70	.32	.07
☐ 80	**Nick Pietrosante**, Detroit Lions	.70	.32	.07
☐ 81	**Howard Cassady**, Detroit Lions	.80	.40	.08
☐ 82	**Jim Gibbons**, Detroit Lions	.50	.22	.05
☐ 83	**Gail Cogdill**, Detroit Lions	.50	.22	.05
☐ 84	**Dick Lane**, Detroit Lions	1.75	.85	.17
☐ 85	**Yale Lary**, Detroit Lions	1.75	.85	.17
☐ 86	**Joe Schmidt**, Detroit Lions	2.25	1.00	.22
☐ 87	**Darris McCord**, Detroit Lions	.50	.22	.05
☐ 88	**Bart Starr**, Green Bay Packers	7.50	3.50	.75

		MINT	VG-E	F-G
☐	89 **Jim Taylor**, Green Bay Packers	4.00	1.85	.40
☐	90 **Paul Hornung**, Green Bay Packers	6.00	2.80	.60
☐	91 **Tom Moore**, Green Bay Packers	.50	.22	.05
☐	92 **Boyd Dowler**, Green Bay Packers	.70	.32	.07
☐	93 **Max McGee**, Green Bay Packers	.70	.32	.07
☐	94 **Forrest Gregg**, Green Bay Packers	2.00	.90	.20
☐	95 **Jerry Kramer**, Green Bay Packers	1.25	.60	.12
☐	96 **Jim Ringo**, Green Bay Packers	1.75	.85	.17
☐	97 **Bill Forester**, Green Bay Packers	.80	.40	.08
☐	98 **Frank Ryan**, Los Angeles Rams	1.25	.60	.12
☐	99 **Ollie Matson**, Los Angeles Rams	2.50	1.15	.25
☐	100 **Jon Arnett**, Los Angeles Rams	.80	.40	.08
☐	101 **Dick Bass**, Los Angeles Rams	.70	.32	.07
☐	102 **Jim Phillips**, Los Angeles Rams	.50	.22	.05
☐	103 **Del Shofner**, Los Angeles Rams	.80	.40	.08
☐	104 **Art Hunter**, Los Angeles Rams	.50	.22	.05
☐	105 **Lindon Crow**, Los Angeles Rams	.50	.22	.05
☐	106 **Les Richter**, Los Angeles Rams	.60	.28	.06
☐	107 **Lou Michaels**, Los Angeles Rams	.60	.28	.06
☐	108 **Ralph Guglielmi**, Washington Redskins	.70	.32	.07
☐	109 **Don Bosseler**, Washington Redskins	.50	.22	.05
☐	110 **John Olszewski**, Washington Redskins	.50	.22	.05
☐	111 **Bill Anderson**, Washington Redskins	.50	.22	.05
☐	112 **Joe Walton**, Washington Redskins	.80	.40	.08
☐	113 **Jim Schrader**, Washington Redskins	.50	.22	.05
☐	114 **Gary Glick**, Washington Redskins	.50	.22	.05
☐	115 **Ralph Felton**, Washington Redskins	.50	.22	.05
☐	116 **Bob Toneff**, Washington Redskins	.50	.22	.05
☐	117 **Bobby Layne**, Pittsburgh Steelers	7.00	3.25	.70
☐	118 **John Henry Johnson**, Pittsburgh Steelers	1.25	.60	.12
☐	119 **Tom Tracy**, Pittsburgh Steelers	.60	.28	.06
☐	120 **Jimmy Orr**, Pittsburgh Steelers	.70	.32	.07
☐	121 **John Nisby**, Pittsburgh Steelers	.50	.22	.05
☐	122 **Dean Derby**, Pittsburgh Steelers	.50	.22	.05
☐	123 **John Reger**, Pittsburgh Steelers	.50	.22	.05
☐	124 **George Tarasovic**, Pittsburgh Steelers	.50	.22	.05
☐	125 **Ernie Stautner**, Pittsburgh Steelers	2.25	1.00	.22
☐	126 **George Shaw**, Minnesota Vikings	.70	.32	.07
☐	127 **Hugh McElhenny**, Minnesota Vikings	2.50	1.15	.25
☐	128 **Dick Haley**, Minnesota Vikings	.50	.22	.05
☐	129 **Dave Middleton**, Minnesota Vikings	.50	.22	.05
☐	130 **Perry Richards**, Minnesota Vikings	.50	.22	.05
☐	131 **Gene Johnson**, Minnesota Vikings	.50	.22	.05
☐	132 **Don Joyce**, Minnesota Vikings	.50	.22	.05
☐	133 **John Chuck Green**, Buffalo Bills	.90	.40	.09
☐	134 **Wray Carlton**, Buffalo Bills	.90	.40	.09

		MINT	VG-E	F-G
☐ 135	**Richie Lucas,** Buffalo Bills	1.25	.60	.12
☐ 136	**Elbert Dubenion,** Buffalo Bills	1.25	.60	.12
☐ 137	**Tom Rychlec,** Buffalo Bills	.90	.40	.09
☐ 138	**Mack Yoho,** Buffalo Bills	.90	.40	.09
☐ 139	**Phil Blazer,** Buffalo Bills	.90	.40	.09
☐ 140	**Dan McGrew,** Buffalo Bills	.90	.40	.09
☐ 141	**Bill Atkins,** Buffalo Bills	.90	.40	.09
☐ 142	**Archie Matsos,** Buffalo Bills	.90	.40	.09
☐ 143	**Gene Grabosky,** Buffalo Bills	.90	.40	.09
☐ 144	**Frank Tripucka,** Denver Broncos	1.25	.60	.12
☐ 145	**Al Carmichael,** Denver Broncos	.90	.40	.09
☐ 146	**Bob McNamara,** Denver Broncos	.90	.40	.09
☐ 147	**Lionel Taylor,** Denver Broncos	2.00	.90	.20
☐ 148	**Eldon Danenhauer,** Denver Broncos	.90	.40	.09
☐ 149	**Willie Smith,** Denver Broncos	.90	.40	.09
☐ 150	**Carl Larpenter,** Denver Broncos	.90	.40	.09
☐ 151	**Ken Adamson,** Denver Broncos	.90	.40	.09
☐ 152	**Goose Gonsoulin,** Denver Broncos	.90	.40	.09
☐ 153	**Joe Young,** Denver Broncos	.90	.40	.09
☐ 154	**Gordy Molz,** Denver Broncos	.90	.40	.09
☐ 155	**Jack Kemp,** San Diego Chargers	13.00	6.00	1.30
☐ 156	**Charlie Flowers,** San Diego Chargers	.90	.40	.09
☐ 157	**Paul Lowe,** San Diego Chargers	2.00	.90	.20
☐ 158	**Don Norton,** San Diego Chargers	.90	.40	.09
☐ 159	**Howard Clark,** San Diego Chargers	.90	.40	.09
☐ 160	**Paul Maguire,** San Diego Chargers	1.25	.60	.12
☐ 161	**Ernie Wright,** San Diego Chargers	.90	.40	.09
☐ 162	**Ron Mix,** San Diego Chargers	3.00	1.40	.30
☐ 163	**Fred Cole,** San Diego Chargers	.90	.40	.09
☐ 164	**Jim Sears,** San Diego Chargers	.90	.40	.09
☐ 165	**Volney Peters,** San Diego Chargers	.90	.40	.09
☐ 166	**George Blanda,** Houston Oilers	8.00	3.75	.80
☐ 167	**Jacky Lee,** Houston Oilers	1.25	.60	.12
☐ 168	**Bob White,** Houston Oilers	.90	.40	.09
☐ 169	**Doug Cline,** Houston Oilers	.90	.40	.09
☐ 170	**Dave Smith,** Houston Oilers	.90	.40	.09
☐ 171	**Billy Cannon,** Houston Oilers	2.00	.90	.20
☐ 172	**Bill Groman,** Houston Oilers	1.25	.60	.12
☐ 173	**Al Jamison,** Houston Oilers	.90	.40	.09
☐ 174	**Jim Norton,** Houston Oilers	.90	.40	.09
☐ 175	**Dennit Morris,** Houston Oilers	.90	.40	.09
☐ 176	**Don Floyd,** Houston Oilers	.90	.40	.09
☐ 177	**Butch Songin,** Boston Patriots	.90	.40	.09
☐ 178	**Ron Burton,** Boston Patriots	1.25	.60	.12
☐ 179	**Billy Lott,** Boston Patriots	.90	.40	.09
☐ 180	**Jim Colclough,** Boston Patriots	.90	.40	.09

		MINT	VG-E	F-G
☐ 181	**Charley Leo,** Boston Patriots	.90	.40	.09
☐ 182	**Walt Cudzik,** Boston Patriots	.90	.40	.09
☐ 183	**Fred Bruney,** Boston Patriots	.90	.40	.09
☐ 184	**Ross O'Hanley,** Boston Patriots	.90	.40	.09
☐ 185	**Tony Sardisco,** Boston Patriots	.90	.40	.09
☐ 186	**Harry Jacobs,** Boston Patriots	.90	.40	.09
☐ 187	**Bob Dee,** Boston Patriots	.90	.40	.09
☐ 188	**Tom Flores,** Oakland Raiders	2.50	1.15	.25
☐ 189	**Jack Larsheid,** Oakland Raiders	.90	.40	.09
☐ 190	**Dick Christy,** Oakland Raiders	.90	.40	.09
☐ 191	**Alan Miller,** Oakland Raiders	.90	.40	.09
☐ 192	**Jim Smith,** Oakland Raiders	.90	.40	.09
☐ 193	**Gerald Burch,** Oakland Raiders	.90	.40	.09
☐ 194	**Gene Prebola,** Oakland Raiders	.90	.40	.09
☐ 195	**Alan Goldstein,** Oakland Raiders	.90	.40	.09
☐ 196	**Don Manoukian,** Oakland Raiders	.90	.40	.09
☐ 197	**Jim Otto,** Oakland Raiders	5.00	2.35	.50
☐ 198	**Wayne Crow,** Oakland Raiders	.90	.40	.09
☐ 199	**Cotton Davidson,** Dallas Texans	1.25	.60	.12
☐ 200	**Randy Duncan,** Dallas Texans	1.25	.60	.12
☐ 201	**Jack Spikes,** Dallas Texans	.90	.40	.09
☐ 202	**Johnny Robinson,** Dallas Texans	1.50	.70	.15
☐ 203	**Abner Haynes,** Dallas Texans	2.00	.90	.20
☐ 204	**Chris Burford,** Dallas Texans	.90	.40	.09
☐ 205	**Bill Krisher,** Dallas Texans	.90	.40	.09
☐ 206	**Marvin Terrell,** Dallas Texans	.90	.40	.09
☐ 207	**Jimmy Harris,** Dallas Texans	.90	.40	.09
☐ 208	**Mel Branch,** Dallas Texans	.90	.40	.09
☐ 209	**Paul Miller,** Dallas Texans	.90	.40	.09
☐ 210	**Al Dorow,** New York Titans	.90	.40	.09
☐ 211	**Dick Jamieson,** New York Titans	.90	.40	.09
☐ 212	**Pete Hart,** New York Titans	.90	.40	.09
☐ 213	**Bill Shockley,** New York Titans	.90	.40	.09
☐ 214	**Dewey Bohling,** New York Titans	.90	.40	.09
☐ 215	**Don Maynard,** New York Titans	5.00	2.35	.50
☐ 216	**Bob Mischak,** New York Titans	.90	.40	.09
☐ 217	**Mike Hudock,** New York Titans	.90	.40	.09
☐ 218	**Bob Reifsnyder,** New York Titans	.90	.40	.09
☐ 219	**Tom Saidock,** New York Titans	.90	.40	.09
☐ 220	**Sid Youngelman,** New York Titans	1.50	.50	.10

1962 FLEER

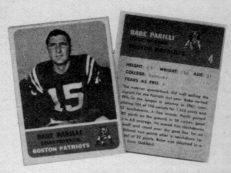

The 1962 Fleer set contains 88 cards featuring AFL players only. The cards measure 2 ½" by 3 ½". The card backs are printed in black and blue on a white card stock.

		MINT	VG-E	F-G
	COMPLETE SET	90.00	40.00	8.00
	COMMON PLAYER (1-88)	.70	.32	.07
☐ 1	**Billy Lott**, Boston Patriots	1.50	.40	.10
☐ 2	**Ron Burton**, Boston Patriots	1.00	.45	.10
☐ 3	**Gino Cappelletti**, Boston Patriots	2.00	.90	.20
☐ 4	**Babe Parilli**, Boston Patriots	1.50	.70	.15
☐ 5	**Jim Colclough**, Boston Patriots	.70	.32	.07
☐ 6	**Tony Sardisco**, Boston Patriots	.70	.32	.07
☐ 7	**Walt Cudzik**, Boston Patriots	.70	.32	.07
☐ 8	**Bob Dee**, Boston Patriots	.70	.32	.07
☐ 9	**Tommy Addison**, Boston Patriots	.70	.32	.07
☐ 10	**Harry Jacobs**, Boston Patriots	.70	.32	.07
☐ 11	**Ross O'Hanley**, Boston Patriots	.70	.32	.07
☐ 12	**Art Baker**, Buffalo Bills	.70	.32	.07
☐ 13	**John Chuck Green**, Buffalo Bills	.70	.32	.07
☐ 14	**Elbert Dubenion**, Buffalo Bills	1.00	.45	.10
☐ 15	**Tom Rychlec**, Buffalo Bills	.70	.32	.07
☐ 16	**Billy Shaw**, Buffalo Bills	.70	.32	.07
☐ 17	**Ken Rice**, Buffalo Bills	.70	.32	.07
☐ 18	**Bill Atkins**, Buffalo Bills	.70	.32	.07
☐ 19	**Richie Lucas**, Buffalo Bills	1.00	.45	.10
☐ 20	**Archie Matsos**, Buffalo Bills	.70	.32	.07

		MINT	VG-E	F-G
☐ 21	**Lavern Torczon,** Buffalo Bills	.70	.32	.07
☐ 22	**Warren Raab,** Buffalo Bills	.70	.32	.07
☐ 23	**Jack Spikes,** Dallas Texans	.70	.32	.07
☐ 24	**Cotton Davidson,** Dallas Texans	1.00	.45	.10
☐ 25	**Abner Haynes,** Dallas Texans	2.00	.90	.20
☐ 26	**Jimmy Saxton,** Dallas Texans	1.00	.45	.10
☐ 27	**Chris Burford,** Dallas Texans	1.00	.45	.10
☐ 28	**Bill Miller,** Dallas Texans	.70	.32	.07
☐ 29	**Sherrill Headrick,** Dallas Texans	1.00	.45	.10
☐ 30	**E.J. Holub,** Dallas Texans	1.00	.45	.10
☐ 31	**Jerry Mays,** Dallas Texans	.70	.32	.07
☐ 32	**Mel Branch,** Dallas Texans	.70	.32	.07
☐ 33	**Paul Rochester,** Dallas Texans	.70	.32	.07
☐ 34	**Frank Tripucka,** Denver Broncos	1.00	.45	.10
☐ 35	**Gene Mingo,** Denver Broncos	.70	.32	.07
☐ 36	**Lionel Taylor,** Denver Broncos	1.50	.70	.15
☐ 37	**Ken Adamson,** Denver Broncos	.70	.32	.07
☐ 38	**Eldon Danehauer,** Denver Broncos	.70	.32	.07
☐ 39	**Goose Gonsoulin,** Denver Broncos	.70	.32	.07
☐ 40	**Gordy Holz,** Denver Broncos	.70	.32	.07
☐ 41	**Bud McFadin,** Denver Broncos	.70	.32	.07
☐ 42	**Jim Stinnette,** Denver Broncos	.70	.32	.07
☐ 43	**Bob Hudson,** Denver Broncos	.70	.32	.07
☐ 44	**George Herring,** Denver Broncos	.70	.32	.07
☐ 45	**Charley Tolar,** Houston Oilers	.70	.32	.07
☐ 46	**George Blanda,** Houston Oilers	8.00	3.75	.80
☐ 47	**Billy Cannon,** Houston Oilers	2.00	.90	.20
☐ 48	**Charlie Hennigan,** Houston Oilers	1.25	.60	.12
☐ 49	**Bill Groman,** Houston Oilers	1.00	.45	.10
☐ 50	**Al Jamison,** Houston Oilers	.70	.32	.07
☐ 51	**Tony Banfield,** Houston Oilers	.70	.32	.07
☐ 52	**Jim Norton,** Houston Oilers	.70	.32	.07
☐ 53	**Dennit Morris,** Houston Oilers	.70	.32	.07
☐ 54	**Don Floyd,** Houston Oilers	.70	.32	.07
☐ 55	**Ed Husmann,** Houston Oilers	.70	.32	.07
☐ 56	**Robert Brooks,** New York Titans	.70	.32	.07
☐ 57	**Al Dorow,** New York Titans	.70	.32	.07
☐ 58	**Dick Christy,** New York Titans	.70	.32	.07
☐ 59	**Don Maynard,** New York Titans	3.50	1.65	.35
☐ 60	**Art Powell,** New York Titans	1.00	.45	.10
☐ 61	**Mike Hudock,** New York Titans	.70	.32	.07
☐ 62	**Bill Mathis,** New York Titans	.70	.32	.07
☐ 63	**Butch Songin,** New York Titans	1.00	.45	.10
☐ 64	**Larry Grantham,** New York Titans	1.00	.45	.10
☐ 65	**Nick Mumley,** New York Titans	.70	.32	.07
☐ 66	**Tom Saidock,** New York Titans	.70	.32	.07

		MINT	VG-E	F-G
☐ 67	**Alan Miller,** Oakland Raiders	.70	.32	.07
☐ 68	**Tom Flores,** Oakland Raiders	1.75	.85	.17
☐ 69	**Bob Coolbaugh,** Oakland Raiders	.70	.32	.07
☐ 70	**George Fleming,** Oakland Raiders	.70	.32	.07
☐ 71	**Wayne Hawkins,** Oakland Raiders	.70	.32	.07
☐ 72	**Jim Otto,** Oakland Raiders	3.50	1.65	.35
☐ 73	**Wayne Crow,** Oakland Raiders	.70	.32	.07
☐ 74	**Fred Williamson,** Oakland Raiders	1.75	.85	.17
☐ 75	**Tom Louderback,** Oakland Raiders	.70	.32	.07
☐ 76	**Vol Peters,** Oakland Raiders	.70	.32	.07
☐ 77	**Charley Powell,** Oakland Raiders	.70	.32	.07
☐ 78	**Don Norton,** San Diego Chargers	.70	.32	.07
☐ 79	**Jack Kemp,** San Diego Chargers	12.00	5.50	1.20
☐ 80	**Paul Lowe,** San Diego Chargers	1.75	.85	.17
☐ 81	**Dave Kocourek,** San Diego Chargers	.70	.32	.07
☐ 82	**Ron Mix,** San Diego Chargers	3.00	1.40	.30
☐ 83	**Ernie Wright,** San Diego Chargers	.70	.32	.07
☐ 84	**Dick Harris,** San Diego Chargers	.70	.32	.07
☐ 85	**Bill Hudson,** San Diego Chargers	.70	.32	.07
☐ 86	**Ernie Ladd,** San Diego Chargers	1.75	.85	.17
☐ 87	**Earl Faison,** San Diego Chargers	.70	.32	.07
☐ 88	**Ron Nery,** San Diego Chargers	1.00	.40	.10

1963 FLEER

The 1963 Fleer set of 88 cards features AFL players only. Cards number 6 and 64 are more difficult to obtain than the other cards in the set; their shortage is believed to be attributable to their possible replacement on the printing sheet by the unnum-

bered checklist. The cards measure 2 ½" by 3 ½". The card backs are printed in red and black on a white card stock. The set price below does not include the checklist card.

		MINT	VG-E	F-G
	COMPLETE SET	250.00	110.00	25.00
	COMMON PLAYER (1-88)	1.50	.70	.15
☐ 1	**Larry Garron**, Boston Patriots	2.25	.75	.15
☐ 2	**Babe Parilli**, Boston Patriots	2.50	1.15	.25
☐ 3	**Ron Burton**, Boston Patriots	1.75	.85	.17
☐ 4	**Jim Colclough**, Boston Patriots	1.50	.70	.15
☐ 5	**Gino Cappelletti**, Boston Patriots	2.00	.90	.20
☐ 6	**Charles Long SP**, Boston Patriots	20.00	9.00	2.00
☐ 7	**Bill Neighbors**, Boston Patriots	1.75	.85	.17
☐ 8	**Dick Felt**, Boston Patriots	1.50	.70	.15
☐ 9	**Tommy Addison**, Boston Patriots	1.50	.70	.15
☐ 10	**Nick Buoniconti**, Boston Patriots	6.50	3.00	.65
☐ 11	**Larry Eisenhauer**, Boston Patriots	1.75	.85	.17
☐ 12	**Bill Mathis**, New York Titans	1.75	.85	.17
☐ 13	**Lee Grosscup**, New York Titans	2.00	.90	.20
☐ 14	**Dick Christy**, New York Titans	1.50	.70	.15
☐ 15	**Don Maynard**, New York Titans	5.50	2.60	.55
☐ 16	**Alex Kroll**, New York Titans	1.50	.70	.15
☐ 17	**Bob Mischak**, New York Titans	1.50	.70	.15
☐ 18	**Dainard Paulson**, New York Titans	1.50	.70	.15
☐ 19	**Lee Riley**, New York Titans	1.50	.70	.15
☐ 20	**Larry Grantham**, New York Titans	1.75	.85	.17
☐ 21	**Hubert Bob**, New York Titans	1.50	.70	.15
☐ 22	**Nick Mumley**, New York Titans	1.50	.70	.15
☐ 23	**Cookie Gilchrist**, Buffalo Bills	3.00	1.40	.30
☐ 24	**Jack Kemp**, Buffalo Bills	20.00	9.00	2.00
☐ 25	**Wray Carlton**, Buffalo Bills	1.75	.85	.17
☐ 26	**Elbert Dubenion**, Buffalo Bills	2.00	.90	.20
☐ 27	**Ernie Warlick**, Buffalo Bills	1.50	.70	.15
☐ 28	**Billy Shaw**, Buffalo Bills	1.50	.70	.15
☐ 29	**Ken Rice**, Buffalo Bills	1.50	.70	.15
☐ 30	**Booker Edgerson**, Buffalo Bills	1.50	.70	.15
☐ 31	**Ray Abbruzzese**, Buffalo Bills	1.50	.70	.15
☐ 32	**Mike Stratton**, Buffalo Bills	1.50	.70	.15
☐ 33	**Tom Sestak**, Buffalo Bills	1.50	.70	.15
☐ 34	**Charley Tolar**, Houston Oilers	1.50	.70	.15
☐ 35	**Dave Smith**, Houston Oilers	1.50	.70	.15
☐ 36	**George Blanda**, Houston Oilers	9.00	4.25	.90
☐ 37	**Billy Cannon**, Houston Oilers	2.50	1.15	.25
☐ 38	**Charlie Hennigan**, Houston Oilers	2.00	.90	.20
☐ 39	**Bob Talamini**, Houston Oilers	1.50	.70	.15

	MINT	VG-E	F-G
☐ 40 **Jim Norton**, Houston Oilers	1.50	.70	.15
☐ 41 **Tony Banfield**, Houston Oilers	1.75	.85	.17
☐ 42 **Doug Cline**, Houston Oilers	1.50	.70	.15
☐ 43 **Don Floyd**, Houston Oilers	1.75	.85	.17
☐ 44 **Ed Husmann**, Houston Oilers	1.50	.70	.15
☐ 45 **Curtis McClinton**, Kansas City Chiefs	2.50	1.15	.25
☐ 46 **Jack Spikes**, Kansas City Chiefs	1.75	.85	.17
☐ 47 **Len Dawson**, Kansas City Chiefs	12.50	5.75	1.25
☐ 48 **Abner Haynes**, Kansas City Chiefs	2.25	1.00	.22
☐ 49 **Chris Burford**, Kansas City Chiefs	1.75	.85	.17
☐ 50 **Fred Arbanas**, Kansas City Chiefs	1.75	.85	.17
☐ 51 **Johnny Robinson**, Kansas City Chiefs	2.25	1.00	.22
☐ 52 **E.J. Holub**, Kansas City Chiefs	1.75	.85	.17
☐ 53 **Sherrill Headrick**, Kansas City Chiefs	1.75	.85	.17
☐ 54 **Mel Branch**, Kansas City Chiefs	1.75	.85	.17
☐ 55 **Jerry Mays**, Kansas City Chiefs	1.75	.85	.17
☐ 56 **Cotton Davidson**, Oakland Raiders	2.00	.90	.20
☐ 57 **Clem Daniels**, Oakland Raiders	2.00	.90	.20
☐ 58 **Bo Roberson**, Oakland Raiders	1.50	.70	.15
☐ 59 **Art Powell**, Oakland Raiders	1.75	.85	.17
☐ 60 **Bob Coolbaugh**, Oakland Raiders	1.50	.70	.15
☐ 61 **Wayne Hawkins**, Oakland Raiders	1.50	.70	.15
☐ 62 **Jim Otto**, Oakland Raiders	5.50	2.60	.55
☐ 63 **Fred Williamson**, Oakland Raiders	2.00	.90	.20
☐ 64 **Bob Dougherty SP**, Oakland Raiders	30.00	14.00	3.00
☐ 65 **Dalva Allen**, Oakland Raiders	1.50	.70	.15
☐ 66 **Chuck McMutry**, Oakland Raiders	1.50	.70	.15
☐ 67 **Gerry McDougall**, San Diego Chargers	1.50	.70	.15
☐ 68 **Tobin Rote**, San Diego Chargers	2.25	1.00	.22
☐ 69 **Paul Lowe**, San Diego Chargers	2.25	1.00	.22
☐ 70 **Keith Lincoln**, San Diego Chargers	3.00	1.40	.30
☐ 71 **Dave Kocourek**, San Diego Chargers	1.50	.70	.15
☐ 72 **Lance Alworth**, San Diego Chargers	10.00	4.75	1.00
☐ 73 **Ron Mix**, San Diego Chargers	4.00	1.85	.40
☐ 74 **Charles McNeil**, San Diego Chargers	1.50	.70	.15
☐ 75 **Emil Karas**, San Diego Chargers	1.50	.70	.15
☐ 76 **Ernie Ladd**, San Diego Chargers	3.00	1.40	.30
☐ 77 **Earl Faison**, San Diego Chargers	1.50	.70	.15
☐ 78 **Jim Stinnette**, Denver Broncos	1.50	.70	.15
☐ 79 **Frank Tripucka**, Denver Broncos	1.75	.85	.17
☐ 80 **Don Stone**, Denver Broncos	1.50	.70	.15
☐ 81 **Bob Scarpitto**, Denver Broncos	1.50	.70	.15
☐ 82 **Lionel Taylor**, Denver Broncos	2.25	1.00	.22
☐ 83 **Jerry Tarr**, Denver Broncos	1.50	.70	.15
☐ 84 **Eldon Danehauer**, Denver Broncos	1.75	.85	.17
☐ 85 **Goose Gonsoulin**, Denver Broncos	1.75	.85	.17

		MINT	VG-E	F-G
☐ 86	**Jim Fraser,** Denver Broncos	1.50	.70	.15
☐ 87	**Chuck Gavin,** Denver Broncos	1.50	.70	.15
☐ 88	**Bud McFadin,** Denver Broncos	2.25	.75	.15
☐ 89	**Unnumbered Checklist**	40.00	10.00	2.00

1964 PHILADELPHIA

The 1964 Philadelphia Gum set of 198 cards, featuring National Football League players, is the first of four annual issues released by the company. The cards measure 2½" by 3½". Each player card has a question about that player in a cartoon at the bottom of the reverse; the answer is given upside down in blue ink. Each team has a team picture card as well as a card diagramming one of the team's plays; this "play card" shows a small black and white picture of the team's coach on the front of the card. The card backs are printed in blue and black on a gray card stock.

		MINT	VG-E	F-G
	COMPLETE SET	165.00	75.00	15.00
	COMMON PLAYER (1-198)	.40	.18	.04
☐ 1	**Raymond Berry,** Baltimore Colts	3.25	1.00	.20
☐ 2	**Tom Gilburg,** Baltimore Colts	.40	.18	.04
☐ 3	**John Mackey,** Baltimore Colts	1.75	.85	.17
☐ 4	**Gino Marchetti,** Baltimore Colts	1.75	.85	.17
☐ 5	**Jim Martin,** Baltimore Colts	.40	.18	.04
☐ 6	**Tom Matte,** Baltimore Colts	.65	.30	.06
☐ 7	**Jimmy Orr,** Baltimore Colts	.50	.22	.05

		MINT	VG-E	F-G
☐	8 Jim Parker, Baltimore Colts	1.75	.85	.17
☐	9 Bill Pellington, Baltimore Colts	.40	.18	.04
☐	10 Alex Sandusky, Baltimore Colts	.40	.18	.04
☐	11 Dick Szymanski, Baltimore Colts	.40	.18	.04
☐	12 John Unitas, Baltimore Colts	8.00	3.75	.80
☐	13 Baltimore Colts Team Card	1.25	.60	.12
☐	14 Baltimore Colts Play Card			
	(Don Shula)	1.25	.60	.12
☐	15 Doug Atkins, Chicago Bears	1.50	.70	.15
☐	16 Ron Bull, Chicago Bears	.50	.22	.05
☐	17 Mike Ditka, Chicago Bears	2.00	.90	.20
☐	18 Joe Fortunato, Chicago Bears	.50	.22	.05
☐	19 Willie Galimore, Chicago Bears	.50	.22	.05
☐	20 Joe Marconi, Chicago Bears	.40	.18	.04
☐	21 Bennie McRae, Chicago Bears	.40	.18	.04
☐	22 Johnny Morris, Chicago Bears	.60	.28	.06
☐	23 Richie Petitbon, Chicago Bears	.50	.22	.05
☐	24 Mike Pyle, Chicago Bears	.40	.18	.04
☐	25 Roosevelt Taylor, Chicago Bears	.50	.22	.05
☐	26 Bill Wade, Chicago Bears	.65	.30	.06
☐	27 Chicago Bears Team Card	1.00	.45	.10
☐	28 Chicago Bears Play Card			
	(George Halas)	.75	.35	.07
☐	29 Johnny Brewer, Cleveland Browns	.50	.22	.05
☐	30 Jim Brown, Cleveland Browns	20.00	9.00	2.00
☐	31 Gary Collins, Cleveland Browns	.60	.28	.06
☐	32 Vince Costello, Cleveland Browns	.40	.18	.04
☐	33 Galen Fiss, Cleveland Browns	.40	.18	.04
☐	34 Bill Glass, Cleveland Browns	.60	.28	.06
☐	35 Ernie Green, Cleveland Browns	.50	.22	.05
☐	36 Rich Kreitling, Cleveland Browns	.40	.18	.04
☐	37 John Morrow, Cleveland Browns	.40	.18	.04
☐	38 Frank Ryan, Cleveland Browns	1.00	.45	.10
☐	39 Charlie Scales, Cleveland Browns	.50	.22	.05
☐	40 Dick Schafrath, Cleveland Browns	.50	.22	.05
☐	41 Cleveland Browns Team Card	1.00	.45	.10
☐	42 Cleveland Browns Play Card			
	(Blanton Collier)	.60	.28	.06
☐	43 Don Bishop, Dallas Cowboys	.50	.22	.05
☐	44 Frank Clarke, Dallas Cowboys	.75	.35	.07
☐	45 Mike Connelly, Dallas Cowboys	.50	.22	.05
☐	46 Lee Folkins, Dallas Cowboys	.50	.22	.05
☐	47 Cornell Green, Dallas Cowboys	.75	.35	.07
☐	48 Bob Lilly, Dallas Cowboys	3.00	1.40	.30
☐	49 Amos Marsh, Dallas Cowboys	.50	.22	.05
☐	50 Tommy McDonald, Dallas Cowboys	.75	.35	.07

		MINT	VG-E	F-G
☐ 51	**Don Meredith,** Dallas Cowboys	6.50	3.00	.65
☐ 52	**Pettis Norman,** Dallas Cowboys	.50	.22	.05
☐ 53	**Don Perkins,** Dallas Cowboys	1.25	.60	.12
☐ 54	**Guy Reese,** Dallas Cowboys	.50	.22	.05
☐ 55	**Dallas Cowboys Team Card**	1.25	.60	.12
☐ 56	**Dallas Cowboys Play Card (Tom Landry)**	.90	.40	.09
☐ 57	**Terry Barr,** Detroit Lions	.40	.18	.04
☐ 58	**Roger Brown,** Detroit Lions	.50	.22	.05
☐ 59	**Gail Cogdill,** Detroit Lions	.40	.18	.04
☐ 60	**John Gordy,** Detroit Lions	.40	.18	.04
☐ 61	**Dick Lane,** Detroit Lions	1.50	.70	.15
☐ 62	**Yale Lary,** Detroit Lions	1.50	.70	.15
☐ 63	**Dan Lewis,** Detroit Lions	.40	.18	.04
☐ 64	**Darris McCord,** Detroit Lions	.40	.18	.04
☐ 65	**Earl Morrall,** Detroit Lions	1.25	.60	.12
☐ 66	**Joe Schmidt,** Detroit Lions	1.75	.85	.17
☐ 67	**Pat Studstill,** Detroit Lions	.60	.28	.06
☐ 68	**Wayne Walker,** Detroit Lions	.60	.28	.06
☐ 69	**Detroit Lions Team Card**	1.00	.45	.10
☐ 70	**Detroit Lions Play Card (George Wilson)**	.60	.28	.06
☐ 71	**Herb Adderly,** Green Bay Packers	3.00	1.40	.30
☐ 72	**Willie Davis,** Green Bay Packers	3.00	1.40	.30
☐ 73	**Forrest Gregg,** Green Bay Packers	1.75	.85	.17
☐ 74	**Paul Hornung,** Green Bay Packers	4.50	2.10	.45
☐ 75	**Henry Jordan,** Green Bay Packers	.75	.35	.07
☐ 76	**Jerry Kramer,** Green Bay Packers	1.25	.60	.12
☐ 77	**Tom Moore,** Green Bay Packers	.50	.22	.05
☐ 78	**Jim Ringo,** Green Bay Packers	1.75	.85	.17
☐ 79	**Bart Starr,** Green Bay Packers	6.50	3.00	.65
☐ 80	**Jim Taylor,** Green Bay Packers	3.00	1.40	.30
☐ 81	**Jess Whitten ton,** Green Bay Packers	.50	.22	.05
☐ 82	**Willie Wood,** Green Bay Packers	1.50	.70	.15
☐ 83	**Green Bay Packers Team Card**	1.25	.60	.12
☐ 84	**Green Bay Packers Play Card (Vince Lombardi)**	1.50	.70	.15
☐ 85	**Jon Arnett,** Los Angeles Rams	.75	.35	.07
☐ 86	**Pervis Atkins,** Los Angeles Rams	.50	.22	.05
☐ 87	**Dick Bass,** Los Angeles Rams	.60	.28	.06
☐ 88	**Carroll Dale,** Los Angeles Rams	.50	.22	.05
☐ 89	**Roman Gabriel,** Los Angeles Rams	2.50	1.15	.25
☐ 90	**Ed Meador,** Los Angeles Rams	.60	.28	.06
☐ 91	**Merlin Olsen,** Los Angeles Rams	6.00	2.80	.60
☐ 92	**Jack Pardee,** Los Angeles Rams	1.25	.60	.12
☐ 93	**Jim Phillips,** Los Angeles Rams	.50	.22	.05

		MINT	VG-E	F-G
☐ 94	Carver Shannon, Los Angeles Rams	.40	.18	.04
☐ 95	Frank Varrichione, Los Angeles Rams	.40	.18	.04
☐ 96	Danny Villanueva, Los Angeles Rams	.40	.18	.04
☐ 97	Los Angeles Rams Team Card	1.00	.45	.10
☐ 98	Los Angeles Rams Play Card			
	(Harland Svare)	.60	.28	.06
☐ 99	Grady Alderman, Minnesota Vikings	.40	.18	.04
☐ 100	Larry Bowie, Minnesota Vikings	.40	.18	.04
☐ 101	Bill Brown, Minnesota Vikings	.60	.28	.06
☐ 102	Paul Flatley, Minnesota Vikings	.60	.28	.06
☐ 103	Rip Hawkins, Minnesota Vikings	.40	.18	.04
☐ 104	Jim Marshall, Minnesota Vikings	1.50	.70	.15
☐ 105	Tommy Mason, Minnesota Vikings	.60	.28	.06
☐ 106	Jim Prestel, Minnesota Vikings	.40	.18	.04
☐ 107	Jerry Reichow, Minnesota Vikings	.40	.18	.04
☐ 108	Ed Sharockman, Minnesota Vikings	.40	.18	.04
☐ 109	Fran Tarkenton, Minnesota Vikings	7.00	3.25	.70
☐ 110	Mick Tingelhoff, Minnesota Vikings	.80	.40	.08
☐ 111	Minnesota Vikings Team Card	1.00	.45	.10
☐ 112	Minnesota Vikings Play Card			
	(Norm Van Brocklin)	.75	.35	.07
☐ 113	Erich Barnes, New York Giants	.50	.22	.05
☐ 114	Roosevelt Brown, New York Giants	1.50	.70	.15
☐ 115	Don Chandler, New York Giants	.40	.18	.04
☐ 116	Darrell Dess, New York Giants	.40	.18	.04
☐ 117	Frank Gifford, New York Giants	11.00	5.25	1.10
☐ 118	Dick James, New York Giants	.40	.18	.04
☐ 119	Jim Katcavage, New York Giants	.40	.18	.04
☐ 120	John Lovetere, New York Giants	.40	.18	.04
☐ 121	Dick Lynch, New York Giants	.50	.22	.05
☐ 122	Jim Patton, New York Giants	.50	.22	.05
☐ 123	Del Shofner, New York Giants	.60	.28	.06
☐ 124	Y.A. Tittle, New York Giants	4.50	2.10	.45
☐ 125	New York Giants Team Card	1.00	.45	.10
☐ 126	New York Giants Play Card			
	(Allie Sherman)	.60	.28	.06
☐ 127	Sam Baker, Philadelphia Eagles	.50	.22	.05
☐ 128	Maxie Baughan, Philadelphia Eagles	.50	.22	.05
☐ 129	Tim Brown, Philadelphia Eagles	.60	.28	.06
☐ 130	Mike Clark, Philadelphia Eagles	.40	.18	.04
☐ 131	Irv Cross, Philadelphia Eagles	1.00	.45	.10
☐ 132	Ted Dean, Philadelphia Eagles	.40	.18	.04
☐ 133	Ron Goodwin, Philadelphia Eagles	.50	.22	.05
☐ 134	King Hill, Philadelphia Eagles	.60	.28	.06
☐ 135	Clarence Peaks, Philadelphia Eagles	.40	.18	.04
☐ 136	Pete Retzlaff, Philadelphia Eagles	.50	.22	.05

		MINT	VG-E	F-G
☐ 137	**Jim Schrader**, Philadelphia Eagles	.40	.18	.04
☐ 138	**Norm Snead**, Philadelphia Eagles	1.00	.45	.10
☐ 139	**Philadelphia Eagles Team Card**	1.00	.45	.10
☐ 140	**Philadelphia Eagles Play Card** (Nick Skorich)	.60	.28	.06
☐ 141	**Gary Ballman**, Pittsburgh Steelers	.60	.28	.06
☐ 142	**Charley Bradshaw**, Pittsburgh Steelers	.40	.18	.04
☐ 143	**Ed Brown**, Pittsburgh Steelers	.60	.28	.06
☐ 144	**John Henry Johnson**, Pittsburgh Steelers	1.00	.45	.10
☐ 145	**Joe Krupa**, Pittsburgh Steelers	.40	.18	.04
☐ 146	**Bill Mack**, Pittsburgh Steelers	.40	.18	.04
☐ 147	**Lou Michaels**, Pittsburgh Steelers	.50	.22	.05
☐ 148	**Buzz Nutter**, Pittsburgh Steelers	.40	.18	.04
☐ 149	**Myron Pottios**, Pittsburgh Steelers	.50	.22	.05
☐ 150	**John Reger**, Pittsburgh Steelers	.40	.18	.04
☐ 151	**Mike Sandusky**, Pittsburgh Steelers	.40	.18	.04
☐ 152	**Clendon Thomas**, Pittsburgh Steelers	.40	.18	.04
☐ 153	**Pittsburgh Steelers Team Card**	1.00	.45	.10
☐ 154	**Pittsburgh Steelers Play Card** (Buddy Parker)	.60	.28	.06
☐ 155	**Kermit Alexander**, San Francisco 49ers	.60	.28	.06
☐ 156	**Bernie Casey**, San Francisco 49ers	.75	.35	.07
☐ 157	**Dan Colchico**, San Francisco 49ers	.40	.18	.04
☐ 158	**Clyde Conner**, San Francisco 49ers	.40	.18	.04
☐ 159	**Tommy Davis**, San Francisco 49ers	.40	.18	.04
☐ 160	**Matt Hazeltine**, San Francisco 49ers	.40	.18	.04
☐ 161	**Jim Johnson**, San Francisco 49ers	.60	.28	.06
☐ 162	**Don Lisbon**, San Francisco 49ers	.40	.18	.04
☐ 163	**Lamar McHan**, San Francisco 49ers	.60	.28	.06
☐ 164	**Bob St. Clair**, San Francisco 49ers	.40	.18	.04
☐ 165	**J.D. Smith**, San Francisco 49ers	.40	.18	.04
☐ 166	**Abe Woodson**, San Francisco 49ers	.50	.22	.05
☐ 167	**San Francisco 49ers Team Card**	1.00	.45	.10
☐ 168	**San Francisco 49ers Play Card** (Red Hickey)	.75	.35	.07
☐ 169	**Garland Boyette**, St. Louis Cardinals	.40	.18	.04
☐ 170	**Bobby Joe Conrad**, St. Louis Cardinals	.60	.28	.06
☐ 171	**Bob DeMarco**, St. Louis Cardinals	.40	.18	.04
☐ 172	**Ken Gray**, St. Louis Cardinals	.40	.18	.04
☐ 173	**Jimmy Hill**, St. Louis Cardinals	.40	.18	.04
☐ 174	**Charlie Johnson**, St. Louis Cardinals	1.25	.60	.12
☐ 175	**Ernie McMillan**, St. Louis Cardinals	.40	.18	.04
☐ 176	**Dale Meinert**, St. Louis Cardinals	.40	.18	.04
☐ 177	**Luke Owens**, St. Louis Cardinals	.40	.18	.04
☐ 178	**Sonny Randle**, St. Louis Cardinals	.60	.28	.06
☐ 179	**Joe Robb**, St. Louis Cardinals	.40	.18	.04

		MINT	VG-E	F-G
☐ 180	**Bill Stacy,** St. Louis Cardinals	.40	.18	.04
☐ 181	**St. Louis Cardinal Team Card**	1.00	.45	.10
☐ 182	**St. Louis Cardinals Play Card**			
	(Wally Lemm)	.60	.28	.06
☐ 183	**Bill Barnes,** Washington Redskins	.40	.18	.04
☐ 184	**Don Bosseler,** Washington Redskins	.40	.18	.04
☐ 185	**Sam Huff,** Washington Redskins	1.75	.85	.17
☐ 186	**Sonny Jurgensen,** Washington Redskins	4.50	2.10	.45
☐ 187	**Ed Khayat,** Washington Redskins	.40	.18	.04
☐ 188	**Riley Mattson,** Washington Redskins	.40	.18	.04
☐ 189	**Bobby Mitchell,** Washington Redskins	2.50	1.15	.25
☐ 190	**John Nisby,** Washington Redskins	.40	.18	.04
☐ 191	**Vince Promuto,** Washington Redskins	.40	.18	.04
☐ 192	**Joe Rutgens,** Washington Redskins	.40	.18	.04
☐ 193	**Lonnie Sanders,** Washington Redskins	.40	.18	.04
☐ 194	**Jim Steffen,** Washington Redskins	.40	.18	.04
☐ 195	**Washington Redskins Team Card**	1.00	.45	.10
☐ 196	**Washington Redskins Play Card**			
	(Bill McPeak)	.60	.28	.06
☐ 197	**Checklist 1**	4.50	1.00	.10
☐ 198	**Checklist 2**	9.00	1.50	.15

1965 PHILADELPHIA

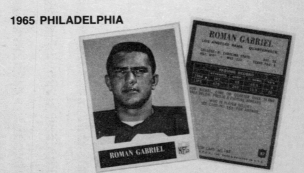

The 1965 Philadelphia Gum set of NFL players is complete at 198 cards. The cards measure 2½" by 3½". The card backs show (when rubbed with a coin) a question and answer interrelated to other cards. Each team has a team picture card as well

as a card featuring a diagram of one of the team's plays; this play card shows a small coach's picture in black and white on the front of the card. The card backs are printed in maroon on a gray card stock.

		MINT	VG-E	F-G
	COMPLETE SET	150.00	70.00	15.00
	COMMON PLAYER (1-198)	.40	.18	.04
☐ 1	Baltimore Colts Team Card	1.25	.50	.10
☐ 2	Raymond Berry, Baltimore Colts	3.00	1.40	.30
☐ 3	Bob Boyd, Baltimore Colts	.40	.18	.04
☐ 4	Wendell Harris, Baltimore Colts	.40	.18	.04
☐ 5	Jerry Logan, Baltimore Colts	.40	.18	.04
☐ 6	Tony Lorick, Baltimore Colts	.40	.18	.04
☐ 7	Lou Michaels, Baltimore Colts	.50	.22	.05
☐ 8	Lenny Moore, Baltimore Colts	2.50	1.15	.25
☐ 9	Jimmy Orr, Baltimore Colts	.60	.28	.06
☐ 10	Jim Parker, Baltimore Colts	1.50	.70	.15
☐ 11	Dick Szymanski, Baltimore Colts	.40	.18	.04
☐ 12	John Unitas, Baltimore Colts	8.00	3.75	.80
☐ 13	Bob Vogel, Baltimore Colts	.40	.18	.04
☐ 14	Baltimore Colts Play Card (Don Shula)	.90	.40	.09
☐ 15	Chicago Bears Team Card	1.00	.45	.10
☐ 16	Jon Arnett, Chicago Bears	.65	.30	.06
☐ 17	Doug Atkins, Chicago Bears	1.50	.70	.15
☐ 18	Rudy Bukich, Chicago Bears	.60	.28	.06
☐ 19	Mike Ditka, Chicago Bears	2.00	.90	.20
☐ 20	Dick Evey, Chicago Bears	.40	.18	.04
☐ 21	Joe Fortunato, Chicago Bears	.50	.22	.05
☐ 22	Bobby Joe Green, Chicago Bears	.40	.18	.04
☐ 23	Johnny Morris, Chicago Bears	.65	.30	.06
☐ 24	Mike Pyle, Chicago Bears	.40	.18	.04
☐ 25	Roosevelt Taylor, Chicago Bears	.50	.22	.05
☐ 26	Bill Wade, Chicago Bears	.60	.28	.06
☐ 27	Bob Wetoska, Chicago Bears	.40	.18	.04
☐ 28	Chicago Bears Play Card (George Halas)	.80	.40	.08
☐ 29	Cleveland Browns Team Card	1.00	.45	.10
☐ 30	Walter Beach, Cleveland Browns	.40	.18	.04
☐ 31	Jim Brown, Cleveland Browns	20.00	9.00	2.00
☐ 32	Gary Collins, Cleveland Browns	.60	.28	.06
☐ 33	Bill Glass, Cleveland Browns	.60	.28	.06
☐ 34	Ernie Green, Cleveland Browns	.50	.22	.05
☐ 35	Jim Houston, Cleveland Browns	.50	.22	.05
☐ 36	Dick Modzelewski, Cleveland Browns	.50	.22	.05
☐ 37	Bernie Parrish, Cleveland Browns	.40	.18	.04

			MINT	VG-E	F-G
☐	38	**Walter Roberts**, Cleveland Browns	.40	.18	.04
☐	39	**Frank Ryan**, Cleveland Browns	1.00	.45	.10
☐	40	**Dick Schafrath**, Cleveland Browns	.50	.22	.05
☐	41	**Paul Warfield**, Cleveland Browns	6.00	2.80	.60
☐	42	**Cleveland Browns Play Card** (Blanton Collier)	.60	.28	.06
☐	43	**Dallas Cowboys Team Card**	1.25	.60	.12
☐	44	**Frank Clarke**, Dallas Cowboys	.75	.35	.07
☐	45	**Mike Connelly**, Dallas Cowboys	.50	.22	.05
☐	46	**Buddy Dial**, Dallas Cowboys	.75	.35	.07
☐	47	**Bob Lilly**, Dallas Cowboys	2.50	1.15	.25
☐	48	**Tony Liscio**, Dallas Cowboys	.50	.22	.05
☐	49	**Tommy McDonald**, Dallas Cowboys	.75	.35	.07
☐	50	**Don Meredith**, Dallas Cowboys	6.50	3.00	.65
☐	51	**Pettis Norman**, Dallas Cowboys	.50	.22	.05
☐	52	**Don Perkins**, Dallas Cowboys	1.00	.45	.10
☐	53	**Mel Renfro**, Dallas Cowboys	2.00	.90	.20
☐	54	**Jim Ridlon**, Dallas Cowboys	.50	.22	.05
☐	55	**Jerry Tubbs**, Dallas Cowboys	.65	.30	.06
☐	56	**Dallas Cowboys Play Card** (Tom Landry)	.90	.40	.09
☐	57	**Detroit Lions Team Card**	1.00	.45	.10
☐	58	**Terry Barr**, Detroit Lions	.40	.18	.04
☐	59	**Roger Brown**, Detroit Lions	.40	.18	.04
☐	60	**Gail Cogdill**, Detroit Lions	.40	.18	.04
☐	61	**Jim Gibbons**, Detroit Lions	.40	.18	.04
☐	62	**John Gordy**, Detroit Lions	.40	.18	.04
☐	63	**Yale Lary**, Detroit Lions	1.50	.70	.15
☐	64	**Dick LeBeau**, Detroit Lions	.50	.22	.05
☐	65	**Earl Morrall**, Detroit Lions	1.25	.60	.12
☐	66	**Nick Pietrosante**, Detroit Lions	.60	.28	.06
☐	67	**Pat Studstill**, Detroit Lions	.60	.28	.06
☐	68	**Wayne Walker**, Detroit Lions	.60	.28	.06
☐	69	**Tom Watkins**, Detroit Lions	.40	.18	.04
☐	70	**Detroit Lions Play Card** (George Wilson)	.60	.28	.06
☐	71	**Green Bay Packers Team Card**	1.25	.60	.12
☐	72	**Herb Adderly**, Green Bay Packers	1.75	.85	.17
☐	73	**Willie Davis**, Green Bay Packers	1.75	.85	.17
☐	74	**Boyd Dowler**, Green Bay Packers	.60	.28	.06
☐	75	**Forrest Gregg**, Green Bay Packers	1.75	.85	.17
☐	76	**Paul Hornung**, Green Bay Packers	4.50	2.10	.45
☐	77	**Henry Jordan**, Green Bay Packers	.75	.35	.07
☐	78	**Tom Moore**, Green Bay Packers	.40	.18	.04
☐	79	**Ray Nitschke**, Green Bay Packers	2.00	.90	.20
☐	80	**Elijah Pitts**, Green Bay Packers	.40	.18	.04

		MINT	VG-E	F-G
☐ 81	**Bart Starr**, Green Bay Packers	6.50	3.00	.65
☐ 82	**Jim Taylor**, Green Bay Packers	3.00	1.40	.30
☐ 83	**Willie Wood**, Green Bay Packers	1.25	.60	.12
☐ 84	**Green Bay Packers Play Card** (Vince Lombardi)	.90	.40	.09
☐ 85	**Los Angeles Rams Team Card**	1.00	.45	.10
☐ 86	**Dick Bass**, Los Angeles Rams	.60	.28	.06
☐ 87	**Roman Gabriel**, Los Angeles Rams	2.25	1.00	.22
☐ 88	**Roosevelt Grier**, Los Angeles Rams	1.50	.70	.15
☐ 89	**Deacon Jones**, Los Angeles Rams	1.75	.85	.17
☐ 90	**Lamar Lundy**, Los Angeles Rams	.40	.18	.04
☐ 91	**Marlin McKeever**, Los Angeles Rams	.40	.18	.04
☐ 92	**Ed Meador**, Los Angeles Rams	.50	.22	.05
☐ 93	**Bill Munson**, Los Angeles Rams	.65	.30	.06
☐ 94	**Merlin Olsen**, Los Angeles Rams	2.50	1.15	.25
☐ 95	**Bobby Smith**, Los Angeles Rams	.40	.18	.04
☐ 96	**Frank Varrichione**, Los Angeles Rams	.40	.18	.04
☐ 97	**Ben Wilson**, Los Angeles Rams	.40	.18	.04
☐ 98	**Los Angeles Rams Play Card** (Harland Svare)	.60	.28	.06
☐ 99	**Minnesota Vikings Team Card**	1.00	.45	.10
☐ 100	**Grady Alderman**, Minnesota Vikings	.40	.18	.04
☐ 101	**Hal Bedsole**, Minnesota Vikings	.40	.18	.04
☐ 102	**Bill Brown**, Minnesota Vikings	.60	.28	.06
☐ 103	**Bill Butler**, Minnesota Vikings	.40	.18	.04
☐ 104	**Fred Cox**, Minnesota Vikings	1.00	.45	.10
☐ 105	**Carl Eller**, Minnesota Vikings	2.25	1.00	.22
☐ 106	**Paul Flatley**, Minnesota Vikings	.60	.28	.06
☐ 107	**Jim Marshall**, Minnesota Vikings	1.50	.70	.15
☐ 108	**Tommy Mason**, Minnesota Vikings	.60	.28	.06
☐ 109	**George Rose**, Minnesota Vikings	.40	.18	.04
☐ 110	**Fran Tarkenton**, Minnesota Vikings	7.00	3.25	.70
☐ 111	**Mick Tingelhoff**, Minnesota Vikings	.70	.32	.07
☐ 112	**Minnesota Vikings Play Card** (Norm Van Brocklin)	.70	.32	.07
☐ 113	**New York Giants Team Card**, New York Giants	1.00	.45	.10
☐ 114	**Erich Barnes**, New York Giants	.50	.22	.05
☐ 115	**Roosevelt Brown**, New York Giants	1.50	.70	.15
☐ 116	**Clarence Childs**, New York Giants	.40	.18	.04
☐ 117	**Jerry Hillebrand**, New York Giants	.40	.18	.04
☐ 118	**Greg Larson**, New York Giants	.40	.18	.04
☐ 119	**Dick Lynch**, New York Giants	.50	.22	.05
☐ 120	**Joe Morrison**, New York Giants	1.00	.45	.10
☐ 121	**Lou Slaby**, New York Giants	.40	.18	.04
☐ 122	**Aaron Thomas**, New York Giants	.40	.18	.04
☐ 123	**Steve Thurlow**, New York Giants	.40	.18	.04

		MINT	VG-E	F-G
☐ 124	Ernie Wheelwright, New York Giants	.40	.18	.04
☐ 125	Gary Wood, New York Giants	.50	.22	.05
☐ 126	New York Giants Play Card			
	(Allie Sherman)	.60	.28	.06
☐ 127	Philadelphia Eagles Team Card	1.00	.45	.10
☐ 128	Sam Baker, Philadelphia Eagles	.50	.22	.05
☐ 129	Maxie Baughan, Philadelphia Eagles	.50	.22	.05
☐ 130	Tim Brown, Philadelphia Eagles	.60	.28	.06
☐ 131	Jack Concannon, Philadelphia Eagles	.65	.30	.06
☐ 132	Irv Cross, Philadelphia Eagles	1.00	.45	.10
☐ 133	Earl Gros, Philadelphia Eagles	.40	.18	.04
☐ 134	Dave Lloyd, Philadelphia Eagles	.40	.18	.04
☐ 135	Floyd Peters, Philadelphia Eagles	.40	.18	.04
☐ 136	Nate Ramsey, Philadelphia Eagles	.40	.18	.04
☐ 137	Pete Retzlaff, Philadelphia Eagles	.50	.22	.05
☐ 138	Jim Ringo, Philadelphia Eagles	1.50	.70	.15
☐ 139	Norm Snead, Philadelphia Eagles	1.00	.45	.10
☐ 140	Philadelphia Eagles Play Card			
	(Joe Kuharich)	.60	.28	.06
☐ 141	Pittsburgh Steelers Team Card	1.00	.45	.10
☐ 142	John Baker, Pittsburgh Steelers	.40	.18	.04
☐ 143	Gary Ballman, Pittsburgh Steelers	.60	.28	.06
☐ 144	Charley Bradshaw, Pittsburgh Steelers	.40	.18	.04
☐ 145	Ed Brown, Pittsburgh Steelers	.60	.28	.06
☐ 146	Dick Haley, Pittsburgh Steelers	.40	.18	.04
☐ 147	John Henry Johnson, Pittsburgh Steelers ...	1.00	.45	.10
☐ 148	Brady Keys, Pittsburgh Steelers	.40	.18	.04
☐ 149	Ray Lemek, Pittsburgh Steelers	.40	.18	.04
☐ 150	Ben McGee, Pittsburgh Steelers	.40	.18	.04
☐ 151	Clarence Peaks, Pittsburgh Steelers	.40	.18	.04
☐ 152	Myron Pottios, Pittsburgh Steelers	.50	.22	.05
☐ 153	Clendon Thomas, Pittsburgh Steelers	.40	.18	.04
☐ 154	Pittsburgh Steelers Play Card			
	(Buddy Parker)	.60	.28	.06
☐ 155	St. Louis Cardinals Team Card	1.00	.45	.10
☐ 156	Jim Bakken, St. Louis Cardinals	1.00	.45	.10
☐ 157	Joe Childress, St. Louis Cardinals	.40	.18	.04
☐ 158	Bobby Joe Conrad, St. Louis Cardinals	.60	.28	.06
☐ 159	Bob DeMarco, St. Louis Cardinals	.40	.18	.04
☐ 160	Pat Fischer, St. Louis Cardinals	.75	.35	.07
☐ 161	Irv Goode, St. Louis Cardinals	.40	.18	.04
☐ 162	Ken Gray, St. Louis Cardinals	.40	.18	.04
☐ 163	Charlie Johnson, St. Louis Cardinals	1.25	.60	.12
☐ 164	Bill Koman, St. Louis Cardinals	.40	.18	.04
☐ 165	Dale Meinert, St. Louis Cardinals	.40	.18	.04
☐ 166	Jerry Stovall, St. Louis Cardinals	.75	.35	.07

		MINT	VG-E	F-G
☐ 167	Abe Woodson, St. Louis Cardinals	.50	.22	.05
☐ 168	St. Louis Cardinals Play Card (Wally Lemm)	.60	.28	.06
☐ 169	San Francisco 49ers Team Card	1.00	.45	.10
☐ 170	Kermit Alexander, San Francisco 49ers	.50	.22	.05
☐ 171	John Brodie, San Francisco 49ers	3.00	1.40	.30
☐ 172	Bernie Casey, San Francisco 49ers	.75	.35	.07
☐ 173	John David Crow, San Francisco 49ers	.60	.28	.06
☐ 174	Tommy Davis, San Francisco 49ers	.40	.18	.04
☐ 175	Matt Hazeltine, San Francisco 49ers	.40	.18	.04
☐ 176	Jim Johnson, San Francisco 49ers	.60	.28	.06
☐ 177	Charlie Krueger, San Francisco 49ers	.40	.18	.04
☐ 178	Roland Lakes, San Francisco 49ers	.40	.18	.04
☐ 179	George Mira, San Francisco 49ers	.90	.40	.09
☐ 180	Dave Parks, San Francisco 49ers	.60	.28	.06
☐ 181	John Thomas, San Francisco 49ers	.40	.18	.04
☐ 182	San Francisco 49ers Play Card (Jack Christiansen)	.65	.30	.06
☐ 183	Washington Redskins Team Card	1.00	.45	.10
☐ 184	Pervis Atkins, Washington Redskins	.40	.18	.04
☐ 185	Preston Carpenter, Washington Redskins	.40	.18	.04
☐ 186	Angelo Coia, Washington Redskins	.40	.18	.04
☐ 187	Sam Huff, Washington Redskins	1.75	.85	.17
☐ 188	Sonny Jurgensen, Washington Redskins	4.00	1.85	.40
☐ 189	Paul Krause, Washington Redskins	.75	.35	.07
☐ 190	Jim Martin, Washington Redskins	.40	.18	.04
☐ 191	Bobby Mitchell, Washington Redskins	2.50	1.15	.25
☐ 192	John Nisby, Washington Redskins	.40	.18	.04
☐ 193	John Paluck, Washington Redskins	.40	.18	.04
☐ 194	Vince Promuto, Washington Redskins	.40	.18	.04
☐ 195	Charley Taylor, Washington Redskins	5.00	2.35	.50
☐ 196	Washington Redskins Play Card (Bill McPeak)	.60	.28	.06
☐ 197	Checklist 1	4.50	1.00	.10
☐ 198	Checklist 2	9.00	1.50	.15

1966 PHILADELPHIA

The 1966 Philadelphia Gum football card set contains 198 cards featuring NFL players. The cards measure 2 ½" by 3 ½". The backs contain the player's name, a card number, a short biography, and a "Guess Who" quiz. The quiz answer is found on another card. The last two cards in the set are checklist cards. Each team's "play card" shows a color photo of actual game action, described on the back. The card backs are printed in green and black on a white card stock.

		MINT	VG-E	F-G
	COMPLETE SET	140.00	65.00	14.00
	COMMON PLAYER (1-198)	.35	.15	.03
☐ 1	Atlanta Falcons Insignia	1.50	.40	.10
☐ 2	Larry Benz, Atlanta Falcons	.35	.15	.03
☐ 3	Dennis Claridge, Atlanta Falcons	.35	.15	.03
☐ 4	Perry Lee Dunn, Atlanta Falcons	.35	.15	.03
☐ 5	Dan Grimm, Atlanta Falcons	.35	.15	.03
☐ 6	Alex Hawkins, Atlanta Falcons	.55	.25	.05
☐ 7	Ralph Heck, Atlanta Falcons	.35	.15	.03
☐ 8	Frank Lasky, Atlanta Falcons	.35	.15	.03
☐ 9	Guy Reese, Atlanta Falcons	.35	.15	.03
☐ 10	Bob Richards, Atlanta Falcons	.35	.15	.03
☐ 11	Ron Smith, Atlanta Falcons	.35	.15	.03
☐ 12	Ernie Wheelwright, Atlanta Falcons	.35	.15	.03
☐ 13	Atlanta Falcons Roster	.90	.40	.09
☐ 14	Baltimore Colts Team Card	1.00	.45	.10
☐ 15	Raymond Berry, Baltimore Colts	2.25	1.00	.22
☐ 16	Bob Boyd, Baltimore Colts	.35	.15	.03
☐ 17	Jerry Logan, Baltimore Colts	.35	.15	.03

		MINT	VG-E	F-G
☐	18 **John Mackey,** Baltimore Colts	.90	.40	.09
☐	19 **Tom Matte,** Baltimore Colts	.55	.25	.05
☐	20 **Lou Michaels,** Baltimore Colts	.45	.20	.04
☐	21 **Lenny Moore,** Baltimore Colts	2.00	.90	.20
☐	22 **Jimmy Orr,** Baltimore Colts	.55	.25	.05
☐	23 **Jim Parker,** Baltimore Colts	1.50	.70	.15
☐	24 **John Unitas,** Baltimore Colts	7.50	3.50	.75
☐	25 **Bob Vogel,** Baltimore Colts	.35	.15	.03
☐	26 **Baltimore Colts Play Card**	.55	.25	.05
☐	27 **Chicago Bears Team Card**	.90	.40	.09
☐	28 **Doug Atkins,** Chicago Bears	1.50	.70	.15
☐	29 **Rudy Bukich,** Chicago Bears	.65	.30	.06
☐	30 **Ron Bull,** Chicago Bears	.55	.25	.05
☐	31 **Dick Butkus,** Chicago Bears	9.00	4.25	.90
☐	32 **Mike Ditka,** Chicago Bears	1.50	.70	.15
☐	33 **Joe Fortunato,** Chicago Bears	.45	.20	.04
☐	34 **Bobby Joe Green,** Chicago Bears	.35	.15	.03
☐	35 **Roger LeClerc,** Chicago Bears	.35	.15	.03
☐	36 **Johnny Morris,** Chicago Bears	.65	.30	.06
☐	37 **Mike Pyle,** Chicago Bears	.35	.15	.03
☐	38 **Gale Sayers,** Chicago Bears	28.00	12.00	2.50
☐	39 **Chicago Bears Play Card**	.55	.25	.05
☐	40 **Cleveland Browns Team Card**	.90	.40	.09
☐	41 **Jim Brown,** Cleveland Browns	18.00	8.50	1.80
☐	42 **Gary Collins,** Cleveland Browns	.55	.25	.05
☐	43 **Ross Fichtner,** Cleveland Browns	.35	.15	.03
☐	44 **Ernie Green,** Cleveland Browns	.35	.15	.03
☐	45 **Gene Hickerson,** Cleveland Browns	.35	.15	.03
☐	46 **Jim Houston,** Cleveland Browns	.45	.20	.04
☐	47 **John Morrow,** Cleveland Browns	.35	.15	.03
☐	48 **Walter Roberts,** Cleveland Browns	.35	.15	.03
☐	49 **Frank Ryan,** Cleveland Browns	1.00	.45	.10
☐	50 **Dick Schafrath,** Cleveland Browns	.45	.20	.04
☐	51 **Paul Wiggin,** Cleveland Browns	.55	.25	.05
☐	52 **Cleveland Browns Play Card** (Ernie Green sweep)	.55	.25	.05
☐	53 **Dallas Cowboys Team Card**	1.25	.60	.12
☐	54 **George Andrie,** Dallas Cowboys	.45	.20	.04
☐	55 **Frank Clarke,** Dallas Cowboys	.65	.30	.06
☐	56 **Mike Connelly,** Dallas Cowboys	.35	.15	.03
☐	57 **Cornell Green,** Dallas Cowboys	.65	.30	.06
☐	58 **Bob Hayes,** Dallas Cowboys	1.50	.70	.15
☐	59 **Chuck Howley,** Dallas Cowboys	1.00	.45	.10
☐	60 **Bob Lilly,** Dallas Cowboys	2.25	1.00	.22
☐	61 **Don Meredith,** Dallas Cowboys	6.00	2.80	.60
☐	62 **Don Perkins,** Dallas Cowboys	.90	.40	.09

		MINT	VG-E	F-G
☐ 63	**Mel Renfro**, Dallas Cowboys	1.00	.45	.10
☐ 64	**Danny Villanueva**, Dallas Cowboys	.45	.20	.04
☐ 65	**Dallas Cowboys Play Card**	.65	.30	.06
☐ 66	**Detroit Lions Team Card**	.90	.40	.09
☐ 67	**Roger Brown**, Detroit Lions	.35	.15	.03
☐ 68	**John Gordy**, Detroit Lions	.35	.15	.03
☐ 69	**Alex Karras**, Detroit Lions	2.00	.90	.20
☐ 70	**Dick LeBeau**, Detroit Lions	.45	.20	.04
☐ 71	**Amos Marsh**, Detroit Lions	.35	.15	.03
☐ 72	**Milt Plum**, Detroit Lions	.90	.40	.09
☐ 73	**Bobby Smith**, Detroit Lions	.35	.15	.03
☐ 74	**Wayne Rasmussen**, Detroit Lions	.35	.15	.03
☐ 75	**Pat Studstill**, Detroit Lions	.55	.25	.05
☐ 76	**Wayne Walker**, Detroit Lions	.55	.25	.05
☐ 77	**Tom Watkins**, Detroit Lions	.35	.15	.03
☐ 78	**Detroit Lions Play Card** (George Izo pass)	.55	.25	.05
☐ 79	**Green Bay Packers Team Card**	1.25	.60	.12
☐ 80	**Herb Adderly**, Green Bay Packers	1.50	.70	.15
☐ 81	**Lee Roy Caffey**, Green Bay Packers	.45	.20	.04
☐ 82	**Don Chandler**, Green Bay Packers	.45	.20	.04
☐ 83	**Willie Davis**, Green Bay Packers	1.50	.70	.15
☐ 84	**Boyd Dowler**, Green Bay Packers	.55	.25	.05
☐ 85	**Forrest Gregg**, Green Bay Packers	1.50	.70	.15
☐ 86	**Tom Moore**, Green Bay Packers	.35	.15	.03
☐ 87	**Ray Nitschke**, Green Bay Packers	1.75	.85	.17
☐ 88	**Bart Starr**, Green Bay Packers	6.00	2.80	.60
☐ 89	**Jim Taylor**, Green Bay Packers	3.00	1.40	.30
☐ 90	**Willie Wood**, Green Bay Packers	1.25	.60	.12
☐ 91	**Green Bay Packers Play Card** (Don Chandler FG)	.65	.30	.06
☐ 92	**Los Angeles Rams Team Card**	.90	.40	.09
☐ 93	**Willie Brown (flanker)**, Los Angeles Rams	.35	.15	.03
☐ 94	**Dick Bass and Roman Gabriel**, Los Angeles Rams	1.50	.70	.15
☐ 95	**Bruce Gossett**, Los Angeles Rams	.45	.20	.04
☐ 96	**Deacon Jones**, Los Angeles Rams	1.75	.85	.17
☐ 97	**Tommy McDonald**, Los Angeles Rams	.55	.25	.05
☐ 98	**Marlin McKeever**, Los Angeles Rams	.35	.15	.03
☐ 99	**Aaron Martin**, Los Angeles Rams	.35	.15	.03
☐ 100	**Ed Meador**, Los Angeles Rams	.45	.20	.04
☐ 101	**Bill Munson**, Los Angeles Rams	.65	.30	.06
☐ 102	**Merlin Olsen**, Los Angeles Rams	2.50	1.15	.25
☐ 103	**Jim Stiger**, Los Angeles Rams	.35	.15	.03
☐ 104	**Los Angeles Rams Play Card** (Willie Brown run)	.55	.25	.05

		MINT	VG-E	F-G
☐ 105	**Minnesota Vikings Team Card**	.90	.40	.09
☐ 106	**Grady Alderman**, Minnesota Vikings	.35	.15	.03
☐ 107	**Bill Brown**, Minnesota Vikings	.55	.25	.05
☐ 108	**Fred Cox**, Minnesota Vikings	.55	.25	.05
☐ 109	**Paul Flatley**, Minnesota Vikings	.45	.20	.04
☐ 110	**Rip Hawkins**, Minnesota Vikings	.35	.15	.03
☐ 111	**Tommy Mason**, Minnesota Vikings	.55	.25	.05
☐ 112	**Ed Sharockman**, Minnesota Vikings	.35	.15	.03
☐ 113	**Gordon Smith**, Minnesota Vikings	.35	.15	.03
☐ 114	**Fran Tarkenton**, Minnesota Vikings	6.50	3.00	.65
☐ 115	**Mick Tingelhoff**, Minnesota Vikings	.65	.30	.06
☐ 116	**Bobby Walden**, Minnesota Vikings	.35	.15	.03
☐ 117	**Minnesota Vikings Play Card** (Bill Brown run)	.55	.25	.05
☐ 118	**New York Giants Team Card**	.90	.40	.09
☐ 119	**Roosevelt Brown**, New York Giants	1.50	.70	.15
☐ 120	**Henry Carr**, New York Giants	.45	.20	.04
☐ 121	**Clarence Childs**, New York Giants	.35	.15	.03
☐ 122	**Tucker Frederickson**, New York Giants	.65	.30	.06
☐ 123	**Jerry Hillebrand**, New York Giants	.35	.15	.03
☐ 124	**Greg Larson**, New York Giants	.35	.15	.03
☐ 125	**Carl Spider Lockhart**, New York Giants	.45	.20	.04
☐ 126	**Dick Lynch**, New York Giants	.45	.20	.04
☐ 127	**Earl Morrall & Bob Scholtz**, New York Giants	1.25	.60	.12
☐ 128	**Joe Morrison**, New York Giants	.55	.25	.05
☐ 129	**Steve Thurlow**, New York Giants	.35	.15	.03
☐ 130	**New York Giants Play Card** (Chuck Mercein over)	.55	.25	.05
☐ 131	**Philadelphia Eagles Team Card**	.90	.40	.09
☐ 132	**Sam Baker**, Philadelphia Eagles	.45	.20	.04
☐ 133	**Maxie Baughan**, Philadelphia Eagles	.45	.20	.04
☐ 134	**Bob Brown**, Philadelphia Eagles	.35	.15	.03
☐ 135	**Tim Brown**, Philadelphia Eagles	.55	.25	.05
☐ 136	**Irv Cross**, Philadelphia Eagles	.90	.40	.09
☐ 137	**Earl Gros**, Philadelphia Eagles	.35	.15	.03
☐ 138	**Ray Poage**, Philadelphia Eagles	.35	.15	.03
☐ 139	**Nate Ramsey**, Philadelphia Eagles	.35	.15	.03
☐ 140	**Pete Retzlaff**, Philadelphia Eagles	.45	.20	.04
☐ 141	**Jim Ringo**, Philadelphia Eagles	1.50	.70	.15
☐ 142	**Norm Snead**, Philadelphia Eagles	.90	.40	.09
☐ 143	**Philadelphia Eagles Play Card** (Earl Gros tackled)	.55	.25	.05
☐ 144	**Pittsburgh Steelers Team Card**	.90	.40	.09
☐ 145	**Gary Ballman**, Pittsburgh Steelers	.55	.25	.05
☐ 146	**Charley Bradshaw**, Pittsburgh Steelers	.35	.15	.03
☐ 147	**Jim Butler**, Pittsburgh Steelers	.35	.15	.03

			MINT	VG-E	F-G
☐ 148	**Mike Clark,** Pittsburgh Steelers		.35	.15	.03
☐ 149	**Dick Hoak,** Pittsburgh Steelers		.35	.15	.03
☐ 150	**Roy Jefferson,** Pittsburgh Steelers		.55	.25	.05
☐ 151	**Frank Lambert,** Pittsburgh Steelers		.35	.15	.03
☐ 152	**Mike Lind,** Pittsburgh Steelers		.35	.15	.03
☐ 153	**Bill Nelsen,** Pittsburgh Steelers		1.00	.45	.10
☐ 154	**Clarence Peaks,** Pittsburgh Steelers		.35	.15	.03
☐ 155	**Clendon Thomas,** Pittsburgh Steelers		.35	.15	.03
☐ 156	**Pittsburgh Steelers Play Card** (Gary Ballman scores)		.55	.25	.05
☐ 157	**St. Louis Cardinals Team Card**		.90	.40	.09
☐ 158	**Jim Bakken,** St. Louis Cardinals		.55	.25	.05
☐ 159	**Bobby Joe Conrad,** St. Louis Cardinals		.55	.25	.05
☐ 160	**Willis Crenshaw,** St. Louis Cardinals		.35	.15	.03
☐ 161	**Bob DeMarco,** St. Louis Cardinals		.35	.15	.03
☐ 162	**Pat Fischer,** St. Louis Cardinals		.55	.25	.05
☐ 163	**Charlie Johnson,** St. Louis Cardinals		1.00	.45	.10
☐ 164	**Dale Meinert,** St. Louis Cardinals		.35	.15	.03
☐ 165	**Sonny Randle,** St. Louis Cardinals		.55	.25	.05
☐ 166	**Sam Silas,** St. Louis Cardinals		.35	.15	.03
☐ 167	**Bill Triplett,** St. Louis Cardinals		.35	.15	.03
☐ 168	**Larry Wilson,** St. Louis Cardinals		1.50	.70	.15
☐ 169	**St. Louis Cardinals Play Card**		.55	.25	.05
☐ 170	**San Francisco 49ers Team Card**		.90	.40	.09
☐ 171	**Kermit Alexander,** San Francisco 49ers		.45	.20	.04
☐ 172	**Bruce Bosley,** San Francisco 49ers		.35	.15	.03
☐ 173	**John Brodie,** San Francisco 49ers		2.50	1.15	.25
☐ 174	**Bernie Casey,** San Francisco 49ers		.65	.30	.06
☐ 175	**John David Crow,** San Francisco 49ers		.55	.25	.05
☐ 176	**Tommy Davis,** San Francisco 49ers		.35	.15	.03
☐ 177	**Jim Johnson,** San Francisco 49ers		.45	.20	.04
☐ 178	**Gary Lewis,** San Francisco 49ers		.35	.15	.03
☐ 179	**Dave Parks,** San Francisco 49ers		.45	.20	.04
☐ 180	**Walter Rock,** San Francisco 49ers		.35	.15	.03
☐ 181	**Ken Willard,** San Francisco 49ers		.55	.25	.05
☐ 182	**San Francisco 49ers Play Card** (Tommy Davis FG)		.55	.25	.05
☐ 183	**Washington Redskins Team Card**		.90	.40	.09
☐ 184	**Rickie Harris,** Washington Redskins		.35	.15	.03
☐ 185	**Sonny Jurgensen,** Washington Redskins		3.25	1.50	.32
☐ 186	**Paul Krause,** Washington Redskins		.55	.25	.05
☐ 187	**Bobby Mitchell,** Washington Redskins		2.00	.90	.20
☐ 188	**Vince Promuto,** Washington Redskins		.35	.15	.03
☐ 189	**Pat Richter,** Washington Redskins		.45	.20	.04
☐ 190	**Joe Rutgens,** Washington Redskins		.35	.15	.03
☐ 191	**John Sample,** Washington Redskins		.35	.15	.03

		MINT	VG-E	F-G
☐ 192	**Lonnie Sanders,** Washington Redskins	.35	.15	.03
☐ 193	**Jim Steffen,** Washington Redskins	.35	.15	.03
☐ 194	**Charley Taylor,** Washington Redskins	2.00	.90	.20
☐ 195	**Washington Redskins Play Card**	.55	.25	.05
☐ 196	**Referee Signals**	.90	.40	.09
☐ 197	**Checklist 1**	2.00	.40	.05
☐ 198	**Checklist 2**	8.00	1.00	.10

1967 PHILADELPHIA

The 1967 Philadelphia Gum set of NFL players is complete at 198 cards and is Philadelphia Gum's last issue. This set is easily distinguished from the other Philadelphia Gum football sets by its yellow border on the fronts of the cards. The cards measure 2½" by 3½". The card backs are printed in brown on a white card stock.

		MINT	VG-E	F-G
	COMPLETE SET	115.00	50.00	10.00
	COMMON PLAYER (1-198)	.30	.12	.03
☐ 1	**Atlanta Falcons Team Card**	1.25	.35	.07
☐ 2	**Junior Coffey,** Atlanta Falcons	.40	.18	.04
☐ 3	**Alex Hawkins,** Atlanta Falcons	.50	.22	.05
☐ 4	**Randy Johnson,** Atlanta Falcons	.60	.28	.06
☐ 5	**Lou Kirouac,** Atlanta Falcons	.30	.12	.03
☐ 6	**Billy Martin,** Atlanta Falcons	.30	.12	.03
☐ 7	**Tommy Nobis,** Atlanta Falcons	1.75	.85	.17

		MINT	VG-E	F-G
☐	8 Jerry Richardson, Atlanta Falcons	.30	.12	.03
☐	9 Marion Rushing, Atlanta Falcons	.30	.12	.03
☐	10 Ron Smith, Atlanta Falcons	.30	.12	.03
☐	11 Ernie Wheelwright, Atlanta Falcons	.30	.12	.03
☐	12 Atlanta Falcons Insignia	.55	.25	.05
☐	13 Baltimore Colts Team Card	1.00	.45	.10
☐	14 Raymond Berry (photo actually Bob Boyd), Baltimore Colts	2.00	.90	.20
☐	15 Bob Boyd, Baltimore Colts	.30	.12	.03
☐	16 Ordell Braase, Baltimore Colts	.30	.12	.03
☐	17 Alvin Haymond, Baltimore Colts	.30	.12	.03
☐	18 Tony Lorick, Baltimore Colts	.30	.12	.03
☐	19 Lenny Lyles, Baltimore Colts	.30	.12	.03
☐	20 John Mackey, Baltimore Colts	.90	.40	.09
☐	21 Tom Matte, Baltimore Colts	.60	.28	.06
☐	22 Lou Michaels, Baltimore Colts	.40	.18	.04
☐	23 John Unitas, Baltimore Colts	8.00	3.75	.80
☐	24 Baltimore Colts Insignia	.55	.25	.05
☐	25 Chicago Bears Team Card	.90	.40	.09
☐	26 Rudy Bukich, Chicago Bears	.60	.28	.06
☐	27 Ron Bull, Chicago Bears	.50	.22	.05
☐	28 Dick Butkus, Chicago Bears	3.50	1.65	.35
☐	29 Mike Ditka, Chicago Bears	1.50	.70	.15
☐	30 Dick Gordon, Chicago Bears	.40	.18	.04
☐	31 Roger LeClerc, Chicago Bears	.40	.18	.04
☐	32 Bennie McRae, Chicago Bears	.30	.12	.03
☐	33 Richie Petitbon, Chicago Bears	.40	.18	.04
☐	34 Mike Pyle, Chicago Bears	.30	.12	.03
☐	35 Gale Sayers, Chicago Bears	12.00	5.50	1.20
☐	36 Chicago Bears Insignia	.55	.25	.05
☐	37 Cleveland Browns Team Card	.90	.40	.09
☐	38 Johnny Brewer, Cleveland Browns	.30	.12	.03
☐	39 Gary Collins, Cleveland Browns	.50	.22	.05
☐	40 Ross Fichtner, Cleveland Browns	.30	.12	.03
☐	41 Ernie Green, Cleveland Browns	.40	.18	.04
☐	42 Gene Hickerson, Cleveland Browns	.40	.18	.04
☐	43 Leroy Kelly, Cleveland Browns	2.50	1.15	.25
☐	44 Frank Ryan, Cleveland Browns	1.00	.45	.10
☐	45 Dick Schafrath, Cleveland Browns	.40	.18	.04
☐	46 Paul Warfield, Cleveland Browns	2.00	.90	.20
☐	47 John Wooten, Cleveland Browns	.30	.12	.03
☐	48 Cleveland Browns Insignia	.55	.25	.05
☐	49 Dallas Cowboys Team Card	1.25	.60	.12
☐	50 George Andrie, Dallas Cowboys	.50	.22	.05
☐	51 Cornell Green, Dallas Cowboys	.60	.28	.06
☐	52 Bob Hayes, Dallas Cowboys	1.00	.45	.10

		MINT	VG-E	F-G
☐	53 **Chuck Howley**, Dallas Cowboys	.90	.40	.09
☐	54 **Lee Roy Jordan**, Dallas Cowboys	2.00	.90	.20
☐	55 **Bob Lilly**, Dallas Cowboys	2.25	1.00	.22
☐	56 **Dave Manders**, Dallas Cowboys	.50	.22	.05
☐	57 **Don Meredith**, Dallas Cowboys	6.00	2.80	.60
☐	58 **Dan Reeves**, Dallas Cowboys	1.50	.70	.15
☐	59 **Mel Renfro**, Dallas Cowboys	1.00	.45	.10
☐	60 **Dallas Cowboys Insignia**	.65	.30	.06
☐	61 **Detroit Lions Team Card**	.90	.40	.09
☐	62 **Roger Brown**, Detroit Lions	.30	.12	.03
☐	63 **Gail Cogdill**, Detroit Lions	.30	.12	.03
☐	64 **John Gordy**, Detroit Lions	.30	.12	.03
☐	65 **Ron Kramer**, Detroit Lions	.30	.12	.03
☐	66 **Dick LeBeau**, Detroit Lions	.30	.12	.03
☐	67 **Mike Lucci**, Detroit Lions	.50	.22	.05
☐	68 **Amos Marsh**, Detroit Lions	.30	.12	.03
☐	69 **Tom Nowatzke**, Detroit Lions	.30	.12	.03
☐	70 **Pat Studstill**, Detroit Lions	.50	.22	.05
☐	71 **Karl Sweetan**, Detroit Lions	.50	.22	.05
☐	72 **Detroit Lions Insignia**	.55	.25	.05
☐	73 **Green Bay Packers Team Card**	1.00	.45	.10
☐	74 **Herb Adderly**, Green Bay Packers	1.50	.70	.15
☐	75 **Lee Roy Caffey**, Green Bay Packers	.40	.18	.04
☐	76 **Willie Davis**, Green Bay Packers	1.50	.70	.15
☐	77 **Forrest Gregg**, Green Bay Packers	1.50	.70	.15
☐	78 **Henry Jordan**, Green Bay Packers	.75	.35	.07
☐	79 **Ray Nitschke**, Green Bay Packers	1.75	.85	.17
☐	80 **Dave Robinson**, Green Bay Packers	.60	.28	.06
☐	81 **Bob Skoronski**, Green Bay Packers	.30	.12	.03
☐	82 **Bart Starr**, Green Bay Packers	6.00	2.80	.60
☐	83 **Willie Wood**, Green Bay Packers	1.00	.45	.10
☐	84 **Green Bay Packers Insignia**	.65	.30	.06
☐	85 **Los Angeles Rams Team Card**	.90	.40	.09
☐	86 **Dick Bass**, Los Angeles Rams	.50	.22	.05
☐	87 **Maxie Baughan**, Los Angeles Rams	.50	.22	.05
☐	88 **Roman Gabriel**, Los Angeles Rams	1.75	.85	.17
☐	89 **Bruce Gossett**, Los Angeles Rams	.30	.12	.03
☐	90 **Deacon Jones**, Los Angeles Rams	1.75	.85	.17
☐	91 **Tommy McDonald**, Los Angeles Rams	.50	.22	.05
☐	92 **Marlin McKeever**, Los Angeles Rams	.30	.12	.03
☐	93 **Tom Moore**, Los Angeles Rams	.30	.12	.03
☐	94 **Merlin Olsen**, Los Angeles Rams	2.25	1.00	.22
☐	95 **Clancy Williams**, Los Angeles Rams	.30	.12	.03
☐	96 **Los Angeles Rams Insignia**	.55	.25	.05
☐	97 **Minnesota Vikings Team Card**	.90	.40	.09
☐	98 **Grady Alderman**, Minnesota Vikings	.30	.12	.03

		MINT	VG-E	F-G
☐ 99	Bill Brown, Minnesota Vikings	.55	.25	.05
☐ 100	Fred Cox, Minnesota Vikings	.55	.25	.05
☐ 101	Paul Flatley, Minnesota Vikings	.45	.20	.04
☐ 102	Dale Hackbart, Minnesota Vikings	.30	.12	.03
☐ 103	Jim Marshall, Minnesota Vikings	1.50	.70	.15
☐ 104	Tommy Mason, Minnesota Vikings	.55	.25	.05
☐ 105	Milt Sunde, Minnesota Vikings	.30	.12	.03
☐ 106	Fran Tarkenton, Minnesota Vikings	6.50	3.00	.65
☐ 107	Mick Tingelhoff, Minnesota Vikings	.65	.30	.06
☐ 108	Minnesota Vikings Insignia	.55	.25	.05
☐ 109	New York Giants Team Card	.90	.40	.09
☐ 110	Henry Carr, New York Giants	.40	.18	.04
☐ 111	Clarence Childs, New York Giants	.30	.12	.03
☐ 112	Allen Jacobs, New York Giants	.30	.12	.03
☐ 113	Homer Jones, New York Giants	.40	.18	.04
☐ 114	Tom Kennedy, New York Giants	.40	.18	.04
☐ 115	Carl Spider Lockhart, New York Giants	.40	.18	.04
☐ 116	Joe Morrison, New York Giants	.65	.30	.06
☐ 117	Francis Peay, New York Giants	.30	.12	.03
☐ 118	Jeff Smith, New York Giants	.30	.12	.03
☐ 119	Aaron Thomas, New York Giants	.30	.12	.03
☐ 120	New York Giants Insignia	.55	.25	.05
☐ 121	New Orleans Saints Insignia (see Card 132)	.90	.40	.09
☐ 122	Charley Bradshaw, New Orleans Saints	.30	.12	.03
☐ 123	Paul Hornung, New Orleans Saints	4.50	2.10	.45
☐ 124	Elbert Kimbrough, New Orleans Saints	.30	.12	.03
☐ 125	Earl Leggett, New Orleans Saints	.30	.12	.03
☐ 126	Obert Logan, New Orleans Saints	.30	.12	.03
☐ 127	Riley Mattson, New Orleans Saints	.30	.12	.03
☐ 128	John Morrow, New Orleans Saints	.30	.12	.03
☐ 129	Bob Scholtz, New Orleans Saints	.30	.12	.03
☐ 130	Dave Whitsell, New Orleans Saints	.30	.12	.03
☐ 131	Gary Wood, New Orleans Saints	.50	.22	.05
☐ 132	New Orleans Saints Roster (has 121 on back)	.90	.40	.09
☐ 133	Philadelphia Eagles Team Card	.90	.40	.09
☐ 134	Sam Baker, Philadelphia Eagles	.40	.18	.04
☐ 135	Bob Brown, Philadelphia Eagles	.30	.12	.03
☐ 136	Tim Brown, Philadelphia Eagles	.50	.22	.05
☐ 137	Earl Gros, Philadelphia Eagles	.30	.12	.03
☐ 138	Dave Lloyd, Philadelphia Eagles	.30	.12	.03
☐ 139	Floyd Peters, Philadelphia Eagles	.30	.12	.03
☐ 140	Pete Retzlaff, Philadelphia Eagles	.40	.18	.04
☐ 141	Joe Scarpati, Philadelphia Eagles	.30	.12	.03
☐ 142	Norm Snead, Philadelphia Eagles	.90	.40	.09

	MINT	VG-E	F-G
☐ 143 **Jim Skaggs**, Philadelphia Eagles	.30	.12	.03
☐ 144 **Philadelphia Eagles Insignia**	.55	.25	.05
☐ 145 **Pittsburgh Steelers Team Card**	.90	.40	.09
☐ 146 **Bill Asbury**, Pittsburgh Steelers	.30	.12	.03
☐ 147 **John Baker**, Pittsburgh Steelers	.30	.12	.03
☐ 148 **Gary Ballman**, Pittsburgh Steelers	.50	.22	.05
☐ 149 **Mike Clark**, Pittsburgh Steelers	.30	.12	.03
☐ 150 **Riley Gunnels**, Pittsburgh Steelers	.30	.12	.03
☐ 151 **John Hilton**, Pittsburgh Steelers	.30	.12	.03
☐ 152 **Roy Jefferson**, Pittsburgh Steelers	.50	.22	.05
☐ 153 **Brady Keys**, Pittsburgh Steelers	.30	.12	.03
☐ 154 **Ben McGee**, Pittsburgh Steelers	.30	.12	.03
☐ 155 **Bill Nelsen**, Pittsburgh Steelers	.90	.40	.09
☐ 156 **Pittsburgh Steelers Insignia**	.55	.25	.05
☐ 157 **St. Louis Cardinals Team Card**	.90	.40	.09
☐ 158 **Jim Bakken**, St. Louis Cardinals	.50	.22	.05
☐ 159 **Bobby Joe Conrad**, St. Louis Cardinals	.50	.22	.05
☐ 160 **Ken Gray**, St. Louis Cardinals	.30	.12	.03
☐ 161 **Charlie Johnson**, St. Louis Cardinals	.90	.40	.09
☐ 162 **Joe Robb**, St. Louis Cardinals	.30	.12	.03
☐ 163 **Johnny Roland**, St. Louis Cardinals	.60	.28	.06
☐ 164 **Roy Shivers**, St. Louis Cardinals	.30	.12	.03
☐ 165 **Jackie Smith**, St. Louis Cardinals	.60	.28	.06
☐ 166 **Jerry Stovall**, St. Louis Cardinals	.60	.28	.06
☐ 167 **Larry Wilson**, St. Louis Cardinals	1.50	.70	.15
☐ 168 **St. Louis Cardinals Insignia**	.55	.25	.05
☐ 169 **San Francisco 49ers Team Card**	.90	.40	.09
☐ 170 **Kermit Alexander**, San Francisco 49ers	.40	.18	.04
☐ 171 **Bruce Bosley**, San Francisco 49ers	.30	.12	.03
☐ 172 **John Brodie**, San Francisco 49ers	2.50	1.15	.25
☐ 173 **Bernie Casey**, San Francisco 49ers	.65	.30	.06
☐ 174 **Tommy Davis**, San Francisco 49ers	.30	.12	.03
☐ 175 **Howard Mudd**, San Francisco 49ers	.30	.12	.03
☐ 176 **Dave Parks**, San Francisco 49ers	.50	.22	.05
☐ 177 **John Thomas**, San Francisco 49ers	.30	.12	.03
☐ 178 **Dave Wilcox**, San Francisco 49ers	.50	.22	.05
☐ 179 **Ken Willard**, San Francisco 49ers	.55	.25	.05
☐ 180 **San Francisco 49ers Insignia**	.55	.25	.05
☐ 181 **Washington Redskins Team Card**	.90	.40	.09
☐ 182 **Charlie Gogolak**, Washington Redskins	.60	.28	.06
☐ 183 **Chris Hanburger**, Washington Redskins	.60	.28	.06
☐ 184 **Len Hauss**, Washington Redskins	.30	.12	.03
☐ 185 **Sonny Jurgensen**, Washington Redskins	3.00	1.40	.30
☐ 186 **Bobby Mitchell**, Washington Redskins	2.00	.90	.20
☐ 187 **Brig Owens**, Washington Redskins	.30	.12	.03
☐ 188 **Jim Shorter**, Washington Redskins	.30	.12	.03

	MINT	VG-E	F-G
☐ 189 Jerry Smith, Washington Redskins	.50	.22	.05
☐ 190 Charley Taylor, Washington Redskins	2.00	.90	.20
☐ 191 A.D. Whitfield, Washington Redskins	.30	.12	.03
☐ 192 Washington Redskins Insignia	.55	.25	.05
☐ 193 Cleveland Browns Play Card (Leroy Kelly)	.70	.32	.07
☐ 194 New York Giants Play Card (Joe Morrison)	.60	.28	.06
☐ 195 Atlanta Falcons Play Card (Ernie Wheelright)	.50	.22	.05
☐ 196 Referee Signals	.90	.40	.09
☐ 197 Checklist 1	3.00	.50	.10
☐ 198 Checklist 2	7.50	.75	.15

1962 POST CEREAL

The 1962 Post Cereal set of 200 cards is Post's only American football issue. The cards were distributed on the back panels of various flavors of Post Cereals. As is typical of the Post package-back issues, the cards are blank-backed and are frequently found poorly cut from the cereal box. The cards (when properly trimmed) measure 2½" by 3½". The cards are grouped in order of the team's 1961 season finish. Certain cards printed only on unpopular types of cereal are relatively difficult to obtain . Twenty-nine such cards are known and are indicated by an SP (short-printed) in the checklist.

	MINT	VG-E	F-G
COMPLETE SET	900.00	400.00	90.00
COMMON PLAYER (1-200)	1.00	.45	.10

		MINT	VG-E	F-G
☐	1 Dan Currie, Green Bay Packers	1.00	.45	.10
☐	2 Boyd Dowler, Green Bay Packers	1.25	.60	.12
☐	3 Bill Forester, Green Bay Packers	1.25	.60	.12
☐	4 Forrest Gregg, Green Bay Packers	2.50	1.15	.25
☐	5 Dave Hanner, Green Bay Packers	1.00	.45	.10
☐	6 Paul Hornung, Green Bay Packers	5.00	2.35	.50
☐	7 Henry Jordan, Green Bay Packers	1.50	.70	.15
☐	8 Jerry Kramer SP, Green Bay Packers	10.00	4.75	1.00
☐	9 Max McGee, Green Bay Packers	1.25	.60	.12
☐	10 Tom Moore SP, Green Bay Packers	40.00	18.00	4.00
☐	11 Jim Ringo, Green Bay Packers	2.50	1.15	.25
☐	12 Bart Starr, Green Bay Packers	7.50	3.50	.75
☐	13 Jim Taylor, Green Bay Packers	3.50	1.65	.35
☐	14 Fuzzy Thurston, Green Bay Packers	1.25	.60	.12
☐	15 Jess Whittenton, Green Bay Packers	1.00	.45	.10
☐	16 Erich Barnes, New York Giants	1.00	.45	.10
☐	17 Roosevelt Brown, New York Giants	2.50	1.15	.25
☐	18 Bob Gaiters, New York Giants	1.00	.45	.10
☐	19 Roosevelt Grier, New York Giants	2.50	1.15	.25
☐	20 Sam Huff, New York Giants	3.50	1.65	.35
☐	21 Jim Katcavage, New York Giants	1.00	.45	.10
☐	22 Cliff Livingston, New York Giants	1.00	.45	.10
☐	23 Dick Lynch, New York Giants	1.00	.45	.10
☐	24 Joe Morrison SP, New York Giants	15.00	7.00	1.50
☐	25 Dick Nolan SP, New York Giants	15.00	7.00	1.50
☐	26 Andy Robustelli, New York Giants	2.50	1.15	.25
☐	27 Kyle Rote, New York Giants	3.50	1.65	.35
☐	28 Del Shofner SP, New York Giants	15.00	7.00	1.50
☐	29 Y.A. Tittle SP, New York Giants	25.00	11.00	2.50
☐	30 Alex Webster, New York Giants	1.25	.60	.12
☐	31 Bill Barnes, Philadelphia Eagles	1.00	.45	.10
☐	32 Maxie Baughan, Philadelphia Eagles	1.25	.60	.12
☐	33 Chuck Bednarik, Philadelphia Eagles	3.50	1.65	.35
☐	34 Tom Brookshier, Philadelphia Eagles	2.00	.90	.20
☐	35 Jimmy Carr, Philadelphia Eagles	1.00	.45	.10
☐	36 Ted Dean, Philadelphia Eagles	1.00	.45	.10
☐	37 Sonny Jurgensen, Philadelphia Eagles	5.00	2.35	.50
☐	38 Tommy McDonald, Philadelphia Eagles	1.25	.60	.12
☐	39 Clarence Peaks, Philadelphia Eagles	1.00	.45	.10
☐	40 Pete Retzlaff, Philadelphia Eagles	1.25	.60	.12
☐	41 Jesse Richardson SP, Philadelphia Eagles	15.00	7.00	1.50
☐	42 Leo Sugar, Philadelphia Eagles	1.00	.45	.10
☐	43 Bobby Walston SP, Philadelphia Eagles	20.00	9.00	2.00
☐	44 Chuck Weber, Philadelphia Eagles	1.00	.45	.10
☐	45 Ed Khayat, Philadelphia Eagles	1.00	.45	.10
☐	46 Howard Cassady, Detroit Lions	1.25	.60	.12

			MINT	VG-E	F-G
☐	47	**Gail Cogdill,** Detroit Lions	1.00	.45	.10
☐	48	**Jim Gibbons,** Detroit Lions	1.00	.45	.10
☐	49	**Bill Glass,** Detroit Lions	1.25	.60	.12
☐	50	**Alex Karras,** Detroit Lions	4.00	1.85	.40
☐	51	**Dick Lane,** Detroit Lions	2.50	1.15	.25
☐	52	**Yale Lary,** Detroit Lions	2.50	1.15	.25
☐	53	**Dan Lewis,** Detroit Lions	1.00	.45	.10
☐	54	**Darris McCord SP,** Detroit Lions	30.00	14.00	3.00
☐	55	**Jim Martin,** Detroit Lions	1.00	.45	.10
☐	56	**Earl Morrall,** Detroit Lions	2.50	1.15	.25
☐	57	**Jim Ninowski,** Detroit Lions	1.25	.60	.12
☐	58	**Nick Pietrosante,** Detroit Lions	1.25	.60	.12
☐	59	**Joe Schmidt SP,** Detroit Lions	15.00	7.00	1.50
☐	60	**Harley Sewell,** Detroit Lions	1.00	.45	.10
☐	61	**Jim Brown,** Cleveland Browns	30.00	14.00	3.00
☐	62	**Galen Fiss SP,** Cleveland Browns	10.00	4.75	1.00
☐	63	**Bob Gain,** Cleveland Browns	1.00	.45	.10
☐	64	**Jim Houston,** Cleveland Browns	1.00	.45	.10
☐	65	**Mike McCormack,** Cleveland Browns	2.50	1.15	.25
☐	66	**Gene Hickerson,** Cleveland Browns	1.00	.45	.10
☐	67	**Bobby Mitchell,** Cleveland Browns	3.50	1.65	.35
☐	68	**John Morrow,** Cleveland Browns	1.00	.45	.10
☐	69	**Bernie Parrish,** Cleveland Browns	1.00	.45	.10
☐	70	**Milt Plum,** Cleveland Browns	1.50	.70	.15
☐	71	**Ray Renfro,** Cleveland Browns	1.25	.60	.12
☐	72	**Dick Schafrath,** Cleveland Browns	1.00	.45	.10
☐	73	**Jim Ray Smith,** Cleveland Browns	1.00	.45	.10
☐	74	**Sam Baker SP,** Cleveland Browns	50.00	22.00	5.00
☐	75	**Paul Wiggin,** Cleveland Browns	1.25	.60	.12
☐	76	**Raymond Berry,** Baltimore Colts	4.00	1.85	.40
☐	77	**Bob Boyd,** Baltimore Colts	1.00	.45	.10
☐	78	**Ordell Braase,** Baltimore Colts	1.00	.45	.10
☐	79	**Art Donovan,** Baltimore Colts	2.50	1.15	.25
☐	80	**Dee Mackey,** Baltimore Colts	1.00	.45	.10
☐	81	**Gino Marchetti,** Baltimore Colts	3.50	1.65	.35
☐	82	**Lenny Moore,** Baltimore Colts	4.00	1.85	.40
☐	83	**Jim Mutscheller,** Baltimore Colts	1.00	.45	.10
☐	84	**Steve Myhra,** Baltimore Colts	1.00	.45	.10
☐	85	**Jimmy Orr,** Baltimore Colts	1.25	.60	.12
☐	86	**Jim Parker,** Baltimore Colts	2.50	1.15	.25
☐	87	**Bill Pellington,** Baltimore Colts	1.00	.45	.10
☐	88	**Alex Sandusky,** Baltimore Colts	1.00	.45	.10
☐	89	**Dick Szymanski,** Baltimore Colts	1.00	.45	.10
☐	90	**John Unitas,** Baltimore Colts	7.50	3.50	.75
☐	91	**Bruce Bosley,** San Francisco 49ers	1.00	.45	.10
☐	92	**John Brodie,** San Francisco 49ers	5.00	2.35	.50

		MINT	VG-E	F-G
☐ 93	**Dave Baker SP**, San Francisco 49ers	25.00	11.00	2.50
☐ 94	**Tommy Davis**, San Francisco 49ers	1.00	.45	.10
☐ 95	**Bob Harrison**, San Francisco 49ers	1.00	.45	.10
☐ 96	**Matt Hazeltine**, San Francisco 49ers	1.00	.45	.10
☐ 97	**Jim Johnson SP**, San Francisco 49ers	10.00	4.75	1.00
☐ 98	**Bill Kilmer**, San Francisco 49ers	2.50	1.15	.25
☐ 99	**Jerry Mertens**, San Francisco 49ers	1.00	.45	.10
☐ 100	**Frank Morze**, San Francisco 49ers	1.00	.45	.10
☐ 101	**R.C. Owens**, San Francisco 49ers	1.00	.45	.10
☐ 102	**J.D. Smith**, San Francisco 49ers	1.00	.45	.10
☐ 103	**Bob St. Clair SP**, San Francisco 49ers	20.00	9.00	2.00
☐ 104	**Monty Stickles**, San Francisco 49ers	1.00	.45	.10
☐ 105	**Abe Woodson**, San Francisco 49ers	1.00	.45	.10
☐ 106	**Doug Atkins**, Chicago Bears	2.50	1.15	.25
☐ 107	**Ed Brown**, Chicago Bears	1.25	.60	.12
☐ 108	**J.C. Caroline**, Chicago Bears	1.00	.45	.10
☐ 109	**Rick Casares**, Chicago Bears	1.25	.60	.12
☐ 110	**Angelo Coia SP**, Chicago Bears	50.00	22.00	5.00
☐ 111	**Mike Ditka**, Chicago Bears	2.50	1.15	.25
☐ 112	**Joe Fortunato**, Chicago Bears	1.00	.45	.10
☐ 113	**Willie Galimore**, Chicago Bears	1.25	.60	.12
☐ 114	**Bill George**, Chicago Bears	2.50	1.15	.25
☐ 115	**Stan Jones**, Chicago Bears	1.00	.45	.10
☐ 116	**Johnny Morris**, Chicago Bears	1.25	.60	.12
☐ 117	**Larry Morris SP**, Chicago Bears	15.00	7.00	1.50
☐ 118	**Richie Petitbon**, Chicago Bears	1.00	.45	.10
☐ 119	**Bill Wade**, Chicago Bears	1.25	.60	.12
☐ 120	**Maury Youmans**, Chicago Bears	1.00	.45	.10
☐ 121	**Preston Carpenter**, Pittsburgh Steelers	1.00	.45	.10
☐ 122	**Buddy Dial**, Pittsburgh Steelers	1.25	.60	.12
☐ 123	**Bobby Joe Green**, Pittsburgh Steelers	1.00	.45	.10
☐ 124	**Mike Henry**, Pittsburgh Steelers	1.50	.70	.15
☐ 125	**John Henry Johnson**, Pittsburgh Steelers	1.50	.70	.15
☐ 126	**Bobby Layne**, Pittsburgh Steelers	7.50	3.50	.75
☐ 127	**Gene Lipscomb**, Pittsburgh Steelers	1.50	.70	.15
☐ 128	**Lou Michaels**, Pittsburgh Steelers	1.00	.45	.10
☐ 129	**John Nisby**, Pittsburgh Steelers	1.00	.45	.10
☐ 130	**John Reger**, Pittsburgh Steelers	1.00	.45	.10
☐ 131	**Mike Sandusky**, Pittsburgh Steelers	1.00	.45	.10
☐ 132	**George Tarasovic**, Pittsburgh Steelers	1.00	.45	.10
☐ 133	**Tom Tracy SP**, Pittsburgh Steelers	20.00	9.00	2.00
☐ 134	**Glynn Gregory**, Dallas Cowboys	1.00	.45	.10
☐ 135	**Frank Clarke SP**, Dallas Cowboys	15.00	7.00	1.50
☐ 136	**Mike Connelly SP**, Dallas Cowboys	15.00	7.00	1.50
☐ 137	**L.G. Dupre**, Dallas Cowboys	1.00	.45	.10
☐ 138	**Bob Fry**, Dallas Cowboys	1.00	.45	.10

		MINT	VG-E	F-G
☐ 139	**Allen Green SP**, Dallas Cowboys	30.00	14.00	3.00
☐ 140	**Bill Howton**, Dallas Cowboys	1.25	.60	.12
☐ 141	**Bob Lilly**, Dallas Cowboys	5.00	2.35	.50
☐ 142	**Don Meredith**, Dallas Cowboys	7.50	3.50	.75
☐ 143	**Dick Moegle**, Dallas Cowboys	1.00	.45	.10
☐ 144	**Don Perkins**, Dallas Cowboys	1.75	.85	.17
☐ 145	**Jerry Tubbs SP**, Dallas Cowboys	30.00	14.00	3.00
☐ 146	**J.W. Lockett**, Dallas Cowboys	1.00	.45	.10
☐ 147	**Ed Cook**, St. Louis Cardinals	1.00	.45	.10
☐ 148	**John David Crow**, St. Louis Cardinals	1.25	.60	.12
☐ 149	**Sam Etcheverry**, St. Louis Cardinals	1.25	.60	.12
☐ 150	**Frank Fuller**, St. Louis Cardinals	1.00	.45	.10
☐ 151	**Prentice Gautt**, St. Louis Cardinals	1.25	.60	.12
☐ 152	**Jimmy Hill**, St. Louis Cardinals	1.00	.45	.10
☐ 153	**Bill Koman SP**, St. Louis Cardinals	15.00	7.00	1.50
☐ 154	**Larry Wilson**, St. Louis Cardinals	2.50	1.15	.25
☐ 155	**Dale Meinert**, St. Louis Cardinals	1.00	.45	.10
☐ 156	**Ed Henke**, St. Louis Cardinals	1.00	.45	.10
☐ 157	**Sonny Randle**, St. Louis Cardinals	1.25	.60	.12
☐ 158	**Ralph Guglielmi SP**, St. Louis Cardinals ..	15.00	7.00	1.50
☐ 159	**Joe Childress**, St. Louis Cardinals	1.00	.45	.10
☐ 160	**Jon Arnett**, Los Angeles Rams	1.25	.60	.12
☐ 161	**Dick Bass**, Los Angeles Rams	1.25	.60	.12
☐ 162	**Zeke Bratkowski**, Los Angeles Rams	1.50	.70	.15
☐ 163	**Carroll Dale**, Los Angeles Rams	1.00	.45	.10
☐ 164	**Art Hunter**, Los Angeles Rams	1.00	.45	.10
☐ 165	**John Lovetere**, Los Angeles Rams	1.00	.45	.10
☐ 166	**Lamar Lundy**, Los Angeles Rams	1.00	.45	.10
☐ 167	**Ollie Matson**, Los Angeles Rams	3.50	1.65	.35
☐ 168	**Ed Meador**, Los Angeles Rams	1.25	.60	.12
☐ 169	**Jack Pardee SP**, Los Angeles Rams	15.00	7.00	1.50
☐ 170	**Jim Phillips**, Los Angeles Rams	1.00	.45	.10
☐ 171	**Les Richter**, Los Angeles Rams	1.25	.60	.12
☐ 172	**Frank Ryan**, Los Angeles Rams	1.75	.85	.17
☐ 173	**Frank Varrichione**, Los Angeles Rams	1.00	.45	.10
☐ 174	**Grady Alderman**, Minnesota Vikings	1.00	.45	.10
☐ 175	**Rip Hawkins**, Minnesota Vikings	1.00	.45	.10
☐ 176	**Don Joyce SP**, Minnesota Vikings	25.00	11.00	2.50
☐ 177	**Bill Lapham**, Minnesota Vikings	1.00	.45	.10
☐ 178	**Tommy Mason**, Minnesota Vikings	1.25	.60	.12
☐ 179	**Hugh McElhenny**, Minnesota Vikings	3.00	1.40	.30
☐ 180	**Dave Middleton**, Minnesota Vikings	1.00	.45	.10
☐ 181	**Dick Pesonen**, Minnesota Vikings	1.00	.45	.10
☐ 182	**Karl Rubke**, Minnesota Vikings	1.00	.45	.10
☐ 183	**George Shaw**, Minnesota Vikings	1.25	.60	.12
☐ 184	**Fran Tarkenton**, Minnesota Vikings	12.00	5.50	1.20

		MINT	VG-E	F-G
☐ 185	**Mel Triplett**, Minnesota Vikings	1.00	.45	.10
☐ 186	**Frank Youso SP**, Minnesota Vikings	15.00	7.00	1.50
☐ 187	**Bill Bishop**, Washington Redskins	1.00	.45	.10
☐ 188	**Bill Anderson SP**, Washington Redskins	20.00	9.00	2.00
☐ 189	**Don Bosseler**, Washington Redskins	1.00	.45	.10
☐ 190	**Fred Hageman**, Washington Redskins	1.00	.45	.10
☐ 191	**Sam Horner**, Washington Redskins	1.00	.45	.10
☐ 192	**Jim Kerr**, Washington Redskins	1.00	.45	.10
☐ 193	**Joe Krakoski SP**, Washington Redskins	40.00	18.00	4.00
☐ 194	**Fred Dugan**, Washington Redskins	1.00	.45	.10
☐ 195	**John Paluck**, Washington Redskins	1.00	.45	.10
☐ 196	**Vince Promuto**, Washington Redskins	1.00	.45	.10
☐ 197	**Joe Rutgens**, Washington Redskins	1.00	.45	.10
☐ 198	**Norm Snead**, Washington Redskins	1.50	.70	.15
☐ 199	**Andy Stynchula**, Washington Redskins	1.00	.45	.10
☐ 200	**Bob Toneff**, Washington Redskins	1.00	.45	.10

1956 TOPPS

The 1956 Topps set of 120 cards contains NFL players. The cards measure 2⅝" by 3⅝". The first football team cards (produced by Topps) were included in this set. Players from the Washington Redskins and the Chicago Cardinals were apparently produced in lesser quantities, as they are more difficult to find compared to the other teams. The card backs were printed in red and black on gray card stock. Statistical information from the immediate past season and career totals are given at the bottom of the reverse. A checklist card and two contest cards were also *issued along with this set, although in much lesser quantities. The complete set price below refers to the 120 numbered cards, i.e., not including the unnumbered checklist card.*

		MINT	VG-E	F-G
	COMPLETE SET	180.00	85.00	18.00
	COMMON PLAYER (1-120)	.70	.32	.07
☐	1 Jack Carson, Washington Redskins	4.00	1.00	.20
☐	2 Gordon Soltau, San Francisco 49ers	.70	.32	.07
☐	3 Frank Varrichione, Pittsburgh Steelers	.70	.32	.07
☐	4 Eddie Bell, Philadelphia Eagles	.70	.32	.07
☐	5 Alex Webster, New York Giants	1.50	.70	.15
☐	6 Norm Van Brocklin, Los Angeles Rams	7.50	3.50	.75
☐	7 Green Bay Packers Team Card	2.00	.90	.20
☐	8 Lou Creekmur, Detroit Lions	.70	.32	.07
☐	9 Lou Groza, Cleveland Browns	5.50	2.60	.55
☐	10 Tom Bienemann, Chicago Cardinals	2.00	.90	.20
☐	11 George Blanda, Chicago Bears	8.00	3.75	.80
☐	12 Alan Ameche, Baltimore Colts	1.50	.70	.15
☐	13 Vic Janowicz, Washington Redskins	1.50	.70	.15
☐	14 Dick Moegle, San Francisco 49ers	.70	.32	.07
☐	15 Fran Rogel, Pittsburgh Steelers	.70	.32	.07
☐	16 Harold Giancanelli, Philadelphia Eagles	.70	.32	.07
☐	17 Emlen Tunnell, New York Giants	3.50	1.65	.35
☐	18 Tank Younger, Los Angeles Rams	1.25	.60	.12
☐	19 Bill Howton, Green Bay Packers	1.00	.45	.10
☐	20 Jack Christiansen, Detroit Lions	3.50	1.65	.35
☐	21 Darrell Brewster, Cleveland Browns	.70	.32	.07
☐	22 Chicago Cardinals Team Card	2.50	1.15	.25
☐	23 Ed Brown, Chicago Bears	1.00	.45	.10
☐	24 Joe Campanella, Baltimore Colts	.70	.32	.07
☐	25 Leon Heath, Washington Redskins	1.50	.70	.15
☐	26 San Francisco 49ers Team Card	1.75	.85	.17
☐	27 Dick Flanagan, Pittsburgh Steelers	.70	.32	.07
☐	28 Chuck Bednarik, Philadelphia Eagles	5.00	2.35	.50
☐	29 Kyle Rote, New York Giants	4.50	2.10	.45
☐	30 Les Richter, Los Angeles Rams	1.00	.45	.10
☐	31 Howard Ferguson, Green Bay Packers	.70	.32	.07
☐	32 Dorne Dibble, Detroit Lions	.70	.32	.07
☐	33 Kenny Konz, Cleveland Browns	.70	.32	.07
☐	34 Dave Mann, Chicago Cardinals	2.00	.90	.20
☐	35 Rick Casares, Chicago Bears	1.00	.45	.10
☐	36 Art Donovan, Baltimore Colts	3.50	1.65	.35
☐	37 Chuck Drazenovich, Washington Redskins	1.50	.70	.15
☐	38 Joe Arenas, San Francisco 49ers	.70	.32	.07
☐	39 Lynn Chandnois, Pittsburgh Steelers	.70	.32	.07

		MINT	VG-E	F-G
☐ 40	Philadelphia Eagles Team Card	1.75	.85	.17
☐ 41	Roosevelt Brown, New York Giants	3.50	1.65	.35
☐ 42	Tom Fears, Los Angeles Rams	3.50	1.65	.35
☐ 43	Gary Knafelc, Green Bay Packers	.70	.32	.07
☐ 44	Joe Schmidt, Detroit Lions	5.00	2.35	.50
☐ 45	Cleveland Browns Team Card	2.00	.90	.20
☐ 46	Len Teeuws, Chicago Cardinals	2.00	.90	.20
☐ 47	Bill George, Chicago Bears	4.00	1.85	.40
☐ 48	Baltimore Colts Team Card	2.00	.90	.20
☐ 49	Eddie LeBaron, Washington Redskins	2.00	.90	.20
☐ 50	Hugh McElhenny, San Francisco 49ers	5.00	2.35	.50
☐ 51	Ted Marchibroda, Pittsburgh Steelers	1.00	.45	.10
☐ 52	Adrian Burk, Philadelphia Eagles	.70	.32	.07
☐ 53	Frank Gifford, New York Giants	18.00	8.50	1.80
☐ 54	Charley Toogood, Los Angeles Rams	.70	.32	.07
☐ 55	Tobin Rote, Green Bay Packers	1.50	.70	.15
☐ 56	Bill Stits, Detroit Lions	.70	.32	.07
☐ 57	Don Colo, Cleveland Browns	.70	.32	.07
☐ 58	Ollie Matson, Chicago Cardinals	5.00	2.35	.50
☐ 59	Harlon Hill, Chicago Bears	1.00	.45	.10
☐ 60	Lenny Moore, Baltimore Colts	8.00	3.75	.80
☐ 61	Washington Redskins Team Card	2.50	1.15	.25
☐ 62	Billy Wilson, San Francisco 49ers	1.00	.45	.10
☐ 63	Pittsburgh Steelers Team Card	2.00	.90	.20
☐ 64	Bob Pellegrini, Philadelphia Eagles	.70	.32	.07
☐ 65	Ken MacAfee, New York Giants	1.00	.45	.10
☐ 66	Willard Sherman, Los Angeles Rams	.70	.32	.07
☐ 67	Roger Zatkoff, Green Bay Packers	.70	.32	.07
☐ 68	Dave Middleton, Detroit Lions	.70	.32	.07
☐ 69	Ray Renfro, Cleveland Browns	1.00	.45	.10
☐ 70	Don Stonesifer, Chicago Cardinals	2.00	.90	.20
☐ 71	Stan Jones, Chicago Bears	.70	.32	.07
☐ 72	Jim Mutscheller, Baltimore Colts	.70	.32	.07
☐ 73	Volney Peters, Washington Redskins	1.50	.70	.15
☐ 74	Leo Nomellini, San Francisco 49ers	3.50	1.65	.35
☐ 75	Ray Mathews, Pittsburgh Steelers	.70	.32	.07
☐ 76	Dick Bielski, Philadelphia Eagles	.70	.32	.07
☐ 77	Charley Conerly, New York Giants	4.00	1.85	.40
☐ 78	Elroy Hirsch, Los Angeles Rams	5.00	2.35	.50
☐ 79	Bill Forester, Green Bay Packers	1.00	.45	.10
☐ 80	Jim Doran, Detroit Lions	.70	.32	.07
☐ 81	Fred Morrison, Cleveland Browns	.70	.32	.07
☐ 82	Jack Simmons, Chicago Cardinals	2.00	.90	.20
☐ 83	Bill McColl, Chicago Bears	.70	.32	.07
☐ 84	Bert Rechichar, Baltimore Colts	.70	.32	.07
☐ 85	Joe Scudero, Washington Redskins	1.50	.70	.15

			MINT	VG-E	F-G
☐	86	**Y.A. Tittle**, San Francisco 49ers	7.50	3.50	.75
☐	87	**Ernie Stautner**, Pittsburgh Steelers	3.50	1.65	.35
☐	88	**Norm Willey**, Philadelphia Eagles	.70	.32	.07
☐	89	**Bob Schnelker**, New York Giants	1.00	.45	.10
☐	90	**Dan Towler**, Los Angeles Rams	1.00	.45	.10
☐	91	**John Martinkovic**, Green Bay Packers	.70	.32	.07
☐	92	**Detroit Lions Team Card**	2.00	.90	.20
☐	93	**George Ratterman**, Cleveland Browns	1.00	.45	.10
☐	94	**Chuck Ulrich**, Chicago Cardinals	2.00	.90	.20
☐	95	**Bobby Watkins**, Chicago Bears	.70	.32	.07
☐	96	**Buddy Young**, Baltimore Colts	1.25	.60	.12
☐	97	**Billy Wells**, Washington Redskins	1.50	.70	.15
☐	98	**Bob Toneff**, San Francisco 49ers	.70	.32	.07
☐	99	**Bill McPeak**, Pittsburgh Steelers	.70	.32	.07
☐	100	**Bobby Thomason**, Philadelphia Eagles	1.00	.45	.10
☐	101	**Roosevelt Grier**, New York Giants	3.00	1.40	.30
☐	102	**Ron Waller**, Los Angeles Rams	.70	.32	.07
☐	103	**Bobby Dillon**, Green Bay Packers	1.00	.45	.10
☐	104	**Leon Hart**, Detroit Lions	1.50	.70	.15
☐	105	**Mike McCormack**, Cleveland Browns	3.00	1.40	.30
☐	106	**John Olszewski**, Chicago Cardinals	2.00	.90	.20
☐	107	**Bill Wightkin**, Chicago Bears	.70	.32	.07
☐	108	**George Shaw**, Baltimore Colts	1.00	.45	.10
☐	109	**Dale Atkeson**, Washington Redskins	1.50	.70	.15
☐	110	**Joe Perry**, San Francisco 49ers	5.00	2.35	.50
☐	111	**Dale Dodrill**, Pittsburgh Steelers	.70	.32	.07
☐	112	**Tom Scott**, Philadelphia Eagles	.70	.32	.07
☐	113	**New York Giants Team Card**	2.00	.90	.20
☐	114	**Los Angeles Rams Team Card**	1.75	.85	.17
☐	115	**Al Carmichael**, Green Bay Packers	.70	.32	.07
☐	116	**Bobby Layne**, Detroit Lions	7.50	3.50	.75
☐	117	**Ed Modzeleski**, Cleveland Browns	.70	.32	.07
☐	118	**Lamar McHan**, Chicago Cardinals	2.00	.90	.20
☐	119	**Chicago Bears Team Card**	2.00	.90	.20
☐	120	**Billy Vessels**, Baltimore Colts	1.50	.50	.10
☐	121	**Checklist card (unnumbered)**	40.00	10.00	2.00

1957 TOPPS

BACK-LIONS

JACK RISTIANSEN — DETROIT LIONS

The 1957 set contains 154 cards, each measuring 2½" by 3½". The second series (89-144) is more difficult to obtain than the first series. The fronts include both a bust and an action picture. The card backs were printed in red and black on gray card stock. Statistical information from the immediate past season and career totals are given at the bottom of the reverse. The rookie cards of Unitas, Starr, and Hornung are included in this set. A checklist card was also issued along with this set. The complete set price below refers to the 154 numbered cards, i.e., not including the unnumbered checklist card.

		MINT	VG-E	F-G
	COMPLETE SET	250.00	110.00	25.00
	COMMON PLAYER (1-88)	.65	.30	.06
	COMMON PLAYER (89-154)	.90	.40	.09
☐ 1	Eddie LeBaron, Washington Redskins	1.50	.50	.10
☐ 2	Pete Retzlaff, Philadelphia Eagles	.90	.40	.09
☐ 3	Mike McCormack, Cleveland Browns	2.25	1.00	.22
☐ 4	Lou Baldacci, Pittsburgh Steelers	.65	.30	.06
☐ 5	Gino Marchetti, Baltimore Colts	3.50	1.65	.35
☐ 6	Leo Nomellini, San Francisco 49ers	2.50	1.15	.25
☐ 7	Bobby Watkins, Chicago Bears	.65	.30	.06
☐ 8	Dave Middleton, Detroit Lions	.65	.30	.06
☐ 9	Bobby Dan Dillon, Green Bay Packers	.90	.40	.09
☐ 10	Les Richter, Los Angeles Rams	.90	.40	.09
☐ 11	Roosevelt Brown, New York Giants	2.50	1.15	.25
☐ 12	Lavern Torgeson, Washington Redskins	.65	.30	.06
☐ 13	Dick Bielski, Philadelphia Eagles	.65	.30	.06

		MINT	VG-E	F-G
☐	14 **Pat Summerall**, Chicago Cardinals	3.00	1.40	.30
☐	15 **Jack Butler**, Pittsburgh Steelers	.65	.30	.06
☐	16 **John Henry Johnson**, San Francisco 49ers ...	1.50	.70	.15
☐	17 **Art Spinney**, Baltimore Colts	.65	.30	.06
☐	18 **Bob St. Clair**, San Francisco 49ers	.65	.30	.06
☐	19 **Perry Jeter**, Chicago Bears	.65	.30	.06
☐	20 **Lou Creekmur**, Detroit Lions	.65	.30	.06
☐	21 **Dave Hanner**, Green Bay Packers	.90	.40	.09
☐	22 **Norm Van Brocklin**, Los Angeles Rams	6.50	3.00	.65
☐	23 **Don Chandler**, New York Giants	.65	.30	.06
☐	24 **Al Dorow**, Washington Redskins	.65	.30	.06
☐	25 **Tom Scott**, Philadelphia Eagles	.65	.30	.06
☐	26 **Ollie Matson**, Chicago Cardinals	3.00	1.40	.30
☐	27 **Fran Rogel**, Pittsburgh Steelers	.65	.30	.06
☐	28 **Lou Groza**, Cleveland Browns	4.50	2.10	.45
☐	29 **Billy Vessels**, Baltimore Colts	.65	.30	.06
☐	30 **Y.A. Tittle**, San Francisco 49ers	6.50	3.00	.65
☐	31 **George Blanda**, Chicago Bears	7.50	3.50	.75
☐	32 **Bobby Layne**, Detroit Lions	6.50	3.00	.65
☐	33 **Bill Howton**, Green Bay Packers	.90	.40	.09
☐	34 **Bill Wade**, Los Angeles Rams	1.00	.45	.10
☐	35 **Emlen Tunnell**, New York Giants	3.00	1.40	.30
☐	36 **Leo Elter**, Washington Redskins	.65	.30	.06
☐	37 **Clarence Peaks**, Philadelphia Eagles	.65	.30	.06
☐	38 **Don Stonesifer**, Chicago Cardinals	.65	.30	.06
☐	39 **George Tarasovic**, Pittsburgh Steelers	.65	.30	.06
☐	40 **Darrell Brewster**, Cleveland Browns	.65	.30	.06
☐	41 **Bert Rechichar**, Baltimore Colts	.65	.30	.06
☐	42 **Billy Wilson**, San Francisco 49ers	.90	.40	.09
☐	43 **Ed Brown**, Chicago Bears	1.00	.45	.10
☐	44 **Gene Gedman**, Detroit Lions	.65	.30	.06
☐	45 **Gary Knafelc**, Green Bay Packers	.65	.30	.06
☐	46 **Elroy Hirsch**, Los Angeles Rams	4.50	2.10	.45
☐	47 **Don Heinrich**, New York Giants	1.00	.45	.10
☐	48 **Gene Brito**, Washington Redskins	.65	.30	.06
☐	49 **Chuck Bednarik**, Philadelphia Eagles	4.50	2.10	.45
☐	50 **Dave Mann**, Chicago Cardinals	.65	.30	.06
☐	51 **Bill McPeak**, Pittsburgh Steelers	.65	.30	.06
☐	52 **Kenny Konz**, Cleveland Browns	.65	.30	.06
☐	53 **Alan Ameche**, Baltimore Colts	1.50	.70	.15
☐	54 **Gordon Soltau**, San Francisco 49ers	.65	.30	.06
☐	55 **Rick Casares**, Chicago Bears	1.00	.45	.10
☐	56 **Charlie Ane**, Detroit Lions	.65	.30	.06
☐	57 **Al Carmichael**, Green Bay Packers	.65	.30	.06
☐	58 **Willard Sherman**, Los Angeles Rams	1.25	.60	.12
☐	59 **Kyle Rote**, New York Giants	3.00	1.40	.30

		MINT	VG-E	F-G
☐ 60	**Chuck Drazenovich**, Washington Redskins ...	.65	.30	.06
☐ 61	**Bobby Walston**, Philadelphia Eagles	.65	.30	.06
☐ 62	**John Olszewski**, Chicago Cardinals	.65	.30	.06
☐ 63	**Ray Mathews**, Pittsburgh Steelers	.65	.30	.06
☐ 64	**Maurice Bassett**, Cleveland Browns	.65	.30	.06
☐ 65	**Art Donovan**, Baltimore Colts	2.50	1.15	.25
☐ 66	**Joe Arenas**, San Francisco 49ers	.65	.30	.06
☐ 67	**Harlon Hill**, Chicago Bears	1.00	.45	.10
☐ 68	**Yale Lary**, Detroit Lions	2.50	1.15	.25
☐ 69	**Bill Forester**, Green Bay Packers	1.00	.45	.10
☐ 70	**Bob Boyd**, Los Angeles Rams	.65	.30	.06
☐ 71	**Andy Robustelli**, New York Giants	2.50	1.15	.25
☐ 72	**Sam Baker**, Washington Redskins	1.00	.45	.10
☐ 73	**Bob Pellegrini**, Philadelphia Eagles	.65	.30	.06
☐ 74	**Leo Sanford**, Chicago Cardinals	.65	.30	.06
☐ 75	**Sid Watson**, Pittsburgh Steelers	.65	.30	.06
☐ 76	**Ray Renfro**, Cleveland Browns	1.00	.45	.10
☐ 77	**Carl Taseff**, Baltimore Colts	.65	.30	.06
☐ 78	**Clyde Conner**, San Francisco 49ers	.65	.30	.06
☐ 79	**J.C. Caroline**, Chicago Bears	.65	.30	.06
☐ 80	**Howard Cassady**, Detroit Lions	1.50	.70	.15
☐ 81	**Tobin Rote**, Green Bay Packers	1.50	.70	.15
☐ 82	**Ron Waller**, Los Angeles Rams	.65	.30	.06
☐ 83	**Jim Patton**, New York Giants	.65	.30	.06
☐ 84	**Volney Peters**, Washington Redskins	.65	.30	.06
☐ 85	**Dick Lane**, Chicago Cardinals	4.50	2.10	.45
☐ 86	**Royce Womble**, Baltimore Colts	.65	.30	.06
☐ 87	**Duane Putnam**, Los Angeles Rams	.65	.30	.06
☐ 88	**Frank Gifford**, New York Giants	15.00	7.00	1.50
☐ 89	**Steve Meilinger**, Washington Redskins	.90	.40	.09
☐ 90	**Buck Lansford**, Philadelphia Eagles	.90	.40	.09
☐ 91	**Lindon Crow**, Chicago Cardinals	.90	.40	.09
☐ 92	**Ernie Stautner**, Pittsburgh Steelers	3.00	1.40	.30
☐ 93	**Preston Carpenter**, Cleveland Browns	.90	.40	.09
☐ 94	**Raymond Berry**, Baltimore Colts	9.00	4.25	.90
☐ 95	**Hugh McElhenny**, San Francisco 49ers	4.50	2.10	.45
☐ 96	**Stan Jones**, Chicago Bears	.90	.40	.09
☐ 97	**Dorne Dibble**, Detroit Lions	.90	.40	.09
☐ 98	**Joe Scudero**, Washington Redskins	.90	.40	.09
☐ 99	**Eddie Bell**, Philadelphia Eagles	.90	.40	.09
☐ 100	**Joe Childress**, Chicago Cardinals	.90	.40	.09
☐ 101	**Elbert Nickel**, Pittsburgh Steelers	.90	.40	.09
☐ 102	**Walt Michaels**, Cleveland Browns	1.50	.70	.15
☐ 103	**Jim Mutscheller**, Baltimore Colts	.90	.40	.09
☐ 104	**Earl Morrall**, San Francisco 49ers	4.50	2.10	.45
☐ 105	**Larry Strickland**, Chicago Bears	.90	.40	.09

		MINT	VG-E	F-G
☐ 106	Jack Christiansen, Detroit Lions	3.50	1.65	.35
☐ 107	Fred Cone, Green Bay Packers	.90	.40	.09
☐ 108	Bud McFadin, Los Angeles Rams	.90	.40	.09
☐ 109	Charley Conerly, New York Giants	3.50	1.65	.35
☐ 110	Tom Runnels, Washington Redskins	.90	.40	.09
☐ 111	Ken Keller, Philadelphia Eagles	.90	.40	.09
☐ 112	James Root, Chicago Cardinals	.90	.40	.09
☐ 113	Ted Marchibroda, Pittsburgh Steelers	1.25	.60	.12
☐ 114	Don Paul, Cleveland Browns	.90	.40	.09
☐ 115	George Shaw, Baltimore Colts	1.25	.60	.12
☐ 116	Dick Moegle, San Francisco 49ers	.90	.40	.09
☐ 117	Don Bingham, Chicago Bears	.90	.40	.09
☐ 118	Leon Hart, Detroit Lions	1.50	.70	.15
☐ 119	Bart Starr, Green Bay Packers	32.00	15.00	3.20
☐ 120	Paul Miller, Los Angeles Rams	.90	.40	.09
☐ 121	Alex Webster, New York Giants	1.50	.70	.15
☐ 122	Ray Wietecha, New York Giants	.90	.40	.09
☐ 123	Tommy Carson, Washington Redskins	.90	.40	.09
☐ 124	Tommy McDonald, Philadelphia Eagles	1.50	.70	.15
☐ 125	Jerry Tubbs, Chicago Cardinals	1.50	.70	.15
☐ 126	Jack Scarbath, Pittsburgh Steelers	.90	.40	.09
☐ 127	Ed Modzelewski, Cleveland Browns	.90	.40	.09
☐ 128	Lenny Moore, Baltimore Colts	5.00	2.35	.50
☐ 129	Joe Perry, San Francisco 49ers	5.00	2.35	.50
☐ 130	Bill Wightkin, Chicago Bears	.90	.40	.09
☐ 131	Jim Doran, Detroit Lions	.90	.40	.09
☐ 132	Howard Ferguson, Green Bay Packers	.90	.40	.09
☐ 133	Tom Wilson, Los Angeles Rams	.90	.40	.09
☐ 134	Dick James, Washington Redskins	.90	.40	.09
☐ 135	Jimmy Harris, Philadelphia Eagles	.90	.40	.09
☐ 136	Chuck Ulrich, Chicago Cardinals	.90	.40	.09
☐ 137	Lynn Chandnois, Pittsburgh Steelers	.90	.40	.09
☐ 138	John Unitas, Baltimore Colts	40.00	18.00	4.00
☐ 139	Jim Ridlon, San Francisco 49ers	.90	.40	.09
☐ 140	Zeke Bratkowski, Chicago Bears	1.50	.70	.15
☐ 141	Ray Krouse, Detroit Lions	.90	.40	.09
☐ 142	John Martinkovic, Green Bay Packers	.90	.40	.09
☐ 143	Jim Cason, Los Angeles Rams	.90	.40	.09
☐ 144	Ken MacAfee, New York Giants	.90	.40	.09
☐ 145	Sid Youngelman, Philadelphia Eagles	.90	.40	.09
☐ 146	Paul Larson, Chicago Cardinals	.90	.40	.09
☐ 147	Len Ford, Cleveland Browns	3.50	1.65	.35
☐ 148	Bob Toneff, San Francisco 49ers	.90	.40	.09
☐ 149	Ronnie Knox, Chicago Bears	1.25	.60	.12
☐ 150	Jim David, Detroit Lions	.90	.40	.09
☐ 151	Paul Hornung, Green Bay Packers	32.00	15.00	3.20

		MINT	VG-E	F-G
☐ 152	**Tank Younger,** Los Angeles Rams	1.50	.70	.15
☐ 153	**Bill Svoboda,** New York Giants	.90	.40	.09
☐ 154	**Fred Morrison,** Cleveland Browns	2.00	.50	.10
☐ 155	**Unnumbered Checklist**	60.00	12.00	2.00

1958 TOPPS

The 1958 Topps set of 132 cards contains NFL players. After a one-year interruption, team cards are back in the Topps football set. The cards measure 2½" by 3½". The rookie cards of Jim Brown and Sonny Jurgensen are included in this set. The backs are easily distinguished from other years, as they are printed in bright red ink on white stock. The right-hand side of the reverse gives a trivia question; the answer could be obtained by rubbing with a coin over the blank space.

		MINT	VG-E	F-G
	COMPLETE SET	165.00	75.00	15.00
	COMMON PLAYER (1-132)	.50	.22	.05
☐ 1	**Gene Filipski,** New York Giants	2.50	.50	.10
☐ 2	**Bobby Layne,** Detroit Lions	5.50	2.60	.55
☐ 3	**Joe Schmidt,** Detroit Lions	2.50	1.15	.25
☐ 4	**Bill Barnes,** Philadelphia Eagles	.50	.22	.05
☐ 5	**Milt Plum,** Cleveland Browns	1.25	.60	.12
☐ 6	**Bill Howton,** Green Bay Packers	.65	.30	.06
☐ 7	**Howard Cassady,** Detroit Lions	.75	.35	.07
☐ 8	**Jim Dooley,** Chicago Bears	.65	.30	.06
☐ 9	**Cleveland Browns Team Card**	1.25	.60	.12
☐ 10	**Lenny Moore,** Baltimore Colts	4.00	1.85	.40

		MINT	VG-E	F-G
☐ 11	**Darrell Brewster,** Cleveland Browns	.50	.22	.05
☐ 12	**Alan Ameche,** Baltimore Colts	1.25	.60	.12
☐ 13	**Jim David,** Detroit Lions	.50	.22	.05
☐ 14	**Jim Mutscheller,** Baltimore Colts	.50	.22	.05
☐ 15	**Andy Robustelli,** New York Giants	2.00	.90	.20
☐ 16	**Gino Marchetti,** Baltimore Colts	2.50	1.15	.25
☐ 17	**Ray Renfro,** Cleveland Browns	.75	.35	.07
☐ 18	**Yale Lary,** Detroit Lions	2.00	.90	.20
☐ 19	**Gary Glick,** Pittsburgh Steelers	.50	.22	.05
☐ 20	**Jon Arnett,** Los Angeles Rams	1.00	.45	.10
☐ 21	**Bob Boyd,** Los Angeles Rams	.50	.22	.05
☐ 22	**John Unitas,** Baltimore Colts	14.00	6.50	1.40
☐ 23	**Zeke Bratkowski,** Chicago Bears	1.00	.45	.10
☐ 24	**Sid Youngelman,** Philadelphia Eagles	.50	.22	.05
☐ 25	**Leo Elter,** Pittsburgh Steelers	.50	.22	.05
☐ 26	**Kenny Konz,** Cleveland Browns	.50	.22	.05
☐ 27	**Washington Redskins Team Card**	1.25	.60	.12
☐ 28	**Carl Brettschneider,** Chicago Cardinals	.50	.22	.05
☐ 29	**Chicago Bears Team Card**	1.25	.60	.12
☐ 30	**Alex Webster,** New York Giants	1.25	.60	.12
☐ 31	**Al Carmichael,** Green Bay Packers	.50	.22	.05
☐ 32	**Bobby Dan Dillon,** Green Bay Packers	.65	.30	.06
☐ 33	**Steve Meilinger,** Green Bay Packers	.50	.22	.05
☐ 34	**Sam Baker,** Washington Redskins	.65	.30	.06
☐ 35	**Chuck Bednarik,** Philadelphia Eagles	4.00	1.85	.40
☐ 36	**Bert Vic Zucco,** Chicago Bears	.50	.22	.05
☐ 37	**George Tarasovic,** Pittsburgh Steelers	.50	.22	.05
☐ 38	**Bill Wade,** Los Angeles Rams	.75	.35	.07
☐ 39	**Dick Stanfel,** Washington Redskins	.50	.22	.05
☐ 40	**Jerry Norton,** Philadelphia Eagles	.50	.22	.05
☐ 41	**San Francisco 49ers Team**	1.25	.60	.12
☐ 42	**Emlen Tunnell,** New York Giants	2.00	.90	.20
☐ 43	**Jim Doran,** Detroit Lions	.50	.22	.05
☐ 44	**Ted Marchibroda,** Chicago Cardinals	.65	.30	.06
☐ 45	**Chet Hanulak,** Cleveland Browns	.50	.22	.05
☐ 46	**Dale Dodrill,** Pittsburgh Steelers	.50	.22	.05
☐ 47	**Johnny Carson,** Washington Redskins	.50	.22	.05
☐ 48	**Dick Deschaine,** Cleveland Browns	.50	.22	.05
☐ 49	**Billy Wells,** Philadelphia Eagles	.50	.22	.05
☐ 50	**Larry Morris,** Los Angeles Rams	.50	.22	.05
☐ 51	**Jack McClairen,** Pittsburgh Steelers	.50	.22	.05
☐ 52	**Lou Groza,** Cleveland Browns	4.00	1.85	.40
☐ 53	**Rick Casares,** Chicago Bears	.75	.35	.07
☐ 54	**Don Chandler,** New York Giants	.50	.22	.05
☐ 55	**Duane Putnam,** Los Angeles Rams	.50	.22	.05
☐ 56	**Gary Knafelc,** Green Bay Packers	.50	.22	.05

			MINT	VG-E	F-G
☐	57	**Earl Morrall,** Pittsburgh Steelers	1.75	.85	.17
☐	58	**Ron Kramer,** Green Bay Packers	.65	.30	.06
☐	59	**Mike McCormack,** Cleveland Browns	2.00	.90	.20
☐	60	**Gern Nagler,** Chicago Bears	.50	.22	.05
☐	61	**New York Giants Team Card**	1.25	.60	.12
☐	62	**Jim Brown,** Cleveland Browns	50.00	22.00	5.00
☐	63	**Joe Marconi,** Los Angeles Rams	.50	.22	.05
☐	64	**R.C. Owens (photo actually Don Owens),** San Francisco 49ers	.65	.30	.06
☐	65	**Jimmy Carr,** Chicago Cardinals	.50	.22	.05
☐	66	**Bart Starr,** Green Bay Packers	9.00	4.25	.90
☐	67	**Tom Wilson,** Los Angeles Rams	.50	.22	.05
☐	68	**Lamar McHan,** Chicago Cardinals	.65	.30	.06
☐	69	**Chicago Cardinals Team Card**	1.25	.60	.12
☐	70	**Jack Christiansen,** Detroit Lions	2.00	.90	.20
☐	71	**Don McIlhenny,** Green Bay Packers	.50	.22	.05
☐	72	**Ron Waller,** Los Angeles Rams	.50	.22	.05
☐	73	**Frank Gifford,** New York Giants	12.50	5.75	1.25
☐	74	**Bert Rechichar,** Baltimore Colts	.50	.22	.05
☐	75	**John Henry Johnson,** Detroit Lions	1.25	.60	.12
☐	76	**Jack Butler,** Pittsburgh Steelers	.50	.22	.05
☐	77	**Frank Varrichione,** Pittsburgh Steelers	.50	.22	.05
☐	78	**Ray Mathews,** Pittsburgh Steelers	.50	.22	.05
☐	79	**Marv Matuszak,** San Francisco 49ers	.50	.22	.05
☐	80	**Harlon Hill,** Chicago Bears	.75	.35	.07
☐	81	**Lou Creekmur,** Detroit Lions	.50	.22	.05
☐	82	**Woodley Lewis,** Chicago Cardinals	.50	.22	.05
☐	83	**Don Heinrich,** New York Giants	.75	.35	.07
☐	84	**Charley Conerly,** New York Giants	2.50	1.15	.25
☐	85	**Los Angeles Rams Team Card**	1.25	.60	.12
☐	86	**Y.A. Tittle,** San Francisco 49ers	5.50	2.60	.55
☐	87	**Bobby Walston,** Philadelphia Eagles	.50	.22	.05
☐	88	**Earl Putman,** Chicago Cardinals	.50	.22	.05
☐	89	**Leo Nomellini,** San Francisco 49ers	2.00	.90	.20
☐	90	**Sonny Jurgensen,** Philadelphia Eagles	15.00	7.00	1.50
☐	91	**Don Paul,** Cleveland Browns	.50	.22	.05
☐	92	**Paige Cothren,** Los Angeles Rams	.50	.22	.05
☐	93	**Joe Perry,** San Francisco 49ers	4.00	1.85	.40
☐	94	**Tobin Rote,** Detroit Lions	1.00	.45	.10
☐	95	**Billy Wilson,** San Francisco 49ers	.65	.30	.06
☐	96	**Green Bay Packers Team Card**	1.25	.60	.12
☐	97	**Lavern Torgenson,** Washington Redskins	.50	.22	.05
☐	98	**Milt Davis,** Baltimore Colts	.50	.22	.05
☐	99	**Larry Strickland,** Chicago Bears	.50	.22	.05
☐	100	**Matt Hazeltine,** San Francisco 49ers	.50	.22	.05
☐	101	**Walt Yowarski,** San Francisco 49ers	.50	.22	.05

		MINT	VG-E	F-G
☐ 102	**Roosevelt Brown**, New York Giants	2.00	.90	.20
☐ 103	**Jim Ringo**, Green Bay Packers	2.00	.90	.20
☐ 104	**Joe Krupa**, Pittsburgh Steelers	.50	.22	.05
☐ 105	**Les Richter**, Los Angeles Rams	.65	.30	.06
☐ 106	**Art Donovan**, Baltimore Colts	2.00	.90	.20
☐ 107	**John Olszewski**, Washington Redskins	.50	.22	.05
☐ 108	**Ken Keller**, Philadelphia Eagles	.50	.22	.05
☐ 109	**Philadelphia Eagles Team Card**	1.25	.60	.12
☐ 110	**Baltimore Colts Team Card**	1.25	.60	.12
☐ 111	**Dick Bielski**, Philadelphia Eagles	.50	.22	.05
☐ 112	**Eddie LeBaron**, Washington Redskins	1.00	.45	.10
☐ 113	**Gene Brito**, Washington Redskins	.50	.22	.05
☐ 114	**Willie Galimore**, Chicago Bears	.65	.30	.06
☐ 115	**Detroit Lions Team Card**	1.25	.60	.12
☐ 116	**Pittsburgh Steelers Team Card**	1.25	.60	.12
☐ 117	**L.G. Dupre**, Baltimore Colts	.50	.22	.05
☐ 118	**Babe Parilli**, Green Bay Packers	1.25	.60	.12
☐ 119	**Bill George**, Chicago Bears	2.00	.90	.20
☐ 120	**Raymond Berry**, Baltimore Colts	4.00	1.85	.40
☐ 121	**Jim Podoley (photo actually Volney Peters)**, Washington Redskins	.50	.22	.05
☐ 122	**Hugh McElhenny**, San Francisco 49ers	3.00	1.40	.30
☐ 123	**Ed Brown**, Chicago Bears	.75	.35	.07
☐ 124	**Dick Moegle**, San Francisco 49ers	.50	.22	.05
☐ 125	**Tom Scott**, Philadelphia Eagles	.50	.22	.05
☐ 126	**Tommy McDonald**, Philadelphia Eagles	1.00	.45	.10
☐ 127	**Ollie Matson**, Chicago Cardinals	3.00	1.40	.30
☐ 128	**Preston Carpenter**, Cleveland Browns	.50	.22	.05
☐ 129	**George Blanda**, Chicago Bears	6.00	2.80	.60
☐ 130	**Gordon Soltau**, San Francisco 49ers	.50	.22	.05
☐ 131	**Dick Nolan**, Chicago Cardinals	1.25	.60	.12
☐ 132	**Don Bosseler**, Washington Redskins	1.50	.40	.08

1959 TOPPS

The 1959 Topps set contains 176 cards which were issued in two series. The cards measure 2½" by 3½". Card backs include a scratch-off quiz. Team cards (with checklist backs), as well as team pennant cards, are included in the set. The card backs were printed in gray on white card stock. Statistical information from the immediate past season and career totals are given on the reverse.

		MINT	VG-E	F-G
	COMPLETE SET	150.00	70.00	15.00
	COMMON PLAYER (1-88)	.40	.18	.04
	COMMON PLAYER (89-176)	.30	.12	.03
☐	1 Johnny Unitas, Baltimore Colts	12.50	4.00	1.00
☐	2 Gene Brito, Los Angeles Rams	.40	.18	.04
☐	3 Detroit Lions Team Card	1.10	.30	.05
☐	4 Max McGee, Green Bay Packers	1.00	.45	.10
☐	5 Hugh McElhenny, San Francisco 49ers	2.50	1.15	.25
☐	6 Joe Schmidt, Detroit Lions	2.00	.90	.20
☐	7 Kyle Rote, New York Giants	2.00	.90	.20
☐	8 Clarence Peaks, Philadelphia Eagles	.40	.18	.04
☐	9 Pittsburgh Steelers Pennant	.60	.28	.06
☐	10 Jim Brown, Cleveland Browns	20.00	9.00	2.00
☐	11 Ray Mathews, Pittsburgh Steelers	.40	.18	.04
☐	12 Bobby Dan Dillon, Green Bay Packers	.50	.22	.05
☐	13 Joe Childress, Chicago Cardinals	.40	.18	.04
☐	14 Terry Barr, Detroit Lions	.40	.18	.04
☐	15 Del Shofner, Los Angeles Rams	.90	.40	.09
☐	16 Bob Pellegrini, Philadelphia Eagles	.40	.18	.04
☐	17 Baltimore Colts Team Card	1.10	.30	.05

		MINT	VG-E	F-G
☐ 18	Preston Carpenter, Cleveland Browns	.40	.18	.04
☐ 19	Leo Nomellini, San Francisco 49ers	1.75	.85	.17
☐ 20	Frank Gifford, New York Giants	11.00	5.25	1.10
☐ 21	Charlie Ane, Detroit Lions	.40	.18	.04
☐ 22	Jack Butler, Pittsburgh Steelers	.40	.18	.04
☐ 23	Bart Starr, Green Bay Packers	7.50	3.50	.75
☐ 24	Chicago Cardinals Team Pennant	.60	.28	.06
☐ 25	Bill Barnes, Philadelphia Eagles	.40	.18	.04
☐ 26	Walt Michaels, Cleveland Browns	.75	.35	.07
☐ 27	Clyde Conner, San Francisco 49ers	.40	.18	.04
☐ 28	Paige Cothren, Philadelphia Eagles	.40	.18	.04
☐ 29	Roosevelt Grier, New York Giants	1.75	.85	.17
☐ 30	Alan Ameche, Baltimore Colts	1.00	.45	.10
☐ 31	Philadelphia Eagles Team	1.10	.30	.05
☐ 32	Dick Nolan, New York Giants	1.00	.45	.10
☐ 33	R.C. Owens, San Francisco 49ers	.40	.18	.04
☐ 34	Dale Dodrill, Pittsburgh Steelers	.40	.18	.04
☐ 35	Gene Gedman, Detroit Lions	.40	.18	.04
☐ 36	Gene Lipscomb, Baltimore Colts	1.75	.85	.17
☐ 37	Ray Renfro, Cleveland Browns	.60	.28	.06
☐ 38	Cleveland Browns Team Pennant	.60	.28	.06
☐ 39	Bill Forester, Green Bay Packers	.60	.28	.06
☐ 40	Bobby Layne, Pittsburgh Steelers	5.00	2.35	.50
☐ 41	Pat Summerall, New York Giants	2.25	1.00	.22
☐ 42	Jerry Mertens, San Francisco 49ers	.40	.18	.04
☐ 43	Steve Myhra, Baltimore Colts	.40	.18	.04
☐ 44	John Henry Johnson, Detroit Lions	1.00	.45	.10
☐ 45	Woodley Lewis, Chicago Cardinals	.40	.18	.04
☐ 46	Green Bay Packers Team Card	1.10	.30	.05
☐ 47	Don Owens, Philadelphia Eagles	.40	.18	.04
☐ 48	Ed Beatty, Pittsburgh Steelers	.40	.18	.04
☐ 49	Don Chandler, New York Giants	.40	.18	.04
☐ 50	Ollie Matson, Los Angeles Rams	2.25	1.00	.22
☐ 51	Sam Huff, New York Giants	4.00	1.85	.40
☐ 52	Tom Miner, Pittsburgh Steelers	.40	.18	.04
☐ 53	New York Giants Team Pennant	.60	.28	.06
☐ 54	Kenny Konz, Cleveland Browns	.40	.18	.04
☐ 55	Raymond Berry, Baltimore Colts	3.50	1.65	.35
☐ 56	Howard Ferguson, Green Bay Packers	.40	.18	.04
☐ 57	Chuck Ulrich, Chicago Cardinals	.40	.18	.04
☐ 58	Bob St. Clair, San Francisco 49ers	.40	.18	.04
☐ 59	Don Burroughs, Los Angeles Rams	.40	.18	.04
☐ 60	Lou Groza, Cleveland Browns	3.50	1.65	.35
☐ 61	San Francisco 49ers Team	1.10	.30	.05
☐ 62	Andy Nelson, Baltimore Colts	.40	.18	.04
☐ 63	Hal Bradley, Philadelphia Eagles	.40	.18	.04

			MINT	VG-E	F-G
☐	64	**Dave Hanner,** Green Bay Packers	.50	.22	.05
☐	65	**Charley Conerly,** New York Giants	2.50	1.15	.25
☐	66	**Gene Cronin,** Detroit Lions	.40	.18	.04
☐	67	**Duane Putnam,** Los Angeles Rams	.40	.18	.04
☐	68	**Baltimore Colts Team Pennant**	.60	.28	.06
☐	69	**Ernie Stautner,** Pittsburgh Steelers	2.25	1.00	.22
☐	70	**Jon Arnett,** Los Angeles Rams	.60	.28	.06
☐	71	**Ken Panfil,** Chicago Cardinals	.40	.18	.04
☐	72	**Matt Hazeltine,** San Francisco 49ers	.40	.18	.04
☐	73	**Harley Sewell,** Detroit Lions	.40	.18	.04
☐	74	**Mike McCormack,** Cleveland Browns	1.75	.85	.17
☐	75	**Jim Ringo,** Green Bay Packers	1.75	.85	.17
☐	76	**Los Angeles Rams Team Card**	1.10	.30	.05
☐	77	**Bob Gain,** Cleveland Browns	.40	.18	.04
☐	78	**Buzz Nutter,** Baltimore Colts	.40	.18	.04
☐	79	**Jerry Norton,** Chicago Cardinals	.40	.18	.04
☐	80	**Joe Perry,** San Francisco 49ers	3.50	1.65	.35
☐	81	**Carl Brettschneider,** Chicago Cardinals	.40	.18	.04
☐	82	**Paul Hornung,** Green Bay Packers	6.00	2.80	.60
☐	83	**Philadelphia Eagles Pennant**	.60	.28	.06
☐	84	**Les Richter,** Los Angeles Rams	.50	.22	.05
☐	85	**Howard Cassady,** Detroit Lions	.60	.28	.06
☐	86	**Art Donovan,** Baltimore Colts	1.75	.85	.17
☐	87	**Jim Patton,** New York Giants	.50	.22	.05
☐	88	**Pete Retzlaff,** Philadelphia Eagles	.50	.22	.05
☐	89	**Jim Mutscheller,** Baltimore Colts	.30	.12	.03
☐	90	**Zeke Bratkowski,** Chicago Bears	.80	.40	.08
☐	91	**Washington Redskins Team Card**	1.10	.30	.05
☐	92	**Art Hunter,** Cleveland Browns	.30	.12	.03
☐	93	**Gern Nagler,** Pittsburgh Steelers	.30	.12	.03
☐	94	**Chuck Weber,** Philadelphia Eagles	.30	.12	.03
☐	95	**Lew Carpenter,** Green Bay Packers	.30	.12	.03
☐	96	**Stan Jones,** Chicago Bears	.30	.12	.03
☐	97	**Ralph Guglielmi,** Washington Redskins	.40	.18	.04
☐	98	**Green Bay Packers Team Pennant**	.60	.28	.06
☐	99	**Ray Wietecha,** New York Giants	.30	.12	.03
☐	100	**Lenny Moore,** Baltimore Colts	2.50	1.15	.25
☐	101	**Jim Ray Smith,** Cleveland Browns	.30	.12	.03
☐	102	**Abe Woodson,** San Francisco 49ers	.40	.18	.04
☐	103	**Alex Karras,** Detroit Lions	6.00	2.80	.60
☐	104	**Chicago Bears Team Card**	1.10	.30	.05
☐	105	**John David Crow,** Chicago Cardinals	.90	.40	.09
☐	106	**Joe Fortunato,** Chicago Bears	.40	.18	.04
☐	107	**Babe Parilli,** Green Bay Packers	.90	.40	.09
☐	108	**Proverb Jacobs,** Philadelphia Eagles	.30	.12	.03
☐	109	**Gino Marchetti,** Baltimore Colts	2.25	1.00	.22

	MINT	VG-E	F-G
☐ 110 **Bill Wade**, Los Angeles Rams	.60	.28	.06
☐ 111 **San Francisco 49ers Pennant**	.60	.28	.06
☐ 112 **Karl Rubke**, San Francisco 49ers	.30	.12	.03
☐ 113 **Dave Middleton**, Detroit Lions	.30	.12	.03
☐ 114 **Roosevelt Brown**, New York Giants	1.75	.85	.17
☐ 115 **John Olszewski**, Washington Redskins	.30	.12	.03
☐ 116 **Jerry Kramer**, Green Bay Packers	2.50	1.15	.25
☐ 117 **King Hill**, Chicago Cardinals	1.00	.45	.10
☐ 118 **Chicago Cardinals Team Card**	1.00	.30	.05
☐ 119 **Frank Varrichione**, Pittsburgh Steelers	.30	.12	.03
☐ 120 **Rick Casares**, Chicago Bears	.60	.28	.06
☐ 121 **George Strugar**, Los Angeles Rams	.30	.12	.03
☐ 122 **Bill Glass**, Detroit Lions	.40	.18	.04
☐ 123 **Don Bosseler**, Washington Redskins	.30	.12	.03
☐ 124 **John Reger**, Pittsburgh Steelers	.30	.12	.03
☐ 125 **Jim Ninowski**, Cleveland Browns	.60	.28	.06
☐ 126 **Los Angeles Rams Team Pennant**	.60	.28	.06
☐ 127 **Willard Sherman**, Los Angeles Rams	.30	.12	.03
☐ 128 **Bob Schnelker**, New York Giants	.50	.22	.05
☐ 129 **Ollie Spencer**, Detroit Lions	.30	.12	.03
☐ 130 **Y.A. Tittle**, San Francisco 49ers	5.00	2.35	.50
☐ 131 **Yale Lary**, Detroit Lions	1.75	.85	.17
☐ 132 **Jim Parker**, Baltimore Colts	3.50	1.65	.35
☐ 133 **New York Giants Team Card**	1.10	.30	.05
☐ 134 **Jim Schrader**, Washington Redskins	.30	.12	.03
☐ 135 **M.C. Reynolds**, Chicago Cardinals	.30	.12	.03
☐ 136 **Mike Sandusky**, Pittsburgh Steelers	.30	.12	.03
☐ 137 **Ed Brown**, Chicago Bears	.60	.28	.06
☐ 138 **Al Barry**, New York Giants	.30	.12	.03
☐ 139 **Detroit Lions Team Pennant**	.60	.28	.06
☐ 140 **Bobby Mitchell**, Cleveland Browns	4.50	2.10	.45
☐ 141 **Larry Morris**, Chicago Bears	.30	.12	.03
☐ 142 **Jim Phillips**, Los Angeles Rams	.30	.12	.03
☐ 143 **Jim David**, Detroit Lions	.30	.12	.03
☐ 144 **Joe Krupa**, Pittsburgh Steelers	.30	.12	.03
☐ 145 **Willie Galimore**, Chicago Bears	.40	.18	.04
☐ 146 **Pittsburgh Steelers Team**	1.10	.30	.05
☐ 147 **Andy Robustelli**, New York Giants	1.75	.85	.17
☐ 148 **Billy Wilson**, San Francisco 49ers	.40	.18	.04
☐ 149 **Leo Sanford**, Baltimore Colts	.30	.12	.03
☐ 150 **Eddie LeBaron**, Washington Redskins	.90	.40	.09
☐ 151 **Bill McColl**, Chicago Bears	.30	.12	.03
☐ 152 **Buck Lansford**, Los Angeles Rams	.30	.12	.03
☐ 153 **Chicago Bears Team Pennant**	.60	.28	.06
☐ 154 **Leo Sugar**, Chicago Cardinals	.30	.12	.03

	MINT	VG-E	F-G
☐ 155 **Jim Taylor (photo actually Jim Taylor Cardinal LB), Green Bay Packers**	3.50	1.65	.35
☐ 156 **Lindon Crow**, New York Giants	.30	.12	.03
☐ 157 **Jack McClairen**, Pittsburgh Steelers	.30	.12	.03
☐ 158 **Vince Costello**, Cleveland Browns	.30	.12	.03
☐ 159 **Stan Wallace**, Chicago Bears	.30	.12	.03
☐ 160 **Mel Triplett**, New York Giants	.30	.12	.03
☐ 161 **Cleveland Browns Team Card**	1.10	.30	.05
☐ 162 **Dan Currie**, Green Bay Packers	.30	.12	.03
☐ 163 **L.G. Dupre**, Baltimore Colts	.30	.12	.03
☐ 164 **John Morrow**, Los Angeles Rams	.30	.12	.03
☐ 165 **Jim Podoley**, Washington Redskins	.30	.12	.03
☐ 166 **Bruce Bosley**, San Francisco 49ers	.30	.12	.03
☐ 167 **Harlon Hill**, Chicago Bears	.50	.22	.05
☐ 168 **Washington Redskins Pennant**	.60	.28	.06
☐ 169 **Junior Wren**, Cleveland Browns	.30	.12	.03
☐ 170 **Tobin Rote**, Detroit Lions	.90	.40	.09
☐ 171 **Art Spinney**, Baltimore Colts	.30	.12	.03
☐ 172 **Chuck Drazenovich**, Washington Redskins ...	.30	.12	.03
☐ 173 **Bobby Joe Conrad**, Chicago Cardinals	.60	.28	.06
☐ 174 **Jesse Richardson**, Philadelphia Eagles	.30	.12	.03
☐ 175 **Sam Baker**, Washington Redskins	.50	.22	.05
☐ 176 **Tom Tracy**, Pittsburgh Steelers	.75	.20	.04

1960 TOPPS

The 1960 Topps set contains 132 cards, each measuring 2½" by 3½". The card backs were printed in green on white card stock. Statistical information from the immediate past season and career totals are given on the reverse. The set marks the debut of the Dallas Cowboys into the National Football League. The backs feature a "Football Funnies" scratch-off quiz; answer was revealed by rubbing with the edge of a coin. Team cards feature checklist backs.

		MINT	VG-E	F-G
	COMPLETE SET	125.00	57.00	12.50
	COMMON PLAYER (1-132)	.35	.15	.03
☐	1 John Unitas, Baltimore Colts	12.50	3.50	.60
☐	2 Alan Ameche, Baltimore Colts	.90	.40	.09
☐	3 Lenny Moore, Baltimore Colts	2.50	1.15	.25
☐	4 Raymond Berry, Baltimore Colts	2.75	1.25	.27
☐	5 Jim Parker, Baltimore Colts	1.75	.85	.17
☐	6 George Preas, Baltimore Colts	.35	.15	.03
☐	7 Art Spinney, Baltimore Colts	.35	.15	.03
☐	8 Bill Pellington, Baltimore Colts	.35	.15	.03
☐	9 John Sample, Baltimore Colts	.35	.15	.03
☐	10 Gene Lipscomb, Baltimore Colts	.90	.40	.09
☐	11 Baltimore Colts Team Card	1.10	.30	.05
☐	12 Ed Brown, Chicago Bears	.55	.25	.05
☐	13 Rick Casares, Chicago Bears	.65	.30	.06
☐	14 Willie Galimore, Chicago Bears	.45	.20	.04
☐	15 Jim Dooley, Chicago Bears	.45	.20	.04
☐	16 Harlon Hill, Chicago Bears	.45	.20	.04
☐	17 Stan Jones, Chicago Bears	.35	.15	.03
☐	18 Bill George, Chicago Bears	1.75	.85	.17
☐	19 Erich Barnes, Chicago Bears	.35	.15	.03
☐	20 Doug Atkins, Chicago Bears	1.75	.85	.17
☐	21 Chicago Bears Team Card	1.10	.30	.05
☐	22 Milt Plum, Cleveland Browns	.90	.40	.09
☐	23 Jim Brown, Cleveland Browns	20.00	9.00	2.00
☐	24 Sam Baker, Cleveland Browns	.45	.20	.04
☐	25 Bobby Mitchell, Cleveland Browns	2.50	1.15	.25
☐	26 Ray Renfro, Cleveland Browns	.45	.20	.04
☐	27 Bill Howton, Cleveland Browns	.45	.20	.04
☐	28 Jim Ray Smith, Cleveland Browns	.35	.15	.03
☐	29 Jim Shofner, Cleveland Browns	.45	.20	.04
☐	30 Bob Gain, Cleveland Browns	.35	.15	.03
☐	31 Cleveland Browns Team Card	1.10	.30	.05
☐	32 Don Heinrich, Dallas Cowboys	.75	.35	.07
☐	33 Ed Modzeleski, Dallas Cowboys	.45	.20	.04
☐	34 Fred Cone, Dallas Cowboys	.45	.20	.04
☐	35 L.G. Dupre, Dallas Cowboys	.45	.20	.04
☐	36 Dick Bielski, Dallas Cowboys	.45	.20	.04

		MINT	VG-E	F-G
☐ 37	**Charlie Ane**, Dallas Cowboys	.45	.20	.04
☐ 38	**Jerry Tubbs**, Dallas Cowboys	.75	.35	.07
☐ 39	**Doyle Nix**, Dallas Cowboys	.45	.20	.04
☐ 40	**Ray Krouse**, Dallas Cowboys	.45	.20	.04
☐ 41	**Earl Morrall**, Detroit Lions	1.50	.70	.15
☐ 42	**Howard Cassady**, Detroit Lions	.55	.25	.05
☐ 43	**Dave Middleton**, Detroit Lions	.35	.15	.03
☐ 44	**Jim Gibbons**, Detroit Lions	.35	.15	.03
☐ 45	**Darris McCord**, Detroit Lions	.35	.15	.03
☐ 46	**Joe Schmidt**, Detroit Lions	2.00	.90	.20
☐ 47	**Terry Barr**, Detroit Lions	.35	.15	.03
☐ 48	**Yale Lary**, Detroit Lions	1.75	.85	.17
☐ 49	**Gil Mains**, Detroit Lions	.35	.15	.03
☐ 50	**Detroit Lions Team Card**	1.10	.30	.05
☐ 51	**Bart Starr**, Green Bay Packers	7.00	3.25	.70
☐ 52	**Jim Taylor (photo actually Jim Taylor Cardinal LB)**, Green Bay Packers	2.50	1.15	.25
☐ 53	**Lew Carpenter**, Green Bay Packers	.35	.15	.03
☐ 54	**Paul Hornung**, Green Bay Packers	5.50	2.60	.55
☐ 55	**Max McGee**, Green Bay Packers	.65	.30	.06
☐ 56	**Forrest Gregg**, Green Bay Packers	2.50	1.15	.25
☐ 57	**Jim Ringo**, Green Bay Packers	1.75	.85	.17
☐ 58	**Bill Forester**, Green Bay Packers	.55	.25	.05
☐ 59	**Dave Hanner**, Green Bay Packers	.55	.25	.05
☐ 60	**Green Bay Packers Team Card**	1.10	.30	.05
☐ 61	**Bill Wade**, Los Angeles Rams	.55	.25	.05
☐ 62	**Frank Ryan**, Los Angeles Rams	1.25	.60	.12
☐ 63	**Ollie Matson**, Los Angeles Rams	2.25	1.00	.22
☐ 64	**Jon Arnett**, Los Angeles Rams	.50	.22	.05
☐ 65	**Del Shofner**, Los Angeles Rams	.60	.28	.06
☐ 66	**Jim Phillips**, Los Angeles Rams	.35	.15	.03
☐ 67	**Art Hunter**, Los Angeles Rams	.35	.15	.03
☐ 68	**Les Richter**, Los Angeles Rams	.45	.20	.04
☐ 69	**Lou Michaels**, Los Angeles Rams	.45	.20	.04
☐ 70	**John Baker**, Los Angeles Rams	.35	.15	.03
☐ 71	**Los Angeles Rams Team Card**	1.10	.30	.05
☐ 72	**Charley Conerly**, New York Giants	2.50	1.15	.25
☐ 73	**Mel Triplett**, New York Giants	.35	.15	.03
☐ 74	**Frank Gifford**, New York Giants	11.00	5.25	1.10
☐ 75	**Alex Webster**, New York Giants	.65	.30	.06
☐ 76	**Bob Schnelker**, New York Giants	.45	.20	.04
☐ 77	**Pat Summerall**, New York Giants	2.00	.90	.20
☐ 78	**Roosevelt Brown**, New York Giants	1.75	.85	.17
☐ 79	**Jim Patton**, New York Giants	.45	.20	.04
☐ 80	**Sam Huff**, New York Giants	2.50	1.15	.25
☐ 81	**Andy Robustelli**, New York Giants	1.75	.85	.17

			MINT	VG-E	F-G
☐	82	**New York Giants Team Card**	1.10	.30	.05
☐	83	**Clarence Peaks**, Philadelphia Eagles	.35	.15	.03
☐	84	**Bill Barnes**, Philadelphia Eagles	.35	.15	.03
☐	85	**Pete Retzlaff**, Philadelphia Eagles	.45	.20	.04
☐	86	**Bobby Walston**, Philadelphia Eagles	.35	.15	.03
☐	87	**Chuck Bednarik**, Philadelphia Eagles	2.50	1.15	.25
☐	88	**Bob Pellegrini**, Philadelphia Eagles	.35	.15	.03
☐	89	**Tom Brookshier**, Philadelphia Eagles	1.25	.60	.12
☐	90	**Marion Campbell**, Philadelphia Eagles	.60	.28	.06
☐	91	**Jesse Richardson**, Philadelphia Eagles	.35	.15	.03
☐	92	**Philadelphia Eagles Team**	1.10	.30	.05
☐	93	**Bobby Layne**, Pittsburgh Steelers	5.00	2.35	.50
☐	94	**John Henry Johnson**, Pittsburgh Steelers	.90	.40	.09
☐	95	**Tom Tracy**, Pittsburgh Steelers	.45	.20	.04
☐	96	**Preston Carpenter**, Pittsburgh Steelers	.35	.15	.03
☐	97	**Frank Varrichione**, Pittsburgh Steelers	.35	.15	.03
☐	98	**John Nisby**, Pittsburgh Steelers	.35	.15	.03
☐	99	**Dean Derby**, Pittsburgh Steelers	.35	.15	.03
☐	100	**George Tarasovic**, Pittsburgh Steelers	.35	.15	.03
☐	101	**Ernie Stautner**, Pittsburgh Steelers	2.00	.90	.20
☐	102	**Pittsburgh Steelers Team Card**	1.10	.30	.05
☐	103	**King Hill**, St. Louis Cardinals	.75	.35	.07
☐	104	**Mal Hammack**, St. Louis Cardinals	.35	.15	.03
☐	105	**John David Crow**, St. Louis Cardinals	.50	.22	.05
☐	106	**Bobby Joe Conrad**, St. Louis Cardinals	.45	.20	.04
☐	107	**Woodley Lewis**, St. Louis Cardinals	.35	.15	.03
☐	108	**Don Gillis**, St. Louis Cardinals	.35	.15	.03
☐	109	**Carl Brettschneider**, St. Louis Cardinals	.35	.15	.03
☐	110	**Leo Sugar**, St. Louis Cardinals	.35	.15	.03
☐	111	**Frank Fuller**, St. Louis Cardinals	.35	.15	.03
☐	112	**St. Louis Cardinals Team Card**	1.10	.30	.05
☐	113	**Y.A. Tittle**, San Francisco 49ers	5.00	2.35	.50
☐	114	**Joe Perry**, San Francisco 49ers	2.50	1.15	.25
☐	115	**J.D. Smith**, San Francisco 49ers	.35	.15	.03
☐	116	**Hugh McElhenny**, San Francisco 49ers	2.50	1.15	.25
☐	117	**Billy Wilson**, San Francisco 49ers	.45	.20	.04
☐	118	**Bob St. Clair**, San Francisco 49ers	.35	.15	.03
☐	119	**Matt Hazeltine**, San Francisco 49ers	.35	.15	.03
☐	120	**Abe Woodson**, San Francisco 49ers	.45	.20	.04
☐	121	**Leo Nomellini**, San Francisco 49ers	1.75	.85	.17
☐	122	**San Francisco 49ers Team Card**	1.10	.30	.05
☐	123	**Ralph Guglielmi**, Washington Redskins	.45	.20	.04
☐	124	**Don Bosseler**, Washington Redskins	.35	.15	.03
☐	125	**John Olszewski**, Washington Redskins	.35	.15	.03
☐	126	**Bill Anderson**, Washington Redskins	.35	.15	.03
☐	127	**Joe Walton**, Washington Redskins	1.00	.45	.10

		MINT	VG-E	F-G
☐ 128	Jim Schrader, Washington Redskins	.35	.15	.03
☐ 129	Ralph Felton, Washington Redskins	.35	.15	.03
☐ 130	Gary Glick, Washington Redskins	.35	.15	.03
☐ 131	Bob Toneff, Washington Redskins	.35	.15	.03
☐ 132	Washington Redskins Team Card	1.50	.30	.05

1961 TOPPS

The 1961 Topps set of 198 contains NFL players (1-132) and AFL players (133-197). The cards measure 2½" by 3½". Card number 198 is a checklist card. The fronts are very similar to the Topps 1961 baseball issue. The card backs were printed in light blue on white card stock. Statistical information from the immediate past season and career totals are given on the reverse. A "coin-rub" picture was featured on the right of the reverse.

		MINT	VG-E	F-G
	COMPLETE SET	175.00	80.00	18.00
	COMMON PLAYER (1-132)	.35	.15	.03
	COMMON PLAYER (133-198)	.55	.25	.05
☐ 1	Johnny Unitas, Baltimore Colts	11.00	3.50	.75
☐ 2	Lenny Moore, Baltimore Colts	2.50	1.15	.25
☐ 3	Alan Ameche, Baltimore Colts	.90	.40	.09
☐ 4	Raymond Berry, Baltimore Colts	2.75	1.25	.27
☐ 5	Jim Mutscheller, Baltimore Colts	.35	.15	.03
☐ 6	Jim Parker, Baltimore Colts	1.75	.85	.17
☐ 7	Gino Marchetti, Baltimore Colts	2.25	1.00	.22

		MINT	VG-E	F-G
☐	8 **Gene Lipscomb**, Baltimore Colts	.90	.40	.09
☐	9 **Baltimore Colts Team Card**	.90	.40	.09
☐	10 **Bill Wade**, Chicago Bears	.55	.25	.05
☐	11 **Johnny Morris**, Chicago Bears	.90	.40	.09
☐	12 **Rick Casares**, Chicago Bears	.60	.28	.06
☐	13 **Harlon Hill**, Chicago Bears	.45	.20	.04
☐	14 **Stan Jones**, Chicago Bears	.35	.15	.03
☐	15 **Doug Atkins**, Chicago Bears	1.50	.70	.15
☐	16 **Bill George**, Chicago Bears	1.50	.70	.15
☐	17 **J.C. Caroline**, Chicago Bears	.35	.15	.03
☐	18 **Chicago Bears Team Card**	.90	.40	.09
☐	19 **Big Time Football Comes To Texas** (Eddie LeBaron)	.90	.40	.09
☐	20 **Eddie LeBaron**, Dallas Cowboys	.90	.40	.09
☐	21 **Don McIlhenny**, Dallas Cowboys	.45	.20	.04
☐	22 **L.G. Dupre**, Dallas Cowboys	.45	.20	.04
☐	23 **Jim Doran**, Dallas Cowboys	.45	.20	.04
☐	24 **Bill Howton**, Dallas Cowboys	.50	.22	.05
☐	25 **Buzz Guy**, Dallas Cowboys	.45	.20	.04
☐	26 **Jack Patera**, Dallas Cowboys	.90	.40	.09
☐	27 **Tom Frankhauser**, Dallas Cowboys	.45	.20	.04
☐	28 **Dallas Cowboys Team Card**	2.25	1.00	.22
☐	29 **Jim Ninowski**, Detroit Lions	.55	.25	.05
☐	30 **Dan Lewis**, Detroit Lions	.35	.15	.03
☐	31 **Nick Pietrosante**, Detroit Lions	.55	.25	.05
☐	32 **Gail Cogdill**, Detroit Lions	.45	.20	.04
☐	33 **Jim Gibbons**, Detroit Lions	.35	.15	.03
☐	34 **Jim Martin**, Detroit Lions	.35	.15	.03
☐	35 **Alex Karras**, Detroit Lions	3.00	1.40	.30
☐	36 **Joe Schmidt**, Detroit Lions	2.00	.90	.20
☐	37 **Detroit Lions Team Card**	.90	.40	.09
☐	38 **Packers' Hornung Sets NFL Scoring Record**	2.00	.90	.20
☐	39 **Bart Starr**, Green Bay Packers	6.50	3.00	.65
☐	40 **Paul Hornung**, Green Bay Packers	5.00	2.35	.50
☐	41 **Jim Taylor**, Green Bay Packers	3.50	1.65	.35
☐	42 **Max McGee**, Green Bay Packers	.65	.30	.06
☐	43 **Boyd Dowler**, Green Bay Packers	.55	.25	.05
☐	44 **Jim Ringo**, Green Bay Packers	1.75	.85	.17
☐	45 **Henry Jordan**, Green Bay Packers	.90	.40	.09
☐	46 **Bill Forester**, Green Bay Packers	.60	.28	.06
☐	47 **Green Bay Packers Team**	1.00	.45	.10
☐	48 **Frank Ryan**, Los Angeles Rams	.90	.40	.09
☐	49 **Jon Arnett**, Los Angeles Rams	.55	.25	.05
☐	50 **Ollie Matson**, Los Angeles Rams	2.25	1.00	.22
☐	51 **Jim Red Phillips**, Los Angeles Rams	.35	.15	.03
☐	52 **Del Shofner**, Los Angeles Rams	.50	.22	.05

		MINT	VG-E	F-G
☐ 53	**Art Hunter**, Los Angeles Rams	.35	.15	.03
☐ 54	**Gene Brito**, Los Angeles Rams	.35	.15	.03
☐ 55	**Lindon Crow**, Los Angeles Rams	.35	.15	.03
☐ 56	**Los Angeles Rams Team Card**	.90	.40	.09
☐ 57	**Colts' Unitas 25 TD Passes**	2.75	1.25	.27
☐ 58	**Y.A. Tittle**, San Francisco 49ers	5.00	2.35	.50
☐ 59	**John Brodie**, San Francisco 49ers	6.50	3.00	.65
☐ 60	**J.D. Smith**, San Francisco 49ers	.35	.15	.03
☐ 61	**R.C. Owens**, San Francisco 49ers	.35	.15	.03
☐ 62	**Clyde Conner**, San Francisco 49ers	.35	.15	.03
☐ 63	**Bob St. Clair**, San Francisco 49ers	.35	.15	.03
☐ 64	**Leo Nomellini**, San Francisco 49ers	1.75	.85	.17
☐ 65	**Abe Woodson**, San Francisco 49ers	.45	.20	.04
☐ 66	**San Francisco 49ers Team Card**	.90	.40	.09
☐ 67	**Checklist**	6.00	.60	.10
☐ 68	**Milt Plum**, Cleveland Browns	.90	.40	.09
☐ 69	**Ray Renfro**, Cleveland Browns	.50	.22	.05
☐ 70	**Bobby Mitchell**, Cleveland Browns	2.50	1.15	.25
☐ 71	**Jim Brown**, Cleveland Browns	20.00	9.00	2.00
☐ 72	**Mike McCormack**, Cleveland Browns	1.50	.70	.15
☐ 73	**Jim Ray Smith**, Cleveland Browns	.35	.15	.03
☐ 74	**Sam Baker**, Cleveland Browns	.45	.20	.04
☐ 75	**Walt Michaels**, Cleveland Browns	.75	.35	.07
☐ 76	**Cleveland Browns Team Card**	.90	.40	.09
☐ 77	**Jimmy Brown Gains 1257 Yards**	6.50	3.00	.65
☐ 78	**George Shaw**, Minnesota Vikings	.45	.20	.04
☐ 79	**Hugh McElhenny**, Minnesota Vikings	2.25	1.00	.22
☐ 80	**Clancy Osborne**, Minnesota Vikings	.35	.15	.03
☐ 81	**Dave Middleton**, Minnesota Vikings	.35	.15	.03
☐ 82	**Frank Youso**, Minnesota Vikings	.35	.15	.03
☐ 83	**Don Joyce**, Minnesota Vikings	.35	.15	.03
☐ 84	**Ed Culpepper**, Minnesota Vikings	.35	.15	.03
☐ 85	**Charley Conerly**, New York Giants	2.50	1.15	.25
☐ 86	**Mel Triplett**, New York Giants	.35	.15	.03
☐ 87	**Kyle Rote**, New York Giants	2.25	1.00	.22
☐ 88	**Roosevelt Brown**, New York Giants	1.75	.85	.17
☐ 89	**Ray Wietecha**, New York Giants	.35	.15	.03
☐ 90	**Andy Robustelli**, New York Giants	1.75	.85	.17
☐ 91	**Sam Huff**, New York Giants	2.25	1.00	.22
☐ 92	**Jim Patton**, New York Giants	.45	.20	.04
☐ 93	**New York Giants Team Card**	.90	.40	.09
☐ 94	**Charlie Conerly Leads Giants For 13th Year**	2.00	.90	.20
☐ 95	**Sonny Jurgensen**, Philadelphia Eagles	3.50	1.65	.35
☐ 96	**Tommy McDonald**, Philadelphia Eagles	.55	.25	.05
☐ 97	**Bill Barnes**, Philadelphia Eagles	.35	.15	.03
☐ 98	**Bobby Walston**, Philadelphia Eagles	.35	.15	.03

		MINT	VG-E	F-G
☐ 99	Pete Retzlaff, Philadelphia Eagles	.45	.20	.04
☐ 100	Jim McCusker, Philadelphia Eagles	.35	.15	.03
☐ 101	Chuck Bednarik, Philadelphia Eagles	2.50	1.15	.25
☐ 102	Tom Brookshier, Philadelphia Eagles	1.00	.45	.10
☐ 103	Philadelphia Eagles Team Card	.90	.40	.09
☐ 104	Bobby Layne, Pittsburgh Steelers	5.00	2.35	.50
☐ 105	John Henry Johnson, Pittsburgh Steelers	.90	.40	.09
☐ 106	Tom Tracy, Pittsburgh Steelers	.45	.20	.04
☐ 107	Buddy Dial, Pittsburgh Steelers	.55	.25	.05
☐ 108	Jimmy Orr, Pittsburgh Steelers	.55	.25	.05
☐ 109	Mike Sandusky, Pittsburgh Steelers	.35	.15	.03
☐ 110	John Reger, Pittsburgh Steelers	.35	.15	.03
☐ 111	Junior Wren, Pittsburgh Steelers	.35	.15	.03
☐ 112	Pittsburgh Steelers Team Card	.90	.40	.09
☐ 113	Bobby Layne Sets New Passing Record	2.25	1.00	.22
☐ 114	John Roach, St. Louis Cardinals	.35	.15	.03
☐ 115	Sam Etcheverry, St. Louis Cardinals	.50	.22	.05
☐ 116	John David Crow, St. Louis Cardinals	.50	.22	.05
☐ 117	Mal Hammack, St. Louis Cardinals	.35	.15	.03
☐ 118	Sonny Randle, St. Louis Cardinals	.50	.22	.05
☐ 119	Leo Sugar, St. Louis Cardinals	.35	.15	.03
☐ 120	Jerry Norton, St. Louis Cardinals	.35	.15	.03
☐ 121	St. Louis Cardinals Team	.90	.40	.09
☐ 122	Checklist	6.00	.60	.10
☐ 123	Ralph Guglielmi, Washington Redskins	.45	.20	.04
☐ 124	Dick James, Washington Redskins	.35	.15	.03
☐ 125	Don Bosseler, Washington Redskins	.35	.15	.03
☐ 126	Joe Walton, Washington Redskins	.75	.35	.07
☐ 127	Bill Anderson, Washington Redskins	.35	.15	.03
☐ 128	Vince Promuto, Washington Redskins	.35	.15	.03
☐ 129	Bob Toneff, Washington Redskins	.35	.15	.03
☐ 130	John Paluck, Washington Redskins	.35	.15	.03
☐ 131	Washington Redskins Team Card	.90	.40	.09
☐ 132	Browns' Plum Wins NFL Passing Title	.55	.25	.05

AFL PLAYERS

☐ 133	Abner Haynes, Dallas Texans	1.75	.85	.17
☐ 134	Mel Branch, Dallas Texans	.75	.35	.07
☐ 135	Jerry Cornelison, Dallas Texans	.55	.25	.05
☐ 136	Bill Krisher, Dallas Texans	.55	.25	.05
☐ 137	Paul Miller, Dallas Texans	.55	.25	.05
☐ 138	Jack Spikes, Dallas Texans	.75	.35	.07

		MINT	VG-E	F-G
☐ 139	**Johnny Robinson**, Dallas Texans	1.25	.60	.12
☐ 140	**Cotton Davidson**, Dallas Texans	1.00	.45	.10
☐ 141	**Dave Smith**, Houston Oilers	.55	.25	.05
☐ 142	**Bill Groman**, Houston Oilers	.90	.40	.09
☐ 143	**Rich Michael**, Houston Oilers	.55	.25	.05
☐ 144	**Mike Dukes**, Houston Oilers	.55	.25	.05
☐ 145	**George Blanda**, Houston Oilers	7.00	3.25	.70
☐ 146	**Billy Cannon**, Houston Oilers	2.25	1.00	.22
☐ 147	**Dennit Morris**, Houston Oilers	.55	.25	.05
☐ 148	**Jacky Lee**, Houston Oilers	.90	.40	.09
☐ 149	**Al Dorow**, New York Titans	.75	.35	.07
☐ 150	**Don Maynard**, New York Titans	6.50	3.00	.65
☐ 151	**Art Powell**, New York Titans	1.00	.45	.10
☐ 152	**Sid Youngelman**, New York Titans	.55	.25	.05
☐ 153	**Bob Mischak**, New York Titans	.55	.25	.05
☐ 154	**Larry Grantham**, New York Titans	.75	.35	.07
☐ 155	**Tom Saidock**, New York Titans	.55	.25	.05
☐ 156	**Roger Donnahoo**, New York Titans	.55	.25	.05
☐ 157	**Lavern Torczon**, Buffalo Bills	.55	.25	.05
☐ 158	**Archie Matsos**, Buffalo Bills	.75	.35	.07
☐ 159	**Elbert Dubenion**, Buffalo Bills	1.00	.45	.10
☐ 160	**Wray Carlton**, Buffalo Bills	.75	.35	.07
☐ 161	**Rich McCabe**, Buffalo Bills	.55	.25	.05
☐ 162	**Ken Rice**, Buffalo Bills	.55	.25	.05
☐ 163	**Art Baker**, Buffalo Bills	.55	.25	.05
☐ 164	**Tom Rychlec**, Buffalo Bills	.55	.25	.05
☐ 165	**Mack Yoho**, Buffalo Bills	.55	.25	.05
☐ 166	**Jack Kemp**, San Diego Chargers	16.00	7.50	1.60
☐ 167	**Paul Lowe**, San Diego Chargers	2.00	.90	.20
☐ 168	**Ron Mix**, San Diego Chargers	3.00	1.40	.30
☐ 169	**Paul Maguire**, San Diego Chargers	1.25	.60	.12
☐ 170	**Volney Peters**, San Diego Chargers	.55	.25	.05
☐ 171	**Ernie Wright**, San Diego Chargers	.55	.25	.05
☐ 172	**Ron Nery**, San Diego Chargers	.55	.25	.05
☐ 173	**Dave Kocourek**, San Diego Chargers	.55	.25	.05
☐ 174	**Jim Colclough**, Boston Patriots	.55	.25	.05
☐ 175	**Babe Parilli**, Boston Patriots	1.00	.45	.10
☐ 176	**Billy Lott**, Boston Patriots	.55	.25	.05
☐ 177	**Fred Bruney**, Boston Patriots	.55	.25	.05
☐ 178	**Ross O'Hanley**, Boston Patriots	.55	.25	.05
☐ 179	**Walt Cudzik**, Boston Patriots	.55	.25	.05
☐ 180	**Charley Leo**, Boston Patriots	.55	.25	.05
☐ 181	**Bob Dee**, Boston Patriots	.55	.25	.05
☐ 182	**Jim Otto**, Oakland Raiders	6.50	3.00	.65
☐ 183	**Eddie Macon**, Oakland Raiders	.55	.25	.05
☐ 184	**Dick Christy**, Oakland Raiders	.55	.25	.05

	MINT	VG-E	F-G
☐ 185 **Alan Miller**, Oakland Raiders	.55	.25	.05
☐ 186 **Tom Flores**, Oakland Raiders	2.50	1.15	.25
☐ 187 **Joe Cannavino**, Oakland Raiders	.55	.25	.05
☐ 188 **Don Manoukian**, Oakland Raiders	.55	.25	.05
☐ 189 **Bob Collbaugh**, Oakland Raiders	.55	.25	.05
☐ 190 **Lionel Taylor**, Denver Broncos	2.00	.90	.20
☐ 191 **Bud McFadin**, Denver Broncos	.55	.25	.05
☐ 192 **Goose Gonsoulin**, Denver Broncos	.75	.35	.07
☐ 193 **Frank Tripucka**, Denver Broncos	.90	.40	.09
☐ 194 **Gene Mingo**, Denver Broncos	.55	.25	.05
☐ 195 **Eldon Danenhauer**, Denver Broncos	.55	.25	.05
☐ 196 **Bob McNamara**, Denver Broncos	.55	.25	.05
☐ 197 **Dave Rolle**, Denver Broncos	.55	.25	.05
☐ 198 **Checklist**	9.00	.90	.15

1962 TOPPS

*The 1962 Topps set contains 176 black-bordered cards. The cards measure 2½"
by 3½". In designing the 1962 set, Topps chose a horizontally oriented card front
for the first time since 1957. The black borders make it exceedingly difficult to
complete a set in perfect mint condition. The asterisked cards are in shorter supply
than the others; the shortage is probably attributable to the fact that the set size is
not the standard 132-card, single-sheet size; hence all cards were not printed in
equal amounts.*

	MINT	VG-E	F-G
COMPLETE SET	200.00	85.00	18.00
COMMON PLAYER (1-176)	.45	.18	.04
☐ 1 **John Unitas**, Baltimore Colts	12.00	3.50	.75

		MINT	VG-E	F-G
☐	2 Lenny Moore, Baltimore Colts	2.50	1.15	.25
☐	3 Alex Hawkins*, Baltimore Colts	2.00	.90	.20
☐	4 Joe Perry, Baltimore Colts	2.50	1.15	.25
☐	5 Raymond Berry*, Baltimore Colts	3.50	1.65	.35
☐	6 Steve Myhra, Baltimore Colts	.45	.18	.04
☐	7 Tom Gilburg*, Baltimore Colts	2.00	.90	.20
☐	8 Gino Marchetti, Baltimore Colts	2.25	1.00	.22
☐	9 Bill Pellington, Baltimore Colts	.45	.18	.04
☐	10 Andy Nelson, Baltimore Colts	.45	.18	.04
☐	11 Wendell Harris*, Baltimore Colts	2.00	.90	.20
☐	12 Baltimore Colts Team Card	.90	.40	.09
☐	13 Bill Wade*, Chicago Bears	2.25	1.00	.22
☐	14 Willie Galimore, Chicago Bears	.55	.25	.05
☐	15 Johnny Morris*, Chicago Bears	2.25	1.00	.22
☐	16 Rick Casares, Chicago Bears	.55	.25	.05
☐	17 Mike Ditka, Chicago Bears	4.00	1.85	.40
☐	18 Stan Jones, Chicago Bears	.45	.18	.04
☐	19 Roger Leclerc, Chicago Bears	.45	.18	.04
☐	20 Angelo Coia, Chicago Bears	.45	.18	.04
☐	21 Doug Atkins, Chicago Bears	1.50	.70	.15
☐	22 Bill George, Chicago Bears	1.50	.70	.15
☐	23 Richie Petitbon, Chicago Bears	.45	.18	.04
☐	24 Ron Bull*, Los Angeles Rams	2.00	.90	.20
☐	25 Chicago Bears Team Card	.90	.40	.09
☐	26 Howard Cassady, Cleveland Browns	.55	.25	.05
☐	27 Ray Renfro*, Cleveland Browns	2.00	.90	.20
☐	28 Jim Brown, Cleveland Browns	22.00	10.00	2.20
☐	29 Rich Kreitling, Cleveland Browns	.45	.18	.04
☐	30 Jim Ray Smith, Cleveland Browns	.45	.18	.04
☐	31 John Morrow, Cleveland Browns	.45	.18	.04
☐	32 Lou Groza, Cleveland Browns	3.50	1.65	.35
☐	33 Bob Gain, Cleveland Browns	.45	.18	.04
☐	34 Bernie Parrish, Cleveland Browns	.45	.18	.04
☐	35 Jim Shofner, Cleveland Browns	.55	.25	.05
☐	36 Ernie Davis*, Cleveland Browns	7.50	3.50	.75
☐	37 Cleveland Browns Team Card	.90	.40	.09
☐	38 Eddie LeBaron, Dallas Cowboys	.90	.40	.09
☐	39 Don Meredith*, Dallas Cowboys	9.00	4.25	.90
☐	40 J.W. Lockett, Dallas Cowboys	2.00	.90	.20
☐	41 Don Perkins, Dallas Cowboys	.90	.40	.09
☐	42 Bill Howton, Dallas Cowboys	.65	.30	.06
☐	43 Dick Bielski, Dallas Cowboys	.55	.25	.05
☐	44 Mike Connelly, Dallas Cowboys	.55	.25	.05
☐	45 Jerry Tubbs*, Dallas Cowboys	2.25	1.00	.22
☐	46 Don Bishop*, Dallas Cowboys	2.00	.90	.20

		MINT	VG-E	F-G
☐	47 **Dick Moegle**, Dallas Cowboys	.55	.25	.05
☐	48 **Bobby Plummer***, Dallas Cowboys	2.00	.90	.20
☐	49 **Dallas Cowboys Team Card**	2.00	.90	.20
☐	50 **Milt Plum**, Detroit Lions	.90	.40	.09
☐	51 **Dan Lewis**, Detroit Lions	.45	.18	.04
☐	52 **Nick Pietrosante***, Detroit Lions	2.00	.90	.20
☐	53 **Gail Cogdill**, Detroit Lions	.45	.18	.04
☐	54 **Jim Gibbons**, Detroit Lions	.45	.18	.04
☐	55 **Jim Martin**, Detroit Lions	.45	.18	.04
☐	56 **Yale Lary**, Detroit Lions	1.50	.70	.15
☐	57 **Darris McCord**, Detroit Lions	.45	.18	.04
☐	58 **Alex Karras**, Detroit Lions	2.75	1.25	.27
☐	59 **Joe Schmidt**, Detroit Lions	2.00	.90	.20
☐	60 **Dick Lane**, Detroit Lions	1.50	.70	.15
☐	61 **John Lomakoski***, Detroit Lions	2.00	.90	.20
☐	62 **Detroit Lions Team Card***	2.50	1.15	.25
☐	63 **Bart Starr***, Green Bay Packers	8.00	3.75	.80
☐	64 **Paul Hornung***, Green Bay Packers	7.00	3.25	.70
☐	65 **Tom Moore***, Green Bay Packers	2.00	.90	.20
☐	66 **Jim Taylor***, Green Bay Packers	5.00	2.35	.50
☐	67 **Max McGee***, Green Bay Packers	2.25	1.00	.22
☐	68 **Jim Ringo***, Green Bay Packers	3.50	1.65	.35
☐	69 **Fuzzy Thurston***, Green Bay Packers	2.25	1.00	.22
☐	70 **Forrest Gregg**, Green Bay Packers	1.75	.85	.17
☐	71 **Boyd Dowler**, Green Bay Packers	.55	.25	.05
☐	72 **Henry Jordan***, Green Bay Packers	2.50	1.15	.25
☐	73 **Bill Forester***, Green Bay Packers	2.25	1.00	.22
☐	74 **Earl Gros***, Green Bay Packers	2.00	.90	.20
☐	75 **Green Bay Packers Team Card***	3.00	1.40	.30
☐	76 **Checklist***	10.00	1.00	.10
☐	77 **Zeke Bratkowski***, Los Angeles Rams	2.25	1.00	.22
☐	78 **Jon Arnett***, Los Angeles Rams	2.25	1.00	.22
☐	79 **Ollie Matson***, Los Angeles Rams	3.50	1.65	.35
☐	80 **Dick Bass***, Los Angeles Rams	2.25	1.00	.22
☐	81 **Jim Phillips**, Los Angeles Rams	.45	.18	.04
☐	82 **Carroll Daie**, Los Angeles Rams	.45	.18	.04
☐	83 **Frank Varrichione**, Los Angeles Rams	.45	.18	.04
☐	84 **Art Hunter**, Los Angeles Rams	.45	.18	.04
☐	85 **Danny Villanueva**, Los Angeles Rams	.45	.18	.04
☐	86 **Les Richter***, Los Angeles Rams	2.25	1.00	.22
☐	87 **Lindon Crow**, Los Angeles Rams	.45	.18	.04
☐	88 **Roman Gabriel***, Los Angeles Rams	5.00	2.35	.50
☐	89 **Los Angeles Rams Team Card***	2.75	1.25	.27
☐	90 **Fran Tarkenton***, Minnesota Vikings	35.00	16.50	3.50
☐	91 **Jerry Reichow***, Minnesota Vikings	2.00	.90	.20

		MINT	VG-E	F-G
☐ 92	Hugh McElhenny*, Minnesota Vikings	3.50	1.65	.35
☐ 93	Mel Triplett*, Minnesota Vikings	2.00	.90	.20
☐ 94	Tommy Mason*, Minnesota Vikings	2.25	1.00	.22
☐ 95	Dave Middleton*, Minnesota Vikings	2.00	.90	.20
☐ 96	Frank Youso*, Minnesota Vikings	2.00	.90	.20
☐ 97	Mike Mercer*, Minnesota Vikings	2.00	.90	.20
☐ 98	Rip Hawkins*, Minnesota Vikings	2.00	.90	.20
☐ 99	Cliff Livingston*, Minnesota Vikings	2.00	.90	.20
☐ 100	Roy Winston*, Minnesota Vikings	2.00	.90	.20
☐ 101	Minnesota Vikings Team Card*	3.50	1.65	.35
☐ 102	Y.A. Tittle, New York Giants	5.00	2.35	.50
☐ 103	Joe Walton, New York Giants	.75	.35	.07
☐ 104	Frank Gifford, New York Giants	11.00	5.25	1.10
☐ 105	Alex Webster, New York Giants	.65	.30	.06
☐ 106	Del Shofner, New York Giants	.65	.30	.06
☐ 107	Don Chandler, New York Giants	.45	.18	.04
☐ 108	Andy Robustelli, New York Giants	1.75	.85	.17
☐ 109	Jim Katcavage, New York Giants	.45	.18	.04
☐ 110	Sam Huff*, New York Giants	4.00	1.85	.40
☐ 111	Erich Barnes, New York Giants	.45	.18	.04
☐ 112	Jim Patton, New York Giants	.55	.25	.05
☐ 113	Jerry Hillebrand*, New York Giants	2.00	.90	.20
☐ 114	New York Giants Team Card	.90	.40	.09
☐ 115	Sonny Jurgensen, Philadelphia Eagles	3.50	1.65	.35
☐ 116	Tommy McDonald, Philadelphia Eagles	.60	.28	.06
☐ 117	Ted Dean*, Philadelphia Eagles	2.00	.90	.20
☐ 118	Clarence Peaks, Philadelphia Eagles	.45	.18	.04
☐ 119	Bobby Walston, Philadelphia Eagles	.45	.18	.04
☐ 120	Pete Retzlaff*, Philadelphia Eagles	2.00	.90	.20
☐ 121	Jim Schrader*, Philadelphia Eagles	2.00	.90	.20
☐ 122	J.D. Smith, Philadelphia Eagles	.45	.18	.04
☐ 123	King Hill, Philadelphia Eagles	.65	.30	.06
☐ 124	Maxie Baughan, Philadelphia Eagles	.55	.25	.05
☐ 125	Pete Case*, Philadelphia Eagles	2.00	.90	.20
☐ 126	Philadelphia Eagles Team Card	.90	.40	.09
☐ 127	Bobby Layne, Pittsburgh Steelers	5.00	2.35	.50
☐ 128	Tom Tracy, Pittsburgh Steelers	.45	.18	.04
☐ 129	John Henry Johnson, Pittsburgh Steelers	.90	.40	.09
☐ 130	Buddy Dial*, Pittsburgh Steelers	2.25	1.00	.22
☐ 131	Preston Carpenter, Pittsburgh Steelers	.45	.18	.04
☐ 132	Lou Michaels*, Pittsburgh Steelers	2.25	1.00	.22
☐ 133	Gene Lipscomb*, Pittsburgh Steelers	2.25	1.00	.22
☐ 134	Ernie Stautner*, Pittsburgh Steelers	3.50	1.65	.35
☐ 135	John Reger*, Pittsburgh Steelers	2.00	.90	.20
☐ 136	Myron Pottios, Pittsburgh Steelers	.45	.18	.04
☐ 137	Bob Ferguson*, Pittsburgh Steelers	2.00	.90	.20

		MINT	VG-E	F-G
☐ 138	**Pittsburgh Steelers Team Card***	2.50	1.15	.25
☐ 139	**Sam Etcheverry**, St. Louis Cardinals	.55	.25	.05
☐ 140	**John David Crow***, St. Louis Cardinals	2.25	1.00	.22
☐ 141	**Bobby Joe Conrad***, St. Louis Cardinals	2.25	1.00	.22
☐ 142	**Prentice Gautt***, St. Louis Cardinals	2.00	.90	.20
☐ 143	**Frank Mestnick**, St. Louis Cardinals	.45	.18	.04
☐ 144	**Sonny Randle**, St. Louis Cardinals	.55	.25	.05
☐ 145	**Gerry Perry**, St. Louis Cardinals	.45	.18	.04
☐ 146	**Jerry Norton**, St. Louis Cardinals	.45	.18	.04
☐ 147	**Jimmy Hill**, St. Louis Cardinals	.45	.18	.04
☐ 148	**Bill Stacy**, St. Louis Cardinals	.45	.18	.04
☐ 149	**Fate Echols***, St. Louis Cardinals	2.00	.90	.20
☐ 150	**St. Louis Cardinals Team Card**	.90	.40	.09
☐ 151	**Bill Kilmer**, San Francisco 49ers	2.50	1.15	.25
☐ 152	**John Brodie**, San Francisco 49ers	3.50	1.65	.35
☐ 153	**J.D. Smith**, San Francisco 49ers	.45	.18	.04
☐ 154	**C.R. Roberts***, San Francisco 49ers	2.00	.90	.20
☐ 155	**Monty Stickles**, San Francisco 49ers	.45	.18	.04
☐ 156	**Clyde Conner**, San Francisco 49ers	.45	.18	.04
☐ 157	**Bob St. Clair**, San Francisco 49ers	.45	.18	.04
☐ 158	**Tommy Davis**, San Francisco 49ers	.45	.18	.04
☐ 159	**Leo Nomellini**, San Francisco 49ers	1.50	.70	.15
☐ 160	**Matt Hazeltine**, San Francisco 49ers	.45	.18	.04
☐ 161	**Abe Woodson**, San Francisco 49ers	.45	.18	.04
☐ 162	**Dave Baker**, San Francisco 49ers	.45	.18	.04
☐ 163	**San Francisco 49ers Team Card**	.90	.40	.09
☐ 164	**Norm Snead***, Washington Redskins	2.50	1.15	.25
☐ 165	**Dick James**, Washington Redskins	.45	.18	.04
☐ 166	**Bobby Mitchell**, Washington Redskins	2.50	1.15	.25
☐ 167	**Sam Horner**, Washington Redskins	.45	.18	.04
☐ 168	**Bill Barnes**, Washington Redskins	.45	.18	.04
☐ 169	**Bill Anderson**, Washington Redskins	.45	.18	.04
☐ 170	**Fred Dugan**, Washington Redskins	.45	.18	.04
☐ 171	**John Aveni***, Washington Redskins	2.00	.90	.20
☐ 172	**Bob Toneff**, Washington Redskins	.45	.18	.04
☐ 173	**Jim Kerr**, Washington Redskins	.45	.18	.04
☐ 174	**Leroy Jackson***, Washington Redskins	2.00	.90	.20
☐ 175	**Washington Redskins Team Card**	.90	.40	.09
☐ 176	**Checklist**	6.50	.75	.10

1963 TOPPS

The 1963 Topps set contains 170 cards of NFL players, grouped together by teams. The cards measure 2½″ by 3½″. The card backs were printed in light orange ink on white card stock. Statistical information from the immediate past season and career totals are given on the reverse. The illustrated trivia question on the reverse could be answered by placing red paper over the card. The 76 asterisked cards are in shorter supply than the others because the set size is not the standard 132-card, single-sheet size; hence all cards were not printed in equal amounts.

		MINT	VG-E	F-G
	COMPLETE SET	185.00	80.00	18.00
	COMMON PLAYER (1-170)	.35	.15	.03
☐	1 John Unitas, Baltimore Colts	10.00	3.00	.60
☐	2 Lenny Moore, Baltimore Colts	2.50	1.15	.25
☐	3 Jimmy Orr, Baltimore Colts	.50	.22	.05
☐	4 Raymond Berry, Baltimore Colts	2.50	1.15	.25
☐	5 Jim Parker, Baltimore Colts	1.50	.70	.15
☐	6 Alex Sandusky, Baltimore Colts	.35	.15	.03
☐	7 Dick Szymanski, Baltimore Colts	.35	.15	.03
☐	8 Gino Marchetti, Baltimore Colts	2.00	.90	.20
☐	9 Billy Ray Smith, Baltimore Colts	.45	.20	.04
☐	10 Bill Pellington, Baltimore Colts	.35	.15	.03
☐	11 Bob Boyd, Baltimore Colts	.35	.15	.03
☐	12 Baltimore Colts Team Card*	2.50	1.15	.25
☐	13 Frank Ryan*, Cleveland Browns	2.50	1.15	.25
☐	14 Jim Brown*, Cleveland Browns	25.00	11.00	2.50
☐	15 Ray Renfro*, Cleveland Browns	2.00	.90	.20
☐	16 Rich Kreitling*, Cleveland Browns	2.00	.90	.20

			MINT	VG-E	F-G
☐	17	Mike McCormack*, Cleveland Browns	2.50	1.15	.25
☐	18	Jim Ray Smith*, Cleveland Browns	2.00	.90	.20
☐	19	Lou Groza*, Cleveland Browns	5.00	2.35	.50
☐	20	Bill Glass*, Cleveland Browns	2.00	.90	.20
☐	21	Galen Fiss*, Cleveland Browns	2.00	.90	.20
☐	22	Don Fleming*, Cleveland Browns	2.00	.90	.20
☐	23	Bob Gain*, Cleveland Browns	2.00	.90	.20
☐	24	Cleveland Browns Team Card*	2.50	1.15	.25
☐	25	Milt Plum, Detroit Lions	.90	.40	.09
☐	26	Dan Lewis, Detroit Lions	.35	.15	.03
☐	27	Nick Pietrosante, Detroit Lions	.55	.25	.05
☐	28	Gail Cogdill, Detroit Lions	.35	.15	.03
☐	29	Harley Sewell, Detroit Lions	.35	.15	.03
☐	30	Jim Gibbons, Detroit Lions	.35	.15	.03
☐	31	Carl Brettschneider, Detroit Lions	.35	.15	.03
☐	32	Dick Lane, Detroit Lions	1.50	.70	.15
☐	33	Yale Lary, Detroit Lions	1.50	.70	.15
☐	34	Roger Brown, Detroit Lions	.35	.15	.03
☐	35	Joe Schmidt, Detroit Lions	1.75	.85	.17
☐	36	Detroit Lions Team Card*	2.50	1.15	.25
☐	37	Roman Gabriel, Los Angeles Rams	2.25	1.00	.22
☐	38	Zeke Bratkowski, Los Angeles Rams	.90	.40	.09
☐	39	Dick Bass, Los Angeles Rams	.50	.22	.05
☐	40	Jon Arnett, Los Angeles Rams	.50	.22	.05
☐	41	Jim Phillips, Los Angeles Rams	.35	.15	.03
☐	42	Frank Varrichione, Los Angeles Rams	.35	.15	.03
☐	43	Danny Villanueva, Los Angeles Rams	.35	.15	.03
☐	44	Deacon Jones, Los Angeles Rams	3.50	1.65	.35
☐	45	Lindon Crow, Los Angeles Rams	.35	.15	.03
☐	46	Marlin McKeever, Los Angeles Rams	.35	.15	.03
☐	47	Ed Meador, Los Angeles Rams	.45	.20	.04
☐	48	Los Angeles Rams Team Card	.90	.40	.09
☐	49	Y.A. Tittle*, New York Giants	6.50	3.00	.65
☐	50	Del Shofner*, New York Giants	2.25	1.00	.22
☐	51	Alex Webster*, New York Giants	2.25	1.00	.22
☐	52	Phil King*, New York Giants	2.00	.90	.20
☐	53	Jack Stroud*, New York Giants	2.00	.90	.20
☐	54	Darrell Dess*, New York Giants	2.00	.90	.20
☐	55	Jim Katcavage*, New York Giants	2.00	.90	.20
☐	56	Roosevelt Grier*, New York Giants	2.50	1.15	.25
☐	57	Erich Barnes*, New York Giants	2.00	.90	.20
☐	58	Jim Patton*, New York Giants	2.00	.90	.20
☐	59	Sam Huff*, New York Giants	3.00	1.40	.30
☐	60	New York Giants Team Card	.90	.40	.09
☐	61	Bill Wade, Chicago Bears	.55	.25	.05
☐	62	Mike Ditka, Chicago Bears	1.50	.70	.15

			MINT	VG-E	F-G
☐	63	Johnny Morris, Chicago Bears	.55	.25	.05
☐	64	Roger Leclerc, Chicago Bears	.35	.15	.03
☐	65	Roger Davis, Chicago Bears	.35	.15	.03
☐	66	Joe Marconi, Chicago Bears	.35	.15	.03
☐	67	Herman Lee, Chicago Bears	.35	.15	.03
☐	68	Doug Atkins, Chicago Bears	1.50	.70	.15
☐	69	Joe Fortunato, Chicago Bears	.45	.20	.04
☐	70	Bill George, Chicago Bears	1.50	.70	.15
☐	71	Richie Pettibon, Chicago Bears	.35	.15	.03
☐	72	Chicago Bears Team Card*	2.50	1.15	.25
☐	73	Eddie LeBaron*, Dallas Cowboys	2.50	1.15	.25
☐	74	Don Meredith*, Dallas Cowboys	9.00	4.25	.90
☐	75	Don Perkins*, Dallas Cowboys	2.25	1.00	.22
☐	76	Amos Marsh*, Dallas Cowboys	2.00	.90	.20
☐	77	Bill Howton*, Dallas Cowboys	2.25	1.00	.22
☐	78	Andy Cverko*, Dallas Cowboys	2.00	.90	.20
☐	79	Sam Baker*, Dallas Cowboys	2.25	1.00	.22
☐	80	Jerry Tubbs*, Dallas Cowboys	2.25	1.00	.22
☐	81	Don Bishop*, Dallas Cowboys	2.00	.90	.20
☐	82	Bob Lilly*, Dallas Cowboys	9.00	4.25	.90
☐	83	Jerry Norton*, Dallas Cowboys	2.00	.90	.20
☐	84	Dallas Cowboys Team Card*	3.50	1.65	.35
☐	85	Checklist	3.00	.40	.05
☐	86	Bart Starr, Green Bay Packers	6.50	3.00	.65
☐	87	Jim Taylor, Green Bay Packers	2.50	1.15	.25
☐	88	Boyd Dowler, Green Bay Packers	.45	.20	.04
☐	89	Forrest Gregg, Green Bay Packers	1.75	.85	.17
☐	90	Fuzzy Thurston, Green Bay Packers	.50	.22	.05
☐	91	Jim Ringo, Green Bay Packers	1.50	.70	.15
☐	92	Ron Kramer, Green Bay Packers	.35	.15	.03
☐	93	Henry Jordan, Green Bay Packers	.65	.30	.06
☐	94	Bill Forester, Green Bay Packers	.55	.25	.05
☐	95	Willie Wood, Green Bay Packers	2.00	.90	.20
☐	96	Ray Nitschke, Green Bay Packers	6.00	2.80	.60
☐	97	Green Bay Packers Team Card	.90	.40	.09
☐	98	Fran Tarkenton, Minnesota Vikings	8.50	4.00	.85
☐	99	Tommy Mason, Minnesota Vikings	.45	.20	.04
☐	100	Mel Triplett, Minnesota Vikings	.35	.15	.03
☐	101	Jerry Reichow, Minnesota Vikings	.35	.15	.03
☐	102	Frank Youso, Minnesota Vikings	.35	.15	.03
☐	103	Hugh McElhenny, Minnesota Vikings	2.00	.90	.20
☐	104	Gerry Huth, Minnesota Vikings	.35	.15	.03
☐	105	Ed Sharockman, Minnesota Vikings	.35	.15	.03
☐	106	Rip Hawkins, Minnesota Vikings	.35	.15	.03
☐	107	Jim Marshall, Minnesota Vikings	2.00	.90	.20
☐	108	Jim Prestel, Minnesota Vikings	.35	.15	.03

		MINT	VG-E	F-G
☐ 109	**Minnesota Vikings Team Card**	.90	.40	.09
☐ 110	**Sonny Jurgensen***, Philadelphia Eagles	5.00	2.35	.50
☐ 111	**Tim Brown***, Philadelphia Eagles	2.25	1.00	.22
☐ 112	**Tommy McDonald***, Philadelphia Eagles	2.25	1.00	.22
☐ 113	**Clarence Peaks***, Philadelphia Eagles	2.00	.90	.20
☐ 114	**Pete Retzlaff***, Philadelphia Eagles	2.25	1.00	.22
☐ 115	**Jim Schrader***, Philadelphia Eagles	2.00	.90	.20
☐ 116	**Jim McCusker***, Philadelphia Eagles	2.00	.90	.20
☐ 117	**Don Burroughs***, Philadelphia Eagles	2.00	.90	.20
☐ 118	**Maxie Baughan***, Philadelphia Eagles	2.25	1.00	.22
☐ 119	**Riley Gunnels***, Philadelphia Eagles	2.00	.90	.20
☐ 120	**Jimmy Carr***, Philadelphia Eagles	2.00	.90	.20
☐ 121	**Philadelphia Eagles Team Card***	2.50	1.15	.25
☐ 122	**Ed Brown***, Pittsburgh Steelers	2.00	.90	.20
☐ 123	**J.H. Johnson***, Pittsburgh Steelers	2.50	1.15	.25
☐ 124	**Buddy Dial***, Pittsburgh Steelers	2.25	1.00	.22
☐ 125	**Red Mack***, Pittsburgh Steelers	2.00	.90	.20
☐ 126	**Preston Carpenter***, Pittsburgh Steelers	2.00	.90	.20
☐ 127	**Ray Lemek***, Pittsburgh Steelers	2.00	.90	.20
☐ 128	**Buzz Nutter***, Pittsburgh Steelers	2.00	.90	.20
☐ 129	**Ernie Stautner***, Pittsburgh Steelers	3.50	1.65	.35
☐ 130	**Lou Michaels***, Pittsburgh Steelers	2.25	1.00	.22
☐ 131	**Clendon Thomas***, Pittsburgh Steelers	2.00	.90	.20
☐ 132	**Tom Bettis***, Pittsburgh Steelers	2.00	.90	.20
☐ 133	**Pittsburgh Steelers Team Card***	2.50	1.15	.25
☐ 134	**John Brodie**, San Francisco 49ers	3.50	1.65	.35
☐ 135	**J.D. Smith**, San Francisco 49ers	.35	.15	.03
☐ 136	**Bill Kilmer**, San Francisco 49ers	2.00	.90	.20
☐ 137	**Bernie Casey**, San Francisco 49ers	.65	.30	.06
☐ 138	**Tommy Davis**, San Francisco 49ers	.35	.15	.03
☐ 139	**Ted Connolly**, San Francisco 49ers	.35	.15	.03
☐ 140	**Bob St. Clair**, San Francisco 49ers	.35	.15	.03
☐ 141	**Abe Woodson**, San Francisco 49ers	.45	.20	.04
☐ 142	**Matt Hazeltine**, San Francisco 49ers	.35	.15	.03
☐ 143	**Leo Nomellini**, San Francisco 49ers	1.50	.70	.15
☐ 144	**Dan Colchico**, San Francisco 49ers	.35	.15	.03
☐ 145	**San Francisco 49ers Team Card***	2.50	1.15	.25
☐ 146	**Charlie Johnson**, St. Louis Cardinals	2.00	.90	.20
☐ 147	**John David Crow**, St. Louis Cardinals	.55	.25	.05
☐ 148	**Bobby Joe Conrad**, St. Louis Cardinals	.50	.22	.05
☐ 149	**Sonny Randle**, St. Louis Cardinals	.50	.22	.05
☐ 150	**Prentice Gautt**, St. Louis Cardinals	.35	.15	.03
☐ 151	**Taz Anderson**, St. Louis Cardinals	.35	.15	.03
☐ 152	**Ernie McMillan**, St. Louis Cardinals	.35	.15	.03
☐ 153	**Jimmy Hill**, St. Louis Cardinals	.35	.15	.03
☐ 154	**Bill Koman**, St. Louis Cardinals	.35	.15	.03

			MINT	VG-E	F-G
☐ 155	**Larry Wilson,** St. Louis Cardinals	....	3.50	1.65	.35
☐ 156	**Don Owens,** St. Louis Cardinals	....	.35	.15	.03
☐ 157	**St. Louis Cardinals Team Card***	....	2.50	1.15	.25
☐ 158	**Norm Snead*,** Washington Redskins	....	2.50	1.15	.25
☐ 159	**Bobby Mitchell*,** Washington Redskins	....	3.50	1.65	.35
☐ 160	**Bill Barnes*,** Washington Redskins	....	2.00	.90	.20
☐ 161	**Fred Dugan*,** Washington Redskins	....	2.00	.90	.20
☐ 162	**Don Bossler*,** Washington Redskins	....	2.00	.90	.20
☐ 163	**John Nisby*,** Washington Redskins	....	2.00	.90	.20
☐ 164	**Riley Mattson*,** Washington Redskins	....	2.00	.90	.20
☐ 165	**Bob Toneff*,** Washington Redskins	....	2.00	.90	.20
☐ 166	**Rod Breedlove*,** Washington Redskins	....	2.00	.90	.20
☐ 167	**Dick James*,** Washington Redskins	....	2.00	.90	.20
☐ 168	**Claud Crabb*,** Washington Redskins	....	2.00	.90	.20
☐ 169	**Washington Redskins Team Card***	....	2.50	1.15	.25
☐ 170	**Checklist**	....	4.50	.50	.05

1964 TOPPS

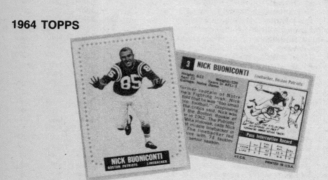

The 1964 Topps football set contains 176 American Football League player cards. The cards measure 2½" by 3½". The players are grouped by teams. Because the cards were not printed in a standard 132-card sheet, some cards are printed in lesser quantities than others. These cards are marked in the checklist with an asterisk. The backs of these cards contain the card number, vital statistics, a short biography, the player's record for the past year and his career, and a cartoon illustrated question-and-answer section.

		MINT	VG-E	F-G
	COMPLETE SET	175.00	80.00	17.00
	COMMON PLAYER (1-176)	.40	.18	.04
☐ 1	**Tommy Addison***, Boston Patriots	3.00	1.00	.20
☐ 2	**Houston Antwine**, Boston Patriots	.40	.18	.04
☐ 3	**Nick Buoniconti**, Boston Patriots	2.25	1.00	.22
☐ 4	**Ron Burton***, Boston Patriots	2.00	.90	.20
☐ 5	**Gino Cappelletti**, Boston Patriots	.90	.40	.09
☐ 6	**Jim Colclough***, Boston Patriots	2.00	.90	.20
☐ 7	**Bob Dee***, Boston Patriots	2.00	.90	.20
☐ 8	**Larry Eisenhauer***, Boston Patriots	.55	.25	.05
☐ 9	**Dick Felt***, Boston Patriots	2.00	.90	.20
☐ 10	**Larry Garron**, Boston Patriots	.40	.18	.04
☐ 11	**Art Graham**, Boston Patriots	.40	.18	.04
☐ 12	**Ron Hall**, Boston Patriots	.40	.18	.04
☐ 13	**Charles Long**, Boston Patriots	.40	.18	.04
☐ 14	**Don McKinnon**, Boston Patriots	.40	.18	.04
☐ 15	**Don Oakes***, Boston Patriots	2.00	.90	.20
☐ 16	**Ross O'Hanley***, Boston Patriots	2.00	.90	.20
☐ 17	**Babe Parilli***, Boston Patriots	2.50	1.15	.25
☐ 18	**Jesse Richardson***, Boston Patriots	2.00	.90	.20
☐ 19	**Jack Rudolph***, Boston Patriots	2.00	.90	.20
☐ 20	**Don Webb**, Boston Patriots	.40	.18	.04
☐ 21	**Boston Patriots Team Card**	.80	.40	.08
☐ 22	**Ray Abbruzzese**, Buffalo Bills	.40	.18	.04
☐ 23	**Stew Barber**, Buffalo Bills	.40	.18	.04
☐ 24	**Dave Behrman**, Buffalo Bills	.40	.18	.04
☐ 25	**Al Bemiller**, Buffalo Bills	.40	.18	.04
☐ 26	**Elbert Dubenion***, Buffalo Bills	2.00	.90	.20
☐ 27	**Jim Dunaway***, Buffalo Bills	2.00	.90	.20
☐ 28	**Booker Edgerson***, Buffalo Bills	2.00	.90	.20
☐ 29	**Cookie Gilchrist***, Buffalo Bills	2.50	1.15	.25
☐ 30	**Jack Kemp***, Buffalo Bills	15.00	7.00	1.50
☐ 31	**Daryle Lamonica***, Buffalo Bills	2.50	1.15	.25
☐ 32	**Bill Miller**, Buffalo Bills	.40	.18	.04
☐ 33	**Herb Paterra**, Buffalo Bills	.40	.18	.04
☐ 34	**Ken Rice***, Buffalo Bills	2.00	.90	.20
☐ 35	**Ed Rutkowski**, Buffalo Bills	.40	.18	.04
☐ 36	**George Saimes**, Buffalo Bills	.65	.30	.06
☐ 37	**Tom Sestak**, Buffalo Bills	.40	.18	.04
☐ 38	**Billy Shaw***, Buffalo Bills	2.00	.90	.20
☐ 39	**Mike Stratton**, Buffalo Bills	.40	.18	.04
☐ 40	**Gene Sykes**, Buffalo Bills	.40	.18	.04
☐ 41	**John Tracey***, Buffalo Bills	2.00	.90	.20
☐ 42	**Sid Youngelman***, Buffalo Bills	2.00	.90	.20
☐ 43	**Buffalo Bills Team Card**	.80	.40	.08

		MINT	VG-E	F-G
☐ 44	Eldon Danenhauer*, Denver Broncos	2.00	.90	.20
☐ 45	Jim Fraser*, Denver Broncos	2.00	.90	.20
☐ 46	Chuck Gavin*, Denver Broncos	2.00	.90	.20
☐ 47	Goose Gonsoulin*, Denver Broncos	2.00	.90	.20
☐ 48	Ernie Barnes, Denver Broncos	.40	.18	.04
☐ 49	Tom Janik, Denver Broncos	.40	.18	.04
☐ 50	Billy Joe, Denver Broncos	.55	.25	.05
☐ 51	Ike Lassiter, Denver Broncos	.40	.18	.04
☐ 52	John McCormick*, Denver Broncos	2.00	.90	.20
☐ 53	Lewis Bud McFadin*, Denver Broncos	2.00	.90	.20
☐ 54	Gene Mingo*, Denver Broncos	2.00	.90	.20
☐ 55	Charlie Mitchell, Denver Broncos	.40	.18	.04
☐ 56	John Nocera*, Denver Broncos	2.00	.90	.20
☐ 57	Tom Nomina, Denver Broncos	.40	.18	.04
☐ 58	Harold Olson*, Denver Broncos	2.00	.90	.20
☐ 59	Bob Scarpitto, Denver Broncos	.40	.18	.04
☐ 60	John Sklopan, Denver Broncos	.40	.18	.04
☐ 61	Mickey Slaughter, Denver Broncos	.55	.25	.05
☐ 62	Don Stone, Denver Broncos	.40	.18	.04
☐ 63	Jerry Sturm, Denver Broncos	.40	.18	.04
☐ 64	Lionel Taylor*, Denver Broncos	2.50	1.15	.25
☐ 65	Denver Broncos Team Card*	2.50	1.15	.25
☐ 66	Scott Appleton, Houston Oilers	.55	.25	.05
☐ 67	Tony Banfield*, Houston Oilers	2.00	.90	.20
☐ 68	George Blanda*, Houston Oilers	10.00	4.75	1.00
☐ 69	Billy Cannon, Houston Oilers	1.75	.85	.17
☐ 70	Doug Cline*, Houston Oilers	2.00	.90	.20
☐ 71	Gary Cutsinger*, Houston Oilers	2.00	.90	.20
☐ 72	Willard Dewveall*, Houston Oilers	2.00	.90	.20
☐ 73	Don Floyd*, Houston Oilers	2.00	.90	.20
☐ 74	Freddy Glick*, Houston Oilers	2.00	.90	.20
☐ 75	Charlie Hennigan*, Houston Oilers	2.50	1.15	.25
☐ 76	Ed Husmann*, Houston Oilers	2.00	.90	.20
☐ 77	Bobby Jancik*, Houston Oilers	2.00	.90	.20
☐ 78	Jacky Lee*, Houston Oilers	2.50	1.15	.25
☐ 79	Bob McLeod*, Houston Oilers	2.00	.90	.20
☐ 80	Rich Michael*, Houston Oilers	2.00	.90	.20
☐ 81	Larry Onesti, Houston Oilers	.40	.18	.04
☐ 82	Checklist	2.50	.40	.05
☐ 83	Bob Schmidt*, Houston Oilers	2.00	.90	.20
☐ 84	Walt Suggs*, Houston Oilers	2.00	.90	.20
☐ 85	Bob Talamini*, Houston Oilers	2.00	.90	.20
☐ 86	Charley Tolar*, Houston Oilers	2.00	.90	.20
☐ 87	Don Trull, Houston Oilers	.65	.30	.06
☐ 88	Houston Oilers Team Card	.80	.40	.08
☐ 89	Fred Arbanas, Kansas City Chiefs	.55	.25	.05

		MINT	VG-E	F-G
☐ 90	**Bobby Bell**, Kansas City Chiefs	3.00	1.40	.30
☐ 91	**Mel Branch***, Kansas City Chiefs	2.00	.90	.20
☐ 92	**Buck Buchanan**, Kansas City Chiefs	1.00	.45	.10
☐ 93	**Ed Budde**, Kansas City Chiefs	.55	.25	.05
☐ 94	**Chris Burford***, Kansas City Chiefs	2.00	.90	.20
☐ 95	**Walt Corey**, Kansas City Chiefs	.40	.18	.04
☐ 96	**Len Dawson***, Kansas City Chiefs	9.00	4.25	.90
☐ 97	**Dave Grayson**, Kansas City Chiefs	.55	.25	.05
☐ 98	**Abner Haynes**, Kansas City Chiefs	1.75	.85	.17
☐ 99	**Sherrill Headrick***, Kansas City Chiefs	2.00	.90	.20
☐ 100	**E.J. Holub**, Kansas City Chiefs	.65	.30	.06
☐ 101	**Bobby Hunt**, Kansas City Chiefs	.40	.18	.04
☐ 102	**Frank Jackson***, Kansas City Chiefs	2.00	.90	.20
☐ 103	**Curtis McClinton**, Kansas City Chiefs	.90	.40	.09
☐ 104	**Jerry Mays***, Kansas City Chiefs	2.00	.90	.20
☐ 105	**Johnny Robinson***, Kansas City Chiefs	2.50	1.15	.25
☐ 106	**Jack Spikes***, Kansas City Chiefs	2.00	.90	.20
☐ 107	**Smokey Stover***, Kansas City Chiefs	2.00	.90	.20
☐ 108	**Jim Tyrer**, Kansas City Chiefs	.55	.25	.05
☐ 109	**Duane Wood***, Kansas City Chiefs	2.00	.90	.20
☐ 110	**Kansas City Chiefs Team Card**	.80	.40	.08
☐ 111	**Dick Christy***, New York Jets	2.00	.90	.20
☐ 112	**Dan Ficca***, New York Jets	2.00	.90	.20
☐ 113	**Larry Grantham**, New York Jets	.55	.25	.05
☐ 114	**Curley Johnson***, New York Jets	2.00	.90	.20
☐ 115	**Gene Heeter**, New York Jets	.40	.18	.04
☐ 116	**Jack Klotz**, New York Jets	.40	.18	.04
☐ 117	**Pete Liske**, New York Jets	.65	.30	.06
☐ 118	**Bob McAdam**, New York Jets	.40	.18	.04
☐ 119	**Dee Mackey***, New York Jets	2.00	.90	.20
☐ 120	**Bill Mathis***, New York Jets	2.00	.90	.20
☐ 121	**Don Maynard**, New York Jets	2.75	1.25	.27
☐ 122	**Dainard Paulson***, New York Jets	2.00	.90	.20
☐ 123	**Gerry Philbin**, New York Jets	.55	.25	.05
☐ 124	**Mark Smolinski***, New York Jets	2.00	.90	.20
☐ 125	**Matt Snell**, New York Jets	1.00	.45	.10
☐ 126	**Mike Taliaferro**, New York Jets	.55	.25	.05
☐ 127	**Bake Turner***, New York Jets	2.50	1.15	.25
☐ 128	**Jeff Ware**, New York Jets	.40	.18	.04
☐ 129	**Clyde Washington**, New York Jets	.40	.18	.04
☐ 130	**Dick Wood**, New York Jets	.55	.25	.05
☐ 131	**New York Jets Team Card**	.90	.40	.09
☐ 132	**Dalva Allen***, Oakland Raiders	2.00	.90	.20
☐ 133	**Dan Birdwell**, Oakland Raiders	.40	.18	.04
☐ 134	**Dave Costa**, Oakland Raiders	.40	.18	.04
☐ 135	**Dobie Craig**, Oakland Raiders	.40	.18	.04

		MINT	VG-E	F-G
☐ 136	Clem Daniels, Oakland Raiders	.65	.30	.06
☐ 137	Cotton Davidson*, Oakland Raiders	2.25	1.00	.22
☐ 138	Claude Gibson, Oakland Raiders	.40	.18	.04
☐ 139	Tom Flores*, Oakland Raiders	2.50	1.15	.25
☐ 140	Wayne Hawkins*, Oakland Raiders	2.00	.90	.20
☐ 141	Ken Herock, Oakland Raiders	.40	.18	.04
☐ 142	Jon Jelacic*, Oakland Raiders	2.00	.90	.20
☐ 143	Joe Krakoski, Oakland Raiders	.40	.18	.04
☐ 144	Archie Matsos*, Oakland Raiders	2.00	.90	.20
☐ 145	Mike Mercer, Oakland Raiders	.40	.18	.04
☐ 146	Alan Miller*, Oakland Raiders	2.00	.90	.20
☐ 147	Bob Mischak*, Oakland Raiders	2.00	.90	.20
☐ 148	Jim Otto*, Oakland Raiders	3.50	1.65	.35
☐ 149	Clancy Osborne*, Oakland Raiders	2.00	.90	.20
☐ 150	Art Powell*, Oakland Raiders	2.25	1.00	.22
☐ 151	Bo Roberson, Oakland Raiders	.40	.18	.04
☐ 152	Fred Williamson*, Oakland Raiders	2.50	1.15	.25
☐ 153	Oakland Raiders Team Card	.80	.40	.08
☐ 154	Chuck Allen*, San Diego Chargers	2.00	.90	.20
☐ 155	Lance Alworth, San Diego Chargers	3.50	1.65	.35
☐ 156	George Blair, San Diego Chargers	.40	.18	.04
☐ 157	Earl Faison, San Diego Chargers	.55	.25	.05
☐ 158	Sam Gruniesen, San Diego Chargers	.40	.18	.04
☐ 159	John Hadl, San Diego Chargers	3.50	1.65	.35
☐ 160	Dick Harris*, San Diego Chargers	2.00	.90	.20
☐ 161	Emil Karas*, San Diego Chargers	2.00	.90	.20
☐ 162	Dave Kocourek*, San Diego Chargers	2.00	.90	.20
☐ 163	Ernie Ladd, San Diego Chargers	1.75	.85	.17
☐ 164	Keith Lincoln, San Diego Chargers	.90	.40	.09
☐ 165	Paul Lowe*, San Diego Chargers	2.50	1.15	.25
☐ 166	Charles McNeil, San Diego Chargers	.40	.18	.04
☐ 167	Jacque MacKinnon*, San Diego Chargers	2.00	.90	.20
☐ 168	Ron Mix*, San Diego Chargers	3.00	1.40	.30
☐ 169	Don Norton*, San Diego Chargers	2.00	.90	.20
☐ 170	Don Rogers*, San Diego Chargers	2.00	.90	.20
☐ 171	Tobin Rote*, San Diego Chargers	2.50	1.15	.25
☐ 172	Henry Schmidt*, San Diego Chargers	2.00	.90	.20
☐ 173	Bud Whitehead, San Diego Chargers	.40	.18	.04
☐ 174	Ernie Wright*, San Diego Chargers	2.00	.90	.20
☐ 175	San Diego Chargers Team Card	.80	.40	.08
☐ 176	Checklist*	12.50	2.00	.25

1965 TOPPS

The 1965 Topps football card set contains 176 oversized (2½″ by 4¹¹⁄₁₆″) cards of American Football League players. The cards are grouped together by teams. Since this set was not printed in the standard fashion, many of the cards were printed in lesser quantities than others. These cards are marked in the checklist with an asterisk. This set is somewhat significant in that it contains the rookie card of Joe Namath.

		MINT	VG-E	F-G
	COMPLETE SET	450.00	200.00	45.00
	COMMON PLAYER (1-176)	.90	.40	.09
☐	1 Tommy Addison*, Boston Patriots	3.00	1.10	.25
☐	2 Houston Antwine*, Boston Patriots	2.25	1.00	.22
☐	3 Nick Buoniconti*, Boston Patriots	4.00	1.85	.40
☐	4 Ron Burton*, Boston Patriots	2.25	1.00	.22
☐	5 Gino Cappelletti*, Boston Patriots	3.00	1.40	.30
☐	6 Jim Colclough, Boston Patriots	.90	.40	.09
☐	7 Bob Dee*, Boston Patriots	2.25	1.00	.22
☐	8 Larry Eisenhauer, Boston Patriots	.90	.40	.09
☐	9 J.D. Garrett, Boston Patriots	.90	.40	.09
☐	10 Larry Garron, Boston Patriots	.90	.40	.09
☐	11 Art Graham*, Boston Patriots	2.25	1.00	.22
☐	12 Ron Hall, Boston Patriots	.90	.40	.09
☐	13 Charles Long, Boston Patriots	.90	.40	.09
☐	14 Jon Morris, Boston Patriots	.90	.40	.09
☐	15 Bill Neighbors*, Boston Patriots	2.25	1.00	.22
☐	16 Ross O'Hanley, Boston Patriots	.90	.40	.09

			MINT	VG-E	F-G
☐	17	Babe Parilli*, Boston Patriots	3.00	1.40	.30
☐	18	Tony Romeo*, Boston Patriots	2.25	1.00	.22
☐	19	Jack Rudolph*, Boston Patriots	2.25	1.00	.22
☐	20	Bob Schmidt, Boston Patriots	.90	.40	.09
☐	21	Don Webb*, Boston Patriots	2.25	1.00	.22
☐	22	Jim Whalen*, Boston Patriots	2.25	1.00	.22
☐	23	Stew Barber, Buffalo Bills	.90	.40	.09
☐	24	Glenn Bass*, Buffalo Bills	2.25	1.00	.22
☐	25	Al Bemiller*, Buffalo Bills	2.25	1.00	.22
☐	26	Wray Carlton*, Buffalo Bills	2.25	1.00	.22
☐	27	Tom Day, Buffalo Bills	.90	.40	.09
☐	28	Elbert Dubenion*, Buffalo Bills	2.50	1.15	.25
☐	29	Jim Dunaway, Buffalo Bills	.90	.40	.09
☐	30	Pete Gogolak*, Buffalo Bills	3.00	1.40	.30
☐	31	Dick Hudson*, Buffalo Bills	2.25	1.00	.22
☐	32	Harry Jacobs*, Buffalo Bills	2.25	1.00	.22
☐	33	Billy Joe*, Buffalo Bills	2.25	1.00	.22
☐	34	Tom Keating*, Buffalo Bills	2.25	1.00	.22
☐	35	Jack Kemp*, Buffalo Bills	25.00	11.00	2.50
☐	36	Daryle Lamonica*, Buffalo Bills	4.00	1.85	.40
☐	37	Paul Maguire*, Buffalo Bills	3.00	1.40	.30
☐	38	Ron McDole*, Buffalo Bills	2.50	1.15	.25
☐	39	George Saimes*, Buffalo Bills	2.50	1.15	.25
☐	40	Tom Sestak*, Buffalo Bills	2.25	1.00	.22
☐	41	Billy Shaw*, Buffalo Bills	2.25	1.00	.22
☐	42	Mike Stratton*, Buffalo Bills	2.25	1.00	.22
☐	43	John Tracey*, Buffalo Bills	2.25	1.00	.22
☐	44	Ernie Warlick*, Buffalo Bills	.90	.40	.09
☐	45	Odell Barry, Denver Broncos	.90	.40	.09
☐	46	Willie Brown*, Denver Broncos	8.00	3.75	.80
☐	47	Gerry Bussell*, Denver Broncos	2.25	1.00	.22
☐	48	Eldon Danenhauer*, Denver Broncos	2.25	1.00	.22
☐	49	Al Denson*, Denver Broncos	2.25	1.00	.22
☐	50	Hewritt Dixon*, Denver Broncos	2.50	1.15	.25
☐	51	Cookie Gilchrist*, Denver Broncos	3.00	1.40	.30
☐	52	Goose Gonsoulin*, Denver Broncos	2.25	1.00	.22
☐	53	Abner Haynes*, Denver Broncos	3.00	1.40	.30
☐	54	Jerry Hopkins, Denver Broncos	.90	.40	.09
☐	55	Ray Jacobs*, Denver Broncos	2.25	1.00	.22
☐	56	Jacky Lee*, Denver Broncos	2.50	1.15	.25
☐	57	John McCormick, Denver Broncos	.90	.40	.09
☐	58	Bob McCullough*, Denver Broncos	2.25	1.00	.22
☐	59	John McGeever, Denver Broncos	.90	.40	.09
☐	60	Charlie Mitchell*, Denver Broncos	2.25	1.00	.22
☐	61	Jim Perkins*, Denver Broncos	2.25	1.00	.22
☐	62	Bob Scarpitto*, Denver Broncos	2.25	1.00	.22

		MINT	VG-E	F-G
☐ 63	Mickey Slaughter*, Denver Broncos	2.50	1.15	.25
☐ 64	Jerry Sturm*, Denver Broncos	2.25	1.00	.22
☐ 65	Lionel Taylor*, Denver Broncos	3.00	1.40	.30
☐ 66	Scott Appleton*, Houston Oilers	2.50	1.15	.25
☐ 67	Johnny Baker*, Houston Oilers	2.25	1.00	.22
☐ 68	Sonny Bishop*, Houston Oilers	2.25	1.00	.22
☐ 69	George Blanda*, Houston Oilers	20.00	9.00	2.00
☐ 70	Sid Blanks*, Houston Oilers	2.25	1.00	.22
☐ 71	Ode Burrell*, Houston Oilers	2.25	1.00	.22
☐ 72	Doug Cline*, Houston Oilers	2.25	1.00	.22
☐ 73	Willard Dewveall, Houston Oilers	.90	.40	.09
☐ 74	Larry Elkins, Houston Oilers	.90	.40	.09
☐ 75	Don Floyd*, Houston Oilers	2.25	1.00	.22
☐ 76	Freddy Glick, Houston Oilers	.90	.40	.09
☐ 77	Tom Goode*, Houston Oilers	2.25	1.00	.22
☐ 78	Charlie Hennigan*, Houston Oilers	2.50	1.15	.25
☐ 79	Ed Husmann, Houston Oilers	.90	.40	.09
☐ 80	Bobby Jancik*, Houston Oilers	2.25	1.00	.22
☐ 81	Bud McFadin*, Houston Oilers	2.25	1.00	.22
☐ 82	Bob McLeod*, Houston Oilers	2.25	1.00	.22
☐ 83	Jim Norton*, Houston Oilers	2.25	1.00	.22
☐ 84	Walt Suggs, Houston Oilers	.90	.40	.09
☐ 85	Bob Talamini, Houston Oilers	.90	.40	.09
☐ 86	Charley Tolar*, Houston Oilers	2.25	1.00	.22
☐ 87	Checklist 1-88*, Houston Oilers	12.00	1.50	.15
☐ 88	Don Trull*, Houston Oilers	2.50	1.15	.25
☐ 89	Fred Arbanas*, Kansas City Chiefs	2.50	1.15	.25
☐ 90	Pete Beathard*, Kansas City Chiefs	3.00	1.40	.30
☐ 91	Bobby Bell*, Kansas City Chiefs	4.00	1.85	.40
☐ 92	Mel Branch*, Kansas City Chiefs	2.25	1.00	.22
☐ 93	Tommy Brooker*, Kansas City Chiefs	2.25	1.00	.22
☐ 94	Buck Buchanan*, Kansas City Chiefs	3.00	1.40	.30
☐ 95	Ed Budde*, Kansas City Chiefs	2.50	1.15	.25
☐ 96	Chris Burford*, Kansas City Chiefs	2.50	1.15	.25
☐ 97	Walt Corey, Kansas City Chiefs	.90	.40	.09
☐ 98	Jerry Cornelison, Kansas City Chiefs	.90	.40	.09
☐ 99	Len Dawson*, Kansas City Chiefs	10.00	4.75	1.00
☐ 100	Jon Gilliam*, Kansas City Chiefs	2.25	1.00	.22
☐ 101	Sherrill Headrick*, Kansas City Chiefs	2.50	1.15	.25
☐ 102	Dave Hill*, Kansas City Chiefs	2.25	1.00	.22
☐ 103	E.J. Holub*, Kansas City Chiefs	2.50	1.15	.25
☐ 104	Bobby Hunt*, Kansas City Chiefs	2.25	1.00	.22
☐ 105	Frank Jackson*, Kansas City Chiefs	2.25	1.00	.22
☐ 106	Jerry Mays, Kansas City Chiefs	.90	.40	.09
☐ 107	Curtis McClinton*, Kansas City Chiefs	2.50	1.15	.25
☐ 108	Bobby Ply*, Kansas City Chiefs	2.25	1.00	.22

		MINT	VG-E	F-G
☐ 109	Johnny Robinson*, Kansas City Chiefs	3.00	1.40	.30
☐ 110	Jim Tyrer*, Kansas City Chiefs	2.50	1.15	.25
☐ 111	Bill Baird*, New York Jets	2.25	1.00	.22
☐ 112	Ralph Baker*, New York Jets	2.25	1.00	.22
☐ 113	Sam DeLuca*, New York Jets	2.25	1.00	.22
☐ 114	Larry Grantham*, New York Jets	2.50	1.15	.25
☐ 115	Gene Heeter*, New York Jets	2.25	1.00	.22
☐ 116	Winston Hill*, New York Jets	2.25	1.00	.22
☐ 117	John Huarte*, New York Jets	4.00	1.85	.40
☐ 118	Cosmo Iacavazzi*, New York Jets	2.25	1.00	.22
☐ 119	Curley Johnson*, New York Jets	2.25	1.00	.22
☐ 120	Dee Mackey, New York Jets	.90	.40	.09
☐ 121	Don Maynard, New York Jets	4.00	1.85	.40
☐ 122	Joe Namath*, New York Jets	150.00	70.00	15.00
☐ 123	Dainard Paulson, New York Jets	.90	.40	.09
☐ 124	Gerry Philbin*, New York Jets	2.25	1.00	.22
☐ 125	Sherman Plunkett*, New York Jets	2.25	1.00	.22
☐ 126	Mark Smolinski, New York Jets	.90	.40	.09
☐ 127	Matt Snell*, New York Jets	3.00	1.40	.30
☐ 128	Mike Taliaferro*, New York Jets	2.50	1.15	.25
☐ 129	Bake Turner*, New York Jets	3.00	1.40	.30
☐ 130	Clyde Washington*, New York Jets	2.25	1.00	.22
☐ 131	Verlon Biggs*, New York Jets	2.25	1.00	.22
☐ 132	Dalva Allen, Oakland Raiders	.90	.40	.09
☐ 133	Fred Biletnikoff*, Oakland Raiders	10.00	4.75	1.00
☐ 134	Billy Cannon*, Oakland Raiders	3.00	1.40	.30
☐ 135	Dave Costa*, Oakland Raiders	2.25	1.00	.22
☐ 136	Clem Daniels*, Oakland Raiders	2.50	1.15	.25
☐ 137	Ben Davidson*, Oakland Raiders	4.00	1.85	.40
☐ 138	Cotton Davidson*, Oakland Raiders	2.50	1.15	.25
☐ 139	Tom Flores*, Oakland Raiders	3.00	1.40	.30
☐ 140	Claude Gibson, Oakland Raiders	.90	.40	.09
☐ 141	Wayne Hawkins, Oakland Raiders	.90	.40	.09
☐ 142	Archie Matsos*, Oakland Raiders	2.25	1.00	.22
☐ 143	Mike Mercer*, Oakland Raiders	2.25	1.00	.22
☐ 144	Bob Mischak*, Oakland Raiders	2.25	1.00	.22
☐ 145	Jim Otto, Oakland Raiders	4.00	1.85	.40
☐ 146	Art Powell*, Oakland Raiders	2.50	1.15	.25
☐ 147	Warren Powers*, Oakland Raiders	2.25	1.00	.22
☐ 148	Ken Rice*, Oakland Raiders	2.25	1.00	.22
☐ 149	Bo Roberson*, Oakland Raiders	2.25	1.00	.22
☐ 150	Harry Schuh, Oakland Raiders	.90	.40	.09
☐ 151	Larry Todd*, Oakland Raiders	2.25	1.00	.22
☐ 152	Fred Williamson*, Oakland Raiders	2.50	1.15	.25
☐ 153	J.R. Williamson, Oakland Raiders	.90	.40	.09
☐ 154	Chuck Allen, San Diego Chargers	.90	.40	.09

	MINT	VG-E	F-G
☐ 155 Lance Alworth, San Diego Chargers	6.50	3.00	.65
☐ 156 Frank Buncom, San Diego Chargers	.90	.40	.09
☐ 157 Steve DeLong*, San Diego Chargers	2.25	1.00	.22
☐ 158 Earl Faison*, San Diego Chargers	2.25	1.00	.22
☐ 159 Kenny Graham*, San Diego Chargers	2.25	1.00	.22
☐ 160 George Gross*, San Diego Chargers	2.25	1.00	.22
☐ 161 John Hadl*, San Diego Chargers	6.00	2.80	.60
☐ 162 Emil Karas*, San Diego Chargers	2.25	1.00	.22
☐ 163 Dave Kocourek*, San Diego Chargers	2.25	1.00	.22
☐ 164 Ernie Ladd*, San Diego Chargers	3.00	1.40	.30
☐ 165 Keith Lincoln*, San Diego Chargers	3.00	1.40	.30
☐ 166 Paul Lowe*, San Diego Chargers	3.00	1.40	.30
☐ 167 Jacque MacKinnon, San Diego Chargers	.90	.40	.09
☐ 168 Ron Mix, San Diego Chargers	3.00	1.40	.30
☐ 169 Don Norton*, San Diego Chargers	2.25	1.00	.22
☐ 170 Bob Petrich, San Diego Chargers	.90	.40	.09
☐ 171 Rick Redman*, San Diego Chargers	2.25	1.00	.22
☐ 172 Pat Shea, San Diego Chargers	.90	.40	.09
☐ 173 Walt Sweeney*, San Diego Chargers	2.25	1.00	.22
☐ 174 Dick Westmoreland, San Diego Chargers	.90	.40	.09
☐ 175 Ernie Wright*, San Diego Chargers	2.25	1.00	.22
☐ 176 Checklist 89-176*	21.00	2.00	.25

1966 TOPPS

The 1966 Topps set of 132 cards contains AFL players grouped together by teams. The cards measure 2½" by 3½". The card backs are printed in black and pink on white card stock. In actuality, card number 15 is not a football card at all but a "Funny Ring" checklist card; nevertheless, it is considered part of the set and is now considered the toughest card in the set to find in mint condition.

		MINT	VG-E	F-G
	COMPLETE SET	150.00	70.00	15.00
	COMMON PLAYER (1-132)	.40	.18	.04
☐	1 Tommy Addison, Boston Patriots	1.00	.25	.05
☐	2 Houston Antwine, Boston Patriots	.40	.18	.04
☐	3 Nick Buoniconti, Boston Patriots	2.00	.90	.20
☐	4 Gino Cappelletti, Boston Patriots	.80	.40	.08
☐	5 Bob Dee, Boston Patriots	.40	.18	.04
☐	6 Larry Garron, Boston Patriots	.40	.18	.04
☐	7 Art Graham, Boston Patriots	.40	.18	.04
☐	8 Ron Hall, Boston Patriots	.40	.18	.04
☐	9 Charles Long, Boston Patriots	.40	.18	.04
☐	10 Jon Morris, Boston Patriots	.40	.18	.04
☐	11 Don Oakes, Boston Patriots	.40	.18	.04
☐	12 Babe Parilli, Boston Patriots	.90	.40	.09
☐	13 Don Webb, Boston Patriots	.40	.18	.04
☐	14 Jim Whalen, Boston Patriots	.40	.18	.04
☐	15 Funny Ring Checklist, Boston Patriots	40.00	10.00	2.00
☐	16 Stew Barber, Buffalo Bills	.40	.18	.04
☐	17 Glenn Bass, Buffalo Bills	.40	.18	.04
☐	18 Dave Behrmann, Buffalo Bills	.40	.18	.04
☐	19 Al Bemiller, Buffalo Bills	.40	.18	.04
☐	20 Butch Byrd, Buffalo Bills	.50	.22	.05
☐	21 Wray Carlton, Buffalo Bills	.50	.22	.05
☐	22 Tom Day, Buffalo Bills	.40	.18	.04
☐	23 Elbert Dubenion, Buffalo Bills	.60	.28	.06
☐	24 Jim Dunaway, Buffalo Bills	.50	.22	.05
☐	25 Dick Hudson, Buffalo Bills	.40	.18	.04
☐	26 Jack Kemp, Buffalo Bills	10.00	4.50	1.00
☐	27 Daryle Lamonica, Buffalo Bills	1.75	.85	.17
☐	28 Tom Sestak, Buffalo Bills	.40	.18	.04
☐	29 Billy Shaw, Buffalo Bills	.50	.22	.05
☐	30 Mike Stratton, Buffalo Bills	.50	.22	.05
☐	31 Eldon Danenhauer, Denver Broncos	.40	.18	.04
☐	32 Cookie Gilchrist, Denver Broncos	1.75	.85	.17
☐	33 Goose Gonsoulin, Denver Broncos	.50	.22	.05
☐	34 Wendell Hayes, Denver Broncos	.50	.22	.05
☐	35 Abner Haynes, Denver Broncos	.80	.40	.08
☐	36 Jerry Hopkins, Denver Broncos	.40	.18	.04
☐	37 Ray Jacobs, Denver Broncos	.40	.18	.04

			MINT	VG-E	F-G
☐	38	Charlie Janerette, Denver Broncos	.40	.18	.04
☐	39	Ray Kubala, Denver Broncos	.40	.18	.04
☐	40	John McCormick, Denver Broncos	.40	.18	.04
☐	41	Leroy Moore, Denver Broncos	.40	.18	.04
☐	42	Bob Scarpitto, Denver Broncos	.40	.18	.04
☐	43	Mickey Slaughter, Denver Broncos	.50	.22	.05
☐	44	Jerry Sturm, Denver Broncos	.40	.18	.04
☐	45	Lionel Taylor, Denver Broncos	.90	.40	.09
☐	46	Scott Appleton, Houston Oilers	.50	.22	.05
☐	47	Johnny Baker, Houston Oilers	.40	.18	.04
☐	48	George Blanda, Houston Oilers	6.50	3.00	.65
☐	49	Sid Blanks, Houston Oilers	.40	.18	.04
☐	50	Danny Brabham, Houston Oilers	.40	.18	.04
☐	51	Ode Burrell, Houston Oilers	.40	.18	.04
☐	52	Gary Cutsinger, Houston Oilers	.40	.18	.04
☐	53	Larry Elkins, Houston Oilers	.50	.22	.05
☐	54	Don Floyd, Houston Oilers	.50	.22	.05
☐	55	Willie Frazier, Houston Oilers	.50	.22	.05
☐	56	Freddy Glick, Houston Oilers	.50	.22	.05
☐	57	Charlie Hennigan, Houston Oilers	.75	.35	.07
☐	58	Bobby Jancik, Houston Oilers	.50	.22	.05
☐	59	Rich Michael, Houston Oilers	.40	.18	.04
☐	60	Don Trull, Houston Oilers	.60	.28	.06
☐	61	Checklist	4.00	.40	.05
☐	62	Fred Arbanas, Kansas City Chiefs	.50	.22	.05
☐	63	Pete Beathard, Kansas City Chiefs	.90	.40	.09
☐	64	Bobby Bell, Kansas City Chiefs	2.00	.90	.20
☐	65	Ed Budde, Kansas City Chiefs	.50	.22	.05
☐	66	Chris Burford, Kansas City Chiefs	.50	.22	.05
☐	67	Len Dawson, Kansas City Chiefs	3.50	1.65	.35
☐	68	Jon Gilliam, Kansas City Chiefs	.40	.18	.04
☐	69	Sherrill Headrick, Kansas City Chiefs	.50	.22	.05
☐	70	E.J. Holub, Kansas City Chiefs	.50	.22	.05
☐	71	Bobby Hunt, Kansas City Chiefs	.40	.18	.04
☐	72	Curtis McClinton, Kansas City Chiefs	.90	.40	.09
☐	73	Jerry Mays, Kansas City Chiefs	.50	.22	.05
☐	74	Johnny Robinson, Kansas City Chiefs	1.00	.45	.10
☐	75	Otis Taylor, Kansas City Chiefs	2.00	.90	.20
☐	76	Tom Erlandson, Miami Dolphins	.40	.18	.04
☐	77	Norm Evans, Miami Dolphins	.40	.18	.04
☐	78	Tom Goode, Miami Dolphins	.40	.18	.04
☐	79	Mike Hudock, Miami Dolphins	.40	.18	.04
☐	80	Frank Jackson, Miami Dolphins	.40	.18	.04
☐	81	Billy Joe, Miami Dolphins	.50	.22	.05
☐	82	Dave Kocourek, Miami Dolphins	.40	.18	.04

			MINT	VG-E	F-G
☐	83	Bo Roberson, Miami Dolphins	.40	.18	.04
☐	84	Jack Spikes, Miami Dolphins	.50	.22	.05
☐	85	Jim Warren, Miami Dolphins	.40	.18	.04
☐	86	Willie West, Miami Dolphins	.40	.18	.04
☐	87	Dick Westmoreland, Miami Dolphins	.40	.18	.04
☐	88	Eddie Wilson, Miami Dolphins	.40	.18	.04
☐	89	Dick Wood, Miami Dolphins	.50	.22	.05
☐	90	Verlon Biggs, New York Jets	.40	.18	.04
☐	91	Sam DeLuca, New York Jets	.40	.18	.04
☐	92	Winston Hill, New York Jets	.40	.18	.04
☐	93	Dee Mackey, New York Jets	.40	.18	.04
☐	94	Bill Mathis, New York Jets	.50	.22	.05
☐	95	Don Maynard, New York Jets	2.50	1.15	.25
☐	96	Joe Namath, New York Jets	20.00	9.00	2.00
☐	97	Dainard Paulson, New York Jets	.40	.18	.04
☐	98	Gerry Philbin, New York Jets	.50	.22	.05
☐	99	Sherman Plunkett, New York Jets	.40	.18	.04
☐	100	Paul Rochester, New York Jets	.40	.18	.04
☐	101	George Sauer Jr., New York Jets	.50	.22	.05
☐	102	Matt Snell, New York Jets	.90	.40	.09
☐	103	Jim Turner, New York Jets	.90	.40	.09
☐	104	Fred Biletnikoff, Oakland Raiders	2.50	1.15	.25
☐	105	Bill Budness, Oakland Raiders	.40	.18	.04
☐	106	Billy Cannon, Oakland Raiders	1.75	.85	.17
☐	107	Clem Daniels, Oakland Raiders	.60	.28	.06
☐	108	Ben Davidson, Oakland Raiders	1.00	.45	.10
☐	109	Cotton Davidson, Oakland Raiders	.50	.22	.05
☐	110	Claude Gibson, Oakland Raiders	.40	.18	.04
☐	111	Wayne Hawkins, Oakland Raiders	.40	.18	.04
☐	112	Ken Herock, Oakland Raiders	.40	.18	.04
☐	113	Bob Mischak, Oakland Raiders	.40	.18	.04
☐	114	Gus Otto, Oakland Raiders	.40	.18	.04
☐	115	Jim Otto, Oakland Raiders	2.50	1.15	.25
☐	116	Art Powell, Oakland Raiders	.60	.28	.06
☐	117	Harry Schuh, Oakland Raiders	.40	.18	.04
☐	118	Chuck Allen, San Diego Chargers	.40	.18	.04
☐	119	Lance Alworth, San Diego Chargers	3.50	1.65	.35
☐	120	Frank Buncom, San Diego Chargers	.40	.18	.04
☐	121	Steve DeLong, San Diego Chargers	.40	.18	.04
☐	122	John Farris, San Diego Chargers	.40	.18	.04
☐	123	Kenny Graham, San Diego Chargers	.40	.18	.04
☐	124	Sam Gruniesen, San Diego Chargers	.40	.18	.04
☐	125	John Hadl, San Diego Chargers	2.50	1.15	.25
☐	126	Walt Sweeney, San Diego Chargers	.50	.22	.05
☐	127	Keith Lincoln, San Diego Chargers	.90	.40	.09
☐	128	Ron Mix, San Diego Chargers	2.25	1.00	.22

		MINT	VG-E	F-G
☐ 129 **Don Norton,** San Diego Chargers		.40	.18	.04
☐ 130 **Pat Shea,** San Diego Chargers		.40	.18	.04
☐ 131 **Ernie Wright,** San Diego Chargers		.40	.18	.04
☐ 132 **Checklist**		6.00	.60	.10

1967 TOPPS

The 1967 Topps set of 132 cards contains AFL players only, with players grouped together by teams. The cards measure 2½" by 3½". The card backs are printed in gold and black on white card stock. A question (with upside down answer) is given on the bottom of the reverse.

		MINT	VG-E	F-G
	COMPLETE SET	115.00	50.00	10.00
	COMMON PLAYER (1-132)	.35	.15	.03
☐	1 **John Huarte,** Boston Patriots	1.50	.50	.10
☐	2 **Babe Parilli,** Boston Patriots	.90	.40	.09
☐	3 **Gino Cappelletti,** Boston Patriots	.75	.35	.07
☐	4 **Larry Garron,** Boston Patriots	.35	.15	.03
☐	5 **Tommy Addison,** Boston Patriots	.35	.15	.03
☐	6 **Jon Morris,** Boston Patriots	.35	.15	.03
☐	7 **Houston Antwine,** Boston Patriots	.35	.15	.03
☐	8 **Don Oakes,** Boston Patriots	.35	.15	.03
☐	9 **Larry Eisenhauer,** Boston Patriots	.35	.15	.03
☐	10 **Jim Hunt,** Boston Patriots	.35	.15	.03

			MINT	VG-E	F-G
☐	11	**Jim Whalen**, Boston Patriots	.35	.15	.03
☐	12	**Art Graham**, Boston Patriots	.35	.15	.03
☐	13	**Nick Buoniconti**, Boston Patriots	1.75	.85	.17
☐	14	**Bob Dee**, Boston Patriots	.35	.15	.03
☐	15	**Keith Lincoln**, Buffalo Bills	.90	.40	.09
☐	16	**Tom Flores**, Buffalo Bills	.90	.40	.09
☐	17	**Art Powell**, Buffalo Bills	.60	.28	.06
☐	18	**Stew Barber**, Buffalo Bills	.35	.15	.03
☐	19	**Wray Carlton**, Buffalo Bills	.45	.20	.04
☐	20	**Elbert Dubenion**, Buffalo Bills	.55	.25	.05
☐	21	**Jim Dunaway**, Buffalo Bills	.45	.20	.04
☐	22	**Dick Hudson**, Buffalo Bills	.35	.15	.03
☐	23	**Harry Jacobs**, Buffalo Bills	.35	.15	.03
☐	24	**Jack Kemp**, Buffalo Bills	9.00	4.25	.90
☐	25	**Ron McDole**, Buffalo Bills	.35	.15	.03
☐	26	**George Saimes**, Buffalo Bills	.55	.25	.05
☐	27	**Tom Sestak**, Buffalo Bills	.35	.15	.03
☐	28	**Billy Shaw**, Buffalo Bills	.45	.20	.04
☐	29	**Mike Stratton**, Buffalo Bills	.45	.20	.04
☐	30	**Nemiah Wilson**, Denver Broncos	.45	.20	.04
☐	31	**John McCormick**, Denver Broncos	.35	.15	.03
☐	32	**Rex Mirich**, Denver Broncos	.35	.15	.03
☐	33	**Dave Costa**, Denver Broncos	.35	.15	.03
☐	34	**Goose Gonsoulin**, Denver Broncos	.45	.20	.04
☐	35	**Abner Haynes**, Denver Broncos	.80	.40	.08
☐	36	**Wendell Hayes**, Denver Broncos	.45	.20	.04
☐	37	**Archie Matsos**, Denver Broncos	.35	.15	.03
☐	38	**John Bramlett**, Denver Broncos	.35	.15	.03
☐	39	**Jerry Sturm**, Denver Broncos	.35	.15	.03
☐	40	**Max Leetzow**, Denver Broncos	.35	.15	.03
☐	41	**Bob Scarpitto**, Denver Broncos	.35	.15	.03
☐	42	**Lionel Taylor**, Denver Broncos	.90	.40	.09
☐	43	**Al Denson**, Denver Broncos	.35	.15	.03
☐	44	**Miller Farr**, Houston Oilers	.55	.25	.05
☐	45	**Don Trull**, Houston Oilers	.55	.25	.05
☐	46	**Jacky Lee**, Houston Oilers	.55	.25	.05
☐	47	**Bobby Jancik**, Houston Oilers	.45	.20	.04
☐	48	**Ode Burrell**, Houston Oilers	.35	.15	.03
☐	49	**Larry Elkins**, Houston Oilers	.45	.20	.04
☐	50	**W.K. Hicks**, Houston Oilers	.35	.15	.03
☐	51	**Sid Blanks**, Houston Oilers	.35	.15	.03
☐	52	**Jim Norton**, Houston Oilers	.35	.15	.03
☐	53	**Bobby Maples**, Houston Oilers	.35	.15	.03
☐	54	**Bob Talamini**, Houston Oilers	.35	.15	.03
☐	55	**Walt Suggs**, Houston Oilers	.35	.15	.03
☐	56	**Gary Cutsinger**, Houston Oilers	.35	.15	.03

		MINT	VG-E	F-G
☐ 57	**Danny Brabham**, Houston Oilers	.35	.15	.03
☐ 58	**Ernie Ladd**, Houston Oilers	.90	.40	.09
☐ 59	**Checklist**	4.00	.60	.10
☐ 60	**Pete Beathard**, Kansas City Chiefs	.90	.40	.09
☐ 61	**Len Dawson**, Kansas City Chiefs	3.50	1.65	.35
☐ 62	**Bobby Hunt**, Kansas City Chiefs	.35	.15	.03
☐ 63	**Bert Coan**, Kansas City Chiefs	.35	.15	.03
☐ 64	**Curtis McClinton**, Kansas City Chiefs	.55	.25	.05
☐ 65	**Johnny Robinson**, Kansas City Chiefs	.90	.40	.09
☐ 66	**E.J. Holub**, Kansas City Chiefs	.55	.25	.05
☐ 67	**Jerry Mays**, Kansas City Chiefs	.45	.20	.04
☐ 68	**Jim Tyrer**, Kansas City Chiefs	.45	.20	.04
☐ 69	**Bobby Bell**, Kansas City Chiefs	1.75	.85	.17
☐ 70	**Fred Arbanas**, Kansas City Chiefs	.45	.20	.04
☐ 71	**Buck Buchanan**, Kansas City Chiefs	.90	.40	.09
☐ 72	**Chris Burford**, Kansas City Chiefs	.45	.20	.04
☐ 73	**Otis Taylor**, Kansas City Chiefs	.90	.40	.09
☐ 74	**Cookie Gilchrist**, Miami Dolphins	.80	.40	.08
☐ 75	**Earl Faison**, Miami Dolphins	.45	.20	.04
☐ 76	**George Wilson**, Miami Dolphins	.35	.15	.03
☐ 77	**Rick Norton**, Miami Dolphins	.35	.15	.03
☐ 78	**Frank Jackson**, Miami Dolphins	.35	.15	.03
☐ 79	**Joe Auer**, Miami Dolphins	.35	.15	.03
☐ 80	**Willie West**, Miami Dolphins	.35	.15	.03
☐ 81	**Jim Warren**, Miami Dolphins	.35	.15	.03
☐ 82	**Wahoo McDaniel**, Miami Dolphins	3.00	1.40	.30
☐ 83	**Ernie Park**, Miami Dolphins	.35	.15	.03
☐ 84	**Bill Neighbors**, Miami Dolphins	.45	.20	.04
☐ 85	**Norm Evans**, Miami Dolphins	.35	.15	.03
☐ 86	**Tom Nomina**, Miami Dolphins	.35	.15	.03
☐ 87	**Rich Zecher**, Miami Dolphins	.35	.15	.03
☐ 88	**Dave Kocourek**, Miami Dolphins	.35	.15	.03
☐ 89	**Bill Baird**, New York Jets	.35	.15	.03
☐ 90	**Ralph Baker**, New York Jets	.35	.15	.03
☐ 91	**Verlon Biggs**, New York Jets	.35	.15	.03
☐ 92	**Sam DeLuca**, New York Jets	.35	.15	.03
☐ 93	**Larry Grantham**, New York Jets	.45	.20	.04
☐ 94	**Jim Harris**, New York Jets	.35	.15	.03
☐ 95	**Winston Hill**, New York Jets	.35	.15	.03
☐ 96	**Bill Mathis**, New York Jets	.45	.20	.04
☐ 97	**Don Maynard**, New York Jets	2.50	1.15	.25
☐ 98	**Joe Namath**, New York Jets	15.00	7.00	1.50
☐ 99	**Gerry Philbin**, New York Jets	.45	.20	.04
☐ 100	**Paul Rochester**, New York Jets	.35	.15	.03
☐ 101	**George Sauer Jr.**, New York Jets	.45	.20	.04
☐ 102	**Matt Snell**, New York Jets	.80	.40	.08

		MINT	VG-E	F-G
☐ 103	**Daryle Lamonica,** Oakland Raiders	1.50	.70	.15
☐ 104	**Glenn Bass,** Oakland Raiders	.35	.15	.03
☐ 105	**Jim Otto,** Oakland Raiders	2.50	1.15	.25
☐ 106	**Fred Biletnikoff,** Oakland Raiders	2.50	1.15	.25
☐ 107	**Cotton Davidson,** Oakland Raiders	.55	.25	.05
☐ 108	**Larry Todd,** Oakland Raiders	.35	.15	.03
☐ 109	**Billy Cannon,** Oakland Raiders	1.50	.70	.15
☐ 110	**Clem Daniels,** Oakland Raiders	.80	.40	.08
☐ 111	**Dave Grayson,** Oakland Raiders	.45	.20	.04
☐ 112	**Kent McCloughan,** Oakland Raiders	.35	.15	.03
☐ 113	**Bob Svihus,** Oakland Raiders	.35	.15	.03
☐ 114	**Ike Lassiter,** Oakland Raiders	.35	.15	.03
☐ 115	**Harry Schuh,** Oakland Raiders	.35	.15	.03
☐ 116	**Ben Davidson,** Oakland Raiders	.90	.40	.09
☐ 117	**Tom Day,** San Diego Chargers	.35	.15	.03
☐ 118	**Scott Appleton,** San Diego Chargers	.45	.20	.04
☐ 119	**Steve Tensi,** San Diego Chargers	.90	.40	.09
☐ 120	**John Hadl,** San Diego Chargers	2.25	1.00	.22
☐ 121	**Paul Lowe,** San Diego Chargers	.90	.40	.09
☐ 122	**Jim Allison,** San Diego Chargers	.35	.15	.03
☐ 123	**Lance Alworth,** San Diego Chargers	3.50	1.65	.35
☐ 124	**Jacque MacKinnon,** San Diego Chargers	.35	.15	.03
☐ 125	**Ron Mix,** San Diego Chargers	2.25	1.00	.22
☐ 126	**Bob Petrich,** San Diego Chargers	.35	.15	.03
☐ 127	**Howard Kindig,** San Diego Chargers	.35	.15	.03
☐ 128	**Steve DeLong,** San Diego Chargers	.35	.15	.03
☐ 129	**Chuck Allen,** San Diego Chargers	.35	.15	.03
☐ 130	**Frank Buncom,** San Diego Chargers	.35	.15	.03
☐ 131	**Speedy Duncan,** San Diego Chargers	.45	.20	.04
☐ 132	**Checklist,** San Diego Chargers	5.00	.75	.10

1968 TOPPS

The 1968 Topps set of 219 cards is Topps' first set in five years (since 1963) to contain NFL players. In fact, the set also includes AFL players even though the two rival leagues didn't formally merge until 1969. The second series (133-219) is slightly more difficult to obtain than the first series. The cards measure 2½" by 3½".

	MINT	VG-E	F-G
COMPLETE SET	125.00	57.00	12.50
COMMON PLAYER (1-132)	.25	.10	.02
COMMON PLAYER (133-219)	.35	.15	.03
1 **Bart Starr**, Green Bay Packers	7.00	2.50	.50
2 **Dick Bass**, Los Angeles Rams	.35	.15	.03
3 **Grady Alderman**, Minnesota Vikings	.25	.10	.02
4 **Obert Logan**, New Orleans Saints	.25	.10	.02
5 **Ernie Koy**, New York Giants	.25	.10	.02
6 **Don Hultz**, Philadelphia Eagles	.25	.10	.02
7 **Earl Gros**, Pittsburgh Steelers	.25	.10	.02
8 **Jim Bakken**, St. Louis Cardinals	.40	.18	.04
9 **George Mira**, San Francisco 49ers	.40	.18	.04
10 **Carl Kammerer**, Washington Redskins ..	.25	.10	.02
11 **Willie Frazier**, San Diego Chargers	.35	.15	.03
12 **Kent McCloughan**, Oakland Raiders	.25	.10	.02
13 **George Sauer Jr.**, New York Jets	.35	.15	.03
14 **Jack Clancy**, Miami Dolphins	.25	.10	.02
15 **Jim Tyrer**, Kansas City Chiefs	.25	.10	.02
16 **Bobby Maples**, Houston Oilers	.25	.10	.02
17 **Bo Hickey**, Denver Broncos	.25	.10	.02

	MINT	VG-E	F-G
☐ 18 Frank Buncom, San Diego Chargers	.25	.10	.02
☐ 19 Keith Lincoln, Buffalo Bills	.65	.30	.06
☐ 20 Jim Whalen, Boston Patriots	.25	.10	.02
☐ 21 Junior Coffey, Atlanta Falcons	.25	.10	.02
☐ 22 Billy Ray Smith, Baltimore Colts	.25	.10	.02
☐ 23 Johnny Morris, Chicago Bears	.50	.22	.05
☐ 24 Ernie Green, Cleveland Browns	.25	.10	.02
☐ 25 Don Meredith, Dallas Cowboys	5.50	2.60	.55
☐ 26 Wayne Walker, Detroit Lions	.35	.15	.03
☐ 27 Carroll Dale, Green Bay Packers	.35	.15	.03
☐ 28 Bernie Casey, Los Angeles Rams	.50	.22	.05
☐ 29 Dave Osborn, Minnesota Vikings	.35	.15	.03
☐ 30 Ray Poage, New Orleans Saints	.25	.10	.02
☐ 31 Homer Jones, New York Jets	.35	.15	.03
☐ 32 Sam Baker, Philadelphia Eagles	.35	.15	.03
☐ 33 Bill Saul, Pittsburgh Steelers	.25	.10	.02
☐ 34 Ken Willard, San Francisco 49ers	.40	.18	.04
☐ 35 Bobby Mitchell, Washington Redskins	2.00	.90	.20
☐ 36 Gary Garrison, San Diego Chargers	.35	.15	.03
☐ 37 Billy Cannon, Oakland Raiders	1.00	.45	.10
☐ 38 Ralph Baker, New York Jets	.25	.10	.02
☐ 39 Howard Twilley, Miami Dolphins	.40	.18	.04
☐ 40 Wendell Hayes, Kansas City Chiefs	.35	.15	.03
☐ 41 Jim Norton, Atlanta Falcons	.25	.10	.02
☐ 42 Tom Beer, Denver Broncos	.25	.10	.02
☐ 43 Chris Burford, Kansas City Chiefs	.35	.15	.03
☐ 44 Stew Barber, Buffalo Bills	.25	.10	.02
☐ 45 Leroy Mitchell, Boston Patriots	.25	.10	.02
☐ 46 Dan Grimm, Atlanta Falcons	.25	.10	.02
☐ 47 Jerry Logan, Baltimore Colts	.25	.10	.02
☐ 48 Andy Livingston, Chicago Bears	.25	.10	.02
☐ 49 Paul Warfield, Cleveland Browns	2.00	.90	.20
☐ 50 Don Perkins, Dallas Cowboys	.65	.30	.06
☐ 51 Ron Kramer, Detroit Lions	.25	.10	.02
☐ 52 Bob Jeter, Green Bay Packers	.35	.15	.03
☐ 53 Les Josephson, Los Angeles Rams	.25	.10	.02
☐ 54 Bobby Walden, Minnesota Vikings	.25	.10	.02
☐ 55 Checklist	2.50	.30	.05
☐ 56 Walter Roberts, New Orleans Saints	.25	.10	.02
☐ 57 Henry Carr, New York Giants	.35	.15	.03
☐ 58 Gary Ballman, Philadelphia Eagles	.35	.15	.03
☐ 59 J.R. Wilburn, Pittsburgh Steelers	.25	.10	.02
☐ 60 Jim Hart, St. Louis Cardinals	2.50	1.15	.25
☐ 61 Jim Johnson, San Francisco 49ers	.35	.15	.03
☐ 62 Chris Hanburger, Washington Redskins	.35	.15	.03
☐ 63 John Hadl, San Diego Chargers	1.50	.70	.15

		MINT	VG-E	F-G
☐ 64	Hewritt Dixon, Oakland Raiders	.40	.18	.04
☐ 65	Joe Namath, New York Jets	12.00	5.50	1.20
☐ 66	Jim Warren, Miami Dolphins	.25	.10	.02
☐ 67	Curtis McClinton, Kansas City Chiefs	.40	.18	.04
☐ 68	Bob Talamini, Houston Oilers	.25	.10	.02
☐ 69	Steve Tensi, Denver Broncos	.40	.18	.04
☐ 70	Dick Van Raaphorst, San Diego Chargers	.25	.10	.02
☐ 71	Art Powell, Buffalo Bills	.35	.15	.03
☐ 72	Jim Nance, Boston Patriots	.45	.20	.04
☐ 73	Bob Riggle, Atlanta Falcons	.25	.10	.02
☐ 74	John Mackey, Baltimore Colts	.65	.30	.06
☐ 75	Gale Sayers, Chicago Bears	10.00	4.75	1.00
☐ 76	Gene Hickerson, Cleveland Browns	.25	.10	.02
☐ 77	Dan Reeves, Dallas Cowboys	1.25	.60	.12
☐ 78	Tom Nowatzke, Detroit Lions	.25	.10	.02
☐ 79	Elijah Pitts, Green Bay Packers	.25	.10	.02
☐ 80	Lamar Lundy, Los Angeles Rams	.25	.10	.02
☐ 81	Paul Flatley, Minnesota Vikings	.35	.15	.03
☐ 82	Dave Whitsell, New Orleans Saints	.25	.10	.02
☐ 83	Spider Lockhart, New York Giants	.25	.10	.02
☐ 84	Dave Lloyd, Philadelphia Eagles	.25	.10	.02
☐ 85	Roy Jefferson, Pittsburgh Steelers	.35	.15	.03
☐ 86	Jackie Smith, St. Louis Cardinals	.40	.18	.04
☐ 87	John David Crow, San Francisco 49ers	.40	.18	.04
☐ 88	Sonny Jurgensen, Washington Redskins	2.50	1.15	.25
☐ 89	Ron Mix, San Diego Chargers	1.50	.70	.15
☐ 90	Clem Daniels, Oakland Raiders	.50	.22	.05
☐ 91	Cornell Gordon, New York Jets	.25	.10	.02
☐ 92	Tom Goode, Miami Dolphins	.25	.10	.02
☐ 93	Bobby Bell, Kansas City Chiefs	1.50	.70	.15
☐ 94	Walt Suggs, Houston Oilers	.25	.10	.02
☐ 95	Eric Crabtree, Denver Broncos	.25	.10	.02
☐ 96	Sherrill Headrick, Kansas City Chiefs	.35	.15	.03
☐ 97	Wray Carlton, Buffalo Bills	.35	.15	.03
☐ 98	Gino Cappelletti, Boston Patriots	.60	.28	.06
☐ 99	Tommy McDonald, Atlanta Falcons	.45	.20	.04
☐ 100	John Unitas, Baltimore Colts	7.00	3.25	.70
☐ 101	Richie Petitbon, Chicago Bears	.25	.10	.02
☐ 102	Erich Barnes, Cleveland Browns	.25	.10	.02
☐ 103	Bob Hayes, Dallas Cowboys	.90	.40	.09
☐ 104	Milt Plum, Detroit Lions	.60	.28	.06
☐ 105	Boyd Dowler, Green Bay Packers	.35	.15	.03
☐ 106	Ed Meador, Los Angeles Rams	.35	.15	.03
☐ 107	Fred Cox, Minnesota Vikings	.45	.20	.04
☐ 108	Steve Stonebreaker, New Orleans Saints	.25	.10	.02
☐ 109	Aaron Thomas, New York Giants	.25	.10	.02

		MINT	VG-E	F-G
☐ 110	**Norm Snead**, Philadelphia Eagles	.65	.30	.06
☐ 111	**Paul Martha**, Pittsburgh Steelers	.50	.22	.05
☐ 112	**Jerry Stovall**, St. Louis Cardinals	.45	.20	.04
☐ 113	**Kay McFarland**, San Francisco 49ers	.25	.10	.02
☐ 114	**Pat Richter**, Washington Redskins	.25	.10	.02
☐ 115	**Rick Redman**, San Diego Chargers	.25	.10	.02
☐ 116	**Tom Keating**, Oakland Raiders	.25	.10	.02
☐ 117	**Matt Snell**, New York Jets	.65	.30	.06
☐ 118	**Dick Westmoreland**, Miami Dolphins	.25	.10	.02
☐ 119	**Jerry Mays**, Kansas City Chiefs	.25	.10	.02
☐ 120	**Sid Blanks**, Houston Oilers	.25	.10	.02
☐ 121	**Al Denson**, Denver Broncos	.25	.10	.02
☐ 122	**Bobby Hunt**, Kansas City Chiefs	.25	.10	.02
☐ 123	**Mike Mercer**, Buffalo Bills	.25	.10	.02
☐ 124	**Nick Buoniconti**, Boston Patriots	1.25	.60	.12
☐ 125	**Ron Vanderkelen**, Minnesota Vikings	.45	.20	.04
☐ 126	**Ordell Braase**, Baltimore Colts	.25	.10	.02
☐ 127	**Dick Butkus**, Cleveland Browns	3.50	1.65	.35
☐ 128	**Gary Collins**, Cleveland Browns	.35	.15	.03
☐ 129	**Mel Renfro**, Dallas Cowboys	.75	.35	.07
☐ 130	**Alex Karras**, Detroit Lions	1.75	.85	.17
☐ 131	**Herb Adderly**, Green Bay Packers	1.50	.70	.15
☐ 132	**Roman Gabriel**, Los Angeles Rams	1.50	.70	.15
☐ 133	**Bill Brown**, Minnesota Vikings	.45	.20	.04
☐ 134	**Kent Kramer**, New Orleans Saints	.35	.15	.03
☐ 135	**Tucker Frederickson**, New York Giants	.50	.22	.05
☐ 136	**Nate Ramsey**, Philadelphia Eagles	.35	.15	.03
☐ 137	**Marv Woodson**, Pittsburgh Steelers	.35	.15	.03
☐ 138	**Ken Gray**, St. Louis Cardinals	.35	.15	.03
☐ 139	**John Brodie**, San Francisco 49ers	2.75	1.25	.27
☐ 140	**Jerry Smith**, Pittsburgh Steelers	.45	.20	.04
☐ 141	**Brad Hubbert**, San Diego Chargers	.35	.15	.03
☐ 142	**George Blanda**, Oakland Raiders	4.50	2.10	.45
☐ 143	**Pete Lammons**, New York Jets	.35	.15	.03
☐ 144	**Doug Moreau**, Miami Dolphins	.35	.15	.03
☐ 145	**E.J. Holub**, Kansas City Chiefs	.45	.20	.04
☐ 146	**Ode Burrell**, Houston Oilers	.35	.15	.03
☐ 147	**Bob Scarpitto**, Denver Broncos	.35	.15	.03
☐ 148	**Andre White**, Denver Broncos	.35	.15	.03
☐ 149	**Jack Kemp**, Buffalo Bills	9.00	4.25	.90
☐ 150	**Art Graham**, Boston Patriots	.35	.15	.03
☐ 151	**Tommy Nobis**, Atlanta Falcons	1.00	.45	.10
☐ 152	**Willie Richardson**, Baltimore Colts	.45	.20	.04
☐ 153	**Jack Concannon**, Chicago Bears	.45	.20	.04
☐ 154	**Bill Glass**, Cleveland Browns	.45	.20	.04
☐ 155	**Craig Morton**, Dallas Cowboys	2.50	1.15	.25

		MINT	VG-E	F-G
☐ 156	Pat Studstill, Detroit Lions	.45	.20	.04
☐ 157	Ray Nitschke, Green Bay Packers	1.75	.85	.17
☐ 158	Roger Brown, Los Angeles Rams	.35	.15	.03
☐ 159	Joe Kapp, Minnesota Vikings	1.50	.70	.15
☐ 160	Jim Taylor, New Orleans Saints	2.25	1.00	.22
☐ 161	Fran Tarkenton, New York Giants	6.00	2.80	.60
☐ 162	Mike Ditka, Philadelphia Eagles	1.25	.60	.12
☐ 163	Andy Russell, Pittsburgh Steelers	.45	.20	.04
☐ 164	Larry Wilson, St. Louis Cardinals	1.50	.70	.15
☐ 165	Tommy Davis, San Francisco 49ers	.35	.15	.03
☐ 166	Paul Krause, Washington Redskins	.45	.20	.04
☐ 167	Speedy Duncan, San Diego Chargers	.35	.15	.03
☐ 168	Fred Biletnikoff, Oakland Raiders	2.00	.90	.20
☐ 169	Don Maynard, New York Giants	2.00	.90	.20
☐ 170	Frank Emanuel, Miami Dolphins	.35	.15	.03
☐ 171	Len Dawson, Kansas City Chiefs	3.00	1.40	.30
☐ 172	Miller Farr, Houston Oilers	.45	.20	.04
☐ 173	Floyd Little, Denver Broncos	1.50	.70	.15
☐ 174	Lonnie Wright, Cincinnati Bengals	.35	.15	.03
☐ 175	Paul Costa, Buffalo Bills	.35	.15	.03
☐ 176	Don Trull, Houston Oilers	.45	.20	.04
☐ 177	Jerry Simmons, New Orleans Saints	.35	.15	.03
☐ 178	Tom Matte, Baltimore Colts	.45	.20	.04
☐ 179	Bennie McRae, Chicago Bears	.35	.15	.03
☐ 180	Jim Kanicki, Cleveland Browns	.35	.15	.03
☐ 181	Bob Lilly, Dallas Cowboys	2.50	1.15	.25
☐ 182	Tom Watkins, Detroit Lions	.35	.15	.03
☐ 183	Jim Grabowski, Green Bay Packers	.45	.20	.04
☐ 184	Jack Snow, Los Angeles Rams	.45	.20	.04
☐ 185	Gary Cuozzo, New Orleans Saints	.45	.20	.04
☐ 186	Bill Kilmer, New Orleans Saints	1.50	.70	.15
☐ 187	Jim Katcavage, New York Giants	.35	.15	.03
☐ 188	Floyd Peters, Philadelphia Eagles	.35	.15	.03
☐ 189	Bill Nelsen, Pittsburgh Steelers	.75	.35	.07
☐ 190	Bobby Joe Conrad, St. Louis Cardinals	.45	.20	.04
☐ 191	Kermit Alexander, San Francisco 49ers	.45	.20	.04
☐ 192	Charley Taylor, Washington Redskins	2.00	.90	.20
☐ 193	Lance Alworth, San Diego Chargers	2.00	.90	.20
☐ 194	Daryle Lamonica, Oakland Raiders	1.50	.70	.15
☐ 195	Al Atkinson, New York Jets	.35	.15	.03
☐ 196	Bob Griese, Miami Dolphins	13.00	6.00	1.30
☐ 197	Buck Buchanan, Kansas City Chiefs	.75	.35	.07
☐ 198	Pete Beathard, Kansas City Chiefs	.65	.30	.06
☐ 199	Nemiah Wilson, Denver Broncos	.45	.20	.04
☐ 200	Ernie Wright, San Diego Chargers	.35	.15	.03
☐ 201	George Saimes, Buffalo Bills	.45	.20	.04

		MINT	VG-E	F-G
☐ 202	John Charles, Boston Patriots	.35	.15	.03
☐ 203	Randy Johnson, Atlanta Falcons	.45	.20	.04
☐ 204	Tony Lorick, Baltimore Colts	.35	.15	.03
☐ 205	Dick Evey, Chicago Bears	.35	.15	.03
☐ 206	Leroy Kelly, Cleveland Browns	1.75	.85	.17
☐ 207	Lee Roy Jordan, Dallas Cowboys	1.00	.45	.10
☐ 208	Jim Gibbons, Detroit Lions	.35	.15	.03
☐ 209	Donny Anderson, Green Bay Packers	.75	.35	.07
☐ 210	Maxie Baughan, Los Angeles Rams	.45	.20	.04
☐ 211	Joe Morrison, New York Giants	.50	.22	.05
☐ 212	Jim Snowden, Washington Redskins	.35	.15	.03
☐ 213	Lenny Lyles, Baltimore Colts	.35	.15	.03
☐ 214	Bobby Joe Green, Chicago Bears	.35	.15	.03
☐ 215	Frank Ryan, Cleveland Browns	.75	.35	.07
☐ 216	Cornell Green, Dallas Cowboys	.50	.22	.05
☐ 217	Karl Sweetan, Detroit Lions	.45	.20	.04
☐ 218	Dave Williams, St. Louis Cardinals	.35	.15	.03
☐ 219	Checklist	3.50	.40	.08

1969 TOPPS

The 1969 Topps set of 263 cards contains 132 borderless cards (1-132), whereas the remaining 131 cards do have white borders. The lack of borders makes the first series especially difficult to find in mint condition. The cards measure 2½" by 3½". This set is distinctive in that it contains the late Brian Piccolo's only card. The backs of the cards are predominantly black but with a green and white accent.

	MINT	VG-E	F-G
COMPLETE SET	115.00	50.00	10.00
COMMON PLAYER (1-132)	.25	.10	.02
COMMON PLAYER (133-263)	.30	.12	.03

		MINT	VG-E	F-G
☐	1 Leroy Kelly, Cleveland Browns	2.50	.50	.10
☐	2 Paul Flatley, Atlanta Falcons	.35	.15	.03
☐	3 Jim Cadile, Chicago Bears	.25	.10	.02
☐	4 Erich Barnes, Cleveland Browns	.25	.10	.02
☐	5 Willie Richardson, Baltimore Colts	.35	.15	.03
☐	6 Bob Hayes, Dallas Cowboys	.90	.40	.09
☐	7 Bob Jeter, Green Bay Packers	.35	.15	.03
☐	8 Jim Colclough, Boston Patriots	.25	.10	.02
☐	9 Sherrill Headrick, Cincinnati Bengals	.25	.10	.02
☐	10 Jim Dunaway, Buffalo Bills	.25	.10	.02
☐	11 Bill Munson, Detroit Lions	.50	.22	.05
☐	12 Jack Pardee, Los Angeles Rams	.60	.28	.06
☐	13 Jim Lindsey, Minnesota Vikings	.25	.10	.02
☐	14 Dave Whitsell, New Orleans Saints	.25	.10	.02
☐	15 Tucker Frederickson, New York Giants	.40	.18	.04
☐	16 Alvin Haymond, Philadelphia Eagles	.25	.10	.02
☐	17 Andy Russell, Pittsburgh Steelers	.35	.15	.03
☐	18 Tom Beer, Denver Broncos	.25	.10	.02
☐	19 Bobby Maples, Houston Oilers	.25	.10	.02
☐	20 Len Dawson, Kansas City Chiefs	2.75	1.25	.27
☐	21 Willis Crenshaw, St. Louis Cardinals	.25	.10	.02
☐	22 Tommy Davis, San Francisco 49ers	.25	.10	.02
☐	23 Rickie Harris, Washington Redskins	.25	.10	.02
☐	24 Jerry Simmons, Atlanta Falcons	.25	.10	.02
☐	25 John Unitas, Baltimore Colts	6.50	3.00	.65
☐	26 Brian Piccolo, Chicago Bears	16.00	7.50	1.60
☐	27 Bob Matheson, Cleveland Browns	.25	.10	.02
☐	28 Howard Twilley, Miami Dolphins	.40	.18	.04
☐	29 Jim Turner, New York Jets	.40	.18	.04
☐	30 Pete Banaszak, Oakland Raiders	.25	.10	.02
☐	31 Lance Rentzel, Dallas Cowboys	.40	.18	.04
☐	32 Bill Triplett, Detroit Lions	.25	.10	.02
☐	33 Boyd Dowler, Green Bay Packers	.35	.15	.03
☐	34 Merlin Olsen, Los Angeles Rams	2.25	1.00	.22
☐	35 Joe Kapp, Minnesota Vikings	1.00	.45	.10
☐	36 Dan Abramowicz, New Orleans Saints	.45	.20	.04
☐	37 Spider Lockhart, New York Giants	.25	.10	.02
☐	38 Tom Day, Buffalo Bills	.25	.10	.02
☐	39 Art Graham, Boston Patriots	.25	.10	.02
☐	40 Bob Cappadona, Buffalo Bills	.25	.10	.02
☐	41 Gary Ballman, Philadelphia Eagles	.35	.15	.03
☐	42 Clendon Thomas, Pittsburgh Steelers	.25	.10	.02

		MINT	VG-E	F-G
☐ 43	**Jackie Smith**, St. Louis Cardinals	.40	.18	.04
☐ 44	**Dave Wilcox**, San Francisco 49ers	.35	.15	.03
☐ 45	**Jerry Smith**, Washington Redskins	.35	.15	.03
☐ 46	**Dan Grimm**, Baltimore Colts	.25	.10	.02
☐ 47	**Tom Matte**, Baltimore Colts	.45	.20	.04
☐ 48	**John Stofa**, Cincinnati Bengals	.25	.10	.02
☐ 49	**Rex Mirich**, Denver Broncos	.25	.10	.02
☐ 50	**Miller Farr**, Houston Oilers	.35	.15	.03
☐ 51	**Gale Sayers**, Chicago Bears	9.00	4.25	.90
☐ 52	**Bill Nelsen**, Cleveland Browns	.65	.30	.06
☐ 53	**Bob Lilly**, Dallas Cowboys	2.00	.90	.20
☐ 54	**Wayne Walker**, Detroit Lions	.35	.15	.03
☐ 55	**Ray Nitschke**, Green Bay Packers	1.75	.85	.17
☐ 56	**Ed Meador**, Los Angeles Rams	.35	.15	.03
☐ 57	**Lonnie Warwick**, Minnesota Vikings	.25	.10	.02
☐ 58	**Wendell Hayes**, Kansas City Chiefs	.35	.15	.03
☐ 59	**Dick Anderson**, Kansas City Chiefs	.45	.20	.04
☐ 60	**Don Maynard**, New York Jets	1.75	.85	.17
☐ 61	**Tony Lorick**, New Orleans Saints	.25	.10	.02
☐ 62	**Pete Gogolak**, New York Giants	.35	.15	.03
☐ 63	**Nate Ramsey**, Philadelphia Eagles	.25	.10	.02
☐ 64	**Dick Shiner**, Pittsburgh Steelers	.35	.15	.03
☐ 65	**Larry Wilson**, St. Louis Cardinals	1.50	.70	.15
☐ 66	**Ken Willard**, San Francisco 49ers	.35	.15	.03
☐ 67	**Charley Taylor**, Washington Redskins	2.00	.90	.20
☐ 68	**Billy Cannon**, Oakland Raiders	.90	.40	.09
☐ 69	**Lance Alworth**, San Diego Chargers	2.00	.90	.20
☐ 70	**Jim Nance**, Boston Patriots	.45	.20	.04
☐ 71	**Nick Rassas**, Atlanta Falcons	.25	.10	.02
☐ 72	**Lenny Lyles**, Chicago Bears	.25	.10	.02
☐ 73	**Bennie McRae**, Chicago Bears	.25	.10	.02
☐ 74	**Bill Glass**, Cleveland Browns	.35	.15	.03
☐ 75	**Don Meredith**, Dallas Cowboys	5.00	2.35	.50
☐ 76	**Dick LeBeau**, Detroit Lions	.25	.10	.02
☐ 77	**Carroll Dale**, Green Bay Packers	.25	.10	.02
☐ 78	**Ron McDole**, Buffalo Bills	.25	.10	.02
☐ 79	**Charley King**, Cincinnati Bengals	.25	.10	.02
☐ 80	**Checklist 1-132**	2.00	.30	.05
☐ 81	**Dick Bass**, Los Angeles Rams	.35	.15	.03
☐ 82	**Roy Winston**, Minnesota Vikings	.25	.10	.02
☐ 83	**Don McCall**, New Orleans Saints	.25	.10	.02
☐ 84	**Jim Katcavage**, New York Giants	.25	.10	.02
☐ 85	**Norm Snead**, Philadelphia Eagles	.55	.25	.05
☐ 86	**Earl Gros**, Pittsburgh Steelers	.25	.10	.02
☐ 87	**Don Brumm**, St. Louis Cardinals	.25	.10	.02
☐ 88	**Sonny Bishop**, Houston Oilers	.25	.10	.02

			MINT	VG-E	F-G
☐	89	Fred Arbanas, Kansas City Chiefs	.35	.15	.03
☐	90	Karl Noonan, Miami Dolphins	.25	.10	.02
☐	91	Dick Witcher, San Francisco 49ers	.25	.10	.02
☐	92	Vince Promuto, Washington Redskins	.25	.10	.02
☐	93	Tommy Nobis, Atlanta Falcons	1.00	.45	.10
☐	94	Jerry Hill, Baltimore Colts	.25	.10	.02
☐	95	Ed O'Bradovich, Chicago Bears	.25	.10	.02
☐	96	Ernie Kellerman, Cleveland Browns	.25	.10	.02
☐	97	Chuck Howley, Dallas Cowboys	.75	.35	.07
☐	98	Hewritt Dixon, Oakland Raiders	.40	.18	.04
☐	99	Ron Mix, San Diego Chargers	1.50	.70	.15
☐	100	Joe Namath, New York Jets	10.00	4.75	1.00
☐	101	Billy Gambrell, Detroit Lions	.25	.10	.02
☐	102	Elijah Pitts, Green Bay Packers	.25	.10	.02
☐	103	Billy Truax, Los Angeles Rams	.25	.10	.02
☐	104	Ed Sharockman, Minnesota Vikings	.25	.10	.02
☐	105	Doug Atkins, New Orleans Saints	1.50	.70	.15
☐	106	Greg Larson, New York Giants	.25	.10	.02
☐	107	Israel Lang, Philadelphia Eagles	.25	.10	.02
☐	108	Houston Antwine, Boston Patriots	.25	.10	.02
☐	109	Paul Guidry, Buffalo Bills	.25	.10	.02
☐	110	Al Denson, Denver Broncos	.25	.10	.02
☐	111	Roy Jefferson, Pittsburgh Steelers	.35	.15	.03
☐	112	Chuck LaTourette, St. Louis Cardinals	.25	.10	.02
☐	113	Jim Johnson, San Francisco 49ers	.35	.15	.03
☐	114	Bobby Mitchell, Washington Redskins	2.00	.90	.20
☐	115	Randy Johnson, Atlanta Falcons	.35	.15	.03
☐	116	Lou Michaels, Baltimore Colts	.25	.10	.02
☐	117	Rudy Kuechenberg, Chicago Bears	.25	.10	.02
☐	118	Walt Suggs, Houston Oilers	.25	.10	.02
☐	119	Goldie Sellers, Kansas City Chiefs	.25	.10	.02
☐	120	Larry Csonka, Miami Dolphins	7.50	3.50	.75
☐	121	Jim Houston, Cleveland Browns	.25	.10	.02
☐	122	Craig Baynham, Dallas Cowboys	.25	.10	.02
☐	123	Alex Karras, Detroit Lions	1.75	.85	.17
☐	124	Jim Grabowski, Green Bay Packers	.35	.15	.03
☐	125	Roman Gabriel, Los Angeles Rams	1.50	.70	.15
☐	126	Larry Bowie, Minnesota Vikings	.25	.10	.02
☐	127	Dave Parks, New Orleans Saints	.35	.15	.03
☐	128	Ben Davidson, Oakland Raiders	.90	.40	.09
☐	129	Steve DeLong, San Diego Chargers	.25	.10	.02
☐	130	Fred Hill, Philadelphia Eagles	.25	.10	.02
☐	131	Ernie Koy, New York Giants	.25	.10	.02
☐	132	Checklist 133-263	2.00	.30	.05
		(two variations)			
☐	133	Dick Hoak, Pittsburgh Steelers	.30	.12	.03

		MINT	VG-E	F-G
☐ 134	**Larry Stallings**, St. Louis Cardinals	.30	.12	.03
☐ 135	**Clifton McNeil**, San Francisco 49ers	.30	.12	.03
☐ 136	**Walter Rock**, Washington Redskins	.30	.12	.03
☐ 137	**Billy Lothridge**, Atlanta Falcons	.30	.12	.03
☐ 138	**Bob Vogel**, Baltimore Colts	.30	.12	.03
☐ 139	**Dick Butkus**, Chicago Bears	3.50	1.65	.35
☐ 140	**Frank Ryan**, Cleveland Browns	.65	.30	.06
☐ 141	**Larry Garron**, Boston Patriots	.30	.12	.03
☐ 142	**George Saimes**, Buffalo Bills	.40	.18	.04
☐ 143	**Frank Buncom**, Cincinnati Bengals	.30	.12	.03
☐ 144	**Don Perkins**, Dallas Cowboys	.75	.35	.07
☐ 145	**Johnny Robinson**, Kansas City Chiefs	.75	.35	.07
☐ 146	**Lee Roy Caffey**, Green Bay Packers	.40	.18	.04
☐ 147	**Bernie Casey**, Los Angeles Rams	.50	.22	.05
☐ 148	**Billy Martin**, Minnesota Vikings	.30	.12	.03
☐ 149	**Gene Howard**, New Orleans Saints	.30	.12	.03
☐ 150	**Fran Tarkenton**, New York Giants	6.00	2.80	.60
☐ 151	**Eric Crabtree**, Denver Broncos	.30	.12	.03
☐ 152	**W.K. Hicks**, Houston Oilers	.30	.12	.03
☐ 153	**Bobby Bell**, Kansas City Chiefs	1.50	.70	.15
☐ 154	**Sam Baker**, Philadelphia Eagles	.30	.12	.03
☐ 155	**Marv Woodson**, Pittsburgh Steelers	.40	.18	.04
☐ 156	**Dave Williams**, St. Louis Cardinals	.30	.12	.03
☐ 157	**Bruce Bosley**, San Francisco 49ers	.30	.12	.03
☐ 158	**Carl Kammerer**, Washington Redskins	.30	.12	.03
☐ 159	**Jim Burson**, Atlanta Falcons	.30	.12	.03
☐ 160	**Roy Hilton**, Baltimore Colts	.30	.12	.03
☐ 161	**Bob Griese**, Miami Dolphins	4.00	1.85	.40
☐ 162	**Bob Talamini**, Miami Dolphins	.30	.12	.03
☐ 163	**Jim Otto**, Oakland Raiders	1.75	.85	.17
☐ 164	**Ron Bull**, Chicago Bears	.40	.18	.04
☐ 165	**Walter Johnson**, Cleveland Browns	.30	.12	.03
☐ 166	**Lee Roy Jordan**, Dallas Cowboys	.75	.35	.07
☐ 167	**Mike Lucci**, Detroit Lions	.40	.18	.04
☐ 168	**Willie Wood**, Green Bay Packers	.75	.35	.07
☐ 169	**Maxie Baughan**, Los Angeles Rams	.40	.18	.04
☐ 170	**Bill Brown**, Minnesota Vikings	.40	.18	.04
☐ 171	**John Hadl**, San Diego Chargers	1.50	.70	.15
☐ 172	**Gino Cappelletti**, Boston Patriots	.60	.28	.06
☐ 173	**George Byrd**, Buffalo Bills	.40	.18	.04
☐ 174	**Steve Stonebreaker**, New Orleans Saints	.30	.12	.03
☐ 175	**Joe Morrison**, New York Giants	.50	.22	.05
☐ 176	**Joe Scarpati**, Philadelphia Eagles	.30	.12	.03
☐ 177	**Bobby Walden**, Pittsburgh Steelers	.30	.12	.03
☐ 178	**Roy Shivers**, St. Louis Cardinals	.30	.12	.03
☐ 179	**Kermit Alexander**, San Francisco 49ers	.40	.18	.04

	MINT	VG-E	F-G
☐ 180 **Pat Richter**, Washington Redskins	.30	.12	.03
☐ 181 **Pete Perreault**, Cincinnati Bengals	.30	.12	.03
☐ 182 **Pete Duranko**, Denver Broncos	.30	.12	.03
☐ 183 **Leroy Mitchell**, Boston Patriots	.30	.12	.03
☐ 184 **Jim Simon**, Atlanta Falcons	.30	.12	.03
☐ 185 **Billy Ray Smith**, Baltimore Colts	.30	.12	.03
☐ 186 **Jack Concannon**, Chicago Bears	.40	.18	.04
☐ 187 **Ben Davis**, Cleveland Browns	.30	.12	.03
☐ 188 **Mike Clark**, Dallas Cowboys	.30	.12	.03
☐ 189 **Jim Gibbons**, Detroit Lions	.30	.12	.03
☐ 190 **Dave Robinson**, Green Bay Packers	.45	.20	.04
☐ 191 **Otis Taylor**, Kansas City Chiefs	.90	.40	.09
☐ 192 **Nick Buoniconti**, Boston Patriots	1.25	.60	.12
☐ 193 **Matt Snell**, New York Jets	.65	.30	.06
☐ 194 **Bruce Gossett**, Los Angeles Rams	.30	.12	.03
☐ 195 **Mick Tingelhoff**, Minnesota Vikings	.55	.25	.05
☐ 196 **Earl Leggett**, New Orleans Saints	.30	.12	.03
☐ 197 **Pete Case**, New York Giants	.30	.12	.03
☐ 198 **Tom Woodeshick**, Philadelphia Eagles	.30	.12	.03
☐ 199 **Ken Kortas**, Pittsburgh Steelers	.30	.12	.03
☐ 200 **Jim Hart**, St. Louis Cardinals	1.50	.70	.15
☐ 201 **Fred Biletnikoff**, Oakland Raiders	2.00	.90	.20
☐ 202 **Jacque MacKinnon**, San Diego Chargers	.30	.12	.03
☐ 203 **Jim Whalen**, Boston Patriots	.30	.12	.03
☐ 204 **Matt Hazeltine**, San Francisco 49ers	.30	.12	.03
☐ 205 **Charlie Gogolak**, Washington Redskins	.40	.18	.04
☐ 206 **Ray Ogden**, Atlanta Falcons	.30	.12	.03
☐ 207 **John Mackey**, Baltimore Colts	.65	.30	.06
☐ 208 **Roosevelt Taylor**, Chicago Bears	.30	.12	.03
☐ 209 **Gene Hickerson**, Cleveland Browns	.30	.12	.03
☐ 210 **Dave Edwards**, Dallas Cowboys	.30	.12	.03
☐ 211 **Tom Sestak**, Buffalo Bills	.30	.12	.03
☐ 212 **Ernie Wright**, Cincinnati Bengals	.30	.12	.03
☐ 213 **Dave Costa**, Denver Broncos	.30	.12	.03
☐ 214 **Tom Vaughn**, Detroit Lions	.30	.12	.03
☐ 215 **Bart Starr**, Green Bay Packers	6.00	2.80	.60
☐ 216 **Les Josephson**, Los Angeles Rams	.30	.12	.03
☐ 217 **Fred Cox**, Minnesota Vikings	.45	.20	.04
☐ 218 **Mike Tilleman**, New Orleans Saints	.30	.12	.03
☐ 219 **Darrell Dess**, New York Giants	.30	.12	.03
☐ 220 **Dave Lloyd**, Philadelphia Eagles	.30	.12	.03
☐ 221 **Pete Beathard**, Houston Oilers	.60	.28	.06
☐ 222 **Buck Buchanan**, Kansas City Chiefs	.75	.35	.07
☐ 223 **Frank Emanuel**, Miami Dolphins	.30	.12	.03
☐ 224 **Paul Martha**, Pittsburgh Steelers	.50	.22	.05
☐ 225 **Johnny Roland**, St. Louis Cardinals	.50	.22	.05

		MINT	VG-E	F-G
☐ 226	**Gary Lewis**, San Francisco 49ers	.30	.12	.03
☐ 227	**Sonny Jurgensen**, Washington Redskins	2.50	1.15	.25
☐ 228	**Jim Butler**, Atlanta Falcons	.30	.12	.03
☐ 229	**Mike Curtis**, Baltimore Colts	.65	.30	.06
☐ 230	**Richie Petitbon**, Chicago Bears	.30	.12	.03
☐ 231	**George Sauer Jr.**, New York Jets	.40	.18	.04
☐ 232	**George Blanda**, Oakland Raiders	4.00	1.85	.40
☐ 233	**Gary Garrison**, San Diego Chargers	.40	.18	.04
☐ 234	**Gary Collins**, Cleveland Browns	.40	.18	.04
☐ 235	**Craig Morton**, Dallas Cowboys	1.50	.70	.15
☐ 236	**Tom Nowatzke**, Detroit Lions	.30	.12	.03
☐ 237	**Donny Anderson**, Green Bay Packers	.50	.22	.05
☐ 238	**Deacon Jones**, Los Angeles Rams	1.75	.85	.17
☐ 239	**Grady Alderman**, Minnesota Vikings	.30	.12	.03
☐ 240	**Bill Kilmer**, New Orleans Saints	1.50	.70	.15
☐ 241	**Mike Taliaferro**, Boston Patriots	.30	.12	.03
☐ 242	**Stew Barber**, Buffalo Bills	.30	.12	.03
☐ 243	**Bobby Hunt**, Kansas City Chiefs	.30	.12	.03
☐ 244	**Homer Jones**, New York Giants	.40	.18	.04
☐ 245	**Bob Brown**, Pittsburgh Steelers	.30	.12	.03
☐ 246	**Bill Asbury**, Pittsburgh Steelers	.30	.12	.03
☐ 247	**Charlie Johnson**, St. Louis Cardinals	.75	.35	.07
☐ 248	**Chris Hanburger**, Washington Redskins	.40	.18	.04
☐ 249	**John Brodie**, San Francisco 49ers	2.75	1.25	.27
☐ 250	**Earl Morrall**, Baltimore Colts	1.50	.70	.15
☐ 251	**Floyd Little**, Denver Broncos	1.00	.45	.10
☐ 252	**Jerrel Wilson**, Kansas City Chiefs	.40	.18	.04
☐ 253	**Jim Keyes**, Miami Dolphins	.30	.12	.03
☐ 254	**Mel Renfro**, Dallas Cowboys	.75	.35	.07
☐ 255	**Herb Adderly**, Green Bay Packers	1.50	.70	.15
☐ 256	**Jack Snow**, Los Angeles Rams	.40	.18	.04
☐ 257	**Charlie Durkee**, New Orleans Saints	.30	.12	.03
☐ 258	**Charlie Harper**, New York Giants	.30	.12	.03
☐ 259	**J.R. Wilburn**, Pittsburgh Steelers	.30	.12	.03
☐ 260	**Charlie Krueger**, San Francisco 49ers	.30	.12	.03
☐ 261	**Pete Jacques**, Denver Broncos	.30	.12	.03
☐ 262	**Gerry Philbin**, New York Jets	.30	.12	.03
☐ 263	**Daryle Lamonica**, Oakland Raiders	1.50	.50	.10

1970 TOPPS

The 1970 Topps set contains 263 cards. The cards measure 2½" by 3½". The second series was printed in slightly lesser quantities than the first series. There are no scarcities, although O.J. Simpson's rookie card appears in this set. The card backs are done in orange, purple, and white.

		MINT	VG-E	F-G
	COMPLETE SET	110.00	50.00	11.00
	COMMON PLAYER (1-132)	.20	.09	.02
	COMMON PLAYER (133-263)	.30	.12	.03
☐	1 Len Dawson, Kansas City Chiefs	3.00	1.00	.20
☐	2 Doug Hart, Green Bay Packers	.20	.09	.02
☐	3 Verlon Biggs, New York Jets	.20	.09	.02
☐	4 Ralph Neely, Dallas Cowboys	.30	.12	.03
☐	5 Harmon Wages, Atlanta Falcons	.20	.09	.02
☐	6 Dan Conners, Oakland Raiders	.20	.09	.02
☐	7 Gino Cappelletti, Boston Patriots	.60	.28	.06
☐	8 Erich Barnes, Cleveland Browns	.20	.09	.02
☐	9 Checklist 1-132	2.50	.35	.05
☐	10 Bob Griese, Miami Dolphins	3.00	1.40	.30
☐	11 Ed Flanagan, Detroit Lions	.20	.09	.02
☐	12 George Seals, Chicago Bears	.20	.09	.02
☐	13 Harry Jacobs, New Orleans Saints	.20	.09	.02
☐	14 Mike Haffner, Cincinnati Bengals	.20	.09	.02
☐	15 Bob Vogel, Baltimore Colts	.20	.09	.02
☐	16 Bill Peterson, Cincinnati Bengals	.20	.09	.02
☐	17 Spider Lockhart, New York Giants	.20	.09	.02

		MINT	VG-E	F-G
☐	18 **Billy Truax**, Dallas Cowboys	.20	.09	.02
☐	19 **Jim Beirne**, Houston Oilers	.20	.09	.02
☐	20 **Leroy Kelly**, Cleveland Browns	1.25	.60	.12
☐	21 **Dave Lloyd**, Philadelphia Eagles	.20	.09	.02
☐	22 **Mike Tilleman**, Houston Oilers	.20	.09	.02
☐	23 **Gary Garrison**, San Diego Chargers	.20	.09	.02
☐	24 **Larry Brown**, Washington Redskins	1.00	.45	.10
☐	25 **Jan Stenerud**, Kansas City Chiefs	1.00	.45	.10
☐	26 **Rolf Krueger**, St. Louis Cardinals	.20	.09	.02
☐	27 **Roland Lakes**, San Francisco 49ers	.20	.09	.02
☐	28 **Dick Hoak**, Pittsburgh Steelers	.20	.09	.02
☐	29 **Gene Washington**, Minnesota Vikings	.30	.12	.03
☐	30 **Bart Starr**, Green Bay Packers	5.00	2.35	.50
☐	31 **Dave Grayson**, Oakland Raiders	.20	.09	.02
☐	32 **Jerry Rush**, Detroit Lions	.20	.09	.02
☐	33 **Len St. Jean**, Boston Patriots	.20	.09	.02
☐	34 **Randy Edmunds**, Miami Dolphins	.20	.09	.02
☐	35 **Matt Snell**, New York Jets	.55	.25	.05
☐	36 **Paul Costa**, Buffalo Bills	.20	.09	.02
☐	37 **Mike Pyle**, Chicago Bears	.20	.09	.02
☐	38 **Roy Hilton**, Baltimore Colts	.20	.09	.02
☐	39 **Steve Tensi**, Denver Broncos	.30	.12	.03
☐	40 **Tommy Nobis**, Atlanta Falcons	.90	.40	.09
☐	41 **Pete Case**, New York Giants	.20	.09	.02
☐	42 **Andy Rice**, San Diego Chargers	.20	.09	.02
☐	43 **Elvin Bethea**, Houston Oilers	.30	.12	.03
☐	44 **Jack Snow**, Los Angeles Rams	.30	.12	.03
☐	45 **Mel Renfro**, Dallas Cowboys	.65	.30	.06
☐	46 **Andy Livingston**, New Orleans Saints	.20	.09	.02
☐	47 **Gary Ballman**, Philadelphia Eagles	.30	.12	.03
☐	48 **Bob DeMarco**, Miami Dolphins	.20	.09	.02
☐	49 **Steve DeLong**, San Diego Chargers	.20	.09	.02
☐	50 **Daryle Lamonica**, Oakland Raiders	.90	.40	.09
☐	51 **Jim Lynch**, Kansas City Chiefs	.20	.09	.02
☐	52 **Mel Farr**, Detroit Lions	.35	.15	.03
☐	53 **Bob Long**, Los Angeles Rams	.20	.09	.02
☐	54 **John Elliott**, New York Jets	.20	.09	.02
☐	55 **Ray Nitschke**, Green Bay Packers	1.50	.70	.15
☐	56 **Jim Shorter**, Pittsburgh Steelers	.20	.09	.02
☐	57 **Dave Wilcox**, San Francisco 49ers	.30	.12	.03
☐	58 **Eric Crabtree**, Cincinnati Bengals	.20	.09	.02
☐	59 **Alan Page**, Minnesota Vikings	1.50	.70	.15
☐	60 **Jim Nance**, Boston Patriots	.35	.15	.03
☐	61 **Glen Ray Hines**, Houston Oilers	.20	.09	.02
☐	62 **John Mackey**, Baltimore Colts	.60	.28	.06
☐	63 **Ron McDole**, Buffalo Bills	.20	.09	.02

		MINT	VG-E	F-G
☐ 64	Tom Beier, Miami Dolphins	.20	.09	.02
☐ 65	Bill Nelsen, Los Angeles Rams	.60	.28	.06
☐ 66	Paul Flatley, Atlanta Falcons	.30	.12	.03
☐ 67	Sam Brunelli, Denver Broncos	.20	.09	.02
☐ 68	Jack Pardee, Los Angeles Rams	.50	.22	.05
☐ 69	Brig Owens, Washington Redskins	.20	.09	.02
☐ 70	Gale Sayers, Chicago Bears	7.50	3.50	.75
☐ 71	Lee Roy Jordan, Dallas Cowboys	.75	.35	.07
☐ 72	Harold Jackson, Philadelphia Eagles	2.00	.90	.20
☐ 73	John Hadl, San Diego Chargers	1.50	.70	.15
☐ 74	Dave Parks, New Orleans Saints	.30	.12	.03
☐ 75	Lem Barney, Detroit Lions	.75	.35	.07
☐ 76	Johnny Roland, St. Louis Cardinals	.35	.15	.03
☐ 77	Ed Budde, Kansas City Chiefs	.20	.09	.02
☐ 78	Ben McGee, Pittsburgh Steelers	.20	.09	.02
☐ 79	Ken Bowman, Green Bay Packers	.20	.09	.02
☐ 80	Fran Tarkenton, New York Giants	6.00	2.80	.60
☐ 81	Gene Washington, San Francisco 49ers	.50	.22	.05
☐ 82	Larry Grantham, New York Jets	.30	.12	.03
☐ 83	Bill Brown, Minnesota Vikings	.30	.12	.03
☐ 84	John Charles, Minnesota Vikings	.20	.09	.02
☐ 85	Fred Biletnikoff, Oakland Raiders	1.50	.70	.15
☐ 86	Royce Berry, Cincinnati Bengals	.20	.09	.02
☐ 87	Bob Lilly, Dallas Cowboys	1.50	.70	.15
☐ 88	Earl Morrall, Baltimore Colts	1.25	.60	.12
☐ 89	Jerry LeVias, Houston Oilers	.30	.12	.03
☐ 90	O.J. Simpson, Buffalo Bills	18.00	8.50	1.80
☐ 91	Mike Howell, Cleveland Browns	.20	.09	.02
☐ 92	Ken Gray, Houston Oilers	.20	.09	.02
☐ 93	Chris Hanburger, Washington Redskins	.30	.12	.03
☐ 94	Larry Seiple, Miami Dolphins	.20	.09	.02
☐ 95	Rich Jackson, Denver Broncos	.20	.09	.02
☐ 96	Rockne Freitas, Detroit Lions	.20	.09	.02
☐ 97	Dick Post, San Diego Chargers	.20	.09	.02
☐ 98	Ben Hawkins, Philadelphia Eagles	.20	.09	.02
☐ 99	Ken Reaves, Atlanta Falcons	.20	.09	.02
☐ 100	Roman Gabriel, Los Angeles Rams	1.50	.70	.15
☐ 101	Dave Rowe, Boston Patriots	.20	.09	.02
☐ 102	Dave Robinson, Green Bay Packers	.35	.15	.03
☐ 103	Otis Taylor, Kansas City Chiefs	.60	.28	.06
☐ 104	Jim Turner, New York Jets	.35	.15	.03
☐ 105	Joe Morrison, New York Jets	.40	.18	.04
☐ 106	Dick Evey, Los Angeles Rams	.20	.09	.02
☐ 107	Ray Mansfield, Pittsburgh Steelers	.20	.09	.02
☐ 108	Grady Alderman, Minnesota Vikings	.20	.09	.02
☐ 109	Bruce Gossett, San Francisco 49ers	.20	.09	.02

		MINT	VG-E	F-G
☐ 110	**Bob Trumpy**, Cincinnati Bengals	1.00	.45	.10
☐ 111	**Jim Hunt**, Boston Patriots	.20	.09	.02
☐ 112	**Larry Stallings**, St. Louis Cardinals	.20	.09	.02
☐ 113	**Lance Rentzel**, Los Angeles Rams	.35	.15	.03
☐ 114	**Bubba Smith**, Baltimore Colts	2.00	.90	.20
☐ 115	**Norm Snead**, Philadelphia Eagles	.50	.22	.05
☐ 116	**Jim Otto**, Oakland Raiders	1.50	.70	.15
☐ 117	**Bo Scott**, Cleveland Browns	.20	.09	.02
☐ 118	**Rick Redman**, San Diego Chargers	.20	.09	.02
☐ 119	**George Byrd**, Buffalo Bills	.30	.12	.03
☐ 120	**George Webster**, Houston Oilers	.35	.15	.03
☐ 121	**Chuck Walton**, Detroit Lions	.20	.09	.02
☐ 122	**Dave Costa**, Denver Broncos	.20	.09	.02
☐ 123	**Al Dodd**, New Orleans Saints	.20	.09	.02
☐ 124	**Len Hauss**, Washington Redskins	.20	.09	.02
☐ 125	**Deacon Jones**, Los Angeles Rams	1.50	.70	.15
☐ 126	**Randy Johnson**, Atlanta Falcons	.30	.12	.03
☐ 127	**Ralph Heck**, New York Giants	.20	.09	.02
☐ 128	**Emerson Boozer**, New York Jets	.20	.09	.02
☐ 129	**Johnny Robinson**, Kansas City Chiefs	.45	.20	.04
☐ 130	**John Brodie**, San Francisco 49ers	2.50	1.15	.25
☐ 131	**Gale Gillingham**, Green Bay Packers	.20	.09	.02
☐ 132	**Checklist 133-263**	1.25	.25	.05
	(double print)			
☐ 133	**Chuck Walker**, St. Louis Cardinals	.30	.12	.03
☐ 134	**Bennie McRae**, Chicago Bears	.30	.12	.03
☐ 135	**Paul Warfield**, Miami Dolphins	2.00	.90	.20
☐ 136	**Dan Darragh**, Buffalo Bills	.30	.12	.03
☐ 137	**Paul Robinson**, Cincinnati Bengals	.30	.12	.03
☐ 138	**Ed Philpott**, Boston Patriots	.30	.12	.03
☐ 139	**Craig Morton**, Dallas Cowboys	1.25	.60	.12
☐ 140	**Tom Dempsey**, Philadelphia Eagles	.40	.18	.04
☐ 141	**Al Nelson**, Philadelphia Eagles	.30	.12	.03
☐ 142	**Tom Matte**, Baltimore Colts	.45	.20	.04
☐ 143	**Dick Schafrath**, Cleveland Browns	.30	.12	.03
☐ 144	**Willie Brown**, Oakland Raiders	1.75	.85	.17
☐ 145	**Charley Taylor**, Washington Redskins	2.00	.90	.20
☐ 146	**John Huard**, Denver Broncos	.30	.12	.03
☐ 147	**Dave Osborn**, Minnesota Vikings	.30	.12	.03
☐ 148	**Gene Mingo**, Pittsburgh Steelers	.30	.12	.03
☐ 149	**Larry Hand**, Detroit Lions	.30	.12	.03
☐ 150	**Joe Namath**, New York Jets	9.00	4.25	.90
☐ 151	**Tom Mack**, Los Angeles Rams	.40	.18	.04
☐ 152	**Kenny Graham**, San Diego Chargers	.30	.12	.03
☐ 153	**Don Herrmann**, New York Giants	.30	.12	.03
☐ 154	**Bobby Bell**, Kansas City Chiefs	1.50	.70	.15

		MINT	VG-E	F-G
☐ 155	**Hoyle Granger**, Houston Oilers	.30	.12	.03
☐ 156	**Claude Humphrey**, Atlanta Falcons	.50	.22	.05
☐ 157	**Clifton McNeil**, New York Giants	.30	.12	.03
☐ 158	**Mick Tingelhoff**, Minnesota Vikings	.45	.20	.04
☐ 159	**Don Horn**, Denver Broncos	.40	.18	.04
☐ 160	**Larry Wilson**, Minnesota Vikings	1.50	.70	.15
☐ 161	**Tom Neville**, Boston Patriots	.30	.12	.03
☐ 162	**Larry Csonka**, Miami Dolphins	1.75	.85	.17
☐ 163	**Doug Buffone**, Chicago Bears	.30	.12	.03
☐ 164	**Cornell Green**, Dallas Cowboys	.45	.20	.04
☐ 165	**Haven Moses**, Buffalo Bills	.40	.18	.04
☐ 166	**Bill Kilmer**, New Orleans Saints	1.50	.70	.15
☐ 167	**Tim Rossovich**, Philadelphia Eagles	.40	.18	.04
☐ 168	**Bill Bergey**, Cincinnati Bengals	1.00	.45	.10
☐ 169	**Gary Collins**, Cleveland Browns	.40	.18	.04
☐ 170	**Floyd Little**, Denver Broncos	1.00	.45	.10
☐ 171	**Tom Keating**, Oakland Raiders	.30	.12	.03
☐ 172	**Pat Fischer**, Washington Redskins	.40	.18	.04
☐ 173	**Walt Sweeney**, San Diego Chargers	.30	.12	.03
☐ 174	**Greg Larson**, New York Giants	.30	.12	.03
☐ 175	**Carl Eller**, Minnesota Vikings	1.50	.70	.15
☐ 176	**George Sauer Jr.**, New York Jets	.40	.18	.04
☐ 177	**Jim Hart**, St. Louis Cardinals	1.50	.70	.15
☐ 178	**Bob Brown**, Los Angeles Rams	.30	.12	.03
☐ 179	**Mike Garrett**, Kansas City Chiefs	1.00	.45	.10
☐ 180	**John Unitas**, Baltimore Colts	6.00	2.80	.60
☐ 181	**Tom Regner**, Houston Oilers	.30	.12	.03
☐ 182	**Bob Jeter**, Green Bay Packers	.40	.18	.04
☐ 183	**Gail Cogdill**, Atlanta Falcons	.30	.12	.03
☐ 184	**Earl Gros**, New Orleans Saints	.30	.12	.03
☐ 185	**Dennis Partee**, San Diego Chargers	.30	.12	.03
☐ 186	**Charles Krueger**, San Francisco 49ers	.30	.12	.03
☐ 187	**Martin Baccaglio**, Cincinnati Bengals	.30	.12	.03
☐ 188	**Charles Long**, Boston Patriots	.30	.12	.03
☐ 189	**Bob Hayes**, Dallas Cowboys	.90	.40	.09
☐ 190	**Dick Butkus**, Chicago Bears	3.25	1.50	.32
☐ 191	**Al Bemiller**, Buffalo Bills	.30	.12	.03
☐ 192	**Dick Westmoreland**, Miami Dolphins	.30	.12	.03
☐ 193	**Joe Scarpatti**, New Orleans Saints	.30	.12	.03
☐ 194	**Ron Snidow**, Cleveland Browns	.30	.12	.03
☐ 195	**Earl McCullough**, Detroit Lions	.40	.18	.04
☐ 196	**Jake Kupp**, New Orleans Saints	.30	.12	.03
☐ 197	**Bob Lurtsema**, New York Giants	.30	.12	.03
☐ 198	**Mike Current**, Denver Broncos	.30	.12	.03
☐ 199	**Charlie Smith**, Oakland Raiders	.30	.12	.03
☐ 200	**Sonny Jurgensen**, Washington Redskins	2.50	1.15	.25

		MINT	VG-E	F-G
☐ 201	**Mike Curtis**, Baltimore Colts	.40	.18	.04
☐ 202	**Aaron Brown**, Kansas City Chiefs	.30	.12	.03
☐ 203	**Richie Petitbon**, Washington Redskins	.30	.12	.03
☐ 204	**Walt Suggs**, Houston Oilers	.30	.12	.03
☐ 205	**Roy Jefferson**, Baltimore Colts	.40	.18	.04
☐ 206	**Russ Washington**, San Diego Chargers	.30	.12	.03
☐ 207	**Woody Peoples**, San Francisco 49ers	.30	.12	.03
☐ 208	**Dave Williams**, St. Louis Cardinals	.30	.12	.03
☐ 209	**John Zook**, Atlanta Falcons	.40	.18	.04
☐ 210	**Tom Woodeshick**, Philadelphia Eagles	.30	.12	.03
☐ 211	**Howard Fest**, Cincinnati Bengals	.30	.12	.03
☐ 212	**Jack Concannon**, Chicago Bears	.40	.18	.04
☐ 213	**Jim Marshall**, Minnesota Vikings	1.00	.45	.10
☐ 214	**Jon Morris**, Boston Patriots	.30	.12	.03
☐ 215	**Dan Abramowicz**, New Orleans Saints	.40	.18	.04
☐ 216	**Paul Martha**, Denver Broncos	.40	.18	.04
☐ 217	**Ken Willard**, San Francisco 49ers	.40	.18	.04
☐ 218	**Walter Rock**, Washington Redskins	.30	.12	.03
☐ 219	**Garland Boyette**, Houston Oilers	.30	.12	.03
☐ 220	**Buck Buchanan**, Kansas City Chiefs	.65	.30	.06
☐ 221	**Bill Munson**, Detroit Lions	.50	.22	.05
☐ 222	**David Lee**, Baltimore Colts	.30	.12	.03
☐ 223	**Karl Noonan**, Miami Dolphins	.30	.12	.03
☐ 224	**Harry Schuh**, Oakland Raiders	.30	.12	.03
☐ 225	**Jackie Smith**, St. Louis Cardinals	.40	.18	.04
☐ 226	**Gerry Philbin**, New York Jets	.30	.12	.03
☐ 227	**Ernie Koy**, New York Giants	.30	.12	.03
☐ 228	**Chuck Howley**, Dallas Cowboys	.50	.22	.05
☐ 229	**Billy Shaw**, Buffalo Bills	.30	.12	.03
☐ 230	**Jerry Hillebrand**, Pittsburgh Steelers	.30	.12	.03
☐ 231	**Bill Thompson**, Denver Broncos	.40	.18	.04
☐ 232	**Carroll Dale**, Green Bay Packers	.30	.12	.03
☐ 233	**Gene Hickerson**, Cleveland Browns	.30	.12	.03
☐ 234	**Jim Butler**, Atlanta Falcons	.30	.12	.03
☐ 235	**Greg Cook**, Cincinnati Bengals	.75	.35	.07
☐ 236	**Lee Roy Caffey**, Chicago Bears	.30	.12	.03
☐ 237	**Merlin Olsen**, Los Angeles Rams	2.25	1.00	.22
☐ 238	**Fred Cox**, Minnesota Vikings	.45	.20	.04
☐ 239	**Nate Ramsey**, Philadelphia Eagles	.30	.12	.03
☐ 240	**Lance Alworth**, San Diego Chargers	2.00	.90	.20
☐ 241	**Chuck Hinton**, Pittsburgh Steelers	.30	.12	.03
☐ 242	**Jerry Smith**, Washington Redskins	.30	.12	.03
☐ 243	**Tony Baker**, New Orleans Saints	.30	.12	.03
☐ 244	**Nick Buoniconti**, Miami Dolphins	1.00	.45	.10
☐ 245	**Jim Johnson**, San Francisco 49ers	.40	.18	.04
☐ 246	**Willie Richardson**, Miami Dolphins	.40	.18	.04

		MINT	VG-E	F-G
☐ 247	**Fred Dryer**, New York Giants	1.50	.70	.15
☐ 248	**Bobby Maples**, Houston Oilers	.30	.12	.03
☐ 249	**Alex Karras**, Detroit Lions	1.75	.85	.17
☐ 250	**Joe Kapp**, Boston Patriots	.90	.40	.09
☐ 251	**Ben Davidson**, Oakland Raiders	.90	.40	.09
☐ 252	**Mike Stratton**, Buffalo Bills	.30	.12	.03
☐ 253	**Les Josephson**, Los Angeles Rams	.30	.12	.03
☐ 254	**Don Maynard**, New York Jets	1.50	.70	.15
☐ 255	**Houston Antwine**, Boston Patriots	.30	.12	.03
☐ 256	**Mac Percival**, Chicago Bears	.30	.12	.03
☐ 257	**George Goeddeke**, Denver Broncos	.30	.12	.03
☐ 258	**Homer Jones**, Cleveland Browns	.30	.12	.03
☐ 259	**Bob Berry**, Atlanta Falcons	.40	.18	.04
☐ 260	**Calvin Hill**, Dallas Cowboys	1.25	.60	.12
☐ 261	**Willie Wood**, Green Bay Packers	.75	.35	.07
☐ 262	**Ed Weisacosky**, Miami Dolphins	.30	.12	.03
☐ 263	**Jim Tyrer**, Kansas City Chiefs	.45	.15	.03

1971 TOPPS

The 1971 Topps set contains 263 cards. The cards measure 2½" by 3½". The second series was printed in slightly lesser quantities than the first series. There are no known scarcities, although the first cards of two Steeler greats, Terry Bradshaw and Mean Joe Greene, occur in this set. The card backs are printed in black ink with a gold accent on gray card stock.

		MINT	VG-E	F-G
	COMPLETE SET	90.00	42.00	9.00
	COMMON PLAYER (1-132)	.16	.07	.01
	COMMON PLAYER (133-263)	.25	.10	.02
☐ 1	John Unitas, Baltimore Colts	6.50	2.50	.40
☐ 2	Jim Butler, Atlanta Falcons	.16	.07	.01
☐ 3	Marty Schottenheimer, Boston Patriots	.25	.10	.02
☐ 4	Joe O'Donnell, Buffalo Bills	.16	.07	.01
☐ 5	Tom Dempsey, New Orleans Saints	.25	.10	.02
☐ 6	Chuck Allen, Pittsburgh Steelers	.16	.07	.01
☐ 7	Ernie Kellerman, Cleveland Browns	.16	.07	.01
☐ 8	Walt Garrison, Dallas Cowboys	.60	.28	.06
☐ 9	Bill Van Heusen, Denver Broncos	.16	.07	.01
☐ 10	Lance Alworth, Dallas Cowboys	1.50	.70	.15
☐ 11	Greg Landry, Detroit Lions	1.00	.45	.10
☐ 12	Larry Krause, Green Bay Packers	.16	.07	.01
☐ 13	Buck Buchanan, Kansas City Chiefs	.60	.28	.06
☐ 14	Roy Gerela, Pittsburgh Steelers	.16	.07	.01
☐ 15	Clifton McNeil, New York Giants	.16	.07	.01
☐ 16	Bob Brown, Los Angeles Rams	.16	.07	.01
☐ 17	Lloyd Mumphord, Miami Dolphins	.16	.07	.01
☐ 18	Gary Cuozzo, Minnesota Vikings	.25	.10	.02
☐ 19	Don Maynard, New York Jets	1.50	.70	.15
☐ 20	Larry Wilson, St. Louis Cardinals	1.25	.60	.12
☐ 21	Charlie Smith, Oakland Raiders	.16	.07	.01
☐ 22	Ken Avery, Cincinnati Bengals	.16	.07	.01
☐ 23	Billy Walik, Philadelphia Eagles	.16	.07	.01
☐ 24	Jim Johnson, San Francisco 49ers	.25	.10	.02
☐ 25	Dick Butkus, Chicago Bears	2.50	1.15	.25
☐ 26	Charley Taylor, Washington Redskins	1.50	.70	.15
☐ 27	Checklist 1-132	2.00	.30	.05
☐ 28	Lionel Aldridge, Green Bay Packers	.16	.07	.01
☐ 29	Billy Lothridge, Atlanta Falcons	.16	.07	.01
☐ 30	Terry Hanratty, Pittsburgh Steelers	.50	.22	.05
☐ 31	Lee Roy Jordan, Dallas Cowboys	.75	.35	.07
☐ 32	Rick Volk, Baltimore Colts	.16	.07	.01
☐ 33	Howard Kindig, Buffalo Bills	.16	.07	.01
☐ 34	Carl Garrett, New England Patriots	.16	.07	.01
☐ 35	Bobby Bell, Kansas City Chiefs	1.25	.60	.12
☐ 36	Gene Hickerson, Cleveland Browns	.16	.07	.01
☐ 37	Dave Parks, New Orleans Saints	.16	.07	.01
☐ 38	Paul Martha, Denver Broncos	.30	.12	.03
☐ 39	George Blanda, Oakland Raiders	3.00	1.40	.30
☐ 40	Tom Woodeshick, Philadelphia Eagles	.16	.07	.01
☐ 41	Alex Karras, Detroit Lions	1.50	.70	.15
☐ 42	Rick Redman, San Diego Chargers	.16	.07	.01

		MINT	VG-E	F-G
☐ 43	**Zeke Moore**, Houston Oilers	.16	.07	.01
☐ 44	**Jack Snow**, Los Angeles Rams	.25	.10	.02
☐ 45	**Larry Csonka**, Miami Dolphins	1.50	.70	.15
☐ 46	**Karl Kassulke**, Minnesota Vikings	.16	.07	.01
☐ 47	**Jim Hart**, St. Louis Cardinals	1.00	.45	.10
☐ 48	**Al Atkinson**, New York Jets	.16	.07	.01
☐ 49	**Horst Muhlmann**, Cincinnati Bengals	.16	.07	.01
☐ 50	**Sonny Jurgensen**, Washington Redskins	2.00	.90	.20
☐ 51	**Ron Johnson**, New York Giants	.30	.12	.03
☐ 52	**Cas Banaszek**, San Francisco 49ers	.16	.07	.01
☐ 53	**Bubba Smith**, Baltimore Colts	1.25	.60	.12
☐ 54	**Bobby Douglass**, Chicago Bears	.25	.10	.02
☐ 55	**Willie Wood**, Green Bay Packers	.60	.28	.06
☐ 56	**Bake Turner**, Boston Patriots	.25	.10	.02
☐ 57	**Mike Morgan**, New Orleans Saints	.16	.07	.01
☐ 58	**George Byrd**, Denver Broncos	.16	.07	.01
☐ 59	**Don Horn**, Denver Broncos	.16	.07	.01
☐ 60	**Tommy Nobis**, Atlanta Falcons	.90	.40	.09
☐ 61	**Jan Stenerud**, Kansas City Chiefs	.50	.22	.05
☐ 62	**Altie Taylor**, Detroit Lions	.16	.07	.01
☐ 63	**Gary Pettigrew**, Philadelphia Eagles	.16	.07	.01
☐ 64	**Spike Jones**, Buffalo Bills	.16	.07	.01
☐ 65	**Duane Thomas**, Dallas Cowboys	.60	.28	.06
☐ 66	**Marty Domres**, San Diego Chargers	.16	.07	.01
☐ 67	**Dick Anderson**, Miami Dolphins	.30	.12	.03
☐ 68	**Ken Iman**, Los Angeles Rams	.16	.07	.01
☐ 69	**Miller Farr**, St. Louis Cardinals	.16	.07	.01
☐ 70	**Daryle Lamonica**, Oakland Raiders	.75	.35	.07
☐ 71	**Alan Page**, Minnesota Vikings	1.00	.45	.10
☐ 72	**Pat Matson**, Cincinnati Bengals	.16	.07	.01
☐ 73	**Emerson Boozer**, New York Jets	.16	.07	.01
☐ 74	**Pat Fischer**, Washington Redskins	.25	.10	.02
☐ 75	**Gary Collins**, Cleveland Browns	.25	.10	.02
☐ 76	**John Fuqua**, Pittsburgh Steelers	.16	.07	.01
☐ 77	**Bruce Gossett**, San Francisco 49ers	.16	.07	.01
☐ 78	**Ed O'Bradovich**, Chicago Bears	.16	.07	.01
☐ 79	**Bob Tucker**, New York Giants	.30	.12	.03
☐ 80	**Mike Curtis**, Baltimore Colts	.30	.12	.03
☐ 81	**Rich Jackson**, Denver Broncos	.16	.07	.01
☐ 82	**Tom Janik**, New England Patriots	.16	.07	.01
☐ 83	**Gale Gillingham**, Green Bay Packers	.16	.07	.01
☐ 84	**Jim Mitchell**, Atlanta Falcons	.16	.07	.01
☐ 85	**Charlie Johnson**, Houston Oilers	.60	.28	.06
☐ 86	**Edgar Chandler**, Buffalo Bills	.16	.07	.01
☐ 87	**Cyril Pinder**, Chicago Bears	.16	.07	.01
☐ 88	**Johnny Robinson**, Kansas City Chiefs	.40	.18	.04

			MINT	VG-E	F-G
☐ 89	**Ralph Neely**, Dallas Cowboys		.25	.10	.02
☐ 90	**Dan Abramowicz**, New Orleans Saints		.25	.10	.02
☐ 91	**Mercury Morris**, Miami Dolphins		.50	.22	.05
☐ 92	**Steve DeLong**, San Diego Chargers		.16	.07	.01
☐ 93	**Larry Stallings**, St. Louis Cardinals		.16	.07	.01
☐ 94	**Tom Mack**, Los Angeles Rams		.25	.10	.02
☐ 95	**Hewritt Dixon**, Oakland Raiders		.30	.12	.03
☐ 96	**Fred Cox**, Minnesota Vikings		.35	.15	.03
☐ 97	**Chris Hanburger**, Washington Redskins		.30	.12	.03
☐ 98	**Gerry Philbin**, New York Jets		.25	.10	.02
☐ 99	**Ernie Wright**, Cincinnati Bengals		.16	.07	.01
☐ 100	**John Brodie**, San Francisco 49ers		2.50	1.15	.25
☐ 101	**Tucker Frederickson**, New York Giants		.30	.12	.03
☐ 102	**Bobby Walden**, Pittsburgh Steelers		.16	.07	.01
☐ 103	**Dick Gordon**, Chicago Bears		.25	.10	.02
☐ 104	**Walter Johnson**, Cleveland Browns		.16	.07	.01
☐ 105	**Mike Lucci**, Detroit Lions		.25	.10	.02
☐ 106	**Checklist 133-263**		1.00	.20	.04
	(double print)				
☐ 107	**Ron Berger**, New England Patriots		.16	.07	.01
☐ 108	**Dan Sullivan**, Baltimore Colts		.16	.07	.01
☐ 109	**George Kunz**, Atlanta Falcons		.25	.10	.02
☐ 110	**Floyd Little**, Denver Broncos		.60	.28	.06
☐ 111	**Zeke Bratkowski**, Green Bay Packers		.45	.20	.04
☐ 112	**Haven Moses**, Buffalo Bills		.25	.10	.02
☐ 113	**Ken Houston**, Houston Oilers		.50	.22	.05
☐ 114	**Willie Lanier**, Kansas City Chiefs		.75	.35	.07
☐ 115	**Larry Brown**, Washington Redskins		.50	.22	.05
☐ 116	**Tim Rossovich**, Philadelphia Eagles		.25	.10	.02
☐ 117	**Errol Linden**, New Orleans Saints		.16	.07	.01
☐ 118	**Mel Renfro**, Dallas Cowboys		.60	.28	.06
☐ 119	**Mike Garrett**, San Diego Chargers		.35	.15	.03
☐ 120	**Fran Tarkenton**, New York Giants		5.00	2.35	.50
☐ 121	**Garo Yepremian**, Miami Dolphins		.50	.22	.05
☐ 122	**Glen Condren**, Atlanta Falcons		.16	.07	.01
☐ 123	**Johnny Roland**, St. Louis Cardinals		.30	.12	.03
☐ 124	**Dave Herman**, New York Jets		.16	.07	.01
☐ 125	**Merlin Olsen**, Los Angeles Rams		1.75	.85	.17
☐ 126	**Doug Buffone**, Chicago Bears		.16	.07	.01
☐ 127	**Earl McCullouch**, Detroit Lions		.25	.10	.02
☐ 128	**Spider Lockhart**, New York Giants		.16	.07	.01
☐ 129	**Ken Willard**, San Francisco 49ers		.25	.10	.02
☐ 130	**Gene Washington**, Minnesota Vikings		.25	.10	.02
☐ 131	**Mike Phipps**, Cleveland Browns		.50	.22	.05
☐ 132	**Andy Russell**, Pittsburgh Steelers		.25	.10	.02
☐ 133	**Ray Nitschke**, Green Bay Packers		1.50	.70	.15

		MINT	VG-E	F-G
☐ 134	**Jerry Logan**, Baltimore Colts	.25	.10	.02
☐ 135	**MacArthur Lane**, St. Louis Cardinals	.35	.15	.03
☐ 136	**Jim Turner**, Denver Broncos	.35	.15	.03
☐ 137	**Kent McCloughan**, Oakland Raiders	.25	.10	.02
☐ 138	**Paul Guidry**, Buffalo Bills	.25	.10	.02
☐ 139	**Otis Taylor**, Kansas City Chiefs	.60	.28	.06
☐ 140	**Virgil Carter**, Cincinnati Bengals	.35	.15	.03
☐ 141	**Joe Dawkins**, Houston Oilers	.25	.10	.02
☐ 142	**Steve Preece**, Philadelphia Eagles	.25	.10	.02
☐ 143	**Mike Bragg**, Washington Redskins	.25	.10	.02
☐ 144	**Bob Lilly**, Dallas Cowboys	1.75	.85	.17
☐ 145	**Joe Kapp**, Boston Patriots	.90	.40	.09
☐ 146	**Al Dodd**, New Orleans Saints	.25	.10	.02
☐ 147	**Nick Buoniconti**, Miami Dolphins	1.25	.60	.12
☐ 148	**Speedy Duncan**, Washington Redskins	.25	.10	.02
☐ 149	**Cedric Hardman**, San Francisco 49ers	.25	.10	.02
☐ 150	**Gale Sayers**, Chicago Bears	6.00	2.80	.60
☐ 151	**Jim Otto**, Oakland Raiders	1.75	.85	.17
☐ 152	**Billy Truax**, Dallas Cowboys	.25	.10	.02
☐ 153	**John Elliott**, New York Jets	.25	.10	.02
☐ 154	**Dick LeBeau**, Detroit Lions	.25	.10	.02
☐ 155	**Bill Bergey**, Cincinnati Bengals	.55	.25	.05
☐ 156	**Terry Bradshaw**, Pittsburgh Steelers	9.00	4.25	.90
☐ 157	**Leroy Kelly**, Cleveland Browns	1.25	.60	.12
☐ 158	**Paul Krause**, Minnesota Vikings	.35	.15	.03
☐ 159	**Ted Vector**, Washington Redskins	.25	.10	.02
☐ 160	**Bob Griese**, Miami Dolphins	3.00	1.40	.30
☐ 161	**Ernie McMillan**, St. Louis Cardinals	.25	.10	.02
☐ 162	**Donny Anderson**, Green Bay Packers	.40	.18	.04
☐ 163	**John Pitts**, Buffalo Bills	.25	.10	.02
☐ 164	**Dave Costa**, Denver Broncos	.25	.10	.02
☐ 165	**Gene Washington**, San Francisco 49ers	.40	.18	.04
☐ 166	**John Zook**, Atlanta Falcons	.35	.15	.03
☐ 167	**Pete Gogolak**, New York Giants	.35	.15	.03
☐ 168	**Erich Barnes**, Cleveland Browns	.25	.10	.02
☐ 169	**Alvin Reed**, Houston Oilers	.25	.10	.02
☐ 170	**Jim Nance**, New England Patriots	.35	.15	.03
☐ 171	**Craig Morton**, Dallas Cowboys	1.25	.60	.12
☐ 172	**Gary Garrison**, San Diego Chargers	.25	.10	.02
☐ 173	**Joe Scarpati**, New Orleans Saints	.25	.10	.02
☐ 174	**Adrian Young**, Philadelphia Eagles	.25	.10	.02
☐ 175	**John Mackey**, Baltimore Colts	.50	.22	.05
☐ 176	**Mac Percival**, Chicago Bears	.25	.10	.02
☐ 177	**Preston Pearson**, Pittsburgh Steelers	.50	.22	.05
☐ 178	**Fred Biletnikoff**, Oakland Raiders	1.50	.70	.15
☐ 179	**Mike Battle**, New York Jets	.25	.10	.02

		MINT	VG-E	F-G
☐ 180	**Len Dawson**, Kansas City Chiefs	2.50	1.15	.25
☐ 181	**Les Josephson**, Los Angeles Rams	.25	.10	.02
☐ 182	**Royce Berry**, Cincinnati Bengals	.25	.10	.02
☐ 183	**Herman Weaver**, Detroit Lions	.25	.10	.02
☐ 184	**Norm Snead**, Minnesota Vikings	.45	.20	.04
☐ 185	**Sam Brunelli**, Denver Broncos	.25	.10	.02
☐ 186	**Jim Kiick**, Miami Dolphins	.35	.15	.03
☐ 187	**Austin Denney**, Buffalo Bills	.25	.10	.02
☐ 188	**Roger Wehrli**, St. Louis Cardinals	.40	.18	.04
☐ 189	**Dave Wilcox**, San Francisco 49ers	.35	.15	.03
☐ 190	**Bob Hayes**, Dallas Cowboys	.85	.40	.08
☐ 191	**Joe Morrison**, New York Giants	.40	.18	.04
☐ 192	**Manny Sistrunk**, Washington Redskins	.25	.10	.02
☐ 193	**Don Cockroft**, Cleveland Browns	.25	.10	.02
☐ 194	**Lee Bouggess**, Philadelphia Eagles	.25	.10	.02
☐ 195	**Bob Berry**, Atlanta Falcons	.35	.15	.03
☐ 196	**Ron Sellers**, New England Patriots	.25	.10	.02
☐ 197	**George Webster**, Houston Oilers	.35	.15	.03
☐ 198	**Hoyle Granger**, New Orleans Saints	.25	.10	.02
☐ 199	**Bob Vogel**, Baltimore Colts	.25	.10	.02
☐ 200	**Bart Starr**, Green Bay Packers	5.00	2.35	.50
☐ 201	**Mike Mercer**, San Diego Chargers	.25	.10	.02
☐ 202	**Dave Smith**, Pittsburgh Steelers	.25	.10	.02
☐ 203	**Lee Roy Caffey**, Dallas Cowboys	.25	.10	.02
☐ 204	**Mick Tingelhoff**, Minnesota Vikings	.45	.20	.04
☐ 205	**Matt Snell**, New York Jets	.55	.25	.05
☐ 206	**Jim Tyrer**, Kansas City Chiefs	.25	.10	.02
☐ 207	**Willie Brown**, Oakland Raiders	1.75	.85	.17
☐ 208	**Bob Johnson**, Cincinnati Bengals	.25	.10	.02
☐ 209	**Deacon Jones**, Los Angeles Rams	1.75	.85	.17
☐ 210	**Charlie Sanders**, Detroit Lions	.35	.15	.03
☐ 211	**Jake Scott**, Miami Dolphins	.50	.22	.05
☐ 212	**Bob Anderson**, Denver Broncos	.35	.15	.03
☐ 213	**Charlie Krueger**, San Francisco 49ers	.25	.10	.02
☐ 214	**Jim Bakken**, St. Louis Cardinals	.40	.18	.04
☐ 215	**Harold Jackson**, Philadelphia Eagles	.75	.35	.07
☐ 216	**Bill Brundige**, Washington Redskins	.25	.10	.02
☐ 217	**Calvin Hill**, Dallas Cowboys	.75	.35	.07
☐ 218	**Claude Humphrey**, Atlanta Falcons	.35	.15	.03
☐ 219	**Glen Ray Hines**, New Orleans Saints	.25	.10	.02
☐ 220	**Bill Nelson**, Los Angeles Rams	.60	.28	.06
☐ 221	**Roy Hilton**, Baltimore Colts	.25	.10	.02
☐ 222	**Don Herrmann**, New York Giants	.25	.10	.02
☐ 223	**John Bramlett**, Atlanta Falcons	.25	.10	.02
☐ 224	**Ken Ellis**, Green Bay Packers	.25	.10	.02
☐ 225	**Dave Osborn**, Minnesota Vikings	.25	.10	.02

		MINT	VG-E	F-G
☐ 226	Edd Hargett, New Orleans Saints	.35	.15	.03
☐ 227	Gene Mingo, Pittsburgh Steelers	.25	.10	.02
☐ 228	Larry Grantham, New York Jets	.35	.15	.03
☐ 229	Dick Post, Denver Broncos	.25	.10	.02
☐ 230	Roman Gabriel, Los Angeles Rams	1.50	.70	.15
☐ 231	Mike Eischeid, Oakland Raiders	.25	.10	.02
☐ 232	Jim Lynch, Kansas City Chiefs	.25	.10	.02
☐ 233	Lemarr Parrish, Cincinnati Bengals	.25	.10	.02
☐ 234	Cecil Turner, Chicago Bears	.25	.10	.02
☐ 235	Dennis Shaw, Buffalo Bills	.25	.10	.02
☐ 236	Mel Farr, Detroit Lions	.35	.15	.03
☐ 237	Curt Knight, Washington Redskins	.25	.10	.02
☐ 238	Chuck Howley, Dallas Cowboys	.45	.20	.04
☐ 239	Bruce Taylor, San Francisco 49ers	.35	.15	.03
☐ 240	Jerry LeVias, San Diego Chargers	.25	.10	.02
☐ 241	Bob Lurtsema, New York Giants	.25	.10	.02
☐ 242	Earl Morrall, Baltimore Colts	1.25	.60	.12
☐ 243	Kermit Alexander, Los Angeles Rams	.35	.15	.03
☐ 244	Jackie Smith, St. Louis Cardinals	.35	.15	.03
☐ 245	Joe Greene, New York Giants	5.00	2.35	.50
☐ 246	Harmon Wages, Atlanta Falcons	.25	.10	.02
☐ 247	Errol Mann, Detroit Lions	.25	.10	.02
☐ 248	Mike McCoy, Green Bay Packers	.25	.10	.02
☐ 249	Milt Morin, Cleveland Browns	.25	.10	.02
☐ 250	Joe Namath, New York Jets	9.00	4.25	.90
☐ 251	Jackie Burkett, New Orleans Saints	.25	.10	.02
☐ 252	Steve Chomyszak, Cincinnati Bengals	.25	.10	.02
☐ 253	Ed Sharockman, Minnesota Vikings	.25	.10	.02
☐ 254	Robert Holmes, Kansas City Chiefs	.25	.10	.02
☐ 255	John Hadl, San Diego Chargers	1.25	.60	.12
☐ 256	Cornell Gordon, Denver Broncos	.25	.10	.02
☐ 257	Mark Moseley, Houston Oilers	.60	.28	.06
☐ 258	Gus Otto, Oakland Raiders	.25	.10	.02
☐ 259	Mike Taliaferro, Boston Patriots	.25	.10	.02
☐ 260	O. J. Simpson, Buffalo Bills	8.00	3.75	.80
☐ 261	Paul Warfield, Miami Dolphins	1.75	.85	.17
☐ 262	Jack Concannon, Chicago Bears	.35	.15	.03
☐ 263	Tom Matte, Baltimore Colts	.45	.15	.03

1972 TOPPS

The 1972 Topps set contains 351 cards. The cards measure 2½" by 3½". The second series was printed in slightly lesser quantities than the first series. The third series (264-351) is considerably more difficult to obtain than cards in the first two series. In Action cards (IA in the checklist below) are included, as are All Pro selections (AP below). The card backs are printed in blue and green on gray card stock.

		MINT	VG-E	F-G
	COMPLETE SET	275.00	130.00	25.00
	COMMON PLAYER (1-132)	.15	.06	.01
	COMMON PLAYER (133-263)	.20	.09	.02
	COMMON PLAYER (264-351)	2.25	1.00	.22
☐ 1	**AFC Rushing Leaders** . . . . Floyd Little Larry Csonka Marv Hubbard	1.00	.25	.05
☐ 2	**NFC Rushing Leaders** . . . . John Brockington Steve Owens Willie Ellison	.30	.12	.03
☐ 3	**AFC Passing Leaders** . . . . Bob Griese Len Dawson Virgil Carter	.55	.25	.05
☐ 4	**NFC Passing Leaders** . . . . Roger Staubach Greg Landry Bill Kilmer	1.00	.45	.10

		MINT	VG-E	F-G
☐	5 **AFC Receiving Leaders**	.50	.22	.05
	Fred Biletnikoff			
	Otis Taylor			
	Randy Vataha			
☐	6 **NFC Receiving Leaders**	.30	.12	.03
	Bob Tucker			
	Ted Kwalick			
	Harold Jackson			
	Roy Jefferson			
☐	7 **AFC Scoring Leaders**	.30	.12	.03
	Garo Yepremian			
	Jan Stenerud			
	Jim O'Brien			
☐	8 **NFC Scoring Leaders**	.25	.10	.02
	Curt Knight			
	Errol Mann			
	Bruce Gossett			
☐	9 **Jim Kiick**, Miami Dolphins	.25	.10	.02
☐	10 **Otis Taylor**, Kansas City Chiefs	.50	.22	.05
☐	11 **Bobby Joe Green**, Chicago Bears	.15	.06	.01
☐	12 **Ken Ellis**, Green Bay Packers	.15	.06	.01
☐	13 **John Riggins**, New York Jets	5.00	2.25	.50
☐	14 **Dave Parks**, New Orleans Saints	.25	.10	.02
☐	15 **John Hadl**, San Diego Chargers	1.00	.45	.10
☐	16 **Ron Hornsby**, New York Giants	.15	.06	.01
☐	17 **Chip Myers**, Cincinnati Bengals	.15	.06	.01
☐	18 **Bill Kilmer**, Washington Redskins	1.00	.45	.10
☐	19 **Fred Hoaglin**, Cleveland Browns	.15	.06	.01
☐	20 **Carl Eller**, Minnesota Vikings	1.00	.45	.10
☐	21 **Steve Zabel**, Philadelphia Eagles	.15	.06	.01
☐	22 **Vic Washington**, San Francisco 49ers	.15	.06	.01
☐	23 **Len St. Jean**, New England Patriots	.15	.06	.01
☐	24 **Bill Thompson**, Denver Broncos	.15	.06	.01
☐	25 **Steve Owens**, Detroit Lions	.50	.22	.05
☐	26 **Ken Burrough**, Houston Oilers	.25	.10	.02
☐	27 **Mike Clark**, Dallas Cowboys	.15	.06	.01
☐	28 **Willie Brown**, Oakland Raiders	1.50	.70	.15
☐	29 **Checklist 1-132**	1.50	.25	.05
☐	30 **Marlin Briscoe**, Buffalo Bills	.25	.10	.02
☐	31 **Jerry Logan**, Baltimore Colts	.15	.06	.01
☐	32 **Donny Anderson**, St. Louis Cardinals	.30	.12	.03
☐	33 **Rich McGeorge**, Green Bay Packers	.15	.06	.01
☐	34 **Charlie Durkee**, New Orleans Saints	.15	.06	.01
☐	35 **Willie Lanier**, Kansas City Chiefs	.60	.28	.06
☐	36 **Chris Farasopoulos**, New York Jets	.15	.06	.01
☐	37 **Ron Shanklin**, Pittsburgh Steelers	.15	.06	.01

		MINT	VG-E	F-G
☐	38 **Forrest Blue**, San Francisco 49ers	.15	.06	.01
☐	39 **Ken Reaves**, Atlanta Falcons	.15	.06	.01
☐	40 **Roman Gabriel**, Los Angeles Rams	1.00	.45	.10
☐	41 **Mac Percival**, Chicago Bears	.15	.06	.01
☐	42 **Lem Barney**, Detroit Lions	.30	.12	.03
☐	43 **Nick Buoniconti**, Miami Dolphins	1.00	.45	.10
☐	44 **Charlie Gogolak**, New England Patriots	.25	.10	.02
☐	45 **Bill Bradley**, Philadelphia Eagles	.30	.12	.03
☐	46 **Joe Jones**, Cleveland Browns	.15	.06	.01
☐	47 **Dave Williams**, St. Louis Cardinals	.15	.06	.01
☐	48 **Pete Athas**, New York Giants	.15	.06	.01
☐	49 **Virgil Carter**, Cincinnati Bengals	.30	.12	.03
☐	50 **Floyd Little**, Denver Broncos	.60	.28	.06
☐	51 **Curt Knight**, Washington Redskins	.15	.06	.01
☐	52 **Bobby Maples**, Pittsburgh Steelers	.15	.06	.01
☐	53 **Charlie West**, Minnesota Vikings	.15	.06	.01
☐	54 **Marv Hubbard**, Oakland Raiders	.25	.10	.02
☐	55 **Archie Manning**, Oakland Raiders	2.00	.90	.20
☐	56 **Jim O'Brien**, Baltimore Colts	.15	.06	.01
☐	57 **Wayne Patrick**, Buffalo Bills	.15	.06	.01
☐	58 **Ken Bowman**, Green Bay Packers	.15	.06	.01
☐	59 **Roger Wehrli**, St. Louis Cardinals	.30	.12	.03
☐	60 **Charlie Sanders**, Detroit Lions	.25	.10	.02
☐	61 **Jan Stenerud**, Kansas City Chiefs	.30	.12	.03
☐	62 **Willie Ellison**, Los Angeles Rams	.15	.06	.01
☐	63 **Walt Sweeney**, San Diego Chargers	.15	.06	.01
☐	64 **Ron Smith**, Chicago Bears	.15	.06	.01
☐	65 **Jim Plunkett**, New England Patriots	3.00	1.40	.30
☐	66 **Herb Adderly**, Dallas Cowboys	1.25	.60	.12
☐	67 **Mike Reid**, Cincinnati Bengals	.25	.10	.02
☐	68 **Richard Caster**, New York Jets	.35	.15	.03
☐	69 **Dave Wilcox**, San Francisco 49ers	.25	.10	.02
☐	70 **Leroy Kelly**, Cleveland Browns	.75	.35	.07
☐	71 **Bob Lee**, Minnesota Vikings	.25	.10	.02
☐	72 **Verlon Biggs**, Washington Redskins	.15	.06	.01
☐	73 **Henry Allison**, Philadelphia Eagles	.15	.06	.01
☐	74 **Steve Ramsey**, Denver Broncos	.15	.06	.01
☐	75 **Claude Humphrey**, Atlanta Falcons	.25	.10	.02
☐	76 **Bob Grim**, Minnesota Vikings	.15	.06	.01
☐	77 **John Fuqua**, Pittsburgh Steelers	.15	.06	.01
☐	78 **Ken Houston**, Houston Oilers	.40	.18	.04
☐	79 **Checklist 133-263 (double print)**	1.00	.20	.04
☐	80 **Bob Griese**, Miami Dolphins	3.00	1.40	.30
☐	81 **Lance Rentzel**, Los Angeles Rams	.30	.12	.03
☐	82 **Ed Podolak**, Kansas City Chiefs	.30	.12	.03
☐	83 **Ike Hill**, Buffalo Bills	.15	.06	.01

		MINT	VG-E	F-G
☐ 84	**George Farmer**, Chicago Bears	.15	.06	.01
☐ 85	**John Brockington**, Green Bay Packers	.65	.30	.06
☐ 86	**Jim Otto**, Oakland Raiders	1.00	.45	.10
☐ 87	**Richard Neal**, New Orleans Saints	.15	.06	.01
☐ 88	**Jim Hart**, St. Louis Cardinals	1.00	.45	.10
☐ 89	**Bob Babich**, San Diego Chargers	.15	.06	.01
☐ 90	**Gene Washington**, San Francisco 49ers	.30	.12	.03
☐ 91	**John Zook**, Atlanta Falcons	.25	.10	.02
☐ 92	**Bobby Duhon**, New York Giants	.15	.06	.01
☐ 93	**Ted Hendricks**, Baltimore Colts	1.00	.45	.10
☐ 94	**Rockne Freitas**, Detroit Lions	.15	.06	.01
☐ 95	**Larry Brown**, Washington Redskins	.60	.28	.06
☐ 96	**Mike Phipps**, Cleveland Browns	.45	.20	.04
☐ 97	**Julius Adams**, New England Patriots	.15	.06	.01
☐ 98	**Dick Anderson**, Miami Dolphins	.30	.12	.03
☐ 99	**Fred Willis**, Cincinnati Bengals	.15	.06	.01
☐ 100	**Joe Namath**, New York Jets	7.50	3.50	.75
☐ 101	**L.C. Greenwood**, Pittsburgh Steelers	.90	.40	.09
☐ 102	**Mark Nordquist**, Philadelphia Eagles	.15	.06	.01
☐ 103	**Robert Holmes**, Kansas City Chiefs	.15	.06	.01
☐ 104	**Ron Yary**, Minnesota Vikings	.25	.10	.02
☐ 105	**Bob Hayes**, Dallas Cowboys	.75	.35	.07
☐ 106	**Lyle Alzado**, Denver Broncos	2.50	1.15	.25
☐ 107	**Bob Berry**, Atlanta Falcons	.25	.10	.02
☐ 108	**Phil Villapiano**, Oakland Raiders	.35	.15	.03
☐ 109	**Dave Elmendorf**, Los Angeles Rams	.15	.06	.01
☐ 110	**Gale Sayers**, Chicago Bears	5.00	2.35	.50
☐ 111	**Jim Tyrer**, Kansas City Chiefs	.15	.06	.01
☐ 112	**Mel Gray**, St. Louis Cardinals	.60	.28	.06
☐ 113	**Gerry Philbin**, New York Jets	.15	.06	.01
☐ 114	**Bob James**, Buffalo Bills	.15	.06	.01
☐ 115	**Garo Yepremian**, Miami Dolphins	.30	.12	.03
☐ 116	**Dave Robinson**, Green Bay Packers	.30	.12	.03
☐ 117	**Jeff Queen**, San Diego Chargers	.15	.06	.01
☐ 118	**Norm Snead**, Minnesota Vikings	.40	.18	.04

IN ACTION CARDS

☐ 119	**Jim Nance IA**, New England Patriots	.25	.10	.02
☐ 120	**Terry Bradshaw IA**, Pittsburgh Steelers	2.00	.90	.20
☐ 121	**Jim Kiick IA**, Miami Dolphins	.25	.10	.02
☐ 122	**Roger Staubach IA**, Dallas Cowboys	3.00	1.40	.30
☐ 123	**Bo Scott IA**, Cleveland Browns	.15	.06	.01
☐ 124	**John Brodie IA**, San Francisco 49ers	1.50	.70	.15

	MINT	VG-E	F-G
☐ 125 **Rick Volk IA**, Baltimore Colts	.15	.06	.01
☐ 126 **John Riggins IA**, Baltimore Colts	1.50	.70	.15
☐ 127 **Bubba Smith IA**, Baltimore Colts	.50	.22	.05
☐ 128 **Roman Gabriel IA**, Los Angeles Rams	.90	.40	.09
☐ 129 **Calvin Hill IA**, Dallas Cowboys	.30	.12	.03
☐ 130 **Bill Nelson IA**, Cleveland Browns	.25	.10	.02
☐ 131 **Tom Matte IA**, Baltimore Colts	.25	.10	.02
☐ 132 **Bob Griese IA**, Miami Dolphins	1.75	.85	.17

PLAYOFF CARDS

	MINT	VG-E	F-G
☐ 133 **AFC Semi-Final** .... Dolphins 27, Chiefs 24	.45	.20	.04
☐ 134 **NFC Semi-Final** .... Cowboys 20, Vikings 12 (Duane Thomas getting tackled)	.45	.20	.04
☐ 135 **AFC Semi-Final** .... Colts 20, Browns 3 (Don Nottingham)	.45	.20	.04
☐ 136 **NFC Semi-Final** .... 49ers 24, Redskins 20	.45	.20	.04
☐ 137 **AFC Title Game** .... Dolphins 21, Colts 0 (Johnny Unitas getting tackled)	.90	.40	.09
☐ 138 **NFC Title Game** .... Cowboys 14, 49ers 3 (Bob Lilly making tackle)	.90	.40	.09
☐ 139 **Super Bowl** .... Cowboys 24, Dolphins 3 (Roger Staubach rolling out)	1.75	.85	.17
☐ 140 **Larry Csonka**, Miami Dolphins	1.00	.45	.10
☐ 141 **Rick Volk**, Baltimore Colts	.20	.09	.02
☐ 142 **Roy Jefferson**, Washington Redskins	.25	.10	.02
☐ 143 **Raymond Chester**, Oakland Raiders	.30	.12	.03
☐ 144 **Bobby Douglass**, Chicago Bears	.30	.12	.03
☐ 145 **Bob Lilly**, Dallas Cowboys	1.50	.70	.15
☐ 146 **Harold Jackson**, Philadelphia Eagles	.60	.28	.06
☐ 147 **Pete Gogolak**, New York Giants	.25	.10	.02
☐ 148 **Art Malone**, Atlanta Falcons	.20	.09	.02

		MINT	VG-E	F-G
☐ 149	**Ed Flanagan**, Detroit Lions	.20	.09	.02
☐ 150	**Terry Bradshaw**, Pittsburgh Steelers	4.50	2.10	.45
☐ 151	**MacArthur Lane**, St. Louis Cardinals	.30	.12	.03
☐ 152	**Jack Snow**, Los Angeles Rams	.30	.12	.03
☐ 153	**Al Beauchamp**, Cincinnati Bengals	.20	.09	.02
☐ 154	**Bob Anderson**, Denver Broncos	.30	.12	.03
☐ 155	**Ted Kwalick**, San Francisco 49ers	.30	.12	.03
☐ 156	**Dan Pastorini**, Houston Oilers	.90	.40	.09
☐ 157	**Emmitt Thomas**, Kansas City Chiefs	.30	.12	.03
☐ 158	**Randy Vataha**, New England Patriots	.30	.12	.03
☐ 159	**Al Atkinson**, New York Jets	.20	.09	.02
☐ 160	**O.J. Simpson**, Buffalo Bills	6.00	2.80	.60
☐ 161	**Jackie Smith**, St. Louis Cardinals	.30	.12	.03
☐ 162	**Ernie Kellerman**, Cleveland Browns	.20	.09	.02
☐ 163	**Dennis Partee**, San Diego Chargers	.20	.09	.02
☐ 164	**Jake Kupp**, New Orleans Saints	.20	.09	.02
☐ 165	**John Unitas**, Baltimore Colts	5.00	2.35	.50
☐ 166	**Clint Jones**, Minnesota Vikings	.20	.09	.02
☐ 167	**Paul Warfield**, Miami Dolphins	1.50	.70	.15
☐ 168	**Ron McDole**, Washington Redskins	.20	.09	.02
☐ 169	**Daryle Lamonica**, Oakland Raiders	.75	.35	.07
☐ 170	**Dick Butkus**, Chicago Bears	2.50	1.15	.25
☐ 171	**Jim Butler**, Atlanta Falcons	.20	.09	.02
☐ 172	**Mike McCoy**, Green Bay Packers	.20	.09	.02
☐ 173	**Dave Smith**, Pittsburgh Steelers	.20	.09	.02
☐ 174	**Greg Landry**, Detroit Lions	.45	.20	.04
☐ 175	**Tom Dempsey**, Philadelphia Eagles	.30	.12	.03
☐ 176	**John Charles**, Houston Oilers	.20	.09	.02
☐ 177	**Bobby Bell**, Kansas City Chiefs	1.00	.45	.10
☐ 178	**Don Horn**, Denver Broncos	.20	.09	.02
☐ 179	**Bob Trumpy**, Cincinnati Bengals	.40	.18	.04
☐ 180	**Duane Thomas**, Dallas Cowboys	.50	.22	.05
☐ 181	**Merlin Olsen**, Los Angeles Rams	1.75	.85	.17
☐ 182	**Dave Herman**, New York Jets	.20	.09	.02
☐ 183	**Jim Nance**, New England Patriots	.30	.12	.03
☐ 184	**Pete Beathard**, St. Louis Cardinals	.35	.15	.03
☐ 185	**Bob Tucker**, New York Giants	.30	.12	.03
☐ 186	**Gene Upshaw**, Oakland Raiders	.35	.15	.03
☐ 187	**Bo Scott**, Cleveland Browns	.20	.09	.02
☐ 188	**J.D. Hill**, Buffalo Bills	.20	.09	.02
☐ 189	**Bruce Gossett**, San Francisco 49ers	.20	.09	.02
☐ 190	**Bubba Smith**, Baltimore Colts	1.00	.45	.10

		MINT	VG-E	F-G
☐ 191	Edd Hargett, New Orleans Saints	.30	.12	.03
☐ 192	Gary Garrison, San Diego Chargers	.20	.09	.02
☐ 193	Jake Scott, Miami Dolphins	.35	.15	.03
☐ 194	Fred Cox, Minnesota Vikings	.35	.15	.03
☐ 195	Sonny Jurgensen, Washington Redskins	2.00	.90	.20
☐ 196	Greg Brezina, Atlanta Falcons	.20	.09	.02
☐ 197	Ed O'Bradovich, Chicago Bears	.20	.09	.02
☐ 198	John Rowser, Pittsburgh Steelers	.20	.09	.02
☐ 199	Altie Taylor, Detroit Lions	.20	.09	.02
☐ 200	Roger Staubach, Dallas Cowboys	11.00	5.25	1.10
☐ 201	Leroy Keyes, Philadelphia Eagles	.30	.12	.03
☐ 202	Garland Boyette, Houston Oilers	.20	.09	.02
☐ 203	Tom Beer, New England Patriots	.20	.09	.02
☐ 204	Buck Buchanan, Kansas City Chiefs	.50	.22	.05
☐ 205	Larry Wilson, St. Louis Cardinals	1.00	.45	.10
☐ 206	Scott Hunter, Green Bay Packers	.45	.20	.04
☐ 207	Ron Johnson, New York Giants	.30	.12	.03
☐ 208	Sam Brunelli, Denver Broncos	.20	.09	.02
☐ 209	Deacon Jones, Los Angeles Rams	1.50	.70	.15
☐ 210	Fred Biletnikoff, Oakland Raiders	1.50	.70	.15
☐ 211	Bill Nelsen, Cleveland Browns	.50	.22	.05
☐ 212	George Nock, New York Jets	.20	.09	.02
☐ 213	Dan Abramowicz, New Orleans Saints	.30	.12	.03
☐ 214	Irv Goode, St. Louis Cardinals	.20	.09	.02
☐ 215	Isiah Robertson, Los Angeles Rams	.30	.12	.03
☐ 216	Tom Matte, Baltimore Colts	.35	.15	.03
☐ 217	Pat Fischer, Washington Redskins	.30	.12	.03
☐ 218	Gene Washington, San Francisco 49ers	.35	.15	.03
☐ 219	Paul Robinson, Cincinnati Bengals	.20	.09	.02
☐ 220	John Brodie, San Francisco 49ers	2.00	.90	.20
☐ 221	Manny Fernandez, Miami Dolphins	.20	.09	.02
☐ 222	Errol Mann, Detroit Lions	.20	.09	.02
☐ 223	Dick Gordon, Chicago Bears	.20	.09	.02
☐ 224	Calvin Hill, Dallas Cowboys	.50	.22	.05
☐ 225	Fran Tarkenton, New York Giants	5.00	2.35	.50
☐ 226	Jim Turner, Denver Broncos	.35	.15	.03
☐ 227	Jim Mitchell, Atlanta Falcons	.20	.09	.02
☐ 228	Pete Liske, Philadelphia Eagles	.20	.09	.02
☐ 229	Carl Garrett, New England Patriots	.20	.09	.02
☐ 230	Mean Joe Greene, Pittsburgh Steelers	1.75	.85	.17
☐ 231	Gale Gillingham, Green Bay Packers	.20	.09	.02
☐ 232	Norm Bulaich, Baltimore Colts	.30	.12	.03
☐ 233	Spider Lockhart, New York Giants	.20	.09	.02
☐ 234	Ken Willard, San Francisco 49ers	.30	.12	.03
☐ 235	George Blanda, Oakland Raiders	3.00	1.40	.30
☐ 236	Wayne Mulligan, St. Louis Cardinals	.20	.09	.02

		MINT	VG-E	F-G
☐ 237	**Dave Lewis**, Cincinnati Bengals	.20	.09	.02
☐ 238	**Dennis Shaw**, Buffalo Bills	.20	.09	.02
☐ 239	**Fair Hooker**, Cleveland Browns	.20	.09	.02
☐ 240	**Larry Little**, Miami Dolphins	.30	.12	.03
☐ 241	**Mike Garrett**, San Diego Chargers	.35	.15	.03
☐ 242	**Glen Ray Hines**, New Orleans Saints	.20	.09	.02
☐ 243	**Myron Pottios**, Washington Redskins	.20	.09	.02
☐ 244	**Charlie Joiner**, Houston Oilers	2.00	.90	.20
☐ 245	**Len Dawson**, Kansas City Chiefs	2.00	.90	.20
☐ 246	**W.K. Hicks**, New York Jets	.20	.09	.02
☐ 247	**Les Josephson**, Los Angeles Rams	.20	.09	.02
☐ 248	**Lance Alworth**, Dallas Cowboys	1.50	.70	.15
☐ 249	**Frank Nunley**, San Francisco 49ers	.20	.09	.02

IN ACTION CARDS

		MINT	VG-E	F-G
☐ 250	**Mel Farr IA**, Detroit Lions	.25	.10	.02
☐ 251	**Johnny Unitas IA**, Baltimore Colts	2.25	1.00	.22
☐ 252	**George Farmer IA**, Chicago Bears	.20	.09	.02
☐ 253	**Duane Thomas IA**, Dallas Cowboys	.30	.12	.03
☐ 254	**John Hadl IA**, San Diego Chargers	.60	.28	.06
☐ 255	**Vic Washington IA**, San Francisco 49ers	.20	.09	.02
☐ 256	**Don Horn IA**, Denver Broncos	.20	.09	.02
☐ 257	**L.C. Greenwood IA**, Pittsburgh Steelers	.30	.12	.03
☐ 258	**Bob Lee IA**, Minnesota Vikings	.20	.09	.02
☐ 259	**Larry Csonka IA**, Miami Dolphins	.75	.35	.07
☐ 260	**Mike McCoy IA**, Green Bay Packers	.20	.09	.02
☐ 261	**Greg Landry IA**, Detroit Lions	.40	.18	.04
☐ 262	**Ray May IA**, Baltimore Colts	.20	.09	.02
☐ 263	**Bobby Douglass IA**, Chicago Bears	.25	.10	.02

ALL PRO CARDS

		MINT	VG-E	F-G
☐ 264	**Charlie Sanders AP**, Detroit Lions	2.50	1.15	.25
☐ 265	**Ron Yary AP**, Minnesota Vikings	2.50	1.15	.25
☐ 266	**Rayfield Wright AP**, Dallas Cowboys	2.50	1.15	.25
☐ 267	**Larry Little AP**, Miami Dolphins	2.50	1.15	.25
☐ 268	**John Niland AP**, Dallas Cowboys	2.50	1.15	.25
☐ 269	**Forrest Blue AP**, San Francisco 49ers	2.50	1.15	.25
☐ 270	**Otis Taylor AP**, Kansas City Chiefs	2.50	1.15	.25
☐ 271	**Paul Warfield AP**, Miami Dolphins	4.00	1.85	.40

	MINT	VG-E	F-G
☐ 272 Bob Griese AP, Miami Dolphins	5.50	2.60	.55
☐ 273 John Brockington AP, Green Bay Packers	2.50	1.15	.25
☐ 274 Floyd Little AP, Denver Broncos	2.50	1.15	.25
☐ 275 Garo Yepremian AP, Miami Dolphins	2.50	1.15	.25
☐ 276 Jerrell Wilson AP, Kansas City Chiefs	2.50	1.15	.25
☐ 277 Carl Eller AP, Minnesota Vikings	3.00	1.40	.30
☐ 278 Bubba Smith AP, Baltimore Colts	3.00	1.40	.30
☐ 279 Alan Page AP, Minnesota Vikings	3.00	1.40	.30
☐ 280 Bob Lilly AP, Dallas Cowboys	4.00	1.85	.40
☐ 281 Ted Hendricks AP, Baltimore Colts	2.75	1.25	.27
☐ 282 Dave Wilcox AP, San Francisco 49ers	2.50	1.15	.25
☐ 283 Willie Lanier AP, Kansas City Chiefs	2.75	1.25	.27
☐ 284 Jim Johnson AP, San Francisco 49ers	2.50	1.15	.25
☐ 285 Willie Brown AP, Oakland Raiders	3.50	1.65	.35
☐ 286 Bill Bradley AP, Philadelphia Eagles	2.50	1.15	.25
☐ 287 Ken Houston AP, Houston Oilers	2.75	1.25	.27
☐ 288 Mel Farr, Detroit Lions	2.25	1.00	.22
☐ 289 Kermit Alexander, Los Angeles Rams	2.25	1.00	.22
☐ 290 John Gilliam, St. Louis Cardinals	2.25	1.00	.22
☐ 291 Steve Spurrier, San Francisco 49ers	3.00	1.40	.30
☐ 292 Walter Johnson, Cleveland Browns	2.25	1.00	.22
☐ 293 Jack Pardee, Washington Redskins	2.50	1.15	.25
☐ 294 Checklist 264-351	5.00	1.00	.20
☐ 295 Winston Hill, New York Jets	2.25	1.00	.22
☐ 296 Hugo Hollas, New Orleans Saints	2.25	1.00	.22
☐ 297 Ray May, Baltimore Colts	2.25	1.00	.22
☐ 298 Jim Bakken, St. Louis Cardinals	2.50	1.15	.25
☐ 299 Larry Carwell, New England Patriots	2.25	1.00	.22
☐ 300 Alan Page, Minnesota Vikings	3.00	1.40	.30
☐ 301 Walt Garrison, Dallas Cowboys	2.75	1.25	.27
☐ 302 Mike Lucci, Detroit Lions	2.50	1.15	.25
☐ 303 Nemiah Wilson, Oakland Raiders	2.25	1.00	.22
☐ 304 Carroll Dale, Green Bay Packers	2.25	1.00	.22
☐ 305 Jim Kanicki, New York Giants	2.25	1.00	.22
☐ 306 Preston Pearson, Pittsburgh Steelers	2.75	1.25	.27
☐ 307 Lemar Parrish, Cincinnati Bengals	2.25	1.00	.22
☐ 308 Earl Morrall, Baltimore Colts	3.00	1.40	.30
☐ 309 Tommy Nobis, Atlanta Falcons	3.00	1.40	.30
☐ 310 Rich Jackson, Denver Broncos	2.25	1.00	.22
☐ 311 Doug Cunningham, San Francisco 49ers	2.25	1.00	.22
☐ 312 Jim Marsalis, Kansas City Chiefs	2.25	1.00	.22
☐ 313 Jim Beirne, Houston Oilers	2.25	1.00	.22
☐ 314 Tom McNeill, Philadelphia Eagles	2.25	1.00	.22
☐ 315 Milt Morin, Cleveland Browns	2.25	1.00	.22
☐ 316 Rayfield Wright, Dallas Cowboys	2.25	1.00	.22
☐ 317 Jerry LeVias, San Diego Chargers	2.25	1.00	.22

		MINT	VG-E	F-G
☐ 318	**Travis Williams**, Los Angeles Rams	2.50	1.15	.25
☐ 319	**Edgar Chandler**, Buffalo Bills	2.25	1.00	.22
☐ 320	**Bob Wallace**, Chicago Bears	2.25	1.00	.22
☐ 321	**Delles Howell**, New Orleans Saints	2.25	1.00	.22
☐ 322	**Emerson Boozer**, New York Jets	2.25	1.00	.22
☐ 323	**George Atkinson**, Oakland Raiders	2.25	1.00	.22
☐ 324	**Mike Montler**, New England Patriots	2.25	1.00	.22
☐ 325	**Randy Johnson**, New York Jets	2.25	1.00	.22
☐ 326	**Mike Curtis**, Baltimore Colts	2.50	1.15	.25
☐ 327	**Miller Farr**, St. Louis Cardinals	2.25	1.00	.22
☐ 328	**Horst Muhlmann**, Cincinnati Bengals	2.25	1.00	.22
☐ 329	**John Niland**, Dallas Cowboys	2.25	1.00	.22
☐ 330	**Andy Russell**, Pittsburgh Steelers	2.50	1.15	.25
☐ 331	**Mercury Morris**, Miami Dolphins	2.50	1.15	.25
☐ 332	**Jim Johnson**, San Francisco 49ers	2.50	1.15	.25
☐ 333	**Jerrel Wilson**, Kansas City Chiefs	2.25	1.00	.22
☐ 334	**Charley Taylor**, Washington Redskins	4.50	2.10	.45
☐ 335	**Dick LeBeau**, Detroit Lions	2.25	1.00	.22
☐ 336	**Jim Marshall**, Minnesota Vikings	3.00	1.40	.30
☐ 337	**Tom Mack**, Los Angeles Rams	2.50	1.15	.25

IN ACTION CARDS

☐ 338	**Steve Spurrier IA**, San Francisco 49ers	2.50	1.15	.25
☐ 339	**Floyd Little IA**, Denver Broncos	2.50	1.15	.25
☐ 340	**Len Dawson IA**, Kansas City Chiefs	4.00	1.85	.40
☐ 341	**Dick Butkus IA**, Chicago Bears	5.00	2.35	.50
☐ 342	**Larry Brown IA**, Washington Redskins	2.50	1.15	.25
☐ 343	**Joe Namath IA**, New York Jets	11.00	5.25	1.10
☐ 344	**Jim Turner IA**, Denver Broncos	2.25	1.00	.22
☐ 345	**Doug Cunningham IA**, San Francisco 49ers ..	2.25	1.00	.22
☐ 346	**Edd Hargett IA**, New Orleans Saints	2.25	1.00	.22
☐ 347	**Steve Owens IA**, Detroit Lions	2.25	1.00	.22
☐ 348	**George Blanda IA**, Oakland Raiders	6.50	3.00	.65
☐ 349	**Ed Podolak IA**, Kansas City Chiefs	2.25	1.00	.22
☐ 350	**Rich Jackson IA**, Denver Broncos	2.25	1.00	.22
☐ 351	**Ken Willard IA**, San Francisco 49ers	2.50	1.15	.25

1973 TOPPS

The 1973 Topps set marks the first of ten years in a row that Topps settled on a 528-card football set. This is Topps' first large football set which was not issued in series. The cards measure 2½" by 3½". The first six cards in the set are statistical league leader cards. Cards 265-267 are Kid Pictures (KP), showing the player in a boyhood photo. No known scarcities exist. The card backs are printed with blue ink with a red background on gray card stock. The bottom portion of each card back gives a cartoon and trivia question; the question's answer is given, but upside down.

	MINT	VG-E	F-G
COMPLETE SET	70.00	30.00	7.00
COMMON PLAYER (1-528)	.13	.06	.01
☐ 1 **Rushing Leaders**	1.25	.35	.07
Larry Brown			
O.J. Simpson			
☐ 2 **Passing Leaders**	.35	.15	.03
Norm Snead			
Earl Morrall			
☐ 3 **Receiving Leaders**	.40	.18	.04
Harold Jackson			
Fred Biletnikoff			
☐ 4 **Scoring Leaders**	.20	.09	.02
Chester Marcol			
Bobby Howfield			
☐ 5 **Interception Leaders**	.20	.09	.02
Bill Bradley			
Mike Sensibaugh			

		MINT	VG-E	F-G
☐	6 **Punting Leaders**	.20	.09	.02
	Dave Chapple			
	Jerrell Wilson			
☐	7 **Bob Trumpy**, Cincinnati Bengals	.40	.18	.04
☐	8 **Mel Tom**, Philadelphia Eagles	.13	.06	.01
☐	9 **Clarence Ellis**, Atlanta Falcons	.13	.06	.01
☐	10 **John Niland**, Dallas Cowboys	.13	.06	.01
☐	11 **Randy Jackson**, San Francisco 49ers	.13	.06	.01
☐	12 **Greg Landry**, Detroit Lions	.35	.15	.03
☐	13 **Cid Edwards**, San Diego Chargers	.13	.06	.01
☐	14 **Phil Olsen**, Los Angeles Rams	.13	.06	.01
☐	15 **Terry Bradshaw**, Pittsburgh Steelers	3.50	1.65	.35
☐	16 **Al Cowlings**, Houston Oilers	.13	.06	.01
☐	17 **Walker Gillette**, St. Louis Cardinals	.13	.06	.01
☐	18 **Bob Atkins**, Houston Oilers	.13	.06	.01
☐	19 **Diron Talbert**, Washington Redskins	.13	.06	.01
☐	20 **Jim Johnson**, San Francisco 49ers	.20	.09	.02
☐	21 **Howard Twilley**, Miami Dolphins	.20	.09	.02
☐	22 **Dick Enderle**, New York Giants	.13	.06	.01
☐	23 **Wayne Colman**, New Orleans Saints	.13	.06	.01
☐	24 **John Schmitt**, New York Jets	.13	.06	.01
☐	25 **George Blanda**, Oakland Raiders	2.50	1.15	.25
☐	26 **Milt Morin**, Cleveland Browns	.13	.06	.01
☐	27 **Mike Current**, Denver Broncos	.13	.06	.01
☐	28 **Rex Kern**, Baltimore Colts	.20	.09	.02
☐	29 **MacArthur Lane**, Green Bay Packers	.20	.09	.02
☐	30 **Alan Page**, Minnesota Vikings	.75	.35	.07
☐	31 **Randy Vataha**, New England Patriots	.20	.09	.02
☐	32 **Jim Kearney**, Kansas City Chiefs	.13	.06	.01
☐	33 **Steve Smith**, Philadelphia Eagles	.13	.06	.01
☐	34 **Ken Anderson**, Cincinnati Bengals	3.00	1.40	.30
☐	35 **Calvin Hill**, Dallas Cowboys	.40	.18	.04
☐	36 **Andy Maurer**, Atlanta Falcons	.13	.06	.01
☐	37 **Joe Taylor**, Chicago Bears	.13	.06	.01
☐	38 **Deacon Jones**, San Diego Chargers	1.00	.45	.10
☐	39 **Mike Weger**, Detroit Lions	.13	.06	.01
☐	40 **Roy Gerela**, Pittsburgh Steelers	.13	.06	.01
☐	41 **Les Josephson**, Los Angeles Rams	.13	.06	.01
☐	42 **Dave Washington**, Buffalo Bills	.13	.06	.01
☐	43 **Bill Curry**, Houston Oilers	.13	.06	.01
☐	44 **Fred Heron**, St. Louis Cardinals	.13	.06	.01
☐	45 **John Brodie**, San Francisco 49ers	1.50	.70	.15
☐	46 **Roy Winston**, Minnesota Vikings	.13	.06	.01
☐	47 **Mike Bragg**, Washington Redskins	13	.06	.01
☐	48 **Mercury Morris**, Miami Dolphins	.40	.18	.04
☐	49 **Jim Files**, New York Giants	.13	.06	.01

			MINT	VG-E	F-G
☐	50	**Gene Upshaw,** Oakland Raiders	.20	.09	.02
☐	51	**Hugo Hollas,** New Orleans Saints	.13	.06	.01
☐	52	**Rod Sherman,** Los Angeles Rams	.13	.06	.01
☐	53	**Ron Snidow,** Cleveland Browns	.13	.06	.01
☐	54	**Steve Tannen,** New York Jets	.13	.06	.01
☐	55	**Jim Carter,** Green Bay Packers	.13	.06	.01
☐	56	**Lydell Mitchell,** Baltimore Colts	.75	.35	.07
☐	57	**Jack Rudnay,** Kansas City Chiefs	.13	.06	.01
☐	58	**Halvor Hagen,** Buffalo Bills	.13	.06	.01
☐	59	**Tom Dempsey,** Philadelphia Eagles	.20	.09	.02
☐	60	**Fran Tarkenton,** Minnesota Vikings	4.00	1.85	.40
☐	61	**Lance Alworth,** Dallas Cowboys	1.00	.45	.10
☐	62	**Vern Holland,** Cincinnati Bengals	.13	.06	.01
☐	63	**Steve DeLong,** Chicago Bears	.13	.06	.01
☐	64	**Art Malone,** Atlanta Falcons	.13	.06	.01
☐	65	**Isiah Robertson,** Los Angeles Rams	.20	.09	.02
☐	66	**Jerry Rush,** Detroit Lions	.13	.06	.01
☐	67	**Bryant Salter,** San Diego Chargers	.13	.06	.01
☐	68	**Checklist 1-132**	1.00	.20	.04
☐	69	**J.D. Hill,** Buffalo Bills	.13	.06	.01
☐	70	**Forrest Blue,** San Francisco 49ers	.13	.06	.01
☐	71	**Myron Pottios,** Washington Redskins	.13	.06	.01
☐	72	**Norm Thompson,** St. Louis Cardinals	.13	.06	.01
☐	73	**Paul Robinson,** Houston Oilers	.13	.06	.01
☐	74	**Larry Grantham,** New York Jets	.20	.09	.02
☐	75	**Manny Fernandez,** Miami Dolphins	.13	.06	.01
☐	76	**Kent Nix,** Houston Oilers	.13	.06	.01
☐	77	**Art Shell,** Oakland Raiders	.20	.09	.02
☐	78	**George Saimes,** Denver Broncos	.20	.09	.02
☐	79	**Don Cockroft,** Cleveland Browns	.13	.06	.01
☐	80	**Bob Tucker,** New York Giants	.25	.10	.02
☐	81	**Don McCauley,** Baltimore Colts	.13	.06	.01
☐	82	**Bob Brown,** Green Bay Packers	.13	.06	.01
☐	83	**Larry Carwell,** New England Patriots	.13	.06	.01
☐	84	**Mo Moorman,** Kansas City Chiefs	.13	.06	.01
☐	85	**John Gilliam,** Minnesota Vikings	.20	.09	.02
☐	86	**Wade Key,** Philadelphia Eagles	.13	.06	.01
☐	87	**Ross Brupbacher,** Chicago Bears	.13	.06	.01
☐	88	**Dave Lewis,** Cincinnati Bengals	.13	.06	.01
☐	89	**Franco Harris,** Pittsburgh Steelers	6.00	2.80	.60
☐	90	**Tom Mack,** Los Angeles Rams	.20	.09	.02
☐	91	**Mike Tilleman,** Atlanta Falcons	.13	.06	.01
☐	92	**Carl Mauck,** San Diego Chargers	.13	.06	.01
☐	93	**Larry Hand,** Detroit Lions	.13	.06	.01
☐	94	**Dave Foley,** Buffalo Bills	.13	.06	.01
☐	95	**Frank Nunley,** San Francisco 49ers	.13	.06	.01

		MINT	VG-E	F-G
☐ 96	**John Charles,** Houston Oilers	.13	.06	.01
☐ 97	**Jim Bakken,** St. Louis Cardinals	.30	.12	.03
☐ 98	**Pat Fischer,** Washington Redskins	.20	.09	.02
☐ 99	**Randy Rasmussen,** New York Jets	.13	.06	.01
☐ 100	**Larry Csonka,** Miami Dolphins	1.00	.45	.10
☐ 101	**Mike Siani,** Oakland Raiders	.13	.06	.01
☐ 102	**Tom Roussel,** Philadelphia Eagles	.13	.06	.01
☐ 103	**Clarence Scott,** Cleveland Browns	.13	.06	.01
☐ 104	**Charlie Johnson,** Denver Broncos	.45	.20	.04
☐ 105	**Rick Volk,** Baltimore Colts	.13	.06	.01
☐ 106	**Willie Young,** Miami Dolphins	.13	.06	.01
☐ 107	**Emmitt Thomas,** Kansas City Chiefs	.13	.06	.01
☐ 108	**Jon Morris,** New England Patriots	.13	.06	.01
☐ 109	**Clarence Williams,** Green Bay Packers	.13	.06	.01
☐ 110	**Rayfield Wright,** Dallas Cowboys	.13	.06	.01
☐ 111	**Norm Bulaich,** Philadelphia Eagles	.20	.09	.02
☐ 112	**Mike Eischeid,** Minnesota Vikings	.13	.06	.01
☐ 113	**Speedy Thomas,** New Orleans Saints	.13	.06	.01
☐ 114	**Glen Holloway,** Chicago Bears	.13	.06	.01
☐ 115	**Jack Ham,** Pittsburgh Steelers	1.00	.45	.10
☐ 116	**Jim Nettles,** Los Angeles Rams	.13	.06	.01
☐ 117	**Errol Mann,** Detroit Lions	.13	.06	.01
☐ 118	**John Mackey,** San Diego Chargers	.40	.18	.04
☐ 119	**George Kunz,** Atlanta Falcons	.20	.09	.02
☐ 120	**Bob James,** Buffalo Bills	.13	.06	.01
☐ 121	**Garland Boyette,** Houston Oilers	.13	.06	.01
☐ 122	**Mel Phillips,** San Francisco 49ers	.13	.06	.01
☐ 123	**Johnny Roland,** New York Giants	.25	.10	.02
☐ 124	**Doug Swift,** Miami Dolphins	.13	.06	.01
☐ 125	**Archie Manning,** New Orleans Saints	.90	.40	.09
☐ 126	**Dave Herman,** New York Jets	.13	.06	.01
☐ 127	**Carlton Oats,** Green Bay Packers	.13	.06	.01
☐ 128	**Bill Van Heusen,** Denver Broncos	.13	.06	.01
☐ 129	**Rich Jackson,** Cleveland Browns	.13	.06	.01
☐ 130	**Len Hauss,** Washington Redskins	.13	.06	.01
☐ 131	**Billy Parks,** Houston Oilers	.13	.06	.01
☐ 132	**Ray May,** Baltimore Colts	.13	.06	.01
☐ 133	**NFC Semi-Final**	1.00	.45	.10
	Cowboys 30, 49ers 28 (Roger Staubach dropping back)			
☐ 134	**AFC Semi-Final**	.35	.15	.03
	Steelers 13, Raiders 7 (line play)			
☐ 135	**NFC Semi-Final**	.35	.15	.03
	Redskins 16, Packers 3 (Redskins defense)			

		MINT	VG-E	F-G
☐ 136	**AFC Semi-Final**	.75	.35	.07
	Dolphins 20, Browns 14			
	(Bob Griese handing off to Larry Csonka)			
☐ 137	**NFC Title Game**	.65	.30	.06
	Redskins 26, Cowboys 3			
	(Bill Kilmer handing off to Larry Brown)			
☐ 138	**AFC Title Game**	.35	.15	.03
	Dolphins 21, Steelers 17			
	(Miami defense stops Fuqua)			
☐ 139	**Super Bowl**	.65	.30	.06
	Dolphins 14, Redskins 7			
	(Miami defense)			
☐ 140	**Dwight White**, Pittsburgh Steelers	.20	.09	.02
☐ 141	**Jim Marsalis**, Kansas City Chiefs	.13	.06	.01
☐ 142	**Doug Van Horn**, New York Giants	.13	.06	.01
☐ 143	**Al Matthews**, Green Bay Packers	.13	.06	.01
☐ 144	**Bob Windsor**, New England Patriots	.13	.06	.01
☐ 145	**Dave Hampton**, Atlanta Falcons	.13	.06	.01
☐ 146	**Horst Muhlmann**, Cincinnati Bengals	.13	.06	.01
☐ 147	**Wally Hilgenberg**, Minnesota Vikings	.13	.06	.01
☐ 148	**Ron Smith**, San Diego Chargers	.13	.06	.01
☐ 149	**Coy Bacon**, San Diego Chargers	.13	.06	.01
☐ 150	**Winston Hill**, New York Jets	.13	.06	.01
☐ 151	**Ron Jessie**, Detroit Lions	.20	.09	.02
☐ 152	**Ken Iman**, Los Angeles Rams	.13	.06	.01
☐ 153	**Ron Saul**, Houston Oilers	.13	.06	.01
☐ 154	**Jim Braxton**, Buffalo Bills	.13	.06	.01
☐ 155	**Bubba Smith**, Oakland Raiders	.75	.35	.07
☐ 156	**Gary Cuozzo**, St. Louis Cardinals	.20	.09	.02
☐ 157	**Charlie Krueger**, San Francisco 49ers	.13	.06	.01
☐ 158	**Tim Foley**, Miami Dolphins	.13	.06	.01
☐ 159	**Lee Roy Jordan**, Dallas Cowboys	.50	.22	.05
☐ 160	**Bob Brown**, Oakland Raiders	.13	.06	.01
☐ 161	**Margene Adkins**, New York Jets	.13	.06	.01
☐ 162	**Ron Widby**, Green Bay Packers	.13	.06	.01
☐ 163	**Jim Houston**, Cleveland Browns	.13	.06	.01
☐ 164	**Joe Dawkins**, Denver Broncos	.13	.06	.01
☐ 165	**L.C. Greenwood**, Pittsburgh Steelers	.40	.18	.04
☐ 166	**Richmond Flowers**, New York Giants	.13	.06	.01
☐ 167	**Curley Culp**, Kansas City Chiefs	.20	.09	.02
☐ 168	**Len St. Jean**, New England Patriots	.13	.06	.01
☐ 169	**Walter Rock**, Washington Redskins	.13	.06	.01
☐ 170	**Bill Bradley**, Philadelphia Eagles	.20	.09	.02
☐ 171	**Ken Riley**, Cincinnati Bengals	.20	.09	.02
☐ 172	**Rich Coady**, Chicago Bears	.13	.06	.01
☐ 173	**Don Hansen**, Atlanta Falcons	.13	.06	.01

	MINT	VG-E	F-G
☐ 174 **Lionel Aldridge**, San Diego Chargers	.13	.06	.01
☐ 175 **Don Maynard**, St. Louis Cardinals	1.00	.45	.10
☐ 176 **Dave Osborn**, Minnesota Vikings	.13	.06	.01
☐ 177 **Jim Bailey**, Baltimore Colts	.13	.06	.01
☐ 178 **John Pitts**, Buffalo Bills	.13	.06	.01
☐ 179 **Dave Parks**, New Orleans Saints	.20	.09	.02
☐ 180 **Chester Marcol**, Green Bay Packers	.20	.09	.02
☐ 181 **Len Rohde**, San Francisco 49ers	.13	.06	.01
☐ 182 **Jeff Staggs**, St. Louis Cardinals	.13	.06	.01
☐ 183 **Gene Hickerson**, Cleveland Browns	.13	.06	.01
☐ 184 **Charlie Evans**, New York Giants	.13	.06	.01
☐ 185 **Mel Renfro**, Dallas Cowboys	.40	.18	.04
☐ 186 **Marvin Upshaw**, Kansas City Chiefs	.13	.06	.01
☐ 187 **George Atkinson**, Oakland Raiders	.13	.06	.01
☐ 188 **Norm Evans**, Miami Dolphins	.13	.06	.01
☐ 189 **Steve Ramsey**, Denver Broncos	.13	.06	.01
☐ 190 **Dave Chapple**, Los Angeles Rams	.13	.06	.01
☐ 191 **Gerry Mullins**, Pittsburgh Steelers	.13	.06	.01
☐ 192 **John Didion**, New Orleans Saints	.13	.06	.01
☐ 193 **Bob Gladieux**, New England Patriots	.13	.06	.01
☐ 194 **Don Hultz**, Philadelphia Eagles	.13	.06	.01
☐ 195 **Mike Lucci**, Detroit Lions	.20	.09	.02
☐ 196 **John Wilbur**, Washington Redskins	.13	.06	.01
☐ 197 **George Farmer**, Chicago Bears	.13	.06	.01
☐ 198 **Tommy Casanova**, Cincinnati Bengals	.20	.09	.02
☐ 199 **Russ Washington**, San Diego Chargers	.13	.06	.01
☐ 200 **Claude Humphrey**, Atlanta Falcons	.20	.09	.02
☐ 201 **Pat Hughes**, New York Jets	.13	.06	.01
☐ 202 **Zeke Moore**, Houston Oilers	.13	.06	.01
☐ 203 **Chip Glass**, Cleveland Browns	.13	.06	.01
☐ 204 **Glenn Ressler**, Baltimore Colts	.13	.06	.01
☐ 205 **Willie Ellison**, Kansas City Chiefs	.13	.06	.01
☐ 206 **John Leypoldt**, Buffalo Bills	.13	.06	.01
☐ 207 **Johnny Fuller**, San Francisco 49ers	.13	.06	.01
☐ 208 **Bill Hayhoe**, Green Bay Packers	.13	.06	.01
☐ 209 **Ed Bell**, New York Jets	.13	.06	.01
☐ 210 **Willie Brown**, Oakland Raiders	1.00	.45	.10
☐ 211 **Carl Eller**, Minnesota Vikings	.75	.35	.07
☐ 212 **Mark Nordquist**, Philadelphia Eagles	.13	.06	.01
☐ 213 **Larry Willingham**, St. Louis Cardinals	.13	.06	.01
☐ 214 **Nick Buoniconti**, Miami Dolphins	.75	.35	.07
☐ 215 **John Hadl**, Los Angeles Rams	.75	.35	.07
☐ 216 **Jethro Pugh**, Dallas Cowboys	.40	.18	.04
☐ 217 **Leroy Mitchell**, Denver Broncos	.13	.06	.01
☐ 218 **Billy Newsome**, New Orleans Saints	.13	.06	.01
☐ 219 **John McMakin**, Pittsburgh Steelers	.13	.06	.01

		MINT	VG-E	F-G
☐ 220	**Larry Brown**, Washington Redskins	.40	.18	.04
☐ 221	**Clarence Scott**, New England Patriots	.13	.06	.01
☐ 222	**Paul Naumoff**, Detroit Lions	.13	.06	.01
☐ 223	**Ted Fritsch Jr.**, Atlanta Falcons	.13	.06	.01
☐ 224	**Checklist 133-264**	1.00	.20	.04
☐ 225	**Dan Pastorini**, Houston Oilers	.60	.28	.06
☐ 226	**Joe Beauchamp**, Cincinnati Bengals	.13	.06	.01
☐ 227	**Pat Matson**, Cincinnati Bengals	.13	.06	.01
☐ 228	**Tony McGee**, Chicago Bears	.13	.06	.01
☐ 229	**Mike Phipps**, Cleveland Browns	.40	.18	.04
☐ 230	**Harold Jackson**, Los Angeles Rams	.50	.22	.05
☐ 231	**Willie Williams**, New York Giants	.13	.06	.01
☐ 232	**Spike Jones**, Buffalo Bills	.13	.06	.01
☐ 233	**Jim Tyrer**, Kansas City Chiefs	.13	.06	.01
☐ 234	**Roy Hilton**, Baltimore Colts	.13	.06	.01
☐ 235	**Phil Villapiano**, Oakland Raiders	.20	.09	.02
☐ 236	**Charley Taylor**, Washington Redskins	1.00	.45	.10
☐ 237	**Malcolm Snider**, Green Bay Packers	.13	.06	.01
☐ 238	**Vic Washington**, San Francisco 49ers	.13	.06	.01
☐ 239	**Grady Alderman**, Minnesota Vikings	.13	.06	.01
☐ 240	**Dick Anderson**, Miami Dolphins	.25	.10	.02
☐ 241	**Ron Yankowski**, St. Louis Cardinals	.13	.06	.01
☐ 242	**Billy Masters**, Denver Broncos	.13	.06	.01
☐ 243	**Herb Adderly**, Dallas Cowboys	1.00	.45	.10
☐ 244	**David Ray**, Los Angeles Rams	.13	.06	.01
☐ 245	**John Riggins**, New York Jets	1.50	.70	.15
☐ 246	**Mike Wagner**, Pittsburgh Steelers	.20	.09	.02
☐ 247	**Don Morrison**, New Orleans Saints	.13	.06	.01
☐ 248	**Earl McCullouch**, Detroit Lions	.20	.09	.02
☐ 249	**Dennis Wirgowski**, Philadelphia Eagles	.13	.06	.01
☐ 250	**Chris Hanburger**, Washington Redskins	.20	.09	.02
☐ 251	**Pat Sullivan**, Atlanta Falcons	.35	.15	.03
☐ 252	**Walt Sweeney**, San Diego Chargers	.13	.06	.01
☐ 253	**Willie Alexander**, Houston Oilers	.13	.06	.01
☐ 254	**Doug Dressler**, Cincinnati Bengals	.13	.06	.01
☐ 255	**Walter Johnson**, Cleveland Browns	.13	.06	.01
☐ 256	**Ron Hornsby**, New York Giants	.13	.06	.01
☐ 257	**Ben Hawkins**, Philadelphia Eagles	.13	.06	.01
☐ 258	**Donnie Green**, Buffalo Bills	.13	.06	.01
☐ 259	**Fred Hoaglin**, Baltimore Colts	.13	.06	.01
☐ 260	**Jerrel Wilson**, Kansas City Chiefs	.13	.06	.01
☐ 261	**Horace Jones**, Oakland Raiders	.13	.06	.01
☐ 262	**Woody Peoples**, San Francisco 49ers	.13	.06	.01
☐ 263	**Jim Hill**, Green Bay Packers	.13	.06	.01
☐ 264	**John Fuqua**, Pittsburgh Steelers	.13	.06	.01

	MINT	VG-E	F-G

KID PICTURES

		MINT	VG-E	F-G
☐ 265	**Donny Anderson,** St. Louis Cardinals	.20	.09	.02
☐ 266	**Roman Gabriel,** Philadelphia Eagles	.50	.22	.05
☐ 267	**Mike Garrett,** San Diego Chargers	.20	.09	.02
☐ 268	**Rufus Mayes,** Cincinnati Bengals	.13	.06	.01
☐ 269	**Chip Myrtle,** Denver Broncos	.13	.06	.01
☐ 270	**Bill Stanfill,** Miami Dolphins	.20	.09	.02
☐ 271	**Clint Jones,** San Diego Chargers	.13	.06	.01
☐ 272	**Miller Farr,** Detroit Lions	.13	.06	.01
☐ 273	**Harry Schuh,** Los Angeles Rams	.13	.06	.01
☐ 274	**Bob Hayes,** Dallas Cowboys	.50	.22	.05
☐ 275	**Bobby Douglass,** Chicago Bears	.20	.09	.02
☐ 276	**Gus Hollomon,** New York Jets	.13	.06	.01
☐ 277	**Del Williams,** New Orleans Saints	.13	.06	.01
☐ 278	**Julius Adams,** New England Patriots	.13	.06	.01
☐ 279	**Herman Weaver,** Detroit Lions	.13	.06	.01
☐ 280	**Joe Greene,** Pittsburgh Steelers	1.50	.70	.15
☐ 281	**Wes Chesson,** Atlanta Falcons	.13	.06	.01
☐ 282	**Charlie Harraway,** Washington Redskins	.13	.06	.01
☐ 283	**Paul Guidry,** Houston Oilers	.13	.06	.01
☐ 284	**Terry Owens,** Los Angeles Chargers	.13	.06	.01
☐ 285	**Jan Stenerud,** Kansas City Chiefs	.25	.10	.02
☐ 286	**Pete Athas,** New York Giants	.13	.06	.01
☐ 287	**Dale Lindsey,** Los Angeles Raiders	.13	.06	.01
☐ 288	**Jack Tatum,** Oakland Raiders	.40	.18	.04
☐ 289	**Floyd Little,** Denver Broncos	.50	.22	.05
☐ 290	**Bob Johnson,** Cincinnati Bengals	.13	.06	.01
☐ 291	**Tommy Hart,** San Francisco 49ers	.13	.06	.01
☐ 292	**Tom Mitchell,** Baltimore Colts	.13	.06	.01
☐ 293	**Walt Patulski,** Buffalo Bills	.13	.06	.01
☐ 294	**Jim Skaggs,** Philadelphia Eagles	.13	.06	.01
☐ 295	**Bob Griese,** Miami Dolphins	2.50	1.15	.25
☐ 296	**Mike McCoy,** Green Bay Packers	.13	.06	.01
☐ 297	**Mel Gray,** St. Louis Cardinals	.30	.12	.03
☐ 298	**Bobby Bryant,** Minnesota Vikings	.13	.06	.01
☐ 299	**Blaine Nye,** Dallas Cowboys	.13	.06	.01
☐ 300	**Dick Butkus,** Chicago Bears	2.00	.90	.20
☐ 301	**Charlie Cowan,** Los Angeles Rams	.13	.06	.01
☐ 302	**Mark Lomas,** New York Jets	.13	.06	.01
☐ 303	**Josh Ashton,** New England Patriots	.13	.06	.01
☐ 304	**Happy Feller,** New Orleans Saints	.13	.06	.01
☐ 305	**Ron Shanklin,** Pittsburgh Steelers	.13	.06	.01
☐ 306	**Wayne Rasmussen,** Detroit Lions	.13	.06	.01

		MINT	VG-E	F-G
☐ 307	**Jerry Smith**, Washington Redskins	.20	.09	.02
☐ 308	**Ken Reaves**, Atlanta Falcons	.13	.06	.01
☐ 309	**Ron East**, San Diego Chargers	.13	.06	.01
☐ 310	**Otis Taylor**, Kansas City Chiefs	.40	.18	.04
☐ 311	**John Garlington**, Cleveland Browns	.13	.06	.01
☐ 312	**Lyle Alzado**, Denver Broncos	1.25	.60	.12
☐ 313	**Remi Prudhomme**, Buffalo Bills	.13	.06	.01
☐ 314	**Cornelius Johnson**, Baltimore Colts	.13	.06	.01
☐ 315	**Lemar Parrish**, Cincinnati Bengals	.13	.06	.01
☐ 316	**Jim Kiick**, Miami Dolphins	.20	.09	.02
☐ 317	**Steve Zabel**, Philadelphia Eagles	.13	.06	.01
☐ 318	**Alden Roche**, Green Bay Packers	.13	.06	.01
☐ 319	**Tom Blanchard**, New York Giants	.13	.06	.01
☐ 320	**Fred Biletnikoff**, Oakland Raiders	1.00	.45	.10
☐ 321	**Ralph Neely**, Dallas Cowboys	.20	.09	.02
☐ 322	**Dan Dierdorf**, St. Louis Cardinals	.20	.09	.02
☐ 323	**Richard Caster**, New York Jets	.25	.10	.02
☐ 324	**Gene Howard**, Los Angeles Rams	.13	.06	.01
☐ 325	**Elvin Bethea**, Houston Oilers	.20	.09	.02
☐ 326	**Carl Garrett**, Chicago Bears	.13	.06	.01
☐ 327	**Ron Billingsley**, New Orleans Saints	.13	.06	.01
☐ 328	**Charlie West**, Minnesota Vikings	.13	.06	.01
☐ 329	**Tom Neville**, New England Patriots	.13	.06	.01
☐ 330	**Ted Kwalick**, San Francisco 49ers	.20	.09	.02
☐ 331	**Rudy Redmond**, Detroit Lions	.13	.06	.01
☐ 332	**Henry Davis**, Pittsburgh Steelers	.13	.06	.01
☐ 333	**John Zook**, Atlanta Falcons	.20	.09	.02
☐ 334	**Jim Turner**, Denver Broncos	.25	.10	.02
☐ 335	**Len Dawson**, Kansas City Chiefs	1.50	.70	.15
☐ 336	**Bob Chandler**, Buffalo Bills	.20	.09	.02
☐ 337	**Al Beauchamp**, Cincinnati Bengals	.13	.06	.01
☐ 338	**Tom Matte**, San Diego Chargers	.25	.10	.02
☐ 339	**Paul Laaveg**, Washington Redskins	.13	.06	.01
☐ 340	**Ken Ellis**, Green Bay Packers	.13	.06	.01
☐ 341	**Jim Langer**, Miami Dolphins	.13	.06	.01
☐ 342	**Ron Porter**, Minnesota Vikings	.13	.06	.01
☐ 343	**Jack Youngblood**, Los Angeles Rams	1.25	.60	.12
☐ 344	**Cornell Green**, Dallas Cowboys	.30	.12	.03
☐ 345	**Marv Hubbard**, Oakland Raiders	.20	.09	.02
☐ 346	**Bruce Taylor**, San Francisco 49ers	.20	.09	.02
☐ 347	**Sam Havrilak**, Baltimore Colts	.13	.06	.01
☐ 348	**Walt Sumner**, Cleveland Browns	.13	.06	.01
☐ 349	**Steve O'Neal**, New Orleans Saints	.13	.06	.01
☐ 350	**Ron Johnson**, New York Giants	.25	.10	.02
☐ 351	**Rockne Freitas**, Detroit Lions	.13	.06	.01
☐ 352	**Larry Stallings**, St. Louis Cardinals	.13	.06	.01

	MINT	VG-E	F-G
☐ 353 **Jim Cadile**, Chicago Bears	.13	.06	.01
☐ 354 **Ken Burrough**, Houston Oilers	.20	.09	.02
☐ 355 **Jim Plunkett**, New England Patriots	1.00	.45	.10
☐ 356 **Dave Long**, New Orleans Saints	.13	.06	.01
☐ 357 **Ralph Anderson**, New England Patriots	.13	.06	.01
☐ 358 **Checklist 265-396**	1.00	.20	.04
☐ 359 **Gene Washington**, San Francisco 49ers	.30	.12	.03
☐ 360 **Dave Wilcox**, San Francisco 49ers	.20	.09	.02
☐ 361 **Paul Smith**, Denver Broncos	.13	.06	.01
☐ 362 **Alvin Wyatt**, Houston Oilers	.13	.06	.01
☐ 363 **Charlie Smith**, Oakland Raiders	.13	.06	.01
☐ 364 **Royce Berry**, Cincinnati Bengals	.13	.06	.01
☐ 365 **Dave Elmendorf**, Los Angeles Rams	.13	.06	.01
☐ 366 **Scott Hunter**, Green Bay Packers	.35	.15	.03
☐ 367 **Bob Kuechenberg**, Miami Dolphins	.13	.06	.01
☐ 368 **Pete Gogolak**, New York Giants	.20	.09	.02
☐ 369 **Dave Edwards**, Dallas Cowboys	.13	.06	.01
☐ 370 **Lem Barney**, Detroit Lions	.20	.09	.02
☐ 371 **Verlon Biggs**, Washington Redskins	.13	.06	.01
☐ 372 **John Reaves**, Philadelphia Eagles	.20	.09	.02
☐ 373 **Ed Podolak**, Kansas City Chiefs	.20	.09	.02
☐ 374 **Chris Farasopoulos**, New York Jets	.13	.06	.01
☐ 375 **Gary Garrison**, San Diego Chargers	.13	.06	.01
☐ 376 **Tom Funchess**, Houston Oilers	.13	.06	.01
☐ 377 **Bobby Joe Green**, Chicago Bears	.13	.06	.01
☐ 378 **Don Brumm**, St. Louis Cardinals	.13	.06	.01
☐ 379 **Jim O'Brien**, Detroit Lions	.13	.06	.01
☐ 380 **Paul Krause**, Minnesota Vikings	.20	.09	.02
☐ 381 **Leroy Kelly**, Cleveland Browns	.45	.20	.04
☐ 382 **Ray Mansfield**, Pittsburgh Steelers	.13	.06	.01
☐ 383 **Dan Abramowicz**, New Orleans Saints	.20	.09	.02
☐ 384 **John Outlaw**, Philadelphia Eagles	.13	.06	.01
☐ 385 **Tommy Nobis**, Atlanta Falcons	.75	.35	.07
☐ 386 **Tom Domres**, Denver Broncos	.13	.06	.01
☐ 387 **Ken Willard**, San Francisco 49ers	.25	.10	.02
☐ 388 **Mike Stratton**, San Diego Chargers	.13	.06	.01
☐ 389 **Fred Dryer**, Los Angeles Rams	.75	.35	.07
☐ 390 **Jake Scott**, Miami Dolphins	.20	.09	.02
☐ 391 **Rich Houston**, New York Giants	.13	.06	.01
☐ 392 **Virgil Carter**, Cincinnati Bengals	.20	.09	.02
☐ 393 **Tody Smith**, Houston Oilers	.13	.06	.01
☐ 394 **Ernie Calloway**, Philadelphia Eagles	.13	.06	.01
☐ 395 **Charlie Sanders**, Detroit Lions	.20	.09	.02
☐ 396 **Fred Willis**, Houston Oilers	.13	.06	.01
☐ 397 **Curt Knight**, Washington Redskins	.13	.06	.01
☐ 398 **Nemiah Wilson**, Oakland Raiders	.13	.06	.01

	MINT	VG-E	F-G
☐ 399 **Carroll Dale**, Minnesota Vikings	.13	.06	.01
☐ 400 **Joe Namath**, New York Jets	5.50	2.60	.55
☐ 401 **Wayne Mulligan**, St. Louis Cardinals	.13	.06	.01
☐ 402 **Jim Harrison**, Chicago Bears	.13	.06	.01
☐ 403 **Tim Rossovich**, San Diego Chargers	.20	.09	.02
☐ 404 **David Lee**, Baltimore Colts	.13	.06	.01
☐ 405 **Frank Pitts**, Cleveland Browns	.13	.06	.01
☐ 406 **Jim Marshall**, Minnesota Vikings	.75	.35	.07
☐ 407 **Bob Brown**, New Orleans Saints	.13	.06	.01
☐ 408 **John Rowser**, Pittsburgh Steelers	.13	.06	.01
☐ 409 **Mike Montler**, Buffalo Bills	.13	.06	.01
☐ 410 **Willie Lanier**, Kansas City Chiefs	.50	.22	.05
☐ 411 **Bill Bell**, New England Patriots	.13	.06	.01
☐ 412 **Cedric Hardman**, San Francisco 49ers	.20	.09	.02
☐ 413 **Bob Anderson**, Denver Broncos	.20	.09	.02
☐ 414 **Earl Morrall**, Miami Dolphins	.75	.35	.07
☐ 415 **Ken Houston**, Washington Redskins	.30	.12	.03
☐ 416 **Jack Snow**, Los Angeles Rams	.20	.09	.02
☐ 417 **Dick Cunningham**, Philadelphia Eagles	.13	.06	.01
☐ 418 **Greg Larson**, New York Giants	.13	*.06	.01
☐ 419 **Mike Bass**, Washington Redskins	.13	.06	.01
☐ 420 **Mike Reid**, Cincinnati Bengals	.20	.09	.02
☐ 421 **Walt Garrison**, Dallas Cowboys	.40	.18	.04
☐ 422 **Pete Liske**, Philadelphia Eagles	.20	.09	.02
☐ 423 **Jim Yarbrough**, Detroit Lions	.13	.06	.01
☐ 424 **Rich McGeorge**, Green Bay Packers	.13	.06	.01
☐ 425 **Bobby Howfield**, New York Jets	.13	.06	.01
☐ 426 **Pete Banaszak**, Oakland Raiders	.13	.06	.01
☐ 427 **Willie Holman**, Chicago Bears	.13	.06	.01
☐ 428 **Dale Hackbart**, Denver Broncos	.13	.06	.01
☐ 429 **Fair Hooker**, Cleveland Browns	.13	.06	.01
☐ 430 **Ted Hendricks**, Baltimore Colts	.40	.18	.04
☐ 431 **Mike Garrett**, San Diego Chargers	.25	.10	.02
☐ 432 **Glen Ray Hines**, Pittsburgh Steelers	.13	.06	.01
☐ 433 **Fred Cox**, Minnesota Vikings	.25	.10	.02
☐ 434 **Bobby Walden**, Pittsburgh Steelers	.13	.06	.01
☐ 435 **Bobby Bell**, Kansas City Chiefs	1.00	.45	.10
☐ 436 **Dave Rowe**, New England Patriots	.13	.06	.01
☐ 437 **Bob Berry**, Minnesota Vikings	.20	.09	.02
☐ 438 **Bill Thompson**, Denver Broncos	.20	.09	.02
☐ 439 **Jim Beirne**, Houston Oilers	.13	.06	.01
☐ 440 **Larry Little**, Miami Dolphins	.20	.09	.02
☐ 441 **Rocky Thompson**, New York Giants	.13	.06	.01
☐ 442 **Brig Owens**, Washington Redskins	.13	.06	.01
☐ 443 **Richard Neal**, New York Jets	.13	.06	.01
☐ 444 **Al Nelson**, Philadelphia Eagles	.13	.06	.01

		MINT	VG-E	F-G
☐ 445	**Chip Myers**, Cincinnati Bengals	.13	.06	.01
☐ 446	**Ken Bowman**, Green Bay Packers	.13	.06	.01
☐ 447	**Jim Purnell**, Los Angeles Rams	.13	.06	.01
☐ 448	**Altie Taylor**, Detroit Lions	.13	.06	.01
☐ 449	**Linzy Cole**, Buffalo Bills	.13	.06	.01
☐ 450	**Bob Lilly**, Dallas Cowboys	1.25	.60	.12
☐ 451	**Charlie Ford**, Chicago Bears	.13	.06	.01
☐ 452	**Milt Sunde**, Minnesota Vikings	.13	.06	.01
☐ 453	**Doug Wyatt**, Detroit Lions	.13	.06	.01
☐ 454	**Don Nottingham**, Baltimore Colts	.13	.06	.01
☐ 455	**John Unitas**, San Diego Chargers	4.00	1.85	.40
☐ 456	**Frank Lewis**, Pittsburgh Steelers	.35	.15	.03
☐ 457	**Roger Wehrli**, St. Louis Cardinals	.25	.10	.02
☐ 458	**Jim Cheyunski**, Buffalo Bills	.13	.06	.01
☐ 459	**Jerry Sherk**, Cleveland Browns	.20	.09	.02
☐ 460	**Gene Washington**, San Francisco 49ers	.25	.10	.02
☐ 461	**Jim Otto**, Oakland Raiders	1.00	.45	.10
☐ 462	**Ed Budde**, Kansas City Chiefs	.20	.09	.02
☐ 463	**Jim Mitchell**, Atlanta Falcons	.13	.06	.01
☐ 464	**Emerson Boozer**, New York Jets	.20	.09	.02
☐ 465	**Garo Yepremian**, Miami Dolphins	.25	.10	.02
☐ 466	**Pete Duranko**, Denver Broncos	.13	.06	.01
☐ 467	**Charlie Joiner**, Cincinnati Bengals	1.00	.45	.10
☐ 468	**Spider Lockhart**, New York Giants	.13	.06	.01
☐ 469	**Marty Domres**, Baltimore Colts	.20	.09	.02
☐ 470	**John Brockington**, Green Bay Packers	.30	.12	.03
☐ 471	**Ed Flanagan**, Detroit Lions	.13	.06	.01
☐ 472	**Roy Jefferson**, Washington Redskins	.20	.09	.02
☐ 473	**Julian Fagan**, New York Jets	.13	.06	.01
☐ 474	**Bill Brown**, Minnesota Vikings	.20	.09	.02
☐ 475	**Roger Staubach**, Dallas Cowboys	4.50	2.10	.45
☐ 476	**Jan White**, Buffalo Bills	.13	.06	.01
☐ 477	**Pat Holmes**, Kansas City Chiefs	.13	.06	.01
☐ 478	**Bob DeMarco**, Cleveland Browns	.13	.06	.01
☐ 479	**Merlin Olsen**, Los Angeles Rams	1.25	.60	.12
☐ 480	**Andy Russell**, Pittsburgh Steelers	.20	.09	.02
☐ 481	**Steve Spurrier**, San Francisco 49ers	.40	.18	.04
☐ 482	**Nate Ramsey**, New Orleans Saints	.13	.06	.01
☐ 483	**Dennis Partee**, San Diego Chargers	.13	.06	.01
☐ 484	**Jerry Simmons**, Denver Broncos	.13	.06	.01
☐ 485	**Donny Anderson**, St. Louis Cardinals	.25	.10	.02
☐ 486	**Ralph Baker**, New York Jets	.13	.06	.01
☐ 487	**Ken Stabler**, Oakland Raiders	2.50	1.15	.25
☐ 488	**Ernie McMillan**, St. Louis Cardinals	.13	.06	.01
☐ 489	**Ken Burrow**, Atlanta Falcons	.13	.06	.01
☐ 490	**Jack Gregory**, New York Giants	.20	.09	.02

	MINT	VG-E	F-G
☐ 491 **Larry Sieple**, Miami Dolphins	.13	.06	.01
☐ 492 **Mick Tingelhoff**, Minnesota Vikings	.30	.12	.03
☐ 493 **Craig Morton**, Dallas Cowboys	.90	.40	.09
☐ 494 **Cecil Turner**, Chicago Bears	.13	.06	.01
☐ 495 **Steve Owens**, Detroit Lions	.30	.12	.03
☐ 496 **Rickie Harris**, New England Patriots	.13	.06	.01
☐ 497 **Buck Buchanan**, Kansas City Chiefs	.40	.18	.04
☐ 498 **Checklist 397-528**	1.00	.20	.04
☐ 499 **Bill Kilmer**, Washington Redskins	.75	.35	.07
☐ 500 **O.J. Simpson**, Buffalo Bills	4.50	2.10	.45
☐ 501 **Bruce Gossett**, San Francisco 49ers	.13	.06	.01
☐ 502 **Art Thoms**, Oakland Raiders	.13	.06	.01
☐ 503 **Larry Kaminski**, Denver Broncos	.13	.06	.01
☐ 504 **Larry Smith**, Houston Oilers	.13	.06	.01
☐ 505 **Bruce Van Dyke**, Pittsburgh Steelers	.13	.06	.01
☐ 506 **Alvin Reed**, Washington Redskins	.13	.06	.01
☐ 507 **Delles Howell**, New York Jets	.13	.06	.01
☐ 508 **Leroy Keyes**, Kansas City Chiefs	.20	.09	.02
☐ 509 **Bo Scott**, Cleveland Browns	.13	.06	.01
☐ 510 **Ron Yary**, Minnesota Vikings	.20	.09	.02
☐ 511 **Paul Warfield**, Miami Dolphins	1.00	.45	.10
☐ 512 **Mac Percival**, Chicago Bears	.13	.06	.01
☐ 513 **Essex Johnson**, Cincinnati Bengals	.13	.06	.01
☐ 514 **Jackie Smith**, St. Louis Cardinals	.25	.10	.02
☐ 515 **Norm Snead**, New York Giants	.35	.15	.03
☐ 516 **Charlie Stukes**, Los Angeles Rams	.13	.06	.01
☐ 517 **Reggie Rucker**, New England Patriots	.20	.09	.02
☐ 518 **Bill Sandeman**, Atlanta Falcons	.13	.06	.01
☐ 519 **Mel Farr**, Detroit Lions	.20	.09	.02
☐ 520 **Raymond Chester**, Baltimore Colts	.25	.10	.02
☐ 521 **Fred Carr**, Green Bay Packers	.13	.06	.01
☐ 522 **Jerry LeVias**, San Diego Chargers	.13	.06	.01
☐ 523 **Jim Strong**, New Orleans Saints	.13	.06	.01
☐ 524 **Ron McDole**, Washington Redskins	.13	.06	.01
☐ 525 **Dennis Shaw**, Buffalo Bills	.13	.06	.01
☐ 526 **Dave Manders**, Dallas Cowboys	.13	.06	.01
☐ 527 **Skip Vanderbundt**, San Francisco 49ers	.13	.06	.01
☐ 528 **Mike Sensibaugh**, Kansas City Chiefs	.20	.09	.02

1974 TOPPS

The 1974 Topps set contains 528 cards. The cards measure 2½" by 3½". Cards 328-333 present the statistical league leaders from each league. This set contains the rookie card of Bert Jones. No known scarcities exist. The card backs are printed in blue and yellow on gray card stock. The bottom of the reverse provided part of a simulated football game which could be played by drawing cards.

		MINT	VG-E	F-G
	COMPLETE SET	65.00	30.00	6.50
	COMMON PLAYER (1-528)	.12	.05	.01
☐	1 O.J. Simpson, Buffalo Bills	4.50	1.50	.30
☐	2 Blaine Nye, Dallas Cowboys	.12	.05	.01
☐	3 Don Hansen, Atlanta Falcons	.12	.05	.01
☐	4 Ken Bowman, Green Bay Packers	.12	.05	.01
☐	5 Carl Eller, Minnesota Vikings	.75	.35	.07
☐	6 Jerry Smith, Washington Redskins	.20	.09	.02
☐	7 Ed Podolak, Kansas City Chiefs	.20	.09	.02
☐	8 Mel Gray, St. Louis Cardinals	.25	.10	.02
☐	9 Pat Matson, Cincinnati Bengals	.12	.05	.01
☐	10 Floyd Little, Denver Broncos	.45	.20	.04
☐	11 Frank Pitts, Cleveland Browns	.12	.05	.01
☐	12 Vern Den Herder, Miami Dolphins	.12	.05	.01
☐	13 John Fuqua, Pittsburgh Steelers	.12	.05	.01
☐	14 Jack Tatum, Oakland Raiders	.30	.12	.03
☐	15 Winston Hill, New York Jets	.12	.05	.01
☐	16 John Beasley, New Orleans Saints	.12	.05	.01
☐	17 David Lee, Baltimore Colts	.12	.05	.01
☐	18 Rich Coady, Chicago Bears	.12	.05	.01

		MINT	VG-E	F-G
☐	19 **Ken Willard,** San Francisco 49ers	.20	.09	.02
☐	20 **Coy Bacon,** San Diego Chargers	.12	.05	.01
☐	21 **Ben Hawkins,** Philadelphia Eagles	.12	.05	.01
☐	22 **Paul Guidry,** Houston Oilers	.12	.05	.01
☐	23 **Norm Snead,** New York Giants	.35	.15	.03
☐	24 **Jim Yarbrough,** Detroit Lions	.12	.05	.01
☐	25 **Jack Reynolds,** Los Angeles Rams	.12	.05	.01
☐	26 **Josh Ashton,** New England Patriots	.12	.05	.01
☐	27 **Donnie Green,** Buffalo Bills	.12	.05	.01
☐	28 **Bob Hayes,** Dallas Cowboys	.50	.22	.05
☐	29 **John Zook,** Atlanta Falcons	.20	.09	.02
☐	30 **Bobby Bryant,** Minnesota Vikings	.12	.05	.01
☐	31 **Scott Hunter,** Green Bay Packers	.30	.12	.03
☐	32 **Dan Dierdorf,** St. Louis Cardinals	.20	.09	.02
☐	33 **Curt Knight,** Washington Redskins	.12	.05	.01
☐	34 **Elmo Wright,** Kansas City Chiefs	.20	.09	.02
☐	35 **Essex Johnson,** Cincinnati Bengals	.12	.05	.01
☐	36 **Walt Sumner,** Cleveland Browns	.12	.05	.01
☐	37 **Marv Montgomery,** Denver Broncos	.12	.05	.01
☐	38 **Tim Foley,** Miami Dolphins	.12	.05	.01
☐	39 **Mike Siani,** Oakland Raiders	.12	.05	.01
☐	40 **Joe Greene,** Pittsburgh Steelers	1.25	.60	.12
☐	41 **Bobby Howfield,** New York Jets	.12	.05	.01
☐	42 **Del Williams,** New Orleans Saints	.12	.05	.01
☐	43 **Don McCauley,** Baltimore Colts	.12	.05	.01
☐	44 **Randy Jackson,** San Francisco 49ers	.12	.05	.01
☐	45 **Ron Smith,** San Diego Chargers	.12	.05	.01
☐	46 **Gene Washington,** San Francisco 49ers	.25	.10	.02
☐	47 **Po James,** Philadelphia Eagles	.12	.05	.01
☐	48 **Solomon Freelon,** Houston Oilers	.12	.05	.01
☐	49 **Bob Windsor,** New England Patriots	.12	.05	.01
☐	50 **John Hadl,** Los Angeles Rams	.75	.35	.07
☐	51 **Greg Larson,** New York Giants	.12	.05	.01
☐	52 **Steve Owens,** Detroit Lions	.25	.10	.02
☐	53 **Jim Cheyunski,** Buffalo Bills	.12	.05	.01
☐	54 **Rayfield Wright,** Dallas Cowboys	.12	.05	.01
☐	55 **Dave Hampton,** Atlanta Falcons	.12	.05	.01
☐	56 **Ron Widby,** Green Bay Packers	.12	.05	.01
☐	57 **Milt Sunde,** Minnesota Vikings	.12	.05	.01
☐	58 **Bill Kilmer,** Washington Redskins	.75	.35	.07
☐	59 **Bobby Bell,** Kansas City Chiefs	.75	.35	.07
☐	60 **Jim Bakken,** St. Louis Cardinals	.25	.10	.02
☐	61 **Rufus Mayes,** Cincinnati Bengals	.12	.05	.01
☐	62 **Vic Washington,** San Francisco 49ers	.12	.05	.01
☐	63 **Gene Washington,** Minnesota Vikings	.20	.09	.02
☐	64 **Clarence Scott,** Cleveland Browns	.12	.05	.01

		MINT	VG-E	F-G
☐ 65	**Gene Upshaw**, Oakland Raiders	.20	.09	.02
☐ 66	**Larry Seiple**, Miami Dolphins	.12	.05	.01
☐ 67	**John McMakin**, Pittsburgh Steelers	.12	.05	.01
☐ 68	**Ralph Baker**, New York Jets	.12	.05	.01
☐ 69	**Lydell Mitchell**, Baltimore Colts	.35	.15	.03
☐ 70	**Archie Manning**, New Orleans Saints	.90	.40	.09
☐ 71	**George Farmer**, Chicago Bears	.12	.05	.01
☐ 72	**Ron East**, San Diego Chargers	.12	.05	.01
☐ 73	**Al Nelson**, Philadelphia Eagles	.12	.05	.01
☐ 74	**Pat Hughes**, New York Giants	.12	.05	.01
☐ 75	**Fred Willis**, Houston Oilers	.12	.05	.01
☐ 76	**Larry Walton**, Detroit Lions	.12	.05	.01
☐ 77	**Tom Neville**, New England Patriots	.12	.05	.01
☐ 78	**Ted Kwalick**, San Francisco 49ers	.20	.09	.02
☐ 79	**Walt Patulski**, Buffalo Bills	.12	.05	.01
☐ 80	**John Niland**, Dallas Cowboys	.12	.05	.01
☐ 81	**Ted Fritsch Jr.**, Atlanta Falcons	.12	.05	.01
☐ 82	**Paul Krause**, Minnesota Vikings	.20	.09	.02
☐ 83	**Jack Snow**, Los Angeles Rams	.20	.09	.02
☐ 84	**Mike Bass**, Washington Redskins	.12	.05	.01
☐ 85	**Jim Tyrer**, Kansas City Chiefs	.12	.05	.01
☐ 86	**Ron Yankowski**, St. Louis Cardinals	.12	.05	.01
☐ 87	**Mike Phipps**, Cleveland Browns	.35	.15	.03
☐ 88	**Al Beauchamp**, Cincinnati Bengals	.12	.05	.01
☐ 89	**Riley Odoms**, Denver Broncos	.40	.18	.04
☐ 90	**McArthur Lane**, Green Bay Packers	.20	.09	.02
☐ 91	**Art Thoms**, Oakland Raiders	.12	.05	.01
☐ 92	**Marlin Briscoe**, Miami Dolphins	.20	.09	.02
☐ 93	**Bruce Van Dyke**, Pittsburgh Steelers	.12	.05	.01
☐ 94	**Tom Myers**, New Orleans Saints	.12	.05	-.01
☐ 95	**Calvin Hill**, Dallas Cowboys	.40	.18	.04
☐ 96	**Bruce Laird**, Baltimore Colts	.12	.05	.01
☐ 97	**Tony McGee**, Chicago Bears	.12	.05	.01
☐ 98	**Len Rohde**, San Francisco 49ers	.12	.05	.01
☐ 99	**Tom McNeill**, Philadelphia Eagles	.12	.05	.01
☐ 100	**Delles Howell**, New York Jets	.12	.05	.01
☐ 101	**Gary Garrison**, San Diego Chargers	.12	.05	.01
☐ 102	**Dan Goich**, New York Giants	.12	.05	.01
☐ 103	**Len St. Jean**, New England Patriots	.12	.05	.01
☐ 104	**Zeke Moore**, Houston Oilers	.12	.05	.01
☐ 105	**Ahmad Rashad**, St. Louis Cardinals	1.00	.45	.10
☐ 106	**Mel Renfro**, Dallas Cowboys	.40	.18	.04
☐ 107	**Jim Mitchell**, Detroit Lions	.12	.05	.01
☐ 108	**Ed Budde**, Kansas City Chiefs	.12	.05	.01
☐ 109	**Harry Schuh**, Los Angeles Rams	.12	.05	.01
☐ 110	**Greg Pruitt**, Cleveland Browns	.75	.35	.07

	MINT	VG-E	F-G
☐ 111 **Ed Flanagan**, Detroit Lions	.12	.05	.01
☐ 112 **Larry Stallings**, St. Louis Cardinals	.12	.05	.01
☐ 113 **Chuck Foreman**, Minnesota Vikings	.90	.40	.09
☐ 114 **Royce Berry**, Cincinnati Bengals	.12	.05	.01
☐ 115 **Gale Gillingham**, Green Bay Packers	.12	.05	.01
☐ 116 **Charlie Johnson**, Denver Broncos	.50	.22	.05
☐ 117 **Checklist 1-132**	.90	.15	.03
☐ 118 **Bill Butler**, Houston Oilers	.12	.05	.01
☐ 119 **Roy Jefferson**, Washington Redskins	.20	.09	.02
☐ 120 **Bobby Douglass**, Chicago Bears	.20	.09	.02

ALL PROS 121-144

	MINT	VG-E	F-G
☐ 121 **Harold Carmichael AP**, Philadelphia Eagles ..	1.25	.60	.12
☐ 122 **George Kunz AP**, Atlanta Falcons	.20	.09	.02
☐ 123 **Larry Little AP**, Miami Dolphins	.20	.09	.02
☐ 124 **Forrest Blue AP**, San Francisco 49ers	.20	.09	.02
☐ 125 **Ron Yary AP**, Minnesota Vikings	.20	.09	.02
☐ 126 **Tom Mack AP**, Los Angeles Rams	.20	.09	.02
☐ 127 **Bob Tucker AP**, New York Giants	.20	.09	.02
☐ 128 **Paul Warfield AP**, Miami Dolphins	1.00	.45	.10
☐ 129 **Fran Tarkenton AP**, Minnesota Vikings	3.50	1.65	.35
☐ 130 **O.J. Simpson AP**, Buffalo Bills	4.00	1.85	.40
☐ 131 **Larry Csonka AP**, Miami Dolphins	1.00	.45	.10
☐ 132 **Bruce Gossett AP**, San Francisco 49ers	.20	.09	.02
☐ 133 **Bill Stanfill AP**, Miami Dolphins	.20	.09	.02
☐ 134 **Alan Page AP**, Minnesota Vikings	.75	.35	.07
☐ 135 **Paul Smith AP**, Denver Broncos	.12	.05	.01
☐ 136 **Claude Humphrey AP**, Atlanta Falcons	.12	.05	.01
☐ 137 **Jack Ham AP**, Pittsburgh Steelers	.40	.18	.04
☐ 138 **Lee Roy Jordan AP**, Dallas Cowboys	.40	.18	.04
☐ 139 **Phil Villapiano AP**, Oakland Raiders	.20	.09	.02
☐ 140 **Ken Ellis AP**, Green Bay Packers	.20	.09	.02
☐ 141 **Willie Brown AP**, Oakland Raiders	1.00	.45	.10
☐ 142 **Dick Anderson AP**, Miami Dolphins	.20	.09	.02
☐ 143 **Bill Bradley AP**, Philadelphia Eagles	.20	.09	.02
☐ 144 **Jerrel Wilson AP**, Kansas City Chiefs	.12	.05	.01
☐ 145 **Reggie Rucker**, New England Patriots	.20	.09	.02
☐ 146 **Marty Domres**, Baltimore Colts	.20	.09	.02
☐ 147 **Bob Kowalkowski**, Detroit Lions	.12	.05	.01
☐ 148 **John Matuszak**, Houston Oilers	.65	.30	.06
☐ 149 **Mike Adamle**, New York Jets	.20	.09	.02
☐ 150 **John Unitas**, San Diego Chargers	3.50	1.65	.35

		MINT	VG-E	F-G
☐ 151	**Charlie Ford**, Chicago Bears	.12	.05	.01
☐ 152	**Bob Klein**, Los Angeles Rams	.12	.05	.01
☐ 153	**Jim Merlo**, New Orleans Saints	.12	.05	.01
☐ 154	**Willie Young**, New York Giants	.12	.05	.01
☐ 155	**Donny Anderson**, St. Louis Cardinals	.25	.10	.02
☐ 156	**Brig Owens**, Washington Redskins	.12	.05	.01
☐ 157	**Bruce Jarvis**, Buffalo Bills	.12	.05	.01
☐ 158	**Ron Carpenter**, Cincinnati Bengals	.12	.05	.01
☐ 159	**Don Cockroft**, Cleveland Browns	.12	.05	.01
☐ 160	**Tommy Nobis**, Atlanta Falcons	.60	.28	.06
☐ 161	**Craig Morton**, Dallas Cowboys	.75	.35	.07
☐ 162	**John Staggers**, Green Bay Packers	.12	.05	.01
☐ 163	**Mike Eischeid**, Minnesota Vikings	.12	.05	.01
☐ 164	**Jerry Sisemore**, Philadelphia Eagles	.12	.05	.01
☐ 165	**Cedric Hardman**, San Francisco 49ers	.12	.05	.01
☐ 166	**Bill Thompson**, Denver Broncos	.12	.05	.01
☐ 167	**Jim Lynch**, Kansas City Chiefs	.12	.05	.01
☐ 168	**Bob Moore**, Oakland Raiders	.12	.05	.01
☐ 169	**Glen Edwards**, Pittsburgh Steelers	.12	.05	.01
☐ 170	**Mercury Morris**, Miami Dolphins	.35	.15	.03
☐ 171	**Julius Adams**, New England Patriots	.12	.05	.01
☐ 172	**Cotton Speyrer**, Baltimore Colts	.12	.05	.01
☐ 173	**Bill Munson**, Detroit Lions	.30	.12	.03
☐ 174	**Benny Johnson**, Houston Oilers	.12	.05	.01
☐ 175	**Burgess Owens**, New York Jets	.12	.05	.01
☐ 176	**Cid Edwards**, San Diego Chargers	.12	.05	.01
☐ 177	**Doug Buffone**, Chicago Bears	.12	.05	.01
☐ 178	**Charlie Cowan**, Los Angeles Rams	.12	.05	.01
☐ 179	**Bob Newland**, New Orleans Saints	.12	.05	.01
☐ 180	**Ron Johnson**, New York Giants	.20	.09	.02
☐ 181	**Bob Rowe**, St. Louis Cardinals	.12	.05	.01
☐ 182	**Len Hauss**, Washington Redskins	.12	.05	.01
☐ 183	**Joe DeLamielleure**, Buffalo Bills	.20	.09	.02
☐ 184	**Sherman White**, Cincinnati Bengals	.12	.05	.01
☐ 185	**Fair Hooker**, Cleveland Browns	.12	.05	.01
☐ 186	**Nick Mike-Mayer**, Atlanta Falcons	.12	.05	.01
☐ 187	**Ralph Neely**, Dallas Cowboys	.12	.05	.01
☐ 188	**Rich McGeorge**, Green Bay Packers	.12	.05	.01
☐ 189	**Ed Marinaro**, Minnesota Vikings	.90	.40	.09
☐ 190	**Dave Wilcox**, San Francisco 49ers	.20	.09	.02
☐ 191	**Joe Owens**, New Orleans Saints	.12	.05	.01
☐ 192	**Bill Van Heusen**, Denver Broncos	.12	.05	.01
☐ 193	**Jim Kearney**, Kansas City Chiefs	.12	.05	.01
☐ 194	**Otis Sistrunk**, Oakland Raiders	.20	.09	.02
☐ 195	**Ron Shanklin**, Pittsburgh Steelers	.12	.05	.01

		MINT	VG-E	F-G
☐ 196	**Bill Lenkaitis**, New England Patriots	.12	.05	.01
☐ 197	**Tom Drougas**, Baltimore Colts	.12	.05	.01
☐ 198	**Larry Hand**, Denver Broncos	.12	.05	.01
☐ 199	**Mack Alston**, Houston Oilers	.12	.05	.01
☐ 200	**Bob Griese**, Miami Dolphins	2.00	.90	.20
☐ 201	**Earlie Thomas**, New York Jets	.12	.05	.01
☐ 202	**Carl Gerbach**, San Diego Chargers	.12	.05	.01
☐ 203	**Jim Harrison**, Chicago Bears	.12	.05	.01
☐ 204	**Jake Kupp**, New Orleans Saints	.12	.05	.01
☐ 205	**Merlin Olsen**, Los Angeles Rams	1.25	.60	.12
☐ 206	**Spider Lockhart**, New York Giants	.12	.05	.01
☐ 207	**Walker Gillette**, New York Giants	.12	.05	.01
☐ 208	**Verlon Biggs**, Washington Redskins	.12	.05	.01
☐ 209	**Bob James**, Buffalo Bills	.12	.05	.01
☐ 210	**Bob Trumpy**, Cincinnati Bengals	.35	.15	.03
☐ 211	**Jerry Sherk**, Cleveland Browns	.20	.09	.02
☐ 212	**Andy Maurer**, Atlanta Falcons	.12	.05	.01
☐ 213	**Fred Carr**, Green Bay Packers	.12	.05	.01
☐ 214	**Mick Tingelhoff**, Minnesota Vikings	.30	.12	.03
☐ 215	**Steve Spurrier**, San Francisco 49ers	.40	.18	.04
☐ 216	**Richard Harris**, Philadelphia Eagles	.12	.05	.01
☐ 217	**Charlie Greer**, Denver Broncos	.12	.05	.01
☐ 218	**Buck Buchanan**, Kansas City Chiefs	.40	.18	.04
☐ 219	**Ray Guy**, Oakland Raiders	.75	.35	.07
☐ 220	**Franco Harris**, Pittsburgh Steelers	2.00	.90	.20
☐ 221	**Darryl Stingley**, New England Patriots	.40	.18	.04
☐ 222	**Rex Kern**, Baltimore Colts	.20	.09	.02
☐ 223	**Toni Fritsch**, Dallas Cowboys	.20	.09	.02
☐ 224	**Levi Johnson**, Detroit Lions	.12	.05	.01
☐ 225	**Bob Kuechenberg**, Miami Dolphins	.12	.05	.01
☐ 226	**Elvin Bethea**, Houston Oilers	.20	.09	.02
☐ 227	**Al Woodall**, New York Jets	.12	.05	.01
☐ 228	**Terry Owens**, San Diego Chargers	.12	.05	.01
☐ 229	**Bivian Lee**, New Orleans Saints	.12	.05	.01
☐ 230	**Dick Butkus**, Chicago Bears	2.00	.90	.20
☐ 231	**Jim Bertelsen**, Los Angeles Rams	.12	.05	.01
☐ 232	**John Mendenhall**, New York Giants	.12	.05	.01
☐ 233	**Conrad Dobler**, St. Louis Cardinals	.20	.09	.02
☐ 234	**J.D. Hill**, Buffalo Bills	.12	.05	.01
☐ 235	**Ken Houston**, Washington Redskins	.30	.12	.03
☐ 236	**Dave Lewis**, Cincinnati Bengals	.12	.05	.01
☐ 237	**John Garlington**, Cleveland Browns	.12	.05	.01
☐ 238	**Bill Sandeman**, Atlanta Falcons	.12	.05	.01
☐ 239	**Alden Roche**, Green Bay Packers	.12	.05	.01
☐ 240	**John Gilliam**, Minnesota Vikings	.20	.09	.02
☐ 241	**Bruce Taylor**, San Francisco 49ers	.20	.09	.02

		MINT	VG-E	F-G
☐ 242	Vern Winfield, Philadelphia Eagles	.12	.05	.01
☐ 243	Bobby Maples, Denver Broncos	.12	.05	.01
☐ 244	Wendell Hayes, Kansas City Chiefs	.20	.09	.02
☐ 245	George Blanda, Oakland Raiders	2.50	1.15	.25
☐ 246	Dwight White, Pittsburgh Steelers	.20	.09	.02
☐ 247	Sandy Durko, New England Patriots	.12	.05	.01
☐ 248	Tom Mitchell, Baltimore Colts	.12	.05	.01
☐ 249	Chuck Walton, Detroit Lions	.12	.05	.01
☐ 250	Bob Lilly, Dallas Cowboys	1.25	.60	.12
☐ 251	Doug Swift, Miami Dolphins	.12	.05	.01
☐ 252	Lynn Dickey, Houston Oilers	.75	.35	.07
☐ 253	Jerome Barkum, New York Jets	.20	.09	.02
☐ 254	Clint Jones, San Diego Chargers	.12	.05	.01
☐ 255	Billy Newsome, New Orleans Saints	.12	.05	.01
☐ 256	Bob Asher, Chicago Bears	.12	.05	.01
☐ 257	Joe Scibelli, Los Angeles Rams	.12	.05	.01
☐ 258	Tom Blanchard, New York Giants	.12	.05	.01
☐ 259	Norm Thompson, St. Louis Cardinals	.12	.05	.01
☐ 260	Larry Brown, Washington Redskins	.40	.18	.04
☐ 261	Paul Seymour, Buffalo Bills	.12	.05	.01
☐ 262	Checklist 133-264	1.00	.20	.04
☐ 263	Doug Dieken, Cleveland Browns	.12	.05	.01
☐ 264	Lemar Parrish, Cincinnati Bengals	.12	.05	.01
☐ 265	Bob Lee, Atlanta Falcons	.20	.09	.02
☐ 266	Bob Brown, Green Bay Packers	.12	.05	.01
☐ 267	Roy Winston, Minnesota Vikings	.12	.05	.01
☐ 268	Randy Beisler, San Francisco 49ers	.12	.05	.01
☐ 269	Joe Dawkins, Denver Broncos	.12	.05	.01
☐ 270	Tom Dempsey, Philadelphia Eagles	.20	.09	.02
☐ 271	Jack Rudnay, Kansas City Chiefs	.12	.05	.01
☐ 272	Art Shell, Oakland Raiders	.20	.09	.02
☐ 273	Mike Wagner, Pittsburgh Steelers	.20	.09	.02
☐ 274	Rick Cash, New England Patriots	.12	.05	.01
☐ 275	Greg Landry, Detroit Lions	.35	.15	.03
☐ 276	Glen Ressler, Baltimore Colts	.12	.05	.01
☐ 277	Billy Joe DuPree, Dallas Cowboys	.75	.35	.07
☐ 278	Norm Evans, Miami Dolphins	.12	.05	.01
☐ 279	Billy Parks, Houston Oilers	.12	.05	.01
☐ 280	John Riggins, New York Jets	1.25	.60	.12
☐ 281	Lionel Aldridge, San Diego Chargers	.12	.05	.01
☐ 282	Steve O'Neal, New Orleans Saints	.12	.05	.01
☐ 283	Craig Clemons, Chicago Bears	.12	.05	.01
☐ 284	Willie Williams, New York Giants	.12	.05	.01
☐ 285	Isiah Robertson, Los Angeles Rams	.12	.05	.01
☐ 286	Dennis Shaw, Buffalo Bills	.12	.05	.01
☐ 287	Bill Brundige, Washington Redskins	.12	.05	.01

		MINT	VG-E	F-G
☐ 288	John Leypoldt, Buffalo Bills	.12	.05	.01
☐ 289	John DeMarie, Cleveland Browns	.12	.05	.01
☐ 290	Mike Reid, Cincinnati Bengals	.20	.09	.02
☐ 291	Greg Brezina, Atlanta Falcons	.12	.05	.01
☐ 292	Willie Buchanon, Green Bay Packers	.20	.09	.02
☐ 293	Dave Osborn, Minnesota Vikings	.12	.05	.01
☐ 294	Mel Phillips, San Francisco 49ers	.12	.05	.01
☐ 295	Haven Moses, Denver Broncos	.20	.09	.02
☐ 296	Wade Key, Philadelphia Eagles	.12	.05	.01
☐ 297	Marvin Upshaw, Kansas City Chiefs	.12	.05	.01
☐ 298	Ray Mansfield, Pittsburgh Steelers	.12	.05	.01
☐ 299	Edgar Chandler, New England Patriots	.12	.05	.01
☐ 300	Marv Hubbard, Oakland Raiders	.20	.09	.02
☐ 301	Herman Weaver, Detroit Lions	.12	.05	.01
☐ 302	Jim Bailey, Baltimore Colts	.12	.05	.01
☐ 303	D.D. Lewis, Dallas Cowboys	.20	.09	.02
☐ 304	Ken Burrough, Houston Oilers	.20	.09	.02
☐ 305	Jake Scott, Miami Dolphins	.20	.09	.02
☐ 306	Randy Rasmussen, New York Jets	.12	.05	.01
☐ 307	Pettis Norman, San Diego Chargers	.12	.05	.01
☐ 308	Carl Johnson, New Orleans Saints	.12	.05	.01
☐ 309	Joe Taylor, Chicago Bears	.12	.05	.01
☐ 310	Pete Gogolak, New York Giants	.20	.09	.02
☐ 311	Tony Baker, Los Angeles Rams	.12	.05	.01
☐ 312	John Richardson, St. Louis Cardinals	.12	.05	.01
☐ 313	Dave Robinson, Washington Redskins	.20	.09	.02
☐ 314	Reggie McKenzie, Buffalo Bills	.20	.09	.02
☐ 315	Isaac Curtis, Cincinnati Bengals	.35	.15	.03
☐ 316	Tom Darden, Cleveland Browns	.12	.05	.01
☐ 317	Ken Reaves, Atlanta Falcons	.12	.05	.01
☐ 318	Malcolm Snider, Green Bay Packers	.12	.05	.01
☐ 319	Jeff Siemon, Minnesota Vikings	.20	.09	.02
☐ 320	Dan Abramowicz, New Orleans Saints	.20	.09	.02
☐ 321	Lyle Alzado, Denver Broncos	.90	.40	.09
☐ 322	John Reaves, Philadelphia Eagles	.20	.09	.02
☐ 323	Morris Stroud, Kansas City Chiefs	.12	.05	.01
☐ 324	Bobby Walden, Pittsburgh Steelers	.12	.05	.01
☐ 325	Randy Vataha, New England Patriots	.20	.09	.02
☐ 326	Nemiah Wilson, Oakland Raiders	.12	.05	.01
☐ 327	Paul Naumoff, Detroit Lions	.12	.05	.01
☐ 328	Rushing Leaders O.J. Simpson John Brockington	1.00	.45	.10
☐ 329	Passing Leaders Ken Stabler Roger Staubach	1.00	.45	.10

		MINT	VG-E	F-G
☐ 330	**Receiving Leaders**	.20	.09	.02
	Fred Willis			
	Harold Carmichael			
☐ 331	**Scoring Leaders**	.20	.09	.02
	Roy Gerela			
	David Ray			
☐ 332	**Interception Leaders**	.20	.09	.02
	Dick Anderson			
	Mike Wagner			
	Bobby Bryant			
☐ 333	**Punting Leaders**	.20	.09	.02
	Jerrell Wilson			
	Tom Wittum			
☐ 334	**Dennis Nelson**, Baltimore Colts	.12	.05	.01
☐ 335	**Walt Garrison**, Dallas Cowboys	.40	.18	.04
☐ 336	**Tody Smith**, Houston Oilers	.12	.05	.01
☐ 337	**Ed Bell**, New York Jets	.12	.05	.01
☐ 338	**Bryant Salter**, San Diego Chargers	.12	.05	.01
☐ 339	**Wayne Colman**, New Orleans Saints	.12	.05	.01
☐ 340	**Garo Yepremian**, Miami Dolphins	.25	.10	.02
☐ 341	**Bob Newton**, Chicago Bears	.12	.05	.01
☐ 342	**Vince Clements**, New York Jets	.12	.05	.01
☐ 343	**Ken Iman**, Los Angeles Rams	.12	.05	.01
☐ 344	**Jim Tolbert**, St. Louis Cardinals	.12	.05	.01
☐ 345	**Chris Hanburger**, Washington Redskins	.20	.09	.02
☐ 346	**Dave Foley**, Buffalo Bills	.12	.05	.01
☐ 347	**Tommy Casanova**, Cincinnati Bengals ...	.20	.09	.02
☐ 348	**John James**, Atlanta Falcons	.12	.05	.01
☐ 349	**Clarence Williams**, Green Bay Packers ...	.12	.05	.01
☐ 350	**Leroy Kelly**, Cleveland Browns	.50	.22	.05
☐ 351	**Stu Voigt**, Minnesota Vikings	.12	.05	.01
☐ 352	**Skip Vanderbundt**, San Francisco 49ers ...	.12	.05	.01
☐ 353	**Pete Duranko**, Denver Broncos	.12	.05	.01
☐ 354	**John Outlaw**, Philadelphia Eagles	.12	.05	.01
☐ 355	**Jan Stenerud**, Kansas City Chiefs	.25	.10	.02
☐ 356	**Barry Pearson**, Pittsburgh Steelers	.12	.05	.01
☐ 357	**Brian Dowling**, New England Patriots ...	.12	.05	.01
☐ 358	**Dan Conners**, Oakland Raiders	.12	.05	.01
☐ 359	**Bob Bell**, Detroit Lions	.12	.05	.01
☐ 360	**Rick Volk**, Baltimore Colts	.12	.05	.01
☐ 361	**Pat Toomay**, Dallas Cowboys	.12	.05	.01
☐ 362	**Bob Gresham**, Houston Oilers	.12	.05	.01
☐ 363	**John Schmitt**, New York Jets	.12	.05	.01
☐ 364	**Mel Rogers**, San Diego Chargers	.12	.05	.01
☐ 365	**Manny Fernandez**, Miami Dolphins	.12	.05	.01
☐ 366	**Ernie Jackson**, New Orleans Saints	.12	.05	.01

	MINT	VG-E	F-G
☐ 367 **Gary Huff**, Chicago Bears	.20	.09	.02
☐ 368 **Bob Grim**, New York Giants	.12	.05	.01
☐ 369 **Ernie McMillan**, St. Louis Cardinals	.12	.05	.01
☐ 370 **Dave Elmendorf**, Los Angeles Rams	.12	.05	.01
☐ 371 **Mike Bragg**, Washington Redskins	.12	.05	.01
☐ 372 **John Skorupan**, Buffalo Bills	.12	.05	.01
☐ 373 **Howard Fest**, Cincinnati Bengals	.12	.05	.01
☐ 374 **Jerry Tagge**, Green Bay Packers	.20	.09	.02
☐ 375 **Art Malone**, Atlanta Falcons	.12	.05	.01
☐ 376 **Bob Babich**, Cleveland Browns	.12	.05	.01
☐ 377 **Jim Marshall**, Minnesota Vikings	.75	.35	.07
☐ 378 **Bob Hoskins**, San Francisco 49ers	.12	.05	.01
☐ 379 **Don Zimmerman**, Philadelphia Eagles	.12	.05	.01
☐ 380 **Ray May**, Baltimore Colts	.12	.05	.01
☐ 381 **Emmitt Thomas**, Kansas City Chiefs	.20	.09	.02
☐ 382 **Terry Hanratty**, Pittsburgh Steelers	.35	.15	.03
☐ 383 **John Hannah**, New England Patriots	.75	.35	.07
☐ 384 **George Atkinson**, Oakland Raiders	.12	.05	.01
☐ 385 **Ted Hendricks**, Baltimore Colts	.35	.15	.03
☐ 386 **Jim O'Brien**, Detroit Lions	.12	.05	.01
☐ 387 **Jethro Pugh**, Dallas Cowboys	.20	.09	.02
☐ 388 **Elbert Drungo**, Houston Oilers	.12	.05	.01
☐ 389 **Richard Caster**, New York Jets	.20	.09	.02
☐ 390 **Deacon Jones**, San Diego Chargers	.75	.35	.07
☐ 391 **Checklist 265-396**	.90	.15	.03
☐ 392 **Jess Phillips**, Cincinnati Bengals	.12	.05	.01
☐ 393 **Garry Lyle**, Chicago Bears	.12	.05	.01
☐ 394 **Jim Files**, New York Giants	.12	.05	.01
☐ 395 **Jim Hart**, St. Louis Cardinals	.75	.35	.07
☐ 396 **Dave Chapple**, Los Angeles Rams	.12	.05	.01
☐ 397 **Jim Langer**, Miami Dolphins	.12	.05	.01
☐ 398 **John Wilbur**, Washington Redskins	.12	.05	.01
☐ 399 **Dwight Harrison**, Buffalo Bills	.12	.05	.01
☐ 400 **John Brockington**, Green Bay Packers	.30	.12	.03
☐ 401 **Ken Anderson**, Cincinnati Bengals	1.25	.60	.12
☐ 402 **Mike Tilleman**, Atlanta Falcons	.12	.05	.01
☐ 403 **Charlie Hall**, Cleveland Browns	.12	.05	.01
☐ 404 **Tommy Hart**, San Francisco 49ers	.12	.05	.01
☐ 405 **Norm Bulaich**, Philadelphia Eagles	.20	.09	.02
☐ 406 **Jim Turner**, Denver Broncos	.20	.09	.02
☐ 407 **Mo Moorman**, Kansas City Chiefs	.12	.05	.01
☐ 408 **Ralph Anderson**, New England Patriots	.12	.05	.01
☐ 409 **Jim Otto**, Oakland Raiders	1.00	.45	.10
☐ 410 **Andy Russell**, Pittsburgh Steelers	.20	.09	.02
☐ 411 **Glenn Doughty**, Baltimore Colts	.12	.05	.01
☐ 412 **Altie Taylor**, Detroit Lions	.12	.05	.01

		MINT	VG-E	F-G
☐ 413	**Marv Bateman**, Dallas Cowboys	.12	.05	.01
☐ 414	**Willie Alexander**, Houston Oilers	.12	.05	.01
☐ 415	**Bill Zapalac**, New York Jets	.12	.05	.01
☐ 416	**Russ Washington**, San Diego Chargers	.12	.05	.01
☐ 217	**Joe Federspiel**, New Orleans Saints	.12	.05	.01
☐ 418	**Craig Cotton**, Chicago Bears	.12	.05	.01
☐ 419	**Randy Johnson**, New York Giants	.20	.09	.02
☐ 420	**Harold Jackson**, Los Angeles Rams	.45	.20	.04
☐ 421	**Roger Wehrli**, St. Louis Cardinals	.20	.09	.02
☐ 422	**Charlie Harraway**, Washington Redskins	.12	.05	.01
☐ 423	**Spike Jones**, Buffalo Bills	.12	.05	.01
☐ 424	**Bob Johnson**, Cincinnati Bengals	.12	.05	.01
☐ 425	**Mike McCoy**, Green Bay Packers	.12	.05	.01
☐ 426	**Dennis Havig**, Atlanta Falcons	.12	.05	.01
☐ 427	**Bob McKay**, Cleveland Browns	.12	.05	.01
☐ 428	**Steve Zabel**, Philadelphia Eagles	.12	.05	.01
☐ 429	**Horace Jones**, Oakland Raiders	.12	.05	.01
☐ 430	**Jim Johnson**, San Francisco 49ers	.20	.09	.02
☐ 431	**Roy Gerela**, Pittsburgh Steelers	.12	.05	.01
☐ 432	**Tom Graham**, Denver Broncos	.12	.05	.01
☐ 433	**Curley Culp**, Kansas City Chiefs	.20	.09	.02
☐ 434	**Ken Mendenhall**, Baltimore Colts	.12	.05	.01
☐ 435	**Jim Plunkett**, New England Patriots	.80	.40	.08
☐ 436	**Julian Fagan**, New York Jets	.12	.05	.01
☐ 437	**Mike Garrett**, San Diego Chargers	.25	.10	.02
☐ 438	**Bobby Joe Green**, Chicago Bears	.12	.05	.01
☐ 439	**John Gregory**, New York Giants	.20	.09	.02
☐ 440	**Charlie Sanders**, Detroit Lions	.20	.09	.02
☐ 441	**Bill Curry**, Houston Oilers	.12	.05	.01
☐ 442	**Bob Pollard**, New Orleans Saints	.12	.05	.01
☐ 443	**David Ray**, Los Angeles Rams	.12	.05	.01
☐ 444	**Terry Metcalf**, St. Louis Cardinals	.40	.18	.04
☐ 445	**Pat Fischer**, Washington Redskins	.20	.09	.02
☐ 446	**Bob Chandler**, Buffalo Bills	.20	.09	.02
☐ 447	**Bill Bergey**, Cincinnati Bengals	.35	.15	.03
☐ 448	**Walter Johnson**, Cleveland Browns	.12	.05	.01
☐ 449	**Charlie Young**, Philadelphia Eagles	.25	.10	.02
☐ 450	**Chester Marcol**, Green Bay Packers	.12	.05	.01
☐ 451	**Ken Stabler**, Oakland Raiders	1.25	.60	.12
☐ 452	**Preston Pearson**, Pittsburgh Steelers	.30	.12	.03
☐ 453	**Mike Current**, Denver Broncos	.12	.05	.01
☐ 454	**Ron Bolton**, New England Patriots	.12	.05	.01
☐ 455	**Mark Lomas**, New York Jets	.12	.05	.01
☐ 456	**Raymond Chester**, Baltimore Colts	.20	.09	.02
☐ 457	**Jerry LeVias**, San Diego Chargers	.12	.05	.01
☐ 458	**Skip Butler**, Houston Oilers	.12	.05	.01

	MINT	VG-E	F-G
☐ 459 **Mike Livingston**, Kansas City Chiefs	.20	.09	.02
☐ 460 **AFC Semis**	.35	.15	.03
Raiders 33, Steelers 14			
Dolphins 34, Bengals 16			
☐ 461 **NFC Semis**	.75	.35	.07
Vikings 27, Redskins 20			
Cowboys 27, Rams 16			
(Staubach)			
☐ 462 **Playoff Championship**	.75	.35	.07
Dolphins 27, Raiders 10			
Vikings 27, Cowboys 10			
(Stabler/Tarkenton)			
☐ 463 **Super Bowl**	.75	.35	.07
Dolphins 24, Vikings 7			
☐ 464 **Wayne Mulligan**, St. Louis Cardinals	.12	.05	.01
☐ 465 **Horst Muhlmann**, Cincinnati Bengals	.12	.05	.01
☐ 466 **Milt Morin**, Cleveland Browns	.12	.05	.01
☐ 467 **Don Parish**, Kansas City Chiefs	.12	.05	.01
☐ 468 **Richard Neal**, New York Jets	.12	.05	.01
☐ 469 **Ron Jessie**, Detroit Lions	.20	.09	.02
☐ 470 **Terry Bradshaw**, Pittsburgh Steelers	3.00	1.40	.30
☐ 471 **Fred Dryer**, Los Angeles Rams	.50	.22	.05
☐ 472 **Jim Carter**, Green Bay Packers	.12	.05	.01
☐ 473 **Ken Burrow**, Atlanta Falcons	.12	.05	.01
☐ 474 **Wally Chambers**, Chicago Bears	.20	.09	.02
☐ 475 **Dan Pastorini**, Houston Oilers	.60	.28	.06
☐ 476 **Don Morrison**, New Orleans Saints	.12	.05	.01
☐ 477 **Carl Mauck**, San Diego Chargers	.12	.05	.01
☐ 478 **Larry Cole**, Minnesota Vikings	.12	.05	.01
☐ 479 **Jim Kiick**, Miami Dolphins	.20	.09	.02
☐ 480 **Willie Lanier**, Kansas City Chiefs	.45	.20	.04
☐ 481 **Don Herrmann**, New York Giants	.12	.05	.01
☐ 482 **George Hunt**, Baltimore Colts	.12	.05	.01
☐ 483 **Bob Howard**, San Diego Chargers	.12	.05	.01
☐ 484 **Myron Pottios**, Washington Redskins	.12	.05	.01
☐ 485 **Jackie Smith**, St. Louis Cardinals	.20	.09	.02
☐ 486 **Vern Holland**, Cincinnati Bengals	.12	.05	.01
☐ 487 **Jim Braxton**, Buffalo Bills	.12	.05	.01
☐ 488 **Joe Reed**, San Francisco 49ers	.20	.09	.02
☐ 489 **Wally Hilgenberg**, Minnesota Vikings	.12	.05	.01
☐ 490 **Fred Biletnikoff**, Oakland Raiders	.90	.40	.09
☐ 491 **Bob DeMarco**, Cleveland Browns	.12	.05	.01
☐ 492 **Mark Nordquist**, Philadelphia Eagles	.12	.05	.01
☐ 493 **Larry Brooks**, Los Angeles Rams	.12	.05	.01
☐ 494 **Pete Athas**, New York Giants	.12	.05	.01
☐ 495 **Emerson Boozer**, New York Jets	.20	.09	.02

		MINT	VG-E	F-G
☐ 496	**L.C. Greenwood**, Pittsburgh Steelers	.40	.18	.04
☐ 497	**Rockne Freitas**, Detroit Lions	.12	.05	.01
☐ 498	**Checklist 397-528**	.90	.15	.03
☐ 499	**Joe Schmiesing**, Baltimore Colts	.12	.05	.01
☐ 500	**Roger Staubach**, Dallas Cowboys	4.00	1.85	.40
☐ 501	**Al Cowlings**, Houston Oilers	.12	.05	.01
☐ 502	**Sam Cunningham**, New England Patriots	.20	.09	.02
☐ 503	**Dennis Partee**, San Diego Chargers	.12	.05	.01
☐ 504	**John Didion**, New Orleans Saints	.12	.05	.01
☐ 505	**Nick Buoniconti**, Miami Dolphins	.75	.35	.07
☐ 506	**Carl Garrett**, Chicago Bears	.12	.05	.01
☐ 507	**Doug Van Horn**, New York Giants	.12	.05	.01
☐ 508	**Jamie Rivers**, St. Louis Cardinals	.12	.05	.01
☐ 509	**Jack Youngblood**, Los Angeles Rams	.60	.28	.06
☐ 510	**Charley Taylor**, Washington Redskins	1.00	.45	.10
☐ 511	**Ken Riley**, Cincinnati Bengals	.20	.09	.02
☐ 512	**Joe Ferguson**, Buffalo Bills	.75	.35	.07
☐ 513	**Bill Lueck**, Green Bay Packers	.12	.05	.01
☐ 514	**Ray Brown**, Atlanta Falcons	.12	.05	.01
☐ 515	**Fred Cox**, Minnesota Vikings	.20	.09	.02
☐ 516	**Joe Jones**, Cleveland Browns	.12	.05	.01
☐ 517	**Larry Schreiber**, San Francisco 49ers	.12	.05	.01
☐ 518	**Dennis Wirgowski**, Philadelphia Eagles	.12	.05	.01
☐ 519	**Leroy Mitchell**, Denver Broncos	.12	.05	.01
☐ 520	**Otis Taylor**, Kansas City Chiefs	.35	.15	.03
☐ 521	**Henry Davis**, Pittsburgh Steelers	.12	.05	.01
☐ 522	**Bruce Barnes**, New England Patriots	.12	.05	.01
☐ 523	**Charlie Smith**, Oakland Raiders	.12	.05	.01
☐ 524	**Bert Jones**, Baltimore Colts	.90	.40	.09
☐ 525	**Lem Barney**, Detroit Lions	.20	.09	.02
☐ 526	**John Fitzgerald**, Dallas Cowboys	.12	.05	.01
☐ 527	**Tom Fuchess**, Houston Oilers	.12	.05	.01
☐ 528	**Steve Tannen**, New York Jets	.20	.09	.02

1975 TOPPS

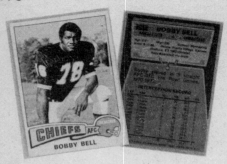

The 1975 Topps set contains 528 cards. The cards measure 2½" by 3½". The first six cards in the set depict the statistical league leaders from each league. Cards 7 and 8 both show George Blanda in a very similar pose but with a different color jersey. Cards 201-225 are the All Pro (AP) selections at each position. Record Breakers (351-356) and Highlights (452-460) are also featured in this set. No known scarcities exist. The card backs are printed in black ink with a green background on gray card stock.

		MINT	VG-E	F-G
	COMPLETE SET	55.00	25.00	5.50
	COMMON PLAYER (1-528)	.10	.04	.01
☐	**1 Rushing Leaders**	.75	.15	.03
	Lawrence McCutcheon			
	Otis Armstrong			
☐	**2 Passing Leaders**	.75	.35	.07
	Sonny Jurgensen			
	Ken Anderson			
☐	**3 Receiving Leaders**	.20	.09	.02
	Charley Young			
	Lydell Mitchell			
☐	**4 Scoring Leaders**	.15	.06	.01
	Chester Marcol			
	Roy Gerela			
☐	**5 Interception Leaders**	.15	.06	.01
	Ray Brown			
	Emmitt Thomas			

		MINT	VG-E	F-G
☐	**6 Punting Leaders**	.20	.09	.02
	Tom Blanchard			
	Ray Guy			
☐	**7 George Blanda**	1.75	.85	.17
	Oakland Raiders			
	(black jersey; highlights on back of card)			
☐	**8 George Blanda**	1.75	.85	.17
	Oakland Raiders			
	(white jersey; career record on back of card)			
☐	**9 Ralph Baker**, New York Jets	.10	.04	.01
☐	**10 Don Woods**, San Diego Chargers	.10	.04	.01
☐	**11 Bob Asher**, Chicago Bears	.10	.04	.01
☐	**12 Mel Blount**, Pittsburgh Steelers	1.00	.45	.10
☐	**13 Sam Cunningham**, New England Patriots	.15	.06	.01
☐	**14 Jackie Smith**, St. Louis Cardinals	.15	.06	.01
☐	**15 Greg Landry**, Detroit Lions	.30	.12	.03
☐	**16 Buck Buchanan**, Kansas City Chiefs	.30	.12	.03
☐	**17 Haven Moses**, Denver Broncos	.15	.06	.01
☐	**18 Clarence Ellis**, Atlanta Falcons	.10	.04	.01
☐	**19 Jim Carter**, Green Bay Packers	.10	.04	.01
☐	**20 Charley Taylor**, Washington Redskins	1.00	.45	.10
☐	**21 Jess Phillips**, New Orleans Saints	.10	.04	.01
☐	**22 Larry Seiple**, Miami Dolphins	.10	.04	.01
☐	**23 Doug Dieken**, Cleveland Browns	.10	.04	.01
☐	**24 Ron Saul**, Houston Oilers	.10	.04	.01
☐	**25 Isaac Curtis**, Cincinnati Bengals	.20	.09	.02
☐	**26 Gary Larsen**, Minnesota Vikings	.10	.04	.01
☐	**27 Bruce Jarvis**, Buffalo Bills	.10	.04	.01
☐	**28 Steve Zabel**, Philadelphia Eagles	.10	.04	.01
☐	**29 John Mendenhall**, New York Giants	.10	.04	.01
☐	**30 Rick Volk**, Baltimore Colts	.10	.04	.01
☐	**31 Checklist 1-132**	.75	.10	.02
☐	**32 Dan Abramowicz**, San Francisco 49ers	.15	.06	.01
☐	**33 Bubba Smith**, Oakland Raiders	.60	.28	.06
☐	**34 David Ray**, Los Angeles Rams	.10	.04	.01
☐	**35 Dan Dierdorf**, St. Louis Cardinals	.15	.06	.01
☐	**36 Randy Rasmussen**, New York Jets	.10	.04	.01
☐	**37 Bob Howard**, New England Patriots	.10	.04	.01
☐	**38 Gary Huff**, Chicago Bears	.15	.06	.01
☐	**39 Rocky Bleier**, Pittsburgh Steelers	.90	.40	.09
☐	**40 Mel Gray**, St. Louis Cardinals	.20	.09	.02
☐	**41 Tony McGee**, New England Patriots	.10	.04	.01
☐	**42 Larry Hand**, Detroit Lions	.10	.04	.01
☐	**43 Wendell Hayes**, Dallas Cowboys	.15	.06	.01
☐	**44 Doug Wilkerson**, San Diego Chargers	.10	.04	.01

		MINT	VG-E	F-G
☐	45 **Paul Smith**, Denver Broncos	.10	.04	.01
☐	46 **Dave Robinson**, Washington Redskins	.15	.06	.01
☐	47 **Bivian Lee**, New York Jets	.10	.04	.01
☐	48 **Jim Mandich**, Miami Dolphins	.10	.04	.01
☐	49 **Greg Pruitt**, Cleveland Browns	.30	.12	.03
☐	50 **Dan Pastorini**, Houston Oilers	.45	.20	.04
☐	51 **Ron Pritchard**, Cincinnati Bengals	.10	.04	.01
☐	52 **Dan Conners**, Oakland Raiders	.10	.04	.01
☐	53 **Fred Cox**, Minnesota Vikings	.20	.09	.02
☐	54 **Tony Greene**, Buffalo Bills	.10	.04	.01
☐	55 **Craig Morton**, Dallas Cowboys	.60	.28	.06
☐	56 **Jerry Sisemore**, Philadelphia Eagles	.10	.04	.01
☐	57 **Glenn Doughty**, Baltimore Colts	.10	.04	.01
☐	58 **Larry Schreiber**, San Francisco 49ers	.10	.04	.01
☐	59 **Charlie Waters**, Dallas Cowboys	.65	.30	.06
☐	60 **Jack Youngblood**, Los Angeles Rams	.50	.22	.05
☐	61 **Bill Lenkaitis**, New England Patriots	.10	.04	.01
☐	62 **Greg Brezina**, Atlanta Falcons	.10	.04	.01
☐	63 **Bob Pollard**, New Orleans Saints	.10	.04	.01
☐	64 **Mack Alston**, Houston Oilers	.10	.04	.01
☐	65 **Drew Pearson**, Dallas Cowboys	1.00	.45	.10
☐	66 **Charlie Stukes**, Los Angeles Rams	.10	.04	.01
☐	67 **Emerson Boozer**, New York Jets	.15	.06	.01
☐	68 **Dennis Partee**, San Diego Chargers	.10	.04	.01
☐	69 **Bob Newton**, Chicago Bears	.10	.04	.01
☐	70 **Jack Tatum**, Oakland Raiders	.25	.10	.02
☐	71 **Frank Lewis**, Pittsburgh Steelers	.20	.09	.02
☐	72 **Bob Young**, St. Louis Cardinals	.10	.04	.01
☐	73 **Julius Adams**, New England Patriots	.10	.04	.01
☐	74 **Paul Naumoff**, Detroit Lions	.10	.04	.01
☐	75 **Otis Taylor**, Kansas City Chiefs	.30	.12	.03
☐	76 **Dave Hampton**, Atlanta Falcons	.10	.04	.01
☐	77 **Mike Current**, Denver Broncos	.10	.04	.01
☐	78 **Brig Owens**, Washington Redskins	.10	.04	.01
☐	79 **Bobby Scott**, New Orleans Saints	.15	.06	.01
☐	80 **Harold Carmichael**, Philadelphia Eagles	.60	.28	.06
☐	81 **Bill Stanfill**, Miami Dolphins	.15	.06	.01
☐	82 **Bob Babich**, Cleveland Browns	.10	.04	.01
☐	83 **Vic Washington**, Houston Oilers	.10	.04	.01
☐	84 **Mick Tingelhoff**, Minnesota Vikings	.20	.09	.02
☐	85 **Bob Trumpy**, Cincinnati Bengals	.30	.12	.03
☐	86 **Earl Edwards**, Buffalo Bills	.10	.04	.01
☐	87 **Ron Hornsby**, New York Giants	.10	.04	.01
☐	88 **Don McCauley**, Baltimore Colts	.10	.04	.01
☐	89 **Jim Johnson**, San Francisco 49ers	.15	.06	.01
☐	90 **Andy Russell**, Pittsburgh Steelers	.15	.06	.01

			MINT	VG-E	F-G
☐	91	Cornell Green, Dallas Cowboys	.20	.09	.02
☐	92	Charlie Cowan, Los Angeles Rams	.10	.04	.01
☐	93	Jon Staggers, Green Bay Packers	.10	.04	.01
☐	94	Billy Newsome, New Orleans Saints	.10	.04	.01
☐	95	Willie Brown, Oakland Raiders	.90	.40	.09
☐	96	Carl Mauck, San Diego Chargers	.10	.04	.01
☐	97	Doug Buffone, Chicago Bears	.10	.04	.01
☐	98	Preston Pearson, Pittsburgh Steelers	.30	.12	.03
☐	99	Jim Bakken, St. Louis Cardinals	.20	.09	.02
☐	100	Bob Griese, Miami Dolphins	1.75	.85	.17
☐	101	Bob Windsor, New England Patriots	.10	.04	.01
☐	102	Rockne Freitas, Detroit Lions	.10	.04	.01
☐	103	Jim Marsalis, Kansas City Chiefs	.10	.04	.01
☐	104	Bill Thompson, Denver Broncos	.10	.04	.01
☐	105	Ken Burrow, Atlanta Falcons	.10	.04	.01
☐	106	Diron Talbert, Washington Redskins	.10	.04	.01
☐	107	Joe Federspiel, New Orleans Saints	.10	.04	.01
☐	108	Norm Bulaich, Philadelphia Eagles	.15	.06	.01
☐	109	Bob DeMarco, Cleveland Browns	.10	.04	.01
☐	110	Tom Wittum, San Francisco 49ers	.10	.04	.01
☐	111	Larry Hefner, Green Bay Packers	.10	.04	.01
☐	112	Tody Smith, Houston Oilers	.10	.04	.01
☐	113	Stu Voight, Minnesota Vikings	.10	.04	.01
☐	114	Horst Muhlmann, Cincinnati Bengals	.10	.04	.01
☐	115	Ahmad Rashad, Buffalo Bills	.60	.28	.06
☐	116	Joe Dawkins, Denver Broncos	.10	.04	.01
☐	117	George Kunz, Atlanta Falcons	.15	.06	.01
☐	118	D.D. Lewis, Dallas Cowboys	.20	.09	.02
☐	119	Levi Johnson, Detroit Lions	.10	.04	.01
☐	120	Len Dawson, Kansas City Chiefs	1.25	.60	.12
☐	121	Jim Bertelsen, Los Angeles Rams	.10	.04	.01
☐	122	Ed Bell, New York Giants	.10	.04	.01
☐	123	Art Thoms, Oakland Raiders	.10	.04	.01
☐	124	Joe Beauchamp, San Diego Chargers	.10	.04	.01
☐	125	Jack Ham, Pittsburgh Steelers	.30	.12	.03
☐	126	Carl Garrett, Chicago Bears	.10	.04	.01
☐	127	Roger Finnie, St. Louis Cardinals	.10	.04	.01
☐	128	Howard Twilley, Miami Dolphins	.15	.06	.01
☐	129	Bruce Barnes, New England Patriots	.10	.04	.01
☐	130	Nate Wright, Minnesota Vikings	.10	.04	.01
☐	131	Jerry Tagge, Green Bay Packers	.15	.06	.01
☐	132	Floyd Little, Denver Broncos	.35	.15	.03
☐	133	John Zook, Atlanta Falcons	.15	.06	.01
☐	134	Len Hauss, Washington Redskins	.10	.04	.01
☐	135	Archie Manning, New Orleans Saints	.75	.35	.07
☐	136	Po James, Philadelphia Eagles	.10	.04	.01

		MINT	VG-E	F-G
☐ 137	**Walt Sumner**, Cleveland Browns	.10	.04	.01
☐ 138	**Randy Beisler**, San Francisco 49ers	.10	.04	.01
☐ 139	**Willie Alexander**, Houston Oilers	.10	.04	.01
☐ 140	**Garo Yepremian**, Miami Dolphins	.20	.09	.02
☐ 141	**Chip Myers**, Cincinnati Bengals	.10	.04	.01
☐ 142	**Jim Braxton**, Buffalo Bills	.10	.04	.01
☐ 143	**Doug Van Horn**, New York Giants	.10	.04	.01
☐ 144	**Stan White**, Baltimore Colts	.10	.04	.01
☐ 145	**Roger Staubach**, Dallas Cowboys	3.50	1.65	.35
☐ 146	**Herman Weaver**, Detroit Lions	.10	.04	.01
☐ 147	**Marvin Upshaw**, Kansas City Chiefs	.10	.04	.01
☐ 148	**Bob Klein**, Los Angeles Rams	.10	.04	.01
☐ 149	**Earlie Thomas**, New York Jets	.10	.04	.01
☐ 150	**John Brockington**, Green Bay Packers	.25	.10	.02
☐ 151	**Mike Siani**, Oakland Raiders	.10	.04	.01
☐ 152	**Sam Davis**, Pittsburgh Steelers	.10	.04	.01
☐ 153	**Mike Wagner**, Pittsburgh Steelers	.15	.06	.01
☐ 154	**Larry Stallings**, St. Louis Cardinals	.10	.04	.01
☐ 155	**Wally Chambers**, Chicago Bears	.15	.06	.01
☐ 156	**Randy Vataha**, New England Patriots	.15	.06	.01
☐ 157	**Jim Marshall**, Minnesota Vikings	.60	.28	.06
☐ 158	**Jim Turner**, Denver Broncos	.15	.06	.01
☐ 159	**Walt Sweeney**, Washington Redskins	.10	.04	.01
☐ 160	**Ken Anderson**, Cincinnati Bengals	1.25	.60	.12
☐ 161	**Ray Brown**, Atlanta Falcons	.10	.04	.01
☐ 162	**John Didion**, New Orleans Saints	.10	.04	.01
☐ 163	**Tom Dempsey**, Philadelphia Eagles	.15	.06	.01
☐ 164	**Clarence Scott**, Cleveland Browns	.10	.04	.01
☐ 165	**Gene Washington**, San Francisco 49ers	.20	.09	.02
☐ 166	**Willie Rogers**, Houston Oilers	.10	.04	.01
☐ 167	**Doug Swift**, Miami Dolphins	.10	.04	.01
☐ 168	**Rufus Mayes**, Cincinnati Bengals	.10	.04	.01
☐ 169	**Marv Bateman**, Dallas Cowboys	.10	.04	.01
☐ 170	**Lydell Mitchell**, Baltimore Colts	.30	.12	.03
☐ 171	**Ron Smith**, San Diego Chargers	.10	.04	.01
☐ 172	**Bill Munson**, Detroit Lions	.30	.12	.03
☐ 173	**Bob Grim**, New York Giants	.10	.04	.01
☐ 174	**Ed Budde**, Kansas City Chiefs	.10	.04	.01
☐ 175	**Bob Lilly**, Dallas Cowboys	1.00	.45	.10
☐ 176	**Jim Youngblood**, Los Angeles Rams	.15	.06	.01
☐ 177	**Steve Tannen**, New York Jets	.10	.04	.01
☐ 178	**Rich McGeorge**, Green Bay Packers	.10	.04	.01
☐ 179	**Jim Tyrer**, Washington Redskins	.10	.04	.01
☐ 180	**Forrest Blue**, San Francisco 49ers	.10	.04	.01
☐ 181	**Jerry LeVias**, San Diego Chargers	.10	.04	.01
☐ 182	**Joe Gilliam**, Pittsburgh Steelers	.20	.09	.02

	MINT	VG-E	F-G
☐ 183 **Jim Otis**, St. Louis Cardinals	.20	.09	.02
☐ 184 **Mel Tom**, Chicago Bears	.10	.04	.01
☐ 185 **Paul Seymour**, Buffalo Bills	.10	.04	.01
☐ 186 **George Webster**, New England Patriots	.15	.06	.01
☐ 187 **Pete Duranko**, Denver Broncos	.10	.04	.01
☐ 188 **Essex Johnson**, Cincinnati Bengals	.10	.04	.01
☐ 189 **Bob Lee**, Atlanta Falcons	.15	.06	.01
☐ 190 **Gene Upshaw**, Oakland Raiders	.15	.06	.01
☐ 191 **Tom Myers**, New Orleans Saints	.10	.04	.01
☐ 192 **Don Zimmerman**, Philadelphia Eagles	.10	.04	.01
☐ 193 **John Garlington**, Cleveland Browns	.10	.04	.01
☐ 194 **Skip Butler**, Houston Oilers	.10	.04	.01
☐ 195 **Tom Mitchell**, San Francisco 49ers	.10	.04	.01
☐ 196 **Jim Langer**, Miami Dolphins	.10	.04	.01
☐ 197 **Ron Carpenter**, Cincinnati Bengals	.10	.04	.01
☐ 198 **Dave Foley**, Buffalo Bills	.10	.04	.01
☐ 199 **Bert Jones**, Baltimore Colts	.60	.28	.06
☐ 200 **Larry Brown**, Kansas City Chiefs	.30	.12	.03

ALL PRO SELECTIONS

	MINT	VG-E	F-G
☐ 201 **All Pro Receivers** .... Charley Taylor Fred Biletnikoff	.65	.30	.06
☐ 202 **All Pro Tackles** .... Rayfield Wright Russ Washington	.15	.06	.01
☐ 203 **All Pro Guards** .... Tom Mack Larry Little	.15	.06	.01
☐ 204 **All Pro Centers** .... Jeff Van Note Jack Rudnay	.15	.06	.01
☐ 205 **All Pro Guards** .... Gale Gillingham John Hannah	.15	.06	.01
☐ 206 **All Pro Tackles** .... Dan Dierdorf Winston Hill	.15	.06	.01
☐ 207 **All Pro Tight Ends** .... Charley Young Riley Odoms	.15	.06	.01
☐ 208 **All Pro Quarterbacks** .... Fran Tarkenton Ken Stabler	1.00	.45	.10

		MINT	VG-E	F-G
☐ 209	**All Pro Backs** .... Lawrence McCutcheon O.J. Simpson	.90	.40	.09
☐ 210	**All Pro Backs** .... Terry Metcalf Otis Armstrong	.25	.10	.02
☐ 211	**All Pro Receivers** .... Mel Gray Isaac Curtis	.25	.10	.02
☐ 212	**All Pro Kickers** .... Chester Marcol Roy Gerela	.15	.06	.01
☐ 213	**All Pro Ends** .... Jack Youngblood Elvin Bethea	.20	.09	.02
☐ 214	**All Pro Tackles** .... Alan Page Otis Sistrunk	.20	.09	.02
☐ 215	**All Pro Tackles** .... Merlin Olsen Mike Reid	.40	.18	.04
☐ 216	**All Pro Ends** .... Carl Eller Lyle Alzado	.40	.18	.04
☐ 217	**All Pro Linebackers** .... Ted Hendricks Phil Villapiano	.20	.09	.02
☐ 218	**All Pro Linebackers** .... Lee Roy Jordan Willie Lanier	.35	.15	.03
☐ 219	**All Pro Linebackers** .... Isiah Robertson Andy Russell	.15	.06	.01
☐ 220	**All Pro Cornerbacks** .... Nate Wright Emmitt Thomas Willie Buchanon Lemar Parrish	.15	.06	.01
☐ 222	**All Pro Safeties** .... Ken Houston Dick Anderson	.20	.09	.02
☐ 223	**All Pro Safeties** .... Cliff Harris Jack Tatum	.25	.10	.02

		MINT	VG-E	F-G
☐ 224	**All Pro Punters**	.25	.10	.02
	Tom Wittum			
	Ray Guy			
☐ 225	**All Pro Returners**	.25	.10	.02
	Terry Metcalf			
	Greg Pruitt			
☐ 226	**Ted Kwalick**, San Francisco 49ers	.15	.06	.01
☐ 227	**Spider Lockhart**, New York Giants	.10	.04	.01
☐ 228	**Mike Livingston**, Kansas City Chiefs	.15	.06	.01
☐ 229	**Larry Cole**, Dallas Cowboys	.10	.04	.01
☐ 230	**Gary Garrison**, San Diego Chargers	.10	.04	.01
☐ 231	**Larry Brooks**, Los Angeles Rams	.10	.04	.01
☐ 232	**Bobby Howfield**, New York Jets	.10	.04	.01
☐ 233	**Fred Carr**, Green Bay Packers	.10	.04	.01
☐ 234	**Norm Evans**, Miami Dolphins	.10	.04	.01
☐ 235	**Dwight White**, Pittsburgh Steelers	.15	.06	.01
☐ 236	**Conrad Dobler**, St. Louis Cardinals	.15	.06	.01
☐ 237	**Garry Lyle**, Chicago Bears	.10	.04	.01
☐ 238	**Darryl Stingley**, New England Patriots	.25	.10	.02
☐ 239	**Tom Graham**, Kansas City Chiefs	.10	.04	.01
☐ 240	**Chuck Foreman**, Minnesota Vikings	.50	.22	.05
☐ 241	**Ken Riley**, Cincinnati Bengals	.15	.06	.01
☐ 242	**Don Morrison**, New Orleans Saints	.10	.04	.01
☐ 243	**Lynn Dickey**, Houston Oilers	.50	.22	.05
☐ 244	**Don Cockroft**, Cleveland Browns	.10	.04	.01
☐ 245	**Claude Humphrey**, Atlanta Falcons	.15	.06	.01
☐ 246	**John Skorupan**, Buffalo Bills	.10	.04	.01
☐ 247	**Ray Chester**, Oakland Raiders	.15	.06	.01
☐ 248	**Cas Banaszak**, San Francisco 49ers	.10	.04	.01
☐ 249	**Art Malone**, Atlanta Falcons	.10	.04	.01
☐ 250	**Ed Flanagan**, Detroit Lions	.10	.04	.01
☐ 251	**Checklist 133-264**	.75	.15	.03
☐ 252	**Nemiah Wilson**, Oakland Raiders	.10	.04	.01
☐ 253	**Ron Jessie**, Detroit Lions	.15	.06	.01
☐ 254	**Jim Lynch**, Kansas City Chiefs	.10	.04	.01
☐ 255	**Bob Tucker**, New York Giants	.15	.06	.01
☐ 256	**Terry Owens**, New York Giants	.10	.04	.01
☐ 257	**John Fitzgerald**, Dallas Cowboys	.10	.04	.01
☐ 258	**Jack Snow**, Los Angeles Rams	.15	.06	.01
☐ 259	**Garry Puetz**, New York Jets	.10	.04	.01
☐ 260	**Mike Phipps**, Cleveland Browns	.25	.10	.02
☐ 261	**Al Matthews**, Green Bay Packers	.10	.04	.01
☐ 262	**Bob Kuechenberg**, Miami Dolphins	.10	.04	.01
☐ 263	**Ron Yankowski**, St. Louis Cardinals	.10	.04	.01
☐ 264	**Ron Shanklin**, Pittsburgh Steelers	.10	.04	.01

	MINT	VG-E	F-G
☐ 265 **Bobby Douglass**, Chicago Bears	.15	.06	.01
☐ 266 **Josh Ashton**, New England Patriots	.10	.04	.01
☐ 267 **Bill Van Heusen**, Denver Broncos	.10	.04	.01
☐ 268 **Jeff Siemon**, Minnesota Vikings	.15	.06	.01
☐ 269 **Bob Newland**, New Orleans Saints	.10	.04	.01
☐ 270 **Gale Gillingham**, Green Bay Packers	.10	.04	.01
☐ 271 **Zeke Moore**, Houston Oilers	.10	.04	.01
☐ 272 **Mike Tilleman**, Atlanta Falcons	.10	.04	.01
☐ 273 **John Leypoldt**, Buffalo Bills	.10	.04	.01
☐ 274 **Ken Mendenhall**, Baltimore Colts	.10	.04	.01
☐ 275 **Norm Snead**, San Francisco 49ers	.25	.10	.02
☐ 276 **Bill Bradley**, Philadelphia Eagles	.15	.06	.01
☐ 277 **Jerry Smith**, Washington Redskins	.15	.06	.01
☐ 278 **Clarence Davis**, Oakland Raiders	.10	.04	.01
☐ 279 **Jim Yarbrough**, Detroit Lions	.10	.04	.01
☐ 280 **Lemar Parrish**, Cincinnati Bengals	.10	.04	.01
☐ 281 **Bobby Bell**, Kansas City Chiefs	.65	.30	.06
☐ 282 **Lynn Swann**, Pittsburgh Steelers	2.25	1.00	.22
☐ 283 **John Hicks**, New York Giants	.10	.04	.01
☐ 284 **Coy Bacon**, San Diego Chargers	.10	.04	.01
☐ 285 **Lee Roy Jordan**, Dallas Cowboys	.35	.15	.03
☐ 286 **Willie Buchanon**, Green Bay Packers	.15	.06	.01
☐ 287 **Al Woodall**, New York Jets	.10	.04	.01
☐ 288 **Reggie Rucker**, New England Patriots	.15	.06	.01
☐ 289 **John Schmitt**, Green Bay Packers	.10	.04	.01
☐ 290 **Carl Eller**, Minnesota Vikings	.60	.28	.06
☐ 291 **Jake Scott**, Miami Dolphins	.15	.06	.01
☐ 292 **Donny Anderson**, St. Louis Cardinals	.20	.09	.02
☐ 293 **Charley Wade**, Chicago Bears	.10	.04	.01
☐ 294 **John Tanner**, New Orleans Saints	.10	.04	.01
☐ 295 **Charlie Johnson**, Denver Broncos	.40	.18	.04
☐ 296 **Tom Blanchard**, New Orleans Saints	.10	.04	.01
☐ 297 **Curley Culp**, Kansas City Chiefs	.15	.06	.01
☐ 298 **Jeff Van Note**, Atlanta Falcons	.10	.04	.01
☐ 299 **Bob James**, Buffalo Bills	.10	.04	.01
☐ 300 **Franco Harris**, Pittsburgh Steelers	1.75	.85	.17
☐ 301 **Tim Berra**, Baltimore Colts	.25	.10	.02
☐ 302 **Bruce Gossett**, San Francisco 49ers	.10	.04	.01
☐ 303 **Verlon Biggs**, Washington Redskins	.10	.04	.01
☐ 304 **Bob Kowalkowski**, Detroit Lions	.10	.04	.01
☐ 305 **Marv Hubbard**, Oakland Raiders	.15	.06	.01
☐ 306 **Ken Avery**, Cincinnati Bengals	.10	.04	.01
☐ 307 **Mike Adamle**, New York Jets	.15	.06	.01
☐ 308 **Don Herrmann**, New York Giants	.10	.04	.01
☐ 309 **Chris Fletcher**, San Diego Chargers	.10	.04	.01
☐ 310 **Roman Gabriel**, Philadelphia Eagles	.75	.35	.07

		MINT	VG-E	F-G
☐ 311	Billy Joe DuPree, Dallas Cowboys	.35	.15	.03
☐ 312	Fred Dryer, Los Angeles Rams	.45	.20	.04
☐ 313	John Riggins, New York Jets	1.00	.45	.10
☐ 314	Bob McKay, Cleveland Browns	.10	.04	.01
☐ 315	Ted Hendricks, Green Bay Packers	.30	.12	.03
☐ 316	Bobby Bryant, Minnesota Vikings	.10	.04	.01
☐ 317	Don Nottingham, Miami Dolphins	.10	.04	.01
☐ 318	John Hannah, New England Patriots	.30	.12	.03
☐ 319	Rich Coady, Chicago Bears	.10	.04	.01
☐ 320	Phil Villapiano, Oakland Raiders	.15	.06	.01
☐ 321	Jim Plunkett, New England Patriots	.90	.40	.09
☐ 322	Lyle Alzado, Denver Broncos	.75	.35	.07
☐ 323	Ernie Jackson, New Orleans Saints	.10	.04	.01
☐ 324	Billy Parks, Houston Oilers	.10	.04	.01
☐ 325	Willie Lanier, Kansas City Chiefs	.40	.18	.04
☐ 326	John James, Atlanta Falcons	.10	.04	.01
☐ 327	Joe Ferguson, Buffalo Bills	.65	.30	.06
☐ 328	Ernie Holmes, Pittsburgh Steelers	.10	.04	.01
☐ 329	Bruce Laird, Baltimore Colts	.10	.04	.01
☐ 330	Chester Marcol, Green Bay Packers	.15	.06	.01
☐ 331	Dave Wilcox, San Francisco 49ers	.15	.06	.01
☐ 332	Pat Fischer, Washington Redskins	.15	.06	.01
☐ 333	Steve Owens, Detroit Lions	.20	.09	.02
☐ 334	Royce Berry, Cincinnati Bengals	.10	.04	.01
☐ 335	Russ Washington, San Diego Chargers	.10	.04	.01
☐ 336	Walker Gillette, New York Giants	.10	.04	.01
☐ 337	Mark Nordquist, Philadelphia Eagles	.10	.04	.01
☐ 338	James Harris, Los Angeles Rams	.60	.28	.06
☐ 339	Warren Koegel, New York Jets	.10	.04	.01
☐ 340	Emmitt Thomas, Kansas City Chiefs	.15	.06	.01
☐ 341	Walt Garrison, Dallas Cowboys	.35	.15	.03
☐ 342	Thom Darden, Cleveland Browns	.10	.04	.01
☐ 343	Mike Eischeid, Minnesota Vikings	.10	.04	.01
☐ 344	Ernie McMillan, St. Louis Cardinals	.10	.04	.01
☐ 345	Nick Buoniconti, Miami Dolphins	.60	.28	.06
☐ 346	George Farmer, Chicago Bears	.10	.04	.01
☐ 347	Sam Adams, New England Patriots	.10	.04	.01
☐ 348	Larry Cipa, New Orleans Saints	.10	.04	.01
☐ 349	Bob Moore, Oakland Raiders	.10	.04	.01
☐ 350	Otis Armstrong, Denver Broncos	.35	.15	.03

	MINT	VG-E	F-G

RECORD BREAKERS

	MINT	VG-E	F-G
☐ 351 RB: George Blanda .... All Time Scoring Leader	1.00	.45	.10
☐ 352 RB: Fred Cox .... Kicks 151 Straight PAT's	.20	.09	.02
☐ 353 RB: Tom Dempsey .... 63 Yard FG	.15	.06	.01
☐ 354 RB: Ken Houston .... 9th Int. for TD	.20	.09	.02
☐ 355 RB: O.J. Simpson .... 2003 Yard Season	1.50	.70	.15
☐ 356 RB: Ron Smith .... All Time Return Yardage Mark	.15	.06	.01
☐ 357 Bob Atkins, Houston Oilers	.10	.04	.01
☐ 358 Pat Sullivan, Atlanta Falcons	.30	.12	.03
☐ 359 Joe DeLamielleure, Buffalo Bills	.15	.06	.01
☐ 360 Lawrence McCutcheon, Los Angeles Rams ...	.40	.18	.04
☐ 361 David Lee, Baltimore Colts	.10	.04	.01
☐ 362 Mike McCoy, Green Bay Packers	.10	.04	.01
☐ 363 Skip Vanderbundt, San Francisco 49ers	.10	.04	.01
☐ 364 Mark Moseley, Washington Redskins	.20	.09	.02
☐ 365 Lem Barney, Detroit Lions	.15	.06	.01
☐ 366 Doug Dressler, Cincinnati Bengals	.10	.04	.01
☐ 367 Dan Fouts, San Diego Chargers	4.00	1.85	.40
☐ 368 Bob Hyland, New York Giants	.10	.04	.01
☐ 369 John Outlaw, Philadelphia Eagles	.10	.04	.01
☐ 370 Roy Gerela, Pittsburgh Steelers	.10	.04	.01
☐ 371 Isiah Robertson, Los Angeles Rams	.10	.04	.01
☐ 372 Jerome Barkum, New York Jets	.15	.06	.01
☐ 373 Ed Podolak, Kansas City Chiefs	.15	.06	.01
☐ 374 Milt Morin, Cleveland Browns	.10	.04	.01
☐ 375 John Niland, Dallas Cowboys	.10	.04	.01
☐ 376 Checklist 265-396	.75	.15	.03
☐ 377 Ken Iman, St. Louis Cardinals	.10	.04	.01
☐ 378 Manny Fernandez, Miami Dolphins	.10	.04	.01
☐ 379 Dave Gallagher, Chicago Bears	.10	.04	.01
☐ 380 Ken Stabler, Oakland Raiders	1.00	.45	.10
☐ 381 Mack Herron, New England Patriots	.10	.04	.01
☐ 382 Bill McClard, New Orleans Saints	.10	.04	.01
☐ 383 Ray May, Baltimore Colts	.10	.04	.01
☐ 384 Don Hansen, Atlanta Falcons	.10	.04	.01
☐ 385 Elvin Bethea, Houston Oilers	.15	.06	.01
☐ 386 Joe Scibelli, Los Angeles Rams	.10	.04	.01

		MINT	VG-E	F-G
☐ 387	**Neal Craig,** Buffalo Bills	.10	.04	.01
☐ 388	**Marty Domres,** Baltimore Colts	.15	.06	.01
☐ 389	**Ken Ellis,** Green Bay Packers	.10	.04	.01
☐ 390	**Charley Young,** Philadelphia Eagles	.15	.06	.01
☐ 391	**Tommy Hart,** San Francisco 49ers	.10	.04	.01
☐ 392	**Moses Denson,** Washington Redskins	.10	.04	.01
☐ 393	**Larry Walton,** Detroit Lions	.10	.04	.01
☐ 394	**Dave Green,** Cincinnati Bengals	.10	.04	.01
☐ 395	**Ron Johnson,** New York Giants	.15	.06	.01
☐ 396	**Ed Bradley,** Pittsburgh Steelers	.10	.04	.01
☐ 397	**J.T. Thomas,** Pittsburgh Steelers	.10	.04	.01
☐ 398	**Jim Bailey,** Baltimore Colts	.10	.04	.01
☐ 399	**Barry Pearson,** Pittsburgh Steelers	.10	.04	.01
☐ 400	**Fran Tarkenton,** Minnesota Vikings	3.00	1.40	.30
☐ 401	**Jack Rudnay,** Kansas City Chiefs	.10	.04	.01
☐ 402	**Rayfield Wright,** Dallas Cowboys	.10	.04	.01
☐ 403	**Roger Wehrli,** St. Louis Cardinals	.15	.06	.01
☐ 404	**Vern Den Herder,** Miami Dolphins	.10	.04	.01
☐ 405	**Fred Biletnikoff,** Oakland Raiders	.75	.35	.07
☐ 406	**Ken Grandberry,** Chicago Bears	.10	.04	.01
☐ 407	**Bob Adams,** New England Patriots	.10	.04	.01
☐ 408	**Jim Merlo,** New Orleans Saints	.10	.04	.01
☐ 409	**John Pitts,** Denver Broncos	.10	.04	.01
☐ 410	**Dave Osborn,** Minnesota Vikings	.10	.04	.01
☐ 411	**Dennis Havig,** Atlanta Falcons	.10	.04	.01
☐ 412	**Bob Johnson,** Cincinnati Bengals	.10	.04	.01
☐ 413	**Ken Burrough,** Houston Oilers	.15	.06	.01
☐ 414	**Jim Cheyunski,** Buffalo Bills	.10	.04	.01
☐ 415	**MacArthur Lane,** Green Bay Packers	.15	.06	.01
☐ 416	**Joe Theismann,** Washington Redskins	3.00	1.40	.30
☐ 417	**Mike Boryla,** Philadelphia Eagles	.15	.06	.01
☐ 418	**Bruce Taylor,** San Francisco 49ers	.15	.06	.01
☐ 419	**Chris Hanburger,** Washington Redskins	.15	.06	.01
☐ 420	**Tom Mack,** Los Angeles Rams	.15	.06	.01
☐ 421	**Errol Mann,** Detroit Lions	.10	.04	.01
☐ 422	**Jack Gregory,** New York Giants	.15	.06	.01
☐ 423	**Harrison Davis,** San Diego Chargers	.10	.04	.01
☐ 424	**Burgess Owens,** New York Jets	.10	.04	.01
☐ 425	**Joe Greene,** Pittsburgh Steelers	1.00	.45	.10
☐ 426	**Morris Stroud,** Kansas City Chiefs	.10	.04	.01
☐ 427	**John DeMarie,** Cleveland Browns	.10	.04	.01
☐ 428	**Mel Renfro,** Dallas Cowboys	.35	.15	.03
☐ 429	**Cid Edwards,** San Diego Chargers	.10	.04	.01
☐ 430	**Mike Reid,** Cincinnati Bengals	.15	.06	.01
☐ 431	**Jack Mildren,** New England Patriots	.15	.06	.01
☐ 432	**Jerry Simmons,** Denver Broncos	.10	.04	.01

		MINT	VG-E	F-G
☐ 433	**Ron Yary**, Minnesota Vikings	.15	.06	.01
☐ 434	**Howard Stevens**, New Orleans Saints	.10	.04	.01
☐ 435	**Ray Guy**, Oakland Raiders	.30	.12	.03
☐ 436	**Tommy Nobis**, Atlanta Falcons	.50	.22	.05
☐ 437	**Solomon Freelon**, Houston Oilers	.10	.04	.01
☐ 438	**J.D. Hill**, Buffalo Bills	.10	.04	.01
☐ 439	**Toni Linhart**, Baltimore Colts	.10	.04	.01
☐ 440	**Dick Anderson**, Miami Dolphins	.15	.06	.01
☐ 441	**Guy Morriss**, Philadelphia Eagles	.10	.04	.01
☐ 442	**Bob Hoskins**, San Francisco 49ers	.10	.04	.01
☐ 443	**John Hadl**, Los Angeles Rams	.60	.28	.06
☐ 444	**Roy Jefferson**, Washington Redskins	.15	.06	.01
☐ 445	**Charlie Sanders**, Detroit Lions	.15	.06	.01
☐ 446	**Pat Curran**, Los Angeles Rams	.10	.04	.01
☐ 447	**David Knight**, New York Jets	.10	.04	.01
☐ 448	**Bob Brown**, San Diego Chargers	.10	.04	.01
☐ 449	**Pete Gogolak**, New York Giants	.15	.06	.01
☐ 450	**Terry Metcalf**, St. Louis Cardinals	.30	.12	.03
☐ 451	**Bill Bergey**, Philadelphia Eagles	.30	.12	.03

HIGHLIGHT CARDS

		MINT	VG-E	F-G
☐ 452	**HL: Dan Abramowicz** 105 Straight Games	.15	.06	.01
☐ 453	**HL: Otis Armstrong** 183 Yard Game	.25	.10	.02
☐ 454	**HL: Cliff Branch** 13 TD Passes	.25	.10	.02
☐ 455	**HL: John James** Record 96 Punts	.15	.06	.01
☐ 456	**HL: Lydell Mitchell** 13 Passes in Game	.25	.10	.02
☐ 457	**HL: Lemarr Parrish** 3 TD Punt Returns	.15	.06	.01
☐ 458	**HL: Ken Stabler** 26 TD Passes in One Season	.35	.15	.03
☐ 459	**HL: Lynn Swann** 577 Yards in Punt Returns	.30	.12	.03
☐ 460	**HL: Emmitt Thomas** 73 Yd. Interception	.15	.06	.01
☐ 461	**Terry Bradshaw**, Pittsburgh Steelers	2.25	1.00	.22
☐ 462	**Jerrel Wilson**, Kansas City Chiefs	.10	.04	.01

		MINT	VG-E	F-G
☐ 463	**Walter Johnson**, Cleveland Browns	.10	.04	.01
☐ 464	**Golden Richards**, Dallas Cowboys	.15	.06	.01
☐ 465	**Tommy Casanova**, Cincinnati Bengals	.15	.06	.01
☐ 466	**Randy Jackson**, Philadelphia Eagles	.10	.04	.01
☐ 467	**Ron Bolton**, Boston Patriots	.10	.04	.01
☐ 468	**Joe Owens**, New Orleans Saints	.10	.04	.01
☐ 469	**Wally Hilgenberg**, Minnesota Vikings	.10	.04	.01
☐ 470	**Riley Odoms**, Denver Broncos	.15	.06	.01
☐ 471	**Otis Sistrunk**, Oakland Raiders	.15	.06	.01
☐ 472	**Eddie Ray**, Atlanta Falcons	.10	.04	.01
☐ 473	**Reggie McKenzie**, Buffalo Bills	.15	.06	.01
☐ 474	**Elbert Drungo**, Houston Oilers	.10	.04	.01
☐ 475	**Mercury Morris**, Miami Dolphins	.30	.12	.03
☐ 476	**Dan Dickel**, Baltimore Colts	.10	.04	.01
☐ 477	**Merritt Kersey**, Philadelphia Eagles	.10	.04	.01
☐ 478	**Mike Holmes**, San Francisco 49ers	.10	.04	.01
☐ 479	**Clarence Williams**, Green Bay Packers	.10	.04	.01
☐ 480	**Bill Kilmer**, Washington Redskins	.60	.28	.06
☐ 481	**Altie Taylor**, Detroit Lions	.10	.04	.01
☐ 482	**Dave Elmendorf**, Los Angeles Rams	.10	.04	.01
☐ 483	**Bob Rowe**, St. Louis Cardinals	.10	.04	.01
☐ 484	**Pete Athas**, New York Giants	.10	.04	.01
☐ 485	**Winston Hill**, New York Jets	.10	.04	.01
☐ 486	**Bo Matthews**, San Diego Chargers	.10	.04	.01
☐ 487	**Earlie Thomas**, New York Jets	.10	.04	.01
☐ 488	**Jan Stenerud**, Kansas City Chiefs	.20	.09	.02
☐ 489	**Steve Holden**, Cleveland Browns	.10	.04	.01
☐ 490	**Cliff Harris**, Dallas Cowboys	.65	.30	.06
☐ 491	**Bobbie Clark**, Cincinnati Bengals	.15	.06	.01
☐ 492	**Joe Taylor**, Chicago Bears	.10	.04	.01
☐ 493	**Tom Neville**, New England Patriots	.10	.04	.01
☐ 494	**Wayne Coleman**, New Orleans Saints	.10	.04	.01
☐ 495	**Jim Mitchell**, Atlanta Falcons	.10	.04	.01
☐ 496	**Paul Krause**, Minnesota Vikings	.15	.06	.01
☐ 497	**Jim Otto**, Oakland Raiders	.90	.40	.09
☐ 498	**John Rowser**, Denver Broncos	.10	.04	.01
☐ 499	**Larry Little**, Miami Dolphins	.15	.06	.01
☐ 567	**O.J. Simpson**, Buffalo Bills	3.25	1.50	.32
☐ 501	**John Dutton**, Baltimore Colts	.15	.06	.01
☐ 502	**Pat Hughes**, New York Giants	.10	.04	.01
☐ 503	**Malcolm Snider**, Cleveland Browns	.10	.04	.01
☐ 504	**Fred Willis**, Houston Oilers	.10	.04	.01
☐ 505	**Harold Jackson**, Los Angeles Rams	.40	.18	.04
☐ 506	**Mike Bragg**, Washington Redskins	.10	.04	.01
☐ 507	**Jerry Sherk**, Cleveland Browns	.15	.06	.01
☐ 508	**Mirro Roder**, Chicago Bears	.10	.04	.01

		MINT	VG-E	F-G
☐ 509	**Tom Sullivan**, Philadelphia Eagles	.10	.04	.01
☐ 510	**Jim Hart**, St. Louis Cardinals	.60	.28	.06
☐ 511	**Cedric Hardman**, San Francisco 49ers	.15	.06	.01
☐ 512	**Blaine Nye**, Dallas Cowboys	.10	.04	.01
☐ 513	**Elmo Wright**, Kansas City Chiefs	.10	.04	.01
☐ 514	**Herb Orvis**, Detroit Lions	.10	.04	.01
☐ 515	**Richard Caster**, New York Jets	.15	.06	.01
☐ 516	**Doug Kotar**, New York Giants	.10	.04	.01
☐ 517	**Checklist 397-528**	.75	.15	.03
☐ 518	**Jesse Freitas**, San Diego Chargers	.10	.04	.01
☐ 519	**Ken Houston**, Washington Redskins	.20	.09	.02
☐ 520	**Alan Page**, Minnesota Vikings	.60	.28	.06
☐ 521	**Tim Foley**, Miami Dolphins	.10	.04	.01
☐ 522	**Bill Olds**, Baltimore Colts	.10	.04	.01
☐ 523	**Bobby Maples**, Denver Broncos	.10	.04	.01
☐ 524	**Cliff Branch**, Oakland Raiders	.80	.40	.08
☐ 525	**Merlin Olsen**, Los Angeles Rams	1.00	.45	.10
☐ 526	**AFC Champs**	.75	.35	.07
	Pittsburgh 24, Oakland 13			
	(Bradshaw and Franco Harris)			
☐ 527	**NFC Champs**	.30	.12	.03
	Minnesota 14, Los Angeles 10			
	(Foreman tackled)			
☐ 528	**Super Bowl**	1.25	.60	.12
	Steelers 16, Vikings 6			
	(Bradshaw watching pass)			

1976 TOPPS

The 1976 Topps set contains 528 cards. The cards measure 2½" by 3½". No known scarcities exist, although Walter Payton's first card is in great demand. The first eight cards are dedicated to record-breaking (RB) performances from the previous season. The card backs are printed in orange and blue on gray card stock.

		MINT	VG-E	F-G
	COMPLETE SET	55.00	25.00	5.50
	COMMON PLAYER (1-528)	.10	.04	.01
☐	1 **RB: George Blanda** First to Score 2000 Points	1.50	.40	.08
☐	2 **RB: Neal Colzie** Punt Returns	.15	.06	.01
☐	3 **RB: Chuck Foreman** Catches 73 Passes	.25	.10	.02
☐	4 **RB: Jim Marshall** 26th Fumble Recovery	.25	.10	.02
☐	5 **RB: Terry Metcalf**	.25	.10	.02
☐	6 **RB: O.J. Simpson** 23 Touchdowns	1.25	.60	.12
☐	7 **RB: Fran Tarkenton**	1.25	.60	.12
☐	8 **RB: Charlie Taylor** Career Receptions	.35	.15	.03
☐	9 **Ernie Holmes**, Pittsburgh Steelers	.10	.04	.01
☐	10 **Ken Anderson**, Cincinnati Bengals	1.00	.45	.10
☐	11 **Bobby Bryant**, Minnesota Vikings	.10	.04	.01
☐	12 **Jerry Smith**, Washington Redskins	.15	.06	.01
☐	13 **David Lee**, Baltimore Colts	.10	.04	.01
☐	14 **Robert Newhouse**, Dallas Cowboys	.35	.15	.03
☐	15 **Vern Den Herder**, Miami Dolphins	.10	.04	.01
☐	16 **John Hannah**, New England Patriots	.30	.12	.03
☐	17 **J.D. Hill**, Buffalo Bills	.10	.04	.01
☐	18 **James Harris**, Los Angeles Rams	.30	.12	.03
☐	19 **Willie Buchanon**, Green Bay Packers	.15	.06	.01
☐	20 **Charlie Young**, Philadelphia Eagles	.15	.06	.01
☐	21 **Jim Yarbrough**, Detroit Lions	.10	.04	.01
☐	22 **Ronnie Coleman**, Houston Oilers	.10	.04	.01
☐	23 **Don Cockroft**, Cleveland Browns	.10	.04	.01
☐	24 **Willie Lanier**, Kansas City Chiefs	.40	.18	.04
☐	25 **Fred Biletnikoff**, Oakland Raiders	.75	.35	.07
☐	26 **Ron Yankowski**, St. Louis Cardinals	.10	.04	.01
☐	27 **Spider Lockhart**, New York Giants	.10	.04	.01
☐	28 **Bob Johnson**, Cincinnati Bengals	.10	.04	.01
☐	29 **J.T. Thomas**, Philadelphia Eagles	.10	.04	.01
☐	30 **Ron Yary**, Minnesota Vikings	.15	.06	.01
☐	31 **Brad Dusek**, Washington Redskins	.10	.04	.01

		MINT	VG-E	F-G
☐	32 **Raymond Chester**, Baltimore Colts	.15	.06	.01
☐	33 **Larry Little**, Miami Dolphins	.15	.06	.01
☐	34 **Pat Leahy**, New York Jets	.10	.04	.01
☐	35 **Steve Bartkowski**, Atlanta Falcons	1.00	.45	.10
☐	36 **Tom Myers**, New Orleans Saints	.10	.04	.01
☐	37 **Bill Van Heusen**, Denver Broncos	.10	.04	.01
☐	38 **Russ Washington**, San Diego Chargers	.10	.04	.01
☐	39 **Tom Sullivan**, Philadelphia Eagles	.10	.04	.01
☐	40 **Curley Culp**, Houston Oilers	.15	.06	.01
☐	41 **Johnnie Gray**, Green Bay Packers	.10	.04	.01
☐	42 **Bob Klein**, Los Angeles Rams	.10	.04	.01
☐	43 **Lem Barney**, Detroit Lions	.15	.06	.01
☐	44 **Harvey Martin**, Dallas Cowboys	.65	.30	.06
☐	45 **Reggie Rucker**, New England Patriots	.15	.06	.01
☐	46 **Neil Clabo**, Minnesota Vikings	.10	.04	.01
☐	47 **Ray Hamilton**, New England Patriots	.10	.04	.01
☐	48 **Joe Ferguson**, Buffalo Bills	.45	.20	.04
☐	49 **Ed Podolak**, Kansas City Chiefs	.15	.06	.01
☐	50 **Ray Guy**, Oakland Raiders	.25	.10	.02
☐	51 **Glen Edwards**, Pittsburgh Steelers	.10	.04	.01
☐	52 **Jim Leclair**, Cincinnati Bengals	.10	.04	.01
☐	53 **Mike Barnes**, Baltimore Colts	.10	.04	.01
☐	54 **Nat Moore**, Miami Dolphins	.20	.09	.02
☐	55 **Bill Kilmer**, Washington Redskins	.50	.22	.05
☐	56 **Larry Stallings**, St. Louis Cardinals	.10	.04	.01
☐	57 **Jack Gregory**, New York Giants	.15	.06	.01
☐	58 **Steve Mike-Mayer**, San Francisco 49ers	.10	.04	.01
☐	59 **Virgil Livers**, Chicago Bears	.10	.04	.01
☐	60 **Jerry Sherk**, Cleveland Browns	.15	.06	.01
☐	61 **Guy Morriss**, Philadelphia Eagles	.10	.04	.01
☐	62 **Barty Smith**, Green Bay Packers	.10	.04	.01
☐	63 **Jerome Barkum**, New York Jets	.15	.06	.01
☐	64 **Ira Gordon**, San Diego Chargers	.10	.04	.01
☐	65 **Paul Krause**, Minnesota Vikings	.15	.06	.01
☐	66 **John McMakin**, Pittsburgh Steelers	.10	.04	.01
☐	67 **Checklist 1-132**	.65	.10	.02
☐	68 **Charley Johnson**, Denver Broncos	.35	.15	.03
☐	69 **Tommy Nobis**, Atlanta Falcons	.50	.22	.05
☐	70 **Lydell Mitchell**, Baltimore Colts	.25	.10	.02
☐	71 **Vern Holland**, Cincinnati Bengals	.10	.04	.01
☐	72 **Tim Foley**, Miami Dolphins	.10	.04	.01
☐	73 **Golden Richards**, Dallas Cowboys	.15	.06	.01
☐	74 **Bryant Salter**, Washington Redskins	.10	.04	.01
☐	75 **Terry Bradshaw**, Pittsburgh Steelers	2.00	.90	.20
☐	76 **Ted Hendricks**, Oakland Raiders	.30	.12	.03
☐	77 **Rich Saul**, Los Angeles Rams	.10	.04	.01

			MINT	VG-E	F-G
☐	78	**John Smith,** New England Patriots	.10	.04	.01
☐	79	**Altie Taylor,** Detroit Lions	.10	.04	.01
☐	80	**Cedrick Hardman,** San Francisco 49ers	.15	.06	.01
☐	81	**Ken Payne,** Green Bay Packers	.10	.04	.01
☐	82	**Zeke Moore,** Houston Oilers	.10	.04	.01
☐	83	**Alvin Maxson,** New Orleans Saints	.10	.04	.01
☐	84	**Wally Hilgenberg,** Minnesota Vikings	.10	.04	.01
☐	85	**John Niland,** Philadelphia Eagles	.10	.04	.01
☐	86	**Mike Sensibaugh,** Kansas City Chiefs	.10	.04	.01
☐	87	**Ron Johnson,** New York Giants	.15	.06	.01
☐	88	**Winston Hill,** New York Jets	.10	.04	.01
☐	89	**Charlie Joiner,** Cincinnati Bengals	.60	.28	.06
☐	90	**Roger Wehrli,** St. Louis Cardinals	.15	.06	.01
☐	91	**Mike Bragg,** Washington Redskins	.10	.04	.01
☐	92	**Dan Dickel,** Baltimore Colts	.10	.04	.01
☐	93	**Earl Morrall,** Miami Dolphins	.50	.22	.05
☐	94	**Pat Toomay,** Buffalo Bills	.10	.04	.01
☐	95	**Gary Garrison,** San Diego Chargers	.10	.04	.01
☐	96	**Ken Geddes,** Los Angeles Rams	.10	.04	.01
☐	97	**Mike Current,** Denver Broncos	.10	.04	.01
☐	98	**Bob Avellini,** Chicago Bears	.20	.09	.02
☐	99	**Dave Pureifory,** Green Bay Packers	.10	.04	.01
☐	100	**Franco Harris,** Pittsburgh Steelers	1.50	.70	.15
☐	101	**Randy Logan,** Philadelphia Eagles	.10	.04	.01
☐	102	**John Fitzgerald,** Dallas Cowboys	.10	.04	.01
☐	103	**Gregg Bingham,** Houston Oilers	.10	.04	.01
☐	104	**Jim Plunkett,** New England Patriots	.75	.35	.07
☐	105	**Carl Eller,** Minnesota Vikings	.60	.28	.06
☐	106	**Larry Walton,** Detroit Lions	.10	.04	.01
☐	107	**Clarence Scott,** Cleveland Browns	.10	.04	.01
☐	108	**Skip Vanderbundt,** San Francisco 49ers	.10	.04	.01
☐	109	**Boobie Clark,** Cincinnati Bengals	.15	.06	.01
☐	110	**Tom Mack,** Los Angeles Rams	.15	.06	.01
☐	111	**Bruce Laird,** Baltimore Colts	.10	.04	.01
☐	112	**Dave Dalby,** Oakland Raiders	.10	.04	.01
☐	113	**John Leypoldt,** Buffalo Bills	.10	.04	.01
☐	114	**Barry Pearson,** Kansas City Chiefs	.10	.04	.01
☐	115	**Larry Brown,** Washington Redskins	.30	.12	.03
☐	116	**Jackie Smith,** St. Louis Cardinals	.15	.06	.01
☐	117	**Pat Hughes,** New York Giants	.10	.04	.01
☐	118	**Al Woodall,** New York Jets	.10	.04	.01
☐	119	**John Zook,** Atlanta Falcons	.15	.06	.01
☐	120	**Jake Scott,** Miami Dolphins	.15	.06	.01
☐	121	**Rich Glover,** Philadelphia Eagles	.10	.04	.01
☐	122	**Ernie Jackson,** New Orleans Saints	.10	.04	.01
☐	123	**Otis Armstrong,** Denver Broncos	.30	.12	.03

		MINT	VG-E	F-G
☐ 124	**Bob Grim**, Chicago Bears	.10	.04	.01
☐ 125	**Jeff Siemon**, Minnesota Vikings	.15	.06	.01
☐ 126	**Harold Hart**, Oakland Raiders	.10	.04	.01
☐ 127	**John Demarie**, Cleveland Browns	.10	.04	.01
☐ 128	**Dan Fouts**, San Diego Chargers	1.75	.85	.17
☐ 129	**Jim Kearney**, Kansas City Chiefs	.10	.04	.01
☐ 130	**John Dutton**, Baltimore Colts	.15	.06	.01
☐ 131	**Calvin Hill**, Washington Redskins	.30	.12	.03
☐ 132	**Toni Fritsch**, Dallas Cowboys	.10	.04	.01
☐ 133	**Ron Jessie**, Los Angeles Rams	.15	.06	.01
☐ 134	**Don Nottingham**, Miami Dolphins	.10	.04	.01
☐ 135	**Lemar Parrish**, Cincinnati Bengals	.10	.04	.01
☐ 136	**Russ Francis**, New England Patriots	.50	.22	.05
☐ 137	**Joe Reed**, Detroit Lions	.15	.06	.01
☐ 138	**C.L. Whittington**, Houston Oilers	.10	.04	.01
☐ 139	**Otis Sistrunk**, Oakland Raiders	.15	.06	.01
☐ 140	**Lynn Swann**, Pittsburgh Steelers	.75	.35	.07
☐ 141	**Jim Carter**, Green Bay Packers	.10	.04	.01
☐ 142	**Mike Montler**, Buffalo Bills	.10	.04	.01
☐ 143	**Walter Johnson**, Cleveland Browns	.10	.04	.01
☐ 144	**Doug Kotar**, New York Giants	.10	.04	.01
☐ 145	**Roman Gabriel**, Philadelphia Eagles	.75	.35	.07
☐ 146	**Billy Newsome**, New York Jets	.10	.04	.01
☐ 147	**Ed Bradley**, Pittsburgh Steelers	.10	.04	.01
☐ 148	**Walter Payton**, Chicago Bears	18.00	7.50	1.50
☐ 149	**Johnny Fuller**, New Orleans Saints	.10	.04	.01
☐ 150	**Alan Page**, Minnesota Vikings	.60	.28	.06
☐ 151	**Frank Grant**, Washington Redskins	.10	.04	.01
☐ 152	**Dave Green**, Cincinnati Bengals	.10	.04	.01
☐ 153	**Nelson Munsey**, Baltimore Colts	.10	.04	.01
☐ 154	**Jim Mandich**, Miami Dolphins	.10	.04	.01
☐ 155	**Lawrence McCutcheon**, Los Angeles Rams	.25	.10	.02
☐ 156	**Steve Ramsey**, Denver Broncos	.15	.06	.01
☐ 157	**Ed Flanagan**, San Diego Chargers	.10	.04	.01
☐ 158	**Randy White**, Dallas Cowboys	1.50	.70	.15
☐ 159	**Gerry Mullins**, Pittsburgh Steelers	.10	.04	.01
☐ 160	**Jan Stenerud**, Kansas City Chiefs	.20	.09	.02
☐ 161	**Steve Odom**, Green Bay Packers	.15	.06	.01
☐ 162	**Roger Finnie**, St. Louis Cardinals	.10	.04	.01
☐ 163	**Norm Snead**, San Francisco 49ers	.25	.10	.02
☐ 164	**Jeff Van Note**, Atlanta Falcons	.10	.04	.01
☐ 165	**Bill Bergey**, Philadelphia Eagles	.25	.10	.02
☐ 166	**Allen Carter**, New England Patriots	.10	.04	.01
☐ 167	**Steve Holden**, Cleveland Browns	.10	.04	.01
☐ 168	**Sherman White**, Cincinnati Bengals	.10	.04	.01
☐ 169	**Bob Berry**, Minnesota Vikings	.15	.06	.01

	MINT	VG-E	F-G
☐ 170 **Ken Houston,** Washington Redskins	.20	.09	.02
☐ 171 **Bill Olds,** Baltimore Colts	.10	.04	.01
☐ 172 **Larry Seiple,** Miami Dolphins	.10	.04	.01
☐ 173 **Cliff Branch,** Oakland Raiders	.30	.12	.03
☐ 174 **Reggie McKenzie,** Buffalo Bills	.15	.06	.01
☐ 175 **Dan Pastorini,** Houston Oilers	.40	.18	.04
☐ 176 **Paul Naumoff,** Detroit Lions	.10	.04	.01
☐ 177 **Checklist 133-264**	.65	.10	.02
☐ 178 **Durwood Keeton,** New England Patriots	.10	.04	.01
☐ 179 **Earl Thomas,** Denver Broncos	.10	.04	.01
☐ 180 **L.C. Greenwood,** Pittsburgh Steelers	.30	.12	.03
☐ 181 **John Outlaw,** Philadelphia Eagles	.10	.04	.01
☐ 182 **Frank Nunley,** San Francisco 49ers	.10	.04	.01
☐ 183 **Dave Jennings,** New York Giants	.15	.06	.01
☐ 184 **MacArthur Lane,** Kansas City Chiefs	.15	.06	.01
☐ 185 **Chester Marcol,** Green Bay Packers	.10	.04	.01
☐ 186 **J.J. Jones,** New York Jets	.10	.04	.01
☐ 187 **Tom DeLeone,** Cleveland Browns	.10	.04	.01
☐ 188 **Steve Zabel,** New England Patriots	.10	.04	.01
☐ 189 **Ken Johnson,** Cincinnati Bengals	.10	.04	.01
☐ 190 **Rayfield Wright,** Dallas Cowboys	.10	.04	.01
☐ 191 **Brent McClanahan,** Minnesota Vikings	.10	.04	.01
☐ 192 **Pat Fischer,** Washington Redskins	.15	.06	.01
☐ 193 **Roger Carr,** Baltimore Colts	.15	.06	.01
☐ 194 **Manny Fernandez,** Miami Dolphins	.10	.04	.01
☐ 195 **Roy Gerela,** Pittsburgh Steelers	.10	.04	.01
☐ 196 **Dave Elmendorf,** Los Angeles Rams	.10	.04	.01
☐ 197 **Bob Kowalkowski,** Detroit Lions	.10	.04	.01
☐ 198 **Phil Villapiano,** Oakland Raiders	.15	.06	.01
☐ 199 **Will Wynn,** Philadelphia Eagles	.10	.04	.01
☐ 200 **Terry Metcalf,** St. Louis Cardinals	.25	.10	.02

STATISTICAL LEADERS

	MINT	VG-E	F-G
☐ 201 **Passing Leaders** .... Ken Anderson Fran Tarkenton	.90	.40	.09
☐ 202 **Receiving Leaders** .... Reggie Rucker Lydell Mitchell Chuck Foreman	.20	.09	.02

	MINT	VG-E	F-G
☐ 203 **Rushing Leaders**	.90	.40	.09
O.J. Simpson			
Jim Otis			
☐ 204 **Scoring Leaders**	.90	.40	.09
O.J. Simpson			
Chuck Foreman			
☐ 205 **Interception Leaders**	.20	.09	.02
Mel Blount			
Paul Krause			
☐ 206 **Punting Leaders**	.20	.09	.02
Ray Guy			
Herman Weaver			
☐ 207 **Ken Ellis**, Green Bay Packers	.10	.04	.01
☐ 208 **Ron Saul**, Houston Oilers	.10	.04	.01
☐ 209 **Toni Linhart**, Baltimore Colts	.10	.04	.01
☐ 210 **Jim Langer**, Miami Dolphins	.10	.04	.01
☐ 211 **Jeff Wright**, Minnesota Vikings	.10	.04	.01
☐ 212 **Moses Denson**, Washington Redskins	.10	.04	.01
☐ 213 **Earl Edwards**, Buffalo Bills	.10	.04	.01
☐ 214 **Walker Gillette**, New York Giants	.10	.04	.01
☐ 215 **Bob Trumpy**, Cincinnati Bengals	.30	.12	.03
☐ 216 **Emmitt Thomas**, Kansas City Chiefs	.15	.06	.01
☐ 217 **Lyle Alzado**, Denver Broncos	.60	.28	.06
☐ 218 **Carl Garrett**, New York Jets	.10	.04	.01
☐ 219 **Van Green**, Cleveland Browns	.10	.04	.01
☐ 220 **Jack Lambert**, Pittsburgh Steelers	1.25	.60	.12
☐ 221 **Spike Jones**, Philadelphia Eagles	.10	.04	.01
☐ 222 **John Hadl**, Green Bay Packers	.60	.28	.06
☐ 223 **Billy Johnson**, Houston Oilers	.35	.15	.03
☐ 224 **Tony McGee**, New England Patriots	.10	.04	.01
☐ 225 **Preston Pearson**, Dallas Cowboys	.30	.12	.03
☐ 226 **Isiah Robertson**, Los Angeles Rams	.10	.04	.01
☐ 227 **Erroll Mann**, Detroit Lions	.10	.04	.01
☐ 228 **Paul Seal**, New Orleans Saints	.10	.04	.01
☐ 229 **Roland Harper**, Chicago Bears	.10	.04	.01
☐ 230 **Ed White**, Minnesota Vikings	.15	.06	.01
☐ 231 **Joe Theismann**, Washington Redskins	1.50	.70	.15
☐ 232 **Jim Cheyunski**, Baltimore Colts	.10	.04	.01
☐ 233 **Bill Stanfill**, Miami Dolphins	.15	.06	.01
☐ 234 **Marv Hubbard**, Oakland Raiders	.15	.06	.01
☐ 235 **Tommy Casanova**, Cincinnati Bengals	.15	.06	.01
☐ 236 **Bob Hyland**, New York Giants	.10	.04	.01
☐ 237 **Jesse Freitas**, San Diego Chargers	.10	.04	.01
☐ 238 **Norm Thompson**, St. Louis Cardinals	.10	.04	.01
☐ 239 **Charlie Smith**, Philadelphia Eagles	.10	.04	.01

		MINT	VG-E	F-G
☐ 240	**John James**, Atlanta Falcons	.10	.04	.01
☐ 241	**Alden Roche**, Green Bay Packers	.10	.04	.01
☐ 242	**Gordon Jolley**, Detroit Lions	.10	.04	.01
☐ 243	**Larry Ely**, Chicago Bears	.10	.04	.01
☐ 244	**Richard Caster**, New York Jets	.15	.06	.01
☐ 245	**Joe Greene**, Pittsburgh Steelers	.75	.35	.07
☐ 246	**Larry Schreiber**, San Francisco 49ers	.10	.04	.01
☐ 247	**Terry Schmidt**, New Orleans Saints	.10	.04	.01
☐ 248	**Jerrel Wilson**, Kansas City Chiefs	.10	.04	.01
☐ 249	**Marty Domres**, Baltimore Colts	.15	.06	.01
☐ 250	**Isaac Curtis**, Cincinnati Bengals	.20	.09	.02
☐ 251	**Harold McLinton**, Washington Redskins	.10	.04	.01
☐ 252	**Fred Dryer**, Los Angeles Rams	.45	.20	.04
☐ 253	**Bill Lenkaitis**, New England Patriots	.10	.04	.01
☐ 254	**Don Hardeman**, Houston Oilers	.10	.04	.01
☐ 255	**Bob Griese**, Miami Dolphins	1.50	.70	.15
☐ 256	**Oscar Roan**, Cleveland Browns	.10	.04	.01
☐ 257	**Randy Gradishar**, Denver Broncos	.60	.28	.06
☐ 258	**Bob Thomas**, Chicago Bears	.10	.04	.01
☐ 259	**Joe Owens**, New Orleans Saints	.10	.04	.01
☐ 260	**Cliff Harris**, Pittsburgh Steelers	.30	.12	.03
☐ 261	**Frank Lewis**, Pittsburgh Steelers	.15	.06	.01
☐ 262	**Mike McCoy**, Green Bay Packers	.10	.04	.01
☐ 263	**Rickey Young**, San Diego Chargers	.15	.06	.01
☐ 264	**Brian Kelley**, New York Giants	.10	.04	.01
☐ 265	**Charlie Sanders**, Detroit Lions	.15	.06	.01
☐ 266	**Jim Hart**, St. Louis Cardinals	.50	.22	.05
☐ 267	**Greg Gantt**, New York Jets	.10	.04	.01
☐ 268	**John Ward**, Minnesota Vikings	.10	.04	.01
☐ 269	**Al Beauchamp**, Cincinnati Bengals	.10	.04	.01
☐ 270	**Jack Tatum**, Oakland Raiders	.20	.09	.02
☐ 271	**Jim Lash**, Minnesota Vikings	.10	.04	.01
☐ 272	**Diron Talbert**, Washington Redskins	.10	.04	.01
☐ 273	**Checklist 265-396**	.65	.10	.02
☐ 274	**Steve Spurrier**, San Francisco 49ers	.30	.12	.03
☐ 275	**Greg Pruitt**, Cleveland Browns	.30	.12	.03
☐ 276	**Jim Mitchell**, Detroit Lions	.10	.04	.01
☐ 277	**Jack Rudnay**, Kansas City Chiefs	.10	.04	.01
☐ 278	**Freddie Solomon**, Miami Dolphins	.30	.12	.03
☐ 279	**Frank Lemaster**, Pittsburgh Steelers	.10	.04	.01
☐ 280	**Wally Chambers**, Chicago Bears	.15	.06	.01
☐ 281	**Mike Collier**, Pittsburgh Steelers	.10	.04	.01
☐ 282	**Clarence Williams**, Green Bay Packers	.10	.04	.01
☐ 283	**Mitch Hoopes**, Dallas Cowboys	.10	.04	.01
☐ 284	**Ron Bolton**, New England Patriots	.10	.04	.01
☐ 285	**Harold Jackson**, Los Angeles Rams	.40	.18	.04

		MINT	VG-E	F-G
☐ 286	**Greg Landry,** Detroit Lions	.30	.12	.03
☐ 287	**Tony Greene,** Buffalo Bills	.10	.04	.01
☐ 288	**Howard Stevens,** Baltimore Colts	.10	.04	.01
☐ 289	**Roy Jefferson,** Washington Redskins	.15	.06	.01
☐ 290	**Jim Bakken,** St. Louis Cardinals	.20	.09	.02
☐ 291	**Doug Sutherland,** Minnesota Vikings	.10	.04	.01
☐ 292	**Marvin Cobb,** Cincinnati Bengals	.10	.04	.01
☐ 293	**Mack Alston,** Houston Oilers	.10	.04	.01
☐ 294	**Rod McNeil,** New Orleans Saints	.10	.04	.01
☐ 295	**Gene Upshaw,** Oakland Raiders	.15	.06	.01
☐ 296	**Dave Gallagher,** New York Giants	.10	.04	.01
☐ 297	**Larry Ball,** Tampa Bay Buccaneers	.10	.04	.01
☐ 298	**Ron Howard,** Dallas Cowboys	.10	.04	.01
☐ 299	**Don Strock,** Miami Dolphins	.50	.22	.05
☐ 300	**O.J. Simpson,** Buffalo Bills	3.25	1.50	.32
☐ 301	**Ray Mansfield,** Pittsburgh Steelers	.10	.04	.01
☐ 302	**Larry Marshall,** Philadelphia Eagles	.10	.04	.01
☐ 303	**Dick Himes,** Green Bay Packers	.10	.04	.01
☐ 304	**Ray Wershing,** San Diego Chargers	.10	.04	.01
☐ 305	**John Riggins,** New York Jets	1.00	.45	.10
☐ 306	**Bob Parsons,** Chicago Bears	.10	.04	.01
☐ 307	**Ray Brown,** Atlanta Falcons	.10	.04	.01
☐ 308	**Len Dawson,** Kansas City Chiefs	1.25	.60	.12
☐ 309	**Andy Maurer,** Minnesota Vikings	.10	.04	.01
☐ 310	**Jack Youngblood,** Los Angeles Rams	.45	.20	.04
☐ 311	**Essex Johnson,** Cincinnati Bengals	.10	.04	.01
☐ 312	**Stan White,** Baltimore Colts	.10	.04	.01
☐ 313	**Drew Pearson,** Dallas Cowboys	.60	.28	.06
☐ 314	**Rockne Freitas,** Detroit Lions	.10	.04	.01
☐ 315	**Mercury Morris,** Miami Dolphins	.25	.10	.02
☐ 316	**Willie Alexander,** Houston Oilers	.10	.04	.01
☐ 317	**Paul Warfield,** Cleveland Browns	1.00	.45	.10
☐ 318	**Bob Chandler,** Buffalo Bills	.15	.06	.01
☐ 319	**Bobby Walden,** Pittsburgh Steelers	.10	.04	.01
☐ 320	**Riley Odoms,** Denver Broncos	.15	.06	.01
☐ 321	**Mike Boryla,** Philadelphia Eagles	.15	.06	.01
☐ 322	**Bruce Van Dyke,** Green Bay Packers	.10	.04	.01
☐ 323	**Pete Banaszak,** Oakland Raiders	.10	.04	.01
☐ 324	**Darryl Stingley,** New England Patriots	.25	.10	.02
☐ 325	**John Mendenhall,** New York Giants	.10	.04	.01
☐ 326	**Dan Dierdorf,** St. Louis Cardinals	.15	.06	.01
☐ 327	**Bruce Taylor,** San Francisco 49ers	.15	.06	.01
☐ 328	**Don McCauley,** Baltimore Colts	.10	.04	.01
☐ 329	**John Reaves,** Cincinnati Bengals	.15	.06	.01
☐ 330	**Chris Hanburger,** Washington Redskins	.15	.06	.01

		MINT	VG-E	F-G
☐ 331	**NFC Champions**	1.25	.60	.12
	Cowboys 37, Rams 7			
	(Roger Staubach)			
☐ 332	**AFC Champions**	.75	.35	.07
	Steelers 16, Raiders 10			
	(Franco Harris)			
☐ 333	**Super Bowl X**	1.00	.45	.10
	Steelers 21 Cowboys 17			
	(Terry Bradshaw)			
☐ 334	**Godwin Turk**, New York Jets	.10	.04	.01
☐ 335	**Dick Anderson**, Miami Dolphins	.15	.06	.01
☐ 336	**Woody Green**, Kansas City Chiefs	.10	.04	.01
☐ 337	**Pat Curran**, San Diego Chargers	.10	.04	.01
☐ 338	**Council Rudolph**, St. Louis Cardinals	.10	.04	.01
☐ 339	**Joe Lavender**, Philadelphia Eagles	.10	.04	.01
☐ 340	**John Gilliam**, Minnesota Vikings	.15	.06	.01
☐ 341	**Steve Furness**, Pittsburgh Steelers	.10	.04	.01
☐ 342	**D.D. Lewis**, Dallas Cowboys	.15	.06	.01
☐ 343	**Duane Carrell**, Los Angeles Rams	.10	.04	.01
☐ 344	**John Morris**, Detroit Lions	.10	.04	.01
☐ 345	**John Brockington**, Green Bay Packers	.20	.09	.02
☐ 346	**Mike Phipps**, Cleveland Browns	.25	.10	.02
☐ 347	**Lyle Blackwood**, Cincinnati Bengals	.15	.06	.01
☐ 348	**Julius Adams**, New England Patriots	.10	.04	.01
☐ 349	**Terry Hermeling**, Washington Redskins	.10	.04	.01
☐ 350	**Rolland Lawrence**, Atlanta Falcons	.15	.06	.01
☐ 351	**Glenn Doughty**, Baltimore Colts	.10	.04	.01
☐ 352	**Doug Swift**, Miami Dolphins	.10	.04	.01
☐ 353	**Mike Strachan**, New Orleans Saints	.10	.04	.01
☐ 354	**Craig Morton**, New York Giants	.60	.28	.06
☐ 355	**George Blanda**, Oakland Raiders	1.75	.85	.17
☐ 356	**Gary Puetz**, New York Jets	.10	.04	.01
☐ 357	**Carl Mauck**, Houston Oilers	.10	.04	.01
☐ 358	**Walt Patulski**, Buffalo Bills	.10	.04	.01
☐ 359	**Stu Voigt**, Minnesota Vikings	.10	.04	.01
☐ 360	**Fred Carr**, Green Bay Packers	.10	.04	.01
☐ 361	**Po James**, Philadelphia Eagles	.10	.04	.01
☐ 362	**Otis Taylor**, Kansas City Chiefs	.25	.10	.02
☐ 363	**Jeff West**, St. Louis Cardinals	.10	.04	.01
☐ 364	**Gary Huff**, Chicago Bears	.15	.06	.01
☐ 365	**Dwight White**, Pittsburgh Steelers	.15	.06	.01
☐ 366	**Dan Ryczek**, Washington Redskins	.10	.04	.01
☐ 367	**Jon Keyworth**, Denver Broncos	.15	.06	.01
☐ 368	**Mel Renfro**, Dallas Cowboys	.30	.12	.03
☐ 369	**Bruce Gossett**, Los Angeles Rams	.10	.04	.01

		MINT	VG-E	F-G
☐ 370	Len Hauss, Washington Redskins	.10	.04	.01
☐ 371	Rick Volk, Baltimore Colts	.10	.04	.01
☐ 372	Howard Twilley, Miami Dolphins	.15	.06	.01
☐ 373	Cullen Bryant, Los Angeles Rams	.10	.04	.01
☐ 374	Bob Babich, Cleveland Browns	.10	.04	.01
☐ 375	Herman Weaver, Detroit Lions	.10	.04	.01
☐ 376	Steve Grogan, New England Patriots	.75	.35	.07
☐ 377	Bubba Smith, Houston Oilers	.60	.28	.06
☐ 378	Burgess Owens, New York Jets	.10	.04	.01
☐ 379	Alvin Matthews, Green Bay Packers	.10	.04	.01
☐ 380	Art Shell, Oakland Raiders	.15	.06	.01
☐ 381	Larry Brown, Pittsburgh Steelers	.10	.04	.01
☐ 382	Horst Muhlmann, Philadelphia Eagles	.10	.04	.01
☐ 383	Ahmad Rashad, Buffalo Bills	.60	.28	.06
☐ 384	Bobby Maples, Denver Broncos	.10	.04	.01
☐ 375	Jim Marshall, Minnesota Vikings	.50	.22	.05
☐ 386	Joe Dawkins, New York Giants	.10	.04	.01
☐ 387	Dennis Partee, San Diego Chargers	.10	.04	.01
☐ 388	Eddie McMillan, Green Bay Packers	.10	.04	.01
☐ 389	Randy Johnson, Washington Redskins	.15	.06	.01
☐ 390	Bob Kuechenberg, Miami Dolphins	.10	.04	.01
☐ 391	Rufus Mayes, Cincinnati Bengals	.10	.04	.01
☐ 392	Lloyd Mumphord, Baltimore Colts	.10	.04	.01
☐ 393	Ike Harris, St. Louis Cardinals	.10	.04	.01
☐ 394	Dave Hampton, Atlanta Falcons	.10	.04	.01
☐ 395	Roger Staubach, Dallas Cowboys	3.00	1.40	.30
☐ 396	Doug Buffone, Chicago Bears	.10	.04	.01
☐ 397	Howard Fest, Cincinnati Bengals	.10	.04	.01
☐ 398	Wayne Mulligan, New York Jets	.10	.04	.01
☐ 399	Bill Bradley, Philadelphia Eagles	.15	.06	.01
☐ 400	Chuck Foreman, Minnesota Vikings	.40	.18	.04
☐ 401	Jack Snow, Los Angeles Rams	.15	.06	.01
☐ 402	Bob Howard, New England Patriots	.10	.04	.01
☐ 403	John Matuszak, Kansas City Chiefs	.25	.10	.02
☐ 404	Bill Munson, Detroit Lions	.25	.10	.02
☐ 405	Andy Russell, Pittsburgh Steelers	.15	.06	.01
☐ 406	Skip Butler, Houston Oilers	.10	.04	.01
☐ 407	Hugh McKinnis, Cleveland Browns	.10	.04	.01
☐ 408	Bob Penchion, San Francisco 49ers	.10	.04	.01
☐ 409	Mike Bass, Washington Redskins	.10	.04	.01
☐ 410	George Kunz, Baltimore Colts	.15	.06	.01
☐ 411	Ron Pritchard, Cincinnati Bengals	.10	.04	.01
☐ 412	Barry Smith, Green Bay Packers	.10	.04	.01
☐ 413	Norm Bulaich, Miami Dolphins	.15	.06	.01
☐ 414	Marv Bateman, Buffalo Bills	.10	.04	.01
☐ 415	Ken Stabler, Oakland Raiders	.90	.40	.09

		MINT	VG-E	F-G
☐ 416	**Conrad Dobler,** St. Louis Cardinals	.15	.06	.01
☐ 417	**Bob Tucker,** New York Giants	.15	.06	.01
☐ 418	**Gene Washington,** San Francisco 49ers	.20	.09	.02
☐ 419	**Ed Marinaro,** Minnesota Vikings	.40	.18	.04
☐ 420	**Jack Ham,** Pittsburgh Steelers	.30	.12	.03
☐ 421	**Jim Turner,** Denver Broncos	.15	.06	.01
☐ 422	**Chris Fletcher,** San Diego Chargers	.10	.04	.01
☐ 423	**Carl Barzilauskas,** New York Jets	.10	.04	.01
☐ 424	**Robert Brazile,** Houston Oilers	.30	.12	.03
☐ 425	**Harold Carmichael,** Philadelphia Eagles	.50	.22	.05
☐ 426	**Ron Jaworski,** Los Angeles Rams	1.00	.45	.10
☐ 427	**Too Tall Jones,** Dallas Cowboys	1.00	.45	.10
☐ 428	**Larry McCarran,** Green Bay Packers	.10	.04	.01
☐ 429	**Mike Thomas,** Washington Redskins	.10	.04	.01
☐ 430	**Joe DeLamielleure,** Buffalo Bills	.15	.06	.01
☐ 431	**Tom Blanchard,** New Orleans Saints	.10	.04	.01
☐ 432	**Ron Carpenter,** Cincinnati Bengals	.10	.04	.01
☐ 433	**Levi Johnson,** Detroit Lions	.10	.04	.01
☐ 434	**Sam Cunningham,** New England Patriots	.15	.06	.01
☐ 435	**Garo Yepremian,** Miami Dolphins	.20	.09	.02
☐ 436	**Mike Livingston,** Kansas City Chiefs	.15	.06	.01
☐ 437	**Larry Csonka,** Miami Dolphins	.90	.40	.09
☐ 438	**Doug Dieken,** Cleveland Browns	.10	.04	.01
☐ 439	**Bill Lueck,** Philadelphia Eagles	.10	.04	.01
☐ 440	**Tom MacLeod,** Baltimore Colts	.10	.04	.01
☐ 441	**Mick Tingelhoff,** Minnesota Vikings	.20	.09	.02
☐ 442	**Terry Hanratty,** Pittsburgh Steelers	.25	.10	.02
☐ 443	**Mike Siani,** Oakland Raiders	.10	.04	.01
☐ 444	**Dwight Harrison,** Buffalo Bills	.10	.04	.01
☐ 445	**Jim Otis,** St. Louis Cardinals	.15	.06	.01
☐ 446	**Jack Reynolds,** Los Angeles Rams	.15	.06	.01
☐ 447	**Jean Fugett,** Dallas Cowboys	.10	.04	.01
☐ 448	**Dave Beverly,** Houston Oilers	.10	.04	.01
☐ 449	**Bernard Jackson,** Cincinnati Bengals	.15	.06	.01
☐ 450	**Charley Taylor,** Washington Redskins	.90	.40	.09

TEAM CHECKLISTS

☐ 451	**Atlanta Falcons**	.30	.07	.01
	Team Checklist			
☐ 452	**Baltimore Colts**	.30	.07	.01
	Team Checklist			
☐ 453	**Buffalo Bills**	.30	.07	.01
	Team Checklist			

		MINT	VG-E	F-G
☐ 454	**Chicago Bears** .... Team Checklist	.30	.07	.01
☐ 455	**Cincinnati Bengals** .... Team Checklist	.30	.07	.01
☐ 456	**Cleveland Browns** .... Team Checklist	.30	.07	.01
☐ 457	**Dallas Cowboys** .... Team Checklist	.50	.10	.01
☐ 458	**Denver Broncos** .... Team Checklist	.30	.07	.01
☐ 459	**Detroit Lions** .... Team Checklist	.30	.07	.01
☐ 460	**Green Bay Packers** .... Team Checklist	.30	.07	.01
☐ 461	**Houston Oilers** .... Team Checklist	.30	.07	.01
☐ 462	**Kansas City Chiefs** .... Team Checklist	.30	.07	.01
☐ 463	**Los Angeles Rams** .... Team Checklist	.30	.07	.01
☐ 464	**Miami Dolphins** .... Team Checklist	.30	.07	.01
☐ 465	**Minnesota Vikings** .... Team Checklist	.30	.07	.01
☐ 466	**New England Patriots** .... Team Checklist	.30	.07	.01
☐ 467	**New Orleans Saints** .... Team Checklist	.30	.07	.01
☐ 468	**New York Giants** .... Team Checklist	.30	.07	.01
☐ 469	**New York Jets** .... Team Checklist	.30	.07	.01
☐ 470	**Oakland Raiders** .... Team Checklist	.30	.07	.01
☐ 471	**Philadelphia Eagles** .... Team Checklist	.30	.07	.01
☐ 472	**Pittsburgh Steelers** .... Team Checklist	.50	.10	.01
☐ 473	**St. Louis Cardinals** .... Team Checklist	.30	.07	.01
☐ 474	**San Diego Chargers** .... Team Checklist	.30	.07	.01
☐ 475	**San Francisco 49ers** .... Team Checklist	.30	.07	.01
☐ 476	**Seattle Seahawks** .... Team Checklist	.30	.07	.01

		MINT	VG-E	F-G
☐ 477	**Tampa Bay Buccaneers** .... Team Checklist	.30	.07	.01
☐ 478	**Washington Redskins** .... Team Checklist	.30	.07	.01
☐ 479	**Fred Cox**, Minnesota Vikings	.20	.09	.02
☐ 480	**Mel Blount**, Pittsburgh Steelers	.35	.15	.03
☐ 481	**John Bunting**, Philadelphia Eagles	.10	.04	.01
☐ 482	**John Mendenhall**, Baltimore Colts	.10	.04	.01
☐ 483	**Will Harrell**, Green Bay Packers	.10	.04	.01
☐ 484	**Marlin Briscoe**, San Diego Chargers	.15	.06	.01
☐ 485	**Archie Manning**, New Orleans Saints	.60	.28	.06
☐ 486	**Tody Smith**, Houston Oilers	.10	.04	.01
☐ 487	**George Hunt**, New York Giants	.10	.04	.01
☐ 488	**Roscoe Word**, New York Jets	.10	.04	.01
☐ 489	**Paul Seymour**, Buffalo Bills	.10	.04	.01
☐ 490	**Lee Roy Jordan**, Dallas Cowboys	.35	.15	.03
☐ 491	**Chip Myers**, Cincinnati Bengals	.10	.04	.01
☐ 492	**Norm Evans**, Miami Dolphins	.10	.04	.01
☐ 493	**Jim Bertelson**, Los Angeles Rams	.10	.04	.01
☐ 494	**Mark Moseley**, Washington Redskins	.20	.09	.02
☐ 495	**George Buehler**, Oakland Raiders	.10	.04	.01
☐ 496	**Charlie Hall**, Cleveland Browns	.10	.04	.01
☐ 497	**Marvin Upshaw**, Kansas City Chiefs	.10	.04	.01
☐ 498	**Tom Banks**, St. Louis Cardinals	.10	.04	.01
☐ 499	**Randy Vataha**, New England Patriots	.10	.04	.01
☐ 500	**Fran Tarkenton**, Minnesota Vikings	3.00	1.40	.30
☐ 501	**Mike Wagner**, Pittsburgh Steelers	.15	.06	.01
☐ 502	**Art Malone**, Philadelphia Eagles	.10	.04	.01
☐ 503	**Fred Cook**, Baltimore Colts	.10	.04	.01
☐ 504	**Rich McGeorge**, Green Bay Packers	.10	.04	.01
☐ 505	**Ken Burrough**, Houston Oilers	.15	.06	.01
☐ 506	**Nick Mike-Mayer**, Atlanta Falcons	.10	.04	.01
☐ 507	**Checklist 397-528**	.65	.10	.02
☐ 508	**Steve Owens**, Detroit Lions	.20	.09	.02
☐ 509	**Brad Van Pelt**, New York Giants	.20	.09	.02
☐ 510	**Ken Riley**, Cincinnati Bengals	.15	.06	.01
☐ 511	**Art Thoms**, Oakland Raiders	.10	.04	.01
☐ 512	**Ed Bell**, New York Jets	.10	.04	.01
☐ 513	**Tom Wittum**, San Francisco 49ers	.10	.04	.01
☐ 514	**Jim Braxton**, Buffalo Bills	.10	.04	.01
☐ 515	**Nick Buoniconti**, Miami Dolphins	.60	.28	.06
☐ 516	**Brian Sipe**, Cleveland Browns	.90	.40	.09
☐ 517	**Jim Lynch**, Kansas City Chiefs	.10	.04	.01
☐ 518	**Prentice McCray**, New England Patriots	.10	.04	.01
☐ 519	**Tom Dempsey**, Los Angeles Rams	.15	.06	.01
☐ 520	**Mel Gray**, St. Louis Cardinals	.20	.09	.02

		MINT	VG-E	F-G
☐ 521	**Nate Wright,** Minnesota Vikings	.10	.04	.01
☐ 522	**Rocky Bleier,** Pittsburgh Steelers	.30	.12	.03
☐ 523	**Dennis Johnson,** Washington Redskins	.10	.04	.01
☐ 524	**Jerry Sisemore,** Philadelphia Eagles	.10	.04	.01
☐ 525	**Bert Jones,** Baltimore Colts	.50	.22	.05
☐ 526	**Perry Smith,** Green Bay Packers	.10	.04	.01
☐ 527	**Blaine Nye,** Dallas Cowboys	.10	.04	.01
☐ 528	**Bob Moore,** Oakland Raiders	.15	.06	.01

1977 TOPPS

The 1977 Topps set contains 528 cards. The cards measure 2½" by 3½". The first six cards in the set are the statistical league leaders from each conference. Cards 451 to 455 are Record Breaker (RB) cards featuring players breaking individual records during the previous season. No known scarcities exist. The card backs are printed in purple and black on gray card stock.

		MINT	VG-E	F-G
	COMPLETE SET	37.00	16.00	3.00
	COMMON PLAYER (1-528)	.07	.03	.01
☐ 1	**Passing Leaders**	.50	.10	.02
	James Harris			
	Ken Stabler			
☐ 2	**Receiving Leaders**	.20	.09	.02
	Drew Pearson			
	MacArthur Lane			

			MINT	VG-E	F-G
☐	3	**Rushing Leaders**	1.25	.60	.12
		Walter Payton			
		O.J. Simpson			
☐	4	**Scoring Leaders**	.10	.04	.01
		Mark Moseley			
		Toni Linhart			
☐	5	**Interception Leaders**	.10	.04	.01
		Monte Jackson			
		Ken Riley			
☐	6	**Punting Leaders**	.10	.04	.01
		John James			
		Marv Bateman			
☐	7	**Mike Phipps**, Cleveland Browns	.20	.09	.02
☐	8	**Rick Volk**, New York Giants	.07	.03	.01
☐	9	**Steve Furness**, Pittsburgh Steelers	.07	.03	.01
☐	10	**Isaac Curtis**, Cincinnati Bengals	.10	.04	.01
☐	11	**Nate Wright**, Minnesota Vikings	.07	.03	.01
☐	12	**Jean Fugett**, Washington Redskins	.07	.03	.01
☐	13	**Ken Mendenhall**, Baltimore Colts	.07	.03	.01
☐	14	**Sam Adams**, New England Patriots	.07	.03	.01
☐	15	**Charlie Waters**, Dallas Cowboys	.25	.10	.02
☐	16	**Bill Stanfill**, Miami Dolphins	.10	.04	.01
☐	17	**John Holland**, Buffalo Bills	.07	.03	.01
☐	18	**Pat Haden**, Los Angeles Rams	.60	.28	.06
☐	19	**Bob Young**, St. Louis Cardinals	.07	.03	.01
☐	20	**Wally Chambers**, Chicago Bears	.10	.04	.01
☐	21	**Lawrence Gaines**, Detroit Lions	.07	.03	.01
☐	22	**Larry McCarren**, Green Bay Packers	.07	.03	.01
☐	23	**Horst Muhlmann**, Philadelphia Eagles	.07	.03	.01
☐	24	**Phil Villapiano**, Oakland Raiders	.10	.04	.01
☐	25	**Greg Pruitt**, Cleveland Browns	.25	.10	.02
☐	26	**Ron Howard**, Seattle Seahawks	.07	.03	.01
☐	27	**Craig Morton**, New York Giants	.50	.22	.05
☐	28	**Rufus Mayes**, Cincinnati Bengals	.07	.03	.01
☐	29	**Lee Roy Selmon**, Tampa Bay Buccaneers	.75	.35	.07
☐	30	**Ed White**, Minnesota Vikings	.07	.03	.01
☐	31	**Harold McLinton**, Washington Redskins	.07	.03	.01
☐	32	**Glenn Doughty**, Baltimore Colts	.07	.03	.01
☐	33	**Bob Kuechenberg**, Miami Dolphins	.07	.03	.01
☐	34	**Duane Carrell**, New York Jets	.07	.03	.01
☐	35	**Riley Odoms**, Denver Broncos	.10	.04	.01
☐	36	**Bobby Scott**, New Orleans Saints	.10	.04	.01
☐	37	**Nick Mike-Mayer**, Atlanta Falcons	.07	.03	.01
☐	38	**Bill Lenkaitis**, New England Patriots	.07	.03	.01
☐	39	**Roland Harper**, Chicago Bears	.10	.04	.01

			MINT	VG-E	F-G
☐	40	**Tommy Hart,** San Francisco 49ers	.07	.03	.01
☐	41	**Mike Sensibaugh,** St. Louis Cardinals	.07	.03	.01
☐	42	**Rusty Jackson,** Los Angeles Rams	.07	.03	.01
☐	43	**Levi Johnson,** Detroit Lions	.07	.03	.01
☐	44	**Mike McCoy,** Green Bay Packers	.07	.03	.01
☐	45	**Roger Staubach,** Dallas Cowboys	2.50	1.15	.25
☐	46	**Fred Cox,** Minnesota Vikings	.15	.06	.01
☐	47	**Bob Babich,** Cleveland Browns	.07	.03	.01
☐	48	**Reggie McKenzie,** Buffalo Bills	.10	.04	.01
☐	49	**Dave Jennings,** New York Giants	.07	.03	.01
☐	50	**Mike Haynes,** New England Patriots	.75	.35	.07
☐	51	**Larry Brown,** Pittsburgh Steelers	.07	.03	.01
☐	52	**Marvin Cobb,** Cincinnati Bengals	.07	.03	.01
☐	53	**Fred Cook,** Baltimore Colts	.07	.03	.01
☐	54	**Freddie Solomon,** Miami Dolphins	.10	.04	.01
☐	55	**John Riggins,** Washington Redskins	.90	.40	.09
☐	56	**John Bunting,** Philadelphia Eagles	.07	.03	.01
☐	57	**Ray Wersching,** San Diego Chargers	.07	.03	.01
☐	58	**Mike Livingston,** Kansas City Chiefs	.10	.04	.01
☐	59	**Billy Johnson,** Houston Oilers	.25	.10	.02
☐	60	**Mike Wagner,** Pittsburgh Steelers	.10	.04	.01
☐	61	**Waymond Bryant,** Chicago Bears	.07	.03	.01
☐	62	**Jim Otis,** St. Louis Cardinals	.10	.04	.01
☐	63	**Ed Galigher,** New York Jets	.07	.03	.01
☐	64	**Randy Vataha,** New England Patriots	.07	.03	.01
☐	65	**Jim Zorn,** Seattle Seahawks	.50	.22	.05
☐	66	**Jon Keyworth,** Denver Broncos	.07	.03	.01
☐	67	**Checklist 1-132**	.40	.06	.01
☐	68	**Henry Childs,** New Orleans Saints	.07	.03	.01
☐	69	**Thom Darden,** Cleveland Browns	.07	.03	.01
☐	70	**George Kunz,** Baltimore Colts	.10	.04	.01
☐	71	**Lenvil Elliott,** Cincinnati Bengals	.07	.03	.01
☐	72	**Curtis Johnson,** Miami Dolphins	.07	.03	.01
☐	73	**Doug Van Horn,** New York Giants	.07	.03	.01
☐	74	**Joe Theismann,** Washington Redskins	1.00	.45	.10
☐	75	**Dwight White,** Pittsburgh Steelers	.10	.04	.01
☐	76	**Scott Laidlaw,** Dallas Cowboys	.07	.03	.01
☐	77	**Monte Johnson,** Oakland Raiders	.07	.03	.01
☐	78	**Dave Beverly,** Green Bay Packers	.07	.03	.01
☐	79	**Jim Mitchell,** Atlanta Falcons	.07	.03	.01
☐	80	**Jack Youngblood,** Los Angeles Rams	.35	.15	.03
☐	81	**Mel Gray,** St. Louis Cardinals	.15	.06	.01
☐	82	**Dwight Harrison,** Buffalo Bills	.07	.03	.01
☐	83	**John Hadl,** Houston Oilers	.50	.22	.05
☐	84	**Matt Blair,** Minnesota Vikings	.10	.04	.01
☐	85	**Charlie Sanders,** Detroit Lions	.10	.04	.01

		MINT	VG-E	F-G
☐	86 **Noah Jackson,** Chicago Bears	.07	.03	.01
☐	87 **Ed Marinaro,** New York Jets	.35	.15	.03
☐	88 **Bob Howard,** New England Patriots	.07	.03	.01
☐	89 **John McDaniel,** Cincinnati Bengals	.07	.03	.01
☐	90 **Dan Dierdorf,** St. Louis Cardinals	.10	.04	.01
☐	91 **Mark Moseley,** Washington Redskins	.15	.06	.01
☐	92 **Cleo Miller,** Cleveland Browns	.07	.03	.01
☐	93 **Andre Tillman,** Miami Dolphins	.07	.03	.01
☐	94 **Bruce Taylor,** San Francisco 49ers	.10	.04	.01
☐	95 **Bert Jones,** Baltimore Colts	.45	.20	.04
☐	96 **Anthony Davis,** Tampa Bay Buccaneers	.25	.10	.02
☐	97 **Don Goode,** San Diego Chargers	.07	.03	.01
☐	98 **Ray Rhodes,** New York Giants	.07	.03	.01
☐	99 **Mike Webster,** Pittsburgh Steelers	.15	.06	.01
☐	100 **O.J. Simpson,** Buffalo Bills	2.75	1.25	.27
☐	101 **Doug Plank,** Chicago Bears	.10	.04	.01
☐	102 **Efren Herrera,** Dallas Cowboys	.07	.03	.01
☐	103 **Charlie Smith,** Philadelphia Eagles	.07	.03	.01
☐	104 **Carlos Brown,** Green Bay Packers	.07	.03	.01
☐	105 **Jim Marshall,** Minnesota Vikings	.50	.22	.05
☐	106 **Paul Naumoff,** Detroit Lions	.07	.03	.01
☐	107 **Walter White,** Kansas City Chiefs	.07	.03	.01
☐	108 **John Cappelletti,** Los Angeles Rams	.60	.28	.06
☐	109 **Chip Myers,** Cincinnati Bengals	.07	.03	.01
☐	110 **Ken Stabler,** Oakland Raiders	.75	.35	.07
☐	111 **Joe Ehrmann,** Baltimore Colts	.07	.03	.01
☐	112 **Rick Engles,** Seattle Seahawks	.07	.03	.01
☐	113 **Jack Dolbin,** Denver Broncos	.07	.03	.01
☐	114 **Ron Bolton,** Cleveland Browns	.07	.03	.01
☐	115 **Mike Thomas,** Washington Redskins	.07	.03	.01
☐	116 **Mike Fuller,** San Diego Chargers	.07	.03	.01
☐	117 **John Hill,** New Orleans Saints	.07	.03	.01
☐	118 **Richard Todd,** New York Jets	.65	.30	.06
☐	119 **Duriel Harris,** Miami Dolphins	.10	.04	.01
☐	120 **John James,** Atlanta Falcons	.07	.03	.01
☐	121 **Lionel Antoine,** Chicago Bears	.07	.03	.01
☐	122 **John Skorupan,** Buffalo Bills	.07	.03	.01
☐	123 **Skip Butler,** Houston Oilers	.07	.03	.01
☐	124 **Bob Tucker,** New York Giants	.10	.04	.01
☐	125 **Paul Krause,** Minnesota Vikings	.10	.04	.01
☐	126 **Dave Hampton,** Philadelphia Eagles	.07	.03	.01
☐	127 **Tom Wittum,** San Francisco 49ers	.07	.03	.01
☐	128 **Gary Huff,** Chicago Bears	.10	.04	.01
☐	129 **Emmitt Thomas,** Kansas City Chiefs	.10	.04	.01
☐	130 **Drew Pearson,** Dallas Cowboys	.45	.20	.04
☐	131 **Ron Saul,** Washington Redskins	.07	.03	.01

		MINT	VG-E	F-G
☐ 132	**Steve Niehaus**, Seattle Seahawks	.07	.03	.01
☐ 133	**Fred Carr**, Green Bay Packers	.07	.03	.01
☐ 134	**Norm Bulaich**, Miami Dolphins	.10	.04	.01
☐ 135	**Bob Trumpy**, Cincinnati Bengals	.25	.10	.02
☐ 136	**Greg Landry**, Detroit Lions	.25	.10	.02
☐ 137	**George Buehler**, Oakland Raiders	.07	.03	.01
☐ 138	**Reggie Rucker**, Cleveland Browns	.15	.06	.01
☐ 139	**Julius Adams**, New England Patriots	.07	.03	.01
☐ 140	**Jack Ham**, Pittsburgh Steelers	.25	.10	.02
☐ 141	**Wayne Morris**, St. Louis Cardinals	.10	.04	.01
☐ 142	**Marv Bateman**, Buffalo Bills	.07	.03	.01
☐ 143	**Bobby Maples**, Denver Broncos	.07	.03	.01
☐ 144	**Harold Carmichael**, Philadelphia Eagles	.45	.20	.04
☐ 145	**Bob Avellini**, Chicago Bears	.10	.04	.01
☐ 146	**Harry Carson**, New York Giants	.50	.22	.05
☐ 147	**Lawrence Pillers**, New York Jets	.07	.03	.01
☐ 148	**Ed Williams**, Tampa Bay Buccaneers	.07	.03	.01
☐ 149	**Dan Pastorini**, Houston Oilers	.40	.18	.04
☐ 150	**Ron Yary**, Minnesota Vikings	.10	.04	.01
☐ 151	**Joe Lavender**, Washington Redskins	.07	.03	.01
☐ 152	**Pat McInally**, Cincinnati Bengals	.15	.06	.01
☐ 153	**Lloyd Mumphord**, Baltimore Colts	.07	.03	.01
☐ 154	**Cullen Bryant**, Los Angeles Rams	.07	.03	.01
☐ 155	**Willie Lanier**, Kansas City Chiefs	.35	.15	.03
☐ 156	**Gene Washington**, San Francisco 49ers	.15	.06	.01
☐ 157	**Scott Hunter**, Atlanta Falcons	.20	.09	.02
☐ 158	**Jim Merlo**, New Orleans Saints	.07	.03	.01
☐ 159	**Randy Grossman**, Pittsburgh Steelers	.07	.03	.01
☐ 160	**Blaine Nye**, Dallas Cowboys	.07	.03	.01
☐ 161	**Ike Harris**, St. Louis Cardinals	.07	.03	.01
☐ 162	**Doug Dieken**, Cleveland Browns	.07	.03	.01
☐ 163	**Guy Morriss**, Philadelphia Eagles	.07	.03	.01
☐ 164	**Bob Parsons**, Chicago Bears	.07	.03	.01
☐ 165	**Steve Grogan**, New England Patriots	.35	.15	.03
☐ 166	**John Brockington**, Green Bay Packers	.20	.09	.02
☐ 167	**Charlie Joiner**, San Diego Chargers	.50	.22	.05
☐ 168	**Ron Carpenter**, Cincinnati Bengals	.07	.03	.01
☐ 169	**Jeff Wright**, Minnesota Vikings	.07	.03	.01
☐ 170	**Chris Hanburger**, Washington Redskins	.10	.04	.01
☐ 171	**Roosevelt Leaks**, Baltimore Colts	.10	.04	.01
☐ 172	**Larry Little**, Miami Dolphins	.10	.04	.01
☐ 173	**John Matuszak**, Oakland Raiders	.15	.06	.01
☐ 174	**Joe Ferguson**, Buffalo Bills	.35	.15	.03
☐ 175	**Brad Van Pelt**, New York Giants	.10	.04	.01
☐ 176	**Dexter Bussey**, Detroit Lions	.10	.04	.01
☐ 177	**Steve Largent**, Seattle Seahawks	.90	.40	.09

		MINT	VG-E	F-G
☐ 178	**Dewey Selmon**, Tampa Bay Buccaneers	.15	.06	.01
☐ 179	**Randy Gradishar**, Denver Broncos	.25	.10	.02
☐ 180	**Mel Blount**, Pittsburgh Steelers	.25	.10	.02
☐ 181	**Dan Neal**, Chicago Bears	.07	.03	.01
☐ 182	**Rich Szaro**, New Orleans Saints	.07	.03	.01
☐ 183	**Mike Boryla**, Philadelphia Eagles	.10	.04	.01
☐ 184	**Steve Jones**, St. Louis Cardinals	.07	.03	.01
☐ 185	**Paul Warfield**, Cleveland Browns	.75	.35	.07
☐ 186	**Greg Buttle**, New York Jets	.10	.04	.01
☐ 187	**Rich McGeorge**, Green Bay Packers	.07	.03	.01
☐ 188	**Leon Gray**, New England Patriots	.10	.04	.01
☐ 189	**John Shinners**, Cincinnati Bengals	.07	.03	.01
☐ 190	**Toni Linhart**, Baltimore Colts	.07	.03	.01
☐ 191	**Robert Miller**, Minnesota Vikings	.07	.03	.01
☐ 192	**Jake Scott**, Washington Redskins	.10	.04	.01
☐ 193	**Jon Morris**, Detroit Lions	.07	.03	.01
☐ 194	**Randy Crowder**, Miami Dolphins	.07	.03	.01
☐ 195	**Lynn Swann**, Pittsburgh Steelers	.60	.28	.06
☐ 196	**Marsh White**, New York Giants	.07	.03	.01
☐ 197	**Rod Perry**, Los Angeles Rams	.10	.04	.01
☐ 198	**Willie Hall**, Oakland Raiders	.07	.03	.01
☐ 199	**Mike Hartenstine**, Chicago Bears	.07	.03	.01
☐ 200	**Jim Bakken**, St. Louis Cardinals	.15	.06	.01
☐ 201	**Atlanta Falcons** Team Checklist	.25	.05	.01
☐ 202	**Baltimore Colts** Team Checklist	.25	.05	.01
☐ 203	**Buffalo Bills** Team Checklist	.25	.05	.01
☐ 204	**Chicago Bears** Team Checklist	.25	.05	.01
☐ 205	**Cincinnati Bengals** Team Checklist	.25	.05	.01
☐ 206	**Cleveland Browns** Team Checklist	.25	.05	.01
☐ 207	**Dallas Cowboys** Team Checklist	.40	.07	.01
☐ 208	**Denver Broncos** Team Checklist	.25	.05	.01
☐ 209	**Detroit Lions** Team Checklist	.25	.05	.01
☐ 210	**Green Bay Packers** Team Checklist	.25	.05	.01
☐ 211	**Houston Oilers** Team Checklist	.25	.05	.01

		MINT	VG-E	F-G
☐ 212	**Kansas City Chiefs** .... Team Checklist	.25	.05	.01
☐ 213	**Los Angeles Rams** .... Team Checklist	.25	.05	.01
☐ 214	**Miami Dolphins** .... Team Checklist	.25	.05	.01
☐ 215	**Minnesota Vikings** .... Team Checklist	.25	.05	.01
☐ 216	**New England Patriots** .... Team Checklist	.25	.05	.01
☐ 217	**New Orleans Saints** .... Team Checklist	.25	.05	.01
☐ 218	**New York Giants** .... Team Checklist	.25	.05	.01
☐ 219	**New York Jets** .... Team Checklist	.25	.05	.01
☐ 220	**Oakland Raiders** .... Team Checklist	.25	.05	.01
☐ 221	**Philadelphia Eagles** .... Team Checklist	.25	.05	.01
☐ 222	**Pittsburgh Steelers** .... Team Checklist	.40	.07	.01
☐ 223	**St. Louis Cardinals** .... Team Checklist	.25	.05	.01
☐ 224	**San Diego Chargers** .... Team Checklist	.25	.05	.01
☐ 225	**San Francisco 49ers** .... Team Checklist	.25	.05	.01
☐ 226	**Seattle Seahawks** .... Team Checklist	.25	.05	.01
☐ 227	**Tampa Bay Bucs** .... Team Checklist	.25	.05	.01
☐ 228	**Washington Redskins** .... Team Checklist	.25	.05	.01
☐ 229	**Sam Cunningham**, New England Patriots	.15	.06	.01
☐ 230	**Alan Page**, Minnesota Vikings	.45	.20	.04
☐ 231	**Eddie Brown**, Washington Redskins	.07	.03	.01
☐ 232	**Stan White**, Baltimore Colts	.07	.03	.01
☐ 233	**Vern Den Herder**, Miami Dolphins	.07	.03	.01
☐ 234	**Clarence Davis**, Oakland Raiders	.07	.03	.01
☐ 235	**Ken Anderson**, Cincinnati Bengals	.75	.35	.07
☐ 236	**Karl Chandler**, New York Giants	.07	.03	.01
☐ 237	**Will Harrell**, Green Bay Packers	.07	.03	.01
☐ 238	**Clarence Scott**, Cleveland Browns	.07	.03	.01
☐ 239	**Bo Rather**, Chicago Bears	.07	.03	.01
☐ 240	**Robert Brazile**, Houston Oilers	.10	.04	.01

		MINT	VG-E	F-G
☐ 241	**Bob Bell**, St. Louis Cardinals	.07	.03	.01
☐ 242	**Rolland Lawrence**, Atlanta Falcons	.10	.04	.01
☐ 243	**Tom Sullivan**, Philadelphia Eagles	.07	.03	.01
☐ 244	**Larry Brunson**, Kansas City Chiefs	.07	.03	.01
☐ 245	**Terry Bradshaw**, Pittsburgh Steelers	1.75	.85	.17
☐ 246	**Rich Saul**, Los Angeles Rams	.07	.03	.01
☐ 247	**Cleveland Elam**, San Francisco 49ers	.07	.03	.01
☐ 248	**Don Woods**, San Diego Chargers	.07	.03	.01
☐ 249	**Bruce Laird**, Baltimore Colts	.07	.03	.01
☐ 250	**Coy Bacon**, Cincinnati Bengals	.07	.03	.01
☐ 251	**Russ Francis**, New England Patriots	.25	.10	.02
☐ 252	**Jim Braxton**, Buffalo Bills	.07	.03	.01
☐ 253	**Terry Smith**, Washington Redskins	.07	.03	.01
☐ 254	**Jerome Barkum**, New York Jets	.10	.04	.01
☐ 255	**Garo Yepremian**, Miami Dolphins	.15	.06	.01
☐ 256	**Checklist 133-264**	.40	.06	.01
☐ 257	**Tony Galbreath**, New Orleans Saints	.15	.06	.01
☐ 258	**Troy Archer**, New York Giants	.10	.04	.01
☐ 259	**Brian Sipe**, Cleveland Browns	.50	.22	.05
☐ 260	**Billy Joe DuPree**, Dallas Cowboys	.25	.10	.02
☐ 261	**Bobby Walden**, Pittsburgh Steelers	.07	.03	.01
☐ 262	**Larry Marshall**, Philadelphia Eagles	.07	.03	.01
☐ 263	**Ted Fritsch**, Washington Redskins	.07	.03	.01
☐ 264	**Larry Hand**, Detroit Lions	.07	.03	.01
☐ 265	**Tom Mack**, Los Angeles Rams	.10	.04	.01
☐ 266	**Ed Bradley**, Seattle Seahawks	.07	.03	.01
☐ 267	**Pat Leahy**, New York Jets	.07	.03	.01
☐ 268	**Louis Carter**, Tampa Bay Buccaneers	.07	.03	.01
☐ 269	**Archie Griffin**, Cincinnati Bengals	.50	.22	.05
☐ 270	**Art Shell**, Oakland Raiders	.10	.04	.01
☐ 271	**Stu Voigt**, Minnesota Vikings	.07	.03	.01
☐ 272	**Prentice McCray**, New England Patriots	.07	.03	.01
☐ 273	**MacArthur Lane**, Kansas City Chiefs	.10	.04	.01
☐ 274	**Dan Fouts**, San Diego Chargers	1.25	.60	.12
☐ 275	**Charlie Young**, Los Angeles Rams	.10	.04	.01
☐ 276	**Wilbur Jackson**, San Francisco 49ers	.10	.04	.01
☐ 277	**John Hicks**, New York Giants	.10	.04	.01
☐ 278	**Nat Moore**, Miami Dolphins	.10	.04	.01
☐ 279	**Virgil Livers**, Chicago Bears	.07	.03	.01
☐ 280	**Curley Culp**, Houston Oilers	.10	.04	.01
☐ 281	**Rocky Bleier**, Pittsburgh Steelers	.25	.10	.02
☐ 282	**John Zook**, St. Louis Cardinals	.10	.04	.01
☐ 283	**Tom DeLeone**, Cleveland Browns	.07	.03	.01
☐ 284	**Danny White**, Dallas Cowboys	1.25	.60	.12
☐ 285	**Otis Armstrong**, Denver Broncos	.25	.10	.02
☐ 286	**Larry Walton**, Detroit Lions	.07	.03	.01

	MINT	VG-E	F-G
☐ 287 **Jim Carter,** Green Bay Packers	.07	.03	.01
☐ 288 **Don McCauley,** Baltimore Colts	.07	.03	.01
☐ 289 **Frank Grant,** Washington Redskins	.07	.03	.01
☐ 290 **Roger Wehrli,** St. Louis Cardinals	.10	.04	.01
☐ 291 **Mick Tinglehoff,** Minnesota Vikings	.15	.06	.01
☐ 292 **Bernard Jackson,** Cincinnati Bengals	.10	.04	.01
☐ 293 **Tom Owen,** New England Patriots	.10	.04	.01
☐ 294 **Mike Esposito,** Atlanta Falcons	.07	.03	.01
☐ 295 **Fred Biletnikoff,** Oakland Raiders	.60	.28	.06
☐ 296 **Revie Sorey,** Chicago Bears	.07	.03	.01
☐ 297 **John McMakin,** Seattle Seahawks	.07	.03	.01
☐ 298 **Dan Ryczek,** Tampa Bay Buccaneers	.07	.03	.01
☐ 299 **Wayne Moore,** Miami Dolphins	.07	.03	.01
☐ 300 **Franco Harris,** Pittsburgh Steelers	1.25	.60	.12
☐ 301 **Rick Upchurch,** Denver Broncos	.35	.15	.03
☐ 302 **Jim Stienke,** New York Giants	.07	.03	.01
☐ 303 **Charlie Davis,** St. Louis Cardinals	.07	.03	.01
☐ 304 **Don Cockroft,** Cleveland Browns	.07	.03	.01
☐ 305 **Ken Burrough,** Houston Oilers	.10	.04	.01
☐ 306 **Clark Gaines,** New York Jets	.07	.03	.01
☐ 307 **Bobby Douglass,** New Orleans Saints	.10	.04	.01
☐ 308 **Ralph Perretta,** San Diego Chargers	.07	.03	.01
☐ 309 **Wally Hilgenberg,** Minnesota Vikings	.07	.03	.01
☐ 310 **Monte Jackson,** Los Angeles Rams	.07	.03	.01
☐ 311 **Chris Bahr,** Cincinnati Bengals	.10	.04	.01
☐ 312 **Jim Cheyunski,** Baltimore Colts	.07	.03	.01
☐ 313 **Mike Patrick,** New England Patriots	.07	.03	.01
☐ 314 **Too Tall Jones,** Dallas Cowboys	.50	.22	.05
☐ 315 **Bill Bradley,** Philadelphia Eagles	.10	.04	.01
☐ 316 **Benny Malone,** Miami Dolphins	.07	.03	.01
☐ 317 **Paul Seymour,** Buffalo Bills	.07	.03	.01
☐ 318 **Jim Laslavic,** Detroit Lions	.07	.03	.01
☐ 319 **Frank Lewis,** Pittsburgh Steelers	.15	.06	.01
☐ 320 **Ray Guy,** Oakland Raiders	.25	.10	.02
☐ 321 **Allan Ellis,** Chicago Bears	.07	.03	.01
☐ 322 **Conrad Dobler,** St. Louis Cardinals	.10	.04	.01
☐ 323 **Chester Marcol,** Green Bay Packers	.07	.03	.01
☐ 324 **Doug Kotar,** New York Giants	.07	.03	.01
☐ 325 **Lemar Parrish,** Cincinnati Bengals	.07	.03	.01
☐ 326 **Steve Holden,** Cleveland Browns	.07	.03	.01
☐ 327 **Jeff Van Note,** Atlanta Falcons	.07	.03	.01
☐ 328 **Howard Stevens,** Baltimore Colts	.07	.03	.01
☐ 329 **Brad Dusek,** Washington Redskins	.07	.03	.01
☐ 330 **Joe DeLamielleure,** Buffalo Bills	.10	.04	.01
☐ 331 **Jim Plunkett,** San Francisco 49ers	.50	.22	.05
☐ 332 **Checklist 265-396**	.40	.06	.01

	MINT	VG-E	F-G
☐ 333 Lou Piccone, New York Jets	.07	.03	.01
☐ 334 Ray Hamilton, New England Patriots	.07	.03	.01
☐ 335 Jan Stenerud, Kansas City Chiefs	.15	.06	.01
☐ 336 Jeris White, Miami Dolphins	.07	.03	.01
☐ 337 Sherman Smith, Seattle Seahawks	.10	.04	.01
☐ 338 Dave Green, Tampa Bay Buccaneers	.07	.03	.01
☐ 339 Terry Schmidt, Chicago Bears	.07	.03	.01
☐ 340 Sammie White, Minnesota Vikings	.25	.10	.02
☐ 341 Jon Kolb, Pittsburgh Steelers	.07	.03	.01
☐ 342 Randy White, Dallas Cowboys	.60	.28	.06
☐ 343 Bob Klein, Los Angeles Rams	.07	.03	.01
☐ 344 Bob Kowalkowski, Detroit Lions	.07	.03	.01
☐ 345 Terry Metcalf, St. Louis Cardinals	.20	.09	.02
☐ 346 Joe Danelo, New York Giants	.07	.03	.01
☐ 347 Ken Payne, Green Bay Packers	.07	.03	.01
☐ 348 Neal Craig, Cleveland Browns	.07	.03	.01
☐ 349 Dennis Johnson, Washington Redskins	.07	.03	.01
☐ 350 Bill Bergey, Philadelphia Eagles	.25	.10	.02
☐ 351 Raymond Chester, Baltimore Colts	.10	.04	.01
☐ 352 Bob Matheson, Miami Dolphins	.10	.04	.01
☐ 353 Mike Kadish, Buffalo Bills	.07	.03	.01
☐ 354 Mark Van Eeghen, Oakland Raiders	.10	.04	.01
☐ 355 L.C. Greenwood, Pittsburgh Steelers	.25	.10	.02
☐ 356 Sam Hunt, New England Patriots	.07	.03	.01
☐ 357 Darrell Austin, New York Jets	.07	.03	.01
☐ 358 Jim Turner, Denver Broncos	.10	.04	.01
☐ 359 Ahmad Rashad, Minnesota Vikings	.45	.20	.04
☐ 360 Walter Payton, Chicago Bears	3.50	1.65	.35
☐ 361 Mark Arneson, St. Louis Cardinals	.07	.03	.01
☐ 362 Jerrel Wilson, Kansas City Chiefs	.07	.03	.01
☐ 363 Steve Bartkowski, Atlanta Falcons	.50	.22	.05
☐ 364 John Watson, San Francisco 49ers	.07	.03	.01
☐ 365 Ken Riley, Cincinnati Bengals	.10	.04	.01
☐ 366 Gregg Bingham, Houston Oilers	.07	.03	.01
☐ 367 Golden Richards, Dallas Cowboys	.10	.04	.01
☐ 368 Clyde Powers, New York Giants	.07	.03	.01
☐ 369 Diron Talbert, Washington Redskins	.07	.03	.01
☐ 370 Lydell Mitchell, Baltimore Colts	.20	.09	.02
☐ 371 Bob Jackson, Cleveland Browns	.07	.03	.01
☐ 372 Jim Mandich, Miami Dolphins	.07	.03	.01
☐ 373 Frank LeMaster, Philadelphia Eagles	.07	.03	.01
☐ 374 Benny Ricardo, Buffalo Bills	.07	.03	.01
☐ 375 Lawrence McCutcheon, Los Angeles Rams ...	.20	.09	.02
☐ 376 Lynn Dickey, Green Bay Packers	.35	.15	.03
☐ 377 Phil Wise, Minnesota Vikings	.07	.03	.01
☐ 378 Tony McGee, New England Patriots	.07	.03	.01

		MINT	VG-E	F-G
☐ 379	**Norm Thompson**, Baltimore Colts	.07	.03	.01
☐ 380	**Dave Casper**, Oakland Raiders	.50	.22	.05
☐ 381	**Glen Edwards**, Pittsburgh Steelers	.07	.03	.01
☐ 382	**Bob Thomas**, Chicago Bears	.07	.03	.01
☐ 383	**Bob Chandler**, Buffalo Bills	.10	.04	.01
☐ 384	**Rickey Young**, San Diego Chargers	.10	.04	.01
☐ 385	**Carl Eller**, Minnesota Vikings	.45	.20	.04
☐ 386	**Lyle Alzado**, Denver Broncos	.55	.25	.05
☐ 387	**John Leypoldt**, Buffalo Bills	.07	.03	.01
☐ 388	**Gordon Bell**, New York Giants	.07	.03	.01
☐ 389	**Mike Bragg**, Washington Redskins	.07	.03	.01
☐ 390	**Jim Langer**, Miami Dolphins	.07	.03	.01
☐ 391	**Vern Holland**, Buffalo Bills	.07	.03	.01
☐ 392	**Nelson Munsey**, Baltimore Colts	.07	.03	.01
☐ 393	**Mack Mitchell**, Cleveland Browns	.07	.03	.01
☐ 394	**Tony Adams**, Kansas City Chiefs	.07	.03	.01
☐ 395	**Preston Pearson**, Dallas Cowboys	.25	.10	.02
☐ 396	**Emanuel Zanders**, New Orleans Saints	.07	.03	.01
☐ 397	**Vince Papale**, Philadelphia Eagles	.07	.03	.01
☐ 398	**Joe Fields**, New York Jets	.07	.03	.01
☐ 399	**Craig Clemons**, Chicago Bears	.07	.03	.01
☐ 400	**Fran Tarkenton**, Minnesota Vikings	2.50	1.15	.25
☐ 401	**Andy Johnson**, New England Patriots	.07	.03	.01
☐ 402	**Willie Buchanon**, Green Bay Packers	.10	.04	.01
☐ 403	**Pat Curran**, San Diego Chargers	.07	.03	.01
☐ 404	**Ray Jarvis**, Detroit Lions	.07	.03	.01
☐ 405	**Joe Greene**, Pittsburgh Steelers	.60	.28	.06
☐ 406	**Bill Simpson**, Los Angeles Rams	.07	.03	.01
☐ 407	**Ronnie Coleman**, Houston Oilers	.07	.03	.01
☐ 408	**J.K. McKay**, Tampa Bay Buccaneers	.10	.04	.01
☐ 409	**Pat Fischer**, Washington Redskins	.10	.04	.01
☐ 410	**John Dutton**, Baltimore Colts	.10	.04	.01
☐ 411	**Boobie Clark**, Cincinnati Bengals	.10	.04	.01
☐ 412	**Pat Tilley**, St. Louis Cardinals	.25	.10	.02
☐ 413	**Don Strock**, Miami Dolphins	.20	.09	.02
☐ 414	**Brian Kelley**, New York Giants	.07	.03	.01
☐ 415	**Gene Upshaw**, Oakland Raiders	.10	.04	.01
☐ 416	**Mike Montler**, Buffalo Bills	.07	.03	.01
☐ 417	**Checklist 397-528**	.40	.06	.01
☐ 418	**John Gilliam**, Atlanta Falcons	.10	.04	.01
☐ 419	**Brent McClanahan**, Minnesota Vikings	.07	.03	.01
☐ 420	**Jerry Sherk**, Cleveland Browns	.10	.04	.01
☐ 421	**Roy Gerela**, Pittsburgh Steelers	.07	.03	.01
☐ 422	**Tim Fox**, New England Patriots	.07	.03	.01
☐ 423	**John Ebersole**, New York Jets	.07	.03	.01
☐ 424	**James Scott**, Chicago Bears	.10	.04	.01

		MINT	VG-E	F-G
☐ 425	**Delvin Williams**, San Francisco 49ers	.25	.10	.02
☐ 426	**Spike Jones**, Philadelphia Eagles	.07	.03	.01
☐ 427	**Harvey Martin**, Dallas Cowboys	.35	.15	.03
☐ 428	**Don Herrmann**, New Orleans Saints	.07	.03	.01
☐ 429	**Calvin Hill**, Washington Redskins	.25	.10	.02
☐ 430	**Isiah Robertson**, Los Angeles Rams	.07	.03	.01
☐ 431	**Tony Greene**, Buffalo Bills	.07	.03	.01
☐ 432	**Bob Johnson**, Cincinnati Bengals	.07	.03	.01
☐ 433	**Lem Barney**, Detroit Lions	.10	.04	.01
☐ 434	**Eric Torkelson**, Green Bay Packers	.07	.03	.01
☐ 435	**John Mendenhall**, New York Giants	.07	.03	.01
☐ 436	**Larry Seiple**, Miami Dolphins	.07	.03	.01
☐ 437	**Art Kuehn**, Seattle Seahawks	.07	.03	.01
☐ 438	**John Vella**, Oakland Raiders	.07	.03	.01
☐ 439	**Greg Latta**, Chicago Bears	.07	.03	.01
☐ 440	**Roger Carr**, Baltimore Colts	.10	.04	.01
☐ 441	**Doug Southerland**, Minnesota Vikings	.07	.03	.01
☐ 442	**Mike Kruczuk**, Pittsburgh Steelers	.10	.04	.01
☐ 443	**Steve Zabel**, New England Patriots	.07	.03	.01
☐ 444	**Mike Pruitt**, Cleveland Browns	.40	.18	.04
☐ 445	**Harold Jackson**, Los Angeles Rams	.35	.15	.03
☐ 446	**George Jakowenko**, Buffalo Bills	.07	.03	.01
☐ 447	**John Fitzgerald**, Dallas Cowboys	.07	.03	.01
☐ 448	**Carey Joyce**, St. Louis Cardinals	.07	.03	.01
☐ 449	**Jim LeClair**, Cincinnati Bengals	.07	.03	.01
☐ 450	**Ken Houston**, Washington Redskins	.15	.06	.01

RECORD BREAKERS

		MINT	VG-E	F-G
☐ 451	**RB: Steve Grogan** Most Touchdowns Rushing by QB, Season	.20	.09	.02
☐ 452	**RB: Jim Marshall** Most Games Played, Lifetime	.25	.10	.02
☐ 453	**RB: O.J. Simpson** Most Yardage, Rushing, Game	1.00	.45	.10
☐ 454	**RB: Fran Tarkenton** Most Yardage, Passing, Lifetime	.80	.40	.08
☐ 455	**RB: Jim Zorn** Most Passing Yards Season, Rookie	.20	.09	.02
☐ 456	**Robert Pratt**, Baltimore Colts	.07	.03	.01
☐ 457	**Walker Gillette**, New York Giants	.07	.03	.01
☐ 458	**Charlie Hall**, Cleveland Browns	.07	.03	.01
☐ 459	**Robert Newhouse**, Dallas Cowboys	.25	.10	.02
☐ 460	**John Hannah**, New England Patriots	.25	.10	.02

		MINT	VG-E	F-G
☐ 461	Ken Reaves, St. Louis Cardinals	.07	.03	.01
☐ 462	Herman Weaver, Detroit Lions	.07	.03	.01
☐ 463	James Harris, Los Angeles Rams	.25	.10	.02
☐ 464	Howard Twilley, Miami Dolphins	.10	.04	.01
☐ 465	Jeff Siemon, Minnesota Vikings	.10	.04	.01
☐ 466	John Outlaw, Philadelphia Eagles	.07	.03	.01
☐ 467	Chuck Muncie, New Orleans Saints	.65	.30	.06
☐ 468	Bob Moore, Tampa Bay Buccaneers	.07	.03	.01
☐ 469	Robert Woods, New York Jets	.07	.03	.01
☐ 470	Cliff Branch, Oakland Raiders	.25	.10	.02
☐ 471	Johnnie Gray, Green Bay Packers	.07	.03	.01
☐ 472	Don Hardeman, Houston Oilers	.07	.03	.01
☐ 473	Steve Ramsey, Denver Broncos	.10	.04	.01
☐ 474	Steve Mike-Mayer, San Francisco 49ers	.07	.03	.01
☐ 475	Gary Garrison, San Diego Chargers	.07	.03	.01
☐ 476	Walter Johnson, Cleveland Browns	.07	.03	.01
☐ 477	Neil Clabo, Minnesota Vikings	.07	.03	.01
☐ 478	Len Hauss, Washington Redskins	.07	.03	.01
☐ 479	Darryl Stingley, New England Patriots	.20	.09	.02
☐ 480	Jack Lambert, Pittsburgh Steelers	.55	.25	.05
☐ 481	Mike Adamle, Chicago Bears	.10	.04	.01
☐ 482	David Lee, Baltimore Colts	.07	.03	.01
☐ 483	Tom Mullen, New York Giants	.07	.03	.01
☐ 484	Claude Humphrey, Atlanta Falcons	.10	.04	.01
☐ 485	Jim Hart, St. Louis Cardinals	.45	.20	.04
☐ 486	Bobby Thompson, Detroit Lions	.07	.03	.01
☐ 487	Jack Rudnay, Kansas City Chiefs	.07	.03	.01
☐ 488	Rich Sowells, New York Jets	.07	.03	.01
☐ 489	Reuben Gant, Buffalo Bills	.07	.03	.01
☐ 490	Cliff Harris, Dallas Cowboys	.25	.10	.02
☐ 491	Bob Brown, Cincinnati Bengals	.07	.03	.01
☐ 492	Don Nottingham, Miami Dolphins	.07	.03	.01
☐ 493	Ron Jessie, Los Angeles Rams	.10	.04	.01
☐ 494	Otis Sistrunk, Oakland Raiders	.10	.04	.01
☐ 495	Bill Kilmer, Washington Redskins	.60	.28	.06
☐ 496	Oscar Roan, Cleveland Browns	.07	.03	.01
☐ 497	Bill Van Heusen, Denver Broncos	.07	.03	.01
☐ 498	Randy Logan, Philadelphia Eagles	.07	.03	.01
☐ 499	John Smith, New England Patriots	.07	.03	.01
☐ 500	Chuck Foreman, Minnesota Vikings	.35	.15	.03
☐ 501	J.T. Thomas, Pittsburgh Steelers	.07	.03	.01
☐ 502	Steve Schubert, Chicago Bears	.07	.03	.01
☐ 503	Mike Barnes, Baltimore Colts	.07	.03	.01
☐ 504	J.V. Cain, St. Louis Cardinals	.07	.03	.01
☐ 505	Larry Csonka, New York Giants	.70	.32	.07
☐ 506	Elvin Bethea, Houston Oilers	.10	.04	.01

		MINT	VG-E	F-G
☐ 507	**Ray Esterling**, Atlanta Falcons	.07	.03	.01
☐ 508	**Joe Reed**, Detroit Lions	.10	.04	.01
☐ 509	**Steve Odom**, Green Bay Packers	.10	.04	.01
☐ 510	**Tommy Casanova**, Cincinnati Bengals	.10	.04	.01
☐ 511	**Dave Dalby**, Oakland Raiders	.07	.03	.01
☐ 512	**Richard Caster**, New York Jets	.10	.04	.01
☐ 513	**Fred Dryer**, Los Angeles Rams	.35	.15	.03
☐ 514	**Jeff Kinney**, Kansas City Chiefs	.07	.03	.01
☐ 515	**Bob Griese**, Miami Dolphins	1.50	.70	.15
☐ 516	**Butch Johnson**, Dallas Cowboys	.25	.10	.02
☐ 517	**Gerald Irons**, Cleveland Browns	.07	.03	.01
☐ 518	**Don Calhoun**, New England Patriots	.07	.03	.01
☐ 519	**Jack Gregory**, New York Giants	.10	.04	.01
☐ 520	**Tom Banks**, St. Louis Cardinals	.07	.03	.01
☐ 521	**Bobby Bryant**, Minnesota Vikings	.07	.03	.01
☐ 522	**Reggie Harrison**, Pittsburgh Steelers	.07	.03	.01
☐ 523	**Terry Hermeling**, Washington Redskins	.07	.03	.01
☐ 524	**David Taylor**, Baltimore Colts	.07	.03	.01
☐ 525	**Brian Baschnagel**, Chicago Bears	.07	.03	.01
☐ 526	**AFC Championship**	.25	.10	.02
	Raiders 24, Steelers 7			
	(Stabler)			
☐ 527	**NFC Championship**	.25	.10	.02
	Vikings 24, Rams 13			
☐ 528	**Superbowl XI**	.45	.20	.04
	Raiders 32, Vikings 14			
	(line play)			

1978 TOPPS

The 1978 Topps set contains 528 cards. The cards measure 2½" by 3½". No known scarcities exist. The first six cards in the set feature Highlights (HL) of the previous season. Cards 501 through 528 are Team Leader (TL) cards depicting typically four individual team (statistical) leaders on the front and a team checklist on the back. The card backs are printed in black and green on gray card stock.

		MINT	VG-E	F-G
	COMPLETE SET	27.00	12.00	2.50
	COMMON PLAYER (1-528)	.05	.02	.00
☐	**1 HL: Gary Huff** .... Huff leads Bucs to First Win	.25	.05	.01
☐	**2 HL: Craig Morton** .... Morton passes Broncos to Super Bowl	.20	.09	.02
☐	**3 HL: Walter Payton** .... Rushes for 275 yards	1.00	.45	.10
☐	**4 HL: O.J. Simpson** .... Reaches 10,000 yards	1.00	.45	.10
☐	**5 HL: Fran Tarkenton** .... Completes 17 of 18	.80	.40	.08
☐	**6 HL: Bob Thomas** .... Thomas' FG sends Bears to Playoffs	.08	.03	.01
☐	**7 Joe Pisarcik**, New York Giants	.08	.03	.01
☐	**8 Skip Thomas**, Oakland Raiders	.05	.02	.00
☐	**9 Roosevelt Leaks**, Baltimore Colts	.08	.03	.01
☐	**10 Ken Houston**, Washington Redskins ..	.15	.06	.01
☐	**11 Tom Blanchard**, New Orleans Saints	.05	.02	.00

		MINT	VG-E	F-G
☐ 12	**Jim Turner,** Denver Broncos	.10	.04	.01
☐ 13	**Tom DeLeone,** Cleveland Browns	.05	.02	.00
☐ 14	**Jim LeClair,** Cincinnati Bengals	.05	.02	.00
☐ 15	**Bob Avellini,** Chicago Bears	.10	.04	.01
☐ 16	**Tony McGee,** New England Patriots	.05	.02	.00
☐ 17	**James Harris,** San Diego Chargers	.20	.09	.02
☐ 18	**Terry Nelson,** Los Angeles Rams	.05	.02	.00
☐ 19	**Rocky Bleier,** Pittsburgh Steelers	.20	.09	.02
☐ 20	**Joe DeLamielleure,** Buffalo Bills	.08	.03	.01
☐ 21	**Richard Caster,** Houston Oilers	.10	.04	.01
☐ 22	**A.J. Duhe,** Miami Dolphins	.40	.18	.04
☐ 23	**John Outlaw,** Pittsburgh Steelers	.05	.02	.00
☐ 24	**Danny White,** Dallas Cowboys	.75	.35	.07
☐ 25	**Larry Csonka,** New York Jets	.50	.22	.05
☐ 26	**David Hill,** Detroit Lions	.05	.02	.00
☐ 27	**Mark Arneson,** St. Louis Cardinals	.05	.02	.00
☐ 28	**Jack Tatum,** Oakland Raiders	.15	.06	.01
☐ 29	**Norm Thompson,** Baltimore Colts	.05	.02	.00
☐ 30	**Sammy White,** Minnesota Vikings	.10	.04	.01
☐ 31	**Dennis Johnson,** Washington Redskins	.05	.02	.00
☐ 32	**Robin Earl,** Chicago Bears	.05	.02	.00
☐ 33	**Don Cockroft,** Cleveland Browns	.05	.02	.00
☐ 34	**Bob Johnson,** Cincinnati Bengals	.05	.02	.00
☐ 35	**John Hannah,** New England Patriots	.20	.09	.02
☐ 36	**Scott Hunter,** Atlanta Falcons	.15	.06	.01
☐ 37	**Ken Burrough,** Houston Oilers	.10	.04	.01
☐ 38	**Wilbur Jackson,** San Francisco 49ers	.10	.04	.01
☐ 39	**Rich McGeorge,** Green Bay Packers	.05	.02	.00
☐ 40	**Lyle Alzado,** Denver Broncos	.40	.18	.04
☐ 41	**John Ebersole,** New York Jets	.05	.02	.00
☐ 42	**Gary Green,** Kansas City Chiefs	.05	.02	.00
☐ 43	**Art Kuehn,** Seattle Seahawks	.05	.02	.00
☐ 44	**Glen Edwards,** San Diego Chargers	.05	.02	.00
☐ 45	**Lawrence McCutcheon,** Los Angeles Rams	.20	.09	.02
☐ 46	**Duriel Harris,** Miami Dolphins	.08	.03	.01
☐ 47	**Rich Szaro,** New Orleans Saints	.05	.02	.00
☐ 48	**Mike Washington,** Tampa Bay Buccaneers	.05	.02	.00
☐ 49	**Stan White,** Baltimore Colts	.05	.02	.00
☐ 50	**Dave Casper,** Oakland Raiders	.20	.09	.02
☐ 51	**Len Hauss,** Washington Redskins	.05	.02	.00
☐ 52	**James Scott,** Chicago Bears	.08	.03	.01
☐ 53	**Brian Sipe,** Cleveland Browns	.40	.18	.04
☐ 54	**Gary Shirk,** New York Giants	.05	.02	.00
☐ 55	**Archie Griffin,** Cincinnati Bengals	.20	.09	.02
☐ 56	**Mike Patrick,** New England Patriots	.05	.02	.00
☐ 57	**Mario Clark,** Buffalo Bills	.05	.02	.00

		MINT	VG-E	F-G
☐	58 **Jeff Siemon**, Minnesota Vikings	.08	.03	.01
☐	59 **Steve Mike-Mayer**, New Orleans Saints	.05	.02	.00
☐	60 **Randy White**, Dallas Cowboys	.45	.20	.04
☐	61 **Darrell Austin**, New York Jets	.05	.02	.00
☐	62 **Tom Sullivan**, Cleveland Browns	.05	.02	.00
☐	63 **Johnny Rodgers**, San Diego Chargers	.25	.10	.02
☐	64 **Ken Reaves**, St. Louis Cardinals	.05	.02	.00
☐	65 **Terry Bradshaw**, Pittsburgh Steelers	1.50	.70	.15
☐	66 **Fred Steinfort**, Atlanta Falcons	.05	.02	.00
☐	67 **Curley Culp**, Houston Oilers	.08	.03	.01
☐	68 **Ted Hendricks**, Oakland Raiders	.20	.09	.02
☐	69 **Raymond Chester**, Oakland Raiders	.10	.04	.01
☐	70 **Jim Langer**, Miami Dolphins	.05	.02	.00
☐	71 **Calvin Hill**, Cleveland Browns	.20	.09	.02
☐	72 **Mike Hartenstein**, Chicago Bears	.05	.02	.00
☐	73 **Gerald Irons**, Cleveland Browns	.05	.02	.00
☐	74 **Billy Brooks**, Cincinnati Bengals	.08	.03	.01
☐	75 **John Mendenhall**, New York Giants	.05	.02	.00
☐	76 **Andy Johnson**, New England Patriots	.05	.02	.00
☐	77 **Tom Wittum**, San Francisco 49ers	.05	.02	.00
☐	78 **Lynn Dickey**, Green Bay Packers	.25	.10	.02
☐	79 **Carl Eller**, Minnesota Vikings	.30	.12	.03
☐	80 **Tom Mack**, Los Angeles Rams	.08	.03	.01
☐	81 **Clark Gaines**, New York Jets	.05	.02	.00
☐	82 **Lem Barney**, Detroit Lions	.08	.03	.01
☐	83 **Mike Montler**, Detroit Lions	.05	.02	.00
☐	84 **Jon Kolb**, Pittsburgh Steelers	.05	.02	.00
☐	85 **Bob Chandler**, Buffalo Bills	.08	.03	.01
☐	86 **Robert Newhouse**, Dallas Cowboys	.20	.09	.02
☐	87 **Frank LeMaster**, Philadelphia Eagles	.05	.02	.00
☐	88 **Jeff West**, San Diego Chargers	.05	.02	.00
☐	89 **Lyle Blackwood**, Baltimore Colts	.05	.02	.00
☐	90 **Gene Upshaw**, Oakland Raiders	.08	.03	.01
☐	91 **Frank Grant**, Washington Redskins	.05	.02	.00
☐	92 **Tom Hicks**, Chicago Bears	.05	.02	.00
☐	93 **Mike Pruitt**, Cleveland Browns	.20	.09	.02
☐	94 **Chris Bahr**, Cincinnati Bengals	.08	.03	.01
☐	95 **Russ Francis**, New England Patriots	.20	.09	.02
☐	96 **Norris Thomas**, Miami Dolphins	.05	.02	.00
☐	97 **Gary Barbaro**, Kansas City Chiefs	.08	.03	.01
☐	98 **Jim Merlo**, New Orleans Saints	.05	.02	.00
☐	99 **Karl Chandler**, Detroit Lions	.05	.02	.00
☐	100 **Fran Tarkenton**, Minnesota Vikings	2.00	.90	.20
☐	101 **Abdul Salaam**, New York Jets	.05	.02	.00
☐	102 **Marty Kellum**, St. Louis Cardinals	.05	.02	.00
☐	103 **Herman Weaver**, Seattle Seahawks	.05	.02	.00

		MINT	VG-E	F-G
☐ 104	**Roy Gerela**, Pittsburgh Steelers	.05	.02	.00
☐ 105	**Harold Jackson**, New England Patriots	.25	.10	.02
☐ 106	**Dewey Selmon**, Tampa Bay Buccaneers	.08	.03	.01
☐ 107	**Checklist 1-132**	.30	.04	.01
☐ 108	**Clarence Davis**, Oakland Raiders	.05	.02	.00
☐ 109	**Robert Pratt**, Baltimore Colts	.05	.02	.00
☐ 110	**Harvey Martin**, Dallas Cowboys	.20	.09	.02
☐ 111	**Brad Dusek**, Washington Redskins	.05	.02	.00
☐ 112	**Greg Latta**, Chicago Bears	.05	.02	.00
☐ 113	**Tony Peters**, Cleveland Browns	.05	.02	.00
☐ 114	**Jim Braxton**, Buffalo Bills	.05	.02	.00
☐ 115	**Ken Riley**, Cincinnati Bengals	.08	.03	.01
☐ 116	**Steve Nelson**, New England Patriots	.05	.02	.00
☐ 117	**Rick Upchurch**, Denver Broncos	.10	.04	.01
☐ 118	**Spike Jones**, Philadelphia Eagles	.05	.02	.00
☐ 119	**Doug Kotar**, New York Giants	.05	.02	.00
☐ 120	**Bob Griese**, Dallas Cowboys	1.00	.45	.10
☐ 121	**Burgess Owens**, New York Jets	.05	.02	.00
☐ 122	**Rolf Benirschke**, San Diego Chargers	.10	.04	.01
☐ 123	**Haskel Stanback**, Atlanta Falcons	.05	.02	.00
☐ 124	**J.T. Thomas**, Pittsburgh Steelers	.05	.02	.00
☐ 125	**Armad Rashad**, Minnesota Vikings	.35	.15	.03
☐ 126	**Rick Kane**, Detroit Lions	.05	.02	.00
☐ 127	**Elvin Bethea**, Houston Oilers	.08	.03	.01
☐ 128	**Dave Dalby**, Oakland Raiders	.05	.02	.00
☐ 129	**Mike Barnes**, Baltimore Colts	.05	.02	.00
☐ 130	**Isiah Robertson**, Los Angeles Rams	.05	.02	.00
☐ 131	**Jim Plunkett**, San Francisco 49ers	.50	.22	.05
☐ 132	**Allan Ellis**, Chicago Bears	.05	.02	.00
☐ 133	**Mike Bragg**, Washington Redskins	.05	.02	.00
☐ 134	**Bob Jackson**, Cleveland Browns	.05	.02	.00
☐ 135	**Coy Bacon**, Washington Redskins	.05	.02	.00
☐ 136	**John Smith**, New England Patriots	.05	.02	.00
☐ 137	**Chuck Muncie**, New Orleans Saints	.20	.09	.02
☐ 138	**Johnnie Gray**, Green Bay Packers	.05	.02	.00
☐ 139	**Jimmy Robertson**, New York Giants	.05	.02	.00
☐ 140	**Tom Banks**, St. Louis Cardinals	.05	.02	.00
☐ 141	**Marvin Powell**, New York Jets	.08	.03	.01
☐ 142	**Jerrel Wilson**, New England Patriots	.05	.02	.00
☐ 143	**Ron Howard**, Seattle Seahawks	.05	.02	.00
☐ 144	**Rob Lytle**, Denver Broncos	.05	.02	.00
☐ 145	**L.C. Greenwood**, Pittsburgh Steelers	.20	.09	.02
☐ 146	**Morris Owens**, Tampa Bay Buccaneers	.05	.02	.00
☐ 147	**Joe Reed**, Detroit Lions	.08	.03	.01
☐ 148	**Mike Kadish**, Buffalo Bills	.05	.02	.00
☐ 149	**Phil Villapiano**, Oakland Raiders	.08	.03	.01

	MINT	VG-E	F-G
☐ 150 **Lydell Mitchell**, San Diego Chargers	.20	.09	.02
☐ 151 **Randy Logan**, Philadelphia Eagles	.05	.02	.00
☐ 152 **Mike Williams**, San Diego Chargers	.05	.02	.00
☐ 153 **Jeff Van Note**, Atlanta Falcons	.08	.03	.01
☐ 154 **Steve Schubert**, Chicago Bears	.05	.02	.00
☐ 155 **Bill Kilmer**, Washington Redskins	.40	.18	.04
☐ 156 **Boobie Clark**, Cincinnati Bengals	.08	.03	.01
☐ 157 **Charlie Hall**, Cleveland Browns	.05	.02	.00
☐ 158 **Raymond Clayborn**, New England Patriots ...	.08	.03	.01
☐ 159 **Jack Gregory**, New York Giants	.08	.03	.01
☐ 160 **Cliff Harris**, Dallas Cowboys	.20	.09	.02
☐ 161 **Joe Fields**, New York Jets	.05	.02	.00
☐ 162 **Don Nottingham**, Miami Dolphins	.05	.02	.00
☐ 163 **Ed White**, San Diego Chargers	.05	.02	.00
☐ 164 **Toni Fritsch**, Houston Oilers	.05	.02	.00
☐ 165 **Jack Lambert**, Pittsburgh Steelers	.35	.15	.03
☐ 166 **NFC Champions**	.35	.15	.03
Cowboys 23, Vikings 6			
☐ 167 **AFC Champions**	.20	.09	.02
Broncos 20, Raiders 17			
(Lytle running)			
☐ 168 **Super Bowl XII**	.55	.25	.05
Cowboys 27, Broncos 10			
☐ 169 **Neal Colzie**, Oakland Raiders	.05	.02	.00
☐ 170 **Cleveland Elam**, San Francisco 49ers	.05	.02	.00
☐ 171 **David Lee**, Baltimore Colts	.05	.02	.00
☐ 172 **Jim Otis**, St. Louis Cardinals	.10	.04	.01
☐ 173 **Archie Manning**, New Orleans Saints	.40	.18	.04
☐ 174 **Jim Carter**, Green Bay Packers	.05	.02	.00
☐ 175 **Jean Fugett**, Washington Redskins	.05	.02	.00
☐ 176 **Willie Parker**, Buffalo Bills	.05	.02	.00
☐ 177 **Haven Moses**, Denver Broncos	.08	.03	.01
☐ 178 **Horace King**, Detroit Lions	.05	.02	.00
☐ 179 **Bob Thomas**, Chicago Bears	.05	.02	.00
☐ 180 **Monty Jackson**, Oakland Raiders	.05	.02	.00
☐ 181 **Steve Zabel**, New England Patriots	.05	.02	.00
☐ 182 **John Fitzgerald**, Dallas Cowboys	.05	.02	.00
☐ 183 **Mike Livingston**, Kansas City Chiefs	.08	.03	.01
☐ 184 **Larry Poole**, Houston Oilers	.05	.02	.00
☐ 185 **Isaac Curtis**, Cincinnati Bengals	.08	.03	.01
☐ 186 **Chuck Ramsey**, New York Jets	.05	.02	.00
☐ 187 **Bob Klein**, San Diego Chargers	.05	.02	.00
☐ 188 **Ray Rhodes**, New York Giants	.05	.02	.00
☐ 189 **Otis Sistrunk**, Oakland Raiders	.08	.03	.01
☐ 190 **Bill Bergey**, Philadelphia Eagles	.20	.09	.02
☐ 191 **Sherman Smith**, Seattle Seahawks	.08	.03	.01

		MINT	VG-E	F-G
☐ 192	**Dave Green**, Tampa Bay Buccaneers	.05	.02	.00
☐ 193	**Carl Mauck**, Houston Oilers	.05	.02	.00
☐ 194	**Reggie Harrison**, Green Bay Packers	.05	.02	.00
☐ 195	**Roger Carr**, Baltimore Colts	.08	.03	.01
☐ 196	**Steve Bartkowski**, Atlanta Falcons	.35	.15	.03
☐ 197	**Ray Wersching**, San Francisco 49ers	.05	.02	.00
☐ 198	**Willie Buchanon**, Green Bay Packers	.08	.03	.01
☐ 199	**Neil Clabo**, Minnesota Vikings	.05	.02	.00
☐ 200	**Walter Payton**, Chicago Bears	2.50	1.15	.25
☐ 201	**Sam Adams**, New England Patriots	.05	.02	.00
☐ 202	**Larry Gordon**, Miami Dolphins	.05	.02	.00
☐ 203	**Pat Tilley**, St. Louis Cardinals	.10	.04	.01
☐ 204	**Mack Mitchell**, Cleveland Browns	.05	.02	.00
☐ 205	**Ken Anderson**, Cincinnati Bengals	.60	.28	.06
☐ 206	**Scott Dierking**, New York Jets	.05	.02	.00
☐ 207	**Jack Rudnay**, Kansas City Chiefs	.05	.02	.00
☐ 208	**Jim Stienke**, Atlanta Falcons	.05	.02	.00
☐ 209	**Bill Simpson**, Los Angeles Rams	.05	.02	.00
☐ 210	**Errol Mann**, Oakland Raiders	.05	.02	.00
☐ 211	**Bucky Dilts**, Denver Broncos	.05	.02	.00
☐ 212	**Reuben Gant**, Buffalo Bills	.05	.02	.00
☐ 213	**Thomas Henderson**, Dallas Cowboys	.20	.09	.02
☐ 214	**Steve Furness**, Pittsburgh Steelers	.05	.02	.00
☐ 215	**John Riggins**, Washington Redskins	.50	.22	.05
☐ 216	**Keith Krepfle**, Philadelphia Eagles	.05	.02	.00
☐ 217	**Fred Dean**, San Diego Chargers	.20	.09	.02
☐ 218	**Emanuel Zanders**, New Orleans Saints	.05	.02	.00
☐ 219	**Don Testerman**, Seattle Seahawks	.05	.02	.00
☐ 220	**George Kunz**, Baltimore Colts	.08	.03	.01
☐ 221	**Darryl Stingley**, New England Patriots	.15	.06	.01
☐ 222	**Ken Sanders**, Detroit Lions	.05	.02	.00
☐ 223	**Gary Huff**, Tampa Bay Buccaneers	.15	.06	.01
☐ 224	**Gregg Bingham**, Houston Oilers	.05	.02	.00
☐ 225	**Jerry Sherk**, Cleveland Browns	.08	.03	.01
☐ 226	**Doug Plank**, Chicago Bears	.05	.02	.00
☐ 227	**Ed Taylor**, New York Jets	.05	.02	.00
☐ 228	**Emery Moorehead**, New York Giants	.05	.02	.00
☐ 229	**Reggie Williams**, Cincinnati Bengals	.10	.04	.01
☐ 230	**Claude Williams**, Atlanta Falcons	.05	.02	.00
☐ 231	**Randy Cross**, San Francisco 49ers	.05	.02	.00
☐ 232	**Jim Hart**, St. Louis Cardinals	.30	.12	.03
☐ 233	**Bobby Bryant**, Minnesota Vikings	.05	.02	.00
☐ 234	**Larry Brown**, Pittsburgh Steelers	.05	.02	.00
☐ 235	**Mark Van Eeghen**, Oakland Raiders	.08	.03	.01
☐ 236	**Terry Hermeling**, Washington Redskins	.05	.02	.00
☐ 237	**Steve Odom**, Green Bay Packers	.05	.02	.00

		MINT	VG-E	F-G
☐ 238	Jan Stenerud, Kansas City Chiefs	.15	.06	.01
☐ 239	Andre Tillman, Miami Dolphins	.05	.02	.00
☐ 240	Tom Jackson, Denver Broncos	.15	.06	.01
☐ 241	Ken Mendenhall, Baltimore Colts	.05	.02	.00
☐ 242	Tim Fox, New England Patriots	.05	.02	.00
☐ 243	Don Hermann, New Orleans Saints	.05	.02	.00
☐ 244	Eddie McMillan, Buffalo Bills	.05	.02	.00
☐ 245	Greg Pruitt, Cleveland Browns	.20	.09	.02
☐ 246	J.K. McKay, Tampa Bay Buccaneers	.05	.02	.00
☐ 247	Larry Keller, New York Jets	.05	.02	.00
☐ 248	Dave Jennings, New York Giants	.08	.03	.01
☐ 249	Bo Harris, Cincinnati Bengals	.05	.02	.00
☐ 250	Revie Sorey, Chicago Bears	.05	.02	.00
☐ 251	Tony Greene, Washington Redskins	.05	.02	.00
☐ 252	Butch Johnson, Dallas Cowboys	.20	.09	.02
☐ 253	Paul Naumoff, Detroit Lions	.05	.02	.00
☐ 254	Rickey Young, Minnesota Vikings	.08	.03	.01
☐ 255	Dwight White, Pittsburgh Steelers	.08	.03	.01
☐ 256	Joe Lavender, Washington Redskins	.05	.02	.00
☐ 257	Checklist 133-264	.30	.04	.01
☐ 258	Ronnie Coleman, Houston Oilers	.05	.02	.00
☐ 259	Charlie Smith, Philadelphia Eagles	.05	.02	.00
☐ 260	Ray Guy, Oakland Raiders	.20	.09	.02
☐ 261	David Taylor, Baltimore Colts	.05	.02	.00
☐ 262	Bill Lenkaitis, New England Patriots	.05	.02	.00
☐ 263	Jim Mitchell, Atlanta Falcons	.05	.02	.00
☐ 264	Delvin Williams, Miami Dolphins	.10	.04	.01
☐ 265	Jack Youngblood, Los Angeles Rams	.30	.12	.03
☐ 266	Chuck Crist, San Francisco 49ers	.05	.02	.00
☐ 267	Richard Todd, New York Jets	.30	.12	.03
☐ 268	Dave Logan, Cleveland Browns	.05	.02	.00
☐ 269	Rufus Mayes, Cincinnati Bengals	.05	.02	.00
☐ 270	Brad Van Pelt, New York Giants	.08	.03	.01
☐ 271	Chester Marcol, Green Bay Packers	.05	.02	.00
☐ 272	J.V. Cain, St. Louis Cardinals	.05	.02	.00
☐ 273	Larry Seiple, Miami Dolphins	.05	.02	.00
☐ 274	Brent McClanahan, Minnesota Vikings	.05	.02	.00
☐ 275	Mike Wagner, Pittsburgh Steelers	.08	.03	.01
☐ 276	Diron Talbert, Washington Redskins	.05	.02	.00
☐ 277	Brian Baschnagel, Chicago Bears	.05	.02	.00
☐ 278	Ed Podolak, Kansas City Chiefs	.08	.03	.01
☐ 279	Don Good, San Diego Chargers	.05	.02	.00
☐ 280	John Dutton, Baltimore Colts	.10	.04	.01
☐ 281	Don Calhoun, New England Patriots	.05	.02	.00
☐ 282	Monte Johnson, Oakland Raiders	.05	.02	.00

	MINT	VG-E	F-G
☐ 283 Ron Jessie, Los Angeles Rams	.08	.03	.01
☐ 284 Jon Morris, Chicago Bears	.05	.02	.00
☐ 285 Riley Odoms, Denver Broncos	.10	.04	.01
☐ 286 Marv Bateman, Buffalo Bills	.05	.02	.00
☐ 287 Joe Klecko, New York Jets	.60	.28	.06
☐ 288 Oliver Davis, Cleveland Browns	.05	.02	.00
☐ 289 John McDaniel, Washington Redskins	.05	.02	.00
☐ 290 Roger Staubach, Dallas Cowboys	2.25	1.00	.22
☐ 291 Brian Kelley, New York Giants	.05	.02	.00
☐ 292 Mike Hogan, Philadelphia Eagles	.05	.02	.00
☐ 293 John Leypoldt, New Orleans Saints	.05	.02	.00
☐ 294 Jack Novak, Tampa Bay Buccaneers	.05	.02	.00
☐ 295 Joe Greene, Pittsburgh Steelers	.40	.18	.04
☐ 296 John Hill, New Orleans Saints	.05	.02	.00
☐ 297 Danny Buggs, Washington Redskins	.05	.02	.00
☐ 298 Ted Albrecht, Chicago Bears	.05	.02	.00
☐ 299 Nelson Munsey, Minnesota Vikings	.05	.02	.00
☐ 300 Chuck Foreman, Minnesota Vikings	.25	.10	.02
☐ 301 Dan Pastorini, Houston Oilers	.25	.10	.02
☐ 302 Tommy Hart, Chicago Bears	.05	.02	.00
☐ 303 Dave Beverly, Green Bay Packers	.05	.02	.00
☐ 304 Tony Reed, Kansas City Chiefs	.15	.06	.01
☐ 305 Cliff Branch, Oakland Raiders	.20	.09	.02
☐ 306 Clarence Duren, San Diego Chargers	.05	.02	.00
☐ 307 Randy Rasmussen, New York Jets	.05	.02	.00
☐ 308 Oscar Roan, Cleveland Browns	.05	.02	.00
☐ 309 Lenvil Elliott, Cincinnati Bengals	.05	.02	.00
☐ 310 Dan Dierdorf, St. Louis Cardinals	.08	.03	.01
☐ 311 Johnny Perkins, New York Giants	.05	.02	.00
☐ 312 Rafael Septien, Dallas Cowboys	.20	.09	.02
☐ 313 Terry Beeson, Seattle Seahawks	.05	.02	.00
☐ 314 LeRoy Selmon, Tampa Bay Buccaneers	.30	.12	.03
☐ 315 Tony Dorsett, Dallas Cowboys	6.00	2.80	.60
☐ 316 Greg Landry, Detroit Lions	.20	.09	.02
☐ 317 Jake Scott, Washington Redskins	.10	.04	.01
☐ 318 Dan Peiffer, Chicago Bears	.05	.02	.00
☐ 319 John Bunting, Philadelphia Eagles	.05	.02	.00
☐ 320 John Stallworth, Pittsburgh Steelers	.40	.18	.04
☐ 321 Rob Howard, Philadelphia Eagles	.05	.02	.00
☐ 322 Larry Little, Miami Dolphins	.08	.03	.01
☐ 323 Reggie McKenzie, Buffalo Bills	.08	.03	.01
☐ 324 Duane Carrell, St. Louis Cardinals	.05	.02	.00
☐ 325 Ed Simonini, Baltimore Colts	.05	.02	.00
☐ 326 John Vella, Oakland Raiders	.05	.02	.00
☐ 327 Wesley Walker, New York Jets	.60	.28	.06

	MINT	VG-E	F-G
☐ 328 **Jon Keyworth**, Denver Broncos	.05	.02	.00
☐ 329 **Ron Bolton**, Cleveland Browns	.05	.02	.00
☐ 330 **Tommy Casanova**, Cincinnati Bengals	.08	.03	.01

STATISTICAL LEADERS

	MINT	VG-E	F-G
☐ 331 **Passing Leaders** .... Bob Griese Roger Staubach	.80	.40	.08
☐ 332 **Receiving Leaders** .... Lydell Mitchell Ahmad Rashad	.20	.09	.02
☐ 333 **Rushing Leaders** .... Mark van Eeghen Walter Payton	.60	.28	.06
☐ 334 **Scoring Leaders** .... Errol Mann Walter Payton	.60	.28	.06
☐ 335 **Interception Leaders** .... Lyle Blackwood Rolland Lawrence	.08	.03	.01
☐ 336 **Punting Leaders** .... Ray Guy Tom Blanchard	.15	.06	.01
☐ 337 **Robert Brazile**, Houston Oilers	.08	.03	.01
☐ 338 **Charlie Joiner**, San Diego Chargers	.30	.12	.03
☐ 339 **Joe Ferguson**, Buffalo Bills	.25	.10	.02
☐ 340 **Bill Thompson**, Denver Broncos	.08	.03	.01
☐ 341 **Sam Cunningham**, New England Patriots	.10	.04	.01
☐ 342 **Curtis Johnson**, Miami Dolphins	.05	.02	.00
☐ 343 **Jim Marshall**, Minnesota Vikings	.30	.12	.03
☐ 344 **Charlie Sanders**, Detroit Lions	.10	.04	.01
☐ 345 **Willie Hall**, Oakland Raiders	.05	.02	.00
☐ 346 **Pat Haden**, Los Angeles Rams	.25	.10	.02
☐ 347 **Jim Bakken**, St. Louis Cardinals	.15	.06	.01
☐ 348 **Bruce Taylor**, San Francisco 49ers	.10	.04	.01
☐ 349 **Barty Smith**, Green Bay Packers	.05	.02	.00
☐ 350 **Drew Pearson**, Dallas Cowboys	.35	.15	.03
☐ 351 **Mike Webster**, Pittsburgh Steelers	.08	.03	.01
☐ 352 **Bobby Hammond**, New York Giants	.05	.02	.00
☐ 353 **Dave Mays**, Buffalo Bills	.05	.02	.00
☐ 354 **Pat McInally**, Cincinnati Bengals	.10	.04	.01
☐ 355 **Toni Linhart**, Baltimore Colts	.05	.02	.00

	MINT	VG-E	F-G
☐ 356 **Larry Hand,** Detroit Lions	.05	.02	.00
☐ 357 **Ted Fritsch,** Washington Redskins	.05	.02	.00
☐ 358 **Larry Marshall,** Philadelphia Eagles	.05	.02	.00
☐ 359 **Waymond Bryant,** Chicago Bears	.05	.02	.00
☐ 360 **Louie Kelcher,** San Diego Chargers	.08	.03	.01
☐ 361 **Stanley Morgan,** New England Patriots	.60	.28	.06
☐ 362 **Bruce Harper,** New York Jets	.05	.02	.00
☐ 363 **Bernard Jackson,** Denver Broncos	.08	.03	.01
☐ 364 **Walter White,** Kansas City Chiefs	.05	.02	.00
☐ 365 **Ken Stabler,** Oakland Raiders	.50	.22	.05
☐ 366 **Fred Dryer,** Los Angeles Rams	.30	.12	.03
☐ 367 **Ike Harris,** New Orleans Saints	.05	.02	.00
☐ 368 **Norm Bulaich,** Miami Dolphins	.08	.03	.01
☐ 369 **Merv Krakau,** Buffalo Bills	.05	.02	.00
☐ 370 **John James,** Atlanta Falcons	.05	.02	.00
☐ 371 **Bennie Cunningham,** Pittsburgh Steelers	.05	.02	.00
☐ 372 **Doug Van Horn,** New York Giants	.05	.02	.00
☐ 373 **Thom Darden,** Cleveland Browns	.05	.02	.00
☐ 374 **Eddie Edwards,** Cincinnati Bengals	.05	.02	.00
☐ 375 **Mike Thomas,** Washington Redskins	.05	.02	.00
☐ 376 **Fred Cook,** Baltimore Colts	.05	.02	.00
☐ 377 **Mike Phipps,** Chicago Bears	.20	.09	.02
☐ 378 **Paul Krause,** Minnesota Vikings	.08	.03	.01
☐ 379 **Harold Carmichael,** Philadelphia Eagles	.30	.12	.03
☐ 380 **Mike Haynes,** New England Patriots	.20	.09	.02
☐ 381 **Wayne Morris,** St. Louis Cardinals	.08	.03	.01
☐ 382 **Greg Buttle,** New York Jets	.08	.03	.01
☐ 383 **Jim Zorn,** Seattle Seahawks	.20	.09	.02
☐ 384 **Jack Dolbin,** Denver Broncos	.05	.02	.00
☐ 385 **Charlie Waters,** Dallas Cowboys	.20	.09	.02
☐ 386 **Dan Ryczek,** Los Angeles Rams	.05	.02	.00
☐ 387 **Joe Washington,** Baltimore Colts	.20	.09	.02
☐ 388 **Checklist 265-396**	.30	.04	.01
☐ 389 **James Hunter,** Detroit Lions	.05	.02	.00
☐ 390 **Billy Johnson,** Houston Oilers	.15	.06	.01
☐ 391 **Jim Allen,** Detroit Lions	.05	.02	.00
☐ 392 **George Buehler,** Oakland Raiders	.05	.02	.00
☐ 393 **Harry Carson,** New York Giants	.20	.09	.02
☐ 394 **Cleo Miller,** Cleveland Browns	.05	.02	.00
☐ 395 **Gary Burley,** Cincinnati Bengals	.05	.02	.00
☐ 396 **Mark Moseley,** Washington Redskins	.10	.04	.01
☐ 397 **Virgil Livers,** Chicago Bears	.05	.02	.00
☐ 398 **Joe Ehrmann,** Baltimore Colts	.05	.02	.00
☐ 399 **Freddie Solomon,** San Francisco 49ers	.10	.04	.01
☐ 400 **O.J. Simpson,** San Francisco 49ers	2.00	.90	.20

	MINT	VG-E	F-G
☐ 401 **Julius Adams,** New England Patriots	.05	.02	.00
☐ 402 **Artimus Parker,** New York Jets	.05	.02	.00
☐ 403 **Gene Washington,** San Francisco 49ers	.10	.04	.01
☐ 404 **Herman Edwards,** Philadelphia Eagles	.05	.02	.00
☐ 405 **Craig Morton,** Denver Broncos	.35	.15	.03
☐ 406 **Alan Page,** Minnesota Vikings	.35	.15	.03
☐ 407 **Larry McCarren,** Green Bay Packers	.05	.02	.00
☐ 408 **Tony Galbreath,** New Orleans Saints	.10	.04	.01
☐ 409 **Roman Gabriel,** Philadelphia Eagles	.45	.20	.04
☐ 410 **Efren Herrera,** Seattle Seahawks	.05	.02	.00
☐ 411 **Jim Smith,** Pittsburgh Steelers	.20	.09	.02
☐ 412 **Bill Bryant,** New York Giants	.05	.02	.00
☐ 413 **Doug Dieken,** Cleveland Browns	.05	.02	.00
☐ 414 **Marvin Cobb,** Cincinnati Bengals	.05	.02	.00
☐ 415 **Fred Biletnikoff,** Oakland Raiders	.35	.15	.03
☐ 416 **Joe Theismann,** Washington Redskins	.90	.40	.09
☐ 417 **Roland Harper,** Chicago Bears	.08	.03	.01
☐ 418 **Derrel Luce,** Baltimore Colts	.05	.02	.00
☐ 419 **Ralph Perretta,** San Diego Chargers	.05	.02	.00
☐ 420 **Louis Wright,** Denver Broncos	.08	.03	.01
☐ 421 **Prentice McCray,** New England Patriots	.05	.02	.00
☐ 422 **Garry Puetz,** New York Jets	.05	.02	.00
☐ 423 **Alfred Jenkins,** Atlanta Falcons	.08	.03	.01
☐ 424 **Paul Seymour,** Buffalo Bills	.05	.02	.00
☐ 425 **Garo Yepremian,** Miami Dolphins	.10	.04	.01
☐ 426 **Emmitt Thomas,** Kansas City Chiefs	.05	.02	.00
☐ 427 **Dexter Bussey,** Detroit Lions	.05	.02	.00
☐ 428 **John Sanders,** Philadelphia Eagles	.05	.02	.00
☐ 429 **Ed Too Tall Jones,** Dallas Cowboys	.35	.15	.03
☐ 430 **Ron Yary,** Minnesota Vikings	.08	.03	.01
☐ 431 **Frank Lewis,** Buffalo Bills	.10	.04	.01
☐ 432 **Jerry Golsteyn,** New York Giants	.08	.03	.01
☐ 433 **Clarence Scott,** Cleveland Browns	.05	.02	.00
☐ 434 **Pete Johnson,** Cincinnati Bengals	.35	.15	.03
☐ 435 **Charley Young,** Los Angeles Rams	.08	.03	.01
☐ 436 **Harold McClinton,** Washington Redskins	.05	.02	.00
☐ 437 **Noah Jackson,** Chicago Bears	.05	.02	.00
☐ 438 **Bruce Laird,** Baltimore Colts	.05	.02	.00
☐ 439 **John Matuszak,** Oakland Raiders	.10	.04	.01
☐ 440 **Nat Moore,** Miami Dolphins	.08	.03	.01
☐ 441 **Leon Gray,** New England Patriots	.08	.03	.01
☐ 442 **Jerome Barkum,** New York Jets	.10	.04	.01
☐ 443 **Steve Largent,** Seattle Seahawks	.30	.12	.03
☐ 444 **John Zook,** St. Louis Cardinals	.08	.03	.01
☐ 445 **Preston Pearson,** Dallas Cowboys	.20	.09	.02
☐ 446 **Conrad Dobler,** New Orleans Saints	.08	.03	.01

	MINT	VG-E	F-G
☐ 447 **Wilbur Summers,** Detroit Lions	.05	.02	.00
☐ 448 **Lou Piccone,** Buffalo Bills	.05	.02	.00
☐ 449 **Ron Jaworski,** Philadelphia Eagles	.45	.20	.04
☐ 450 **Jack Ham,** Pittsburgh Steelers	.20	.09	.02
☐ 451 **Mick Tingelhoff,** Minnesota Vikings	.10	.04	.01
☐ 452 **Clyde Powers,** New York Giants	.05	.02	.00
☐ 453 **John Cappelletti,** Los Angeles Rams	.15	.06	.01
☐ 454 **Dick Ambrose,** Cleveland Browns	.05	.02	.00
☐ 455 **Lemar Parrish,** Washington Redskins	.05	.02	.00
☐ 456 **Ron Saul,** Washington Redskins	.05	.02	.00
☐ 457 **Bob Parsons,** Chicago Bears	.05	.02	.00
☐ 458 **Glenn Doughty,** Baltimore Colts	.05	.02	.00
☐ 459 **Don Woods,** San Diego Chargers	.05	.02	.00
☐ 460 **Art Shell,** Oakland Raiders	.08	.03	.01
☐ 461 **Sam Hunt,** New England Patriots	.05	.02	.00
☐ 462 **Lawrence Pillers,** New York Jets	.05	.02	.00
☐ 463 **Henry Childs,** New Orleans Saints	.05	.02	.00
☐ 464 **Roger Wehrli,** St. Louis Cardinals	.08	.03	.01
☐ 465 **Otis Armstrong,** Denver Broncos	.20	.09	.02
☐ 466 **Bob Baumhower,** Miami Dolphins	.35	.15	.03
☐ 467 **Ray Jarvis,** Detroit Lions	.05	.02	.00
☐ 468 **Guy Morriss,** Philadelphia Eagles	.05	.02	.00
☐ 469 **Matt Blair,** Minnesota Vikings	.08	.03	.01
☐ 470 **Billy Joe DuPree,** Dallas Cowboys	.20	.09	.02
☐ 471 **Roland Hooks,** Buffalo Bills	.05	.02	.00
☐ 472 **Joe Danelo,** New York Giants	.05	.02	.00
☐ 473 **Reggie Rucker,** Cleveland Browns	.10	.04	.01
☐ 474 **Vern Holland,** Cincinnati Bengals	.05	.02	.00
☐ 475 **Mel Blount,** Pittsburgh Steelers	.20	.09	.02
☐ 476 **Eddie Brown,** Los Angeles Rams	.05	.02	.00
☐ 477 **Bo Rather,** Chicago Bears	.05	.02	.00
☐ 478 **Don McCauley,** Baltimore Colts	.05	.02	.00
☐ 479 **Glen Walker,** Los Angeles Rams	.05	.02	.00
☐ 480 **Randy Gradishar,** Denver Broncos	.20	.09	.02
☐ 481 **Dave Rowe,** Oakland Raiders	.05	.02	.00
☐ 482 **Pat Leahy,** New York Jets	.05	.02	.00
☐ 483 **Mike Fuller,** San Diego Chargers	.05	.02	.00
☐ 484 **David Lewis,** Tampa Bay Buccaneers	.05	.02	.00
☐ 485 **Steve Grogan,** New England Patriots	.25	.10	.02
☐ 486 **Mel Gray,** St. Louis Cardinals	.15	.06	.01
☐ 487 **Eddie Payton,** Kansas City Chiefs	.10	.04	.01
☐ 488 **Checklist 397-528**	.30	.04	.01
☐ 489 **Stu Voight,** Minnesota Vikings	.05	.02	.00
☐ 490 **Rolland Lawrence,** Atlanta Falcons	.08	.03	.01
☐ 491 **Nick Mike-Mayer,** Philadelphia Eagles	.05	.02	.00
☐ 492 **Troy Archer,** New York Giants	.05	.02	.00

		MINT	VG-E	F-G
☐ 493	**Benny Malone**, Miami Dolphins	.05	.02	.00
☐ 494	**Golden Richards**, Dallas Cowboys	.08	.03	.01
☐ 495	**Chris Hanburger**, Washington Redskins	.08	.03	.01
☐ 496	**Dwight Harrison**, Baltimore Colts	.05	.02	.00
☐ 497	**Gary Fencik**, Chicago Bears	.05	.02	.00
☐ 498	**Rich Saul**, Los Angeles Rams	.05	.02	.00
☐ 499	**Dan Fouts**, San Diego Chargers	1.00	.45	.10
☐ 500	**Franco Harris**, Pittsburgh Steelers	1.00	.45	.10

TEAM LEADER CARDS

		MINT	VG-E	F-G
☐ 501	**Atlanta Falcons TL**	.20	.05	.01
	Haskel Stanbach			
	Alfred Jenkins			
	Claude Humphrey			
	Jeff Merrow			
	Rolland Lawrence			
☐ 502	**Baltimore Colts TL**	.20	.05	.01
	Lydell Mitchell			
	Lydell Mitchell			
	Lyle Blackwood			
	Fred Cook			
☐ 503	**Buffalo Bills TL**	.50	.10	.01
	O.J. Simpson			
	Bob Chandler			
	Tony Greene			
	Sherman White			
☐ 504	**Chicago Bears TL**	.60	.10	.01
	Walter Payton			
	James Scott			
	Allan Ellis			
	Ron Rydalch			
☐ 505	**Cincinnati Bengals TL**	.20	.05	.01
	Pete Johnson			
	Billy Brooks			
	Lemar Parrish			
	Reggie Williams			
	Gary Burley			
☐ 506	**Cleveland Browns TL**	.20	.05	.01
	Greg Pruitt			
	Reggie Rucker			
	Thom Darden			
	Mack Mitchell			

	MINT	VG-E	F-G
☐ 507 **Dallas Cowboys TL**	.60	.10	.01
Tony Dorsett			
Drew Pearson			
Cliff Harris			
Harvey Martin			
☐ 508 **Denver Broncos TL**	.20	.05	.01
Otis Armstrong			
Haven Moses			
Bill Thompson			
Rick Upchurch			
☐ 509 **Detroit Lions TL**	.20	.05	.01
Horace King			
David Hill			
James Hunter			
Ken Sanders			
☐ 510 **Green Bay Packers TL**	.20	.05	.01
Barty Smith			
Steve Odom			
Steve Luke			
Mike C. McCoy			
Dave Pureifory			
Dave Roller			
☐ 511 **Houston Oilers TL**	.20	.05	.01
Ronnie Coleman			
Ken Burrough			
Mike Reinfeldt			
James Young			
☐ 512 **Kansas City Chiefs TL**	.20	.05	.01
Ed Podolak			
Walter White			
Gary Barbaro			
Wilbur Young			
☐ 513 **Los Angeles Rams TL**	.20	.05	.01
Lawrence McCutcheon			
Harold Jackson			
Bill Simpson			
Jack Youngblood			
☐ 514 **Miami Dolphins TL**	.20	.05	.01
Benny Malone			
Nat Moore			
Curtis Johnson			
A.J. Duhe			

	MINT	VG-E	F-G
☐ 515 **Minnesota Vikings TL**	.20	.05	.01
Chuck Foreman			
Sammie White			
Bobby Bryant			
Carl Eller			
☐ 516 **New England Patriots TL**	.20	.05	.01
Sam Cunningham			
Darryl Stingley			
Mike Haynes			
Tony McGee			
☐ 517 **New Orleans Saints TL**	.20	.05	.01
Chuck Muncie			
Don Herrmann			
Chuck Crist			
Elois Grooms			
☐ 518 **New York Giants TL**	.20	.05	.01
Bobby Hammond			
Jimmy Robinson			
Bill Bryant			
John Mendenhall			
☐ 519 **New York Jets TL**	.20	.05	.01
Clark Gaines			
Wesley Walker			
Burgess Owens			
Joe Klecko			
☐ 520 **Oakland Raiders TL**	.20	.05	.01
Mark van Eeghen			
Dave Casper			
Jack Tatum			
Neal Colzie			
☐ 521 **Philadelphia Eagles TL**	.20	.05	.01
Mike Hogan			
Harold Carmichael			
Herman Edwards			
John Sanders			
Lem Burnham			
☐ 522 **Pittsburgh Steelers TL**	.30	.06	.01
Franco Harris			
Jim Smith			
Mel Blount			
Steve Furness			
☐ 523 **St. Louis Cardinals TL**	.20	.05	.01
Terry Metcalf			
Mel Gray			
Roger Wehrli			
Mike Dawson			

	MINT	VG-E	F-G
☐ 524 **San Diego Chargers TL**	.20	.05	.01
Rickey Young			
Charlie Joiner			
Mike Fuller			
Gary Johnson			
☐ 525 **San Francisco 49ers TL**	.20	.05	.01
Delvin Williams			
Gene Washington			
Mel Phillips			
Dave Washington			
Cleveland Elam			
☐ 526 **Seattle Seahawks TL**	.20	.05	.01
Sherman Smith			
Steve Largent			
Autry Beamon			
Walter Packer			
☐ 527 **Tampa Bay Buccaneers TL**	.20	.05	.01
Morris Owens			
Isaac Hagins			
Mike Washington			
Lee Roy Selmon			
☐ 528 **Washington Redskins TL**	.20	.05	.01
Mike Thomas			
Jean Fugett			
Ken Houston			
Dennis Johnson			

1979 TOPPS

The 1979 Topps set contains 528 cards. The cards measure 2½" by 3½". No known scarcities exist. The first six cards feature the AFC and NFC statistical leaders from the previous season. Distributed throughout the set are Team Leader (TL) cards depicting typically four individual team (statistical) leaders on the front and a team checklist on the back. The set features the first and only Topps cards of Earl Campbell. The card backs are printed in yellow and blue.

		MINT	VG-E	F-G
	COMPLETE SET	25.00	10.00	2.00
	COMMON PLAYER (1-528)	.05	.02	.00
☐	1 **Passing Leaders** .... Roger Staubach Terry Bradshaw	1.00	.25	.05
☐	2 **Receiving Leaders** .... Rickey Young Steve Largent	.15	.06	.01
☐	3 **Rushing Leaders** .... Walter Payton Earl Campbell	1.00	.45	.10
☐	4 **Scoring Leaders** .... Frank Corral Pat Leahy	.08	.03	.01
☐	5 **Interception Leaders** .... Willie Buchanon Ken Stone Thom Darden	.08	.03	.01

		MINT	VG-E	F-G
☐	6 **Punting Leaders**	.08	.03	.01
	Tom Skladany			
	Pat McInally			
☐	7 **Johnny Perkins,** New York Giants	.05	.02	.00
☐	8 **Charles Phillips,** Oakland Raiders	.05	.02	.00
☐	9 **Derrel Luce,** Baltimore Colts	.05	.02	.00
☐	10 **John Riggins,** Washington Redskins	.45	.20	.04
☐	11 **Chester Marcol,** Green Bay Packers	.05	.02	.00
☐	12 **Bernard Jackson,** Denver Broncos	.05	.02	.00
☐	13 **Dave Logan,** Cleveland Browns	.05	.02	.00
☐	14 **Bo Harris,** Cincinnati Bengals	.05	.02	.00
☐	15 **Alan Page,** Minnesota Vikings	.30	.12	.03
☐	16 **John Smith,** New England Patriots	.05	.02	.00
☐	17 **Dwight McDonald,** San Diego Chargers	.05	.02	.00
☐	18 **John Cappelletti,** Los Angeles Rams	.15	.06	.01
☐	19 **Pittsburgh Steelers TL**	.30	.06	.01
	Franco Harris			
	Larry Anderson			
	Tony Dungy			
	L.C. Greenwood			
☐	20 **Bill Bergey,** Philadelphia Eagles	.18	.08	.01
☐	21 **Jerome Barkum,** New York Jets	.10	.04	.01
☐	22 **Larry Csonka,** New York Giants	.45	.20	.04
☐	23 **Joe Ferguson,** Buffalo Bills	.20	.09	.02
☐	24 **Ed Too Tall Jones,** Dallas Cowboys	.30	.12	.03
☐	25 **Dave Jennings,** New York Giants	.08	.03	.01
☐	26 **Horace King,** Detroit Lions	.05	.02	.00
☐	27 **Steve Little,** St. Louis Cardinals	.05	.02	.00
☐	28 **Morris Bradshaw,** Oakland Raiders	.05	.02	.00
☐	29 **Joe Ehrmann,** Baltimore Colts	.05	.02	.00
☐	30 **Ahmad Rashad,** Minnesota Vikings	.25	.10	.02
☐	31 **Joe Lavender,** Washington Redskins	.05	.02	.00
☐	32 **Dan Neal,** Chicago Bears	.05	.02	.00
☐	33 **Johnny Evans,** Cleveland Browns	.05	.02	.00
☐	34 **Pete Johnson,** Cincinnati Bengals	.10	.04	.01
☐	35 **Mike Haynes,** New England Patriots	.15	.06	.01
☐	36 **Tim Mazzetti,** Atlanta Falcons	.05	.02	.00
☐	37 **Mike Barber,** Houston Oilers	.08	.03	.01
☐	38 **San Francisco 49ers TL**	.30	.06	.01
	O.J. Simpson			
	Freddie Solomon			
	Chuck Crist			
	Cedrick Hardman			
☐	39 **Bill Gregory,** Seattle Seahawks	.05	.02	.00
☐	40 **Randy Gradishar,** Denver Broncos	.15	.06	.01
☐	41 **Richard Todd,** New York Jets	.25	.10	.02

		MINT	VG-E	F-G
☐ 42	**Henry Marshall,** Kansas City Chiefs	.05	.02	.00
☐ 43	**John Hill,** New Orleans Saints	.05	.02	.00
☐ 44	**Sidney Thornton,** Pittsburgh Steelers	.05	.02	.00
☐ 45	**Ron Jessie,** Los Angeles Rams	.08	.03	.01
☐ 46	**Bob Baumhower,** Miami Dolphins	.15	.06	.01
☐ 47	**Johnnie Gray,** Green Bay Packers	.05	.02	.00
☐ 48	**Doug Williams,** Tampa Bay Buccaneers	.40	.18	.04
☐ 49	**Don McCauley,** Baltimore Colts	.05	.02	.00
☐ 50	**Ray Guy,** Oakland Raiders	.15	.06	.01
☐ 51	**Bob Klein,** San Diego Chargers	.05	.02	.00
☐ 52	**Golden Richards,** Dallas Cowboys	.08	.03	.01
☐ 53	**Mark Miller,** Cleveland Browns	.05	.02	.00
☐ 54	**John Sanders,** Philadelphia Eagles	.05	.02	.00
☐ 55	**Gary Burley,** Cincinnati Bengals	.05	.02	.00
☐ 56	**Steve Nelson,** New England Patriots	.05	.02	.00
☐ 57	**Buffalo Bills TL**	.20	.05	.01
	Terry Miller			
	Frank Lewis			
	Mario Clark			
	Lucius Sanford			
☐ 58	**Bobby Bryant,** Minnesota Vikings	.05	.02	.00
☐ 59	**Rick Kane,** Detroit Lions	.05	.02	.00
☐ 60	**Larry Little,** Miami Dolphins	.08	.03	.01
☐ 61	**Ted Fritsch,** Washington Redskins	.05	.02	.00
☐ 62	**Larry Mallory,** New York Giants	.05	.02	.00
☐ 63	**Marvin Powell,** New York Jets	.08	.03	.01
☐ 64	**Jim Hart,** St. Louis Cardinals	.25	.10	.02
☐ 65	**Joe Greene,** Pittsburgh Steelers	.40	.18	.04
☐ 66	**Walter White,** Kansas City Chiefs	.05	.02	.00
☐ 67	**Gregg Bingham,** Houston Oilers	.05	.02	.00
☐ 68	**Errol Mann,** Oakland Raiders	.05	.02	.00
☐ 69	**Bruce Laird,** Baltimore Colts	.05	.02	.00
☐ 70	**Drew Pearson,** Dallas Cowboys	.25	.10	.02
☐ 71	**Steve Bartkowski,** Atlanta Falcons	.35	.15	.03
☐ 72	**Ted Albrecht,** Chicago Bears	.05	.02	.00
☐ 73	**Charlie Hall,** Cleveland Browns	.05	.02	.00
☐ 74	**Pat McInally,** Cincinnati Bengals	.10	.04	.01
☐ 75	**Al Bubba Baker,** Detroit Lions	.15	.06	.01
☐ 76	**New England Patriots TL**	.20	.05	.01
	Sam Cunningham			
	Stanley Morgan			
	Mike Haynes			
	Tony McGee			
☐ 77	**Steve DeBerg,** San Francisco 49ers	.25	.10	.02
☐ 78	**John Yarno,** Seattle Seahawks	.05	.02	.00
☐ 79	**Stu Voigt,** Minnesota Vikings	.05	.02	.00

		MINT	VG-E	F-G
☐ 80	**Frank Corral**, Los Angeles Rams	.05	.02	.00
☐ 81	**Troy Archer**, New York Giants	.05	.02	.00
☐ 82	**Bruce Harper**, New York Jets	.05	.02	.00
☐ 83	**Tom Jackson**, Denver Broncos	.08	.03	.01
☐ 84	**Larry Brown**, Pittsburgh Steelers	.05	.02	.00
☐ 85	**Wilbert Montgomery**, Philadelphia Eagles	.50	.22	.05
☐ 86	**Butch Johnson**, Dallas Cowboys	.15	.06	.01
☐ 87	**Mike Kadish**, Buffalo Bills	.05	.02	.00
☐ 88	**Ralph Perretta**, San Diego Chargers	.05	.02	.00
☐ 89	**David Lee**, Baltimore Colts	.05	.02	.00
☐ 90	**Mark Van Eeghen**, Oakland Raiders	.08	.03	.01
☐ 91	**John McDaniel**, Washington Redskins	.05	.02	.00
☐ 92	**Gary Fencik**, Chicago Bears	.05	.02	.00
☐ 93	**Mack Mitchell**, Cleveland Browns	.05	.02	.00
☐ 94	**Cincinnati Bengals TL**	.20	.05	.01
	Pete Johnson			
	Isaac Curtis			
	Dick Jauron			
	Ross Browner			
☐ 95	**Steve Grogan**, New England Patriots	.25	.10	.02
☐ 96	**Garo Yepremian**, Miami Dolphins	.10	.04	.01
☐ 97	**Barty Smith**, Green Bay Packers	.05	.02	.00
☐ 98	**Frank Reed**, Atlanta Falcons	.05	.02	.00
☐ 99	**Jim Clark**, New York Giants	.05	.02	.00
☐ 100	**Chuck Foreman**, Minnesota Vikings	.20	.09	.02
☐ 101	**Joe Klecko**, New York Jets	.20	.09	.02
☐ 102	**Pat Tilley**, St. Louis Cardinals	.10	.04	.01
☐ 103	**Conrad Dobler**, New Orleans Saints	.08	.03	.01
☐ 104	**Craig Colquitt**, Pittsburgh Steelers	.05	.02	.00
☐ 105	**Dan Pastorini**, Houston Oilers	.20	.09	.02
☐ 106	**Rod Perry**, Los Angeles Rams	.05	.02	.00
☐ 107	**Nick Mike-Mayer**, Philadelphia Eagles	.05	.02	.00
☐ 108	**John Matuszak**, Oakland Raiders	.08	.03	.01
☐ 109	**David Taylor**, Baltimore Colts	.05	.02	.00
☐ 110	**Billy Joe DuPree**, Dallas Cowboys	.15	.06	.01
☐ 111	**Harold McLinton**, Washington Redskins	.05	.02	.00
☐ 112	**Virgil Livers**, Chicago Bears	.05	.02	.00
☐ 113	**Cleveland Browns TL**	.20	.05	.01
	Greg Pruitt			
	Reggie Rucker			
	Thom Darden			
	Mack Mitchell			
☐ 114	**Checklist 1-132**	.25	.05	.01
☐ 115	**Ken Anderson**, Cincinnati Bengals	.55	.25	.05
☐ 116	**Bill Lenkaitis**, New Orleans Saints	.05	.02	.00
☐ 117	**Bucky Dilts**, Denver Broncos	.05	.02	.00

		MINT	VG-E	F-G
☐ 118	**Tony Greene**, Buffalo Bills	.05	.02	.00
☐ 119	**Bobby Hammond**, New York Giants	.05	.02	.00
☐ 120	**Nat Moore**, Miami Dolphins	.08	.03	.01
☐ 121	**Pat Leahy**, New York Jets	.05	.02	.00
☐ 122	**James Harris**, San Diego Chargers	.15	.06	.01
☐ 123	**Lee Roy Selmon**, Tampa Bay Buccaneers	.25	.10	.02
☐ 124	**Bennie Cunningham**, Pittsburgh Steelers	.05	.02	.00
☐ 125	**Matt Blair**, Minnesota Vikings	.08	.03	.01
☐ 126	**Jim Allen**, Detroit Lions	.05	.02	.00
☐ 127	**Alfred Jenkins**, Atlanta Falcons	.08	.03	.01
☐ 128	**Arthur Whittington**, Oakland Raiders	.05	.02	.00
☐ 129	**Norm Thompson**, Baltimore Colts	.05	.02	.00
☐ 130	**Pat Haden**, Los Angeles Rams	.20	.09	.02
☐ 131	**Freddie Solomon**, San Francisco 49ers	.08	.03	.01
☐ 132	**Chicago Bears TL**	.40	.08	.01
	Walter Payton			
	James Scott			
	Gary Fencik			
	Alan Page			
☐ 133	**Mark Moseley**, Washington Redskins	.10	.04	.01
☐ 134	**Cleo Miller**, Cleveland Browns	.05	.02	.00
☐ 135	**Ross Browner**, Cincinnati Bengals	.15	.06	.01
☐ 136	**Don Calhoun**, New England Patriots	.05	.02	.00
☐ 137	**David Whitehurst**, Green Bay Packers	.15	.06	.01
☐ 138	**Terry Beeson**, Seattle Seahawks	.05	.02	.00
☐ 139	**Ken Stone**, Tampa Bay Buccaneers	.05	.02	.00
☐ 140	**Brad Van Pelt**, New York Giants	.08	.03	.01
☐ 141	**Wesley Walker**, New York Jets	.15	.06	.01
☐ 142	**Jan Stenerud**, Kansas City Chiefs	.10	.04	.01
☐ 143	**Henry Childs**, New Orleans Saints	.05	.02	.00
☐ 144	**Otis Armstrong**, Denver Broncos	.15	.06	.01
☐ 145	**Dwight White**, Pittsburgh Steelers	.08	.03	.01
☐ 146	**Steve Wilson**, Tampa Bay Buccaneers	.05	.02	.00
☐ 147	**Tom Skladany**, Detroit Lions	.08	.03	.01
☐ 148	**Lou Piccone**, Buffalo Bills	.05	.02	.00
☐ 149	**Monte Johnson**, Oakland Raiders	.05	.02	.00
☐ 150	**Joe Washington**, Baltimore Colts	.15	.06	.01
☐ 151	**Philadelphia Eagles TL**	.20	.05	.01
	Wilbert Montgomery			
	Harold Carmichael			
	Herman Edwards			
	Dennis Harrison			
☐ 152	**Fred Dean**, San Diego Chargers	.10	.04	.01
☐ 153	**Rolland Lawrence**, Atlanta Falcons	.08	.03	.01

		MINT	VG-E	F-G
☐ 154	**Brian Baschnagel,** Chicago Bears	.05	.02	.00
☐ 155	**Joe Theismann,** Washington Redskins	.65	.30	.06
☐ 156	**Marvin Cobb,** Cincinnati Bengals	.05	.02	.00
☐ 157	**Dick Ambrose,** Cleveland Browns	.05	.02	.00
☐ 158	**Mike Patrick,** New England Patriots	.05	.02	.00
☐ 159	**Gary Shirk,** New York Giants	.05	.02	.00
☐ 160	**Tony Dorsett,** Dallas Cowboys	1.25	.60	.12
☐ 161	**Greg Buttle,** New York Jets	.08	.03	.01
☐ 162	**A.J. Duhe,** Miami Dolphins	.15	.06	.01
☐ 163	**Mick Tingelhoff,** Minnesota Vikings	.10	.04	.01
☐ 164	**Ken Burrough,** Houston Oilers	.08	.03	.01
☐ 165	**Mike Wagner,** Pittsburgh Steelers	.08	.03	.01
☐ 166	**AFC Championship**	.30	.12	.03
	Steelers 34, Oilers 5			
	(Franco Harris)			
☐ 167	**NFC Championship**	.15	.06	.01
	Cowboys 28, Rams 0			
	(line of scrimmage)			
☐ 168	**Super Bowl XIII**	.40	.18	.04
	Steelers 35, Cowboys 31			
	(Franco Harris)			
☐ 169	**Oakland Raiders TL**	.20	.05	.01
	Mark van Eeghen			
	Dave Casper			
	Charles Phillips			
	Ted Hendricks			
☐ 170	**O.J. Simpson,** San Francisco 49ers	1.75	.85	.17
☐ 171	**Doug Nettles,** Baltimore Colts	.05	.02	.00
☐ 172	**Dan Dierdorf,** St. Louis Cardinals	.08	.03	.01
☐ 173	**Dave Beverly,** Green Bay Packers	.05	.02	.00
☐ 174	**Jim Zorn,** Seattle Seahawks	.15	.06	.01
☐ 175	**Mike Thomas,** Washington Redskins	.05	.02	.00
☐ 176	**John Outlaw,** Philadelphia Eagles	.05	.02	.00
☐ 177	**Jim Turner,** Denver Broncos	.10	.04	.01
☐ 178	**Freddie Scott,** Detroit Lions	.08	.03	.01
☐ 179	**Mike Phipps,** Chicago Bears	.15	.06	.01
☐ 180	**Jack Youngblood,** Los Angeles Rams	.25	.10	.02
☐ 181	**Sam Hunt,** New England Patriots	.05	.02	.00
☐ 182	**Tony Hill,** Dallas Cowboys	.50	.22	.05
☐ 183	**Gary Barbaro,** Kansas City Chiefs	.08	.03	.01
☐ 184	**Archie Griffin,** Cincinnati Bengals	.15	.06	.01
☐ 185	**Jerry Sherk,** Cleveland Browns	.08	.03	.01
☐ 186	**Bobby Jackson,** New York Jets	.05	.02	.00
☐ 187	**Don Woods,** San Diego Chargers	.05	.02	.00

	MINT	VG-E	F-G
☐ 188 **New York Giants TL**	.20	.05	.01
Doug Kotar			
Jimmy Robinson			
Terry Jackson			
George Martin			
☐ 189 **Raymond Chester**, Oakland Raiders	.10	.04	.01
☐ 190 **Joe DeLamielleure**, Buffalo Bills	.08	.03	.01
☐ 191 **Tony Galbreath**, New Orleans Saints	.08	.03	.01
☐ 192 **Robert Brazile**, Houston Oilers	.08	.03	.01
☐ 193 **Neil O'Donoghue**, Tampa Bay Buccaneers ...	.05	.02	.00
☐ 194 **Mike Webster**, Pittsburgh Steelers	.08	.03	.01
☐ 195 **Ed Simonini**, Baltimore Colts	.05	.02	.00
☐ 196 **Benny Malone**, Miami Dolphins	.05	.02	.00
☐ 197 **Tom Wittum**, San Francisco 49ers	.05	.02	.00
☐ 198 **Steve Largent**, Seattle Seahawks	.20	.09	.02
☐ 199 **Tommy Hart**, Chicago Bears	.05	.02	.00
☐ 200 **Fran Tarkenton**, Minnesota Vikings	1.50	.70	.15
☐ 201 **Leon Gray**, New England Patriots	.08	.03	.01
☐ 202 **Leroy Harris**, Miami Dolphins	.05	.02	.00
☐ 203 **Eric Williams**, St. Louis Cardinals	.05	.02	.00
☐ 204 **Thom Darden**, Cleveland Browns	.05	.02	.00
☐ 205 **Ken Riley**, Cincinnati Bengals	.08	.03	.01
☐ 206 **Clark Gaines**, New York Jets	.05	.02	.00
☐ 207 **Kansas City Chiefs TL**	.20	.05	.01
Tony Reed			
Tony Reed			
Tim Gray			
Art Still			
☐ 208 **Joe Danelo**, New York Giants	.05	.02	.00
☐ 209 **Glen Walker**, Los Angeles Rams	.05	.02	.00
☐ 210 **Art Shell**, Oakland Raiders	.08	.03	.01
☐ 211 **Jon Keyworth**, Denver Broncos	.05	.02	.00
☐ 212 **Herman Edwards**, Philadelphia Eagles	.05	.02	.00
☐ 213 **John Fitzgerald**, Dallas Cowboys	.05	.02	.00
☐ 214 **Jim Smith**, Pittsburgh Steelers	.15	.06	.01
☐ 215 **Coy Bacon**, Washington Redskins	.05	.02	.00
☐ 216 **Dennis Johnson**, Buffalo Bills	.05	.02	.00
☐ 217 **John Jefferson**, San Diego Chargers	.50	.22	.05
☐ 218 **Gary Weaver**, Green Bay Packers	.05	.02	.00
☐ 219 **Tom Blanchard**, New Orleans Saints	.05	.02	.00
☐ 220 **Bert Jones**, Baltimore Colts	.30	.12	.03
☐ 221 **Stanley Morgan**, New England Patriots	.20	.09	.02
☐ 222 **James Hunter**, Detroit Lions	.05	.02	.00
☐ 223 **Jim Obradovich**, Tampa Bay Buccaneers ...	.05	.02	.00
☐ 224 **Carl Mauck**, Houston Oilers	.05	.02	.00
☐ 225 **Chris Bahr**, Cincinnati Bengals	.08	.03	.01

	MINT	VG-E	F-G
☐ 226 **New York Jets TL**	.20	.05	.01
Kevin Long			
Wesley Walker			
Bobby Jackson			
Burgess Owens			
Joe Klecko			
☐ 227 **Roland Harper**, Chicago Bears	.05	.02	.00
☐ 228 **Randy Dean**, New York Giants	.05	.02	.00
☐ 229 **Bob Jackson**, Cleveland Browns	.05	.02	.00
☐ 230 **Sammie White**, Minnesota Vikings	.08	.03	.01
☐ 231 **Mike Dawson**, St. Louis Cardinals	.08	.03	.01
☐ 232 **Checklist 133-264**	.25	.05	.01
☐ 233 **Ken MacAfee**, San Francisco 49ers	.08	.03	.01
☐ 234 **Jon Kolb**, Pittsburgh Steelers	.05	.02	.00
☐ 235 **Willie Hall**, Oakland Raiders	.05	.02	.00
☐ 236 **Ron Saul**, Washington Redskins	.05	.02	.00
☐ 237 **Haskel Stanback**, Atlanta Falcons	.05	.02	.00
☐ 238 **Zenon Andrusyshyn**, Kansas City Chiefs	.05	.02	.00
☐ 239 **Norris Thomas**, Miami Dolphins	.05	.02	.00
☐ 240 **Rick Upchurch**, Denver Broncos	.10	.04	.01
☐ 241 **Robert Pratt**, Baltimore Colts	.05	.02	.00
☐ 242 **Julius Adams**, New England Patriots	.05	.02	.00
☐ 243 **Rich McGeorge**, Green Bay Packers	.05	.02	.00
☐ 244 **Seattle Seahawks TL**	.20	.05	.01
Sherman Smith			
Steve Largent			
Cornell Webster			
Bill Gregory			
☐ 245 **Blair Bush**, Cincinnati Bengals	.05	.02	.00
☐ 246 **Billy Johnson**, Houston Oilers	.15	.06	.01
☐ 247 **Randy Rasmussen**, New York Jets	.05	.02	.00
☐ 248 **Brian Kelley**, New York Giants	.05	.02	.00
☐ 249 **Mike Pruitt**, Cleveland Browns	.15	.06	.01
☐ 250 **Harold Carmichael**, Philadelphia Eagles	.25	.10	.02
☐ 251 **Mike Hartenstine**, Chicago Bears	.05	.02	.00
☐ 252 **Robert Newhouse**, Dallas Cowboys	.15	.06	.01
☐ 253 **Gary Danielson**, Detroit Lions	.15	.06	.01
☐ 254 **Mike Fuller**, San Diego Chargers	.05	.02	.00
☐ 255 **L.C. Greenwood**, Pittsburgh Steelers	.15	.06	.01
☐ 256 **Lemar Parrish**, Washington Redskins	.05	.02	.00
☐ 257 **Ike Harris**, New Orleans Saints	.05	.02	.00
☐ 258 **Ricky Bell**, Tampa Bay Buccaneers	.30	.12	.03
☐ 259 **Willie Parker**, Buffalo Bills	.05	.02	.00
☐ 260 **Gene Upshaw**, Oakland Raiders	.08	.03	.01
☐ 261 **Glenn Doughty**, Baltimore Colts	.05	.02	.00
☐ 262 **Steve Zabel**, New England Patriots	.05	.02	.00

		MINT	VG-E	F-G
☐ 263	**Atlanta Falcons TL**	.20	.05	.01
	Bubba Bean			
	Wallace Francis			
	Rolland Lawrence			
	Greg Brezina			
☐ 264	**Ray Wersching**, San Francisco 49ers	.05	.02	.00
☐ 265	**Lawrence McCutcheon**, Los Angeles Rams ...	.15	.06	.01
☐ 266	**Willie Buchanon**, Green Bay Packers	.08	.03	.01
☐ 267	**Matt Robinson**, Denver Broncos	.10	.04	.01
☐ 268	**Reggie Rucker**, Cleveland Browns	.10	.04	.01
☐ 269	**Doug Van Horn**, New York Giants	.05	.02	.00
☐ 270	**Lydell Mitchell**, San Diego Chargers	.15	.06	.01
☐ 271	**Vern Holland**, Cincinnati Bengals	.05	.02	.00
☐ 272	**Eason Ramson**, St. Louis Cardinals	.05	.02	.00
☐ 273	**Steve Towle**, Miami Dolphins	.05	.02	.00
☐ 274	**Jim Marshall**, Minnesota Vikings	.25	.10	.02
☐ 275	**Mel Blount**, Pittsburgh Steelers	.15	.06	.01
☐ 276	**Bob Kuziel**, Washington Redskins	.05	.02	.00
☐ 277	**James Scott**, Chicago Bears	.08	.03	.01
☐ 278	**Tony Reed**, Kansas City Chiefs	.08	.03	.01
☐ 279	**Dave Green**, Tampa Bay Buccaneers	.05	.02	.00
☐ 280	**Toni Linhart**, Baltimore Colts	.05	.02	.00
☐ 281	**Andy Johnson**, New England Patriots	.05	.02	.00
☐ 282	**Los Angeles Rams TL**	.20	.05	.01
	Cullen Bryant			
	Willie Miller			
	Rod Perry			
	Pat Thomas			
	Larry Brooks			
☐ 283	**Phil Villapiano**, Oakland Raiders	.10	.04	.01
☐ 284	**Dexter Bussey**, Detroit Lions	.05	.02	.00
☐ 285	**Craig Morton**, Denver Broncos	.25	.10	.02
☐ 286	**Guy Morriss**, Philadelphia Eagles	.05	.02	.00
☐ 287	**Lawrence Pillers**, New York Jets	.05	.02	.00
☐ 288	**Gerald Irons**, Cleveland Browns	.05	.02	.00
☐ 289	**Scott Perry**, Cincinnati Bengals	.05	.02	.00
☐ 290	**Randy White**, Dallas Cowboys	.30	.12	.03
☐ 291	**Jack Gregory**, New York Giants	.08	.03	.01
☐ 292	**Bob Chandler**, Buffalo Bills	.08	.03	.01
☐ 293	**Rich Szaro**, New Orleans Saints	.05	.02	.00
☐ 294	**Sherman Smith**, Seattle Seahawks	.05	.02	.00
☐ 295	**Tom Banks**, St. Louis Cardinals	.05	.02	.00
☐ 296	**Revie Sorey**, Chicago Bears	.05	.02	.00
☐ 297	**Ricky Thompson**, Washington Redskins	.05	.02	.00
☐ 298	**Ron Yary**, Minnesota Vikings	.08	.03	.01
☐ 299	**Lyle Blackwood**, Baltimore Colts	.05	.02	.00

	MINT	VG-E	F-G
☐ 300 **Franco Harris**, Pittsburgh Steelers	.90	.40	.09
☐ 301 **Houston Oilers TL**	.50	.10	.01
Earl Campbell			
Ken Burrough			
Willie Alexander			
Elvin Bethea			
☐ 302 **Scott Bull**, San Francisco 49ers	.08	.03	.01
☐ 303 **Dewey Selmon**, Tampa Bay Buccaneers	.08	.03	.01
☐ 304 **Jack Rudnay**, Kansas City Chiefs	.05	.02	.00
☐ 305 **Fred Biletnikoff**, Oakland Raiders	.30	.12	.03
☐ 306 **Jeff West**, San Diego Chargers	.05	.02	.00
☐ 307 **Shafer Suggs**, New York Jets	.05	.02	.00
☐ 308 **Ozzie Newsome**, Cleveland Browns	.50	.22	.05
☐ 309 **Boobie Clark**, Cincinnati Bengals	.08	.03	.01
☐ 310 **James Lofton**, Green Bay Packers	.50	.22	.05
☐ 311 **Joe Pisarcik**, New York Giants	.08	.03	.01
☐ 312 **Bill Simpson**, Los Angeles Rams	.05	.02	.00
☐ 313 **Haven Moses**, Denver Broncos	.08	.03	.01
☐ 314 **Jim Merlo**, New Orleans Saints	.05	.02	.00
☐ 315 **Preston Pearson**, Dallas Cowboys	.15	.06	.01
☐ 316 **Larry Tearry**, Detroit Lions	.05	.02	.00
☐ 317 **Tom Dempsey**, Buffalo Bills	.08	.03	.01
☐ 318 **Greg Latta**, Chicago Bears	.05	.02	.00
☐ 319 **Washington Redskins TL**	.20	.05	.01
John Riggins			
John McDaniel			
Jake Scott			
Coy Bacon			
☐ 320 **Jack Ham**, Pittsburgh Steelers	.15	.06	.01
☐ 321 **Harold Jackson**, New England Patriots	.20	.09	.02
☐ 322 **George Roberts**, Miami Dolphins	.05	.02	.00
☐ 323 **Ron Jaworski**, Philadelphia Eagles	.25	.10	.02
☐ 324 **Jim Otis**, St. Louis Cardinals	.08	.03	.01
☐ 325 **Roger Carr**, Baltimore Colts	.08	.03	.01
☐ 326 **Jack Tatum**, Oakland Raiders	.15	.06	.01
☐ 327 **Derrick Gaffney**, New York Jets	.05	.02	.00
☐ 328 **Reggie Williams**, Cincinnati Bengals	.08	.03	.01
☐ 329 **Doug Dieken**, Cleveland Browns	.05	.02	.00
☐ 330 **Efren Herrera**, Seattle Seahawks	.05	.02	.00

RECORD BREAKERS

	MINT	VG-E	F-G
☐ 331 **RB: Earl Campbell**	1.00	.45	.10
Most Yards Rushing, Rookie			

		MINT	VG-E	F-G
☐ 332 **RB: Tony Galbreath**		.08	.03	.01
Most Receptions, Running Back, Game				
☐ 333 **RB: Bruce Harper**		.08	.03	.01
Most Combined Kick Return Yards, Season				
☐ 334 **RB: John James**		.08	.03	.01
Most Punts, Season				
☐ 335 **RB: Walter Payton**		1.00	.45	.10
Most Combined Attempts, Season				
☐ 336 **RB: Rickey Young**		.08	.03	.01
Most Receptions, Running Back, Season				
☐ 337 **Jeff Van Note**, Atlanta Falcons		.08	.03	.01
☐ 338 **San Diego Chargers TL**		.20	.05	.01
Lydell Mitchell				
John Jefferson				
Mike Fuller				
Fred Dean				
☐ 339 **Stan Walters**, Philadelphia Eagles		.05	.02	.00
☐ 340 **Louis Wright**, Denver Broncos		.08	.03	.01
☐ 341 **Horace Ivory**, New England Patriots		.05	.02	.00
☐ 342 **Andre Tillman**, Miami Dolphins		.05	.02	.00
☐ 343 **Greg Coleman**, Minnesota Vikings		.05	.02	.00
☐ 344 **Doug English**, Detroit Lions		.08	.03	.01
☐ 345 **Ted Hendricks**, Oakland Raiders		.15	.06	.01
☐ 346 **Rich Saul**, Los Angeles Rams		.05	.02	.00
☐ 347 **Mel Gray**, St. Louis Cardinals		.10	.04	.01
☐ 348 **Toni Fritsch**, Houston Oilers		.05	.02	.00
☐ 349 **Cornell Webster**, Seattle Seahawks		.05	.02	.00
☐ 350 **Ken Houston**, Washington Redskins		.15	.06	.01
☐ 351 **Ron Johnson**, Pittsburgh Steelers		.05	.02	.00
☐ 352 **Doug Kotar**, New York Giants		.05	.02	.00
☐ 353 **Brian Sipe**, Cleveland Browns		.30	.12	.03
☐ 354 **Billy Brooks**, Cincinnati Bengals		.08	.03	.01
☐ 355 **John Dutton**, Baltimore Colts		.08	.03	.01
☐ 356 **Don Goode**, San Diego Chargers		.05	.02	.00
☐ 357 **Detroit Lions TL**		.20	.05	.01
Dexter Bussey				
David Hill				
Jim Allen				
Al Baker				
☐ 358 **Reuben Gant**, Buffalo Bills		.05	.02	.00
☐ 359 **Bob Parsons**, Chicago Bears		.05	.02	.00
☐ 360 **Cliff Harris**, Dallas Cowboys		.15	.06	.01
☐ 361 **Raymond Clayborn**, New England Patriots		.08	.03	.01
☐ 362 **Scott Dierking**, New York Jets		.05	.02	.00
☐ 363 **Bill Bryan**, Denver Broncos		.05	.02	.00
☐ 364 **Mike Livingston**, Kansas City Chiefs		.08	.03	.01

	MINT	VG-E	F-G
☐ 365 **Otis Sistrunk**, Oakland Raiders	.08	.03	.01
☐ 366 **Charley Young**, Los Angeles Rams	.08	.03	.01
☐ 367 **Keith Wortman**, St. Louis Cardinals	.05	.02	.00
☐ 368 **Checklist 265-396**	.25	.05	.01
☐ 369 **Mike Michel**, Philadelphia Eagles	.05	.02	.00
☐ 370 **Delvin Williams**, Miami Dolphins	.10	.04	.01
☐ 371 **Steve Furness**, Pittsburgh Steelers	.05	.02	.00
☐ 372 **Emery Moorehead**, New York Giants	.05	.02	.00
☐ 373 **Clarence Scott**, Cleveland Browns	.05	.02	.00
☐ 374 **Rufus Mayes**, Cincinnati Bengals	.05	.02	.00
☐ 375 **Chris Hanburger**, Washington Redskins	.08	.03	.01
☐ 376 **Baltimore Colts TL**	.20	.05	.01
Joe Washington			
Roger Carr			
Norm Thompson			
John Dutton			
☐ 377 **Bob Avellini**, Chicago Bears	.10	.04	.01
☐ 378 **Jeff Siemon**, Minnesota Vikings	.08	.03	.01
☐ 379 **Roland Hooks**, Buffalo Bills	.05	.02	.00
☐ 380 **Russ Francis**, New England Patriots	.15	.06	.01
☐ 381 **Roger Wehrli**, St. Louis Cardinals	.08	.03	.01
☐ 382 **Joe Fields**, New York Jets	.05	.02	.00
☐ 383 **Archie Manning**, New Orleans Saints	.30	.12	.03
☐ 384 **Rob Lytle**, Denver Broncos	.05	.02	.00
☐ 385 **Thomas Henderson**, Dallas Cowboys	.15	.06	.01
☐ 386 **Morris Owens**, Tampa Bay Buccaneers	.05	.02	.00
☐ 387 **Dan Fouts**, San Diego Chargers	1.00	.45	.10
☐ 388 **Chuck Crist**, San Francisco 49ers	.05	.02	.00
☐ 389 **Ed O'Neil**, Detroit Lions	.05	.02	.00
☐ 390 **Earl Campbell**, Houston Oilers	5.00	2.35	.50
☐ 391 **Randy Grossman**, Pittsburgh Steelers	.05	.02	.00
☐ 392 **Monte Jackson**, Oakland Raiders	.05	.02	.00
☐ 393 **John Mendenhall**, New York Giants	.05	.02	.00
☐ 394 **Miami Dolphins TL**	.20	.05	.01
Delvin Williams			
Duriel Harris			
Tim Foley			
Vern Den Herder			
☐ 395 **Isaac Curtis**, Cincinnati Bengals	.08	.03	.01
☐ 396 **Mike Bragg**, Washington Redskins	.05	.02	.00
☐ 397 **Doug Plank**, Chicago Bears	.05	.02	.00
☐ 398 **Mike Barnes**, Baltimore Colts	.05	.02	.00
☐ 399 **Calvin Hill**, Cleveland Browns	.15	.06	.01
☐ 400 **Roger Staubach**, Dallas Cowboys	2.00	.90	.20
☐ 401 **Doug Beaudoin**, New England Patriots	.05	.02	.00
☐ 402 **Chuck Ramsey**, New York Jets	.05	.02	.00

		MINT	VG-E	F-G
☐ 403	**Mike Hogan,** Philadelphia Eagles	.05	.02	.00
☐ 404	**Mario Clark,** Buffalo Bills	.05	.02	.00
☐ 405	**Riley Odoms,** Denver Broncos	.08	.03	.01
☐ 406	**Carl Eller,** Minnesota Vikings	.30	.12	.03
☐ 407	**Green Bay Packers TL**	.20	.05	.01
	Terdell Middleton			
	James Lofton			
	Willie Buchanon			
	Ezra Johnson			
☐ 408	**Mark Arneson,** St. Louis Cardinals	.05	.02	.00
☐ 409	**Vince Ferragamo,** Los Angeles Rams	.35	.15	.03
☐ 410	**Cleveland Elam,** San Francisco 49ers	.05	.02	.00
☐ 411	**Donnie Shell,** Pittsburgh Steelers	.08	.03	.01
☐ 412	**Ray Rhodes,** New York Giants	.05	.02	.00
☐ 413	**Don Cockcroft,** Cleveland Browns	.05	.02	.00
☐ 414	**Don Bass,** Cincinnati Bengals	.05	.02	.00
☐ 415	**Cliff Branch,** Oakland Raiders	.20	.09	.02
☐ 416	**Diron Talbert,** Washington Redskins	.05	.02	.00
☐ 417	**Ron Hicks,** Chicago Bears	.05	.02	.00
☐ 418	**Roosevelt Leaks,** Baltimore Colts	.05	.02	.00
☐ 419	**Charlie Joiner,** San Diego Chargers	.30	.12	.03
☐ 420	**Lyle Alzado,** Denver Broncos	.30	.12	.03
☐ 421	**Sam Cunningham,** New England Patriots	.08	.03	.01
☐ 422	**Larry Keller,** New York Jets	.05	.02	.00
☐ 423	**Jim Mitchell,** Atlanta Falcons	.05	.02	.00
☐ 424	**Randy Logan,** Philadelphia Eagles	.05	.02	.00
☐ 425	**Jim Langer,** Miami Dolphins	.05	.02	.00
☐ 426	**Gary Green,** Kansas City Chiefs	.05	.02	.00
☐ 427	**Luther Blue,** Detroit Lions	.05	.02	.00
☐ 428	**Dennis Johnson,** Buffalo Bills	.05	.02	.00
☐ 429	**Danny White,** Dallas Cowboys	.50	.22	.05
☐ 430	**Roy Gerela,** Pittsburgh Steelers	.05	.02	.00
☐ 431	**Jimmy Robinson,** New York Giants	.05	.02	.00
☐ 432	**Minnesota Vikings TL**	.20	.05	.01
	Chuck Foreman			
	Ahmad Rashad			
	Bobby Bryant			
	Mark Mullaney			
☐ 433	**Oliver Davis,** Cleveland Browns	.05	.02	.00
☐ 434	**Lenvil Elliott,** Cincinnati Bengals	.05	.02	.00
☐ 435	**Willie Miller,** Los Angeles Rams	.05	.02	.00
☐ 436	**Brad Dusek,** Washington Redskins	.05	.02	.00
☐ 437	**Bob Thomas,** Chicago Bears	.05	.02	.00
☐ 438	**Ken Mendenhall,** Baltimore Colts	.05	.02	.00
☐ 439	**Clarence Davis,** Oakland Raiders	.05	.02	.00
☐ 440	**Bob Griese,** Miami Dolphins	1.00	.45	.10

		MINT	VG-E	F-G
☐ 441	**Tony McGee**, New England Patriots	.05	.02	.00
☐ 442	**Ed Taylor**, New York Jets	.05	.02	.00
☐ 443	**Ron Howard**, Seattle Seahawks	.05	.02	.00
☐ 444	**Wayne Morris**, St. Louis Cardinals	.08	.03	.01
☐ 445	**Charlie Waters**, Dallas Cowboys	.15	.06	.01
☐ 446	**Rick Danmeier**, Minnesota Vikings	.05	.02	.00
☐ 447	**Paul Naumoff**, Detroit Lions	.05	.02	.00
☐ 448	**Keith Krepfle**, Philadelphia Eagles	.05	.02	.00
☐ 449	**Rusty Jackson**, Buffalo Bills	.05	.02	.00
☐ 450	**John Stallworth**, Pittsburgh Steelers	.15	.06	.01
☐ 451	**New Orleans Saints TL**	.20	.05	.01
	Tony Galbreath			
	Henry Childs			
	Tom Myers			
	Elex Price			
☐ 452	**Ron Mikolajczyk**, New York Giants	.05	.02	.00
☐ 453	**Fred Dryer**, Los Angeles Rams	.25	.10	.02
☐ 454	**Jim LeClair**, Cincinnati Bengals	.05	.02	.00
☐ 455	**Greg Pruitt**, Cleveland Browns	.20	.09	.02
☐ 456	**Jake Scott**, Washington Redskins	.10	.04	.01
☐ 457	**Steve Schubert**, Chicago Bears	.05	.02	.00
☐ 458	**George Kunz**, Baltimore Colts	.08	.03	.01
☐ 459	**Mike Williams**, San Diego Chargers	.05	.02	.00
☐ 460	**Dave Casper**, Oakland Raiders	.15	.06	.01
☐ 461	**Sam Adams**, New England Patriots	.05	.02	.00
☐ 462	**Abdul Salaam**, New York Jets	.05	.02	.00
☐ 463	**Terdell Middleton**, Green Bay Packers	.05	.02	.00
☐ 464	**Mike Wood**, St. Louis Cardinals	.05	.02	.00
☐ 465	**Bill Thompson**, Denver Broncos	.05	.02	.00
☐ 466	**Larry Gordon**, Miami Dolphins	.05	.02	.00
☐ 467	**Benny Ricardo**, Detroit Lions	.05	.02	.00
☐ 468	**Reggie McKenzie**, Buffalo Bills	.08	.03	.01
☐ 469	**Dallas Cowboys TL**	.40	.08	.01
	Tony Dorsett			
	Tony Hill			
	Benny Barnes			
	Harvey Martin			
	Randy White			
☐ 470	**Rickey Young**, Minnesota Vikings	.08	.03	.01
☐ 471	**Charlie Smith**, Philadelphia Eagles	.05	.02	.00
☐ 472	**Al Dixon**, New York Giants	.05	.02	.00
☐ 473	**Tom DeLeone**, Cleveland Browns	.05	.02	.00
☐ 474	**Louis Breeden**, Cincinnati Bengals	.05	.02	.00
☐ 475	**Jack Lambert**, Pittsburgh Steelers	.30	.12	.03
☐ 476	**Terry Hermeling**, Los Angeles Rams	.05	.02	.00
☐ 477	**J.K. McKay**, Tampa Bay Buccaneers	.05	.02	.00

		MINT	VG-E	F-G
☐ 478	**Stan White,** Baltimore Colts	.05	.02	.00
☐ 479	**Terry Nelson,** Los Angeles Rams	.05	.02	.00
☐ 480	**Walter Payton,** Chicago Bears	2.25	1.00	.22
☐ 481	**Dave Dalby,** Oakland Raiders	.05	.02	.00
☐ 482	**Burgess Owens,** New York Jets	.05	.02	.00
☐ 483	**Rolf Benirschke,** San Diego Chargers	.08	.03	.01
☐ 484	**Jack Dolbin,** Denver Broncos	.05	.02	.00
☐ 485	**John Hannah,** New England Patriots	.15	.06	.01
☐ 486	**Checklist 397-528**	.25	.05	.01
☐ 487	**Greg Landry,** Detroit Lions	.15	.06	.01
☐ 488	**St. Louis Cardinals TL**	.20	.05	.01
	Jim Otis			
	Pat Tilley			
	Ken Stone			
	Mike Dawson			
☐ 489	**Paul Krause,** Minnesota Vikings	.08	.03	.01
☐ 490	**John James,** Atlanta Falcons	.05	.02	.00
☐ 491	**Merv Krakau,** Buffalo Bills	.05	.02	.00
☐ 492	**Dan Doornink,** New York Giants	.05	.02	.00
☐ 493	**Curtis Johnson,** Miami Dolphins	.05	.02	.00
☐ 494	**Rafael Septien,** Dallas Cowboys	.15	.06	.01
☐ 495	**Jean Fugett,** Washington Redskins	.05	.02	.00
☐ 496	**Frank LeMaster,** Philadelphia Eagles	.05	.02	.00
☐ 497	**Allan Ellis,** Chicago Bears	.05	.02	.00
☐ 498	**Billy Waddy,** Los Angeles Rams	.08	.03	.01
☐ 499	**Hank Bauer,** San Diego Chargers	.05	.02	.00
☐ 500	**Terry Bradshaw,** Pittsburgh Steelers	1.25	.60	.12
☐ 501	**Larry McCarren,** Green Bay Packers	.05	.02	.00
☐ 502	**Fred Cook,** Baltimore Colts	.05	.02	.00
☐ 503	**Chuck Muncie,** New Orleans Saints	.20	.09	.02
☐ 504	**Herman Weaver,** Seattle Seahawks	.05	.02	.00
☐ 505	**Eddie Edwards,** Cincinnati Bengals	.05	.02	.00
☐ 506	**Tony Peters,** Cleveland Browns	.05	.02	.00
☐ 507	**Denver Broncos TL**	.20	.05	.01
	Lonnie Perrin			
	Riley Odoms			
	Steve Foley			
	Bernard Jackson			
	Lyle Alzado			
☐ 508	**Jimbo Elrod,** Kansas City Chiefs	.05	.02	.00
☐ 509	**David Hill,** Detroit Lions	.05	.02	.00
☐ 510	**Harvey Martin,** Dallas Cowboys	.20	.09	.02
☐ 511	**Terry Miller,** Buffalo Bills	.15	.06	.01
☐ 512	**June Jones,** Atlanta Falcons	.08	.03	.01
☐ 513	**Randy Cross,** San Francisco 49ers	.05	.02	.00
☐ 514	**Duriel Harris,** Miami Dolphins	.08	.03	.01

		MINT	VG-E	F-G
☐ 515	**Harry Carson**, New York Giants	.15	.06	.01
☐ 516	**Tim Fox**, New England Patriots	.05	.02	.00
☐ 517	**John Zook**, St. Louis Cardinals	.08	.03	.01
☐ 518	**Bob Tucker**, Minnesota Vikings	.08	.03	.01
☐ 519	**Kevin Long**, New York Jets	.05	.02	.00
☐ 520	**Ken Stabler**, Oakland Raiders	.35	.15	.03
☐ 521	**John Bunting**, Philadelphia Eagles	.05	.02	.00
☐ 522	**Rocky Bleier**, Pittsburgh Steelers	.20	.09	.02
☐ 523	**Noah Jackson**, Chicago Bears	.05	.02	.00
☐ 524	**Cliff Parsley**, Houston Oilers	.05	.02	.00
☐ 525	**Louie Kelcher**, San Diego Chargers	.08	.03	.01
☐ 526	**Tampa Bay Bucs TL**	.20	.05	.01
	Ricky Bell			
	Morris Owens			
	Cedric Brown			
	Lee Roy Selmon			
☐ 527	**Bob Brudzinski**, Los Angeles Rams	.08	.03	.01
☐ 528	**Danny Buggs**, Washington Redskins	.08	.03	.01

1980 TOPPS

The 1980 Topps football card set contains 528 cards of NFL players. The cards measure 2½″ by 3½″. The backs of the cards contain vital statistics, year-by-year career records and a cartoon illustrated fact section within a simulated football. No scarcities are known. The first six cards in the set recognize record-breaking (RB)

performances from the previous season. All Pro selections are designated on the player's regular card. Distributed throughout the set are Team Leader (TL) cards depicting, typically, four individual team (statistical) leaders on the front and a team checklist on the back.

		MINT	VG-E	F-G
	COMPLETE SET	18.00	8.50	1.80
	COMMON PLAYER (1-528)	.04	.02	.00
☐ 1	RB: Ottis Anderson Most Yardage Rushing, Rookie	.40	.10	.02
☐ 2	RB: Harold Carmichael Most Consecutive Games, One or More Receptions	.15	.06	.01
☐ 3	RB: Dan Fouts Most Yardage Passing, Season	.40	.18	.04
☐ 4	RB: Paul Krause Most Interceptions Lifetime	.08	.03	.01
☐ 5	RB: Rick Upchurch Most Punt Return Yards, Lifetime	.08	.03	.01
☐ 6	RB: Garo Yepremian Most Consecutive Field Goals	.08	.03	.01
☐ 7	Harold Jackson, New England Patriots	.15	.06	.01
☐ 8	Mike Williams, Kansas City Chiefs	.04	.02	.00
☐ 9	Calvin Hill, Cleveland Browns	.15	.06	.01
☐ 10	Jack Ham AP, Pittsburgh Steelers	.15	.06	.01
☐ 11	Dan Melville, San Francisco 49ers	.04	.02	.00
☐ 12	Matt Robinson, Denver Broncos	.08	.03	.01
☐ 13	Billy Campfield, Philadelphia Eagles	.04	.02	.00
☐ 14	Phil Tabor, New York Giants	.04	.02	.00
☐ 15	Randy Hughes, Dallas Cowboys	.04	.02	.00
☐ 16	Andre Tillman, Miami Dolphins	.04	.02	.00
☐ 17	Isaac Curtis, Cincinnati Bengals	.08	.03	.01
☐ 18	Charley Hannah, Tampa Bay Buccaneers	.04	.02	.00
☐ 19	Washington Redskins TL John Riggins Danny Buggs Joe Lavender Coy Bacon	.15	.04	.01
☐ 20	Jim Zorn, Seattle Seahawks	.15	.06	.01
☐ 21	Brian Baschnagel, Chicago Bears	.04	.02	.00
☐ 22	Jon Keyworth, Denver Broncos	.04	.02	.00
☐ 23	Phil Villapiano, Oakland Raiders	.08	.03	.01
☐ 24	Richard Osborne, St. Louis Cardinals	.04	.02	.00
☐ 25	Rich Saul AP, Washington Redskins	.04	.02	.00
☐ 26	Doug Beaudoin, New England Patriots	.04	.02	.00
☐ 27	Cleveland Elam, Detroit Lions	.04	.02	.00
☐ 28	Charlie Joiner, San Diego Chargers	.25	.10	.02

			MINT	VG-E	F-G
☐	29	**Dick Ambrose,** Cleveland Browns	.04	.02	.00
☐	30	**Mike Reinfeldt AP,** Houston Oilers	.04	.02	.00
☐	31	**Matt Bahr,** Pittsburgh Steelers	.08	.03	.01
☐	32	**Keith Krepfle,** Philadelphia Eagles	.04	.02	.00
☐	33	**Herbert Scott,** Dallas Cowboys	.04	.02	.00
☐	34	**Doug Kotar,** New York Giants	.04	.02	.00
☐	35	**Bob Griese,** Miami Dolphins	.90	.40	.09
☐	36	**Jerry Butler,** Buffalo Bills	.30	.12	.03
☐	37	**Rolland Lawrence,** Atlanta Falcons	.04	.02	.00
☐	38	**Gary Weaver,** Green Bay Packers	.04	.02	.00
☐	39	**Kansas City Chiefs TL**	.15	.04	.01
		Ted McKnight			
		J.T. Smith			
		Gary Barbaro			
		Art Still			
☐	40	**Chuck Muncie,** New Orleans Saints	.15	.06	.01
☐	41	**Mike Hartenstine,** Chicago Bears	.04	.02	.00
☐	42	**Sammie White,** Minnesota Vikings	.08	.03	.01
☐	43	**Ken Clark,** Los Angeles Rams	.04	.02	.00
☐	44	**Clarence Harmon,** Washington Redskins	.04	.02	.00
☐	45	**Bert Jones,** Baltimore Colts	.25	.10	.02
☐	46	**Mike Washington,** Tampa Bay Buccaneers	.04	.02	.00
☐	47	**Joe Fields,** New York Jets	.04	.02	.00
☐	48	**Mike Wood,** San Diego Chargers	.04	.02	.00
☐	49	**Oliver Davis,** Cleveland Browns	.04	.02	.00
☐	50	**Stan Walters AP,** Philadelphia Eagles	.04	.02	.00
☐	51	**Riley Odoms,** Denver Broncos	.08	.03	.01
☐	52	**Steve Pisarkiewicz,** St. Louis Cardinals	.08	.03	.01
☐	53	**Tony Hill,** Dallas Cowboys	.25	.10	.02
☐	54	**Scott Perry,** Cincinnati Bengals	.04	.02	.00
☐	55	**George Martin,** New York Giants	.04	.02	.00
☐	56	**George Roberts,** Miami Dolphins	.04	.02	.00
☐	57	**Seattle Seahawks TL**	.15	.04	.01
		Sherman Smith			
		Steve Largent			
		Dave Brown			
		Manu Tuiasosopo			
☐	58	**Billy Johnson,** Houston Oilers	.15	.06	.01
☐	59	**Reuben Gant,** Buffalo Bills	.04	.02	.00
☐	60	**Dennis Harrah AP,** Los Angeles Rams	.04	.02	.00
☐	61	**Rocky Bleier,** Pittsburgh Steelers	.15	.06	.01
☐	62	**Sam Hunt,** New England Patriots	.04	.02	.00
☐	63	**Allan Ellis,** Chicago Bears	.04	.02	.00
☐	64	**Ricky Thompson,** Washington Redskins	.04	.02	.00
☐	65	**Ken Stabler,** Oakland Raiders	.30	.12	.03
☐	66	**Dexter Bussey,** Detroit Lions	.04	.02	.00

		MINT	VG-E	F-G
☐ 67	**Ken Mendenhall**, Baltimore Colts	.04	.02	.00
☐ 68	**Woodrow Lowe**, San Diego Chargers	.04	.02	.00
☐ 69	**Thom Darden**, Cleveland Browns	.04	.02	.00
☐ 70	**Randy White AP**, Dallas Cowboys	.30	.12	.03
☐ 71	**Ken MacAfee**, San Francisco 49ers	.04	.02	.00
☐ 72	**Ron Jaworski**, Philadelphia Eagles	.20	.09	.02
☐ 73	**William Andrews**, Atlanta Falcons	.50	.22	.05
☐ 74	**Jimmy Robinson**, New York Giants	.04	.02	.00
☐ 75	**Roger Wehrli AP**, St. Louis Cardinals	.08	.03	.01
☐ 76	**Miami Dolphins TL**	.15	.04	.01
	Larry Csonka			
	Nat Moore			
	Neal Colzie			
	Gerald Small			
	Vern Den Herder			
☐ 77	**Jack Rudnay**, Kansas City Chiefs	.04	.02	.00
☐ 78	**James Lofton**, Green Bay Packers	.20	.09	.02
☐ 79	**Robert Brazile**, Houston Oilers	.08	.03	.01
☐ 80	**Russ Francis**, New England Patriots	.15	.06	.01
☐ 81	**Ricky Bell**, Tampa Bay Buccaneers	.15	.06	.01
☐ 82	**Bob Avellini**, Chicago Bears	.10	.04	.01
☐ 83	**Bobby Jackson**, New York Jets	.04	.02	.00
☐ 84	**Mike Bragg**, Washington Redskins	.04	.02	.00
☐ 85	**Cliff Branch**, Oakland Raiders	.15	.06	.01
☐ 86	**Blair Bush**, Cincinnati Bengals	.04	.02	.00
☐ 87	**Sherman Smith**, Seattle Seahawks	.04	.02	.00
☐ 88	**Glen Edwards**, San Diego Chargers	.04	.02	.00
☐ 89	**Don Cockroft**, Cleveland Browns	.04	.02	.00
☐ 90	**Louis Wright AP**, Denver Broncos	.08	.03	.01
☐ 91	**Randy Grossman**, Pittsburgh Steelers	.04	.02	.00
☐ 92	**Carl Hairston**, Philadelphia Eagles	.08	.03	.01
☐ 93	**Archie Manning**, New Orleans Saints	.25	.10	.02
☐ 94	**New York Giants TL**	.15	.04	.01
	Billy Taylor			
	Earnest Gray			
	George Martin			
☐ 95	**Preston Pearson**, Dallas Cowboys	.15	.06	.01
☐ 96	**Rusty Chambers**, Miami Dolphins	.04	.02	.00
☐ 97	**Greg Coleman**, Minnesota Vikings	.04	.02	.00
☐ 98	**Charley Young**, Los Angeles Rams	.08	.03	.01
☐ 99	**Matt Cavanaugh**, New England Patriots	.25	.10	.02
☐ 100	**Jesse Baker**, Houston Oilers	.08	.03	.01
☐ 101	**Doug Plank**, Chicago Bears	.04	.02	.00
☐ 102	**Checklist 1-132**	.20	.04	.01
☐ 103	**Luther Bradley**, Detroit Lions	.04	.02	.00
☐ 104	**Bob Kuziel**, Washington Redskins	.04	.02	.00

			MINT	VG-E	F-G
☐ 105	**Craig Morton**, Denver Broncos		.25	.10	.02
☐ 106	**Sherman White**, Buffalo Bills		.04	.02	.00
☐ 107	**Jim Breech**, Oakland Raiders		.04	.02	.00
☐ 108	**Hank Bauer**, San Diego Chargers		.04	.02	.00
☐ 109	**Tom Blanchard**, Tampa Bay Buccaneers		.04	.02	.00
☐ 110	**Ozzie Newsome AP**, Cleveland Browns		.15	.06	.01
☐ 111	**Steve Furness**, Pittsburgh Steelers		.04	.02	.00
☐ 112	**Frank LeMaster**, Philadelphia Eagles		.04	.02	.00
☐ 113	**Dallas Cowboys TL**		.40	.08	.01
	Tony Dorsett				
	Tony Hill				
	Harvey Martin				
☐ 114	**Doug Van Horn**, New York Giants		.04	.02	.00
☐ 115	**Delvin Williams**, Miami Dolphins		.08	.03	.01
☐ 116	**Lyle Blackwood**, Baltimore Colts		.04	.02	.00
☐ 117	**Derrick Gaffney**, New York Jets		.04	.02	.00
☐ 118	**Cornell Webster**, Seattle Seahawks		.04	.02	.00
☐ 119	**Sam Cunningham**, New England Patriots		.08	.03	.01
☐ 120	**Jim Youngblood AP**, Los Angeles Rams		.04	.02	.00
☐ 121	**Bob Thomas**, Chicago Bears		.04	.02	.00
☐ 122	**Jack Thompson**, Cincinnati Bengals		.15	.06	.01
☐ 123	**Randy Cross**, San Francisco 49ers		.04	.02	.00
☐ 124	**Karl Lorch**, Washington Redskins		.04	.02	.00
☐ 125	**Mel Gray**, St. Louis Cardinals		.10	.04	.01
☐ 126	**John James**, Atlanta Falcons		.04	.02	.00
☐ 127	**Terdell Middleton**, Green Bay Packers		.04	.02	.00
☐ 128	**Leroy Jones**, San Diego Chargers		.04	.02	.00
☐ 129	**Tom DeLeone**, Cleveland Browns		.04	.02	.00
☐ 130	**John Stallworth AP**, Pittsburgh Steelers		.15	.06	.01
☐ 131	**Jimmie Giles**, Tampa Bay Buccaneers		.15	.06	.01
☐ 132	**Philadelphia Eagles TL**		.15	.04	.01
	Wilbert Montgomery				
	Harold Carmichael				
	Brenard Wilson				
	Carl Hairston				
☐ 133	**Gary Green**, Kansas City Chiefs		.04	.02	.00
☐ 134	**John Dutton**, Dallas Cowboys		.08	.03	.01
☐ 135	**Harry Carson AP**, New York Giants		.15	.06	.01
☐ 136	**Bob Kuechenberg**, Miami Dolphins		.04	.02	.00
☐ 137	**Ike Harris**, New Orleans Saints		.04	.02	.00
☐ 138	**Tommy Kramer**, San Francisco 49ers		.50	.22	.05
☐ 139	**Sam Adams**, New England Patriots		.04	.02	.00
☐ 140	**Doug English AP**, Detroit Lions		.08	.03	.01
☐ 141	**Steve Schubert**, Chicago Bears		.04	.02	.00
☐ 142	**Rusty Jackson**, Buffalo Bills		.04	.02	.00
☐ 143	**Reese McCall**, Baltimore Colts		.04	.02	.00

	MINT	VG-E	F-G
☐ 144 **Scott Dierking**, New York Jets	.04	.02	.00
☐ 145 **Ken Houston AP**, Washington Redskins	.10	.04	.01
☐ 146 **Bob Martin**, New York Jets	.04	.02	.00
☐ 147 **Sam McCullum**, Seattle Seahawks	.08	.03	.01
☐ 148 **Tom Banks**, St. Louis Cardinals	.04	.02	.00
☐ 149 **Willie Buchanon**, San Diego Chargers	.08	.03	.01
☐ 150 **Greg Pruitt**, Cleveland Browns	.15	.06	.01
☐ 151 **Denver Broncos TL**	.15	.04	.01
Otis Armstrong			
Rick Upchurch			
Steve Foley			
Brison Manor			
☐ 152 **Don Smith**, Atlanta Falcons	.04	.02	.00
☐ 153 **Pete Johnson**, Cincinnati Bengals	.10	.04	.01
☐ 154 **Charlie Smith**, Philadelphia Eagles	.04	.02	.00
☐ 155 **Mel Blount**, Pittsburgh Steelers	.15	.06	.01
☐ 156 **John Mendenhall**, New York Giants	.04	.02	.00
☐ 157 **Danny White**, Dallas Cowboys	.40	.18	.04
☐ 158 **Jimmy Cefalo**, Miami Dolphins	.04	.02	.00
☐ 159 **Richard Bishop AP**, New England Patriots ...	.04	.02	.00
☐ 160 **Walter Payton AP**, Chicago Bears	1.50	.70	.15
☐ 161 **Dave Dalby**, Oakland Raiders	.04	.02	.00
☐ 162 **Preston Dennard**, Los Angeles Rams	.04	.02	.00
☐ 163 **Johnnie Gray**, Green Bay Packers	.04	.02	.00
☐ 164 **Russell Erxleben**, New Orleans Saints	.04	.02	.00
☐ 165 **Toni Fritsch AP**, Houston Oilers	.04	.02	.00
☐ 166 **Terry Hermeling**, Washington Redskins	.04	.02	.00
☐ 167 **Roland Hooks**, Buffalo Bills	.04	.02	.00
☐ 168 **Roger Carr**, Baltimore Colts	.08	.03	.01
☐ 169 **San Diego Chargers TL**	.15	.04	.01
Clarence Williams			
John Jefferson			
Woodrow Lowe			
Ray Preston			
Wilbur Young			
☐ 170 **Ottis Anderson AP**, St. Louis Cardinals	.90	.40	.09
☐ 171 **Brian Sipe**, Cleveland Browns	.25	.10	.02
☐ 172 **Leonard Thompson**, Detroit Lions	.08	.03	.01
☐ 173 **Tony Reed**, Kansas City Chiefs	.08	.03	.01
☐ 174 **Bob Tucker**, Minnesota Vikings	.08	.03	.01
☐ 175 **Joe Greene**, Pittsburgh Steelers	.30	.12	.03
☐ 176 **Jack Dolbin**, Denver Broncos	.04	.02	.00
☐ 177 **Chuck Ramsey**, New York Jets	.04	.02	.00
☐ 178 **Paul Hofer**, San Francisco 49ers	.04	.02	.00
☐ 179 **Randy Logan**, Philadelphia Eagles	.04	.02	.00
☐ 180 **David Lewis AP**, Tampa Bay Buccaneers	.04	.02	.00

		MINT	VG-E	F-G
☐ 181	**Duriel Harris**, Miami Dolphins	.08	.03	.01
☐ 182	**June Jones**, Atlanta Falcons	.08	.03	.01
☐ 183	**Larry McCarren**, Green Bay Packers	.04	.02	.00
☐ 184	**Ken Johnson**, New York Jets	.04	.02	.00
☐ 185	**Charlie Waters**, Dallas Cowboys	.15	.06	.01
☐ 186	**Noah Jackson**, Chicago Bears	.04	.02	.00
☐ 187	**Reggie Williams**, Cincinnati Bengals	.08	.03	.01
☐ 188	**New England Patriots TL**	.15	.04	.01
	Sam Cunningham			
	Harold Jackson			
	Raymond Clayborn			
	Tony McGee			
☐ 189	**Carl Eller**, Seattle Seahawks	.25	.10	.02
☐ 190	**Ed White AP**, San Diego Chargers	.08	.03	.01
☐ 191	**Mario Clark**, Buffalo Bills	.04	.02	.00
☐ 192	**Roosevelt Leaks**, Baltimore Colts	.04	.02	.00
☐ 193	**Ted McKnight**, Kansas City Chiefs	.04	.02	.00
☐ 194	**Danny Buggs**, Washington Redskins	.04	.02	.00
☐ 195	**Lester Hayes**, Oakland Raiders	.20	.09	.02
☐ 196	**Clarence Scott**, Cleveland Browns	.04	.02	.00
☐ 197	**New Orleans Saints TL**	.15	.04	.01
	Chuck Muncie			
	Wes Chandler			
	Tom Myers			
	Elois Grooms			
	Don Reese			
☐ 198	**Richard Caster**, Houston Oilers	.10	.04	.01
☐ 199	**Louie Giammona**, Philadelphia Eagles	.04	.02	.00
☐ 200	**Terry Bradshaw**, Pittsburgh Steelers	1.00	.45	.10
☐ 201	**Ed Newman**, Miami Dolphins	.04	.02	.00
☐ 202	**Fred Dryer**, Los Angeles Rams	.20	.09	.02
☐ 203	**Dennis Franks**, Detroit Lions	.04	.02	.00
☐ 204	**Bob Breunig**, Dallas Cowboys	.15	.06	.01
☐ 205	**Alan Page**, Chicago Bears	.25	.10	.02
☐ 206	**Earnest Gray**, New York Giants	.08	.03	.01
☐ 207	**Minnesota Vikings TL**	.15	.04	.01
	Rickey Young			
	Ahmad Rashad			
	Tom Hannon			
	Nate Wright			
	Mark Mullaney			
☐ 208	**Horace Ivory**, New England Patriots	.04	.02	.00
☐ 209	**Isaac Hagins**, Tampa Bay Buccaneers	.04	.02	.00
☐ 210	**Gary Johnson AP**, San Diego Chargers	.08	.03	.01
☐ 211	**Kevin Long**, New York Jets	.04	.02	.00
☐ 212	**Bill Thompson**, Denver Broncos	.04	.02	.00

	MINT	VG-E	F-G
☐ 213 **Don Bass**, Cincinnati Bengals	.04	.02	.00
☐ 214 **George Starke**, Washington Redskins	.04	.02	.00
☐ 215 **Efren Herrera**, Seattle Seahawks	.04	.02	.00
☐ 216 **Theo Bell**, Pittsburgh Steelers	.04	.02	.00
☐ 217 **Monte Jackson**, Oakland Raiders	.04	.02	.00
☐ 218 **Reggie McKenzie**, Buffalo Bills	.04	.02	.00
☐ 219 **Bucky Dilts**, Baltimore Colts	.04	.02	.00
☐ 220 **Lyle Alzado**, Cleveland Browns	.25	.10	.02
☐ 221 **Tim Foley**, Miami Dolphins	.04	.02	.00
☐ 222 **Mark Arneson**, St. Louis Cardinals	.04	.02	.00
☐ 223 **Fred Quillan**, San Francisco 49ers	.04	.02	.00
☐ 224 **Benny Ricardo**, Detroit Lions	.04	.02	.00
☐ 225 **Phil Simms**, New York Giants	.50	.22	.05
☐ 226 **Chicago Bears TL**	.40	.08	.01
Walter Payton			
Brian Baschnagel			
Gary Fencik			
Terry Schmidt			
Jim Osborne			
☐ 227 **Max Runager**, Philadelphia Eagles	.04	.02	.00
☐ 228 **Barty Smith**, Green Bay Packers	.04	.02	.00
☐ 229 **Jay Saldi**, Dallas Cowboys	.04	.02	.00
☐ 230 **John Hannah AP**, New England Patriots	.15	.06	.01
☐ 231 **Tim Wilson**, Houston Oilers	.04	.02	.00
☐ 232 **Jeff Van Note**, Atlanta Falcons	.04	.02	.00
☐ 233 **Henry Marshall**, Kansas City Chiefs	.04	.02	.00
☐ 234 **Diron Talbert**, Washington Redskins	.04	.02	.00
☐ 235 **Garo Yepremian**, Buffalo Bills	.08	.03	.01
☐ 236 **Larry Brown**, Pittsburgh Steelers	.04	.02	.00
☐ 237 **Clarence Williams**, San Diego Chargers	.04	.02	.00
☐ 238 **Burgess Owens**, New York Jets	.04	.02	.00
☐ 239 **Vince Ferragamo**, Los Angeles Rams	.20	.09	.02
☐ 240 **Rickey Young**, Minnesota Vikings	.08	.03	.01
☐ 241 **Dave Logan**, Tampa Bay Buccaneers	.04	.02	.00
☐ 242 **Larry Gordon**, Miami Dolphins	.04	.02	.00
☐ 243 **Terry Miller**, Buffalo Bills	.08	.03	.01
☐ 244 **Baltimore Colts TL**	.15	.04	.01
Joe Washington			
Joe Washington			
Fred Cook			
☐ 245 **Steve DeBerg**, San Francisco 49ers	.15	.06	.01
☐ 246 **Checklist 133-264**	.20	.04	.01
☐ 247 **Greg Latta**, Chicago Bears	.04	.02	.00
☐ 248 **Raymond Clayborn**, New England Patriots	.08	.03	.01
☐ 249 **Jim Clark**, New York Giants	.04	.02	.00
☐ 250 **Drew Pearson**, Dallas Cowboys	.25	.10	.02

		MINT	VG-E	F-G
☐ 251	**John Bunting**, Philadelphia Eagles	.04	.02	.00
☐ 252	**Rob Lytle**, Denver Broncos	.04	.02	.00
☐ 253	**Jim Hart**, St. Louis Cardinals	.25	.10	.02
☐ 254	**John McDaniel**, Washington Redskins	.04	.02	.00
☐ 255	**Dave Pear AP**, Oakland Raiders	.04	.02	.00
☐ 256	**Donnie Shell**, Pittsburgh Steelers	.08	.03	.01
☐ 257	**Dan Doornink**, Seattle Seahawks	.04	.02	.00
☐ 258	**Wallace Francis**, Atlanta Falcons	.15	.06	.01
☐ 259	**Dave Beverly**, Green Bay Packers	.04	.02	.00
☐ 260	**Lee Roy Selmon AP**, Tampa Bay Buccaneers	.20	.09	.02
☐ 261	**Doug Dieken**, Cleveland Browns	.04	.02	.00
☐ 262	**Gary Davis**, Miami Dolphins	.04	.02	.00
☐ 263	**Bob Rush**, San Diego Chargers	.04	.02	.00
☐ 264	**Buffalo Bills TL**	.15	.04	.01
	Curtis Brown			
	Frank Lewis			
	Keith Moody			
	Sherman White			
☐ 265	**Greg Landry**, Baltimore Colts	.15	.06	.01
☐ 266	**Jan Stenerud**, Kansas City Chiefs	.10	.04	.01
☐ 267	**Tom Hicks**, Chicago Bears	.04	.02	.00
☐ 268	**Pat McInally**, Cincinnati Bengals	.10	.04	.01
☐ 269	**Tim Fox**, New England Patriots	.08	.03	.01
☐ 270	**Harvey Martin**, Dallas Cowboys	.15	.06	.01
☐ 271	**Dan Lloyd**, St. Louis Cardinals	.04	.02	.00
☐ 272	**Mike Barber**, Houston Oilers	.08	.03	.01
☐ 273	**Wendell Tyler**, Los Angeles Rams	.25	.10	.02
☐ 274	**Jeff Komlo**, Detroit Lions	.15	.06	.01
☐ 275	**Wes Chandler**, New Orleans Saints	.25	.10	.02
☐ 276	**Brad Dusek**, Washington Redskins	.04	.02	.00
☐ 277	**Charlie Johnson**, Philadelphia Eagles	.04	.02	.00
☐ 278	**Dennis Swilley**, Minnesota Vikings	.04	.02	.00
☐ 279	**Johnny Evans**, Cleveland Browns	.04	.02	.00
☐ 280	**Jack Lambert AP**, Pittsburgh Steelers	.25	.10	.02
☐ 281	**Vern Den Herder**, Miami Dolphins	.04	.02	.00
☐ 282	**Tampa Bay Bucs TL**	.15	.04	.01
	Ricky Bell			
	Isaac Hagins			
	Lee Roy Selmon			
☐ 283	**Bob Klein**, San Diego Chargers	.04	.02	.00
☐ 284	**Jim Turner**, Denver Broncos	.08	.03	.01
☐ 285	**Marvin Powell AP**, New York Jets	.08	.03	.01
☐ 286	**Aaron Kyle**, Dallas Cowboys	.04	.02	.00
☐ 287	**Dan Neal**, Chicago Bears	.04	.02	.00
☐ 288	**Wayne Morris**, St. Louis Cardinals	.08	.03	.01
☐ 289	**Steve Bartkowski**, Atlanta Falcons	.25	.10	.02

	MINT	VG-E	F-G
☐ 290 **Dave Jennings AP**, New York Giants	.04	.02	.00
☐ 291 **John Smith**, New England Patriots	.04	.02	.00
☐ 292 **Bill Gregory**, Seattle Seahawks	.04	.02	.00
☐ 293 **Frank Lewis**, Buffalo Bills	.08	.03	.01
☐ 294 **Fred Cook**, Baltimore Colts	.04	.02	.00
☐ 295 **David Hill AP**, Detroit Lions	.04	.02	.00
☐ 296 **Wade Key**, Philadelphia Eagles	.04	.02	.00
☐ 297 **Sidney Thornton**, Pittsburgh Steelers	.04	.02	.00
☐ 298 **Charlie Hall**, Cleveland Browns	.04	.02	.00
☐ 299 **Joe Lavender**, Washington Redskins	.04	.02	.00
☐ 300 **Tom Rafferty**, Dallas Cowboys	.04	.02	.00
☐ 301 **Mike Renfro**, Houston Oilers	.04	.02	.00
☐ 302 **Wilbur Jackson**, San Francisco 49ers	.04	.02	.00
☐ 303 **Green Bay Packers TL**	.15	.04	.01
Terdell Middleton			
James Lofton			
Johnnie Gray			
Robert Barber			
Ezra Johnson			
☐ 304 **Henry Childs**, New Orleans Saints	.04	.02	.00
☐ 305 **Russ Washington AP**, San Diego Chargers ...	.04	.02	.00
☐ 306 **Jim LeClair**, Cincinnati Bengals	.04	.02	.00
☐ 307 **Tommy Hart**, Chicago Bears	.04	.02	.00
☐ 308 **Gary Barbaro**, Kansas City Chiefs	.08	.03	.01
☐ 309 **Billy Taylor**, New York Giants	.08	.03	.01
☐ 310 **Ray Guy**, Oakland Raiders	.15	.06	.01
☐ 311 **Don Hasselbeck**, New England Patriots	.04	.02	.00
☐ 312 **Doug Williams**, Tampa Bay Buccaneers	.20	.09	.02
☐ 313 **Nick Mike-Mayer**, Buffalo Bills	.04	.02	.00
☐ 314 **Don McCauley**, Baltimore Colts	.04	.02	.00
☐ 315 **Wesley Walker**, New York Jets	.15	.06	.01
☐ 316 **Dan Dierdorf**, St. Louis Cardinals	.08	.03	.01
☐ 317 **Dave Brown**, Seattle Seahawks	.04	.02	.00
☐ 318 **Leroy Harris**, Philadelphia Eagles	.04	.02	.00
☐ 319 **Pittsburgh Steelers TL**	.30	.06	.01
Franco Harris			
John Stallworth			
Jack Lambert			
Steve Furness			
L.C. Greenwood			
☐ 320 **Mark Moseley AP**, Washington Redskins	.10	.04	.01
☐ 321 **Mark Dennard**, Miami Dolphins	.04	.02	.00
☐ 322 **Terry Nelson**, Los Angeles Rams	.04	.02	.00
☐ 323 **Tom Jackson**, Denver Broncos	.08	.03	.01
☐ 324 **Rick Kane**, Detroit Lions	.04	.02	.00
☐ 325 **Jerry Sherk**, Cleveland Browns	.08	.03	.01

		MINT	VG-E	F-G
☐ 326	**Ray Preston**, San Diego Chargers	.04	.02	.00
☐ 327	**Golden Richards**, Denver Broncos	.08	.03	.01
☐ 328	**Randy Dean**, New York Giants	.04	.02	.00
☐ 329	**Rick Danmeier**, Minnesota Vikings	.04	.02	.00
☐ 330	**Tony Dorsett**, Dallas Cowboys	1.00	.45	.10

STATISTICAL LEADERS

		MINT	VG-E	F-G
☐ 331	**Passing Leaders** .... Dan Fouts Roger Staubach	.65	.30	.06
☐ 332	**Receiving Leaders** .... Joe Washington Ahmad Rashad	.15	.06	.01
☐ 333	**Sacks Leaders** .... Jesse Baker Al Baker Jack Youngblood	.15	.06	.01
☐ 334	**Scoring Leaders** .... John Smith Mark Moseley	.08	.03	.01
☐ 335	**Interception Leaders** .... Mike Reinfeldt Lemar Parrish	.08	.03	.01
☐ 336	**Punting Leaders** .... Bob Grupp Dave Jennings	.08	.03	.01
☐ 337	**Freddie Solomon**, San Francisco 49ers	.08	.03	.01
☐ 338	**Cincinnati Bengals TL** .... Pete Johnson Don Bass Dick Jauron Gary Burley	.15	.04	.01
☐ 339	**Ken Stone**, St. Louis Cardinals	.04	.02	.00
☐ 340	**Greg Buttle AP**, New York Jets	.08	.03	.01
☐ 341	**Bob Baumhower**, Miami Dolphins	.08	.03	.01
☐ 342	**Billy Waddy**, Los Angeles Rams	.04	.02	.00
☐ 343	**Cliff Parsley**, Houston Oilers	.04	.02	.00
☐ 344	**Walter White**, Kansas City Chiefs	.04	.02	.00
☐ 345	**Mike Thomas**, San Diego Chargers	.04	.02	.00
☐ 346	**Neil O'Donoghue**, Tampa Bay Buccaneers ...	.04	.02	.00
☐ 347	**Freddie Scott**, Detroit Lions	.08	.03	.01
☐ 348	**Joe Ferguson**, Buffalo Bills	.20	.09	.02

		MINT	VG-E	F-G
☐ 349	**Doug Nettles**, Baltimore Colts	.04	.02	.00
☐ 350	**Mike Webster AP**, Pittsburgh Steelers	.08	.03	.01
☐ 351	**Ron Saul**, Washington Redskins	.04	.02	.00
☐ 352	**Julius Adams**, New England Patriots	.04	.02	.00
☐ 353	**Rafael Septien**, Dallas Cowboys	.15	.06	.01
☐ 354	**Cleo Miller**, Cleveland Browns	.04	.02	.00
☐ 355	**Keith Simpson AP**, Seattle Seahawks	.04	.02	.00
☐ 356	**Johnny Perkins**, New York Jets	.04	.02	.00
☐ 357	**Jerry Sisemore**, Philadelphia Eagles	.04	.02	.00
☐ 358	**Arthur Whittington**, Oakland Raiders	.04	.02	.00
☐ 359	**St. Louis Cardinals TL**	.15	.04	.01
	Ottis Anderson			
	Pat Tilley			
	Ken Stone			
	Bob Pollard			
☐ 360	**Rick Upchurch**, Denver Broncos	.10	.04	.01
☐ 361	**Kim Bokamper**, Miami Dolphins	.04	.02	.00
☐ 362	**Roland Harper**, Chicago Bears	.04	.02	.00
☐ 363	**Pat Leahy**, New York Jets	.04	.02	.00
☐ 364	**Louis Breeden**, Cincinnati Bengals	.04	.02	.00
☐ 365	**John Jefferson**, San Diego Chargers	.20	.09	.02
☐ 366	**Jerry Eckwood**, Tampa Bay Buccaneers	.08	.03	.01
☐ 367	**David Whitehurst**, Green Bay Packers	.08	.03	.01
☐ 368	**Willie Parker**, Buffalo Bills	.04	.02	.00
☐ 369	**Ed Simonini**, Baltimore Colts	.04	.02	.00
☐ 370	**Jack Youngblood AP**, Los Angeles Rams	.20	.09	.02
☐ 371	**Don Warren**, Washington Redskins	.04	.02	.00
☐ 372	**Andy Johnson**, New England Patriots	.04	.02	.00
☐ 373	**D.D. Lewis**, Dallas Cowboys	.10	.04	.01
☐ 374	**Beasley Reece**, Tampa Bay Buccaneers	.04	.02	.00
☐ 375	**L.C. Greenwood**, Pittsburgh Steelers	.15	.06	.01
☐ 376	**Cleveland Browns TL**	.15	.04	.01
	Mike Pruitt			
	Dave Logan			
	Thom Darden			
	Jerry Sherk			
☐ 377	**Herman Edwards**, Philadelphia Eagles	.04	.02	.00
☐ 378	**Rob Carpenter**, Houston Oilers	.08	.03	.01
☐ 379	**Herman Weaver**, Seattle Seahawks	.04	.02	.00
☐ 380	**Gary Fencik AP**, Chicago Bears	.04	.02	.00
☐ 381	**Don Strock**, Miami Dolphins	.15	.06	.01
☐ 382	**Art Shell**, Oakland Raiders	.08	.03	.01
☐ 383	**Tim Mazzetti**, Atlanta Falcons	.04	.02	.00
☐ 384	**Bruce Harper**, New York Jets	.04	.02	.00
☐ 385	**Al Bubba Baker**, Detroit Lions	.08	.03	.01
☐ 386	**Conrad Dobler**, New Orleans Saints	.08	.03	.01

	MINT	VG-E	F-G
☐ 387 **Stu Voigt**, Minnesota Vikings	.04	.02	.00
☐ 388 **Ken Anderson**, Cincinnati Bengals	.50	.22	.05
☐ 389 **Pat Tilley**, St. Louis Cardinals	.10	.04	.01
☐ 390 **John Riggins**, Washington Redskins	.40	.18	.04
☐ 391 **Checklist 265-396**	.20	.04	.01
☐ 392 **Fred Dean AP**, San Diego Chargers	.08	.03	.01
☐ 393 **Benny Barnes**, Dallas Cowboys	.04	.02	.00
☐ 394 **Los Angeles Rams TL**	.15	.04	.01
Wendell Tyler			
Preston Dennard			
Nolan Cromwell			
Jim Youngblood			
Jack Youngblood			
☐ 395 **Brad Van Pelt**, New York Giants	.08	.03	.01
☐ 396 **Eddie Hare**, New England Patriots	.04	.02	.00
☐ 397 **John Sciarra**, Philadelphia Eagles	.04	.02	.00
☐ 398 **Bob Jackson**, Cleveland Browns	.04	.02	.00
☐ 399 **John Yarno**, Seattle Seahawks	.04	.02	.00
☐ 400 **Franco Harris AP**, Pittsburgh Steelers	.75	.35	.07
☐ 401 **Ray Wersching**, San Francisco 49ers	.04	.02	.00
☐ 402 **Virgil Livers**, Chicago Bears	.04	.02	.00
☐ 403 **Raymond Chester**, Oakland Raiders	.08	.03	.01
☐ 404 **Leon Gray**, Houston Oilers	.08	.03	.01
☐ 405 **Richard Todd**, New York Jets	.20	.09	.02
☐ 406 **Larry Little**, Miami Dolphins	.08	.03	.01
☐ 407 **Ted Fritsch**, Washington Redskins	.04	.02	.00
☐ 408 **Larry Mucker**, Tampa Bay Buccaneers	.04	.02	.00
☐ 409 **Jim Allen**, Detroit Lions	.04	.02	.00
☐ 410 **Randy Gradishar**, Denver Broncos	.15	.06	.01
☐ 411 **Atlanta Falcons TL**	.15	.04	.01
William Andrews			
Wallace Francis			
Rolland Lawrence			
Don Smith			
☐ 412 **Louie Kelcher**, San Diego Chargers	.08	.03	.01
☐ 413 **Robert Newhouse**, Dallas Cowboys	.10	.04	.01
☐ 414 **Gary Shirk**, New York Giants	.04	.02	.00
☐ 415 **Mike Haynes AP**, New England Patriots	.15	.06	.01
☐ 416 **Craig Colquitt**, Pittsburgh Steelers	.04	.02	.00
☐ 417 **Lou Piccone**, Buffalo Bills	.04	.02	.00
☐ 418 **Clay Matthews**, Cleveland Browns	.08	.03	.01
☐ 419 **Marvin Cobb**, Cincinnati Bengals	.04	.02	.00
☐ 420 **Harold Carmichael AP**, Philadelphia Eagles ..	.25	.10	.02
☐ 421 **Uwe von Schamann**, Miami Dolphins	.10	.04	.01
☐ 422 **Mike Phipps**, Chicago Bears	.15	.06	.01
☐ 423 **Nolan Cromwell**, Los Angeles Rams	.25	.10	.02

	MINT	VG-E	F-G
☐ 424 **Glenn Doughty**, Baltimore Colts	.04	.02	.00
☐ 425 **Bob Young** AP, St. Louis Cardinals	.04	.02	.00
☐ 426 **Tony Galbreath**, New Orleans Saints	.08	.03	.01
☐ 427 **Luke Prestridge**, Denver Broncos	.04	.02	.00
☐ 428 **Terry Beeson**, Seattle Seahawks	.04	.02	.00
☐ 429 **Jack Tatum**, Oakland Raiders	.15	.06	.01
☐ 430 **Lemar Parrish** AP, Washington Redskins	.04	.02	.00
☐ 431 **Chester Marcol**, Green Bay Packers	.04	.02	.00
☐ 432 **Houston Oilers TL**	.15	.04	.01
Dan Pastorini			
Ken Burrough			
Mike Reinfeldt			
Jesse Baker			
☐ 433 **John Fitzgerald**, Dallas Cowboys	.04	.02	.00
☐ 434 **Gary Jeter**, New York Giants	.04	.02	.00
☐ 435 **Steve Grogan**, New England Patriots	.20	.09	.02
☐ 436 **Jon Kolb**, Pittsburgh Steelers	.04	.02	.00
☐ 437 **Jim Obradovich**, Tampa Bay Buccaneers	.04	.02	.00
☐ 438 **Gerald Irons**, Cleveland Browns	.04	.02	.00
☐ 439 **Jeff West**, San Diego Chargers	.04	.02	.00
☐ 440 **Wilbert Montgomery**, Philadelphia Eagles	.20	.09	.02
☐ 441 **Norris Thomas**, Miami Dolphins	.04	.02	.00
☐ 442 **James Scott**, Chicago Bears	.04	.02	.00
☐ 443 **Curtis Brown**, Buffalo Bills	.04	.02	.00
☐ 444 **Ken Fantetti**, Detroit Lions	.04	.02	.00
☐ 445 **Pat Haden**, Los Angeles Rams	.15	.06	.01
☐ 446 **Carl Mauck**, Houston Oilers	.04	.02	.00
☐ 447 **Bruce Laird**, Baltimore Colts	.04	.02	.00
☐ 448 **Otis Armstrong**, Denver Broncos	.15	.06	.01
☐ 449 **Gene Upshaw**, Oakland Raiders	.08	.03	.01
☐ 450 **Steve Largent** AP, Seattle Seahawks	.20	.09	.02
☐ 451 **Benny Malone**, Washington Redskins	.04	.02	.00
☐ 452 **Steve Nelson**, New England Patriots	.04	.02	.00
☐ 453 **Mark Cotney**, Tampa Bay Buccaneers	.04	.02	.00
☐ 454 **Joe Danelo**, New York Giants	.04	.02	.00
☐ 455 **Billy Joe DuPree**, Dallas Cowboys	.15	.06	.01
☐ 456 **Ron Johnson**, Pittsburgh Steelers	.04	.02	.00
☐ 457 **Archie Griffin**, Cincinnati Bengals	.15	.06	.01
☐ 458 **Reggie Rucker**, Cleveland Browns	.10	.04	.01
☐ 459 **Claude Humphrey**, Philadelphia Eagles	.08	.03	.01
☐ 460 **Lydell Mitchell**, San Diego Chargers	.15	.06	.01
☐ 461 **Steve Towle**, Miami Dolphins	.04	.02	.00
☐ 462 **Revie Sorey**, Chicago Bears	.04	.02	.00
☐ 463 **Tom Skladany**, Detroit Lions	.08	.03	.01
☐ 464 **Clark Gaines**, New York Jets	.04	.02	.00
☐ 465 **Frank Corral**, Los Angeles Rams	.04	.02	.00

			MINT	VG-E	F-G
☐ 466	**Steve Fuller,** Kansas City Chiefs		.20	.09	.02
☐ 467	**Ahmad Rashad AP,** Minnesota Vikings		.25	.10	.02
☐ 468	**Oakland Raiders TL**		.15	.04	.01
	Mark van Eeghen				
	Cliff Branch				
	Lester Hayes				
	Willie Jones				
☐ 469	**Brian Peets,** Seattle Seahawks		.04	.02	.00
☐ 470	**Pat Donovan AP,** Dallas Cowboys		.08	.03	.01
☐ 471	**Ken Burrough,** Houston Oilers		.08	.03	.01
☐ 472	**Don Calhoun,** New England Patriots		.04	.02	.00
☐ 473	**Bill Bryan,** Denver Broncos		.04	.02	.00
☐ 474	**Terry Jackson,** New York Giants		.04	.02	.00
☐ 475	**Joe Theismann,** Washington Redskins		.60	.28	.06
☐ 476	**Jim Smith,** Pittsburgh Steelers		.08	.03	.01
☐ 477	**Joe DeLamielleure,** Buffalo Bills		.08	.03	.01
☐ 478	**Mike Pruitt AP,** Cleveland Browns		.15	.06	.01
☐ 479	**Steve Mike-Mayer,** Baltimore Colts		.04	.02	.00
☐ 480	**Bill Bergey,** Philadelphia Eagles		.15	.06	.01
☐ 481	**Mike Fuller,** San Diego Chargers		.04	.02	.00
☐ 482	**Bob Parsons,** Chicago Bears		.04	.02	.00
☐ 483	**Billy Brooks,** Cincinnati Bengals		.04	.02	.00
☐ 484	**Jerome Barkum,** New York Jets		.08	.03	.01
☐ 485	**Larry Csonka,** Miami Dolphins		.40	.18	.04
☐ 486	**John Hill,** San Francisco 49ers		.04	.02	.00
☐ 487	**Mike Dawson,** St. Louis Cardinals		.04	.02	.00
☐ 488	**Detroit Lions TL**		.15	.04	.01
	Dexter Bussey				
	Freddie Scott				
	Jim Allen				
	Luther Bradley				
	Al Baker				
☐ 489	**Ted Hendricks,** Oakland Raiders		.15	.06	.01
☐ 490	**Dan Pastorini,** Houston Oilers		.20	.09	.02
☐ 491	**Stanley Morgan,** New England Patriots		.15	.06	.01
☐ 492	**AFC Championship**		.15	.06	.01
	Steelers 27, Oilers 13				
	(R. Bleier running)				
☐ 493	**NFC Championship**		.15	.06	.01
	Rams 9, Buccaneers 0				
	(Vince Ferragamo)				
☐ 494	**Super Bowl XIV**		.20	.09	.02
	Steelers 31, Rams 19				
	(line play)				
☐ 495	**Dwight White,** Pittsburgh Steelers		.08	.03	.01
☐ 496	**Haven Moses,** Denver Broncos		.08	.03	.01

		MINT	VG-E	F-G
☐ 497	**Guy Morriss**, Philadelphia Eagles	.04	.02	.00
☐ 498	**Dewey Selmon**, Tampa Bay Buccaneers	.08	.03	.01
☐ 499	**Dave Butz**, Washington Redskins	.08	.03	.01
☐ 500	**Chuck Foreman**, Minnesota Vikings	.15	.06	.01
☐ 501	**Chris Bahr**, Cincinnati Bengals	.08	.03	.01
☐ 502	**Mark Miller**, Cleveland Browns	.04	.02	.00
☐ 503	**Tony Greene**, Buffalo Bills	.04	.02	.00
☐ 504	**Brian Kelley**, New York Giants	.04	.02	.00
☐ 505	**Joe Washington**, Baltimore Colts	.15	.06	.01
☐ 506	**Butch Johnson**, Dallas Cowboys	.15	.06	.01
☐ 507	**New York Jets TL**	.15	.04	.01
	Clark Gaines			
	Wesley Walker			
	Burgess Owens			
	Joe Klecko			
☐ 508	**Steve Little**, St. Louis Cardinals	.04	.02	.00
☐ 509	**Checklist 397-528**	.20	.04	.01
☐ 510	**Mark van Eeghen**, Oakland Raiders	.08	.03	.01
☐ 511	**Gary Danielson**, Detroit Lions	.15	.06	.01
☐ 512	**Manu Tuiasosopo**, Seattle Seahawks	.04	.02	.00
☐ 513	**Paul Coffman**, Green Bay Packers	.04	.02	.00
☐ 514	**Cullen Bryant**, Los Angeles Rams	.04	.02	.00
☐ 515	**Nat Moore**, Miami Dolphins	.08	.03	.01
☐ 516	**Bill Lenkaitis**, Atlanta Falcons	.04	.02	.00
☐ 517	**Lynn Cain**, Atlanta Falcons	.15	.06	.01
☐ 518	**Gregg Bingham**, Houston Oilers	.04	.02	.00
☐ 519	**Ted Albrecht**, Chicago Bears	.04	.02	.00
☐ 520	**Dan Fouts AP**, San Diego Chargers	.75	.35	.07
☐ 521	**Bernard Jackson**, Denver Broncos	.08	.03	.01
☐ 522	**Coy Bacon**, Washington Redskins	.04	.02	.00
☐ 523	**Tony Franklin**, Philadelphia Eagles	.15	.06	.01
☐ 524	**Bo Harris**, Cincinnati Bengals	.04	.02	.00
☐ 525	**Bob Grupp AP**, Kansas City Chiefs	.04	.02	.00
☐ 526	**San Francisco 49ers TL**	.15	.04	.01
	Paul Hofer			
	Freddie Solomon			
	James Owens			
	Dwaine Board			
☐ 527	**Steve Wilson**, Tampa Bay Buccaneers	.04	.02	.00
☐ 528	**Bennie Cunningham**, Pittsburgh Steelers	.08	.03	.01

1981 TOPPS

The 1981 Topps football card set contains 528 cards of NFL players. The cards measure 2½" by 3½". The backs of the cards contain player vital statistics, year-by-year records and a short biography of the player. The fronts of the cards contain the name Topps in the frame line. The term SA refers to a super action card as stated on the obverse; the SA card is a special card issued in addition to the player's regular card. The first six cards in the set feature statistical league leaders from the previous season. All Pro (AP) selections are designated on the player's regular card, not a special card. Distributed throughout the set are Team Leader (TL) cards typically featuring four individual team statistical leaders on the front as well as a team checklist on the back.

			MINT	VG-E	F-G
	COMPLETE SET		16.00	7.50	1.60
	COMMON PLAYER (1-528)		.04	.02	.00
☐	1	Passing Leaders	.20	.05	.01
		Ron Jaworski			
		Brian Sipe			
☐	2	Receiving Leaders	.10	.04	.01
		Earl Cooper			
		Kellen Winslow			
☐	3	Sack Leaders	.08	.03	.01
		Al Baker			
		Gary Johnson			
☐	4	Scoring Leaders	.08	.03	.01
		Ed Murray			
		John Smith			

		MINT	VG-E	F-G
☐	**5 Interception Leaders**	.10	.04	.01
	Nolan Cromwell			
	Lester Hayes			
☐	**6 Punting Leaders**	.08	.03	.01
	Dave Jennings			
	Luke Prestridge			
☐	**7 Don Calhoun**, New England Patriots	.04	.02	.00
☐	**8 Jack Tatum**, Houston Oilers	.10	.04	.01
☐	**9 Reggie Rucker**, Cleveland Browns	.08	.03	.01
☐	**10 Mike Webster AP**, Pittsburgh Steelers	.08	.03	.01
☐	**11 Vince Evans**, Chicago Bears	.15	.06	.01
☐	**12 Ottis Anderson SA**, St. Louis Cardinals	.20	.09	.02
☐	**13 Leroy Harris**, Philadelphia Eagles	.04	.02	.00
☐	**14 Gordon King**, New York Giants	.04	.02	.00
☐	**15 Harvey Martin**, Dallas Cowboys	.15	.06	.01
☐	**16 Johnny Lam Jones**, New York Jets	.15	.06	.01
☐	**17 Ken Greene**, St. Louis Cardinals	.04	.02	.00
☐	**18 Frank Lewis**, Buffalo Bills	.08	.03	.01
☐	**19 Seattle Seahawks TL**	.15	.04	.01
	Jim Jodat			
	Dave Brown			
	John Harris			
	Steve Largent			
	Jacob Green			
☐	**20 Lester Hayes AP**, Oakland Raiders	.12	.05	.01
☐	**21 Uwe von Schamann**, Miami Dolphins	.08	.03	.01
☐	**22 Joe Washington**, Baltimore Colts	.12	.05	.01
☐	**23 Louie Kelcher**, San Diego Chargers	.08	.03	.01
☐	**24 Willie Miller**, Los Angeles Rams	.04	.02	.00
☐	**25 Steve Grogan**, New England Patriots	.20	.09	.02
☐	**26 John Hill**, New Orleans Saints	.04	.02	.00
☐	**27 Stan White**, Detroit Lions	.04	.02	.00
☐	**28 William Andrews SA**, Atlanta Falcons	.12	.05	.01
☐	**29 Clarence Scott**, Cleveland Browns	.04	.02	.00
☐	**30 Leon Gray AP**, Houston Oilers	.08	.03	.01
☐	**31 Craig Colquitt**, Pittsburgh Steelers	.04	.02	.00
☐	**32 Doug Williams**, Tampa Bay Buccaneers	.20	.09	.02
☐	**33 Bob Breunig**, Dallas Cowboys	.10	.04	.01
☐	**34 Billy Taylor**, New York Giants	.08	.03	.01
☐	**35 Harold Carmichael**, Philadelphia Eagles	.20	.09	.02
☐	**36 Ray Wersching**, San Francisco 49ers	.04	.02	.00
☐	**37 Dennis Johnson**, Minnesota Vikings	.04	.02	.00
☐	**38 Archie Griffin**, Cincinnati Bengals	.12	.05	.01

			MINT	VG-E	F-G
☐	39	**Los Angeles Rams TL**	.15	.04	.01
		Cullen Bryant			
		Billy Waddy			
		Nolan Cromwell			
		Jack Youngblood			
☐	40	**Gary Fencik AP**, Chicago Bears	.04	.02	.00
☐	41	**Lynn Dickey**, Green Bay Packers	.20	.09	.02
☐	42	**Steve Bartkowski SA**, Atlanta Falcons	.15	.06	.01
☐	43	**Art Shell**, Oakland Raiders	.06	.02	.00
☐	44	**Wilbur Jackson**, Washington Redskins	.04	.02	.00
☐	45	**Frank Corral**, Los Angeles Rams	.04	.02	.00
☐	46	**Ted McKnight**, Kansas City Chiefs	.04	.02	.00
☐	47	**Joe Klecko**, New York Jets	.15	.06	.01
☐	48	**Dan Doornink**, Seattle Seahawks	.04	.02	.00
☐	49	**Doug Dieken**, Cleveland Browns	.04	.02	.00
☐	50	**Jerry Robinson AP**, Philadelphia Eagles	.15	.06	.01
☐	51	**Wallace Francis**, Atlanta Falcons	.08	.03	.01
☐	52	**Dave Preston**, Denver Broncos	.04	.02	.00
☐	53	**Jay Saldi**, Dallas Cowboys	.04	.02	.00
☐	54	**Rush Brown**, St. Louis Cardinals	.04	.02	.00
☐	55	**Phil Simms**, New York Giants	.25	.10	.02
☐	56	**Nick Mike-Mayer**, Buffalo Bills	.04	.02	.00
☐	57	**Washington Redskins TL**	.15	.04	.01
		Wilbur Jackson			
		Art Monk			
		Lemar Parrish			
		Coy Bacon			
☐	58	**Mike Renfro**, Houston Oilers	.04	.02	.00
☐	59	**Ted Brown SA**, Minnesota Vikings	.08	.03	.01
☐	60	**Steve Nelson AP**, New England Patriots	.04	.02	.00
☐	61	**Sidney Thornton**, Pittsburgh Steelers	.04	.02	.00
☐	62	**Kent Hill**, Los Angeles Rams	.04	.02	.00
☐	63	**Don Bessillieu**, Miami Dolphins	.04	.02	.00
☐	64	**Fred Cook**, Baltimore Colts	.04	.02	.00
☐	65	**Raymond Chester**, Oakland Raiders	.08	.03	.01
☐	66	**Rick Kane**, Detroit Lions	.04	.02	.00
☐	67	**Mike Fuller**, San Diego Chargers	.04	.02	.00
☐	68	**Dewey Selmon**, Tampa Bay Buccaneers	.08	.03	.01
☐	69	**Charles White**, Cleveland Browns	.25	.10	.02
☐	70	**Jeff Van Note AP**, Atlanta Falcons	.06	.02	.00
☐	71	**Robert Newhouse**, Dallas Cowboys	.10	.04	.01
☐	72	**Roynell Young**, Philadelphia Eagles	.04	.02	.00
☐	73	**Lynn Cain SA**, Atlanta Falcons	.08	.03	.01
☐	74	**Mike Friede**, New York Giants	.04	.02	.00

		MINT	VG-E	F-G
☐ 75 **Earl Cooper**, San Francisco 49ers		.08	.03	.01
☐ 76 **New Orleans Saints TL**		.15	.04	.01
Jimmy Rogers				
Wes Chandler				
Tom Myers				
Elois Grooms				
Derland Moore				
☐ 77 **Rick Danmeier**, Minnesota Vikings		.04	.02	.00
☐ 78 **Darrol Ray**, New York Jets		.08	.03	.01
☐ 79 **Gregg Bingham**, Houston Oilers		.04	.02	.00
☐ 80 **John Hannah AP**, New England Patriots		.12	.05	.01
☐ 81 **Jack Thompson**, Cincinnati Bengals		.12	.05	.01
☐ 82 **Rick Upchurch**, Denver Broncos		.10	.04	.01
☐ 83 **Mike Butler**, Green Bay Packers		.04	.02	.00
☐ 84 **Don Warren**, Washington Redskins		.04	.02	.00
☐ 85 **Mark Van Eeghen**, Oakland Raiders		.08	.03	.01
☐ 86 **J.T. Smith**, Kansas City Chiefs		.04	.02	.00
☐ 87 **Herman Weaver**, Seattle Seahawks		.04	.02	.00
☐ 88 **Terry Bradshaw SA**, Pittsburgh Steelers		.40	.18	.04
☐ 89 **Charlie Hall**, Cleveland Browns		.04	.02	.00
☐ 90 **Donnie Shell**, Pittsburgh Steelers		.08	.03	.01
☐ 91 **Ike Harris**, New Orleans Saints		.04	.02	.00
☐ 92 **Charlie Johnson**, Green Bay Packers		.04	.02	.00
☐ 93 **Rickey Watts**, Chicago Bears		.04	.02	.00
☐ 94 **New England Patriots TL**		.15	.04	.01
Vagas Ferguson				
Stanley Morgan				
Raymond Clayborn				
Julius Adams				
☐ 95 **Drew Pearson**, Dallas Cowboys		.20	.09	.02
☐ 96 **Neil O'Donoghue**, St. Louis Cardinals		.04	.02	.00
☐ 97 **Conrad Dobler**, Buffalo Bills		.06	.02	.00
☐ 98 **Jewerl Thomas**, Los Angeles Rams		.06	.02	.00
☐ 99 **Mike Barber**, Houston Oilers		.08	.03	.01
☐ 100 **Billy Sims AP**, Detroit Lions		1.00	.45	.10
☐ 101 **Vern Den Herder**, Miami Dolphins		.04	.02	.00
☐ 102 **Greg Landry**, Baltimore Colts		.12	.05	.01
☐ 103 **Joe Cribbs SA**, Buffalo Bills		.12	.05	.01
☐ 104 **Mark Murphy**, Washington Redskins		.06	.02	.00
☐ 105 **Chuck Muncie**, San Diego Chargers		.15	.06	.01
☐ 106 **Alfred Jackson**, Atlanta Falcons		.08	.03	.01
☐ 107 **Chris Bahr**, Oakland Raiders		.06	.02	.00
☐ 108 **Gordon Jones**, Tampa Bay Buccaneers		.08	.03	.01
☐ 109 **Willie Harper**, San Francisco 49ers		.04	.02	.00
☐ 110 **Dave Jennings AP**, New York Giants		.06	.02	.00
☐ 111 **Bennie Cunningham**, Pittsburgh Steelers		.04	.02	.00

	MINT	VG-E	F-G
☐ 112 **Jerry Sisemore**, Philadelphia Eagles	.04	.02	.00
☐ 113 **Cleveland Browns TL**	.15	.04	.01
Mike Pruitt			
Dave Logan			
Ron Bolton			
Lyle Alzado			
☐ 114 **Rickey Young**, Minnesota Vikings	.06	.02	.00
☐ 115 **Ken Anderson**, Cincinnati Bengals	.35	.15	.03
☐ 116 **Randy Gradishar**, Denver Broncos	.15	.06	.01
☐ 117 **Eddie Lee Ivery**, Green Bay Packers	.25	.10	.02
☐ 118 **Wesley Walker**, New York Jets	.15	.06	.01
☐ 119 **Chuck Foreman**, New England Patriots	.15	.06	.01
☐ 120 **Nolan Cromwell AP**, Los Angeles Rams	.12	.05	.01
☐ 121 **Curtis Dickey SA**, Baltimore Colts	.12	.05	.01
☐ 122 **Wayne Morris**, St. Louis Cardinals	.06	.02	.00
☐ 123 **Greg Stemrick**, Houston Oilers	.04	.02	.00
☐ 124 **Coy Bacon**, Washington Redskins	.04	.02	.00
☐ 125 **Jim Zorn**, Seattle Seahawks	.15	.06	.01
☐ 126 **Henry Childs**, New Orleans Saints	.04	.02	.00
☐ 127 **Checklist 1-132**	.15	.03	.01
☐ 128 **Len Walterscheid**, Chicago Bears	.04	.02	.00
☐ 129 **Johnny Evans**, Cleveland Browns	.04	.02	.00
☐ 130 **Gary Barbaro AP**, Kansas City Chiefs	.06	.02	.00
☐ 131 **Jim Smith**, Pittsburgh Steelers	.08	.03	.01
☐ 132 **New York Jets TL**	.15	.04	.01
Scott Dierking			
Bruce Harper			
Ken Schroy			
Mark Gastineau			
☐ 133 **Curtis Brown**, Buffalo Bills	.04	.02	.00
☐ 134 **D.D. Lewis**, Dallas Cowboys	.08	.03	.01
☐ 135 **Jim Plunkett**, Oakland Raiders	.30	.12	.03
☐ 136 **Nat Moore**, Miami Dolphins	.08	.03	.01
☐ 137 **Don McCauley**, Baltimore Colts	.04	.02	.00
☐ 138 **Tony Dorsett SA**, Dallas Cowboys	.40	.18	.04
☐ 139 **Julius Adams**, New England Patriots	.04	.02	.00
☐ 140 **Ahmad Rashad AP**, Minnesota Vikings	.25	.10	.02
☐ 141 **Rich Saul**, Los Angeles Rams	.04	.02	.00
☐ 142 **Ken Fantetti**, Detroit Lions	.04	.02	.00
☐ 143 **Kenny Johnson**, Buffalo Bills	.04	.02	.00
☐ 144 **Clark Gaines**, New York Jets	.04	.02	.00
☐ 145 **Mark Moseley**, Washington Redskins	.08	.03	.01
☐ 146 **Vernon Perry**, Houston Oilers	.04	.02	.00
☐ 147 **Jerry Eckwood**, Tampa Bay Buccaneers	.08	.03	.01
☐ 148 **Freddie Solomon**, San Francisco 49ers	.08	.03	.01
☐ 149 **Jerry Sherk**, Cleveland Browns	.06	.02	.00

		MINT	VG-E	F-G
☐ 150	**Kellen Winslow AP**, San Diego Chargers	.50	.22	.05
☐ 151	**Green Bay Packers TL**	.15	.04	.01
	Eddie Lee Ivery			
	James Lofton			
	Johnnie Gray			
	Mike Butler			
☐ 152	**Ross Browner**, Cincinnati Bengals	.08	.03	.01
☐ 153	**Dan Fouts SA**, San Diego Chargers	.35	.15	.03
☐ 154	**Woody Peoples**, Philadelphia Eagles	.04	.02	.00
☐ 155	**Jack Lambert**, Pittsburgh Steelers	.25	.10	.02
☐ 156	**Mike Dennis**, New York Giants	.04	.02	.00
☐ 157	**Rafael Septien**, Dallas Cowboys	.12	.05	.01
☐ 158	**Archie Manning**, New Orleans Saints	.25	.10	.02
☐ 159	**Don Hasselbeck**, New England Patriots	.04	.02	.00
☐ 160	**Alan Page AP**, Chicago Bears	.25	.10	.02
☐ 161	**Arthur Whittington**, Oakland Raiders	.04	.02	.00
☐ 162	**Billy Waddy**, Los Angeles Rams	.04	.02	.00
☐ 163	**Horace Belton**, Kansas City Chiefs	.04	.02	.00
☐ 164	**Luke Prestridge**, Denver Broncos	.04	.02	.00
☐ 165	**Joe Theismann**, Washington Redskins	.55	.25	.05
☐ 166	**Morris Towns**, Houston Oilers	.04	.02	.00
☐ 167	**Dave Brown**, Seattle Seahawks	.04	.02	.00
☐ 168	**Ezra Johnson**, Green Bay Packers	.04	.02	.00
☐ 169	**Tampa Bay Bucs TL**	.15	.04	.01
	Ricky Bell			
	Gordon Jones			
	Mike Washington			
	Lee Roy Selmon			
☐ 170	**Joe DeLamielleure AP**, Cleveland Browns	.06	.02	.00
☐ 171	**Earnest Gray SA**, New York Giants	.06	.02	.00
☐ 172	**Mike Thomas**, San Diego Chargers	.04	.02	.00
☐ 173	**Jim Haslett**, Buffalo Bills	.04	.02	.00
☐ 174	**Dave Woodley**, Miami Dolphins	.20	.09	.02
☐ 175	**Al Baker**, Detroit Lions	.06	.02	.00
☐ 176	**Nesby Glasgow**, Baltimore Colts	.04	.02	.00
☐ 177	**Pat Leahy**, New York Jets	.04	.02	.00
☐ 178	**Tom Brahaney**, St. Louis Cardinals	.04	.02	.00
☐ 179	**Herman Edwards**, Philadelphia Eagles	.04	.02	.00
☐ 180	**Junior Miller AP**, Atlanta Falcons	.08	.03	.01
☐ 181	**Richard Wood**, Tampa Bay Buccaneers	.04	.02	.00
☐ 182	**Lenvil Elliott**, San Francisco 49ers	.04	.02	.00
☐ 183	**Sammy White**, Minnesota Vikings	.08	.03	.01
☐ 184	**Russell Erxleben**, New Orleans Saints	.04	.02	.00
☐ 185	**Ed Too Tall Jones**, Dallas Cowboys	.20	.09	.02
☐ 186	**Ray Guy SA**, Oakland Raiders	.08	.03	.01
☐ 187	**Haven Moses**, Denver Broncos	.06	.02	.00

	MINT	VG-E	F-G
☐ 188 **New York Giants TL**	.15	.04	.01
Billy Taylor			
Earnest Gray			
Mike Dennis			
Gary Jeter			
☐ 189 **David Whitehurst**, Green Bay Packers	.12	.05	.01
☐ 190 **John Jefferson AP**, San Diego Chargers	.20	.09	.02
☐ 191 **Terry Beeson**, Seattle Seahawks	.04	.02	.00
☐ 192 **Dan Ross**, Cincinnati Bengals	.08	.03	.01
☐ 193 **Dave Williams**, Chicago Bears	.04	.02	.00
☐ 194 **Art Monk**, Washington Redskins	.40	.18	.04
☐ 195 **Roger Wehrli**, St. Louis Cardinals	.08	.03	.01
☐ 196 **Ricky Feacher**, Cleveland Browns	.04	.02	.00
☐ 197 **Miami Dolphins TL**	.15	.04	.01
Delvin Williams			
Tony Nathan			
Gerald Small			
Kim Bokamper			
A.J. Duhe			
☐ 198 **Carl Roaches**, Houston Oilers	.08	.03	.01
☐ 199 **Billy Campfield**, Philadelphia Eagles	.04	.02	.00
☐ 200 **Ted Hendricks AP**, Oakland Raiders	.15	.06	.01
☐ 201 **Fred Smerlas**, Buffalo Bills	.04	.02	.00
☐ 202 **Walter Payton SA**, Chicago Bears	.65	.30	.06
☐ 203 **Luther Bradley**, Detroit Lions	.04	.02	.00
☐ 204 **Herbert Scott**, Dallas Cowboys	.04	.02	.00
☐ 205 **Jack Youngblood**, Los Angeles Rams	.20	.09	.02
☐ 206 **Danny Pittman**, New York Giants	.04	.02	.00
☐ 207 **Houston Oilers TL**	.15	.04	.01
Carl Roaches			
Mike Barber			
Jack Tatum			
Jesse Baker			
Robert Brazile			
☐ 208 **Vagas Ferguson**, Buffalo Bills	.25	.10	.02
☐ 209 **Mark Dennard**, Miami Dolphins	.04	.02	.00
☐ 210 **Lemar Parrish AP**, Washington Redskins ...	.04	.02	.00
☐ 211 **Bruce Harper**, New York Jets	.04	.02	.00
☐ 212 **Ed Simonini**, Baltimore Colts	.04	.02	.00
☐ 213 **Nick Lowery**, Kansas City Chiefs	.04	.02	.00
☐ 214 **Kevin House**, Tampa Bay Buccaneers	.08	.03	.01
☐ 215 **Mike Kenn**, Atlanta Falcons	.04	.02	.00
☐ 216 **Joe Montana**, San Francisco 49ers	3.50	1.65	.35
☐ 217 **Joe Senser**, Minnesota Vikings	.08	.03	.01
☐ 218 **Lester Hayes SA**, Oakland Raiders	.06	.02	.00
☐ 219 **Gene Upshaw**, Oakland Raiders	.06	.02	.00

		MINT	VG-E	F-G
☐ 220	**Franco Harris,** Pittsburgh Steelers	.60	.28	.06
☐ 221	**Ron Bolton,** Cleveland Browns	.04	.02	.00
☐ 222	**Charles Alexander,** Cincinnati Bengals	.06	.02	.00
☐ 223	**Matt Robinson,** Denver Broncos	.06	.02	.00
☐ 224	**Ray Oldham,** Detroit Lions	.04	.02	.00
☐ 225	**George Martin,** New York Giants	.04	.02	.00
☐ 226	**Buffalo Bills TL**	.15	.04	.01
	Joe Cribbs			
	Jerry Butler			
	Steve Freeman			
	Ben Williams			
☐ 227	**Tony Franklin,** Philadelphia Eagles	.06	.02	.00
☐ 228	**George Cumby,** Green Bay Packers	.04	.02	.00
☐ 229	**Butch Johnson,** Dallas Cowboys	.12	.05	.01
☐ 230	**Mike Haynes AP,** New England Patriots	.12	.05	.01
☐ 231	**Rob Carpenter,** Houston Oilers	.08	.03	.01
☐ 232	**Steve Fuller,** Kansas City Chiefs	.12	.05	.01
☐ 233	**John Sawyer,** Seattle Seahawks	.04	.02	.00
☐ 234	**Kenny King SA,** Oakland Raiders	.08	.03	.01
☐ 235	**Jack Ham,** Pittsburgh Steelers	.15	.06	.01
☐ 236	**Jimmy Rogers,** New Orleans Saints	.04	.02	.00
☐ 237	**Bob Parsons,** Chicago Bears	.04	.02	.00
☐ 238	**Marty Lyons,** New York Jets	.08	.03	.01
☐ 239	**Pat Tilley,** St. Louis Cardinals	.08	.03	.01
☐ 240	**Dennis Harrah AP,** Los Angeles Rams	.04	.02	.00
☐ 241	**Thom Darden,** Cleveland Browns	.04	.02	.00
☐ 242	**Rolf Benirschke,** San Diego Chargers	.08	.03	.01
☐ 243	**Gerald Small,** Miami Dolphins	.04	.02	.00
☐ 244	**Atlanta Falcons TL**	.15	.04	.01
	William Andrews			
	Alfred Jenkins			
	Al Richardson			
	Joel Williams			
☐ 245	**Roger Carr,** Baltimore Colts	.06	.02	.00
☐ 246	**Sherman White,** Buffalo Bills	.04	.02	.00
☐ 247	**Ted Brown,** Minnesota Vikings	.10	.04	.01
☐ 248	**Matt Cavanaugh,** New England Patriots	.15	.06	.01
☐ 249	**John Dutton,** Dallas Cowboys	.08	.03	.01
☐ 250	**Bill Bergey AP,** Philadelphia Eagles	.15	.06	.01
☐ 251	**Jim Allen,** Detroit Lions	.04	.02	.00
☐ 252	**Mike Nelms SA,** Washington Redskins	.06	.02	.00
☐ 253	**Tom Blanchard,** Tampa Bay Buccaneers	.04	.02	.00
☐ 254	**Ricky Thompson,** Washington Redskins	.04	.02	.00
☐ 255	**John Matuszak,** Oakland Raiders	.08	.03	.01
☐ 256	**Randy Grossman,** Pittsburgh Steelers	.04	.02	.00
☐ 257	**Ray Griffin,** Cincinnati Bengals	.04	.02	.00

	MINT	VG-E	F-G
☐ 258 **Lynn Cain**, Atlanta Falcons	.08	.03	.01
☐ 259 **Checklist 133-264**	.15	.04	.01
☐ 260 **Mike Pruitt AP**, Cleveland Browns	.15	.06	.01
☐ 261 **Chris Ward**, New York Jets	.04	.02	.00
☐ 262 **Fred Steinfort**, Denver Broncos	.04	.02	.00
☐ 263 **James Owens**, San Francisco 49ers	.06	.02	.00
☐ 264 **Chicago Bears TL**	.30	.06	.01
Walter Payton			
James Scott			
Len Walterscheid			
Dan Hampton			
☐ 265 **Dan Fouts**, San Diego Chargers	.65	.30	.06
☐ 266 **Arnold Morgado**, Kansas City Chiefs	.04	.02	.00
☐ 267 **John Jefferson SA**, San Diego Chargers	.12	.05	.01
☐ 268 **Bill Lenkaitis**, New England Patriots	.04	.02	.00
☐ 269 **James Jones**, Dallas Cowboys	.06	.02	.00
☐ 270 **Brad Van Pelt**, New York Giants	.08	.03	.01
☐ 271 **Steve Largent**, Seattle Seahawks	.20	.09	.02
☐ 272 **Elvin Bethea**, Houston Oilers	.08	.03	.01
☐ 273 **Cullen Bryant**, Los Angeles Rams	.04	.02	.00
☐ 272 **Gary Danielson**, Detroit Lions	.15	.06	.01
☐ 275 **Tony Galbreath**, New Orleans Saints	.08	.03	.01
☐ 276 **Dave Butz**, Washington Redskins	.06	.02	.00
☐ 277 **Steve Mike-Mayer**, Baltimore Colts	.04	.02	.00
☐ 278 **Ron Johnson**, Pittsburgh Steelers	.04	.02	.00
☐ 279 **Tom DeLeone**, Cleveland Browns	.04	.02	.00
☐ 280 **Ron Jaworski**, Philadelphia Eagles	.20	.09	.02
☐ 281 **Mel Gray**, St. Louis Cardinals	.08	.03	.01
☐ 282 **San Diego Chargers TL**	.15	.04	.01
Chuck Muncie			
John Jefferson			
Glen Edwards			
Gary Johnson			
☐ 283 **Mark Brammer**, Buffalo Bills	.04	.02	.00
☐ 284 **Alfred Jenkins SA**, Atlanta Falcons	.06	.02	.00
☐ 285 **Greg Buttle**, New York Jets	.06	.02	.00
☐ 286 **Randy Hughes**, Dallas Cowboys	.04	.02	.00
☐ 287 **Delvin Williams**, Miami Dolphins	.08	.03	.01
☐ 288 **Brian Baschnagel**, Chicago Bears	.04	.02	.00
☐ 289 **Gary Jeter**, New York Giants	.06	.02	.00
☐ 290 **Stanley Morgan AP**, New England Patriots ...	.15	.06	.01
☐ 291 **Gerry Ellis**, Green Bay Packers	.04	.02	.00
☐ 292 **Al Richardson**, Atlanta Falcons	.04	.02	.00
☐ 293 **Jimmie Giles**, Tampa Bay Buccaneers	.08	.03	.01
☐ 294 **Dave Jennings SA**, New York Giants	.04	.02	.00
☐ 295 **Wilbert Montgomery**, Philadelphia Eagles	.25	.10	.02

		MINT	VG-E	F-G
☐ 296	**Dave Pureifory**, Detroit Lions	.04	.02	.00
☐ 297	**Greg Hawthorne**, Pittsburgh Steelers	.08	.03	.01
☐ 298	**Dick Ambrose**, Cleveland Browns	.04	.02	.00
☐ 299	**Terry Hermeling**, Washington Redskins	.04	.02	.00
☐ 300	**Danny White**, Dallas Cowboys	.40	.18	.04
☐ 301	**Ken Burrough**, Houston Oilers	.08	.03	.01
☐ 302	**Paul Hofer**, San Francisco 49ers	.04	.02	.00
☐ 303	**Denver Broncos TL**	.15	.04	.01
	Jim Jensen			
	Haven Moses			
	Steve Foley			
	Rulon Jones			
☐ 304	**Eddie Payton**, Minnesota Vikings	.06	.02	.00
☐ 305	**Isaac Curtis**, Cincinnati Bengals	.08	.03	.01
☐ 306	**Benny Ricardo**, New Orleans Saints	.04	.02	.00
☐ 307	**Riley Odoms**, Denver Broncos	.08	.03	.01
☐ 308	**Bob Chandler**, Oakland Raiders	.06	.02	.00
☐ 309	**Larry Heater**, New York Giants	.04	.02	.00
☐ 310	**Art Still AP**, Kansas City Chiefs	.20	.09	.02
☐ 311	**Harold Jackson**, New England Patriots	.15	.06	.01
☐ 312	**Charlie Joiner SA**, San Diego Chargers	.12	.05	.01
☐ 313	**Jeff Nixon**, Buffalo Bills	.04	.02	.00
☐ 314	**Aundra Thompson**, Green Bay Packers	.04	.02	.00
☐ 315	**Richard Todd**, New York Jets	.20	.09	.02
☐ 316	**Dan Hampton**, Chicago Bears	.20	.09	.02
☐ 317	**Doug Marsh**, St. Louis Cardinals	.04	.02	.00
☐ 318	**Louie Giammona**, Philadelphia Eagles	.04	.02	.00
☐ 319	**San Francisco 49ers TL**	.15	.04	.01
	Earl Cooper			
	Dwight Clark			
	Ricky Churchman			
	Dwight Hicks			
	Jim Stuckey			
☐ 320	**Manu Tuiasosopo**, Seattle Seahawks	.04	.02	.00
☐ 321	**Rich Milot**, Washington Redskins	.04	.02	.00
☐ 322	**Mike Guman**, Los Angeles Rams	.04	.02	.00
☐ 323	**Bob Kuechenberg**, Miami Dolphins	.04	.02	.00
☐ 324	**Tom Skladany**, Detroit Lions	.06	.02	.00
☐ 325	**Dave Logan**, Cleveland Browns	.04	.02	.00
☐ 326	**Bruce Laird**, Baltimore Colts	.04	.02	.00
☐ 327	**James Jones SA**, Dallas Cowboys	.06	.02	.00
☐ 328	**Joe Danelo**, New York Giants	.04	.02	.00
☐ 329	**Kenny King**, Oakland Raiders	.15	.06	.01
☐ 330	**Pat Donovan AP**, Dallas Cowboys	.06	.02	.00

	MINT	VG-E	F-G

RECORD BREAKERS

		MINT	VG-E	F-G
☐ 331	**RB: Earl Cooper** .... Most Receptions, Running Back, Season, Rookie	.08	.03	.01
☐ 332	**RB: John Jefferson** .... Most Consecutive Seasons, 1000 Yards Receiving, Start of Career	.10	.04	.01
☐ 333	**RB: Kenny King** .... Longest Pass Caught, Super Bowl History	.08	.03	.01
☐ 334	**RB: Rod Martin** .... Most Interceptions Super Bowl Game	.08	.03	.01
☐ 335	**RB: Jim Plunkett** .... Longest Pass, Super Bowl History	.15	.06	.01
☐ 336	**RB: Bill Thompson** .... Most Touchdowns, Fumble Recoveries, Lifetime	.08	.03	.01
☐ 337	**John Cappelletti**, San Diego Chargers	.12	.05	.01
☐ 338	**Detroit Lions TL** .... Billy Sims Freddie Scott Jim Allen James Hunter Al Baker	.15	.04	.01
☐ 339	**Don Smith**, Atlanta Falcons	.04	.02	.00
☐ 340	**Rod Perry AP**, Los Angeles Rams	.06	.02	.00
☐ 341	**David Lewis**, Tampa Bay Buccaneers ...	.04	.02	.00
☐ 342	**Mark Gastineau**, New York Jets	1.00	.45	.10
☐ 343	**Steve Largent SA**, Seattle Seahawks ...	.10	.04	.01
☐ 344	**Charley Young**, San Francisco 49ers	.06	.02	.00
☐ 345	**Toni Fritsch**, Houston Oilers	.04	.02	.00
☐ 346	**Matt Blair**, Minnesota Vikings	.06	.02	.00
☐ 347	**Don Bass**, Cincinnati Bengals	.04	.02	.00
☐ 348	**Jim Jensen**, Denver Broncos	.04	.02	.00
☐ 349	**Karl Lorch**, Washington Redskins	.04	.02	.00
☐ 350	**Brian Sipe AP**, Cleveland Browns	.25	.10	.02
☐ 351	**Theo Bell**, Pittsburgh Steelers	.04	.02	.00
☐ 352	**Sam Adams**, New Orleans Saints	.04	.02	.00
☐ 353	**Paul Coffman**, Green Bay Packers	.04	.02	.00
☐ 354	**Eric Harris**, Kansas City Chiefs	.04	.02	.00
☐ 355	**Tony Hill**, New York Giants	.20	.09	.02
☐ 356	**J.T. Turner**, New York Giants	.04	.02	.00
☐ 357	**Frank LeMaster**, Philadelphia Eagles ...	.04	.02	.00
☐ 358	**Jim Jodat**, Seattle Seahawks	.04	.02	.00

			MINT	VG-E	F-G
☐ 359	**Oakland Raiders TL**		.15	.04	.01
	Mark van Eeghen				
	Cliff Branch				
	Lester Hayes				
	Cedrick Hardman				
	Ted Hendricks				
☐ 360	**Joe Cribbs AP**, Buffalo Bills		.80	.40	.08
☐ 361	**James Lofton SA**, Green Bay Packers		.12	.05	.01
☐ 362	**Dexter Bussey**, Detroit Lions		.04	.02	.00
☐ 363	**Bobby Jackson**, New York Jets		.04	.02	.00
☐ 364	**Steve DeBerg**, San Francisco 49ers		.15	.06	.01
☐ 365	**Ottis Anderson**, St. Louis Cardinals		.30	.12	.03
☐ 366	**Tom Myers**, New Orleans Saints		.04	.02	.00
☐ 367	**John James**, Atlanta Falcons		.04	.02	.00
☐ 368	**Reese McCall**, Baltimore Colts		.04	.02	.00
☐ 369	**Jack Reynolds**, Los Angeles Rams		.06	.02	.00
☐ 370	**Gary Johnson AP**, San Diego Chargers		.06	.02	.00
☐ 371	**Jimmy Cefalo**, Miami Dolphins		.04	.02	.00
☐ 372	**Horace Ivory**, New England Patriots		.04	.02	.00
☐ 373	**Garo Yepremian**, Tampa Bay Buccaneers		.08	.03	.01
☐ 374	**Brian Kelley**, New York Giants		.04	.02	.00
☐ 375	**Terry Bradshaw**, Pittsburgh Steelers		.75	.35	.07
☐ 376	**Dallas Cowboys TL**		.40	.08	.01
	Tony Dorsett				
	Tony Hill				
	Dennis Thurman				
	Charlie Waters				
	Harvey Martin				
☐ 377	**Randy Logan**, Philadelphia Eagles		.04	.02	.00
☐ 378	**Tim Wilson**, Houston Oilers		.04	.02	.00
☐ 379	**Archie Manning SA**, New Orleans Saints		.15	.06	.01
☐ 380	**Revie Sorey AP**, Chicago Bears		.04	.02	.00
☐ 381	**Randy Holloway**, Minnesota Vikings		.04	.02	.00
☐ 382	**Henry Lawrence**, Oakland Raiders		.04	.02	.00
☐ 383	**Pat McInally**, Cincinnati Bengals		.08	.03	.01
☐ 384	**Kevin Long**, New York Jets		.04	.02	.00
☐ 385	**Louis Wright**, Denver Broncos		.06	.02	.00
☐ 386	**Leonard Thompson**, Detroit Lions		.04	.02	.00
☐ 387	**Jan Stenerud**, Green Bay Packers		.08	.03	.01
☐ 388	**Raymond Butler**, Baltimore Colts		.12	.05	.01
☐ 389	**Checklist 265-396**		.15	.04	.01
☐ 390	**Steve Bartkowski AP**, Atlanta Falcons		.25	.10	.02
☐ 391	**Clarence Harmon**, Washington Redskins		.04	.02	.00
☐ 392	**Wilbert Montgomery SA**, Philadelphia Eagles		.15	.06	.01
☐ 393	**Billy Joe DuPree**, Dallas Cowboys		.15	.06	.01

	MINT	VG-E	F-G
☐ 394 **Kansas City Chiefs TL**	.15	.04	.01
Ted McKnight			
Henry Marshall			
Gary Barbaro			
Art Still			
☐ 395 **Earnest Gray**, New York Giants	.08	.03	.01
☐ 396 **Ray Hamilton**, New England Patriots	.04	.02	.00
☐ 397 **Bernard Wilson**, Philadelphia Eagles	.04	.02	.00
☐ 398 **Calvin Hill**, Cleveland Browns	.15	.06	.01
☐ 399 **Robin Cole**, Pittsburgh Steelers	.04	.02	.00
☐ 400 **Walter Payton AP**, Chicago Bears	1.50	.70	.15
☐ 401 **Jim Hart**, St. Louis Cardinals	.25	.10	.02
☐ 402 **Ron Yary**, Minnesota Vikings	.06	.02	.00
☐ 403 **Cliff Branch**, Oakland Raiders	.15	.06	.01
☐ 404 **Roland Hooks**, Buffalo Bills	.04	.02	.00
☐ 405 **Ken Stabler**, Houston Oilers	.30	.12	.03
☐ 406 **Chuck Ramsey**, New York Jets	.04	.02	.00
☐ 407 **Mike Nelms**, Washington Redskins	.06	.02	.00
☐ 408 **Ron Jaworski SA**, Philadelphia Eagles	.12	.05	.01
☐ 409 **James Hunter**, Detroit Lions	.04	.02	.00
☐ 410 **Lee Roy Selmon AP**, Tampa Bay Buccaneers .	.20	.09	.02
☐ 411 **Baltimore Colts TL**	.15	.04	.01
Curtis Dickey			
Roger Carr			
Bruce Laird			
Mike Barnes			
☐ 412 **Henry Marshall**, Kansas City Chiefs	.04	.02	.00
☐ 413 **Preston Pearson**, Dallas Cowboys	.12	.05	.01
☐ 414 **Richard Bishop**, New England Patriots	.04	.02	.00
☐ 415 **Greg Pruitt**, Cleveland Browns	.15	.06	.01
☐ 416 **Matt Bahr**, Pittsburgh Steelers	.06	.02	.00
☐ 417 **Tom Mullady**, New York Giants	.04	.02	.00
☐ 418 **Glen Edwards**, San Diego Chargers	.04	.02	.00
☐ 419 **Sam McCullum**, Seattle Seahawks	.04	.02	.00
☐ 420 **Stan Walters AP**, Philadelphia Eagles	.04	.02	.00
☐ 421 **George Roberts**, Miami Dolphins	.04	.02	.00
☐ 422 **Dwight Clark**, San Francisco 49ers	.50	.22	.05
☐ 423 **Pat Thomas**, Los Angeles Rams	.04	.02	.00
☐ 424 **Bruce Harper SA**, New York Jets	.04	.02	.00
☐ 425 **Craig Morton**, Denver Broncos	.25	.10	.02
☐ 426 **Derrick Gaffney**, New York Jets	.04	.02	.00
☐ 427 **Pete Johnson**, Cincinnati Bengals	.08	.03	.01
☐ 428 **Wes Chandler**, New Orleans Saints	.12	.05	.01
☐ 429 **Burgess Owens**, Oakland Raiders	.04	.02	.00
☐ 430 **James Lofton AP**, Green Bay Packers	.20	.09	.02

		MINT	VG-E	F-G
☐ 431	**Tony Reed,** Kansas City Chiefs	.06	.02	.00
☐ 432	**Minnesota Vikings TL**	.15	.04	.01
	Ted Brown			
	Ahmad Rashad			
	John Turner			
	Doug Sutherland			
☐ 433	**Ron Springs,** Dallas Cowboys	.06	.02	.00
☐ 434	**Tim Fox,** New England Patriots	.04	.02	.00
☐ 435	**Ozzie Newsome,** Cleveland Browns	.15	.06	.01
☐ 436	**Steve Furness,** Pittsburgh Steelers	.04	.02	.00
☐ 437	**Will Lewis,** Seattle Seahawks	.04	.02	.00
☐ 438	**Mike Hartenstine,** Chicago Bears	.04	.02	.00
☐ 439	**John Bunting,** Philadelphia Eagles	.04	.02	.00
☐ 440	**Ed Murray,** Detroit Lions	.04	.02	.00
☐ 441	**Mike Pruitt SA,** Cleveland Browns	.08	.03	.01
☐ 442	**Larry Swider,** St. Louis Cardinals	.04	.02	.00
☐ 443	**Steve Freeman,** Buffalo Bills	.04	.02	.00
☐ 444	**Bruce Hardy,** Miami Dolphins	.04	.02	.00
☐ 445	**Pat Haden,** Los Angeles Rams	.15	.06	.01
☐ 446	**Curtis Dickey,** Baltimore Colts	.25	.10	.02
☐ 447	**Doug Wilkerson,** San Diego Chargers	.04	.02	.00
☐ 448	**Alfred Jenkins,** Atlanta Falcons	.08	.03	.01
☐ 449	**Dave Dalby,** Oakland Raiders	.04	.02	.00
☐ 450	**Robert Brazile AP,** Houston Oilers	.06	.02	.00
☐ 451	**Bobby Hammond,** Washington Redskins	.04	.02	.00
☐ 452	**Raymond Clayborn,** New England Patriots	.06	.02	.00
☐ 453	**Jim Miller,** San Francisco 49ers	.04	.02	.00
☐ 454	**Roy Simmons,** New York Giants	.04	.02	.00
☐ 455	**Charlie Waters,** Dallas Cowboys	.15	.06	.01
☐ 456	**Ricky Bell,** Tampa Bay Buccaneers	.10	.04	.01
☐ 457	**Ahmad Rashad SA,** Minnesota Vikings	.12	.05	.01
☐ 458	**Don Cockroft,** Cleveland Browns	.04	.02	.00
☐ 459	**Keith Krepfle,** Philadelphia Eagles	.04	.02	.00
☐ 460	**Marvin Powell AP,** New York Jets	.06	.02	.00
☐ 461	**Tommy Kramer,** Minnesota Vikings	.25	.10	.02
☐ 462	**Jim LeClair,** Cincinnati Bengals	.04	.02	.00
☐ 463	**Freddie Scott,** Detroit Lions	.06	.02	.00
☐ 464	**Rob Lytle,** Denver Broncos	.04	.02	.00
☐ 465	**Johnnie Gray,** Green Bay Packers	.04	.02	.00
☐ 466	**Doug France,** Los Angeles Rams	.04	.02	.00
☐ 467	**Carlos Carson,** Kansas City Chiefs	.15	.06	.01

	MINT	VG-E	F-G
☐ 468 **St. Louis Cardinals TL**	.15	.04	.01
Ottis Anderson			
Pat Tilley			
Ken Stone			
Curtis Greer			
Steve Neils			
☐ 469 **Efren Herrera**, Seattle Seahawks	.04	.02	.00
☐ 470 **Randy White AP**, Dallas Cowboys	.25	.10	.02
☐ 471 **Richard Caster**, Houston Oilers	.08	.03	.01
☐ 472 **Andy Johnson**, New England Patriots	.04	.02	.00
☐ 473 **Billy Sims SA**, Detroit Lions	.25	.10	.02
☐ 474 **Joe Lavender**, Washington Redskins	.04	.02	.00
☐ 475 **Harry Carson**, New York Giants	.15	.06	.01
☐ 476 **John Stallworth**, Pittsburgh Steelers	.12	.05	.01
☐ 477 **Bob Thomas**, Chicago Bears	.04	.02	.00
☐ 478 **Keith Wright**, Cleveland Browns	.04	.02	.00
☐ 479 **Ken Stone**, St. Louis Cardinals	.04	.02	.00
☐ 480 **Carl Hairston AP**, Philadelphia Eagles	.06	.02	.00
☐ 481 **Reggie McKenzie**, Buffalo Bills	.06	.02	.00
☐ 482 **Bob Griese**, Miami Dolphins	.60	.28	.06
☐ 483 **Mike Bragg**, Baltimore Colts	.04	.02	.00
☐ 484 **Scott Dierking**, New York Jets	.04	.02	.00
☐ 485 **David Hill**, Detroit Lions	.04	.02	.00
☐ 486 **Brian Sipe SA**, Cleveland Browns	.20	.09	.02
☐ 487 **Rod Martin**, Oakland Raiders	.08	.03	.01
☐ 488 **Cincinnati Bengals TL**	.15	.04	.01
Pete Johnson			
Dan Ross			
Louis Breeden			
Eddie Edwards			
☐ 489 **Preston Dennard**, Los Angeles Rams	.04	.02	.00
☐ 490 **John Smith AP**, New England Patriots	.04	.02	.00
☐ 491 **Mike Reinfeldt**, Houston Oilers	.04	.02	.00
☐ 492 **1980 NFC Champions**	.15	.06	.01
Eagles 20, Cowboys 7			
(Jaworski)			
☐ 493 **1980 AFC Champions**	.15	.06	.01
Raiders 34, Chargers 27			
(Plunkett)			
☐ 494 **Super Bowl XV**	.20	.09	.02
Raiders 27, Eagles 10			
(Plunkett handing off to King)			
☐ 495 **Joe Greene**, Pittsburgh Steelers	.30	.12	.03
☐ 496 **Charlie Joiner**, San Diego Chargers	.20	.09	.02
☐ 497 **Rolland Lawrence**, Atlanta Falcons	.06	.02	.00
☐ 498 **Al Baker SA**, Detroit Lions	.06	.02	.00

	MINT	VG-E	F-G
☐ 499 **Brad Dusek**, Washington Redskins	.04	.02	.00
☐ 500 **Tony Dorsett**, Dallas Cowboys	.75	.35	.07
☐ 501 **Robin Earl**, Chicago Bears	.04	.02	.00
☐ 502 **Theotis Brown**, St. Louis Cardinals	.08	.03	.01
☐ 503 **Joe Ferguson**, Buffalo Bills	.15	.06	.01
☐ 504 **Beasley Reece**, New York Giants	.04	.02	.00
☐ 505 **Lyle Alzado**, Cleveland Browns	.20	.09	.02
☐ 506 **Tony Nathan**, Miami Dolphins	.15	.06	.01
☐ 507 **Philadelphia Eagles TL**	.15	.04	.01
Wilbert Montgomery			
Charlie Smith			
Brenard Wilson			
Claude Humphrey			
☐ 508 **Herb Orvis**, Baltimore Colts	.04	.02	.00
☐ 509 **Clarence Williams**, San Diego Chargers ..	.04	.02	.00
☐ 510 **Ray Guy AP**, Oakland Raiders	.12	.05	.01
☐ 511 **Jeff Komlo**, Detroit Lions	.08	.03	.01
☐ 512 **Freddie Solomon SA**, San Francisco 49ers ...	.06	.02	.00
☐ 513 **Tim Mazzetti**, Atlanta Falcons	.04	.02	.00
☐ 514 **Elvis Peacock**, Los Angeles Rams	.06	.02	.00
☐ 515 **Russ Francis**, New England Patriots	.12	.05	.01
☐ 516 **Roland Harper**, Chicago Bears	.04	.02	.00
☐ 517 **Checklist 397-528**	.15	.04	.01
☐ 518 **Billy Johnson**, Houston Oilers	.12	.05	.01
☐ 519 **Dan Dierdorf**, St. Louis Cardinals	.06	.02	.00
☐ 520 **Fred Dean AP**, San Diego Chargers	.06	.02	.00
☐ 521 **Jerry Butler**, Buffalo Bills	.12	.05	.01
☐ 522 **Ron Saul**, Washington Redskins	.04	.02	.00
☐ 523 **Charlie Smith**, Philadelphia Eagles	.04	.02	.00
☐ 524 **Kellen Winslow SA**, San Diego Chargers	.12	.05	.01
☐ 525 **Bert Jones**, Baltimore Colts	.20	.09	.02
☐ 526 **Pittsburgh Steelers TL**	.25	.05	.01
Franco Harris			
Theo Bell			
Donnie Shell			
L.C. Greenwood			
☐ 527 **Duriel Harris**, Miami Dolphins	.06	.02	.00
☐ 528 **William Andrews**, Atlanta Falcons	.20	.09	.02

1982 TOPPS

The 1982 Topps set features 528 cards. The cards measure 2½" by 3½". The team helmets appear on the fronts for the first time, as Topps apparently received permission from the teams for the use of their insignia. Again, the fronts contain the stylized Topps logo within the frame line. The backs contain blue and yellow-green ink on a gray card stock. Many special cards, e.g., Super Bowl, Record Breakers, Team Leaders, are included in the set. Cards 263-270 feature brothers playing in the NFL. All Pro (AP) selections are denoted on each player's regular card. Some players also have an additional special card with an in-action (IA) pose. Distributed throughout the set are Team Leader (TL) cards typically featuring four individual team statistical leaders on the front, as well as a team checklist on the back. The set is organized in team order alphabetically by team within conference.

		MINT	VG-E	F-G
	COMPLETE SET	14.00	6.50	1.40
	COMMON PLAYER (1-528)	.03	.01	.00
☐	**1 RB: Ken Anderson,** Cincinnati Bengals	.40	.08	.01
	Most Completions Super Bowl Game			
☐	**2 RB: Dan Fouts,** San Diego Chargers	.30	.12	.03
	Most Passing Yards Playoff Game			
☐	**3 RB: Leroy Irvin,** Los Angeles Rams	.06	.02	.00
	Most Punt Return Game Yardage			
☐	**4 RB: Stump Mitchell,** St. Louis Cardinals	.06	.02	.00
	Most Return Season Yardage			
☐	**5 RB: George Rogers,** New Orleans Saints	.20	.09	.02
	Most Rushing Yards Rookie Season			

		MINT	VG-E	F-G
☐ 6	**RB: Dan Ross,** Cincinnati Bengals .... Most Receptions Super Bowl Game	.06	.02	.00
☐ 7	**AFC Championship** .... Bengals 27, Chargers 7 (Ken Anderson handing off to Pete Johnson)	.12	.05	.01
☐ 8	**NFC Championship** .... 49'ers 28, Cowboys 27 (Earl Cooper)	.12	.05	.01
☐ 9	**Super Bowl XVI** .... 49'ers 26, Bengals 7 (Munoz blocking)	.15	.06	.01
☐ 10	**Baltimore Colts TL** .... Curtis Dickey Raymond Butler Larry Braziel Bruce Laird	.12	.03	.01
☐ 11	**Raymond Butler,** Baltimore Colts	.06	.02	.00
☐ 12	**Roger Carr,** Baltimore Colts	.06	.02	.00
☐ 13	**Curtis Dickey,** Baltimore Colts	.12	.05	.01
☐ 14	**Zachary Dixon,** Baltimore Colts	.03	.01	.00
☐ 15	**Nesby Glasgow,** Baltimore Colts	.03	.01	.00
☐ 16	**Bert Jones,** Baltimore Colts	.15	.06	.01
☐ 17	**Bruce Laird,** Baltimore Colts	.03	.01	.00
☐ 18	**Reese McCall,** Baltimore Colts	.03	.01	.00
☐ 19	**Randy McMillan,** Baltimore Colts	.12	.05	.01
☐ 20	**Ed Simonini,** Baltimore Colts	.03	.01	.00
☐ 21	**Buffalo Bills TL** .... Joe Cribbs Frank Lewis Mario Clark Fred Smerlas	.12	.03	.01
☐ 22	**Mark Brammer,** Buffalo Bills	.03	.01	.00
☐ 23	**Curtis Brown,** Buffalo Bills	.03	.01	.00
☐ 24	**Jerry Butler,** Buffalo Bills	.12	.05	.01
☐ 25	**Mario Clark,** Buffalo Bills	.03	.01	.00
☐ 26	**Joe Cribbs,** Buffalo Bills	.20	.09	.02
☐ 27	**Joe Cribbs IA,** Buffalo Bills	.12	.05	.01
☐ 28	**Joe Ferguson,** Buffalo Bills	.15	.06	.01
☐ 29	**Jim Haslett,** Buffalo Bills	.03	.01	.00
☐ 30	**Frank Lewis AP,** Buffalo Bills	.06	.02	.00
☐ 31	**Frank Lewis IA,** Buffalo Bills	.06	.02	.00
☐ 32	**Shane Nelson,** Buffalo Bills	.03	.01	.00
☐ 33	**Charles Romes,** Buffalo Bills	.03	.01	.00
☐ 34	**Bill Simpson,** Buffalo Bills	.03	.01	.00
☐ 35	**Fred Smerlas,** Buffalo Bills	.06	.02	.00

		MINT	VG-E	F-G
☐ 36	**Cincinnati Bengals TL**	.12	.03	.01
	Pete Johnson			
	Cris Collinsworth			
	Ken Riley			
	Reggie Wiliams			
☐ 37	**Charles Alexander**, Cincinnati Bengals	.03	.01	.00
☐ 38	**Ken Anderson AP**, Cincinnati Bengals	.35	.15	.03
☐ 39	**Ken Anderson IA**, Cincinnati Bengals	.15	.06	.01
☐ 40	**Jim Breech**, Cincinnati Bengals	.03	.01	.00
☐ 41	**Jim Breech IA**, Cincinnati Bengals	.03	.01	.00
☐ 42	**Louis Breeden**, Cincinnati Bengals	.03	.01	.00
☐ 43	**Ross Browner**, Cincinnati Bengals	.06	.02	.00
☐ 44	**Cris Collinsworth**, Cincinnati Bengals	.60	.28	.06
☐ 45	**Cris Collinsworth IA**, Cincinnati Bengals	.20	.09	.02
☐ 46	**Isaac Curtis**, Cincinnati Bengals	.06	.02	.00
☐ 47	**Pete Johnson**, Cincinnati Bengals	.06	.02	.00
☐ 48	**Pete Johnson IA**, Cincinnati Bengals	.06	.02	.00
☐ 49	**Steve Kreider**, Cincinnati Bengals	.03	.01	.00
☐ 50	**Pat McInally AP**, Cincinnati Bengals	.06	.02	.00
☐ 51	**Anthony Munoz AP**, Cincinnati Bengals	.15	.06	.01
☐ 52	**Dan Ross**, Cincinnati Bengals	.06	.02	.00
☐ 53	**David Verser**, Cincinnati Bengals	.03	.01	.00
☐ 54	**Reggie Williams**, Cincinnati Bengals	.06	.02	.00
☐ 55	**Cleveland Browns TL**	.12	.03	.01
	Mike Pruitt			
	Ozzie Newsome			
	Clarence Scott			
	Lyle Alzado			
☐ 56	**Lyle Alzado**, Cleveland Browns	.20	.09	.02
☐ 57	**Dick Ambrose**, Cleveland Browns	.03	.01	.00
☐ 58	**Ron Bolton**, Cleveland Browns	.03	.01	.00
☐ 59	**Steve Cox**, Cleveland Browns	.03	.01	.00
☐ 60	**Joe DeLamielliure**, Cleveland Browns	.06	.02	.00
☐ 61	**Tom DeLeone**, Cleveland Browns	.03	.01	.00
☐ 62	**Doug Dieken**, Cleveland Browns	.03	.01	.00
☐ 63	**Ricky Feacher**, Cleveland Browns	.03	.01	.00
☐ 64	**Don Goode**, Cleveland Browns	.03	.01	.00
☐ 65	**Robert L. Jackson**, Cleveland Browns	.03	.01	.00
☐ 66	**Dave Logan**, Cleveland Browns	.03	.01	.00
☐ 67	**Ozzie Newsome**, Cleveland Browns	.12	.05	.01
☐ 68	**Ozzie Newsome IA**, Cleveland Browns	.06	.02	.00
☐ 69	**Greg Pruitt**, Cleveland Browns	.12	.05	.01
☐ 70	**Mike Pruitt**, Cleveland Browns	.12	.05	.01
☐ 71	**Mike Pruitt IA**, Cleveland Browns	.06	.02	.00
☐ 72	**Reggie Rucker**, Cleveland Browns	.06	.02	.00

			MINT	VG-E	F-G
☐	73	**Clarence Scott,** Cleveland Browns	.03	.01	.00
☐	74	**Brian Sipe,** Cleveland Browns	.20	.09	.02
☐	75	**Charles White,** Cleveland Browns	.12	.05	.01
☐	76	**Denver Broncos TL**	.12	.03	.01
		Rick Parros			
		Steve Watson			
		Steve Foley			
		Rulon Jones			
☐	77	**Rubin Carter,** Denver Broncos	.03	.01	.00
☐	78	**Steve Foley,** Denver Broncos	.03	.01	.00
☐	79	**Randy Gradishar,** Denver Broncos	.12	.05	.01
☐	80	**Tom Jackson,** Denver Broncos	.06	.02	.00
☐	81	**Craig Morton,** Denver Broncos	.20	.09	.02
☐	82	**Craig Morton IA,** Denver Broncos	.12	.05	.01
☐	83	**Riley Odoms,** Denver Broncos	.06	.02	.00
☐	84	**Rick Parros,** Denver Broncos	.03	.01	.00
☐	85	**Dave Preston,** Denver Broncos	.03	.01	.00
☐	86	**Tony Reed,** Denver Broncos	.03	.01	.00
☐	87	**Bob Swenson,** Denver Broncos	.03	.01	.00
☐	88	**Bill Thompson,** Denver Broncos	.03	.01	.00
☐	89	**Rick Upchurch,** Denver Broncos	.06	.02	.00
☐	90	**Steve Watson AP,** Denver Broncos	.12	.05	.01
☐	91	**Steve Watson IA,** Denver Broncos	.06	.02	.00
☐	92	**Houston Oilers TL**	.12	.03	.01
		Carl Roaches			
		Ken Burrough			
		Carter Hartwig			
		Greg Stemrick			
		Jesse Baker			
☐	93	**Mike Barber,** Houston Oilers	.06	.02	.00
☐	94	**Elvin Bethea,** Houston Oilers	.06	.02	.00
☐	95	**Gregg Bingham,** Houston Oilers	.03	.01	.00
☐	96	**Robert Brazile AP,** Houston Oilers	.06	.02	.00
☐	97	**Ken Burrough,** Houston Oilers	.06	.02	.00
☐	98	**Toni Fritsch,** Houston Oilers	.03	.01	.00
☐	99	**Leon Gray,** Houston Oilers	.06	.02	.00
☐	100	**Gifford Nielsen,** Houston Oilers	.12	.05	.01
☐	101	**Vernon Perry,** Houston Oilers	.03	.01	.00
☐	102	**Mike Reinfeldt,** Houston Oilers	.03	.01	.00
☐	103	**Mike Renfro,** Houston Oilers	.03	.01	.00
☐	104	**Carl Roaches AP,** Houston Oilers	.06	.02	.00
☐	105	**Ken Stabler,** Houston Oilers	.20	.09	.02
☐	106	**Greg Stemrick,** Houston Oilers	.03	.01	.00
☐	107	**J.C. Wilson,** Houston Oilers	.03	.01	.00
☐	108	**Tim Wilson,** Houston Oilers	.03	.01	.00

		MINT	VG-E	F-G
☐ 109	**Kansas City Chiefs TL**	.12	.03	.01
	Joe Delaney			
	J.T. Smith			
	Eric Harris			
	Ken Kremer			
☐ 110	**Gary Barbaro AP**, Kansas City Chiefs	.06	.02	.00
☐ 111	**Brad Budde**, Kansas City Chiefs	.03	.01	.00
☐ 112	**Joe Delaney AP**, Kansas City Chiefs	.20	.09	.02
☐ 113	**Joe Delaney IA**, Kansas City Chiefs	.06	.02	.00
☐ 114	**Steve Fuller**, Kansas City Chiefs	.12	.05	.01
☐ 115	**Gary Green**, Kansas City Chiefs	.03	.01	.00
☐ 116	**James Hadnot**, Kansas City Chiefs	.06	.02	.00
☐ 117	**Eric Harris**, Kansas City Chiefs	.03	.01	.00
☐ 118	**Billy Jackson**, Kansas City Chiefs	.03	.01	.00
☐ 119	**Bill Kenney**, Kansas City Chiefs	.15	.06	.01
☐ 120	**Nick Lowery AP**, Kansas City Chiefs	.03	.01	.00
☐ 121	**Nick Lowery IA**, Kansas City Chiefs	.03	.01	.00
☐ 122	**Henry Marshall**, Kansas City Chiefs	.03	.01	.00
☐ 123	**J.T. Smith**, Kansas City Chiefs	.03	.01	.00
☐ 124	**Art Still**, Kansas City Chiefs	.06	.02	.00
☐ 125	**Miami Dolphins TL**	.12	.03	.01
	Tony Nathan			
	Duriel Harris			
	Glenn Blackwood			
	Bob Baumhower			
☐ 126	**Bob Baumhower AP**, Miami Dolphins	.06	.02	.00
☐ 127	**Glenn Blackwood**, Miami Dolphins	.03	.01	.00
☐ 128	**Jimmy Cefalo**, Miami Dolphins	.03	.01	.00
☐ 129	**A.J. Duhe**, Miami Dolphins	.12	.05	.01
☐ 130	**Andra Franklin**, Miami Dolphins	.12	.05	.01
☐ 131	**Duriel Harris**, Miami Dolphins	.06	.02	.00
☐ 132	**Nat Moore**, Miami Dolphins	.06	.02	.00
☐ 133	**Tony Nathan**, Miami Dolphins	.10	.04	.01
☐ 134	**Ed Newman**, Miami Dolphins	.03	.01	.00
☐ 135	**Earnie Rhone**, Miami Dolphins	.03	.01	.00
☐ 136	**Don Strock**, Miami Dolphins	.10	.04	.01
☐ 137	**Tommy Vigorito**, Miami Dolphins	.06	.02	.00
☐ 138	**Uwe von Schamann**, Miami Dolphins	.06	.02	.00
☐ 139	**Uwe von Schamann IA**, Miami Dolphins	.03	.01	.00
☐ 140	**Dave Woodley**, Miami Dolphins	.12	.05	.01
☐ 141	**New England Patriots TL**	.12	.03	.01
	Tony Collins			
	Stanley Morgan			
	Tim Fox			
	Rick Sanford			
	Tony McGee			

	MINT	VG-E	F-G
☐ 142 **Julius Adams,** New England Patriots	.03	.01	.00
☐ 143 **Richard Bishop,** New England Patriots	.03	.01	.00
☐ 144 **Matt Cavanaugh,** New England Patriots	.12	.05	.01
☐ 145 **Raymond Clayborn,** New England Patriots ...	.06	.02	.00
☐ 146 **Tony Collins,** New England Patriots	.20	.09	.02
☐ 147 **Vagas Ferguson,** New England Patriots	.06	.02	.00
☐ 148 **Tim Fox,** New England Patriots	.03	.01	.00
☐ 149 **Steve Grogan,** New England Patriots	.15	.06	.01
☐ 150 **John Hannah AP,** New England Patriots	.10	.04	.01
☐ 151 **John Hannah IA,** New England Patriots	.06	.02	.00
☐ 152 **Don Hasselbeck,** New England Patriots	.03	.01	.00
☐ 153 **Mike Haynes,** New England Patriots	.12	.05	.01
☐ 154 **Harold Jackson,** New England Patriots	.12	.05	.01
☐ 155 **Andy Johnson,** New England Patriots	.03	.01	.00
☐ 156 **Stanley Morgan,** New England Patriots	.12	.05	.01
☐ 157 **Stanley Morgan IA,** New England Patriots	.06	.02	.00
☐ 158 **Steve Nelson,** New England Patriots	.03	.01	.00
☐ 159 **Rod Shoate,** New England Patriots	.03	.01	.00
☐ 160 **New York Jets TL**	.15	.03	.01
Freeman McNeil			
Wesley Walker			
Darrol Ray			
Joe Klecko			
☐ 161 **Dan Alexander,** New York Jets	.03	.01	.00
☐ 162 **Mike Augustyniak,** New York Jets	.03	.01	.00
☐ 163 **Jerome Barkum,** New York Jets	.06	.02	.00
☐ 164 **Greg Buttle,** New York Jets	.06	.02	.00
☐ 165 **Scott Dierking,** New York Jets	.03	.01	.00
☐ 166 **Joe Fields,** New York Jets	.03	.01	.00
☐ 167 **Mark Gastineau AP,** New York Jets	.20	.09	.02
☐ 168 **Mark Gastineau IA,** New York Jets	.12	.05	.01
☐ 169 **Bruce Harper,** New York Jets	.06	.02	.00
☐ 170 **Johnny (Lam) Jones,** New York Jets	.10	.04	.01
☐ 171 **Joe Klecko AP,** New York Jets	.12	.05	.01
☐ 172 **Joe Klecko IA,** New York Jets	.06	.02	.00
☐ 173 **Pat Leahy,** New York Jets	.03	.01	.00
☐ 174 **Pat Leahy IA,** New York Jets	.03	.01	.00
☐ 175 **Marty Lyons,** New York Jets	.06	.02	.00
☐ 176 **Freeman McNeil,** New York Jets	.80	.40	.08
☐ 177 **Marvin Powell AP,** New York Jets	.06	.02	.00
☐ 178 **Chuck Ramsey,** New York Jets	.03	.01	.00
☐ 179 **Darrol Ray,** New York Jets	.06	.02	.00
☐ 180 **Abdul Salaam,** New York Jets	.03	.01	.00
☐ 181 **Richard Todd,** New York Jets	.15	.06	.01
☐ 182 **Richard Todd IA,** New York Jets	.10	.04	.01
☐ 183 **Wesley Walker,** New York Jets	.12	.05	.01

		MINT	VG-E	F-G
☐ 184	Chris Ward, New York Jets	.03	.01	.00
☐ 185	Oakland Raiders TL	.12	.03	.01
	Kenny King			
	Derrick Ramsey			
	Lester Hayes			
	Odis McKinney			
	Rod Martin			
☐ 186	Cliff Branch, Oakland Raiders	.12	.05	.01
☐ 187	Bob Chandler, Oakland Raiders	.06	.02	.00
☐ 188	Ray Guy, Oakland Raiders	.12	.05	.01
☐ 189	Lester Hayes AP, Oakland Raiders	.10	.04	.01
☐ 190	Ted Hendricks AP, Oakland Raiders	.12	.05	.01
☐ 191	Monte Jackson, Oakland Raiders	.03	.01	.00
☐ 192	Derrick Jensen, Oakland Raiders	.03	.01	.00
☐ 193	Kenny King, Oakland Raiders	.06	.02	.00
☐ 194	Rod Martin, Oakland Raiders	.03	.01	.00
☐ 195	John Matuszak, Oakland Raiders	.06	.02	.00
☐ 196	Matt Millen, Oakland Raiders	.06	.02	.00
☐ 197	Derrick Ramsey, Oakland Raiders	.03	.01	.00
☐ 198	Art Shell, Oakland Raiders	.06	.02	.00
☐ 199	Mark van Eeghen, Oakland Raiders	.06	.02	.00
☐ 200	Arthur Whittington, Oakland Raiders	.03	.01	.00
☐ 201	Marc Wilson, Oakland Raiders	.30	.12	.03
☐ 202	Pittsburgh Steelers TL	.25	.05	.01
	Franco Harris			
	John Stallworth			
	Mel Blount			
	Jack Lambert			
	Gary Dunn			
☐ 203	Mel Blount AP, Pittsburgh Steelers	.12	.05	.01
☐ 204	Terry Bradshaw, Pittsburgh Steelers	.60	.28	.06
☐ 205	Terry Bradshaw IA, Pittsburgh Steelers	.25	.10	.02
☐ 206	Craig Colquit, Pittsburgh Steelers	.03	.01	.00
☐ 207	Bennie Cunningham, Pittsburgh Steelers	.03	.01	.00
☐ 208	Russell Davis, Pittsburgh Steelers	.03	.01	.00
☐ 209	Gary Dunn, Pittsburgh Steelers	.03	.01	.00
☐ 210	Jack Ham, Pittsburgh Steelers	.12	.05	.01
☐ 211	Franco Harris, Pittsburgh Steelers	.45	.20	.04
☐ 212	Franco Harris IA, Pittsburgh Steelers	.20	.09	.02
☐ 213	Jack Lambert AP, Pittsburgh Steelers	.20	.09	.02
☐ 214	Jack Lambert IA, Pittsburgh Steelers	.12	.05	.01
☐ 215	Mark Malone, Pittsburgh Steelers	.30	.12	.03
☐ 216	Frank Pollard, Pittsburgh Steelers	.06	.02	.00
☐ 217	Donnie Shell AP, Pittsburgh Steelers	.06	.02	.00
☐ 218	Jim Smith, Pittsburgh Steelers	.06	.02	.00
☐ 219	John Stallworth, Pittsburgh Steelers	.12	.05	.01

		MINT	VG-E	F-G
☐ 220	**John Stallworth IA**, Pittsburgh Steelers	.06	.02	.00
☐ 221	**David Trout**, Pittsburgh Steelers	.03	.01	.00
☐ 222	**Mike Webster AP**, Pittsburgh Steelers	.06	.02	.00
☐ 223	**San Diego Chargers TL**	.12	.03	.01
	Chuck Muncie			
	Charlie Joiner			
	Willie Buchanon			
	Gary Johnson			
☐ 224	**Rolf Bernirschke**, San Diego Chargers	.06	.02	.00
☐ 225	**Rolf Bernirschke IA**, San Diego Chargers	.06	.02	.00
☐ 226	**James Brooks**, San Diego Chargers	.10	.04	.01
☐ 227	**Willie Buchanon**, San Diego Chargers	.06	.02	.00
☐ 228	**Wes Chandler**, San Diego Chargers	.10	.04	.01
☐ 229	**Wes Chandler IA**, San Diego Chargers	.06	.02	.00
☐ 230	**Dan Fouts**, San Diego Chargers	.60	.28	.06
☐ 231	**Dan Fouts IA**, San Diego Chargers	.30	.12	.03
☐ 232	**Gary Johnson AP**, San Diego Chargers	.06	.02	.00
☐ 233	**Charlie Joiner**, San Diego Chargers	.20	.09	.02
☐ 234	**Charlie Joiner IA**, San Diego Chargers	.12	.05	.01
☐ 235	**Louie Kelcher**, San Diego Chargers	.06	.02	.00
☐ 236	**Chuck Muncie AP**, San Diego Chargers	.12	.05	.01
☐ 237	**Chuck Muncie IA**, San Diego Chargers	.06	.02	.00
☐ 238	**George Roberts**, San Diego Chargers	.03	.01	.00
☐ 239	**Ed White**, San Diego Chargers	.03	.01	.00
☐ 240	**Doug Wilkerson AP**, San Diego Chargers	.06	.02	.00
☐ 241	**Kellen Winslow AP**, San Diego Chargers	.15	.06	.01
☐ 242	**Kellen Winslow IA**, San Diego Chargers	.10	.04	.01
☐ 243	**Seattle Seahawks TL**	.12	.03	.01
	Theotis Brown			
	Steve Largent			
	John Harris			
	Jacob Green			
☐ 244	**Theotis Brown**, Seattle Seahawks	.06	.02	.00
☐ 245	**Dan Doornink**, Seattle Seahawks	.03	.01	.00
☐ 246	**John Harris**, Seattle Seahawks	.03	.01	.00
☐ 247	**Efren Herrera**, Seattle Seahawks	.03	.01	.00
☐ 248	**David Hughes**, Seattle Seahawks	.03	.01	.00
☐ 249	**Steve Largent**, Seattle Seahawks	.15	.06	.01
☐ 250	**Steve Largent IA**, Seattle Seahawks	.10	.04	.01
☐ 251	**Sam McCullum**, Seattle Seahawks	.06	.02	.00
☐ 252	**Sherman Smith**, Seattle Seahawks	.03	.01	.00
☐ 253	**Manu Tuiasosopo**, Seattle Seahawks	.03	.01	.00
☐ 254	**John Yarno**, Seattle Seahawks	.03	.01	.00
☐ 255	**Jim Zorn**, Seattle Seahawks	.12	.05	.01
☐ 256	**Jim Zorn IA**, Seattle Seahawks	.06	.02	.00

	MINT	VG-E	F-G

STATISTICAL LEADERS

		MINT	VG-E	F-G
☐ 257	**Passing Leaders** .... Ken Anderson Joe Montana	.30	.12	.03
☐ 258	**Receiving Leaders** .... Kellen Winslow Dwight Clark	.15	.06	.01
☐ 259	**QB Sack Leaders** .... Joe Klecko Curtis Greer	.10	.04	.01
☐ 260	**Scoring Leaders** .... Jim Breech Nick Lowery Ed Murray Rafael Septien	.10	.04	.01
☐ 261	**Interception Leaders** .... John Harris Everson Walls	.10	.04	.01
☐ 262	**Punting Leaders** .... Pat McInally Tom Skladany	.06	.02	.00

NFL BROTHERS

		MINT	VG-E	F-G
☐ 263	**Brothers: Bahr** .... Chris and Matt	.06	.02	.00
☐ 264	**Brothers: Blackwood** .... Lyle and Glenn	.06	.02	.00
☐ 265	**Brothers: Brock** .... Pete and Stan	.06	.02	.00
☐ 266	**Brothers: Griffin** .... Archie and Ray	.06	.02	.00
☐ 267	**Brothers: Hannah** .... John and Charlie	.06	.02	.00
☐ 268	**Brothers: Jackson** .... Monte and Terry	.06	.02	.00
☐ 269	**Brothers: Payton** .... Eddie and Walter	.40	.18	.04
☐ 270	**Brothers: Selmon** .... Dewey and LeeRoy	.10	.04	.01

	MINT	VG-E	F-G
☐ 271 **Atlanta Falcons TL**	.12	.03	.01
William Andrews			
Alfred Jenkins			
Tom Pridemore			
Al Richardson			
☐ 272 **William Andrews**, Atlanta Falcons	.15	.06	.01
☐ 273 **William Andrews IA**, Atlanta Falcons	.08	.03	.01
☐ 274 **Steve Bartkowski**, Atlanta Falcons	.20	.09	.02
☐ 275 **Steve Bartkowski IA**, Atlanta Falcons	.10	.04	.01
☐ 276 **Bobby Butler**, Atlanta Falcons	.03	.01	.00
☐ 277 **Lynn Cain**, Atlanta Falcons	.06	.02	.00
☐ 278 **Wallace Francis**, Atlanta Falcons	.06	.02	.00
☐ 279 **Alfred Jackson**, Atlanta Falcons	.06	.02	.00
☐ 280 **John James**, Atlanta Falcons	.03	.01	.00
☐ 281 **Alfred Jenkins AP**, Atlanta Falcons	.06	.02	.00
☐ 282 **Alfred Jenkins IA**, Atlanta Falcons	.06	.02	.00
☐ 283 **Kenny Johnson**, Atlanta Falcons	.03	.01	.00
☐ 284 **Mike Kenn AP**, Atlanta Falcons	.06	.02	.00
☐ 285 **Fulton Kuhkendall**, Atlanta Falcons	.03	.01	.00
☐ 286 **Mick Luckhurst**, Atlanta Falcons	.03	.01	.00
☐ 287 **Mick Luckhurst IA**, Atlanta Falcons	.03	.01	.00
☐ 288 **Junior Miller**, Atlanta Falcons	.06	.02	.00
☐ 289 **Al Richardson**, Atlanta Falcons	.03	.01	.00
☐ 290 **R.C. Thielemann**, Atlanta Falcons	.03	.01	.00
☐ 291 **Jeff Van Note**, Atlanta Falcons	.03	.01	.00
☐ 292 **Chicago Bears TL**	.30	.06	.01
Walter Payton			
Ken Margerum			
Gary Fencik			
Dan Hampton			
Alan Page			
☐ 293 **Brian Baschnagel**, Chicago Bears	.03	.01	.00
☐ 294 **Robin Earl**, Chicago Bears	.03	.01	.00
☐ 295 **Vince Evans**, Chicago Bears	.06	.02	.00
☐ 296 **Gary Fencik AP**, Chicago Bears	.03	.01	.00
☐ 297 **Dan Hampton**, Chicago Bears	.10	.04	.01
☐ 298 **Noah Jackson**, Chicago Bears	.03	.01	.00
☐ 299 **Ken Margerum**, Chicago Bears	.10	.04	.01
☐ 300 **Jim Osborne**, Chicago Bears	.03	.01	.00
☐ 301 **Bob Parsons**, Chicago Bears	.03	.01	.00
☐ 302 **Walter Payton**, Chicago Bears	1.00	.45	.10
☐ 303 **Walter Payton IA**, Chicago Bears	.50	.22	.05
☐ 304 **Revie Sorey**, Chicago Bears	.03	.01	.00
☐ 305 **Matt Suhey**, Chicago Bears	.06	.02	.00
☐ 306 **Rickey Watts**, Chicago Bears	.03	.01	.00

		MINT	VG-E	F-G
☐ 307	**Dallas Cowboys TL**	.40	.08	.01
	Tony Dorsett			
	Tony Hill			
	Everson Walls			
	Harvey Martin			
☐ 308	**Bob Breunig**, Dallas Cowboys	.06	.02	.00
☐ 309	**Doug Cosbie**, Dallas Cowboys	.15	.06	.01
☐ 310	**Pat Donovan AP**, Dallas Cowboys	.06	.02	.00
☐ 311	**Tony Dorsett AP**, Dallas Cowboys	.60	.28	.06
☐ 312	**Tony Dorsett IA**, Dallas Cowboys	.30	.12	.03
☐ 313	**Michael Downs**, Dallas Cowboys	.06	.02	.00
☐ 314	**Billy Joe DuPree**, Dallas Cowboys	.10	.04	.01
☐ 315	**John Dutton**, Dallas Cowboys	.06	.02	.00
☐ 316	**Tony Hill**, Dallas Cowboys	.15	.06	.01
☐ 317	**Butch Johnson**, Dallas Cowboys	.10	.04	.01
☐ 318	**Ed Too Tall Jones AP**, Dallas Cowboys	.15	.06	.01
☐ 319	**James Jones**, Dallas Cowboys	.03	.01	.00
☐ 320	**Harvey Martin**, Dallas Cowboys	.12	.05	.01
☐ 321	**Drew Pearson**, Dallas Cowboys	.20	.09	.02
☐ 322	**Herbert Scott AP**, Dallas Cowboys	.03	.01	.00
☐ 323	**Rafael Septien AP**, Dallas Cowboys	.10	.04	.01
☐ 324	**Rafael Septien IA**, Dallas Cowboys	.06	.02	.00
☐ 325	**Ron Springs**, Dallas Cowboys	.03	.01	.00
☐ 326	**Dennis Thurman**, Dallas Cowboys	.06	.02	.00
☐ 327	**Everson Walls**, Dallas Cowboys	.25	.10	.02
☐ 328	**Everson Walls IA**, Dallas Cowboys	.10	.04	.01
☐ 329	**Danny White**, Dallas Cowboys	.30	.12	.03
☐ 330	**Danny White IA**, Dallas Cowboys	.15	.06	.01
☐ 331	**Randy White AP**, Dallas Cowboys	.25	.10	.02
☐ 332	**Randy White IA**, Dallas Cowboys	.12	.05	.01
☐ 333	**Detroit Lions TL**	.12	.03	.01
	Billy Sims			
	Freddie Scott			
	Jim Allen			
	Dave Pureifory			
☐ 334	**Jim Allen**, Detroit Lions	.03	.01	.00
☐ 335	**Al Bubba Baker**, Detroit Lions	.06	.02	.00
☐ 336	**Dexter Bussey**, Detroit Lions	.03	.01	.00
☐ 337	**Doug English AP**, Detroit Lions	.06	.02	.00
☐ 338	**Ken Fantetti**, Detroit Lions	.03	.01	.00
☐ 339	**William Gay**, Detroit Lions	.03	.01	.00
☐ 340	**David Hill**, Detroit Lions	.03	.01	.00
☐ 341	**Eric Hipple**, Detroit Lions	.15	.06	.01
☐ 342	**Rick Kane**, Detroit Lions	.03	.01	.00
☐ 343	**Ed Murray**, Detroit Lions	.03	.01	.00

	MINT	VG-E	F-G
☐ 344 **Ed Murray IA**, Detroit Lions	.03	.01	.00
☐ 345 **Ray Oldham**, Detroit Lions	.03	.01	.00
☐ 346 **Dave Pureifory**, Detroit Lions	.03	.01	.00
☐ 347 **Freddie Scott**, Detroit Lions	.03	.01	.00
☐ 348 **Freddie Scott IA**, Detroit Lions	.03	.01	.00
☐ 349 **Billy Sims AP**, Detroit Lions	.30	.12	.03
☐ 350 **Billy Sims IA**, Detroit Lions	.15	.06	.01
☐ 351 **Tom Skladany AP**, Detroit Lions	.06	.02	.00
☐ 352 **Leonard Thompson**, Detroit Lions	.06	.02	.00
☐ 353 **Stan White**, Detroit Lions	.03	.01	.00
☐ 354 **Green Bay Packers TL**	.12	.03	.01
Gerry Ellis			
James Lofton			
Maurice Harvey			
Mark Lee			
Mike Butler			
☐ 355 **Paul Coffman**, Green Bay Packers	.03	.01	.00
☐ 356 **George Cumby**, Green Bay Packers	.03	.01	.00
☐ 357 **Lynn Dickey**, Green Bay Packers	.15	.06	.01
☐ 358 **Lynn Dickey IA**, Green Bay Packers	.10	.04	.01
☐ 359 **Gerry Ellis**, Green Bay Packers	.03	.01	.00
☐ 360 **Maurice Harvey**, Green Bay Packers	.03	.01	.00
☐ 361 **Harlan Huckleby**, Green Bay Packers	.10	.04	.01
☐ 362 **John Jefferson**, Green Bay Packers	.15	.06	.01
☐ 363 **Mark Lee**, Green Bay Packers	.03	.01	.00
☐ 364 **James Lofton AP**, Green Bay Packers	.15	.06	.01
☐ 365 **James Lofton IA**, Green Bay Packers	.10	.04	.01
☐ 366 **Jan Stenerud**, Green Bay Packers	.10	.04	.01
☐ 367 **Jan Stenerud IA**, Green Bay Packers	.06	.02	.00
☐ 368 **Rich Wingo**, Green Bay Packers	.03	.01	.00
☐ 369 **Los Angeles Rams TL**	.12	.03	.01
Wendell Tyler			
Preston Dennard			
Nolan Cromwell			
Jack Youngblood			
☐ 370 **Frank Corral**, Los Angeles Rams	.03	.01	.00
☐ 371 **Nolan Cromwell AP**, Los Angeles Rams	.10	.04	.01
☐ 372 **Nolan Cromwell IA**, Los Angeles Rams	.06	.02	.00
☐ 373 **Preston Dennard**, Los Angeles Rams	.03	.01	.00
☐ 374 **Mike Fanning**, Los Angeles Rams	.03	.01	.00
☐ 375 **Doug France**, Los Angeles Rams	.03	.01	.00
☐ 376 **Mike Guman**, Los Angeles Rams	.03	.01	.00
☐ 377 **Pat Haden**, Los Angeles Rams	.15	.06	.01
☐ 378 **Dennis Harrah**, Los Angeles Rams	.03	.01	.00
☐ 379 **Drew Hill**, Los Angeles Rams	.03	.01	.00
☐ 380 **LeRoy Irvin**, Los Angeles Rams	.03	.01	.00

		MINT	VG-E	F-G
☐ 381	**Cody Jones,** Los Angeles Rams	.03	.01	.00
☐ 382	**Rod Perry,** Los Angeles Rams	.03	.01	.00
☐ 383	**Rich Saul AP,** Los Angeles Rams	.03	.01	.00
☐ 384	**Pat Thomas,** Los Angeles Rams	.03	.01	.00
☐ 385	**Wendell Tyler,** Los Angeles Rams	.12	.05	.01
☐ 386	**Wendell Tyler IA,** Los Angeles Rams	.06	.02	.00
☐ 387	**Billy Waddy,** Los Angeles Rams	.03	.01	.00
☐ 388	**Jack Youngblood,** Los Angeles Rams	.15	.06	.01
☐ 389	**Minnesota Vikings TL**	.12	.03	.01
	Ted Brown			
	Joe Senser			
	Tom Hannon			
	Willie Teal			
	Matt Blair			
☐ 390	**Matt Blair AP,** Minnesota Vikings	.06	.02	.00
☐ 391	**Ted Brown,** Minnesota Vikings	.06	.02	.00
☐ 392	**Ted Brown IA,** Minnesota Vikings	.06	.02	.00
☐ 393	**Rick Danmeier,** Minnesota Vikings	.03	.01	.00
☐ 394	**Tommy Kramer,** Minnesota Vikings	.20	.09	.02
☐ 395	**Mark Mullaney,** Minnesota Vikings	.06	.02	.00
☐ 396	**Eddie Payton,** Minnesota Vikings	.06	.02	.00
☐ 397	**Ahmad Rashad,** Minnesota Vikings	.20	.09	.02
☐ 398	**Joe Senser,** Minnesota Vikings	.06	.02	.00
☐ 399	**Joe Senser IA,** Minnesota Vikings	.06	.02	.00
☐ 400	**Sammy White,** Minnesota Vikings	.06	.02	.00
☐ 401	**Sammy White IA,** Minnesota Vikings	.06	.02	.00
☐ 402	**Ron Yary,** Minnesota Vikings	.06	.02	.00
☐ 403	**Rickey Young,** Minnesota Vikings	.06	.02	.00
☐ 404	**New Orleans Saints TL**	.15	.03	.01
	George Rogers			
	Guido Merkens			
	Dave Waymer			
	Rickey Jackson			
☐ 405	**Russell Erxleben,** New Orleans Saints	.03	.01	.00
☐ 406	**Elois Grooms,** New Orleans Saints	.03	.01	.00
☐ 407	**Jack Holmes,** New Orleans Saints	.03	.01	.00
☐ 408	**Archie Manning,** New Orleans Saints	.15	.06	.01
☐ 409	**Derland Moore,** New Orleans Saints	.03	.01	.00
☐ 410	**George Rogers,** New Orleans Saints	.50	.22	.05
☐ 411	**George Rogers IA,** New Orleans Saints	.20	.09	.02
☐ 412	**Toussaint Tyler,** New Orleans Saints	.03	.01	.00
☐ 413	**Dave Waymer,** New Orleans Saints	.03	.01	.00
☐ 414	**Wayne Wilson,** New Orleans Saints	.03	.01	.00

	MINT	VG-E	F-G
☐ 415 **New York Giants TL**	.12	.03	.01
Rob Carpenter			
Johnny Perkins			
Beasley Reece			
George Martin			
☐ 416 **Scott Brunner**, New York Giants	.15	.06	.01
☐ 417 **Rob Carpenter**, New York Giants	.06	.02	.00
☐ 418 **Harry Carson AP**, New York Giants	.12	.05	.01
☐ 419 **Bill Currier**, New York Giants	.03	.01	.00
☐ 420 **Joe Danelo**, New York Giants	.03	.01	.00
☐ 421 **Joe Danelo IA**, New York Giants	.03	.01	.00
☐ 422 **Mark Haynes**, New York Giants	.06	.02	.00
☐ 423 **Terry Jackson**, New York Giants	.03	.01	.00
☐ 424 **Dave Jennings**, New York Giants	.03	.01	.00
☐ 425 **Gary Jeter**, New York Giants	.06	.02	.00
☐ 426 **Brian Kelley**, New York Giants	.03	.01	.00
☐ 427 **George Martin**, New York Giants	.03	.01	.00
☐ 428 **Curtis McGriff**, New York Giants	.03	.01	.00
☐ 429 **Bill Neill**, New York Giants	.03	.01	.00
☐ 430 **Johnny Perkins**, New York Giants	.03	.01	.00
☐ 431 **Beasley Reece**, New York Giants	.03	.01	.00
☐ 432 **Gary Shirk**, New York Giants	.03	.01	.00
☐ 433 **Phil Simms**, New York Giants	.20	.09	.02
☐ 434 **Lawrence Taylor AP**, New York Giants	1.00	.45	.10
☐ 435 **Lawrence Taylor IA**, New York Giants	.25	.10	.02
☐ 436 **Brad Van Pelt**, New York Giants	.06	.02	.00
☐ 437 **Philadelphia Eagles TL**	.12	.03	.01
Wilbert Montgomery			
Harold Carmichael			
Brenard Wilson			
Carl Hairston			
☐ 438 **Johnny Bunting**, Philadelphia Eagles	.03	.01	.00
☐ 439 **Billy Campfield**, Philadelphia Eagles	.03	.01	.00
☐ 440 **Harold Carmichael**, Philadelphia Eagles	.15	.06	.01
☐ 441 **Harold Carmichael IA**, Philadelphia Eagles ...	.10	.04	.01
☐ 442 **Herman Edwards**, Philadelphia Eagles	.03	.01	.00
☐ 443 **Tony Franklin**, Philadelphia Eagles	.03	.01	.00
☐ 444 **Tony Franklin IA**, Philadelphia Eagles	.03	.01	.00
☐ 445 **Carl Hairston**, Philadelphia Eagles	.06	.02	.00
☐ 446 **Dennis Harrison**, Philadelphia Eagles	.03	.01	.00
☐ 447 **Ron Jaworski**, Philadelphia Eagles	.20	.09	.02
☐ 448 **Charlie Johnson**, Philadelphia Eagles	.03	.01	.00
☐ 449 **Keith Krepfle**, Philadelphia Eagles	.03	.01	.00
☐ 450 **Frank LeMaster**, Philadelphia Eagles	.03	.01	.00
☐ 451 **Randy Logan**, Philadelphia Eagles	.03	.01	.00
☐ 452 **Wilbert Montgomery**, Philadelphia Eagles	.20	.09	.02

		MINT	VG-E	F-G
☐ 453	**Wilbert Montgomery IA**, Philadelphia Eagles	.12	.05	.01
☐ 454	**Hubert Oliver**, Philadelphia Eagles	.06	.02	.00
☐ 455	**Jerry Robinson**, Philadelphia Eagles	.06	.02	.00
☐ 456	**Jerry Robinson IA**, Philadelphia Eagles	.06	.02	.00
☐ 457	**Jerry Sisemore**, Philadelphia Eagles	.03	.01	.00
☐ 458	**Charlie Smith**, Philadelphia Eagles	.03	.01	.00
☐ 459	**Stan Walters**, Philadelphia Eagles	.03	.01	.00
☐ 460	**Brenard Wilson**, Philadelphia Eagles	.03	.01	.00
☐ 461	**Roynell Young AP**, Philadelphia Eagles	.03	.01	.00
☐ 462	**St. Louis Cardinals TL**	.12	.03	.01
	Ottis Anderson			
	Pat Tilley			
	Ken Greene			
	Curtis Greer			
☐ 463	**Ottis Anderson**, St. Louis Cardinals	.25	.10	.02
☐ 464	**Ottis Anderson IA**, St. Louis Cardinals	.12	.05	.01
☐ 465	**Carl Birdsong**, St. Louis Cardinals	.03	.01	.00
☐ 466	**Rush Brown**, St. Louis Cardinals	.03	.01	.00
☐ 467	**Mel Gray**, St. Louis Cardinals	.08	.03	.01
☐ 468	**Ken Greene**, St. Louis Cardinals	.03	.01	.00
☐ 469	**Jim Hart**, St. Louis Cardinals	.20	.09	.02
☐ 470	**E.J. Junior**, St. Louis Cardinals	.12	.05	.01
☐ 471	**Neil Lomax**, St. Louis Cardinals	.35	.15	.03
☐ 472	**Stump Mitchell**, St. Louis Cardinals	.10	.04	.01
☐ 473	**Wayne Morris**, St. Louis Cardinals	.06	.02	.00
☐ 474	**Neil O'Donoghue**, St. Louis Cardinals	.03	.01	.00
☐ 475	**Pat Tilley**, St. Louis Cardinals	.08	.03	.01
☐ 476	**Pat Tilley IA**, St. Louis Cardinals	.06	.02	.00
☐ 477	**San Francisco 49ers TL**	.12	.03	.01
	Ricky Patton			
	Dwight Clark			
	Dwight Hicks			
	Fred Dean			
☐ 478	**Dwight Clark**, San Francisco 49ers	.20	.09	.02
☐ 479	**Dwight Clark IA**, San Francisco 49ers	.12	.05	.01
☐ 480	**Earl Cooper**, San Francisco 49ers	.03	.01	.00
☐ 481	**Randy Cross AP**, San Francisco 49ers	.03	.01	.00
☐ 482	**Johnny Davis**, San Francisco 49ers	.03	.01	.00
☐ 483	**Fred Dean**, San Francisco 49ers	.06	.02	.00
☐ 484	**Fred Dean IA**, San Francisco 49ers	.06	.02	.00
☐ 485	**Dwight Hicks**, San Francisco 49ers	.12	.05	.01
☐ 486	**Ronnie Lott AP**, San Francisco 49ers	.30	.12	.03
☐ 487	**Ronnie Lott IA**, San Francisco 49ers	.12	.05	.01
☐ 488	**Joe Montana AP**, San Francisco 49ers	1.00	.45	.10
☐ 489	**Joe Montana IA**, San Francisco 49ers	.35	.15	.03
☐ 490	**Ricky Patton**, San Francisco 49ers	.03	.01	.00

		MINT	VG-E	F-G
☐ 491	**Jack Reynolds,** San Francisco 49ers	.06	.02	.00
☐ 492	**Freddie Solomon,** San Francisco 49ers	.06	.02	.00
☐ 493	**Ray Wersching,** San Francisco 49ers	.03	.01	.00
☐ 494	**Charley Young,** San Francisco 49ers	.06	.02	.00
☐ 495	**Tampa Bay Buccaneers TL**	.12	.03	.01
	Jerry Eckwood			
	Kevin House			
	Cedric Brown			
	Lee Roy Selmon			
☐ 496	**Cedric Brown,** Tampa Bay Buccaneers	.03	.01	.00
☐ 497	**Neal Colzie,** Tampa Bay Buccaneers	.03	.01	.00
☐ 498	**Jerry Eckwood,** Tampa Bay Buccaneers	.06	.02	.00
☐ 499	**Jimmy Giles AP,** Tampa Bay Buccaneers	.06	.02	.00
☐ 500	**Hugh Green,** Tampa Bay Buccaneers	.30	.12	.03
☐ 501	**Kevin House,** Tampa Bay Buccaneers	.06	.02	.00
☐ 502	**Kevin House IA,** Tampa Bay Buccaneers	.06	.02	.00
☐ 503	**Cecil Johnson,** Tampa Bay Buccaneers	.03	.01	.00
☐ 504	**James Owens,** Tampa Bay Buccaneers	.06	.02	.00
☐ 505	**Lee Roy Selmon AP,** Tampa Bay Buccaneers .	.15	.06	.01
☐ 506	**Mike Washington,** Tampa Bay Buccaneers ...	.03	.01	.00
☐ 507	**James Wilder,** Tampa Bay Buccaneers	.40	.18	.04
☐ 508	**Doug Williams,** Tampa Bay Buccaneers	.15	.06	.01
☐ 509	**Washington Redskins TL**	.12	.03	.01
	Joe Washington			
	Art Monk			
	Mark Murphy			
	Perry Brooks			
☐ 510	**Perry Brooks,** Washington Redskins	.03	.01	.00
☐ 511	**Dave Butz,** Washington Redskins	.06	.02	.00
☐ 512	**Wilbur Jackson,** Washington Redskins	.03	.01	.00
☐ 513	**Joe Lavender,** Washington Redskins	.03	.01	.00
☐ 514	**Terry Metcalf,** Washington Redskins	.08	.03	.01
☐ 515	**Art Monk,** Washington Redskins	.12	.05	.01
☐ 516	**Mark Moseley,** Washington Redskins	.08	.03	.01
☐ 517	**Mark Murphy,** Washington Redskins	.03	.01	.00
☐ 518	**Mike Nelms AP,** Washington Redskins	.06	.02	.00
☐ 519	**Lemar Parrish,** Washington Redskins	.03	.01	.00
☐ 520	**John Riggins,** Washington Redskins	.30	.12	.03
☐ 521	**Joe Theismann,** Washington Redskins	.35	.15	.03
☐ 522	**Ricky Thompson,** Washington Redskins	.03	.01	.00
☐ 523	**Don Warren,** Washington Redskins	.03	.01	.00
☐ 524	**Joe Washington,** Washington Redskins	.10	.04	.01

	MINT	VG-E	F-G

CHECKLISTS

		MINT	VG-E	F-G
☐ 525	Checklist 1-132	.10	.02	.00
☐ 526	Checklist 133-264	.10	.02	.00
☐ 527	Checklist 265-396	.10	.02	.00
☐ 528	Checklist 397-528	.10	.02	.00

1983 TOPPS

The 1983 Topps set decreased in number from previous years, as only 396 cards are contained in this year's set. The cards measure 2½" by 3½". Although there are only 396 cards, the set was printed on four sheets; therefore, there are 132 double printings which are denoted in the checklist below by DP. The cards themselves contain the player's name at the bottom in a rectangular area, while the team names are in block letters at the top of the cards. The first nine cards in the set recognize record-breaking (RB) achievements occurring during the previous season. Players who appeared in the Pro Bowl game are identified as such in a rectangular area on the front. The backs of the cards are printed in black ink with red borders and a faintly identifiable helmet of the player's team covering the center of the back in a screened red color. The Team Leader (TL) cards are distributed throughout the set as the first card of the team sequence; this year only one leader (usually the team's rushing leader) is pictured and the backs contain team scoring information from the previous year.

	MINT	VG-E	F-G
COMPLETE SET	11.00	5.25	1.10
COMMON PLAYER (1-396)	.03	.01	.00

		MINT	VG-E	F-G
☐	**1 RB: Ken Anderson**	.25	.05	.01
	20 Consecutive Pass Completions			
☐	**2 RB: Tony Dorsett**	.25	.10	.02
	99 Yard Run			
☐	**3 RB: Dan Fouts**	.25	.10	.02
	30 Games Over 300 Yards Passing			
☐	**4 RB: Joe Montana**	.25	.10	.02
	5 Straight 300 Yard Games			
☐	**5 RB: Mark Moseley**	.06	.02	.00
	21 Straight Field Goals			
☐	**6 RB: Mike Nelms**	.06	.02	.00
	Most Yards Punt Returns, Super Bowl Game			
☐	**7 RB: Darrol Ray**	.06	.02	.00
	Longest Interception Return, Playoff Game			
☐	**8 RB: John Riggins**	.15	.06	.01
	Most Yards Rushing, Super Bowl Game			
☐	**9 RB: Fulton Walker**	.06	.02	.00
	Most Yards Kickoff Returns, Super Bowl Game			
☐	**10 NFC Championship**	.10	.04	.01
	Redskins 31, Cowboys 17			
	(Riggins tackled)			
☐	**11 AFC Championship**	.10	.04	.01
	Dolphins 14, Jets 0			
☐	**12 Super Bowl XVII**	.15	.06	.01
	Redskins 27, Dolphins 17			
	(Riggins running)			
☐	**13 Atlanta Falcons TL**	.10	.04	.01
	William Andrews			
☐	**14 William Andrews DP**, Atlanta Falcons	.06	.02	.00
☐	**15 Steve Bartkowski**, Atlanta Falcons	.20	.09	.02
☐	**16 Bobby Butler**, Atlanta Falcons	.03	.01	.00
☐	**17 Buddy Curry**, Atlanta Falcons	.03	.01	.00
☐	**18 Alfred Jackson DP**, Atlanta Falcons	.03	.01	.00
☐	**19 Alfred Jenkins**, Atlanta Falcons	.06	.02	.00
☐	**20 Kenny Johnson**, Atlanta Falcons	.03	.01	.00
☐	**21 Mike Kenn**, Atlanta Falcons	.03	.01	.00
☐	**22 Mick Luckhurst**, Atlanta Falcons	.03	.01	.00
☐	**23 Junior Miller**, Atlanta Falcons	.06	.02	.00
☐	**24 Al Richardson**, Atlanta Falcons	.03	.01	.00
☐	**25 Gerald Riggs DP**, Atlanta Falcons	.06	.02	.00
☐	**26 R.C. Thielemann**, Atlanta Falcons	.03	.01	.00
☐	**27 Jeff Van Note**, Atlanta Falcons	.03	.01	.00
☐	**28 Chicago Bears TL**	.30	.12	.03
	Walter Payton			
☐	**29 Brian Baschnagel**, Chicago Bears	.03	.01	.00
☐	**30 Dan Hampton**, Chicago Bears	.06	.02	.00

		MINT	VG-E	F-G
☐ 31	**Mike Hartenstine**, Chicago Bears	.03	.01	.00
☐ 32	**Noah Jackson**, Chicago Bears	.03	.01	.00
☐ 33	**Jim McMahon**, Chicago Bears	1.25	.60	.12
☐ 34	**Emery Moorehead DP**, Chicago Bears	.02	.01	.00
☐ 35	**Bob Parsons**, Chicago Bears	.03	.01	.00
☐ 36	**Walter Payton**, Chicago Bears	.60	.28	.06
☐ 37	**Terry Schmidt**, Chicago Bears	.03	.01	.00
☐ 38	**Mike Singletary**, Chicago Bears	.80	.40	.08
☐ 39	**Matt Suhey DP**, Chicago Bears	.02	.01	.00
☐ 40	**Rickey Watts DP**, Chicago Bears	.02	.01	.00
☐ 41	**Otis Wilson DP**, Chicago Bears	.03	.01	.00
☐ 42	**Dallas Cowboys TL**	.25	.10	.02
	Tony Dorsett			
☐ 43	**Bob Breunig**, Dallas Cowboys	.06	.02	.00
☐ 44	**Doug Cosbie**, Dallas Cowboys	.06	.02	.00
☐ 45	**Pat Donovan**, Dallas Cowboys	.03	.01	.00
☐ 46	**Tony Dorsett DP**, Dallas Cowboys	.30	.12	.03
☐ 47	**Tony Hill**, Dallas Cowboys	.10	.04	.01
☐ 48	**Butch Johnson DP**, Dallas Cowboys	.03	.01	.00
☐ 49	**Ed Too Tall Jones DP**, Dallas Cowboys	.10	.04	.01
☐ 50	**Harvey Martin DP**, Dallas Cowboys	.06	.02	.00
☐ 51	**Drew Pearson**, Dallas Cowboys	.15	.06	.01
☐ 52	**Rafael Septien**, Dallas Cowboys	.10	.04	.01
☐ 53	**Ron Springs DP**, Dallas Cowboys	.03	.01	.00
☐ 54	**Dennis Thurman**, Dallas Cowboys	.03	.01	.00
☐ 55	**Everson Walls**, Dallas Cowboys	.10	.04	.01
☐ 56	**Danny White DP**, Dallas Cowboys	.15	.06	.01
☐ 57	**Randy White**, Dallas Cowboys	.18	.08	.01
☐ 58	**Detroit Lions TL**	.12	.05	.01
	Billy Sims			
☐ 59	**Al Baker DP**, Detroit Lions	.03	.01	.00
☐ 60	**Dexter Bussey DP**, Detroit Lions	.02	.01	.00
☐ 61	**Gary Danielson DP**, Detroit Lions	.06	.02	.00
☐ 62	**Keith Dorney DP**, Detroit Lions	.02	.01	.00
☐ 63	**Doug English**, Detroit Lions	.03	.01	.00
☐ 64	**Ken Fantetti DP**, Detroit Lions	.02	.01	.00
☐ 65	**Alvin Hall DP**, Detroit Lions	.02	.01	.00
☐ 66	**David Hill DP**, Detroit Lions	.02	.01	.00
☐ 67	**Eric Hipple**, Detroit Lions	.10	.04	.01
☐ 68	**Ed Murray DP**, Detroit Lions	.02	.01	.00
☐ 69	**Freddie Scott**, Detroit Lions	.03	.01	.00
☐ 70	**Billy Sims DP**, Detroit Lions	.15	.06	.01
☐ 71	**Tom Skladany DP**, Detroit Lions	.02	.01	.00
☐ 72	**Leonard Thompson DP**, Detroit Lions	.02	.01	.00
☐ 73	**Bobby Watkins**, Detroit Lions	.06	.02	.00

		MINT	VG-E	F-G
☐ 74	**Green Bay Packers TL**	.10	.04	.01
	Eddie Lee Ivery			
☐ 75	**John Anderson**, Green Bay Packers	.03	.01	.00
☐ 76	**Paul Coffman**, Green Bay Packers	.03	.01	.00
☐ 77	**Lynn Dickey**, Green Bay Packers	.15	.06	.01
☐ 78	**Mike Douglass DP**, Green Bay Packers	.02	.01	.00
☐ 79	**Eddie Lee Ivery**, Green Bay Packers	.08	.03	.01
☐ 80	**John Jefferson**, Green Bay Packers	.06	.02	.00
☐ 81	**Ezra Johnson**, Green Bay Packers	.03	.01	.00
☐ 82	**Mark Lee**, Green Bay Packers	.03	.01	.00
☐ 83	**James Lofton**, Green Bay Packers	.15	.06	.01
☐ 84	**Larry McCarren**, Green Bay Packers	.03	.01	.00
☐ 85	**Jan Stenerud DP**, Green Bay Packers	.06	.02	.00
☐ 86	**Los Angeles Rams TL**	.10	.04	.01
	Wendell Tyler			
☐ 87	**Bill Bain DP**, Los Angeles Rams	.02	.01	.00
☐ 88	**Nolan Cromwell**, Los Angeles Rams	.08	.03	.01
☐ 89	**Preston Dennard**, Los Angeles Rams	.03	.01	.00
☐ 90	**Vince Ferragamo DP**, Los Angeles Rams	.08	.03	.01
☐ 91	**Mike Guman**, Los Angeles Rams	.03	.01	.00
☐ 92	**Kent Hill**, Los Angeles Rams	.03	.01	.00
☐ 93	**Mike Lansford DP**, Los Angeles Rams	.02	.01	.00
☐ 94	**Rod Perry**, Los Angeles Rams	.03	.01	.00
☐ 95	**Pat Thomas DP**, Los Angeles Rams	.02	.01	.00
☐ 96	**Jack Youngblood**, Los Angeles Rams	.12	.05	.01
☐ 97	**Minnesota Vikings TL**	.10	.04	.01
	Ted Brown			
☐ 98	**Matt Blair**, Minnesota Vikings	.06	.02	.00
☐ 99	**Ted Brown**, Minnesota Vikings	.06	.02	.00
☐ 100	**Greg Coleman**, Minnesota Vikings	.03	.01	.00
☐ 101	**Randy Holloway**, Minnesota Vikings	.03	.01	.00
☐ 102	**Tommy Kramer**, Minnesota Vikings	.15	.06	.01
☐ 103	**Doug Martin DP**, Minnesota Vikings	.02	.01	.00
☐ 104	**Mark Mullaney**, Minnesota Vikings	.03	.01	.00
☐ 105	**Joe Senser**, Minnesota Vikings	.06	.02	.00
☐ 106	**Willie Teal DP**, Minnesota Vikings	.02	.01	.00
☐ 107	**Sammy White**, Minnesota Vikings	.06	.02	.00
☐ 108	**Rickey Young**, Minnesota Vikings	.06	.02	.00
☐ 109	**New Orleans Saints TL**	.10	.04	.01
	George Rogers			
☐ 110	**Stan Brock**, New Orleans Saints	.03	.01	.00
☐ 111	**Bruce Clark**, New Orleans Saints	.06	.02	.00
☐ 112	**Russell Erxleben DP**, New Orleans Saints	.02	.01	.00
☐ 113	**Russell Gary**, New Orleans Saints	.03	.01	.00
☐ 114	**Jeff Groth DP**, New Orleans Saints	.02	.01	.00
☐ 115	**John Hill DP**, New Orleans Saints	.02	.01	.00

		MINT	VG-E	F-G
☐ 116	**Derland Moore,** New Orleans Saints	.03	.01	.00
☐ 117	**George Rogers,** New Orleans Saints	.15	.06	.01
☐ 118	**Ken Stabler,** New Orleans Saints	.20	.09	.02
☐ 119	**Wayne Wilson,** New Orleans Saints	.03	.01	.00
☐ 120	**New York Giants TL**	.10	.04	.01
	Butch Woolfolk			
☐ 121	**Scott Brunner,** New York Giants	.10	.04	.01
☐ 122	**Rob Carpenter,** New York Giants	.06	.02	.00
☐ 123	**Harry Carson,** New York Giants	.10	.04	.01
☐ 124	**Joe Danelo DP,** New York Giants	.02	.01	.00
☐ 125	**Earnest Gray,** New York Giants	.06	.02	.00
☐ 126	**Mark Haynes DP,** New York Giants	.03	.01	.00
☐ 127	**Terry Jackson,** New York Giants	.03	.01	.00
☐ 128	**Dave Jennings,** New York Giants	.03	.01	.00
☐ 129	**Brian Kelley,** New York Giants	.03	.01	.00
☐ 130	**George Martin,** New York Giants	.03	.01	.00
☐ 131	**Tom Mullady,** New York Giants	.03	.01	.00
☐ 132	**Johnny Perkins,** New York Giants	.03	.01	.00
☐ 133	**Lawrence Taylor,** New York Giants	.20	.09	.02
☐ 134	**Brad Van Pelt,** New York Giants	.06	.02	.00
☐ 135	**Butch Woolfolk DP,** New York Giants	.06	.02	.00
☐ 136	**Philadelphia Eagles TL**	.10	.04	.01
	Wilbert Montgomery			
☐ 137	**Harold Carmichael,** Philadelphia Eagles	.12	.05	.01
☐ 138	**Herman Edwards,** Philadelphia Eagles	.03	.01	.00
☐ 139	**Tony Franklin DP,** Philadelphia Eagles	.03	.01	.00
☐ 140	**Carl Hairston DP,** Philadelphia Eagles	.03	.01	.00
☐ 141	**Dennis Harrison DP,** Philadelphia Eagles	.02	.01	.00
☐ 142	**Ron Jaworski DP,** Philadelphia Eagles	.10	.04	.01
☐ 143	**Frank LeMaster,** Philadelphia Eagles	.03	.01	.00
☐ 144	**Wilbert Montgomery DP,** Philadelphia Eagles .	.10	.04	.01
☐ 145	**Guy Morriss,** Philadelphia Eagles	.03	.01	.00
☐ 146	**Jerry Robinson,** Philadelphia Eagles	.06	.02	.00
☐ 147	**Max Runager,** Philadelphia Eagles	.03	.01	.00
☐ 148	**Ron Smith DP,** Philadelphia Eagles	.02	.01	.00
☐ 149	**John Spagnola,** Philadelphia Eagles	.03	.01	.00
☐ 150	**Stan Walters DP,** Philadelphia Eagles	.02	.01	.00
☐ 151	**Roynell Young DP,** Philadelphia Eagles	.02	.01	.00
☐ 152	**St. Louis Cardinals TL**	.10	.04	.01
	Ottis Anderson			
☐ 153	**Ottis Anderson,** St. Louis Cardinals	.20	.09	.02
☐ 154	**Carl Birdsong,** St. Louis Cardinals	.03	.01	.00
☐ 155	**Dan Dierdorf DP,** St. Louis Cardinals	.03	.01	.00
☐ 156	**Roy Green,** St. Louis Cardinals	.25	.10	.02
☐ 157	**Elois Grooms,** St. Louis Cardinals	.03	.01	.00
☐ 158	**Neil Lomax DP,** St. Louis Cardinals	.10	.04	.01

		MINT	VG-E	F-G
☐ 159	**Wayne Morris**, St. Louis Cardinals	.03	.01	.00
☐ 160	**James Robbins**, St. Louis Cardinals	.03	.01	.00
☐ 161	**Luis Sharpe**, St. Louis Cardinals	.03	.01	.00
☐ 162	**Pat Tilley**, St. Louis Cardinals	.06	.02	.00
☐ 163	**San Francisco 49ers TL**	.10	.04	.01
	Jeff Moore			
☐ 164	**Dwight Clark**, San Francisco 49ers	.10	.04	.01
☐ 165	**Randy Cross**, San Francisco 49ers	.03	.01	.00
☐ 166	**Russ Francis**, San Francisco 49ers	.08	.03	.01
☐ 167	**Dwight Hicks**, San Francisco 49ers	.06	.02	.00
☐ 168	**Ronnie Lott**, San Francisco 49ers	.10	.04	.01
☐ 169	**Joe Montana DP**, San Francisco 49ers	.35	.15	.03
☐ 170	**Jeff Moore**, San Francisco 49ers	.06	.02	.00
☐ 171	**Renaldo Nehemiah DP**, San Francisco 49ers	.10	.04	.01
☐ 172	**Freddie Solomon**, San Francisco 49ers	.06	.02	.00
☐ 173	**Ray Wersching DP**, San Francisco 49ers	.02	.01	.00
☐ 174	**Tampa Bay Buccaneers TL**	.10	.04	.01
	James Wilder			
☐ 175	**Cedric Brown**, Tampa Bay Buccaneers	.03	.01	.00
☐ 176	**Bill Capece**, Tampa Bay Buccaneers	.03	.01	.00
☐ 177	**Neal Colzie**, Tampa Bay Buccaneers	.03	.01	.00
☐ 178	**Jimmie Giles**, Tampa Bay Buccaneers	.06	.02	.00
☐ 179	**Hugh Green**, Tampa Bay Buccaneers	.10	.04	.01
☐ 180	**Kevin House DP**, Tampa Bay Buccaneers	.03	.01	.00
☐ 181	**James Owens**, Tampa Bay Buccaneers	.06	.02	.00
☐ 182	**Lee Roy Selmon**, Tampa Bay Buccaneers	.15	.06	.01
☐ 183	**Mike Washington**, Tampa Bay Buccaneers	.03	.01	.00
☐ 184	**James Wilder**, Tampa Bay Buccaneers	.15	.06	.01
☐ 185	**Doug Williams DP**, Tampa Bay Buccaneers	.06	.02	.00
☐ 186	**Washington Redskins TL**	.15	.06	.01
	John Riggins			
☐ 187	**Jeff Bostic DP**, Washington Redskins	.02	.01	.00
☐ 188	**Charlie Brown**, Washington Redskins	.25	.10	.02
☐ 189	**Vernon Dean DP**, Washington Redskins	.03	.01	.00
☐ 190	**Joe Jacoby**, Washington Redskins	.03	.01	.00
☐ 191	**Dexter Manley**, Washington Redskins	.06	.02	.00
☐ 192	**Rich Milot**, Washington Redskins	.03	.01	.00
☐ 193	**Art Monk DP**, Washington Redskins	.06	.02	.00
☐ 194	**Mark Moseley DP**, Washington Redskins	.03	.01	.00
☐ 195	**Mike Nelms**, Washington Redskins	.06	.02	.00
☐ 196	**Neal Olkewicz DP**, Washington Redskins	.02	.01	.00
☐ 197	**Tony Peters**, Washington Redskins	.03	.01	.00
☐ 198	**John Riggins DP**, Washington Redskins	.15	.06	.01
☐ 199	**Joe Theismann**, Washington Redskins	.40	.18	.04
☐ 200	**Don Warren**, Washington Redskins	.03	.01	.00
☐ 201	**Jeris White DP**, Washington Redskins	.02	.01	.00

	MINT	VG-E	F-G

LEAGUE LEADERS

		MINT	VG-E	F-G
☐ 202	**Passing Leaders** .... Joe Theismann Ken Anderson	.20	.09	.02
☐ 203	**Receiving Leaders** .... Dwight Clark Kellen Winslow	.12	.05	.01
☐ 204	**Rushing Leaders** .... Tony Dorsett Freeman McNeil	.25	.10	.02
☐ 205	**Scoring Leaders** .... Wendell Tyler Marcus Allen	.25	.10	.02
☐ 206	**Interception Leaders** .... Everson Walls AFC Tie (Four)	.08	.03	.01
☐ 207	**Punting Leaders** .... Carl Birdsong Luke Prestridge	.06	.02	.00
☐ 208	**Baltimore Colts TL** .... Randy McMillan	.10	.04	.01
☐ 209	**Matt Bouza**, Baltimore Colts	.03	.01	.00
☐ 210	**Johnnie Cooks DP**, Baltimore Colts	.06	.02	.00
☐ 211	**Curtis Dickey**, Baltimore Colts	.10	.04	.01
☐ 212	**Nesby Glasgow DP**, Baltimore Colts	.02	.01	.00
☐ 213	**Derrick Hatchett**, Baltimore Colts	.03	.01	.00
☐ 214	**Randy McMillan**, Baltimore Colts	.06	.02	.00
☐ 215	**Mike Pagel**, Baltimore Colts	.15	.06	.01
☐ 216	**Rohn Stark DP**, Baltimore Colts	.03	.01	.00
☐ 217	**Donnell Thompson**, Baltimore Colts	.02	.01	.00
☐ 218	**Leo Wisniewski DP**, Baltimore Colts	.02	.01	.00
☐ 219	**Buffalo Bills TL** .... Joe Cribbs	.10	.04	.01
☐ 220	**Curtis Brown**, Buffalo Bills	.03	.01	.00
☐ 221	**Jerry Butler**, Buffalo Bills	.10	.04	.01
☐ 222	**Greg Cater DP**, Buffalo Bills	.02	.01	.00
☐ 223	**Joe Cribbs**, Buffalo Bills	.15	.06	.01
☐ 224	**Joe Ferguson**, Buffalo Bills	.15	.06	.01
☐ 225	**Roosevelt Leaks**, Buffalo Bills	.03	.01	.00
☐ 226	**Frank Lewis**, Buffalo Bills	.06	.02	.00
☐ 227	**Eugene Marve**, Buffalo Bills	.03	.01	.00
☐ 228	**Fred Smerlas DP**, Buffalo Bills	.02	.01	.00
☐ 229	**Ben Williams DP**, Buffalo Bills	.02	.01	.00

		MINT	VG-E	F-G
☐ 230	**Cincinnati Bengals TL**	.10	.04	.01
	Pete Johnson			
☐ 231	**Charles Alexander,** Cincinnati Bengals	.03	.01	.00
☐ 232	**Ken Anderson DP,** Cincinnati Bengals	.15	.06	.01
☐ 233	**Jim Breech DP,** Cincinnati Bengals	.02	.01	.00
☐ 234	**Ross Browner,** Cincinnati Bengals	.06	.02	.00
☐ 235	**Cris Collinsworth DP,** Cincinnati Bengals	.06	.02	.00
☐ 236	**Isaac Curtis,** Cincinnati Bengals	.06	.02	.00
☐ 237	**Pete Johnson,** Cincinnati Bengals	.06	.02	.00
☐ 238	**Steve Kreider DP,** Cincinnati Bengals	.02	.01	.00
☐ 239	**Max Montoya DP,** Cincinnati Bengals	.02	.01	.00
☐ 240	**Anthony Munoz,** Cincinnati Bengals	.06	.02	.00
☐ 241	**Ken Riley,** Cincinnati Bengals	.06	.02	.00
☐ 242	**Dan Ross,** Cincinnati Bengals	.06	.02	.00
☐ 243	**Reggie Williams,** Cincinnati Bengals	.06	.02	.00
☐ 244	**Cleveland Browns TL**	.10	.04	.01
	Mike Pruitt			
☐ 245	**Chip Banks DP,** Cleveland Browns	.10	.04	.01
☐ 246	**Tom Cousineau DP,** Cleveland Browns	.15	.06	.01
☐ 247	**Joe DeLamielleure DP,** Cleveland Browns	.03	.01	.00
☐ 248	**Doug Dieken DP,** Cleveland Browns	.02	.01	.00
☐ 249	**Hanford Dixon,** Cleveland Browns	.03	.01	.00
☐ 250	**Ricky Feacher DP,** Cleveland Browns	.02	.01	.00
☐ 251	**Lawrence Johnson DP,** Cleveland Browns	.02	.01	.00
☐ 252	**Dave Logan DP,** Cleveland Browns	.02	.01	.00
☐ 253	**Paul McDonald DP,** Cleveland Browns	.06	.02	.00
☐ 254	**Ozzie Newsome DP,** Cleveland Browns	.06	.02	.00
☐ 255	**Mike Pruitt,** Cleveland Browns	.10	.04	.01
☐ 256	**Clarence Scott DP,** Cleveland Browns	.02	.01	.00
☐ 257	**Brian Sipe DP,** Cleveland Browns	.10	.04	.01
☐ 258	**Dwight Walker DP,** Cleveland Browns	.02	.01	.00
☐ 259	**Charles White,** Cleveland Browns	.10	.04	.01
☐ 260	**Denver Broncos TL**	.10	.04	.01
	Gerald Willhite			
☐ 261	**Steve DeBerg DP,** Denver Broncos	.06	.02	.00
☐ 262	**Randy Gradishar DP,** Denver Broncos	.06	.02	.00
☐ 263	**Rulon Jones DP,** Denver Broncos	.02	.01	.00
☐ 264	**Rick Karlis DP,** Denver Broncos	.02	.01	.00
☐ 265	**Don Latimer,** Denver Broncos	.03	.01	.00
☐ 266	**Rick Parros DP,** Denver Broncos	.02	.01	.00
☐ 267	**Luke Prestridge,** Denver Broncos	.03	.01	.00
☐ 268	**Rick Upchurch,** Denver Broncos	.06	.02	.00
☐ 269	**Steve Watson DP,** Denver Broncos	.03	.01	.00
☐ 270	**Gerald Willhite DP,** Denver Broncos	.03	.01	.00
☐ 271	**Houston Oilers TL**	.10	.04	.01
	Gifford Nielson			

		MINT	VG-E	F-G
☐ 272	**Harold Bailey**, Houston Oilers	.03	.01	.00
☐ 273	**Jesse Baker DP**, Houston Oilers	.03	.01	.00
☐ 274	**Greg Bingham DP**, Houston Oilers	.02	.01	.00
☐ 275	**Robert Brazile DP**, Houston Oilers	.03	.01	.00
☐ 276	**Donnie Craft**, Houston Oilers	.03	.01	.00
☐ 277	**Daryl Hunt**, Houston Oilers	.03	.01	.00
☐ 278	**Archie Manning DP**, Houston Oilers	.10	.04	.01
☐ 279	**Gifford Nielsen**, Houston Oilers	.10	.04	.01
☐ 280	**Mike Renfro**, Houston Oilers	.03	.01	.00
☐ 281	**Carl Roaches DP**, Houston Oilers	.03	.01	.00
☐ 282	**Kansas City Chiefs TL**	.10	.04	.01
	Joe Delaney			
☐ 283	**Gary Barbaro**, Kansas City Chiefs	.06	.02	.00
☐ 284	**Joe Delaney**, Kansas City Chiefs	.10	.04	.01
☐ 285	**Jeff Gossett**, Kansas City Chiefs	.03	.01	.00
☐ 286	**Gary Green DP**, Kansas City Chiefs	.02	.01	.00
☐ 287	**Eric Harris DP**, Kansas City Chiefs	.02	.01	.00
☐ 288	**Billy Jackson DP**, Kansas City Chiefs	.02	.01	.00
☐ 289	**Bill Kenney DP**, Kansas City Chiefs	.06	.02	.00
☐ 290	**Nick Lowery**, Kansas City Chiefs	.03	.01	.00
☐ 291	**Henry Marshall**, Kansas City Chiefs	.03	.01	.00
☐ 292	**Art Still DP**, Kansas City Chiefs	.03	.01	.00
☐ 293	**Los Angeles Raiders TL**	.25	.10	.02
	Marcus Allen			
☐ 294	**Marcus Allen DP**, Los Angeles Raiders	.60	.28	.06
☐ 295	**Lyle Alzado**, Los Angeles Raiders	.15	.06	.01
☐ 296	**Chris Bahr DP**, Los Angeles Raiders	.03	.01	.00
☐ 297	**Cliff Branch**, Los Angeles Raiders	.10	.04	.01
☐ 298	**Todd Christensen**, Los Angeles Raiders	.15	.06	.01
☐ 299	**Ray Guy**, Los Angeles Raiders	.10	.04	.01
☐ 300	**Frank Hawkins DP**, Los Angeles Raiders	.02	.01	.00
☐ 301	**Lester Hayes DP**, Los Angeles Raiders	.06	.02	.00
☐ 302	**Ted Hendricks DP**, Los Angeles Raiders	.06	.02	.00
☐ 303	**Kenny King DP**, Los Angeles Raiders	.03	.01	.00
☐ 304	**Rod Martin**, Los Angeles Raiders	.03	.01	.00
☐ 305	**Matt Millen DP**, Los Angeles Raiders	.03	.01	.00
☐ 306	**Burgess Owens**, Los Angeles Raiders	.03	.01	.00
☐ 307	**Jim Plunkett**, Los Angeles Raiders	.15	.06	.01
☐ 308	**Miami Dolphins TL**	.10	.04	.01
	Andra Franklin			
☐ 309	**Bob Baumhower**, Miami Dolphins	.06	.02	.00
☐ 310	**Glenn Blackwood**, Miami Dolphins	.03	.01	.00
☐ 311	**Lyle Blackwood DP**, Miami Dolphins	.02	.01	.00
☐ 312	**A.J. Duhe**, Miami Dolphins	.10	.04	.01
☐ 313	**Andra Franklin**, Miami Dolphins	.06	.02	.00
☐ 314	**Duriel Harris**, Miami Dolphins	.06	.02	.00

		MINT	VG-E	F-G
☐ 315	**Bob Kuechenberg DP**, Miami Dolphins	.02	.01	.00
☐ 316	**Don McNeal**, Miami Dolphins	.06	.02	.00
☐ 317	**Tony Nathan**, Miami Dolphins	.06	.02	.00
☐ 318	**Ed Newman**, Miami Dolphins	.03	.01	.00
☐ 319	**Earnie Rhone DP**, Miami Dolphins	.02	.01	.00
☐ 320	**Joe Rose DP**, Miami Dolphins	.03	.01	.00
☐ 321	**Don Strock DP**, Miami Dolphins	.06	.02	.00
☐ 322	**Uwe von Schamann**, Miami Dolphins	.06	.02	.00
☐ 323	**David Woodley DP**, Miami Dolphins	.06	.02	.00
☐ 324	**New England Patriots TL** Tony Collins	.10	.04	.01
☐ 325	**Julius Adams**, New England Patriots	.03	.01	.00
☐ 326	**Pete Brock**, New England Patriots	.03	.01	.00
☐ 327	**Rich Camarillo DP**, New England Patriots	.02	.01	.00
☐ 328	**Tony Collins DP**, New England Patriots	.06	.02	.00
☐ 329	**Steve Grogan**, New England Patriots	.15	.06	.01
☐ 330	**John Hannah**, New England Patriots	.10	.04	.01
☐ 331	**Don Hasselbeck**, New England Patriots	.03	.01	.00
☐ 332	**Mike Haynes**, New England Patriots	.10	.04	.01
☐ 333	**Roland James**, New England Patriots	.03	.01	.00
☐ 334	**Stanley Morgan**, New England Patriots	.10	.04	.01
☐ 335	**Steve Nelson**, New England Patriots	.03	.01	.00
☐ 336	**Kenneth Sims DP**, New England Patriots	.10	.04	.01
☐ 337	**Mark van Eeghen**, New England Patriots	.06	.02	.00
☐ 338	**New York Jets TL** Freeman McNeil	.10	.04	.01
☐ 339	**Greg Buttle**, New York Jets	.06	.02	.00
☐ 340	**Joe Fields**, New York Jets	.03	.01	.00
☐ 341	**Mark Gastineau DP**, New York Jets	.10	.04	.01
☐ 342	**Bruce Harper**, New York Jets	.06	.02	.00
☐ 343	**Bobby Jackson**, New York Jets	.03	.01	.00
☐ 344	**Bobby Jones**, New York Jets	.03	.01	.00
☐ 345	**Johnny Lam Jones DP**, New York Jets	.06	.02	.00
☐ 346	**Joe Klecko**, New York Jets	.10	.04	.01
☐ 347	**Marty Lyons**, New York Jets	.06	.02	.00
☐ 348	**Freeman McNeil**, New York Jets	.15	.06	.01
☐ 349	**Lance Mehl**, New York Jets	.03	.01	.00
☐ 350	**Marvin Powell DP**, New York Jets	.03	.01	.00
☐ 351	**Darrol Ray DP**, New York Jets	.03	.01	.00
☐ 352	**Abdul Salaam**, New York Jets	.03	.01	.00
☐ 353	**Richard Todd**, New York Jets	.15	.06	.01
☐ 354	**Wesley Walker**, New York Jets	.10	.04	.01
☐ 355	**Pittsburgh Steelers TL** Franco Harris	.20	.09	.02
☐ 356	**Gary Anderson DP**, Pittsburgh Steelers	.02	.01	.00
☐ 357	**Mel Blount DP**, Pittsburgh Steelers	.03	.01	.00

	MINT	VG-E	F-G
☐ 358 **Terry Bradshaw DP**, Pittsburgh Steelers	.25	.10	.02
☐ 359 **Larry Brown**, Pittsburgh Steelers	.03	.01	.00
☐ 360 **Bennie Cunningham**, Pittsburgh Steelers	.03	.01	.00
☐ 361 **Gary Dunn**, Pittsburgh Steelers	.03	.01	.00
☐ 362 **Franco Harris**, Pittsburgh Steelers	.30	.12	.03
☐ 363 **Jack Lambert**, Pittsburgh Steelers	.20	.09	.02
☐ 364 **Frank Pollard**, Pittsburgh Steelers	.06	.02	.00
☐ 365 **Donnie Shell**, Pittsburgh Steelers	.06	.02	.00
☐ 366 **John Stallworth**, Pittsburgh Steelers	.10	.04	.01
☐ 367 **Loren Toews**, Pittsburgh Steelers	.03	.01	.00
☐ 368 **Mike Webster DP**, Pittsburgh Steelers	.03	.01	.00
☐ 369 **Dwayne Woodruff**, Pittsburgh Steelers	.03	.01	.00
☐ 370 **San Diego Chargers TL**	.10	.04	.01
Chuck Muncie			
☐ 371 **Rolf Bernirschke DP**, San Diego Chargers	.03	.01	.00
☐ 372 **James Brooks**, San Diego Chargers	.06	.02	.00
☐ 373 **Wes Chandler**, San Diego Chargers	.08	.03	.01
☐ 374 **Dan Fouts DP**, San Diego Chargers	.25	.10	.02
☐ 375 **Tim Fox**, San Diego Chargers	.06	.02	.00
☐ 376 **Gary Johnson**, San Diego Chargers	.06	.02	.00
☐ 377 **Charlie Joiner DP**, San Diego Chargers	.06	.02	.00
☐ 378 **Louie Kelcher**, San Diego Chargers	.06	.02	.00
☐ 379 **Chuck Muncie**, San Diego Chargers	.10	.04	.01
☐ 380 **Cliff Thrift**, San Diego Chargers	.03	.01	.00
☐ 381 **Doug Wilkerson**, San Diego Chargers	.03	.01	.00
☐ 382 **Kellen Winslow**, San Diego Chargers	.15	.06	.01
☐ 383 **Seattle Seahawks TL**	.10	.04	.01
Sherman Smith			
☐ 384 **Kenny Easley**, Seattle Seahawks	.25	.10	.02
☐ 385 **Jacob Green**, Seattle Seahawks	.10	.04	.01
☐ 386 **John Harris**, Seattle Seahawks	.03	.01	.00
☐ 387 **Michael Jackson**, Seattle Seahawks	.03	.01	.00
☐ 388 **Norm Johnson**, Seattle Seahawks	.03	.01	.00
☐ 389 **Steve Largent**, Seattle Seahawks	.10	.04	.01
☐ 390 **Keith Simpson**, Seattle Seahawks	.03	.01	.00
☐ 391 **Sherman Smith**, Seattle Seahawks	.03	.01	.00
☐ 392 **Jeff West DP**, Seattle Seahawks	.02	.01	.00
☐ 393 **Jim Zorn DP**, Seattle Seahawks	.06	.02	.00

CHECKLISTS

	MINT	VG-E	F-G
☐ 394 **Checklist 1-132**	.09	.02	.00
☐ 395 **Checklist 133-264**	.09	.02	.00
☐ 396 **Checklist 265-396**	.09	.02	.00

1984 TOPPS

The 1984 Topps Football set contains 396 cards featuring players of the NFL. Cards are standard size, 2½" by 3½". The first six cards in the set recognize record-breaking (RB) achievements during the previous season. The Team Leader (TL) cards are distributed throughout the set as the first card of the team sequence; this year only one leader (usually the team's rushing leader) is pictured and the backs contain team scoring information from the previous year. Instant Replay (IR) cards were issued as a special card for certain players in addition to (and immediately following) their regular card.

		MINT	VG-E	F-G
	COMPLETE SET	11.00	5.00	1.00
	COMMON PLAYER	.03	.01	.00
☐	1 RB: Eric Dickerson .... Sets Rookie Mark With 1808 Yards	.35	.10	.02
☐	2 RB: Ali Haji-Sheikh .... Sets Field Goal Mark as a Rookie	.05	.02	.00
☐	3 RB: Franco Harris .... Records Eighth 1000 Yard Year	.15	.06	.01
☐	4 RB: Mark Moseley .... 161 Points Sets Mark for Kickers	.05	.02	.00
☐	5 RB: John Riggins .... 24 Rushing TD's	.15	.06	.01
☐	6 RB: Jan Stenerud .... 338th Career FG	.05	.02	.00
☐	7 AFC Championship .... Raiders 30, Seahawks 14 (M. Allen running)	.10	.04	.01

		MINT	VG-E	F-G
☐	**8 NFC Championship**	.10	.04	.01
	Redskins 24, 49ers 21			
	(Riggins running)			
☐	**9 Super Bowl XVIII**	.12	.05	.01
	Raiders 38, Redskins 9			
	(hand-off to M. Allen)			
☐	**10 Indianapolis Colts TL**	.09	.04	.01
	Curtis Dickey			
☐	**11 Raul Allegre,** Indianapolis Colts	.06	.02	.00
☐	**12 Curtis Dickey,** Indianapolis Colts	.09	.04	.01
☐	**13 Ray Donaldson,** Indianapolis Colts	.03	.01	.00
☐	**14 Nesby Glasgow,** Indianapolis Colts	.03	.01	.00
☐	**15 Chris Hinton,** Indianapolis Colts	.09	.04	.01
☐	**16 Vernon Maxwell,** Indianapolis Colts	.07	.03	.01
☐	**17 Randy McMillan,** Indianapolis Colts	.05	.02	.00
☐	**18 Mike Pagel,** Indianapolis Colts	.07	.03	.01
☐	**19 Rohn Stark,** Indianapolis Colts	.03	.01	.00
☐	**20 Leo Wisniewski,** Indianapolis Colts	.03	.01	.00
☐	**21 Buffalo Bills TL**	.10	.04	.01
	Joe Cribbs			
☐	**22 Jerry Butler,** Buffalo Bills	.10	.04	.01
☐	**23 Joe Danelo,** Buffalo Bills	.03	.01	.00
☐	**24 Joe Ferguson,** Buffalo Bills	.12	.05	.01
☐	**25 Steve Freeman,** Buffalo Bills	.03	.01	.00
☐	**26 Roosevelt Leaks,** Buffalo Bills	.03	.01	.00
☐	**27 Frank Lewis,** Buffalo Bills	.05	.02	.00
☐	**28 Eugene Marve,** Buffalo Bills	.03	.01	.00
☐	**29 Booker Moore,** Buffalo Bills	.03	.01	.00
☐	**30 Fred Smerlas,** Buffalo Bills	.05	.02	.00
☐	**31 Ben Williams,** Buffalo Bills	.03	.01	.00
☐	**32 Cincinnati Bengals TL**	.08	.03	.01
	Cris Collinsworth			
☐	**33 Charles Alexander,** Cincinnati Bengals	.03	.01	.00
☐	**34 Ken Anderson,** Cincinnati Bengals	.25	.10	.02
☐	**35 Ken Anderson IR,** Cincinnati Bengals	.15	.06	.01
☐	**36 Jim Breech,** Cincinnati Bengals	.03	.01	.00
☐	**37 Cris Collinsworth,** Cincinnati Bengals	.10	.04	.01
☐	**38 Cris Collinsworth IR,** Cincinnati Bengals	.06	.02	.00
☐	**39 Isaac Curtis,** Cincinnati Bengals	.05	.02	.00
☐	**40 Eddie Edwards,** Cincinnati Bengals	.03	.01	.00
☐	**41 Ray Horton,** Cincinnati Bengals	.03	.01	.00
☐	**42 Pete Johnson,** Cincinnati Bengals	.05	.02	.00
☐	**43 Steve Kreider,** Cincinnati Bengals	.03	.01	.00
☐	**44 Max Montoya,** Cincinnati Bengals	.03	.01	.00
☐	**45 Anthon Munoz,** Cincinnati Bengals	.07	.03	.01
☐	**46 Reggie Williams,** Cincinnati Bengals	.05	.02	.00

		MINT	VG-E	F-G
☐ 47	**Cleveland Browns TL** .... Mike Pruitt	.08	.03	.01
☐ 48	**Matt Bahr,** Cleveland Browns	.05	.02	.00
☐ 49	**Chip Banks,** Cleveland Browns	.07	.03	.01
☐ 50	**Tom Cousineau,** Cleveland Browns	.10	.04	.01
☐ 51	**Joe DeLamielleure,** Cleveland Browns	.05	.02	.00
☐ 52	**Doug Dieken,** Cleveland Browns	.03	.01	.00
☐ 53	**Bob Golic,** Cleveland Browns	.03	.01	.00
☐ 54	**Bobby Jones,** Cleveland Browns	.03	.01	.00
☐ 55	**Dave Logan,** Cleveland Browns	.03	.01	.00
☐ 56	**Clay Matthews,** Cleveland Browns	.05	.02	.00
☐ 57	**Paul McDonald,** Cleveland Browns	.05	.02	.00
☐ 58	**Ozzie Newsome,** Cleveland Browns	.08	.03	.01
☐ 59	**Ozzie Newsome IR,** Cleveland Browns	.05	.02	.00
☐ 60	**Mike Pruitt,** Cleveland Browns	.08	.03	.01
☐ 61	**Denver Broncos TL** .... Steve Watson	.08	.03	.01
☐ 62	**Barney Chavous,** Denver Broncos	.03	.01	.00
☐ 63	**John Elway,** Denver Broncos	.60	.28	.06
☐ 64	**Steve Foley,** Denver Broncos	.03	.01	.00
☐ 65	**Tom Jackson,** Denver Broncos	.05	.02	.00
☐ 66	**Rick Karlis,** Denver Broncos	.03	.01	.00
☐ 67	**Luke Prestridge,** Denver Broncos	.03	.01	.00
☐ 68	**Zack Thomas,** Denver Broncos	.03	.01	.00
☐ 69	**Rick Upchurch,** Denver Broncos	.06	.02	.00
☐ 70	**Steve Watson,** Denver Broncos	.05	.02	.00
☐ 71	**Sammy Winder,** Denver Broncos	.09	.04	.01
☐ 72	**Louis Wright,** Denver Broncos	.05	.02	.00
☐ 73	**Houston Oilers TL** .... Tim Smith	.07	.03	.01
☐ 74	**Jesse Baker,** Houston Oilers	.03	.01	.00
☐ 75	**Gregg Bingham,** Houston Oilers	.03	.01	.00
☐ 76	**Robert Brazile,** Houston Oilers	.05	.02	.00
☐ 77	**Steve Brown,** Houston Oilers	.03	.01	.00
☐ 78	**Chris Dressel,** Houston Oilers	.03	.01	.00
☐ 79	**Doug France,** Houston Oilers	.03	.01	.00
☐ 80	**Florian Kempf,** Houston Oilers	.03	.01	.00
☐ 81	**Carl Roaches,** Houston Oilers	.03	.01	.00
☐ 82	**Tim Smith,** Houston Oilers	.05	.02	.00
☐ 83	**Willie Tullis,** Houston Oilers	.03	.01	.00
☐ 84	**Kansas City Chiefs TL** .... Carlos Carson	.08	.03	.01
☐ 85	**Mike Bell,** Kansas City Chiefs	.05	.02	.00
☐ 86	**Theotis Brown,** Kansas City Chiefs	.05	.02	.00
☐ 87	**Carlos Carson,** Kansas City Chiefs	.07	.03	.01
☐ 88	**Carlos Carson IR,** Kansas City Chiefs	.05	.02	.00

			MINT	VG-E	F-G
☐	89	**Deron Cherry**, Kansas City Chiefs	.03	.01	.00
☐	90	**Gary Green**, Kansas City Chiefs	.03	.01	.00
☐	91	**Billy Jackson**, Kansas City Chiefs	.03	.01	.00
☐	92	**Bill Kenney**, Kansas City Chiefs	.10	.04	.01
☐	93	**Bill Kenney IR**, Kansas City Chiefs	.06	.02	.00
☐	94	**Nick Lowery**, Kansas City Chiefs	.03	.01	.00
☐	95	**Henry Marshall**, Kansas City Chiefs	.03	.01	.00
☐	96	**Art Still**, Kansas City Chiefs	.05	.02	.00
☐	97	**Los Angeles Raiders TL** .... Todd Christensen	.08	.03	.01
☐	98	**Marcus Allen**, Los Angeles Raiders	.25	.10	.02
☐	99	**Marcus Allen IR**, Los Angeles Raiders	.12	.05	.01
☐	100	**Lyle Alzado**, Los Angeles Raiders	.10	.04	.01
☐	101	**Lyle Alzado IR**, Los Angeles Raiders	.06	.02	.00
☐	102	**Chris Bahr**, Los Angeles Raiders	.05	.02	.00
☐	103	**Malcolm Barnwell**, Los Angeles Raiders	.05	.02	.00
☐	104	**Cliff Branch**, Los Angeles Raiders	.09	.04	.01
☐	105	**Todd Christensen**, Los Angeles Raiders	.08	.03	.01
☐	106	**Todd Christensen IR**, Los Angeles Raiders ...	.05	.02	.00
☐	107	**Ray Guy**, Los Angeles Raiders	.09	.04	.01
☐	108	**Frank Hawkins**, Los Angeles Raiders	.03	.01	.00
☐	109	**Lester Hayes**, Los Angeles Raiders	.07	.03	.01
☐	110	**Ted Hendricks**, Los Angeles Raiders	.09	.04	.01
☐	111	**Howie Long**, Los Angeles Raiders	.25	.10	.02
☐	112	**Rod Martin**, Los Angeles Raiders	.03	.01	.00
☐	113	**Vann McElroy**, Los Angeles Raiders	.03	.01	.00
☐	114	**Jim Plunkett**, Los Angeles Raiders	.15	.06	.01
☐	115	**Greg Pruitt**, Los Angeles Raiders	.09	.04	.01
☐	116	**Miami Dolphins TL** .... Mark Duper	.10	.04	.01
☐	117	**Bob Baumhower**, Miami Dolphins	.06	.02	.00
☐	118	**Doug Betters**, Miami Dolphins	.10	.04	.01
☐	119	**A.J. Duhe**, Miami Dolphins	.08	.03	.01
☐	120	**Mark Duper**, Miami Dolphins	.40	.18	.04
☐	121	**Andra Franklin**, Miami Dolphins	.05	.02	.00
☐	122	**William Judson**, Miami Dolphins	.03	.01	.00
☐	123	**Dan Marino**, Miami Dolphins	2.00	.90	.20
☐	124	**Dan Marino IR**, Miami Dolphins	.40	.18	.04
☐	125	**Nat Moore**, Miami Dolphins	.05	.02	.00
☐	126	**Ed Newman**, Miami Dolphins	.03	.01	.00
☐	127	**Reggie Roby**, Miami Dolphins	.20	.09	.02
☐	128	**Gerald Small**, Miami Dolphins	.03	.01	.00
☐	129	**Dwight Stephenson**, Miami Dolphins	.05	.02	.00
☐	130	**Uwe von Schamann**, Miami Dolphins	.05	.02	.00
☐	131	**New England Patriots TL** .... Tony Collins	.08	.03	.01

	MINT	VG-E	F-G
☐ 132 **Rich Camarillo**, New England Patriots	.03	.01	.00
☐ 133 **Tony Collins**, New England Patriots	.07	.03	.01
☐ 134 **Tony Collins IR**, New England Patriots	.05	.02	.00
☐ 135 **Bob Cryder**, New England Patriots	.03	.01	.00
☐ 136 **Steve Grogan**, New England Patriots	.12	.05	.01
☐ 137 **John Hannah**, New England Patriots	.08	.03	.01
☐ 138 **Brian Holloway**, New England Patriots	.03	.01	.00
☐ 139 **Roland James**, New England Patriots	.03	.01	.00
☐ 140 **Stanley Morgan**, New England Patriots	.10	.04	.01
☐ 141 **Rick Sanford**, New England Patriots	.03	.01	.00
☐ 142 **Mosi Tatupu**, New England Patriots	.03	.01	.00
☐ 143 **Andre Tippett**, New England Patriots	.15	.06	.01
☐ 144 **New York Jets TL** Wesley Walker	.08	.03	.01
☐ 145 **Jerome Barkum**, New York Jets	.05	.02	.00
☐ 146 **Mark Gastineau**, New York Jets	.15	.06	.01
☐ 147 **Mark Gastineau IR**, New York Jets	.07	.03	.01
☐ 148 **Bruce Harper**, New York Jets	.03	.01	.00
☐ 149 **Johnny Lam Jones**, New York Jets	.05	.02	.00
☐ 150 **Joe Klecko**, New York Jets	.08	.03	.01
☐ 151 **Pat Leahy**, New York Jets	.03	.01	.00
☐ 152 **Freeman McNeil**, New York Jets	.15	.06	.01
☐ 153 **Lance Mehl**, New York Jets	.03	.01	.00
☐ 154 **Marvin Powell**, New York Jets	.05	.02	.00
☐ 155 **Darrol Ray**, New York Jets	.05	.02	.00
☐ 156 **Pat Ryan**, New York Jets	.10	.04	.01
☐ 157 **Kirk Springs**, New York Jets	.03	.01	.00
☐ 158 **Wesley Walker**, New York Jets	.08	.03	.01
☐ 159 **Pittsburgh Steelers TL** Franco Harris	.15	.06	.01
☐ 160 **Walter Abercrombie**, Pittsburgh Steelers	.20	.09	.02
☐ 161 **Gary Anderson**, Pittsburgh Steelers	.03	.01	.00
☐ 162 **Terry Bradshaw**, Pittsburgh Steelers	.35	.15	.03
☐ 163 **Craig Colquitt**, Pittsburgh Steelers	.03	.01	.00
☐ 164 **Bennie Cunningham**, Pittsburgh Steelers	.03	.01	.00
☐ 165 **Franco Harris**, Pittsburgh Steelers	.25	.10	.02
☐ 166 **Franco Harris IR**, Pittsburgh Steelers	.15	.06	.01
☐ 167 **Jack Lambert**, Pittsburgh Steelers	.15	.06	.01
☐ 168 **Jack Lambert IR**, Pittsburgh Steelers	.10	.04	.01
☐ 169 **Frank Pollard**, Pittsburgh Steelers	.05	.02	.00
☐ 170 **Donnie Shell**, Pittsburgh Steelers	.05	.02	.00
☐ 171 **Mike Webster**, Pittsburgh Steelers	.05	.02	.00
☐ 172 **Keith Willis**, Pittsburgh Steelers	.05	.02	.00
☐ 173 **Rick Woods**, Pittsburgh Steelers	.03	.01	.00
☐ 174 **San Diego Chargers TL** Kellen Winslow	.08	.03	.01

		MINT	VG-E	F-G
☐ 175	**Rolf Benirschke**, San Diego Chargers	.05	.02	.00
☐ 176	**James Brooks**, San Diego Chargers	.05	.02	.00
☐ 177	**Maury Buford**, San Diego Chargers	.03	.01	.00
☐ 178	**Wes Chandler**, San Diego Chargers	.07	.03	.01
☐ 179	**Dan Fouts**, San Diego Chargers	.35	.15	.03
☐ 180	**Dan Fouts IR**, San Diego Chargers	.15	.06	.01
☐ 181	**Charlie Joiner**, San Diego Chargers	.10	.04	.01
☐ 182	**Linden King**, San Diego Chargers	.03	.01	.00
☐ 183	**Chuck Muncie**, San Diego Chargers	.09	.04	.01
☐ 184	**Billy Ray Smith**, San Diego Chargers	.12	.05	.01
☐ 185	**Danny Walters**, San Diego Chargers	.08	.03	.01
☐ 186	**Kellen Winslow**, San Diego Chargers	.10	.04	.01
☐ 187	**Kellen Winslow IR**, San Diego Chargers	.07	.03	.01
☐ 188	**Seattle Seahawks TL**	.10	.04	.01
	Curt Warner			
☐ 189	**Steve August**, Seattle Seahawks	.03	.01	.00
☐ 190	**Dave Brown**, Seattle Seahawks	.03	.01	.00
☐ 191	**Zachary Dixon**, Seattle Seahawks	.03	.01	.00
☐ 192	**Kenny Easley**, Seattle Seahawks	.08	.03	.01
☐ 193	**Jacob Green**, Seattle Seahawks	.05	.02	.00
☐ 194	**Norm Johnson**, Seattle Seahawks	.03	.01	.00
☐ 195	**Dave Krieg**, Seattle Seahawks	.30	.12	.03
☐ 196	**Steve Largent**, Seattle Seahawks	.10	.04	.01
☐ 197	**Steve Largent IR**, Seattle Seahawks	.07	.03	.01
☐ 198	**Curt Warner**, Seattle Seahawks	.40	.18	.04
☐ 199	**Curt Warner IR**, Seattle Seahawks	.15	.06	.01
☐ 200	**Jeff West**, Seattle Seahawks	.03	.01	.00
☐ 201	**Charley Young**, Seattle Seahawks	.05	.02	.00
☐ 202	**Passing Leaders**	.35	.15	.03
	Dan Marino			
	Steve Bartkowski			
☐ 203	**Receiving Leaders**	.10	.04	.01
	Todd Christensen			
	Charlie Brown			
	Earnest Gray			
	Roy Green			
☐ 204	**Rushing Leaders**	.30	.12	.03
	Curt Warner			
	Eric Dickerson			
☐ 205	**Scoring Leaders**	.06	.02	.00
	Gary Anderson			
	Mark Moseley			
☐ 206	**Interception Leaders**	.06	.02	.00
	Van McElroy			
	Ken Riley			
	Mark Murphy			

		MINT	VG-E	F-G
☐ 207	**Punting Leaders**	.06	.02	.00
	Rich Camarillo			
☐ 208	**Atlanta Falcons TL**	.08	.03	.01
	William Andrews			
☐ 209	**William Andrews**, Atlanta Falcons	.10	.04	.01
☐ 210	**William Andrews IR**, Atlanta Falcons	.07	.03	.01
☐ 211	**Stacey Bailey**, Atlanta Falcons	.08	.03	.01
☐ 212	**Steve Bartkowski**, Atlanta Falcons	.15	.06	.01
☐ 213	**Steve Bartkowski IR**, Atlanta Falcons	.10	.04	.01
☐ 214	**Ralph Giacomarro**, Atlanta Falcons	.03	.01	.00
☐ 215	**Billy Johnson**, Atlanta Falcons	.05	.02	.00
☐ 216	**Mike Kenn**, Atlanta Falcons	.05	.02	.00
☐ 217	**Mick Luckhurst**, Atlanta Falcons	.03	.01	.00
☐ 218	**Gerald Riggs**, Atlanta Falcons	.08	.03	.01
☐ 219	**R.C. Thielemann**, Atlanta Falcons	.03	.01	.00
☐ 220	**Jeff Van Note**, Atlanta Falcons	.05	.02	.00
☐ 221	**Chicago Bears TL**	.30	.12	.03
	Walter Payton			
☐ 222	**Jim Covert**, Chicago Bears	.12	.05	.01
☐ 223	**Leslie Frazier**, Chicago Bears	.03	.01	.00
☐ 224	**Willie Gault**, Chicago Bears	.25	.10	.02
☐ 225	**Mike Hartenstine**, Chicago Bears	.03	.01	.00
☐ 226	**Noah Jackson**, Chicago Bears	.03	.01	.00
☐ 227	**Jim McMahon**, Chicago Bears	.25	.10	.02
☐ 228	**Walter Payton**, Chicago Bears	.60	.28	.06
☐ 229	**Walter Payton IR**, Chicago Bears	.25	.10	.02
☐ 230	**Mike Richardson**, Chicago Bears	.03	.01	.00
☐ 231	**Terry Schmidt**, Chicago Bears	.03	.01	.00
☐ 232	**Mike Singletary**, Chicago Bears	.12	.05	.01
☐ 233	**Matt Suhey**, Chicago Bears	.03	.01	.00
☐ 234	**Bob Thomas**, Chicago Bears	.03	.01	.00
☐ 235	**Dallas Cowboys TL**	.20	.09	.02
	Tony Dorsett			
☐ 236	**Bob Breunig**, Dallas Cowboys	.06	.02	.00
☐ 237	**Doug Cosbie**, Dallas Cowboys	.06	.02	.00
☐ 238	**Tony Dorsett**, Dallas Cowboys	.35	.15	.03
☐ 239	**Tony Dorsett IR**, Dallas Cowboys	.20	.09	.02
☐ 240	**John Dutton**, Dallas Cowboys	.05	.02	.00
☐ 241	**Tony Hill**, Dallas Cowboys	.10	.04	.01
☐ 242	**Ed Too Tall Jones**, Dallas Cowboys	.12	.05	.01
☐ 243	**Drew Pearson**, Dallas Cowboys	.12	.05	.01
☐ 244	**Rafael Septien**, Dallas Cowboys	.08	.03	.01
☐ 245	**Ron Springs**, Dallas Cowboys	.05	.02	.00
☐ 246	**Dennis Thurman**, Dallas Cowboys	.03	.01	.00
☐ 247	**Everson Walls**, Dallas Cowboys	.07	.03	.01
☐ 248	**Danny White**, Dallas Cowboys	.20	.09	.02

		MINT	VG-E	F-G
☐ 249	**Randy White**, Dallas Cowboys	.18	.08	.01
☐ 250	**Detroit Lions TL**	.12	.05	.01
	Billy Sims			
☐ 251	**Jeff Chadwick**, Detroit Lions	.07	.03	.01
☐ 252	**Garry Cobb**, Detroit Lions	.03	.01	.00
☐ 253	**Doug English**, Detroit Lions	.05	.02	.00
☐ 254	**William Gay**, Detroit Lions	.03	.01	.00
☐ 255	**Eric Hipple**, Detroit Lions	.08	.03	.01
☐ 256	**James Jones**, Detroit Lions	.07	.03	.01
☐ 257	**Bruce McNorton**, Detroit Lions	.03	.01	.00
☐ 258	**Ed Murray**, Detroit Lions	.03	.01	.00
☐ 259	**Ulysses Norris**, Detroit Lions	.03	.01	.00
☐ 260	**Billy Sims**, Detroit Lions	.15	.06	.01
☐ 261	**Billy Sims IR**, Detroit Lions	.10	.04	.01
☐ 262	**Leonard Thompson**, Detroit Lions	.05	.02	.00
☐ 263	**Green Bay Packers TL**	.08	.03	.01
	James Lofton			
☐ 264	**John Anderson**, Green Bay Packers	.03	.01	.00
☐ 265	**Paul Coffman**, Green Bay Packers	.03	.01	.00
☐ 266	**Lynn Dickey**, Green Bay Packers	.10	.04	.01
☐ 267	**Gerry Ellis**, Green Bay Packers	.03	.01	.00
☐ 268	**John Jefferson**, Green Bay Packers	.10	.04	.01
☐ 269	**John Jefferson IR**, Green Bay Packers	.07	.03	.01
☐ 270	**Ezra Johnson**, Green Bay Packers	.03	.01	.00
☐ 271	**Tim Lewis**, Green Bay Packers	.03	.01	.00
☐ 272	**James Lofton**, Green Bay Packers	.12	.05	.01
☐ 273	**James Lofton IR**, Green Bay Packers	.07	.03	.01
☐ 274	**Larry McCarren**, Green Bay Packers	.03	.01	.00
☐ 275	**Jan Stenerud**, Green Bay Packers	.07	.03	.01
☐ 276	**Los Angeles Rams TL**	.25	.10	.02
	Eric Dickerson			
☐ 277	**Mike Barber**, Los Angeles Rams	.03	.01	.00
☐ 278	**Jim Collins**, Los Angeles Rams	.03	.01	.00
☐ 279	**Nolan Cromwell**, Los Angeles Rams	.06	.02	.00
☐ 280	**Eric Dickerson**, Los Angeles Rams	1.50	.70	.15
☐ 281	**Eric Dickerson IR**, Los Angeles Rams	.35	.15	.03
☐ 282	**George Farmer**, Los Angeles Rams	.03	.01	.00
☐ 283	**Vince Ferragamo**, Los Angeles Rams	.10	.04	.01
☐ 284	**Kent Hill**, Los Angeles Rams	.03	.01	.00
☐ 285	**John Misko**, Los Angeles Rams	.03	.01	.00
☐ 286	**Jackie Slater**, Los Angeles Rams	.03	.01	.00
☐ 287	**Jack Youngblood**, Los Angeles Rams	.10	.04	.01
☐ 288	**Minnesota Vikings TL**	.08	.03	.01
	Darrin Nelson			
☐ 289	**Ted Brown**, Minnesota Vikings	.06	.02	.00
☐ 290	**Greg Coleman**, Minnesota Vikings	.03	.01	.00

	MINT	VG-E	F-G
☐ 291 **Steve Dils**, Minnesota Vikings	.06	.02	.00
☐ 292 **Tony Galbreath**, Minnesota Vikings	.05	.02	.00
☐ 293 **Tommy Kramer**, Minnesota Vikings	.12	.05	.01
☐ 294 **Doug Martin**, Minnesota Vikings	.03	.01	.00
☐ 295 **Darrin Nelson**, Minnesota Vikings	.10	.04	.01
☐ 296 **Benny Ricardo**, Minnesota Vikings	.03	.01	.00
☐ 297 **John Swain**, Minnesota Vikings	.03	.01	.00
☐ 298 **John Turner**, Minnesota Vikings	.03	.01	.00
☐ 299 **New Orleans Saints TL** George Rogers	.08	.03	.01
☐ 300 **Morten Andersen**, New Orleans Saints	.03	.01	.00
☐ 301 **Russell Erxleben**, New Orleans Saints	.03	.01	.00
☐ 302 **Jeff Groth**, New Orleans Saints	.03	.01	.00
☐ 303 **Rickey Jackson**, New Orleans Saints	.03	.01	.00
☐ 304 **Johnnie Poe**, New Orleans Saints	.03	.01	.00
☐ 305 **George Rogers**, New Orleans Saints	.15	.06	.01
☐ 306 **Richard Todd**, New Orleans Saints	.12	.05	.01
☐ 307 **Jim Wilks**, New Orleans Saints	.03	.01	.00
☐ 308 **Dave Wilson**, New Orleans Saints	.12	.05	.01
☐ 309 **Wayne Wilson**, New Orleans Saints	.03	.01	.00
☐ 310 **New York Giants TL** Earnest Gray	.08	.03	.01
☐ 311 **Leon Bright**, New York Giants	.03	.01	.00
☐ 312 **Scott Brunner**, New York Giants	.07	.03	.01
☐ 313 **Rob Carpenter**, New York Giants	.05	.02	.00
☐ 314 **Harry Carson**, New York Giants	.08	.03	.01
☐ 315 **Earnest Gray**, New York Giants	.05	.02	.00
☐ 316 **Ali Haji-Sheikh**, New York Giants	.12	.05	.01
☐ 317 **Mark Haynes**, New York Giants	.05	.02	.00
☐ 318 **Dave Jennings**, New York Giants	.03	.01	.00
☐ 319 **Brian Kelley**, New York Giants	.03	.01	.00
☐ 320 **Phil Simms**, New York Giants	.12	.05	.01
☐ 321 **Lawrence Taylor**, New York Giants	.18	.08	.01
☐ 322 **Lawrence Taylor IR**, New York Giants	.10	.04	.01
☐ 323 **Brad Van Pelt**, New York Giants	.05	.02	.00
☐ 324 **Butch Woolfolk**, New York Giants	.05	.02	.00
☐ 325 **Philadelphia Eagles TL** Mike Quick	.08	.03	.01
☐ 326 **Harold Carmichael**, Philadelphia Eagles	.12	.05	.01
☐ 327 **Herman Edwards**, Philadelphia Eagles	.03	.01	.00
☐ 328 **Michael Haddix**, Philadelphia Eagles	.05	.02	.00
☐ 329 **Dennis Harrison**, Philadelphia Eagles	.03	.01	.00
☐ 330 **Ron Jaworski**, Philadelphia Eagles	.12	.05	.01
☐ 331 **Wilbert Montgomery**, Philadelphia Eagles	.12	.05	.01
☐ 332 **Hubert Oliver**, Philadelphia Eagles	.03	.01	.00
☐ 333 **Mike Quick**, Philadelphia Eagles	.20	.09	.02

		MINT	VG-E	F-G
☐ 334	**Jerry Robinson,** Philadelphia Eagles	.07	.03	.01
☐ 335	**Max Runager,** Philadelphia Eagles	.03	.01	.00
☐ 336	**Michael Williams,** Philadelphia Eagles	.03	.01	.00
☐ 337	**St. Louis Cardinals TL**	.10	.04	.01
	Ottis Anderson			
☐ 338	**Ottis Anderson,** St. Louis Cardinals	.20	.09	.02
☐ 339	**Al Bubba Baker,** St. Louis Cardinals	.05	.02	.00
☐ 340	**Carl Birdsong,** St. Louis Cardinals	.03	.01	.00
☐ 341	**David Galloway,** St. Louis Cardinals	.03	.01	.00
☐ 342	**Roy Green,** St. Louis Cardinals	.10	.04	.01
☐ 343	**Roy Green IR,** St. Louis Cardinals	.06	.02	.00
☐ 344	**Curtis Greer,** St. Louis Cardinals	.06	.02	.00
☐ 345	**Neil Lomax,** St. Louis Cardinals	.12	.05	.01
☐ 346	**Doug Marsh,** St. Louis Cardinals	.05	.02	.00
☐ 347	**Stump Mitchell,** St. Louis Cardinals	.06	.02	.00
☐ 348	**Lionel Washington,** St. Louis Cardinals	.03	.01	.00
☐ 349	**San Francisco 49ers TL**	.08	.03	.01
	Dwight Clark			
☐ 350	**Dwaine Board,** San Francisco 49ers	.03	.01	.00
☐ 351	**Dwight Clark,** San Francisco 49ers	.10	.04	.01
☐ 352	**Dwight Clark IR,** San Francisco 49ers	.06	.02	.00
☐ 353	**Roger Craig,** San Francisco 49ers	.30	.12	.03
☐ 354	**Fred Dean,** San Francisco 49ers	.06	.02	.00
☐ 355	**Fred Dean IR,** San Francisco 49ers	.05	.02	.00
☐ 356	**Dwight Hicks,** San Francisco 49ers	.05	.02	.00
☐ 357	**Ronnie Lott,** San Francisco 49ers	.09	.04	.01
☐ 358	**Joe Montana,** San Francisco 49ers	.45	.20	.04
☐ 359	**Joe Montana IR,** San Francisco 49ers	.25	.10	.02
☐ 360	**Freddie Solomon,** San Francisco 49ers	.05	.02	.00
☐ 361	**Wendell Tyler,** San Francisco 49ers	.07	.03	.01
☐ 362	**Ray Wersching,** San Francisco 49ers	.03	.01	.00
☐ 363	**Eric Wright,** San Francisco 49ers	.03	.01	.00
☐ 364	**Tampa Bay Buccaneers TL**	.08	.03	.01
	Kevin House			
☐ 365	**Gerald Carter,** Tampa Bay Buccaneers	.05	.02	.00
☐ 366	**Hugh Green,** Tampa Bay Buccaneers	.10	.04	.01
☐ 367	**Kevin House,** Tampa Bay Buccaneers	.05	.02	.00
☐ 368	**Michael Morton,** Tampa Bay Buccaneers	.03	.01	.00
☐ 369	**James Owens,** Tampa Bay Buccaneers	.05	.02	.00
☐ 370	**Booker Reese,** Tampa Bay Buccaneers	.03	.01	.00
☐ 371	**Lee Roy Selmon,** Tampa Bay Buccaneers	.15	.06	.01
☐ 372	**Jack Thompson,** Tampa Bay Buccaneers	.10	.04	.01
☐ 373	**James Wilder,** Tampa Bay Buccaneers	.15	.06	.01
☐ 374	**Steve Wilson,** Tampa Bay Buccaneers	.03	.01	.00
☐ 375	**Washington Redskins TL**	.15	.06	.01
	John Riggins			

	MINT	VG-E	F-G
☐ 376 **Jeff Bostic**, Washington Redskins	.03	.01	.00
☐ 377 **Charlie Brown**, Washington Redskins	.10	.04	.01
☐ 378 **Charlie Brown IR**, Washington Redskins	.07	.03	.01
☐ 379 **Dave Butz**, Washington Redskins	.05	.02	.00
☐ 380 **Darrell Green**, Washington Redskins	.08	.03	.01
☐ 381 **Russ Grimm**, Washington Redskins	.03	.01	.00
☐ 382 **Joe Jacoby**, Washington Redskins	.03	.01	.00
☐ 383 **Dexter Manley**, Washington Redskins	.03	.01	.00
☐ 384 **Art Monk**, Washington Redskins	.12	.05	.01
☐ 385 **Mark Moseley**, Washington Redskins	.06	.02	.00
☐ 386 **Mark Murphy**, Washington Redskins	.03	.01	.00
☐ 387 **Mike Nelms**, Washington Redskins	.03	.01	.00
☐ 388 **John Riggins**, Washington Redskins	.20	.09	.02
☐ 389 **John Riggins IR**, Washington Redskins	.12	.05	.01
☐ 390 **Joe Theismann**, Washington Redskins	.35	.15	.03
☐ 391 **Joe Theismann IR**, Washington Redskins	.20	.09	.02
☐ 392 **Don Warren**, Washington Redskins	.03	.01	.00
☐ 393 **Joe Washington**, Washington Redskins	.07	.03	.01

CHECKLISTS

☐ 394 **Checklist 1-132**	.07	.01	.00
☐ 395 **Checklist 133-264**	.07	.01	.00
☐ 396 **Checklist 265-396**	.07	.01	.00

1984 TOPPS USFL

The 1984 Topps USFL set contains 132 cards, which were available as a pre-packaged set from Topps, housed in its own specially made box. The cards are in full color and measure the standard 2½″ by 3½″.

		MINT	VG-E	F-G
	COMPLETE SET	15.00	7.00	1.50
	COMMON PLAYER	.07	.03	.01
☐	1 **Luther Bradley**, Arizona Wranglers	.10	.04	.01
☐	2 **Frank Corral**, Arizona Wranglers	.10	.04	.01
☐	3 **Trumaine Johnson**, Arizona Wranglers	.30	.12	.03
☐	4 **Greg Landry**, Arizona Wranglers	.15	.06	.01
☐	5 **Kit Lathrop**, Arizona Wranglers	.10	.04	.01
☐	6 **Kevin Long**, Arizona Wranglers	.07	.03	.01
☐	7 **Tim Spencer**, Arizona Wranglers	.20	.09	.02
☐	8 **Stan White**, Arizona Wranglers	.07	.03	.01
☐	9 **Buddy Aydelette**, Birmingham Stallions	.10	.04	.01
☐	10 **Tom Banks**, Birmingham Stallions	.07	.03	.01
☐	11 **Fred Bohannon**, Birmingham Stallions	.07	.03	.01
☐	12 **Joe Cribbs**, Birmingham Stallions	.25	.10	.02
☐	13 **Joey Jones**, Birmingham Stallions	.10	.04	.01
☐	14 **Scott Norwood**, Birmingham Stallions	.07	.03	.01
☐	15 **Jim Smith**, Birmingham Stallions	.15	.06	.01
☐	16 **Cliff Stoudt**, Birmingham Stallions	.15	.06	.01
☐	17 **Vince Evans**, Chicago Blitz	.15	.06	.01
☐	18 **Vagas Ferguson**, Chicago Blitz	.15	.06	.01
☐	19 **John Gillen**, Chicago Blitz	.07	.03	.01
☐	20 **Kris Haines**, Chicago Blitz	.07	.03	.01
☐	21 **Glenn Hyde**, Chicago Blitz	.07	.03	.01
☐	22 **Mark Keel**, Chicago Blitz	.07	.03	.01
☐	23 **Gary Lewis**, Chicago Blitz	.07	.03	.01
☐	24 **Doug Plank**, Chicago Blitz	.15	.06	.01
☐	25 **Neil Balholm**, Denver Gold	.07	.03	.01
☐	26 **David Dumars**, Denver Gold	.07	.03	.01
☐	27 **David Martin**, Denver Gold	.15	.06	.01
☐	28 **Craig Penrose**, Denver Gold	.15	.06	.01
☐	29 **Dave Stalls**, Denver Gold	.10	.04	.01
☐	30 **Harry Sydney**, Denver Gold	.07	.03	.01
☐	31 **Vincent White**, Denver Gold	.07	.03	.01
☐	32 **George Yarno**, Denver Gold	.07	.03	.01
☐	33 **Kiki DeAyala**, Houston Gamblers	.15	.06	.01
☐	34 **Sam Harrell**, Houston Gamblers	.07	.03	.01
☐	35 **Mike Hawkins**, Houston Gamblers	.07	.03	.01
☐	36 **Jim Kelly**, Houston Gamblers	1.00	.45	.10
☐	37 **Mark Rush**, Houston Gamblers	.07	.03	.01
☐	38 **Ricky Sanders**, Houston Gamblers	.07	.03	.01
☐	39 **Paul Bergmann**, Jacksonville Bulls	.07	.03	.01

			MINT	VG-E	F-G
☐	40	**Tom Dinkel**, Jacksonville Bulls	.07	.03	.01
☐	41	**Wyatt Henderson**, Jacksonville Bulls	.07	.03	.01
☐	42	**Vaughan Johnson**, Jacksonville Bulls	.07	.03	.01
☐	43	**Willie McClendon**, Jacksonville Bulls	.07	.03	.01
☐	44	**Matt Robinson**, Jacksonville Bulls	.15	.06	.01
☐	45	**George Achica**, Los Angeles Express	.10	.04	.01
☐	46	**Mark Adickes**, Los Angeles Express	.10	.04	.01
☐	47	**Howard Carson**, Los Angeles Express	.10	.04	.01
☐	48	**Kevin Nelson**, Los Angeles Express	.07	.03	.01
☐	49	**Jeff Partridge**, Los Angeles Express	.07	.03	.01
☐	50	**Jo Jo Townsell**, Los Angeles Express	.15	.06	.01
☐	51	**Eddie Weaver**, Los Angeles Express	.07	.03	.01
☐	52	**Steve Young**, Los Angeles Express	.65	.30	.06
☐	53	**Derrick Crawford**, Memphis Showboats	.10	.04	.01
☐	54	**Walter Lewis**, Memphis Showboats	.15	.06	.01
☐	55	**Phil McKinnely**, Memphis Showboats	.07	.03	.01
☐	56	**Vic Minore**, Memphis Showboats	.07	.03	.01
☐	57	**Gary Shirk**, Memphis Showboats	.10	.04	.01
☐	58	**Reggie White**, Memphis Showboats	.25	.10	.02
☐	59	**Anthony Carter**, Michigan Panthers	.35	.15	.03
☐	60	**John Corker**, Michigan Panthers	.20	.09	.02
☐	61	**David Greenwood**, Michigan Panthers	.10	.04	.01
☐	62	**Bobby Hebert**, Michigan Panthers	.40	.18	.04
☐	63	**Derek Holloway**, Michigan Panthers	.07	.03	.01
☐	64	**Ken Lacy**, Michigan Panthers	.15	.06	.01
☐	65	**Tyrone McGriff**, Michigan Panthers	.10	.04	.01
☐	66	**Ray Pinney**, Michigan Panthers	.10	.04	.01
☐	67	**Gary Barbaro**, New Jersey Generals	.15	.06	.01
☐	68	**Sam Bowers**, New Jersey Generals	.07	.03	.01
☐	69	**Clarence Collins**, New Jersey Generals	.10	.04	.01
☐	70	**Willie Harper**, New Jersey Generals	.10	.04	.01
☐	71	**Jim LeClair**, New Jersey Generals	.10	.04	.01
☐	72	**Bob Leopold**, New Jersey Generals	.07	.03	.01
☐	73	**Brian Sipe**, New Jersey Generals	.25	.10	.02
☐	74	**Herschel Walker**, New Jersey Generals	2.00	.90	.20
☐	75	**Junior Ah You**, New Orleans Breakers	.07	.03	.01
☐	76	**Marcus Dupree**, New Orleans Breakers	.30	.12	.03
☐	77	**Marcus Marek**, New Orleans Breakers	.15	.06	.01
☐	78	**Tim Mazzetti**, New Orleans Breakers	.10	.04	.01
☐	79	**Mike Robinson**, New Orleans Breakers	.07	.03	.01
☐	80	**Dan Ross**, New Orleans Breakers	.15	.06	.01
☐	81	**Mark Schellen**, New Orleans Breakers	.07	.03	.01
☐	82	**Johnnie Walton**, New Orleans Breakers	.10	.04	.01
☐	83	**Gordon Banks**, Oakland Invaders	.10	.04	.01
☐	84	**Fred Besana**, Oakland Invaders	.10	.04	.01

		MINT	VG-E	F-G
☐ 85	**Dave Browning,** Oakland Invaders	.07	.03	.01
☐ 86	**Eric Jordan,** Oakland Invaders	.07	.03	.01
☐ 87	**Frank Manumaleuga,** Oakland Invaders	.07	.03	.01
☐ 88	**Gary Plummer,** Oakland Invaders	.07	.03	.01
☐ 89	**Stan Talley,** Oakland Invaders	.10	.04	.01
☐ 90	**Arthur Whittington,** Oakland Invaders	.10	.04	.01
☐ 91	**Terry Beeson,** Oklahoma Outlaws	.07	.03	.01
☐ 92	**Mel Gray,** Oklahoma Outlaws	.10	.04	.01
☐ 93	**Mike Katolin,** Oklahoma Outlaws	.07	.03	.01
☐ 94	**Dewey McClain,** Oklahoma Outlaws	.07	.03	.01
☐ 95	**Sidney Thornton,** Oklahoma Outlaws	.10	.04	.01
☐ 96	**Doug Williams,** Oklahoma Outlaws	.20	.09	.02
☐ 97	**Kelvin Bryant,** Philadelphia Stars	.35	.15	.03
☐ 98	**John Bunting,** Philadelphia Stars	.07	.03	.01
☐ 99	**Irv Eatman,** Philadelphia Stars	.20	.09	.02
☐ 100	**Scott Fitzkee,** Philadelphia Stars	.10	.04	.01
☐ 101	**Chuck Fusina,** Philadelphia Stars	.20	.09	.02
☐ 102	**Sean Landeta,** Philadelphia Stars	.10	.04	.01
☐ 103	**David Trout,** Philadelphia Stars	.07	.03	.01
☐ 104	**Scott Woerner,** Philadelphia Stars	.07	.03	.01
☐ 105	**Glenn Carano,** Pittsburgh Maulers	.15	.06	.01
☐ 106	**Ron Crosby,** Pittsburgh Maulers	.07	.03	.01
☐ 107	**Jerry Holmes,** Pittsburgh Maulers	.15	.06	.01
☐ 108	**Bruce Huther,** Pittsburgh Maulers	.07	.03	.01
☐ 109	**Mike Rozier,** Pittsburgh Maulers	.50	.22	.05
☐ 110	**Larry Swider,** Pittsburgh Maulers	.07	.03	.01
☐ 111	**Danny Buggs,** San Antonio Gunslingers	.10	.04	.01
☐ 112	**Putt Choate,** San Antonio Gunslingers	.07	.03	.01
☐ 113	**Rich Garza,** San Antonio Gunslingers	.07	.03	.01
☐ 114	**Joey Hackett,** San Antonio Gunslingers	.07	.03	.01
☐ 115	**Rick Neuheisel,** San Antonio Gunslingers	.15	.06	.01
☐ 116	**Mike St. Clair,** San Antonio Gunslingers	.07	.03	.01
☐ 117	**Gary Anderson,** Tampa Bay Bandits	.40	.18	.04
☐ 118	**Zenon Andrusyshyn,** Tampa Bay Bandits	.10	.04	.01
☐ 119	**Doug Beaudoin,** Tampa Bay Bandits	.07	.03	.01
☐ 120	**Mike Butler,** Tampa Bay Bandits	.07	.03	.01
☐ 121	**Willie Gillespie,** Tampa Bay Bandits	.10	.04	.01
☐ 122	**Fred Nordgren,** Tampa Bay Bandits	.10	.04	.01
☐ 123	**John Reaves,** Tampa Bay Bandits	.15	.06	.01
☐ 124	**Eric Truvillion,** Tampa Bay Bandits	.15	.06	.01
☐ 125	**Reggie Collier,** Washington Federals	.20	.09	.02
☐ 126	**Mike Guess,** Washington Federals	.07	.03	.01
☐ 127	**Mike Hohensee,** Washington Federals	.10	.04	.01
☐ 128	**Craig James,** Washington Federals	.30	.12	.03
☐ 129	**Eric Robinson,** Washington Federals	.07	.03	.01

			MINT	VG-E	F-G
☐ 130	**Billy Taylor,** Washington Federals	....	.07	.03	.01
☐ 131	**Joey Walters,** Washington Federals	....	.10	.04	.01
☐ 132	**Checklist 1-132**	....	.10	.02	.01

1985 TOPPS

The 1985 Topps Football set contains 396 cards featuring players of the NFL. Cards are standard size, 2½" by 3½". The set is distinguished by the black border on the fronts of the cards, as well as the horizontal orientation of the card fronts. The first six cards in the set recognize record-breaking (RB) achievements during the previous season. The Team Leader (TL) cards are distributed throughout the set as the first card of the team sequence; this year, an action scene is pictured and captioned and the backs contain team scoring information from the previous year.

			MINT	VG-E	F-G
	COMPLETE SET	....	10.00	4.75	1.00
	COMMON PLAYER	....	.03	.01	.00
☐ 1	**RB: Mark Clayton**	....	.12	.03	.01
	Most Touchdown Receptions, Season				
☐ 2	**RB: Eric Dickerson**	....	.18	.08	.01
	Most Yards Rushing, Season				
☐ 3	**RB: Charlie Joiner**	....	.07	.03	.01
	Most Receptions, Career				
☐ 4	**RB: Dan Marino**	....	.20	.09	.02
	Most Touchdown Passes, Season				
☐ 5	**RB: Art Monk**	....	.07	.03	.01
	Most Receptions, Season				

	MINT	VG-E	F-G
☐ 6 **RB: Walter Payton**	.20	.09	.02
Most Yards Rushing, Career			
☐ 7 **NFC Championship**	.07	.03	.01
49ers 23, Bears 0			
(Suhey tackled)			
☐ 8 **AFC Championship**	.07	.03	.01
Dolphins 45, Steelers 28			
(Bennett over)			
☐ 9 **Super Bowl XIX**	.08	.03	.01
49ers 38, Dolphins 16			
(Wendell Tyler)			
☐ 10 **Atlanta Falcons TL**	.06	.02	.00
Stretching For The First Down			
(Gerald Riggs)			
☐ 11 **William Andrews**, Atlanta Falcons	.07	.03	.01
☐ 12 **Stacey Bailey**, Atlanta Falcons	.05	.02	.00
☐ 13 **Steve Bartkowski**, Atlanta Falcons	.10	.04	.01
☐ 14 **Rick Bryan**, Atlanta Falcons	.20	.09	.02
☐ 15 **Alfred Jackson**, Atlanta Falcons	.05	.02	.00
☐ 16 **Kenny Johnson**, Atlanta Falcons	.03	.01	.00
☐ 17 **Mike Kenn**, Atlanta Falcons	.05	.02	.00
☐ 18 **Mike Pitts**, Atlanta Falcons	.05	.02	.00
☐ 19 **Gerald Riggs**, Atlanta Falcons	.08	.03	.01
☐ 20 **Sylvester Stamps**, Atlanta Falcons	.03	.01	.00
☐ 21 **R.C. Thielemann**, Atlanta Falcons	.03	.01	.00
☐ 22 **Chicago Bears TL**	.25	.10	.02
Sweetness Sets Record Straight			
(Walter Payton)			
☐ 23 **Todd Bell**, Chicago Bears	.03	.01	.00
☐ 24 **Richard Dent**, Chicago Bears	.65	.30	.06
☐ 25 **Gary Fencik**, Chicago Bears	.03	.01	.00
☐ 26 **Dave Finzer**, Chicago Bears	.03	.01	.00
☐ 27 **Leslie Frazier**, Chicago Bears	.03	.01	.00
☐ 28 **Steve Fuller**, Chicago Bears	.07	.03	.01
☐ 29 **Willie Gault**, Chicago Bears	.07	.03	.01
☐ 30 **Dan Hampton**, Chicago Bears	.07	.03	.01
☐ 31 **Jim McMahon**, Chicago Bears	.20	.09	.02
☐ 32 **Steve McMichael**, Chicago Bears	.03	.01	.00
☐ 33 **Walter Payton**, Chicago Bears	.45	.20	.04
☐ 34 **Mike Singletary**, Chicago Bears	.12	.05	.01
☐ 35 **Matt Suhey**, Chicago Bears	.03	.01	.00
☐ 36 **Bob Thomas**, Chicago Bears	.03	.01	.00
☐ 37 **Dallas Cowboys TL**	.15	.06	.01
Busting Through The Defense			
(Tony Dorsett)			
☐ 38 **Bill Bates**, Dallas Cowboys	.20	.09	.02

	MINT	VG-E	F-G
☐ 39 **Doug Cosbie**, Dallas Cowboys	.06	.02	.00
☐ 40 **Tony Dorsett**, Dallas Cowboys	.30	.12	.03
☐ 41 **Michael Downs**, Dallas Cowboys	.03	.01	.00
☐ 42 **Mike Hegman**, Dallas Cowboys	.03	.01	.00
☐ 43 **Tony Hill**, Dallas Cowboys	.08	.03	.01
☐ 44 **Gary Hogeboom**, Dallas Cowboys	.15	.06	.01
☐ 45 **Jim Jeffcoat**, Dallas Cowboys	.08	.03	.01
☐ 46 **Ed Too Tall Jones**, Dallas Cowboys	.10	.04	.01
☐ 47 **Mike Renfro**, Dallas Cowboys	.03	.01	.00
☐ 48 **Rafael Septien**, Dallas Cowboys	.07	.03	.01
☐ 49 **Dennis Thurman**, Dallas Cowboys	.03	.01	.00
☐ 50 **Everson Walls**, Dallas Cowboys	.06	.02	.00
☐ 51 **Danny White**, Dallas Cowboys	.15	.06	.01
☐ 52 **Randy White**, Dallas Cowboys	.15	.06	.01
☐ 53 **Detroit Lions TL**	.06	.02	.00
Popping One Loose			
(Lions' Defense)			
☐ 54 **Jeff Chadwick**, Detroit Lions	.05	.02	.01
☐ 55 **Mike Cofer**, Detroit Lions	.03	.01	.00
☐ 56 **Gary Danielson**, Detroit Lions	.07	.03	.01
☐ 57 **Keith Dorney**, Detroit Lions	.03	.01	.00
☐ 58 **Doug English**, Detroit Lions	.05	.02	.01
☐ 59 **William Gay**, Detroit Lions	.03	.01	.00
☐ 60 **Ken Jenkins**, Detroit Lions	.03	.01	.00
☐ 61 **James Jones**, Detroit Lions	.07	.03	.01
☐ 62 **Ed Murray**, Detroit Lions	.03	.01	.00
☐ 63 **Billy Sims**, Detroit Lions	.10	.04	.01
☐ 64 **Leonard Thompson**, Detroit Lions	.05	.02	.01
☐ 65 **Bobby Watkins**, Detroit Lions	.03	.01	.00
☐ 66 **Green Bay Packers TL**	.07	.03	.01
Spotting His Deep Receiver			
(Lynn Dickey)			
☐ 67 **Paul Coffman**, Green Bay Packers	.03	.01	.00
☐ 68 **Lynn Dickey**, Green Bay Packers	.10	.04	.01
☐ 69 **Mike Douglass**, Green Bay Packers	.03	.01	.00
☐ 70 **Tom Flynn**, Green Bay Packers	.08	.03	.01
☐ 71 **Eddie Lee Ivery**, Green Bay Packers	.08	.03	.01
☐ 72 **Ezra Johnson**, Green Bay Packers	.03	.01	.00
☐ 73 **Mark Lee**, Green Bay Packers	.03	.01	.00
☐ 74 **Tim Lewis**, Green Bay Packers	.06	.02	.00
☐ 75 **James Lofton**, Green Bay Packers	.10	.04	.01
☐ 76 **Bucky Scribner**, Green Bay Packers	.03	.01	.00
☐ 77 **Los Angeles Rams TL**	.15	.06	.01
Record-Setting Ground Attack			
(Eric Dickerson)			
☐ 78 **Nolan Cromwell**, Los Angeles Rams	.06	.02	.00

			MINT	VG-E	F-G
☐	79	**Eric Dickerson**, Los Angeles Rams	.50	.22	.05
☐	80	**Henry Ellard**, Los Angeles Rams	.10	.04	.01
☐	81	**Kent Hill**, Los Angeles Rams	.03	.01	.00
☐	82	**LeRoy Irvin**, Los Angeles Rams	.03	.01	.00
☐	83	**Jeff Kemp**, Los Angeles Rams	.07	.03	.01
☐	84	**Mike Lansford**, Los Angeles Rams	.03	.01	.00
☐	85	**Barry Redden**, Los Angeles Rams	.03	.01	.00
☐	86	**Jackie Slater**, Los Angeles Rams	.03	.01	.00
☐	87	**Doug Smith**, Los Angeles Rams	.03	.01	.00
☐	88	**Jack Youngblood**, Los Angeles Rams	.08	.03	.01
☐	89	**Minnesota Vikings TL** Smothering The Opposition (Vikings' Defense)	.06	.02	.00
☐	90	**Alfred Anderson**, Minnesota Vikings	.08	.03	.01
☐	91	**Ted Brown**, Minnesota Vikings	.05	.02	.00
☐	92	**Greg Coleman**, Minnesota Vikings	.03	.01	.00
☐	93	**Tommy Hannon**, Minnesota Vikings	.03	.01	.00
☐	94	**Tommy Kramer**, Minnesota Vikings	.12	.05	.01
☐	95	**Leo Lewis**, Minnesota Vikings	.03	.01	.00
☐	96	**Doug Martin**, Minnesota Vikings	.03	.01	.00
☐	97	**Darrin Nelson**, Minnesota Vikings	.07	.03	.01
☐	98	**Jan Stenerud**, Minnesota Vikings	.06	.02	.00
☐	99	**Sammy White**, Minnesota Vikings	.05	.02	.00
☐	100	**New Orleans Saints TL** Hurdling Over Front Line	.06	.02	.00
☐	101	**Morten Anderson**, New Orleans Saints	.03	.01	.00
☐	102	**Hoby Brenner**, New Orleans Saints	.03	.01	.00
☐	103	**Bruce Clark**, New Orleans Saints	.06	.02	.00
☐	104	**Hokie Gajan**, New Orleans Saints	.06	.02	.00
☐	105	**Brian Hansen**, New Orleans Saints	.06	.02	.00
☐	106	**Rickey Jackson**, New Orleans Saints	.03	.01	.00
☐	107	**George Rogers**, New Orleans Saints	.12	.05	.01
☐	108	**Dave Wilson**, New Orleans Saints	.10	.04	.01
☐	109	**Tyrone Young**, New Orleans Saints	.05	.02	.00
☐	110	**New York Giants TL** Engulfing The Quarterback (Giants' Defense)	.07	.03	.01
☐	111	**Carl Banks**, New York Giants	.05	.02	.00
☐	112	**Jim Burt**, New York Giants	.03	.01	.00
☐	113	**Rob Carpenter**, New York Giants	.05	.02	.00
☐	114	**Harry Carson**, New York Giants	.08	.03	.01
☐	115	**Ernest Gray**, New York Giants	.05	.02	.00
☐	116	**Ali Haji-Sheikh**, New York Giants	.05	.02	.00
☐	117	**Mark Haynes**, New York Giants	.05	.02	.00
☐	118	**Bobby Johnson**, New York Giants	.03	.01	.00
☐	119	**Lionel Manuel**, New York Giants	.12	.05	.01

	MINT	VG-E	F-G
☐ 120 **Joe Morris**, New York Giants	.15	.06	.01
☐ 121 **Zeke Mowatt**, New York Giants	.03	.01	.00
☐ 122 **Jeff Rutledge**, New York Giants	.07	.03	.01
☐ 123 **Phil Simms**, New York Giants	.12	.05	.01
☐ 124 **Lawrence Taylor**, New York Giants	.15	.06	.01
☐ 125 **Philadelphia Eagles TL**	.07	.03	.01
Finding The Wide Open Spaces			
(Wilbert Montgomery)			
☐ 126 **Greg Brown**, Philadelphia Eagles	.03	.01	.00
☐ 127 **Ray Ellis**, Philadelphia Eagles	.03	.01	.00
☐ 128 **Dennis Harrison**, Philadelphia Eagles	.03	.01	.00
☐ 129 **Wes Hopkins**, Philadelphia Eagles	.08	.03	.01
☐ 130 **Mike Horan**, Philadelphia Eagles	.03	.01	.00
☐ 131 **Kenny Jackson**, Philadelphia Eagles	.10	.04	.01
☐ 132 **Ron Jaworski**, Philadelphia Eagles	.10	.04	.01
☐ 133 **Paul McFadden**, Philadelphia Eagles	.03	.01	.00
☐ 134 **Wilbert Montgomery**, Philadelphia Eagles	.08	.03	.01
☐ 135 **Mike Quick**, Philadelphia Eagles	.08	.03	.01
☐ 136 **John Spagnola**, Philadelphia Eagles	.03	.01	.00
☐ 137 **St. Louis Cardinals TL**	.08	.03	.01
Exploiting The Air Route			
(Neil Lomax)			
☐ 138 **Ottis Anderson**, St. Louis Cardinals	.15	.06	.01
☐ 139 **Al Bubba Baker**, St. Louis Cardinals	.06	.02	.00
☐ 140 **Roy Green**, St. Louis Cardinals	.08	.03	.01
☐ 141 **Curtis Greer**, St. Louis Cardinals	.07	.03	.01
☐ 142 **E.J. Junior**, St. Louis Cardinals	.07	.03	.01
☐ 143 **Neil Lomax**, St. Louis Cardinals	.12	.05	.01
☐ 144 **Stump Mitchell**, St. Louis Cardinals	.06	.02	.00
☐ 145 **Neil O'Donoghue**, St. Louis Cardinals	.03	.01	.00
☐ 146 **Pat Tilley**, St. Louis Cardinals	.06	.02	.00
☐ 147 **Lionel Washington**, St. Louis Cardinals	.03	.01	.00
☐ 148 **San Francisco 49ers TL**	.15	.06	.01
The Road To Super Bowl XIX			
(Joe Montana)			
☐ 149 **Dwaine Board**, San Francisco 49ers	.03	.01	.00
☐ 150 **Dwight Clark**, San Francisco 49ers	.07	.03	.01
☐ 151 **Roger Craig**, San Francisco 49ers	.10	.04	.01
☐ 152 **Randy Cross**, San Francisco 49ers	.03	.01	.00
☐ 153 **Fred Dean**, San Francisco 49ers	.07	.03	.01
☐ 154 **Keith Fahnhorst**, San Francisco 49ers	.03	.01	.00
☐ 155 **Dwight Hicks**, San Francisco 49ers	.05	.02	.01
☐ 156 **Ronnie Lott**, San Francisco 49ers	.07	.03	.01
☐ 157 **Joe Montana**, San Francisco 49ers	.30	.12	.03
☐ 158 **Renaldo Nehemiah**, San Francisco 49ers	.07	.03	.01
☐ 159 **Fred Quillan**, San Francisco 49ers	.03	.01	.00

		MINT	VG-E	F-G
☐ 160	**Jack Reynolds**, San Francisco 49ers	.05	.02	.00
☐ 161	**Freddie Solomon**, San Francisco 49ers	.05	.02	.00
☐ 162	**Keena Turner**, San Francisco 49ers	.03	.01	.00
☐ 163	**Wendell Tyler**, San Francisco 49ers	.07	.03	.01
☐ 164	**Ray Wersching**, San Francisco 49ers	.03	.01	.00
☐ 165	**Carlton Williamson**, San Francisco 49ers	.03	.01	.00
☐ 166	**Tampa Bay Buccaneers TL** .... Protecting The Quarterback (Steve DeBerg)	.07	.03	.01
☐ 167	**Gerald Carter**, Tampa Bay Buccaneers	.05	.02	.00
☐ 168	**Mark Cotney**, Tampa Bay Buccaneers	.03	.01	.00
☐ 169	**Steve DeBerg**, Tampa Bay Buccaneers	.08	.03	.01
☐ 170	**Sean Farrell**, Tampa Bay Buccaneers	.03	.01	.00
☐ 171	**Hugh Green**, Tampa Bay Buccaneers	.09	.04	.01
☐ 172	**Kevin House**, Tampa Bay Buccaneers	.05	.02	.00
☐ 173	**David Logan**, Tampa Bay Buccaneers	.03	.01	.00
☐ 174	**Michael Morton**, Tampa Bay Buccaneers	.03	.01	.00
☐ 175	**Lee Roy Selmon**, Tampa Bay Buccaneers	.12	.05	.01
☐ 176	**James Wilder**, Tampa Bay Buccaneers	.15	.06	.01
☐ 177	**Washington Redskins TL** .... A Diesel Named Desire (John Riggins)	.12	.05	.01
☐ 178	**Charlie Brown**, Washington Redskins	.08	.03	.01
☐ 179	**Monte Coleman**, Washington Redskins	.03	.01	.00
☐ 180	**Vernon Dean**, Washington Redskins	.03	.01	.00
☐ 181	**Darrell Green**, Washington Redskins	.07	.03	.01
☐ 182	**Russ Grimm**, Washington Redskins	.05	.02	.00
☐ 183	**Joe Jacoby**, Washington Redskins	.05	.02	.00
☐ 184	**Dexter Manley**, Washington Redskins	.03	.01	.00
☐ 185	**Art Monk**, Washington Redskins	.10	.04	.01
☐ 186	**Mark Moseley**, Washington Redskins	.06	.02	.00
☐ 187	**Calvin Muhammad**, Washington Redskins	.05	.02	.00
☐ 188	**Mike Nelms**, Washington Redskins	.03	.01	.00
☐ 189	**John Riggins**, Washington Redskins	.18	.08	.01
☐ 190	**Joe Theismann**, Washington Redskins	.20	.09	.02
☐ 191	**Joe Washington**, Washington Redskins	.07	.03	.01

LEAGUE LEADERS

		MINT	VG-E	F-G
☐ 192	**Passing Leaders** .... Dan Marino Joe Montana	.25	.10	.02
☐ 193	**Receiving Leaders** .... Ozzie Newsome Art Monk	.08	.03	.01

	MINT	VG-E	F-G
☐ 194 **Rushing Leaders**	.15	.06	.01
Earnest Jackson			
Eric Dickerson			
☐ 195 **Scoring Leaders**	.05	.02	.00
Gary Anderson			
Ray Wersching			
☐ 196 **Interception Leaders**	.05	.02	.00
Kenny Easley			
Tom Flynn			
☐ 197 **Punting Leaders**	.05	.02	.00
Jim Arnold			
Brian Hansen			
☐ 198 **Buffalo Bills TL**	.07	.03	.01
Rushing Toward Rookie Stardom			
(Greg Bell)			
☐ 199 **Greg Bell,** Buffalo Bills	.30	.12	.03
☐ 200 **Preston Dennard,** Buffalo Bills	.03	.01	.00
☐ 201 **Joe Ferguson,** Buffalo Bills	.10	.04	.01
☐ 202 **Byron Franklin,** Buffalo Bills	.03	.01	.00
☐ 203 **Steve Freeman,** Buffalo Bills	.03	.01	.00
☐ 204 **Jim Haslett,** Buffalo Bills	.03	.01	.00
☐ 205 **Charles Romes,** Buffalo Bills	.03	.01	.00
☐ 206 **Fred Smerlas,** Buffalo Bills	.05	.02	.00
☐ 207 **Darryl Talley,** Buffalo Bills	.05	.02	.00
☐ 208 **Van Williams,** Buffalo Bills	.03	.01	.00
☐ 209 **Cincinnati Bengals TL**	.08	.03	.01
Advancing The Ball Downfield			
(Anderson/Kinnebrew)			
☐ 210 **Ken Anderson,** Cincinnati Bengals	.15	.06	.01
☐ 211 **Jim Breech,** Cincinnati Bengals	.03	.01	.00
☐ 212 **Louis Breeden,** Cincinnati Bengals	.03	.01	.00
☐ 213 **James Brooks,** Cincinnati Bengals	.05	.02	.00
☐ 214 **Ross Browner,** Cincinnati Bengals	.06	.02	.00
☐ 215 **Eddie Edwards,** Cincinnati Bengals	.03	.01	.00
☐ 216 **M.L. Harris,** Cincinnati Bengals	.03	.01	.00
☐ 217 **Bobby Kemp,** Cincinnati Bengals	.03	.01	.00
☐ 218 **Larry Kinnebrew,** Cincinnati Bengals	.06	.02	.00
☐ 219 **Anthony Munoz,** Cincinnati Bengals	.07	.03	.01
☐ 220 **Reggie Williams,** Cincinnati Bengals	.05	.02	.00
☐ 221 **Cleveland Browns TL**	.07	.03	.01
Evading The Defensive Pursuit			
(Boyce Green)			
☐ 222 **Matt Bahr,** Cleveland Browns	.05	.02	.00
☐ 223 **Chip Banks,** Cleveland Browns	.06	.02	.00
☐ 224 **Reggie Camp,** Cleveland Browns	.03	.01	.00
☐ 225 **Tom Cousineau,** Cleveland Browns	.08	.03	.01

		MINT	VG-E	F-G
☐ 226	**Joe DeLamielleure,** Cleveland Browns	.05	.02	.00
☐ 227	**Ricky Feacher,** Cleveland Browns	.03	.01	.00
☐ 228	**Boyce Green,** Cleveland Browns	.07	.03	.01
☐ 229	**Al Gross,** Cleveland Browns	.03	.01	.00
☐ 230	**Clay Matthews,** Cleveland Browns	.05	.02	.00
☐ 231	**Paul McDonald,** Cleveland Browns	.06	.02	.00
☐ 232	**Ozzie Newsome,** Cleveland Browns	.08	.03	.01
☐ 233	**Mike Pruitt,** Cleveland Browns	.08	.03	.01
☐ 234	**Don Rogers,** Cleveland Browns	.15	.06	.01
☐ 235	**Denver Broncos TL** Thousand Yarder Gets The Ball (Winder/Elway)	.08	.03	.01
☐ 236	**Rubin Carter,** Denver Broncos	.03	.01	.00
☐ 237	**Barney Chavous,** Denver Broncos	.03	.01	.00
☐ 238	**John Elway,** Denver Broncos	.20	.09	.02
☐ 239	**Steve Foley,** Denver Broncos	.03	.01	.00
☐ 240	**Mike Harden,** Denver Broncos	.03	.01	.00
☐ 241	**Tom Jackson,** Denver Broncos	.05	.02	.00
☐ 242	**Butch Johnson,** Denver Broncos	.06	.02	.00
☐ 243	**Rulon Jones,** Denver Broncos	.03	.01	.00
☐ 244	**Rick Karlis,** Denver Broncos	.03	.01	.00
☐ 245	**Steve Watson,** Denver Broncos	.05	.02	.00
☐ 246	**Gerald Willhite,** Denver Broncos	.06	.02	.00
☐ 247	**Sammy Winder,** Denver Broncos	.10	.04	.01
☐ 248	**Houston Oilers TL** Eluding A Traffic Jam (Larry Moriarty)	.06	.02	.00
☐ 249	**Jesse Baker,** Houston Oilers	.03	.01	.00
☐ 250	**Carter Hartwig,** Houston Oilers	.03	.01	.00
☐ 251	**Warren Moon,** Houston Oilers	.20	.09	.02
☐ 252	**Larry Moriarty,** Houston Oilers	.10	.04	.01
☐ 253	**Mike Munchak,** Houston Oilers	.10	.04	.01
☐ 254	**Carl Roaches,** Houston Oilers	.03	.01	.00
☐ 255	**Tim Smith,** Houston Oilers	.03	.01	.00
☐ 256	**Willie Tullis,** Houston Oilers	.03	.01	.00
☐ 257	**Jamie Williams,** Houston Oilers	.03	.01	.00
☐ 258	**Indianapolis Colts TL** Start Of A Long Gainer (Art Schlichter)	.07	.03	.01
☐ 259	**Raymond Butler,** Indianapolis Colts	.08	.03	.01
☐ 260	**Johnie Cooks,** Indianapolis Colts	.05	.02	.00
☐ 261	**Eugene Daniel,** Indianapolis Colts	.03	.01	.00
☐ 262	**Curtis Dickey,** Indianapolis Colts	.07	.03	.01
☐ 263	**Chris Hinton,** Indianapolis Colts	.05	.02	.00
☐ 264	**Vernon Maxwell,** Indianapolis Colts	.05	.02	.00
☐ 265	**Randy McMillan,** Indianapolis Colts	.06	.02	.00

		MINT	VG-E	F-G
☐ 266 **Art Schlichter**, Indianapolis Colts		.10	.04	.01
☐ 267 **Rohn Stark**, Indianapolis Colts		.03	.01	.00
☐ 268 **Leo Wisniewski**, Indianapolis Colts		.03	.01	.00
☐ 269 **Kansas City Chiefs TL**		.06	.02	.00
Pigskin About To Soar Upward				
(Bill Kenney)				
☐ 270 **Jim Arnold**, Kansas City Chiefs		.03	.01	.00
☐ 271 **Mike Bell**, Kansas City Chiefs		.03	.01	.00
☐ 272 **Todd Blackledge**, Kansas City Chiefs		.20	.09	.02
☐ 273 **Carlos Carson**, Kansas City Chiefs		.05	.02	.00
☐ 274 **Deron Cherry**, Kansas City Chiefs		.05	.02	.00
☐ 275 **Herman Heard**, Kansas City Chiefs		.05	.02	.00
☐ 276 **Bill Kenney**, Kansas City Chiefs		.10	.04	.01
☐ 277 **Nick Lowery**, Kansas City Chiefs		.03	.01	.00
☐ 278 **Bill Maas**, Kansas City Chiefs		.07	.03	.01
☐ 279 **Henry Marshall**, Kansas City Chiefs		.03	.01	.00
☐ 280 **Art Still**, Kansas City Chiefs		.05	.02	.00
☐ 281 **Los Angeles Raiders TL**		.15	.06	.01
Diving For The Goal Line				
(Marcus Allen)				
☐ 282 **Marcus Allen**, Los Angeles Raiders		.25	.10	.02
☐ 283 **Lyle Alzado**, Los Angeles Raiders		.10	.04	.01
☐ 284 **Chris Bahr**, Los Angeles Raiders		.05	.02	.00
☐ 285 **Malcolm Barnwell**, Los Angeles Raiders		.05	.02	.00
☐ 286 **Cliff Branch**, Los Angeles Raiders		.08	.03	.01
☐ 287 **Todd Christensen**, Los Angeles Raiders		.08	.03	.01
☐ 288 **Ray Guy**, Los Angeles Raiders		.07	.03	.01
☐ 289 **Lester Hayes**, Los Angeles Raiders		.06	.02	.00
☐ 290 **Mike Haynes**, Los Angeles Raiders		.08	.03	.01
☐ 291 **Henry Lawrence**, Los Angeles Raiders		.03	.01	.00
☐ 292 **Howie Long**, Los Angeles Raiders		.15	.06	.01
☐ 293 **Rod Martin**, Los Angeles Raiders		.03	.01	.00
☐ 294 **Vann McElroy**, Los Angeles Raiders		.03	.01	.00
☐ 295 **Matt Millen**, Los Angeles Raiders		.05	.02	.00
☐ 296 **Bill Pickel**, Los Angeles Raiders		.03	.01	.00
☐ 297 **Jim Plunkett**, Los Angeles Raiders		.12	.05	.01
☐ 298 **Dokie Williams**, Los Angeles Raiders		.10	.04	.01
☐ 299 **Marc Wilson**, Los Angeles Raiders		.12	.05	.01
☐ 300 **Miami Dolphins TL**		.08	.03	.01
Super Duper Performance				
(Mark Duper)				
☐ 301 **Bob Baumhower**, Miami Dolphins		.06	.02	.00
☐ 302 **Doug Betters**, Miami Dolphins		.06	.02	.00
☐ 303 **Glenn Blackwood**, Miami Dolphins		.03	.01	.00
☐ 304 **Lyle Blackwood**, Miami Dolphins		.03	.01	.00
☐ 305 **Kim Bokamper**, Miami Dolphins		.03	.01	.00

	MINT	VG-E	F-G
☐ 306 **Charles Bowser**, Miami Dolphins	.03	.01	.00
☐ 307 **Jimmy Cefalo**, Miami Dolphins	.03	.01	.00
☐ 308 **Mark Clayton**, Miami Dolphins	.35	.15	.03
☐ 309 **A.J. Duhe**, Miami Dolphins	.07	.03	.01
☐ 310 **Mark Duper**, Miami Dolphins	.12	.05	.01
☐ 311 **Andra Franklin**, Miami Dolphins	.05	.02	.00
☐ 312 **Bruce Hardy**, Miami Dolphins	.03	.01	.00
☐ 313 **Pete Johnson**, Miami Dolphins	.06	.02	.00
☐ 314 **Dan Marino**, Miami Dolphins	.50	.22	.05
☐ 315 **Tony Nathan**, Miami Dolphins	.06	.02	.00
☐ 316 **Ed Newman**, Miami Dolphins	.03	.01	.00
☐ 317 **Reggie Roby**, Miami Dolphins	.06	.02	.00
☐ 318 **Dwight Stephenson**, Miami Dolphins	.05	.02	.00
☐ 319 **Uwe Von Schamann**, Miami Dolphins	.05	.02	.00
☐ 320 **New England Patriots TL**	.06	.02	.00
Refusing To Be Denied (Tony Collins)			
☐ 321 **Raymond Clayborn**, New England Patriots	.05	.02	.00
☐ 322 **Tony Collins**, New England Patriots	.06	.02	.00
☐ 323 **Tony Eason**, New England Patriots	.30	.12	.03
☐ 324 **Tony Franklin**, New England Patriots	.03	.01	.00
☐ 325 **Irving Fryar**, New England Patriots	.20	.09	.02
☐ 326 **John Hannah**, New England Patriots	.08	.03	.01
☐ 327 **Brian Holloway**, New England Patriots	.03	.01	.00
☐ 328 **Craig James**, New England Patriots	.15	.06	.01
☐ 329 **Stanley Morgan**, New England Patriots	.09	.04	.01
☐ 330 **Steve Nelson**, New England Patriots	.03	.01	.00
☐ 331 **Derrick Ramsey**, New England Patriots	.05	.02	.00
☐ 332 **Stephen Starring**, New England Patriots	.05	.02	.00
☐ 333 **Mosi Tatupu**, New England Patriots	.03	.01	.00
☐ 334 **Andre Tippett**, New England Patriots	.10	.04	.01
☐ 335 **New York Jets TL**	.07	.03	.01
Thwarting The Passing Game (Gastineau/Ferguson)			
☐ 336 **Russell Carter**, New York Jets	.15	.06	.01
☐ 337 **Mark Gastineau**, New York Jets	.12	.05	.01
☐ 338 **Bruce Harper**, New York Jets	.03	.01	.00
☐ 339 **Bobby Humphrey**, New York Jets	.03	.01	.00
☐ 340 **Johnny Lam Jones**, New York Jets	.06	.02	.00
☐ 341 **Joe Klecko**, New York Jets	.07	.03	.01
☐ 342 **Pat Leahy**, New York Jets	.03	.01	.00
☐ 343 **Marty Lyons**, New York Jets	.05	.02	.00
☐ 344 **Freeman McNeil**, New York Jets	.15	.06	.01
☐ 345 **Lance Mehl**, New York Jets	.03	.01	.00
☐ 346 **Ken O'Brien**, New York Jets	.30	.12	.03
☐ 347 **Marvin Powell**, New York Jets	.05	.02	.00

	MINT	VG-E	F-G
☐ 348 **Pat Ryan,** New York Jets	.10	.04	.01
☐ 349 **Mickey Shuler,** New York Jets	.03	.01	.00
☐ 350 **Wesley Walker,** New York Jets	.07	.03	.01
☐ 351 **Pittsburgh Steelers TL**	.07	.03	.01
Testing Defensive Pass Coverage			
(Mark Malone)			
☐ 352 **Walter Abercrombie,** Pittsburgh Steelers	.06	.02	.00
☐ 353 **Gary Anderson,** Pittsburgh Steelers	.03	.01	.00
☐ 354 **Robin Cole,** Pittsburgh Steelers	.03	.01	.00
☐ 355 **Bennie Cunningham,** Pittsburgh Steelers	.03	.01	.00
☐ 356 **Rich Erenberg,** Pittsburgh Steelers	.03	.01	.00
☐ 357 **Jack Lambert,** Pittsburgh Steelers	.10	.04	.01
☐ 358 **Louis Lipps,** Pittsburgh Steelers	.35	.15	.03
☐ 359 **Mark Malone,** Pittsburgh Steelers	.10	.04	.01
☐ 360 **Mike Merriweather,** Pittsburgh Steelers	.05	.02	.00
☐ 361 **Frank Pollard,** Pittsburgh Steelers	.03	.01	.00
☐ 362 **Donnie Shell,** Pittsburgh Steelers	.05	.02	.00
☐ 363 **John Stallworth,** Pittsburgh Steelers	.08	.03	.01
☐ 364 **Sam Washington,** Pittsburgh Steelers	.03	.01	.00
☐ 365 **Mike Webster,** Pittsburgh Steelers	.05	.02	.00
☐ 366 **Dwayne Woodruff,** Pittsburgh Steelers	.03	.01	.00
☐ 367 **San Diego Chargers TL**	.06	.02	.00
Jarring The Ball Loose			
(Chargers' Defense)			
☐ 368 **Rolf Benirschke,** San Diego Chargers	.05	.02	.00
☐ 369 **Gil Byrd,** San Diego Chargers	.05	.02	.00
☐ 370 **Wes Chandler,** San Diego Chargers	.07	.03	.01
☐ 371 **Bobby Duckworth,** San Diego Chargers	.03	.01	.00
☐ 372 **Dan Fouts,** San Diego Chargers	.25	.10	.02
☐ 373 **Mike Green,** San Diego Chargers	.03	.01	.00
☐ 374 **Pete Holohan,** San Diego Chargers	.05	.02	.00
☐ 375 **Earnest Jackson,** San Diego Chargers	.20	.09	.02
☐ 376 **Lionel James,** San Diego Chargers	.20	.09	.02
☐ 377 **Charlie Joiner,** San Diego Chargers	.10	.04	.01
☐ 378 **Billy Ray Smith,** San Diego Chargers	.06	.02	.00
☐ 379 **Kellen Winslow,** San Diego Chargers	.10	.04	.01
☐ 380 **Seattle Seahawks TL**	.08	.03	.01
Setting Up For The Air Attack			
(Dave Krieg)			
☐ 381 **Dave Brown,** Seattle Seahawks	.03	.01	.00
☐ 382 **Jeff Bryant,** Seattle Seahawks	.03	.01	.00
☐ 383 **Dan Doornink,** Seattle Seahawks	.03	.01	.00
☐ 384 **Kenny Easley,** Seattle Seahawks	.09	.04	.01
☐ 385 **Jacob Green,** Seattle Seahawks	.07	.03	.01
☐ 386 **David Hughes,** Seattle Seahawks	.03	.01	.00
☐ 387 **Norm Johnson,** Seattle Seahawks	.03	.01	.00

	MINT	VG-E	F-G
☐ 388 **Dave Krieg**, Seattle Seahawks	.15	.06	.01
☐ 389 **Steve Largent**, Seattle Seahawks	.09	.04	.01
☐ 390 **Joe Nash**, Seattle Seahawks	.03	.01	.00
☐ 391 **Daryl Turner**, Seattle Seahawks	.05	.02	.00
☐ 392 **Curt Warner**, Seattle Seahawks	.15	.06	.01
☐ 393 **Fredd Young**, Seattle Seahawks	.10	.04	.01

CHECKLISTS

	MINT	VG-E	F-G
☐ 394 **Checklist 1-132**	.07	.02	.00
☐ 395 **Checklist 133-264**	.07	.02	.00
☐ 396 **Checklist 265-396**	.07	.02	.00

1985 TOPPS USFL

The 1985 Topps USFL set contains 132 cards, which were available as a pre-packaged set from Topps, housed in its own specially made box. The cards are in full color and measure the standard 2½" by 3½". The card backs are printed in red and blue on white card stock. The card fronts have a heavy red border with a blue and white stripe in the middle. Card backs describe each player's highlights of the 1985 USFL spring season.

	MINT	VG-E	F-G
COMPLETE SET	9.50	4.50	.75
COMMON PLAYER	.07	.03	.01
☐ 1 **Case DeBruijn**, Arizona Outlaws	.10	.04	.01

		MINT	VG-E	F-G
☐	2 **Mike Katolin**, Arizona Outlaws	.07	.03	.01
☐	3 **Bruce Laird**, Arizona Outlaws	.07	.03	.01
☐	4 **Kit Lathrop**, Arizona Outlaws	.10	.04	.01
☐	5 **Kevin Long**, Arizona Outlaws	.07	.03	.01
☐	6 **Karl Lorch**, Arizona Outlaws	.07	.03	.01
☐	7 **Dave Tipton**, Arizona Outlaws	.07	.03	.01
☐	8 **Doug Williams**, Arizona Outlaws	.15	.06	.01
☐	9 **Luis Zendejas**, Arizona Outlaws	.15	.06	.02
☐	10 **Kelvin Bryant**, Baltimore Stars	.20	.09	.02
☐	11 **Willie Collier**, Baltimore Stars	.10	.04	.01
☐	12 **Irv Eatman**, Baltimore Stars	.15	.06	.01
☐	13 **Scott Fitzkee**, Baltimore Stars	.10	.04	.01
☐	14 **William Fuller**, Baltimore Stars	.10	.04	.01
☐	15 **Chuck Fusina**, Baltimore Stars	.15	.06	.01
☐	16 **Pete Kugler**, Baltimore Stars	.15	.06	.01
☐	17 **Garcia Lane**, Baltimore Stars	.10	.04	.01
☐	18 **Mike Lush**, Baltimore Stars	.07	.03	.01
☐	19 **Sam Mills**, Baltimore Stars	.10	.04	.01
☐	20 **Buddy Aydelette**, Birmingham Stallions	.10	.04	.01
☐	21 **Joe Cribbs**, Birmingham Stallions	.20	.09	.02
☐	22 **David Dumars**, Birmingham Stallions	.07	.03	.01
☐	23 **Robin Earl**, Birmingham Stallions	.10	.04	.01
☐	24 **Joey Jones**, Birmingham Stallions	.10	.04	.01
☐	25 **Leon Perry**, Birmingham Stallions	.07	.03	.01
☐	26 **Dave Pureifory**, Birmingham Stallions	.07	.03	.01
☐	27 **Bill Roe**, Birmingham Stallions	.07	.03	.01
☐	28 **Doug Smith**, Birmingham Stallions	.10	.04	.01
☐	29 **Cliff Stoudt**, Birmingham Stallions	.15	.06	.01
☐	30 **Jeff Delaney**, Denver Gold	.07	.03	.01
☐	31 **Vince Evans**, Denver Gold	.15	.06	.01
☐	32 **Leonard Harris**, Denver Gold	.07	.03	.01
☐	33 **Bill Johnson**, Denver Gold	.07	.03	.01
☐	34 **Marc Lewis**, Denver Gold	.07	.03	.01
☐	35 **David Martin**, Denver Gold	.10	.04	.01
☐	36 **Bruce Thornton**, Denver Gold	.07	.03	.01
☐	37 **Craig Walls**, Denver Gold	.07	.03	.01
☐	38 **Vincent White**, Denver Gold	.07	.03	.01
☐	39 **Luther Bradley**, Houston Gamblers	.10	.04	.01
☐	40 **Pete Catan**, Houston Gamblers	.07	.03	.01
☐	41 **Kiki DeAyala**, Houston Gamblers	.10	.04	.01
☐	42 **Toni Fritsch**, Houston Gamblers	.10	.04	.01
☐	43 **Sam Harrell**, Houston Gamblers	.07	.03	.01
☐	44 **Richard Johnson**, Houston Gamblers	.15	.06	.01
☐	45 **Jim Kelly**, Houston Gamblers	.40	.18	.04
☐	46 **Gerald McNeil**, Houston Gamblers	.15	.06	.01
☐	47 **Clarence Verdin**, Houston Gamblers	.10	.04	.01

		MINT	VG-E	F-G
☐ 48	**Dale Walters**, Houston Gamblers	.07	.03	.01
☐ 49	**Gary Clark**, Jacksonville Bulls	.07	.03	.01
☐ 50	**Tom Dinkel**, Jacksonville Bulls	.07	.03	.01
☐ 51	**Mike Edwards**, Jacksonville Bulls	.07	.03	.01
☐ 52	**Brian Franco**, Jacksonville Bulls	.07	.03	.01
☐ 53	**Bob Gruber**, Jacksonville Bulls	.07	.03	.01
☐ 54	**Robbie Mahfouz**, Jacksonville Bulls	.07	.03	.01
☐ 55	**Mike Rozier**, Jacksonville Bulls	.25	.10	.02
☐ 56	**Brian Sipe**, Jacksonville Bulls	.15	.06	.01
☐ 57	**J.T. Turner**, Jacksonville Bulls	.07	.03	.01
☐ 58	**Howard Carson**, Los Angeles Express	.10	.04	.01
☐ 59	**Wymon Henderson**, Los Angeles Express	.07	.03	.01
☐ 60	**Kevin Nelson**, Los Angeles Express	.07	.03	.01
☐ 61	**Jeff Partridge**, Los Angeles Express	.07	.03	.01
☐ 62	**Ben Rudolph**, Los Angeles Express	.07	.03	.01
☐ 63	**Jojo Townsell**, Los Angeles Express	.10	.04	.01
☐ 64	**Eddie Weaver**, Los Angeles Express	.07	.03	.01
☐ 65	**Steve Young**, Los Angeles Express	.25	.10	.02
☐ 66	**Tony Zendejas**, Los Angeles Express	.15	.06	.01
☐ 67	**Mossy Cade**, Memphis Showboats	.15	.06	.01
☐ 68	**Leonard Coleman**, Memphis Showboats	.15	.06	.01
☐ 69	**John Corker**, Memphis Showboats	.10	.04	.01
☐ 70	**Derrick Crawford**, Memphis Showboats	.10	.04	.01
☐ 71	**Art Kuehn**, Memphis Showboats	.07	.03	.01
☐ 72	**Walter Lewis**, Memphis Showboats	.15	.06	.01
☐ 73	**Tyrone McGriff**, Memphis Showboats	.10	.04	.01
☐ 74	**Tim Spencer**, Memphis Showboats	.15	.06	.01
☐ 75	**Reggie White**, Memphis Showboats	.15	.06	.01
☐ 76	**Henry Williams**, Memphis Showboats	.07	.03	.01
☐ 77	**Sam Bowers**, New Jersey Generals	.07	.03	.01
☐ 78	**Maurice Carthon**, New Jersey Generals	.20	.09	.02
☐ 79	**Clarence Collins**, New Jersey Generals	.10	.04	.01
☐ 80	**Doug Flutie**, New Jersey Generals	.75	.35	.07
☐ 81	**Freddie Gilbert**, New Jersey Generals	.07	.03	.01
☐ 82	**Kerry Justin**, New Jersey Generals	.07	.03	.01
☐ 83	**Dave Lapham**, New Jersey Generals	.07	.03	.01
☐ 84	**Rick Partridge**, New Jersey Generals	.07	.03	.01
☐ 85	**Roger Ruzek**, New Jersey Generals	.07	.03	.01
☐ 86	**Herschel Walker**, New Jersey Generals	.75	.35	.07
☐ 87	**Gordon Banks**, Oakland Invaders	.10	.04	.01
☐ 88	**Monte Bennett**, Oakland Invaders	.07	.03	.01
☐ 89	**Albert Bentley**, Oakland Invaders	.10	.04	.01
☐ 90	**Novo Bojovic**, Oakland Invaders	.10	.04	.01
☐ 91	**Dave Browning**, Oakland Invaders	.07	.03	.01
☐ 92	**Anthony Carter**, Oakland Invaders	.30	.12	.03
☐ 93	**Bobby Hebert**, Oakland Invaders	.20	.09	.02

		MINT	VG-E	F-G
☐ 94	**Ray Pinney,** Oakland Invaders	.10	.04	.01
☐ 95	**Dan Talley,** Oakland Invaders	.10	.04	.01
☐ 96	**Ruben Vaughan,** Oakland Invaders	.07	.03	.01
☐ 97	**Curtis Bledsoe,** Orlando Renegades	.07	.03	.01
☐ 98	**Reggie Collier,** Orlando Renegades	.15	.06	.01
☐ 99	**Jerry Doerger,** Orlando Renegades	.07	.03	.01
☐ 100	**Jerry Golsteyn,** Orlando Renegades	.10	.04	.01
☐ 101	**Bob Niziolek,** Orlando Renegades	.07	.03	.01
☐ 102	**Joel Patten,** Orlando Renegades	.07	.03	.01
☐ 103	**Ricky Simmons,** Orlando Renegades	.07	.03	.01
☐ 104	**Joey Walters,** Orlando Renegades	.10	.04	.01
☐ 105	**Marcus Dupree,** Portland Breakers	.20	.09	.02
☐ 106	**Jeff Gossett,** Portland Breakers	.07	.03	.01
☐ 107	**Frank Lockett,** Portland Breakers	.07	.03	.01
☐ 108	**Marcus Marek,** Portland Breakers	.10	.04	.01
☐ 109	**Kenny Neil,** Portland Breakers	.07	.03	.01
☐ 110	**Robert Pennywell,** Portland Breakers	.07	.03	.01
☐ 111	**Matt Robinson,** Portland Breakers	.10	.04	.01
☐ 112	**Dan Ross,** Portland Breakers	.10	.04	.01
☐ 113	**Doug Woodward,** Portland Breakers	.07	.03	.01
☐ 114	**Danny Buggs,** San Antonio Gunslingers	.10	.04	.01
☐ 115	**Putt Choate,** San Antonio Gunslingers	.07	.03	.01
☐ 116	**Greg Fields,** San Antonio Gunslingers	.07	.03	.01
☐ 117	**Ken Hartley,** San Antonio Gunslingers	.07	.03	.01
☐ 118	**Nick Mike-Mayer,** San Antonio Gunslingers	.07	.03	.01
☐ 119	**Rick Neuheisel,** San Antonio Gunslingers	.10	.04	.01
☐ 120	**Peter Raeford,** San Antonio Gunslingers	.07	.03	.01
☐ 121	**Gary Worthy,** San Antonio Gunslingers	.07	.03	.01
☐ 122	**Gary Anderson,** Tampa Bay Bandits	.25	.10	.02
☐ 123	**Zenon Andrusyshyn,** Tampa Bay Bandits	.10	.04	.01
☐ 124	**Greg Boone,** Tampa Bay Bandits	.07	.03	.01
☐ 125	**Mike Butler,** Tampa Bay Bandits	.07	.03	.01
☐ 126	**Mike Clark,** Tampa Bay Bandits	.07	.03	.01
☐ 127	**Willie Gillespie,** Tampa Bay Bandits	.10	.04	.01
☐ 128	**James Harrell,** Tampa Bay Bandits	.07	.03	.01
☐ 129	**Marvin Harvey,** Tampa Bay Bandits	.07	.03	.01
☐ 130	**John Reaves,** Tampa Bay Bandits	.10	.04	.01
☐ 131	**Eric Truvillion,** Tampa Bay Bandits	.10	.04	.01
☐ 132	**Checklist 1-132**	.10	.02	.00

1986 TOPPS

The 1986 Topps football set contains 396 cards featuring players of the NFL. Cards are standard size, 2½" by 3½". The set is distinguished by the green border on the fronts of the cards. The first seven cards in the set recognize record-breaking (RB) achievements during the previous season.

			MINT	VG-E	F-G
	COMPLETE SET		10.00	4.75	1.00
	COMMON PLAYER		.03	.01	.00
☐	1	RB: **Marcus Allen,** Los Angeles Raiders	.16	.05	.01
		Most Yards From Scrimmage, Season			
☐	2	RB: **Eric Dickerson,** Los Angeles Rams	.15	.06	.01
		Most Yards Rushing, Playoff Game			
☐	3	RB: **Lionel James,** San Diego Chargers	.05	.02	.00
		Most All-Purpose Yards, Season			
☐	4	RB: **Steve Largent,** Seattle Seahawks	.06	.02	.00
		Most Seasons, 50 or More Receptions			
☐	5	RB: **George Martin,** New York Giants	.05	.02	.00
		Most Touchdowns, Def. Lineman, Career			
☐	6	RB: **Stephone Paige,** Kansas City Chiefs	.05	.02	.00
		Most Yards Receiving, Game			
☐	7	RB: **Walter Payton,** Chicago Bears	.15	.06	.01
		Most Consecutive Games, 100 or More Yards Rushing			

		MINT	VG-E	F-G
☐	8 Super Bowl XX	.06	.02	.00
	Bears 46, Patriots 10			
☐	9 Chicago Bears Team Card	.09	.03	.01
☐	10 Jim McMahon, Chicago Bears	.18	.08	.02
☐	11 Walter Payton AP, Chicago Bears	.40	.18	.04
☐	12 Matt Suhey, Chicago Bears	.03	.01	.00
☐	13 William Gault, Chicago Bears	.06	.02	.00
☐	14 Dennis McKinnon, Chicago Bears	.03	.01	.00
☐	15 Emery Moorehead, Chicago Bears	.03	.01	.00
☐	16 Jim Covert AP, Chicago Bears	.15	.06	.01
☐	17 Jay Hilgenberg AP, Chicago Bears	.10	.04	.01
☐	18 Kevin Butler, Chicago Bears	.03	.01	.00
☐	19 Richard Dent AP, Chicago Bears	.10	.04	.01
☐	20 William Perry, Chicago Bears	.90	.35	.08
☐	21 Steve McMichael, Chicago Bears	.03	.01	.00
☐	22 Dan Hampton, Chicago Bears	.06	.02	.00
☐	23 Otis Wilson, Chicago Bears	.06	.02	.00
☐	24 Mike Singletary, Chicago Bears	.10	.04	.01
☐	25 Wilber Marshall, Chicago Bears	.06	.02	.00
☐	26 Leslie Frazier, Chicago Bears	.03	.01	.00
☐	27 Dave Duerson, Chicago Bears	.03	.01	.00
☐	28 Gary Fencik, Chicago Bears	.03	.01	.00
☐	29 New England Patriots Team Card	.06	.02	.00
☐	30 Tony Eason, New England Patriots	.10	.04	.01
☐	31 Steve Grogan, New England Patriots	.07	.03	.01
☐	32 Craig James, New England Patriots	.10	.04	.01
☐	33 Tony Collins, New England Patriots	.06	.02	.00
☐	34 Irving Fryar, New England Patriots	.09	.03	.01
☐	35 Brian Holloway AP, New England Patriots	.05	.02	.00
☐	36 John Hannah AP, New England Patriots	.06	.02	.00
☐	37 Tony Franklin, New England Patriots	.03	.01	.00
☐	38 Garin Veris, New England Patriots	.06	.02	.00
☐	39 Andre Tippett AP, New England Patriots	.07	.03	.01
☐	40 Steve Nelson, New England Patriots	.03	.01	.00
☐	41 Raymond Clayborn, New England Patriots	.03	.01	.00
☐	42 Fred Marion, New England Patriots	.03	.01	.00
☐	43 Rich Camarillo, New England Patriots	.03	.01	.00
☐	44 Miami Dolphins Team Card	.06	.02	.00
☐	45 Dan Marino AP, Miami Dolphins	.40	.18	.04
☐	46 Tony Nathan, Miami Dolphins	.05	.02	.00
☐	47 Ron Davenport, Miami Dolphins	.06	.02	.00
☐	48 Mark Duper, Miami Dolphins	.09	.03	.01
☐	49 Mark Clayton, Miami Dolphins	.09	.03	.01
☐	50 Nat Moore, Miami Dolphins	.05	.02	.00

		MINT	VG-E	F-G
☐ 51	**Bruce Hardy**, Miami Dolphins	.03	.01	.00
☐ 52	**Roy Foster**, Miami Dolphins	.03	.01	.00
☐ 53	**Dwight Stephenson**, Miami Dolphins	.05	.02	.00
☐ 54	**Fuad Reveiz**, Miami Dolphins	.03	.01	.00
☐ 55	**Bob Baumhower**, Miami Dolphins	.06	.02	.00
☐ 56	**Mike Charles**, Miami Dolphins	.03	.01	.00
☐ 57	**Hugh Green**, Miami Dolphins	.07	.03	.01
☐ 58	**Glenn Blackwood**, Miami Dolphins	.03	.01	.00
☐ 59	**Reggie Roby**, Miami Dolphins	.05	.02	.00
☐ 60	**Los Angeles Raiders Team Card**	.06	.02	.00
☐ 61	**Marc Wilson**, Los Angeles Raiders	.08	.03	.01
☐ 62	**Marcus Allen AP**, Los Angeles Raiders	.25	.10	.02
☐ 63	**Dokie Williams**, Los Angeles Raiders	.05	.02	.00
☐ 64	**Todd Christensen**, Los Angeles Raiders	.05	.02	.00
☐ 65	**Chris Bahr**, Los Angeles Raiders	.05	.02	.00
☐ 66	**Fulton Walker**, Los Angeles Raiders	.03	.01	.00
☐ 67	**Howie Long**, Los Angeles Raiders	.09	.03	.01
☐ 68	**Bill Pickel**, Los Angeles Raiders	.03	.01	.00
☐ 69	**Ray Guy**, Los Angeles Raiders	.06	.02	.00
☐ 70	**Greg Townsend**, Los Angeles Raiders	.03	.01	.00
☐ 71	**Rod Martin**, Los Angeles Raiders	.03	.01	.00
☐ 72	**Matt Millen**, Los Angeles Raiders	.03	.01	.00
☐ 73	**Mike Haynes AP**, Los Angeles Raiders	.06	.02	.00
☐ 74	**Lester Hayes**, Los Angeles Raiders	.06	.02	.00
☐ 75	**Vann McElroy**, Los Angeles Raiders	.03	.01	.00
☐ 76	**Los Angeles Rams Team Card**	.06	.02	.00
☐ 77	**Dieter Brock**, Los Angeles Rams	.10	.04	.01
☐ 78	**Eric Dickerson**, Los Angeles Rams	.35	.15	.03
☐ 79	**Henry Ellard**, Los Angeles Rams	.06	.02	.00
☐ 80	**Ron Brown**, Los Angeles Rams	.15	.06	.01
☐ 81	**Tony Hunter**, Los Angeles Rams	.03	.01	.00
☐ 82	**Kent Hill AP**, Los Angeles Rams	.03	.01	.00
☐ 83	**Doug Smith**, Los Angeles Rams	.03	.01	.00
☐ 84	**Dennis Harrah**, Los Angeles Rams	.03	.01	.00
☐ 85	**Jackie Slater**, Los Angeles Rams	.03	.01	.00
☐ 86	**Mike Lansford**, Los Angeles Rams	.03	.01	.00
☐ 87	**Gary Jeter**, Los Angeles Rams	.03	.01	.00
☐ 88	**Mike Wilcher**, Los Angeles Rams	.03	.01	.00
☐ 89	**Jim Collins**, Los Angeles Rams	.03	.01	.00
☐ 90	**LeRoy Irvin**, Los Angeles Rams	.03	.01	.00
☐ 91	**Gary Green**, Los Angeles Rams	.03	.01	.00
☐ 92	**Nolan Cromwell**, Los Angeles Rams	.05	.02	.00
☐ 93	**Dale Hatcher**, Los Angeles Rams	.06	.02	.00
☐ 94	**New York Jets Team Card**	.06	.02	.00
☐ 95	**Ken O'Brien**, New York Jets	.20	.09	.02

		MINT	VG-E	F-G
☐ 96	**Freeman McNeil**, New York Jets	.12	.05	.01
☐ 97	**Tony Paige**, New York Jets	.03	.01	.00
☐ 98	**Johnny Lam Jones**, New York Jets	.05	.02	.00
☐ 99	**Wesley Walker**, New York Jets	.06	.02	.00
☐ 100	**Kurt Sohn**, New York Jets	.03	.01	.00
☐ 101	**Al Toon**, New York Jets	.15	.06	.01
☐ 102	**Mickey Shuler**, New York Jets	.03	.01	.00
☐ 103	**Marvin Powell**, New York Jets	.03	.01	.00
☐ 104	**Pat Leahy**, New York Jets	.03	.01	.00
☐ 105	**Mark Gastineau**, New York Jets	.10	.04	.01
☐ 106	**Joe Klecko AP**, New York Jets	.06	.02	.00
☐ 107	**Marty Lyons**, New York Jets	.05	.02	.00
☐ 108	**Lance Mehl**, New York Jets	.03	.01	.00
☐ 109	**Bobby Jackson**, New York Jets	.03	.01	.00
☐ 110	**Dave Jennings**, New York Jets	.03	.01	.00
☐ 111	**Denver Broncos Team Card**	.06	.02	.00
☐ 112	**John Elway**, Denver Broncos	.18	.08	.02
☐ 113	**Sammy Winder**, Denver Broncos	.07	.03	.01
☐ 114	**Gerald Willhite**, Denver Broncos	.06	.02	.00
☐ 115	**Steve Watson**, Denver Broncos	.05	.02	.00
☐ 116	**Vance Johnson**, Denver Broncos	.06	.02	.00
☐ 117	**Rick Karlis**, Denver Broncos	.03	.01	.00
☐ 118	**Rulon Jones**, Denver Broncos	.03	.01	.00
☐ 119	**Karl Mecklenburg AP**, Denver Broncos	.10	.04	.01
☐ 120	**Louis Wright**, Denver Broncos	.05	.02	.00
☐ 121	**Mark Harden**, Denver Broncos	.03	.01	.00
☐ 122	**Dennis Smith**, Denver Broncos	.03	.01	.00
☐ 123	**Steve Foley**, Denver Broncos	.03	.01	.00
☐ 124	**Dallas Cowboys Team Card**	.07	.03	.01
☐ 125	**Danny White**, Dallas Cowboys	.12	.05	.01
☐ 126	**Tony Dorsett**, Dallas Cowboys	.25	.10	.02
☐ 127	**Timmy Newsome**, Dallas Cowboys	.03	.01	.00
☐ 128	**Mike Renfro**, Dallas Cowboys	.03	.01	.00
☐ 129	**Tony Hill**, Dallas Cowboys	.06	.02	.00
☐ 130	**Doug Cosbie**, Dallas Cowboys	.06	.02	.00
☐ 131	**Rafael Septien**, Dallas Cowboys	.06	.02	.00
☐ 132	**Ed "Too-Tall" Jones**, Dallas Cowboys	.08	.03	.01
☐ 133	**Randy White**, Dallas Cowboys	.10	.04	.01
☐ 134	**Jim Jeffcoat**, Dallas Cowboys	.05	.02	.00
☐ 135	**Everson Walls AP**, Dallas Cowboys	.06	.02	.00
☐ 136	**Dennis Thurman**, Dallas Cowboys	.03	.01	.00
☐ 137	**New York Giants Team Card**	.06	.02	.00
☐ 138	**Phil Simms**, New York Giants	.09	.03	.01
☐ 139	**Joe Morris**, New York Giants	.09	.03	.01
☐ 140	**George Adams**, New York Giants	.09	.03	.01
☐ 141	**Lionel Manuel**, New York Giants	.06	.02	.00

		MINT	VG-E	F-G
☐ 142	**Bobby Johnson,** New York Giants	.03	.01	.00
☐ 143	**Phil McConkey,** New York Giants	.03	.01	.00
☐ 144	**Mark Bavaro,** New York Giants	.06	.02	.00
☐ 145	**Zeke Mowatt,** New York Giants	.03	.01	.00
☐ 146	**Brad Benson,** New York Giants	.03	.01	.00
☐ 147	**Bart Oates,** New York Giants	.03	.01	.00
☐ 148	**Leonard Marshall AP,** New York Giants	.06	.02	.00
☐ 149	**Jim Burt,** New York Giants	.03	.01	.00
☐ 150	**George Martin,** New York Giants	.03	.01	.00
☐ 151	**Lawrence Taylor AP,** New York Giants	.10	.04	.01
☐ 152	**Harry Carson AP,** New York Giants	.06	.02	.00
☐ 153	**Elvis Patterson,** New York Giants	.03	.01	.00
☐ 154	**Sean Landeta,** New York Giants	.03	.01	.00
☐ 155	**San Francisco 49ers Team Card**	.06	.02	.00
☐ 156	**Joe Montana,** San Francisco 49ers	.30	.12	.03
☐ 157	**Roger Craig,** San Francisco 49ers	.08	.03	.01
☐ 158	**Wendell Tyler,** San Francisco 49ers	.06	.02	.00
☐ 159	**Carl Monroe,** San Francisco 49ers	.03	.01	.00
☐ 160	**Dwight Clark,** San Francisco 49ers	.06	.02	.00
☐ 161	**Jerry Rice,** San Francisco 49ers	.15	.06	.01
☐ 162	**Randy Cross,** San Francisco 49ers	.03	.01	.00
☐ 163	**Keith Fahnhorst,** San Francisco 49ers	.03	.01	.00
☐ 164	**Jeff Stover,** San Francisco 49ers	.03	.01	.00
☐ 165	**Michael Carter,** San Francisco 49ers	.07	.03	.01
☐ 166	**Dwaine Board,** San Francisco 49ers	.03	.01	.00
☐ 167	**Eric Wright,** San Francisco 49ers	.03	.01	.00
☐ 168	**Ronnie Lott,** San Francisco 49ers	.06	.02	.00
☐ 169	**Carlton Williamson,** San Francisco 49ers	.03	.01	.00
☐ 170	**Washington Redskins Team Card**	.06	.02	.00
☐ 171	**Joe Theismann,** Washington Redskins	.15	.06	.01
☐ 172	**Jay Schroeder,** Washington Redskins	.10	.04	.01
☐ 173	**George Rogers,** Washington Redskins	.09	.03	.01
☐ 174	**Ken Jenkins,** Washington Redskins	.03	.01	.00
☐ 175	**Art Monk AP,** Washington Redskins	.06	.02	.00
☐ 176	**Gary Clark,** Washington Redskins	.06	.02	.00
☐ 177	**Joe Jacoby,** Washington Redskins	.03	.01	.00
☐ 178	**Russ Grimm,** Washington Redskins	.03	.01	.00
☐ 179	**Mark Moseley,** Washington Redskins	.05	.02	.00
☐ 180	**Dexter Manley,** Washington Redskins	.03	.01	.00
☐ 181	**Charles Mann,** Washington Redskins	.03	.01	.00
☐ 182	**Vernon Dean,** Washington Redskins	.03	.01	.00
☐ 183	**Raphel Cherry,** Washington Redskins	.06	.02	.00
☐ 184	**Curtis Jordan,** Washington Redskins	.03	.01	.00
☐ 185	**Cleveland Browns Team Card**	.06	.02	.00
☐ 186	**Gary Danielson,** Cleveland Browns	.06	.02	.00
☐ 187	**Bernie Kosar,** Cleveland Browns	.35	.15	.03

	MINT	VG-E	F-G
☐ 188 **Kevin Mack,** Cleveland Browns	.15	.06	.01
☐ 189 **Earnest Byner,** Cleveland Browns	.08	.03	.01
☐ 190 **Glen Young,** Cleveland Browns	.03	.01	.00
☐ 191 **Ozzie Newsome,** Cleveland Browns	.06	.02	.00
☐ 192 **Mike Baab,** Cleveland Browns	.03	.01	.00
☐ 193 **Cody Risien,** Cleveland Browns	.03	.01	.00
☐ 194 **Bob Golic,** Cleveland Browns	.05	.02	.00
☐ 195 **Reggie Camp,** Cleveland Browns	.03	.01	.00
☐ 196 **Chip Banks,** Cleveland Browns	.05	.02	.00
☐ 197 **Tom Cousineau,** Cleveland Browns	.06	.02	.00
☐ 198 **Frank Minnifield,** Cleveland Browns	.05	.02	.00
☐ 199 **Al Gross,** Cleveland Browns	.03	.01	.00
☐ 200 **Seattle Seahawks Team Card**	.06	.02	.00
☐ 201 **Dave Krieg,** Seattle Seahawks	.12	.05	.01
☐ 202 **Curt Warner,** Seattle Seahawks	.10	.04	.01
☐ 203 **Steve Largent AP,** Seattle Seahawks	.08	.03	.01
☐ 204 **Norm Johnson,** Seattle Seahawks	.03	.01	.00
☐ 205 **Daryl Turner,** Seattle Seahawks	.03	.01	.00
☐ 206 **Jacob Green,** Seattle Seahawks	.05	.02	.00
☐ 207 **Joe Nash,** Seattle Seahawks	.03	.01	.00
☐ 208 **Jeff Bryant,** Seattle Seahawks	.03	.01	.00
☐ 209 **Randy Edwards,** Seattle Seahawks	.03	.01	.00
☐ 210 **Fredd Young,** Seattle Seahawks	.05	.02	.00
☐ 211 **Kenny Easley,** Seattle Seahawks	.07	.03	.01
☐ 212 **John Harris,** Seattle Seahawks	.03	.01	.00
☐ 213 **Green Bay Packers Team Card**	.06	.02	.00
☐ 214 **Lynn Dickey,** Green Bay Packers	.08	.03	.01
☐ 215 **Gerry Ellis,** Green Bay Packers	.03	.01	.00
☐ 216 **Eddie Lee Ivery,** Green Bay Packers	.06	.02	.00
☐ 217 **Jessie Clark,** Green Bay Packers	.03	.01	.00
☐ 218 **James Lofton,** Green Bay Packers	.08	.03	.01
☐ 219 **Paul Coffman,** Green Bay Packers	.03	.01	.00
☐ 220 **Alphonso Carreker,** Green Bay Packers	.03	.01	.00
☐ 221 **Ezra Johnson,** Green Bay Packers	.03	.01	.00
☐ 222 **Mike Douglass,** Green Bay Packers	.03	.01	.00
☐ 223 **Tim Lewis,** Green Bay Packers	.06	.02	.00
☐ 224 **Mark Murphy,** Green Bay Packers	.03	.01	.00

LEAGUE LEADERS

	MINT	VG-E	F-G
☐ 225 **Passing Leaders:**	.08	.03	.01

Ken O'Brien AFC, New York Jets
Joe Montana NFC, San Francisco 49ers

		MINT	VG-E	F-G
☐ 226	**Receiving Leaders:**	.06	.02	.00
	Lionel James AFC, San Diego Chargers			
	Roger Craig NFC, San Francisco 49ers			
☐ 227	**Rushing Leaders:**	.10	.04	.00
	Marcus Allen AFC, Los Angeles Raiders			
	Gerald Riggs NFC, Atlanta Falcons			
☐ 228	**Scoring Leaders:**	.05	.02	.00
	Gary Anderson AFC, Pittsburgh Steelers			
	Kevin Butler NFC, Chicago Bears			
☐ 229	**Interception Leaders:**	.05	.02	.00
	Eugene Daniel AFC, Indianapolis Colts			
	Albert Lewis AFC, Kansas City Chiefs			
	Everson Walls NFC, Dallas Cowboys			
☐ 230	**San Diego Chargers Team Card**	.06	.02	.00
☐ 231	**Dan Fouts,** San Diego Chargers	.20	.09	.02
☐ 232	**Lionel James,** San Diego Chargers	.08	.03	.01
☐ 233	**Gary Anderson,** San Diego Chargers	.10	.04	.01
☐ 234	**Tim Spencer,** San Diego Chargers	.06	.02	.00
☐ 235	**Wes Chandler,** San Diego Chargers	.06	.02	.00
☐ 236	**Charlie Joiner,** San Diego Chargers	.08	.03	.01
☐ 237	**Kellen Winslow,** San Diego Chargers	.08	.03	.01
☐ 238	**Jim Lachey,** San Diego Chargers	.03	.01	.00
☐ 239	**Bob Thomas,** San Diego Chargers	.03	.01	.00
☐ 240	**Jeffrey Dale,** San Diego Chargers	.03	.01	.00
☐ 241	**Ralph Mojsiejenko,** San Diego Chargers ...	.03	.01	.00
☐ 242	**Detroit Lions Team Card**	.06	.02	.00
☐ 243	**Eric Hipple,** Detroit Lions	.06	.02	.00
☐ 244	**Billy Sims,** Detroit Lions	.09	.03	.01
☐ 245	**James Jones,** Detroit Lions	.05	.02	.00
☐ 246	**Pete Mandley,** Detroit Lions	.03	.01	.00
☐ 247	**Leonard Thompson,** Detroit Lions	.03	.01	.00
☐ 248	**Lomas Brown,** Detroit Lions	.06	.02	.00
☐ 249	**Ed Murray,** Detroit Lions	.03	.01	.00
☐ 250	**Curtis Green,** Detroit Lions	.03	.01	.00
☐ 251	**William Gay,** Detroit Lions	.03	.01	.00
☐ 252	**Jimmy Williams,** Detroit Lions	.03	.01	.00
☐ 253	**Bobby Watkins,** Detroit Lions	.03	.01	.00
☐ 254	**Cincinnati Bengals Team Card**	.06	.02	.00
☐ 255	**Boomer Esiason,** Cincinnati Bengals	.25	.10	.02
☐ 256	**James Brooks,** Cincinnati Bengals	.05	.02	.00
☐ 257	**Larry Kinnebrew,** Cincinnati Bengals	.05	.02	.00
☐ 258	**Cris Collinsworth,** Cincinnati Bengals	.06	.02	.00
☐ 259	**Mike Martin,** Cincinnati Bengals	.03	.01	.00
☐ 260	**Eddie Brown,** Cincinnati Bengals	.20	.09	.02
☐ 261	**Anthony Munoz,** Cincinnati Bengals	.05	.02	.00
☐ 262	**Jim Breech,** Cincinnati Bengals	.03	.01	.00

		MINT	VG-E	F-G
☐ 263	Ross Browner, Cincinnati Bengals	.03	.01	.00
☐ 264	Carl Zander, Cincinnati Bengals	.03	.01	.00
☐ 265	James Griffin, Cincinnati Bengals	.03	.01	.00
☐ 266	Robert Jackson, Cincinnati Bengals	.03	.01	.00
☐ 267	Pat McInally, Cincinnati Bengals	.05	.02	.00
☐ 268	Philadelphia Eagles Team Card	.06	.02	.00
☐ 269	Ron Jaworski, Philadelphia Eagles	.09	.03	.01
☐ 270	Earnest Jackson, Philadelphia Eagles	.06	.02	.00
☐ 271	Mike Quick, Philadelphia Eagles	.07	.03	.01
☐ 272	John Spagnola, Philadelphia Eagles	.03	.01	.00
☐ 273	Mark Dennard, Philadelphia Eagles	.03	.01	.00
☐ 274	Paul McFadden, Philadelphia Eagles	.03	.01	.00
☐ 275	Reggie White, Philadelphia Eagles	.06	.02	.00
☐ 276	Greg Brown, Philadelphia Eagles	.03	.01	.00
☐ 277	Herman Edwards, Philadelphia Eagles	.03	.01	.00
☐ 278	Roynell Young, Philadelphia Eagles	.03	.01	.00
☐ 279	Wes Hopkins AP, Philadelphia Eagles	.05	.02	.00
☐ 280	Pittsburgh Steelers Team Card	.06	.02	.00
☐ 281	Mark Malone, Pittsburgh Steelers	.08	.03	.01
☐ 282	Frank Pollard, Pittsburgh Steelers	.03	.01	.00
☐ 283	Walter Abercrombie, Pittsburgh Steelers	.05	.02	.00
☐ 284	Louis Lipps, Pittsburgh Steelers	.10	.04	.01
☐ 285	John Stallworth, Pittsburgh Steelers	.06	.02	.00
☐ 286	Mike Webster, Pittsburgh Steelers	.05	.02	.00
☐ 287	Gary Anderson AP, Pittsburgh Steelers	.03	.01	.00
☐ 288	Keith Willis, Pittsburgh Steelers	.03	.01	.00
☐ 289	Mike Merriweather, Pittsburgh Steelers	.03	.01	.00
☐ 290	Dwayne Woodruff, Pittsburgh Steelers	.03	.01	.00
☐ 291	Donnie Shell, Pittsburgh Steelers	.05	.02	.00
☐ 292	Minnesota Vikings Team Card	.06	.02	.00
☐ 293	Tommy Kramer, Minnesota Vikings	.09	.03	.01
☐ 294	Darrin Nelson, Minnesota Vikings	.06	.02	.00
☐ 295	Ted Brown, Minnesota Vikings	.05	.02	.00
☐ 296	Buster Rhymes, Minnesota Vikings	.05	.02	.00
☐ 297	Anthony Carter, Minnesota Vikings	.10	.04	.01
☐ 298	Steve Jordan, Minnesota Vikings	.03	.01	.00
☐ 299	Keith Millard, Minnesota Vikings	.03	.01	.00
☐ 300	Joey Browner, Minnesota Vikings	.03	.01	.00
☐ 301	John Turner, Minnesota Vikings	.03	.01	.00
☐ 302	Greg Coleman, Minnesota Vikings	.03	.01	.00
☐ 303	Kansas City Chiefs Team Card	.06	.02	.00
☐ 304	Bill Kenney, Kansas City Chiefs	.08	.03	.01
☐ 305	Herman Heard, Kansas City Chiefs	.03	.01	.00
☐ 306	Stephone Paige, Kansas City Chiefs	.07	.03	.01
☐ 307	Carlos Carson, Kansas City Chiefs	.05	.02	.00
☐ 308	Nick Lowery, Kansas City Chiefs	.03	.01	.00

	MINT	VG-E	F-G
☐ 309 **Mike Bell**, Kansas City Chiefs	.05	.02	.00
☐ 310 **Bill Maas**, Kansas City Chiefs	.05	.02	.00
☐ 311 **Art Still**, Kansas City Chiefs	.05	.02	.00
☐ 312 **Albert Lewis**, Kansas City Chiefs	.06	.02	.00
☐ 313 **Deron Cherry AP**, Kansas City Chiefs	.05	.02	.00
☐ 314 **Indianapolis Colts Team Card**	.06	.02	.00
☐ 315 **Mike Pagel**, Indianapolis Colts	.07	.03	.01
☐ 316 **Randy McMillan**, Indianapolis Colts	.05	.02	.00
☐ 317 **Albert Bentley**, Indianapolis Colts	.06	.02	.00
☐ 318 **George Wonsley**, Indianapolis Colts	.06	.02	.00
☐ 319 **Robbie Martin**, Indianapolis Colts	.03	.01	.00
☐ 320 **Pat Beach**, Indianapolis Colts	.03	.01	.00
☐ 321 **Chris Hinton**, Indianapolis Colts	.05	.02	.00
☐ 322 **Duane Bickett**, Indianapolis Colts	.10	.04	.01
☐ 323 **Eugene Daniel**, Indianapolis Colts	.03	.01	.00
☐ 324 **Cliff Odom**, Indianapolis Colts	.03	.01	.00
☐ 325 **Rohn Stark AP**, Indianapolis Colts	.03	.01	.00
☐ 326 **St. Louis Cardinals Team Card**	.06	.02	.00
☐ 327 **Neil Lomax**, St. Louis Cardinals	.10	.04	.01
☐ 328 **Stump Mitchell**, St. Louis Cardinals	.05	.02	.00
☐ 329 **Ottis Anderson**, St. Louis Cardinals	.12	.05	.01
☐ 330 **J. T. Smith**, St. Louis Cardinals	.03	.01	.00
☐ 331 **Pat Tilley**, St. Louis Cardinals	.05	.02	.00
☐ 332 **Roy Green**, St. Louis Cardinals	.06	.02	.00
☐ 333 **Lance Smith**, St. Louis Cardinals	.03	.01	.00
☐ 334 **Curtis Greer**, St. Louis Cardinals	.05	.02	.00
☐ 335 **Freddie Joe Nunn**, St. Louis Cardinals	.06	.02	.00
☐ 336 **E. J. Junior**, St. Louis Cardinals	.05	.02	.00
☐ 337 **Lonnie Young**, St. Louis Cardinals	.03	.01	.00
☐ 338 **New Orleans Saints Team Card**	.06	.02	.00
☐ 339 **Bobby Hebert**, New Orleans Saints	.12	.05	.01
☐ 340 **Dave Wilson**, New Orleans Saints	.07	.03	.01
☐ 341 **Wayne Wilson**, New Orleans Saints	.03	.01	.00
☐ 342 **Hoby Brenner**, New Orleans Saints	.03	.01	.00
☐ 343 **Stan Brock**, New Orleans Saints	.03	.01	.00
☐ 344 **Morten Andersen**, New Orleans Saints	.03	.01	.00
☐ 345 **Bruce Clark**, New Orleans Saints	.03	.01	.00
☐ 346 **Rickey Jackson**, New Orleans Saints	.03	.01	.00
☐ 347 **Dave Waymer**, New Orleans Saints	.03	.01	.00
☐ 348 **Brian Hansen**, New Orleans Saints	.05	.02	.00
☐ 349 **Houston Oilers Team Card**	.06	.02	.00
☐ 350 **Warren Moon**, Houston Oilers	.12	.05	.01
☐ 351 **Mike Rozier**, Houston Oilers	.15	.06	.01
☐ 352 **Butch Woolfolk**, Houston Oilers	.05	.02	.00
☐ 353 **Drew Hill**, Houston Oilers	.05	.02	.00
☐ 354 **Willie Drewrey**, Houston Oilers	.05	.02	.00

		MINT	VG-E	F-G
☐ 355	**Tim Smith**, Houston Oilers	.05	.02	.00
☐ 356	**Mike Munchak**, Houston Oilers	.05	.02	.00
☐ 357	**Ray Childress**, Houston Oilers	.12	.05	.01
☐ 358	**Frank Bush**, Houston Oilers	.03	.01	.00
☐ 359	**Steve Brown**, Houston Oilers	.03	.01	.00
☐ 360	**Atlanta Falcons Team Card**	.06	.02	.00
☐ 361	**Dave Archer**, Atlanta Falcons	.06	.02	.00
☐ 362	**Gerald Riggs**, Atlanta Falcons	.06	.02	.00
☐ 363	**William Andrews**, Atlanta Falcons	.06	.02	.00
☐ 364	**Billy Johnson**, Atlanta Falcons	.06	.02	.00
☐ 365	**Arthur Cox**, Atlanta Falcons	.03	.01	.00
☐ 366	**Mike Kenn**, Atlanta Falcons	.05	.02	.00
☐ 367	**Bill Fralic**, Atlanta Falcons	.12	.05	.01
☐ 368	**Mick Luckhurst**, Atlanta Falcons	.03	.01	.00
☐ 369	**Rick Bryan**, Atlanta Falcons	.06	.02	.00
☐ 370	**Bobby Butler**, Atlanta Falcons	.03	.01	.00
☐ 371	**Rick Donnelly**, Atlanta Falcons	.03	.01	.00
☐ 372	**Tampa Bay Buccaneers Team Card**	.06	.02	.00
☐ 373	**Steve DeBerg**, Tampa Bay Buccaneers	.06	.02	.00
☐ 374	**Steve Young**, Tampa Bay Buccaneers	.10	.04	.01
☐ 375	**James Wilder**, Tampa Bay Buccaneers	.10	.04	.01
☐ 376	**Kevin House**, Tampa Bay Buccaneers	.03	.01	.00
☐ 377	**Gerald Carter**, Tampa Bay Buccaneers	.03	.01	.00
☐ 378	**Jimmie Giles**, Tampa Bay Buccaneers	.05	.02	.00
☐ 379	**Sean Farrell**, Tampa Bay Buccaneers	.03	.01	.00
☐ 380	**Donald Igwebuike**, Tampa Bay Buccaneers	.03	.01	.00
☐ 381	**David Logan**, Tampa Bay Buccaneers	.03	.01	.00
☐ 382	**Jeremiah Castille**, Tampa Bay Buccaneers	.05	.02	.00
☐ 383	**Buffalo Bills Team Card**	.06	.02	.00
☐ 384	**Bruce Mathison**, Buffalo Bills	.05	.02	.00
☐ 385	**Joe Cribbs**, Buffalo Bills	.06	.02	.00
☐ 386	**Greg Bell**, Buffalo Bills	.08	.03	.01
☐ 387	**Jerry Butler**, Buffalo Bills	.06	.02	.00
☐ 388	**Andre Reed**, Buffalo Bills	.03	.01	.00
☐ 389	**Bruce Smith**, Buffalo Bills	.12	.05	.01
☐ 390	**Fred Smerlas**, Buffalo Bills	.05	.02	.00
☐ 391	**Darryl Talley**, Buffalo Bills	.03	.01	.00
☐ 392	**Jim Haslett**, Buffalo Bills	.03	.01	.00
☐ 393	**Charles Romes**, Buffalo Bills	.03	.01	.00

UNNUMBERED CHECKLISTS

☐ 394	**Checklist 1-132**	.06	.01	.00
☐ 395	**Checklist 133-264**	.06	.01	.00
☐ 396	**Checklist 265-396**	.06	.01	.00

1968 O-PEE-CHEE CFL

The 1968 O-Pee-Chee CFL set of 132 cards received limited distribution and is considered by some to be a test set. The card backs are written in English and French in green ink on yellowish card stock. The cards measure 2½" by 3½". Cards are ordered by teams: Montreal (1-13), Ottawa (14-27), Toronto (28-42), Hamilton (43-57), Winnipeg (58-72), Calgary (73-85), Saskatchewan (86-103), Edmonton (104-117), and B.C. Lions (118-131). A complete checklist is given on card number 132.

		MINT	VG-E	F-G
	COMPLETE SET	300.00	130.00	30.00
	COMMON PLAYER (1-132)	2.00	.90	.20
☐	1 Roger Murphy, Montreal Alouettes	2.00	.90	.20
☐	2 Charlie Parker, Montreal Alouettes	2.00	.90	.20
☐	3 Mike Webster, Montreal Alouettes	2.00	.90	.20
☐	4 Carroll Williams, Montreal Alouettes	2.00	.90	.20
☐	5 Phil Brady, Montreal Alouettes	2.00	.90	.20
☐	6 Dave Lewis, Montreal Alouettes	2.00	.90	.20
☐	7 John Baker, Montreal Alouettes	2.00	.90	.20
☐	8 Basil Bark, Montreal Alouettes	2.00	.90	.20
☐	9 Donnie Davis, Montreal Alouettes	2.00	.90	.20
☐	10 Pierre Desjardins, Montreal Alouettes	2.00	.90	.20
☐	11 Larry Fairholm, Montreal Alouettes	2.00	.90	.20
☐	12 Peter Paquette, Montreal Alouettes	2.00	.90	.20
☐	13 Ray Lychak, Montreal Alouettes	2.00	.90	.20
☐	14 Ted Collins, Ottawa Rough Riders	2.00	.90	.20
☐	15 Margene Adkins, Ottawa Rough Riders	2.50	1.15	.25

		MINT	VG-E	F-G
☐	16 **Ron Stewart**, Ottowa Rough Riders	3.00	1.40	.30
☐	17 **Russ Jackson**, Ottowa Rough Riders	5.00	2.35	.50
☐	18 **Bo Scott**, Ottowa Rough Riders	2.50	1.15	.25
☐	19 **Joe Poirier**, Ottowa Rough Riders	2.00	.90	.20
☐	20 **Wayne Giardino**, Ottowa Rough Riders	2.00	.90	.20
☐	21 **Gene Gaines**, Ottowa Rough Riders	2.00	.90	.20
☐	22 **Bill Joe Booth**, Ottowa Rough Riders	2.00	.90	.20
☐	23 **Whit Tucker**, Ottowa Rough Riders	2.50	1.15	.25
☐	24 **Rick Black**, Ottowa Rough Riders	2.00	.90	.20
☐	25 **Ken Lehmann**, Ottowa Rough Riders	2.50	1.15	.25
☐	26 **Bob Brown**, Ottowa Rough Riders	2.00	.90	.20
☐	27 **Moe Racine**, Ottowa Rough Riders	2.00	.90	.20
☐	28 **Dick Thornton**, Toronto Argonauts	2.50	1.15	.25
☐	29 **Bob Taylor**, Toronto Argonauts	2.00	.90	.20
☐	30 **Mel Profit**, Toronto Argonauts	2.00	.90	.20
☐	31 **Dave Mann**, Toronto Argonauts	2.50	1.15	.25
☐	32 **Marv Luster**, Toronto Argonauts	2.50	1.15	.25
☐	33 **Ed Buchanan**, Toronto Argonauts	2.00	.90	.20
☐	34 **Ed Harrington**, Toronto Argonauts	2.50	1.15	.25
☐	35 **Jim Dilard**, Toronto Argonauts	2.00	.90	.20
☐	36 **Bobby Taylor**, Toronto Argonauts	2.00	.90	.20
☐	37 **Ron Arends**, Toronto Argonauts	2.00	.90	.20
☐	38 **Mike Wadsworth**, Toronto Argonauts	2.00	.90	.20
☐	39 **Wally Gabler**, Toronto Argonauts	2.00	.90	.20
☐	40 **Pete Martin**, Toronto Argonauts	2.00	.90	.20
☐	41 **Danny Nykoluk**, Toronto Argonauts	2.00	.90	.20
☐	42 **Bill Frank**, Toronto Argonauts	2.00	.90	.20
☐	43 **Gordon Christian**, Hamilton Tiger-Cats	2.00	.90	.20
☐	44 **Tommy Joe Coffey**, Hamilton Tiger-Cats	3.00	1.40	.30
☐	45 **Ellison Kelly**, Hamilton Tiger-Cats	2.50	1.15	.25
☐	46 **Angelo Mosca**, Hamilton Tiger-Cats	4.00	1.85	.40
☐	47 **John Barrow**, Hamilton Tiger-Cats	3.00	1.40	.30
☐	48 **Bill Danychuk**, Hamilton Tiger-Cats	2.50	1.15	.25
☐	49 **Jon Hohman**, Hamilton Tiger-Cats	2.00	.90	.20
☐	50 **Bill Redell**, Hamilton Tiger-Cats	2.00	.90	.20
☐	51 **Joe Zuger**, Hamilton Tiger-Cats	2.00	.90	.20
☐	52 **Willie Bethea**, Hamilton Tiger-Cats	2.00	.90	.20
☐	53 **Dick Cohee**, Hamilton Tiger-Cats	2.00	.90	.20
☐	54 **Tommy Grant**, Hamilton Tiger-Cats	2.50	1.15	.25
☐	55 **Garney Henley**, Hamilton Tiger-Cats	3.50	1.65	.35
☐	56 **Ted Page**, Hamilton Tiger-Cats	2.00	.90	.20
☐	57 **Bob Krouse**, Hamilton Tiger-Cats	2.00	.90	.20
☐	58 **Phil Minnick**, Winnepeg Blue Bombers	2.00	.90	.20
☐	59 **Butch Pressley**, Winnepeg Blue Bombers	2.00	.90	.20
☐	60 **Dave Raimey**, Winnepeg Blue Bombers	2.50	1.15	.25
☐	61 **Sherwyn Thorson**, Winnepeg Blue Bombers	2.00	.90	.20

		MINT	VG-E	F-G
☐ 62	**Bill Whisler,** Winnepeg Blue Bombers	2.00	.90	.20
☐ 63	**Roger Hamelin,** Winnepeg Blue Bombers	2.00	.90	.20
☐ 64	**Chuck Harrison,** Winnepeg Blue Bombers	2.00	.90	.20
☐ 65	**Ken Nielsen,** Winnepeg Blue Bombers	2.50	1.15	.25
☐ 66	**Ernie Pitts,** Winnepeg Blue Bombers	2.00	.90	.20
☐ 67	**Mitch Zainasky,** Winnepeg Blue Bombers	2.00	.90	.20
☐ 68	**John Schneider,** Winnepeg Blue Bombers	2.00	.90	.20
☐ 69	**Ron Kirkland,** Winnepeg Blue Bombers	2.00	.90	.20
☐ 70	**Paul Desjardins,** Winnepeg Blue Bombers	2.00	.90	.20
☐ 71	**Luther Selbo,** Winnepeg Blue Bombers	2.00	.90	.20
☐ 72	**Don Gilbert,** Winnepeg Blue Bombers	2.00	.90	.20
☐ 73	**Bob Lueck,** Calgary Stampeders	2.00	.90	.20
☐ 74	**Gerry Shaw,** Calgary Stampeders	2.00	.90	.20
☐ 75	**Chuck Zickefoose,** Calgary Stampeders	2.00	.90	.20
☐ 76	**Frank Andruski,** Calgary Stampeders	2.00	.90	.20
☐ 77	**Lanny Boleski,** Calgary Stampeders	2.00	.90	.20
☐ 78	**Terry Evanshen,** Calgary Stampeders	3.00	1.40	.30
☐ 79	**Jim Furlong,** Calgary Stampeders	2.00	.90	.20
☐ 80	**Wayne Harris,** Calgary Stampeders	3.00	1.40	.30
☐ 81	**Jerry Keeling,** Calgary Stampeders	2.00	.90	.20
☐ 82	**Roger Kramer,** Calgary Stampeders	2.50	1.15	.25
☐ 83	**Peter Liske,** Calgary Stampeders	3.00	1.40	.30
☐ 84	**Dick Suderman,** Calgary Stampeders	2.00	.90	.20
☐ 85	**Granville Liggins,** Calgary Stampeders	2.50	1.15	.25
☐ 86	**George Reed,** Saskatchewan Rough Riders ...	4.00	1.85	.40
☐ 87	**Ron Lancaster,** Saskatchewan Rough Riders .	4.00	1.85	.40
☐ 88	**Alan Ford,** Saskatchewan Rough Riders	2.00	.90	.20
☐ 89	**Gordon Barwell,** Saskatchewan Rough Riders	2.00	.90	.20
☐ 90	**Wayne Shaw,** Saskatchewan Rough Riders ...	2.00	.90	.20
☐ 91	**Bruce Bennett,** Saskatchewan Rough Riders .	2.00	.90	.20
☐ 92	**Henry Dorsch,** Saskatchewan Rough Riders ..	2.00	.90	.20
☐ 93	**Ken Reed,** Saskatchewan Rough Riders	2.00	.90	.20
☐ 94	**Ron Atchison,** Saskatchewan Rough Riders ..	3.00	1.40	.30
☐ 95	**Clyde Brock,** Saskatchewan Rough Riders	2.00	.90	.20
☐ 96	**Alex Benecick,** Saskatchewan Rough Riders ..	2.00	.90	.20
☐ 97	**Ted Urness,** Saskatchewan Rough Riders	2.50	1.15	.25
☐ 98	**Wally Dempsey,** Saskatchewan Rough Riders .	2.00	.90	.20
☐ 99	**Don Gerhardt,** Saskatchewan Rough Riders ..	2.00	.90	.20
☐ 100	**Ted Dushinski,** Saskatchewan Rough Riders ..	2.00	.90	.20
☐ 101	**Ed McQuarters,** Saskatchewan Rough Riders .	2.50	1.15	.25
☐ 102	**Bob Kosid,** Saskatchewan Rough Riders	2.00	.90	.20
☐ 103	**Gary Brandt,** Saskatchewan Rough Riders	2.00	.90	.20
☐ 104	**John Wydareny,** Edmonton Eskimos	2.00	.90	.20
☐ 105	**Jim Thomas,** Edmonton Eskimos	2.00	.90	.20
☐ 106	**Art Perkins,** Edmonton Eskimos	2.00	.90	.20
☐ 107	**Frank Cosentino,** Edmonton Eskimos	2.00	.90	.20

	MINT	VG-E	F-G
☐ 108 **Earl Edwards,** Edmonton Eskimos	2.00	.90	.20
☐ 109 **Garry Lefebvre,** Edmonton Eskimos	2.00	.90	.20
☐ 110 **Greg Pipes,** Edmonton Eskimos	2.00	.90	.20
☐ 111 **Ian MacLeod,** Edmonton Eskimos	2.00	.90	.20
☐ 112 **Dick Dupuis,** Edmonton Eskimos	2.00	.90	.20
☐ 113 **Ron Forwick,** Edmonton Eskimos	2.00	.90	.20
☐ 114 **Jerry Griffin,** Edmonton Eskimos	2.00	.90	.20
☐ 115 **John LaGrone,** Edmonton Eskimos	2.50	1.15	.25
☐ 116 **E.A. Sims,** Edmonton Eskimos	2.00	.90	.20
☐ 117 **Greenard Poles,** Edmonton Eskimos	2.00	.90	.20
☐ 118 **Leroy Sledge,** British Columbia Lions	2.00	.90	.20
☐ 119 **Ken Sugarman,** British Columbia Lions	2.00	.90	.20
☐ 120 **Jim Young,** British Columbia Lions	3.50	1.65	.35
☐ 121 **Garner Ekstran,** British Columbia Lions	2.50	1.15	.25
☐ 122 **Jim Evenson,** British Columbia Lions	2.50	1.15	.25
☐ 123 **Greg Findlay,** British Columbia Lions	2.00	.90	.20
☐ 124 **Ted Gerela,** British Columbia Lions	2.00	.90	.20
☐ 125 **Lach Heron,** British Columbia Lions	2.00	.90	.20
☐ 126 **Mike Martin,** British Columbia Lions	2.00	.90	.20
☐ 127 **Craig Murray,** British Columbia Lions	2.00	.90	.20
☐ 128 **Pete Ohler,** British Columbia Lions	2.00	.90	.20
☐ 129 **Sonny Homer,** British Columbia Lions	2.00	.90	.20
☐ 130 **Bill Lasseter,** British Columbia Lions	2.00	.90	.20
☐ 131 **John McDowell,** British Columbia Lions	2.00	.90	.20
☐ 132 **Checklist**	5.00	1.00	.20

1970 O-PEE-CHEE CFL

The 1970 O-Pee-Chee CFL set features 115 cards ordered by teams: Toronto (1-12), Hamilton (13-24), B.C. Lions (25-36), Ottawa (37-48), Edmonton (49-60), Winnipeg (61-72), Saskatchewan (73-85), Calgary (86-97), and Montreal (98-109). The cards measure 2½" by 3½". The design of these cards is very similar to the 1969 Topps NFL football issue. The card backs are written in French and English; card back is predominantly black with white lettering and green accent. Six miscellaneous feature cards comprise cards numbered 110-115.

		MINT	VG-E	F-G
	COMPLETE SET	60.00	27.00	6.00
	COMMON PLAYER (1-115)	.40	.18	.04
☐	1 Ed Harrington, Toronto Argonauts	.50	.22	.05
☐	2 Danny Nykoluk, Toronto Argonauts	.40	.18	.04
☐	3 Marv Luster, Toronto Argonauts	.40	.18	.04
☐	4 Dave Raimey, Toronto Argonauts	.60	.28	.06
☐	5 Bill Symons, Toronto Argonauts	.50	.22	.05
☐	6 Tom Wilkinson, Toronto Argonauts	.80	.40	.08
☐	7 Mike Wadsworth, Toronto Argonauts	.40	.18	.04
☐	8 Dick Thornton, Toronto Argonauts	.50	.22	.05
☐	9 Jim Tomlin, Toronto Argonauts	.40	.18	.04
☐	10 Mel Profit, Toronto Argonauts	.40	.18	.04
☐	11 Bobby Taylor, Toronto Argonauts	.40	.18	.04
☐	12 Dave Mann, Toronto Argonauts	.50	.22	.05
☐	13 Tommy Joe Coffey, Hamilton Tiger-Cats	1.00	.45	.10
☐	14 Angelo Mosca, Hamilton Tiger-Cats	1.50	.70	.15
☐	15 Joe Zuger, Hamilton Tiger-Cats	.40	.18	.04
☐	16 Garney Henley, Hamilton Tiger-Cats	1.50	.70	.15
☐	17 Mike Strofolino, Hamilton Tiger-Cats	.40	.18	.04
☐	18 Billy Ray Locklin, Hamilton Tiger-Cats	.40	.18	.04
☐	19 Ted Page, Hamilton Tiger-Cats	.40	.18	.04
☐	20 Bill Danychuk, Hamilton Tiger-Cats	.50	.22	.05
☐	21 Bob Krouse, Hamilton Tiger-Cats	.40	.18	.04
☐	22 John Reid, Hamilton Tiger-Cats	.40	.18	.04
☐	23 Dick Wesolowski, Hamilton Tiger-Cats	.40	.18	.04
☐	24 Willie Bethea, Hamilton Tiger-Cats	.40	.18	.04
☐	25 Ken Sugarman, British Columbia Lions	.50	.22	.05
☐	26 Rich Robinson, British Columbia Lions	.40	.18	.04
☐	27 Dave Tobey, British Columbia Lions	.40	.18	.04
☐	28 Paul Brothers, British Columbia Lions	.40	.18	.04
☐	29 Charlie Brown, British Columbia Lions	.40	.18	.04
☐	30 Jerry Bradley, British Columbia Lions	.40	.18	.04
☐	31 Ted Gerela, British Columbia Lions	.40	.18	.04
☐	32 Jim Young, British Columbia Lions	1.25	.60	.12
☐	33 Gary Robinson, British Columbia Lions	.40	.18	.04
☐	34 Bob Howes, British Columbia Lions	.40	.18	.04
☐	35 Greg Findlay, British Columbia Lions	.40	.18	.04

		MINT	VG-E	F-G
☐	36 **Trevor Ekdahl**, British Columbia Lions	.40	.18	.04
☐	37 **Ron Stewart**, Ottowa Rough Riders	.90	.40	.09
☐	38 **Joseph Poirier**, Ottowa Rough Riders	.50	.22	.05
☐	39 **Wayne Giardino**, Ottowa Rough Riders	.40	.18	.04
☐	40 **Tom Schuette**, Ottowa Rough Riders	.40	.18	.04
☐	41 **Roger Perdrix**, Ottowa Rough Riders	.40	.18	.04
☐	42 **Jim Mankins**, Ottowa Rough Riders	.40	.18	.04
☐	43 **Jay Roberts**, Ottowa Rough Riders	.40	.18	.04
☐	44 **Ken Lehmann**, Ottowa Rough Riders	.50	.22	.05
☐	45 **Jerry Campbell**, Ottowa Rough Riders	.40	.18	.04
☐	46 **Billy Joe Booth**, Ottowa Rough Riders	.50	.22	.05
☐	47 **Whit Tucker**, Ottowa Rough Riders	.50	.22	.05
☐	48 **Moe Racine**, Ottowa Rough Riders	.40	.18	.04
☐	49 **Covey Colehour**, Edmonton Eskimos	.40	.18	.04
☐	50 **Dave Gasser**, Edmonton Eskimos	.40	.18	.04
☐	51 **Jerry Griffin**, Edmonton Eskimos	.40	.18	.04
☐	52 **Greg Pipes**, Edmonton Eskimos	.40	.18	.04
☐	53 **Roy Shatzko**, Edmonton Eskimos	.40	.18	.04
☐	54 **Ron Forwick**, Edmonton Eskimos	.40	.18	.04
☐	55 **Ed Molstad**, Edmonton Eskimos	.40	.18	.04
☐	56 **Ken Ferguson**, Edmonton Eskimos	.40	.18	.04
☐	57 **Terry Swarn**, Edmonton Eskimos	.40	.18	.04
☐	58 **Tom Nettles**, British Columbia Lions	.40	.18	.04
☐	59 **John Wydareny**, Edmonton Eskimos	.40	.18	.04
☐	60 **Bayne Norrie**, Edmonton Eskimos	.40	.18	.04
☐	61 **Wally Gabler**, Winnepeg Blue Bombers	.40	.18	.04
☐	62 **Paul Desjardins**, Winnepeg Blue Bombers	.40	.18	.04
☐	63 **Peter Francis**, Winnepeg Blue Bombers	.40	.18	.04
☐	64 **Bill Frank**, Winnepeg Blue Bombers	.40	.18	.04
☐	65 **Chuck Harrison**, Winnepeg Blue Bombers	.40	.18	.04
☐	66 **Gene Lakusiak**, Winnepeg Blue Bombers	.40	.18	.04
☐	67 **Phil Minnick**, Winnepeg Blue Bombers	.40	.18	.04
☐	68 **Doug Strong**, Winnepeg Blue Bombers	.40	.18	.04
☐	69 **Glen Schapansky**, Winnepeg Blue Bombers ..	.40	.18	.04
☐	70 **Ed Ulmer**, Winnepeg Blue Bombers	.40	.18	.04
☐	71 **Bill Whisler**, Winnepeg Blue Bombers	.40	.18	.04
☐	72 **Ted Collins**, Winnepeg Blue Bombers	.40	.18	.04
☐	73 **Larry DeGraw**, Saskatchewan Rough Riders ..	.40	.18	.04
☐	74 **Henry Dorsch**, Saskatchewan Rough Riders ..	.40	.18	.04
☐	75 **Alan Ford**, Saskatchewan Rough Riders	.40	.18	.04
☐	76 **Ron Lancaster**, Saskatchewan Rough Riders	1.50	.70	.15
☐	77 **Bob Kosid**, Saskatchewan Rough Riders	.40	.18	.04
☐	78 **Bobby Thompson**, Saskatchewan Rough Riders	.40	.18	.04
☐	79 **Ted Dushinski**, Saskatchewan Rough Riders ..	.40	.18	.04
☐	80 **Bruce Bennett**, Saskatchewan Rough Riders ..	.40	.18	.04
☐	81 **George Reed**, Saskatchewan Rough Riders ...	1.50	.70	.15

		MINT	VG-E	F-G
☐	82 Wayne Shaw, Saskatchewan Rough Riders ...	.40	.18	.04
☐	83 Cliff Shaw, Saskatchewan Rough Riders	.40	.18	.04
☐	84 Jack Abendschan, Saskatchewan Rough Riders	.40	.18	.04
☐	85 Ed McQuarters, Saskatchewan Rough Riders .	.50	.22	.05
☐	86 Jerry Keeling, Calgary Stampeders	.40	.18	.04
☐	87 Gerry Shaw, Calgary Stampeders	.40	.18	.04
☐	88 Basil Bark, Calgary Stampeders	.40	.18	.04
☐	89 Wayne Harris, Calgary Stampeders	1.50	.70	.15
☐	90 Jim Furlong, Calgary Stampeders	.40	.18	.04
☐	91 Larry Robinson, Calgary Stampeders	.50	.22	.05
☐	92 John Helton, Calgary Stampeders	.60	.28	.06
☐	93 Dave Cranmer, Calgary Stampeders	.40	.18	.04
☐	94 Larry Boleski, Calgary Stampeders	.40	.18	.04
☐	95 Herman Harrison, Calgary Stampeders	.40	.18	.04
☐	96 Granville Liggins, Calgary Stampeders	.50	.22	.05
☐	97 Joe Forzani, Calgary Stampeders	.40	.18	.04
☐	98 Terry Evanshen, Montreal Alouettes	1.50	.70	.15
☐	99 Sonny Wade, Montreal Alouettes	.40	.18	.04
☐	100 Dennis Duncan, Montreal Alouettes	.40	.18	.04
☐	101 Al Phaneuf, Montreal Alouettes	.40	.18	.04
☐	102 Larry Fairholm, Montreal Alouettes	.40	.18	.04
☐	103 Moses Denson, Montreal Alouettes	.40	.18	.04
☐	104 Gino Baretta, Montreal Alouettes	.40	.18	.04
☐	105 Gene Cipetelli, Montreal Alouettes	.40	.18	.04
☐	106 Dick Smith, Montreal Alouettes	.40	.18	.04
☐	107 Gordon Judges, Montreal Alouettes	.40	.18	.04
☐	108 Harry Olszewski, Montreal Alouettes	.40	.18	.04
☐	109 Mike Webster, Montreal Alouettes	.40	.18	.04

SPECIAL CARDS

		MINT	VG-E	F-G
☐	110 Checklist.........................	2.00	.20	.04
☐	111 Outstanding Player	.80	.40	.08
☐	112 Player of the Year	.80	.40	.08
☐	113 Lineman of the Year	.50	.22	.05
☐	114 C.F.L. Coaches	.50	.22	.05
☐	115 Identifying Player	.50	.22	.05

1971 O-PEE-CHEE CFL

The 1971 O-Pee-Chee CFL set features 132 cards ordered by teams: Toronto (1-15), Winnipeg (16-30), B.C. Lions (31-45), Edmonton (46-60), Hamilton (61-75), Ottawa (76-89), Saskatchewan (90-103), Montreal (104-117), and Calgary (118-131). The cards measure 2½" by 3½". The card fronts feature a bright red border. The card backs are written in French and English. A complete checklist is given on card number 132.

		MINT	VG-E	F-G
	COMPLETE SET	36.00	17.00	3.60
	COMMON PLAYER (1-132)	.20	.09	.02
☐	1 **Bill Symons**, Toronto Argonauts	.50	.22	.05
☐	2 **Mel Profit**, Toronto Argonauts	.20	.09	.02
☐	3 **Jim Tomin**, Toronto Argonauts	.20	.09	.02
☐	4 **Ed Harrington**, Toronto Argonauts	.30	.12	.03
☐	5 **Jim Corrigall**, Toronto Argonauts	.30	.12	.03
☐	6 **Chip Barrett**, Toronto Argonauts	.20	.09	.02
☐	7 **Marv Luster**, Toronto Argonauts	.30	.12	.03
☐	8 **Ellison Kelly**, Toronto Argonauts	.40	.18	.04
☐	9 **Charlie Bray**, Toronto Argonauts	.20	.09	.02
☐	10 **Peter Martin**, Toronto Argonauts	.20	.09	.02
☐	11 **Tony Moro**, Toronto Argonauts	.20	.09	.02
☐	12 **Dave Raimey**, Toronto Argonauts	.50	.22	.05
☐	13 **Joe Theismann**, Toronto Argonauts	6.00	2.80	.60
☐	14 **Greg Barton**, Toronto Argonauts	.40	.18	.04
☐	15 **Leon McQuay**, Toronto Argonauts	.30	.12	.03
☐	16 **Don Jonas**, Winnipeg Blue Bombers	.40	.18	.04
☐	17 **Doug Strong**, Winnipeg Blue Bombers	.20	.09	.02

		MINT	VG-E	F-G
☐	18 **Paul Brule,** Winnepeg Blue Bombers	.20	.09	.02
☐	19 **Bill Frank,** Winnepeg Blue Bombers	.20	.09	.02
☐	20 **Joe Critchlow,** Winnepeg Blue Bombers	.20	.09	.02
☐	21 **Chuck Liebrock,** Winnepeg Blue Bombers	.20	.09	.02
☐	22 **Rob McLaren,** Winnepeg Blue Bombers	.20	.09	.02
☐	23 **Bob Swift,** Winnepeg Blue Bombers	.20	.09	.02
☐	24 **Rick Shaw,** Winnepeg Blue Bombers	.20	.09	.02
☐	25 **Ross Richardson,** Winnepeg Blue Bombers	.20	.09	.02
☐	26 **Benji Dial,** Winnepeg Blue Bombers	.20	.09	.02
☐	27 **Jim Heighton,** Winnepeg Blue Bombers	.20	.09	.02
☐	28 **Ed Ulmer,** Winnepeg Blue Bombers	.20	.09	.02
☐	29 **Glen Schapansky,** Winnepeg Blue Bombers	.20	.09	.02
☐	30 **Larry Slagle,** Winnepeg Blue Bombers	.20	.09	.02
☐	31 **Tom Cassese,** British Columbia Lions	.20	.09	.02
☐	32 **Ted Gerela,** British Columbia Lions	.20	.09	.02
☐	33 **Bob Howes,** British Columbia Lions	.20	.09	.02
☐	34 **Ken Sugarman,** British Columbia Lions	.30	.12	.03
☐	35 **A.D. Whitfield,** British Columbia Lions	.20	.09	.02
☐	36 **Jim Young,** British Columbia Lions	.90	.40	.08
☐	37 **Tom Wilkinson,** British Columbia Lions	.50	.22	.05
☐	38 **Lefty Hendrickson,** British Columbia Lions	.20	.09	.02
☐	39 **Dave Golinsky,** British Columbia Lions	.20	.09	.02
☐	40 **Gerry Herron,** British Columbia Lions	.20	.09	.02
☐	41 **Jim Evenson,** British Columbia Lions	.30	.12	.03
☐	42 **Greg Findlay,** British Columbia Lions	.20	.09	.02
☐	43 **Garret Hunsperger,** British Columbia Lions	.20	.09	.02
☐	44 **Jerry Bradley,** British Columbia Lions	.20	.09	.02
☐	45 **Trevor Ekdahl,** British Columbia Lions	.20	.09	.02
☐	46 **Bayne Norrie,** Edmonton Eskimos	.20	.09	.02
☐	47 **Henry King,** Edmonton Eskimos	.20	.09	.02
☐	48 **Terry Swarn,** Edmonton Eskimos	.20	.09	.02
☐	49 **Jim Thomas,** Edmonton Eskimos	.20	.09	.02
☐	50 **Bob Houmard,** Edmonton Eskimos	.20	.09	.02
☐	51 **Don Trull,** Edmonton Eskimos	.30	.12	.03
☐	52 **Dave Cutler,** Edmonton Eskimos	.30	.12	.03
☐	53 **Mike Law,** Edmonton Eskimos	.20	.09	.02
☐	54 **Dick Dupuis,** Edmonton Eskimos	.30	.12	.03
☐	55 **Dave Gasser,** Edmonton Eskimos	.20	.09	.02
☐	56 **Ron Forwick,** Edmonton Eskimos	.20	.09	.02
☐	57 **John LaGrone,** Edmonton Eskimos	.30	.12	.03
☐	58 **Greg Pipes,** Edmonton Eskimos	.30	.12	.03
☐	59 **Ted Page,** Edmonton Eskimos	.20	.09	.02
☐	60 **John Wydareny,** Edmonton Eskimos	.30	.12	.03
☐	61 **Joe Zuger,** Hamilton Tiger-Cats	.20	.09	.02
☐	62 **Tommy Joe Coffey,** Hamilton Tiger-Cats	.75	.35	.07
☐	63 **Rensi Perdoni,** Hamilton Tiger-Cats	.20	.09	.02

		MINT	VG-E	F-G
☐ 64	**Bobby Taylor,** Hamilton Tiger-Cats	.20	.09	.02
☐ 65	**Garney Henley,** Hamilton Tiger-Cats	1.00	.45	.10
☐ 66	**Dick Wesolowski,** Hamilton Tiger-Cats	.20	.09	.02
☐ 67	**Dave Fleming,** Hamilton Tiger-Cats	.20	.09	.02
☐ 68	**Bill Danychuk,** Hamilton Tiger-Cats	.30	.12	.03
☐ 69	**Angelo Mosca,** Hamilton Tiger-Cats	1.50	.70	.15
☐ 70	**Bob Krouse,** Hamilton Tiger-Cats	.20	.09	.02
☐ 71	**Tony Gabriel,** Hamilton Tiger-Cats	1.50	.70	.15
☐ 72	**Wally Gabler,** Hamilton Tiger-Cats	.20	.09	.02
☐ 73	**Bob Steiner,** Hamilton Tiger-Cats	.20	.09	.02
☐ 74	**John Reid,** Hamilton Tiger-Cats	.20	.09	.02
☐ 75	**Jon Hohman,** Hamilton Tiger-Cats	.20	.09	.02
☐ 76	**Barry Ardern,** Ottowa Rough Riders	.20	.09	.02
☐ 77	**Jerry Campbell,** Ottawa Rough Riders	.20	.09	.02
☐ 78	**Billy Cooper,** Ottowa Rough Riders	.20	.09	.02
☐ 79	**Dave Braggins,** Ottawa Rough Riders	.20	.09	.02
☐ 80	**Tom Schuette,** Ottawa Rough Riders	.20	.09	.02
☐ 81	**Dennis Duncan,** Ottawa Rough Riders	.20	.09	.02
☐ 82	**Moe Racine,** Ottawa Rough Riders	.20	.09	.02
☐ 83	**Rod Woodward,** Ottawa Rough Riders	.20	.09	.02
☐ 84	**Al Marcelin,** Ottawa Rough Riders	.30	.12	.03
☐ 85	**Garry Wood,** Ottawa Rough Riders	.20	.09	.02
☐ 86	**Wayne Giardino,** Ottawa Rough Riders	.20	.09	.02
☐ 87	**Roger Perdrix,** Ottawa Rough Riders	.20	.09	.02
☐ 88	**Hugh Oldham,** Ottawa Rough Riders	.20	.09	.02
☐ 89	**Rick Cassata,** Ottowa Rough Riders	.20	.09	.02
☐ 90	**Jack Abendschan,** Saskatchewan Rough Riders	.20	.09	.02
☐ 91	**Don Bahnuik,** Saskatchewan Rough Riders ...	.20	.09	.02
☐ 92	**Bill Baker,** Saskatchewan Rough Riders	.50	.22	.05
☐ 93	**Gordon Barwell,** Saskatchewan Rough Riders	.20	.09	.02
☐ 94	**Gary Brandt,** Saskatchewan Rough Riders	.20	.09	.02
☐ 95	**Henry Dorsch,** Saskatchewan Rough Riders ..	.20	.09	.02
☐ 96	**Ted Dushinski,** Saskatchewan Rough Riders .	.20	.09	.02
☐ 97	**Alan Ford,** Saskatchewan Rough Riders	.20	.09	.02
☐ 98	**Ken Frith,** Saskatchewan Rough Riders	.20	.09	.02
☐ 99	**Ralph Galloway,** Saskatchewan Rough Riders .	.20	.09	.02
☐ 100	**Bob Kosid,** Saskatchewan Rough Riders	.20	.09	.02
☐ 101	**Ron Lancaster,** Saskatchewan Rough Riders .	1.25	.60	.12
☐ 102	**Silas McKinnie,** Saskatchewan Rough Riders .	.20	.09	.02
☐ 103	**George Reed,** Saskatchewan Rough Riders ..	1.25	.60	.12
☐ 104	**Gene Ceppetelli,** Montreal Alouettes	.20	.09	.02
☐ 105	**Merl Code,** Montreal Alouettes	.20	.09	.02
☐ 106	**Peter Dalla Riva,** Montreal Alouettes	.20	.09	.02
☐ 107	**Moses Denson,** Montreal Alouettes	.30	.12	.03
☐ 108	**Pierre Desjardins,** Montreal Alouettes	.20	.09	.02
☐ 109	**Terry Evanshen,** Montreal Alouettes	1.00	.45	.10

	MINT	VG-E	F-G
☐ 110 **Larry Fairholm,** Montreal Alouettes	.20	.09	.02
☐ 111 **Gene Gaines,** Montreal Alouettes	.20	.09	.02
☐ 112 **Ed George,** Montreal Alouettes	.30	.12	.03
☐ 113 **Gordon Judges,** Montreal Alouettes	.20	.09	.02
☐ 114 **Garry Lefebvre,** Montreal Alouettes	.20	.09	.02
☐ 115 **Al Phaneuf,** Montreal Alouettes	.30	.12	.03
☐ 116 **Steve Smear,** Montreal Alouettes	.40	.18	.04
☐ 117 **Sonny Wade,** Montreal Alouettes	.20	.09	.02
☐ 118 **Frank Andruski,** Calgary Stampeders	.20	.09	.02
☐ 119 **Basil Bark,** Calgary Stampeders	.20	.09	.02
☐ 120 **Lanny Boleski,** Calgary Stampeders	.20	.09	.02
☐ 121 **Joe Forzani,** Calgary Stampeders	.30	.12	.03
☐ 122 **Jim Furlong,** Calgary Stampeders	.20	.09	.02
☐ 123 **Wayne Harris,** Calgary Stampeders	1.00	.45	.10
☐ 124 **Herman Harrison,** Calgary Stampeders	.20	.09	.02
☐ 125 **John Helton,** Calgary Stampeders	.40	.18	.04
☐ 126 **Wayne Holm,** Calgary Stampeders	.20	.09	.02
☐ 127 **Fred James,** Calgary Stampeders	.20	.09	.02
☐ 128 **Jerry Keeling,** Calgary Stampeders	.20	.09	.02
☐ 129 **Rudy Linterman,** Calgary Stampeders	.30	.12	.03
☐ 130 **Larry Robinson,** Calgary Stampeders	.30	.12	.03
☐ 131 **Gerry Shaw,** Calgary Stampeders	.20	.09	.02
☐ 132 **Checklist**	1.25	.10	.02

1972 O-PEE-CHEE CFL

The 1972 O-Pee-Chee CFL set of 132 cards is the last O-Pee-Chee CFL issue to date. Cards are ordered by teams: Hamilton (1-13), Montreal (14-26), Toronto (27-39), B.C. Lions (40-52), Calgary (53-65), Ottawa (66-78), Saskatchewan (79-91), Edmonton (92-104), and Winnipeg (105-117). The cards measure 2½" by 3½". The card backs are written in French and English; card back is blue and green print on white card stock. Fourteen Pro Action cards (118-131) and a checklist card (132) complete the set.

			MINT	VG-E	F-G
	COMPLETE SET		30.00	14.00	3.00
	COMMON PLAYER (1-132)		.20	.09	.02
☐	1	Bob Krouse, Hamilton Tiger-Cats	.20	.09	.02
☐	2	John Williams, Hamilton Tiger-Cats	.20	.09	.02
☐	3	Garney Henley, Hamilton Tiger-Cats	1.00	.45	.10
☐	4	Dick Wesolowski, Hamilton Tiger-Cats	.20	.09	.02
☐	5	Paul McKay, Hamilton Tiger-Cats	.20	.09	.02
☐	6	Bill Danychuk, Hamilton Tiger-Cats	.30	.12	.03
☐	7	Angelo Mosca, Hamilton Tiger-Cats	1.50	.70	.15
☐	8	Tommy Joe Coffey, Hamilton Tiger-Cats	.75	.35	.07
☐	9	Tony Gabriel, Hamilton Tiger-Cats	1.50	.70	.15
☐	10	Mike Blum, Hamilton Tiger-Cats	.20	.09	.02
☐	11	Doug Mitchell, Hamilton Tiger-Cats	.20	.09	.02
☐	12	Emery Hicks, Hamilton Tiger-Cats	.20	.09	.02
☐	13	Max Anderson, Hamilton Tiger-Cats	.20	.09	.02
☐	14	Ed George, Montreal Alouettes	.30	.12	.03
☐	15	Mark Kosmos, Montreal Alouettes	.30	.12	.03
☐	16	Ted Collins, Montreal Alouettes	.20	.09	.02
☐	17	Peter Dalla Riva, Montreal Alouettes	.20	.09	.02
☐	18	Pierre Desjardins, Montreal Alouettes	.20	.09	.02
☐	19	Terry Evanshen, Montreal Alouettes	1.00	.45	.10
☐	20	Larry Fairholm, Montreal Alouettes	.20	.09	.02
☐	21	Jim Foley, Montreal Alouettes	.30	.12	.03
☐	22	Gordon Judges, Montreal Alouettes	.20	.09	.02
☐	23	Barry Randall, Montreal Alouettes	.20	.09	.02
☐	24	Brad Upshaw, Montreal Alouettes	.20	.09	.02
☐	25	Jorma Kuisma, Montreal Alouettes	.20	.09	.02
☐	26	Mike Widger, Montreal Alouettes	.20	.09	.02
☐	27	Joe Theismann, Toronto Argonauts	3.00	1.40	.30
☐	28	Greg Barton, Toronto Argonauts	.40	.18	.04
☐	29	Bill Symons, Toronto Argonauts	.30	.12	.03
☐	30	Leon McQuay, Toronto Argonauts	.30	.12	.03
☐	31	Jim Corrigall, Toronto Argonauts	.30	.12	.03
☐	32	Jim Stillwagon, Toronto Argonauts	.50	.22	.05
☐	33	Dick Thornton, Toronto Argonauts	.30	.12	.03
☐	34	Marv Luster, Toronto Argonauts	.30	.12	.03
☐	35	Paul Desjardins, Toronto Argonauts	.20	.09	.02

		MINT	VG-E	F-G
☐	36 **Mike Eben**, Toronto Argonauts	.20	.09	.02
☐	37 **Eric Allen**, Toronto Argonauts	.30	.12	.03
☐	38 **Chip Barrett**, Toronto Argonauts	.20	.09	.02
☐	39 **Noah Jackson**, Toronto Argonauts	.40	.18	.04
☐	40 **Jim Young**, British Columbia Lions	1.00	.45	.10
☐	41 **Trev Ekdahl**, British Columbia Lions	.20	.09	.02
☐	42 **Garret Hunsperger**, British Columbia Lions	.20	.09	.02
☐	43 **Willie Postler**, British Columbia Lions	.20	.09	.02
☐	44 **George Anderson**, British Columbia Lions	.20	.09	.02
☐	45 **Ron Estay**, British Columbia Lions	.20	.09	.02
☐	46 **Johnny Musso**, British Columbia Lions	.75	.35	.07
☐	47 **Eric Guthrie**, British Columbia Lions	.20	.09	.02
☐	48 **Monroe Eley**, British Columbia Lions	.20	.09	.02
☐	49 **Don Bunce**, British Columbia Lions	.40	.18	.04
☐	50 **Jim Evenson**, British Columbia Lions	.30	.12	.03
☐	51 **Ken Sugarman**, British Columbia Lions	.30	.12	.03
☐	52 **Dave Golinsky**, British Columbia Lions	.20	.09	.02
☐	53 **Wayne Harris**, Calgary Stampeders	1.00	.45	.10
☐	54 **Jerry Keeling**, Calgary Stampeders	.20	.09	.02
☐	55 **Herm Harrison**, Calgary Stampeders	.20	.09	.02
☐	56 **Larry Robinson**, Calgary Stampeders	.30	.12	.03
☐	57 **John Helton**, Calgary Stampeders	.40	.18	.04
☐	58 **Gerry Shaw**, Calgary Stampeders	.20	.09	.02
☐	59 **Frank Andruski**, Calgary Stampeders	.20	.09	.02
☐	60 **Basil Bark**, Calgary Stampeders	.20	.09	.02
☐	61 **Joe Forzani**, Calgary Stampeders	.30	.12	.03
☐	62 **Jim Furlong**, Calgary Stampeders	.20	.09	.02
☐	63 **Rudy Linterman**, Calgary Stampeders	.30	.12	.03
☐	64 **Granville Liggins**, Calgary Stampeders	.30	.12	.03
☐	65 **Lanny Boleski**, Calgary Stampeders	.20	.09	.02
☐	66 **Hugh Oldham**, Ottawa Rough Riders	.20	.09	.02
☐	67 **Dave Braggins**, Ottawa Rough Riders	.20	.09	.02
☐	68 **Jerry Campbell**, Ottawa Rough Riders	.20	.09	.02
☐	69 **Al Marcelin**, Ottawa Rough Riders	.30	.12	.03
☐	70 **Tom Pullen**, Ottawa Rough Riders	.20	.09	.02
☐	71 **Rudy Sims**, Ottawa Rough Riders	.20	.09	.02
☐	72 **Marshal Shirk**, Ottawa Rough Riders	.20	.09	.02
☐	73 **Tom Laputka**, Ottawa Rough Riders	.20	.09	.02
☐	74 **Barry Ardern**, Ottawa Rough Riders	.20	.09	.02
☐	75 **Billy Cooper**, Ottawa Rough Riders	.20	.09	.02
☐	76 **Dan Deever**, Ottawa Rough Riders	.20	.09	.02
☐	77 **Wayne Giardino**, Ottawa Rough Riders	.20	.09	.02
☐	78 **Terry Wellesley**, Ottawa Rough Riders	.20	.09	.02
☐	79 **Ron Lancaster**, Saskatchewan Rough Riders	1.00	.45	.10
☐	80 **George Reed**, Saskatchewan Rough Riders	1.00	.45	.10
☐	81 **Bobby Thompson**, Saskatchewan Rough Riders	.20	.09	.02

		MINT	VG-E	F-G
☐ 82	**Jack Abendschan,** Saskatchewan Rough Riders	.20	.09	.02
☐ 83	**Ed McQuarters,** Saskatchewan Rough Riders .	.30	.12	.03
☐ 84	**Bruce Bennett,** Saskatchewan Rough Riders ..	.20	.09	.02
☐ 85	**Bill Baker,** Saskatchewan Rough Riders	.30	.12	.03
☐ 86	**Don Bahnuik,** Saskatchewan Rough Riders	.20	.09	.02
☐ 87	**Gary Brandt,** Saskatchewan Rough Riders	.20	.09	.02
☐ 88	**Henry Dorach,** Saskatchewan Rough Riders ..	.20	.09	.02
☐ 89	**Ted Dushinski,** Saskatchewan Rough Riders ..	.20	.09	.02
☐ 90	**Alan Ford,** Saskatchewan Rough Riders	.20	.09	.02
☐ 91	**Bob Kosid,** Saskatchewan Rough Riders	.20	.09	.02
☐ 92	**Greg Pipes,** Edmonton Eskimos	.30	.12	.03
☐ 93	**John LaGrone,** Edmonton Eskimos	.30	.12	.03
☐ 94	**Dave Gasser,** Edmonton Eskimos	.20	.09	.02
☐ 95	**Bobby Taylor,** Edmonton Eskimos	.20	.09	.02
☐ 96	**Dave Cutler,** Edmonton Eskimos	.30	.12	.03
☐ 97	**Dick Dupuis,** Edmonton Eskimos	.30	.12	.03
☐ 98	**Ron Forwick,** Edmonton Eskimos	.20	.09	.02
☐ 99	**Bayne Norrie,** Edmonton Eskimos	.20	.09	.02
☐ 100	**Jim Henshall,** Edmonton Eskimos	.20	.09	.02
☐ 101	**Charlie Turner,** Edmonton Eskimos	.20	.09	.02
☐ 102	**Fred Dunn,** Edmonton Eskimos	.20	.09	.02
☐ 103	**Sam Scarber,** Edmonton Eskimos	.20	.09	.02
☐ 104	**Bruce Lemmerman,** Edmonton Eskimos	.20	.09	.02
☐ 105	**Don Jonas,** Edmonton Eskimos	.30	.12	.03
☐ 106	**Doug Strong,** Edmonton Eskimos	.20	.09	.02
☐ 107	**Ed Williams,** Edmonton Eskimos	.20	.09	.02
☐ 108	**Paul Markle,** Edmonton Eskimos	.20	.09	.02
☐ 109	**Gene Lakusiak,** Edmonton Eskimos	.20	.09	.02
☐ 110	**Bob LaRose,** Edmonton Eskimos	.20	.09	.02
☐ 111	**Rob McLaren,** Edmonton Eskimos	.20	.09	.02
☐ 112	**Pete Ribbins,** Edmonton Eskimos	.20	.09	.02
☐ 113	**Bill Frank,** Edmonton Eskimos	.20	.09	.02
☐ 114	**Bob Swift,** Edmonton Eskimos	.20	.09	.02
☐ 115	**Chuck Liebrock,** Edmonton Eskimos	.20	.09	.02
☐ 116	**Joe Critchlow,** Edmonton Eskimos	.20	.09	.02
☐ 117	**Paul Williams,** Edmonton Eskimos	.20	.09	.02

PRO ACTION CARDS

		MINT	VG-E	F-G
☐ 118	**Pro Action**	.30	.12	.03
☐ 119	**Pro Action**	.30	.12	.03
☐ 120	**Pro Action**	.30	.12	.03
☐ 121	**Pro Action**	.30	.12	.03

	MINT	VG-E	F-G
☐ 122 Pro Action	.30	.12	.03
☐ 123 Pro Action	.30	.12	.03
☐ 124 Pro Action	.30	.12	.03
☐ 125 Pro Action	.30	.12	.03
☐ 126 Pro Action	.30	.12	.03
☐ 127 Pro Action	.30	.12	.03
☐ 128 Pro Action	.30	.12	.03
☐ 129 Pro Action	.30	.12	.03
☐ 130 Pro Action	.30	.12	.03
☐ 131 Pro Action	.30	.12	.03
☐ 132 Checklist	1.25	.10	.02

☐ Please send me the following price guides—
☐ I would like the most current edition of the books listed below.

THE OFFICIAL PRICE GUIDES TO:

☐ 465-8 American Silver & Silver Plate 4th Ed.	10.95
☐ 482-8 Antique Clocks 3rd Ed.	10.95
☐ 455-0 Antique & Modern Dolls 2nd Ed.	9.95
☐ 483-6 Antique & Modern Firearms 5th Ed.	10.95
☐ 271-X Antiques & Other Collectibles 6th Ed.	9.95
☐ 466-6 Antique Jewelry 4th Ed.	10.95
☐ 270-1 Beer Cans & Collectibles, 3rd Ed.	7.95
☐ 262-0 Bottles Old & New 9th Ed.	10.95
☐ 255-8 Carnival Glass 1st Ed.	10.95
☐ 434 Collectible Cameras 1st Ed.	10.95
☐ 277-9 Collectibles of the Third Reich 2nd Ed.	10.95
☐ 454-2 Collectible Toys 2nd Ed.	9.95
☐ 490-9 Collector Cars 6th Ed.	11.95
☐ 267-1 Collector Handguns 3rd Ed.	11.95
☐ 459-3 Collector Knives 7th Ed.	10.95
☐ 266-3 Collector Plates 3rd Ed.	11.95
☐ 476-3 Collector Prints 6th Ed.	11.95
☐ 489-5 Comic Books & Collectibles 8th Ed.	9.95
☐ 433-X Depression Glass 1st Ed.	9.95
☐ 472-0 Glassware 2nd Ed.	10.95
☐ 492-5 Hummel Figurines & Plates 5th Ed.	9.95
☐ 451-8 Kitchen Collectibles 2nd Ed.	10.95

☐ 460-7 Military Collectibles 4th Ed.	10.95
☐ 268-X Music Collectibles 5th Ed.	11.95
☐ 491-7 Old Books & Autographs 6th Ed.	10.95
☐ 452-6 Oriental Collectibles 2nd Ed.	11.95
☐ 481-5 Paper Collectibles 4th Ed.	10.95
☐ 276-0 Pottery & Porcelain 5th Ed.	11.95
☐ 283-9 Radio, T.V. & Movie Memorabilia 2nd Ed.	11.95
☐ 484-4 Records 6th Ed.	9.95
☐ 485-2 Royal Doulton 4th Ed.	10.95
☐ 418-6 Science Fiction & Fantasy Collectibles 1st Ed.	9.95
☐ 477-1 Wicker 3rd Ed.	10.95

THE OFFICIAL:

☐ 445-3 Price Guide to Collector's Journal 1st Ed.	4.95
☐ 413-5 Identification Guide to Glassware 1st Ed.	9.95
☐ 448-8 Identification Guide to Gunmarks 2nd Ed.	9.95
☐ 412-7 Identification Guide to Pottery & Porcelain 1st Ed.	9.95
☐ 415-1 Identification Guide to Victorian Furniture 1st Ed.	9.95

THE OFFICIAL (POCKET SIZED) PRICE GUIDES TO:

☐ 473-9 Antique & Flea Markets 1st Ed.	3.95
☐ 442-9 Antique Jewelry 2nd Ed.	3.95
☐ 264-7 Baseball Cards 5th Ed.	4.95
☐ 488-7 Bottles 2nd Ed.	4.95

☐ 468-2 Cars & Trucks 2nd Ed.	4.95
☐ 260-4 Collectible Americana 1st Ed.	4.95
☐ 453-1 Collectible Records 2nd Ed.	3.95
☐ 489-0 Collector Guns 2nd Ed.	4.95
☐ 474-7 Comic Books 3rd Ed.	3.95
☐ 496-0 Dolls 3rd Ed.	4.95
☐ 292-2 Football Cards 5th Ed.	4.95
☐ 258-2 Glassware 2nd Ed.	4.95
☐ 487-9 Hummels 3rd Ed.	4.95
☐ 441-0 Military Collectibles 2nd Ed.	3.95
☐ 480-1 Paperbacks & Magazines 3rd Ed.	4.95
☐ 443-7 Pocket Knives 2nd Ed.	3.95
☐ 479-8 Scouting Collectibles 3rd Ed.	3.95
☐ 439-9 Sports Collectibles 1st Ed.	3.95
☐ 494-1 Star Trek/Star Wars Collectibles 3rd Ed.	3.95
☐ 493-3 Toys 3rd Ed.	4.95

THE OFFICIAL BLACKBOOK PRICE GUIDES TO:

☐ 284-1 U.S. Coins 24th Ed.	3.95
☐ 286-8 U.S. Paper Money 18th Ed.	3.95
☐ 285-X U.S. Postage Stamps 8th Ed.	3.95

THE OFFICIAL INVESTORS GUIDE TO BUYING & SELLING:

☐ 496-8 Gold, Silver and Diamonds 2nd Ed.	9.95
☐ 497-6 Gold Coins 2nd Ed.	9.95
☐ 498-4 Silver Coins 2nd Ed.	9.95

TOTAL _____

SEE NEXT PAGE FOR ORDERING INSTRUCTIONS

1986 SERIES

Topps

SPECIAL "1000 YARD CLUB"
GLOSSY CARD INSIDE

NFL

"Officially Licensed by NFL Properties"

"Official NFLPA licensed product"

Football

17 PICTURE CARDS · 1 GLOSSY CARD · 1 STICK BUBBLE GUM

the BEST YET!

SPORTCARDS OF OHIO

Always over a million cards in stock. Featuring Topps, Donruss, Goudeys, Bowmans and Tobacco Issues.

Filling want lists is our specialty. All orders filled the same day they are received so you won't have to wait weeks and even months for your cards.

When ordering, please list cards by year, name, number and condition desired and we will respond immediately with our lowest possible price. All inquiries must include a 22¢ stamp. Money Orders will assure speedy delivery. Allow 10 days for personal checks.

Mastercard and Visa now accepted.

STORE INFORMATION:

SPORTCARDS OF OHIO
1650 State Road
Cuyahoga Falls, OH 44223

Hours of Operation

Monday through Friday 11 AM to 6 PM
Saturdays 10 AM to 5 PM

Phone: (216) 920-1010

We are always interested in buying cards. Nobody beats our buying prices, so if you have cards to sell, just send us a list of the cards you have or give us a call and turn your cards into instant $$$$$$

We wish to extend our appreciation to the over 4,000 customers we served last year and welcome you to visit our store when in the area. Join in America's fastest growing hobby and watch your investment grow each year.

Willie, Mickey and the Duke are always here, as well as Mark, Paul and Tom, owners.

DEN'S COLLECTORS DEN

PLASTIC CARD PROTECTING PAGES
LARGEST SELECTION IN THE HOBBY
FINEST QUALITY PLASTIC SHEETS

TRY **DEN'S**

Featuring:

- NON—MIGRATING PLASTIC IN ALL SHEETS
- PLASTIC THAT DOES NOT STICK TOGETHER
- STIFFNESS TO RESIST CARD CURLING
- INTELLIGENT DESIGN
- RESISTANCE TO CRACKING
- FULL COVERAGE OF CARDS, PHOTOS, ENVELOPES

NO MIX & MATCH

STYLE	POCKETS	RECOMMENDED FOR	PRICE EACH (DOES NOT INCLUDE P & H) 1-24	25-99	100-299	300-600
9	9 / 18	TOPPS (1957-PRESENT), FLEER, DONRUSS, TCMA, KELLOGG, POST CEREAL, LEAF (1960), RECENT NON-SPORTS CARDS, ALL STANDARD 2½" X 3½" CARDS	25	.23	21	.19
8	8 / 16	TOPPS (1952-1956), BOWMAN (1953-55)	25	.23	21	19
12	12 / 24	BOWMAN (1948-50), TOPPS (1951 RED AND BLUE), RECENT TOPPS AND FLEER STICKERS	25	.23	21	19
1	1	PHOTOGRAPHS (8X10)	25	.23	21	19
2	2 / 4	PHOTOGRAPHS (5x7), TOPPS SUPERSTAR PHOTOS	25	.23	21	19
4	4	POSTCARDS, TOPPS SUPER (1964 70.71), EXHIBITS, DONRUSS (ACTION ALL STARS), PEREZ STEELE HOF	25	.23	21	19
18	18 / 36	T CARDS, TOPPS COINS, BAZOOKA (1963-67 INDIVIDUAL CARDS)	35	35	30	27
9G	9 / 18	GOUDEY, DIAMOND STARS, LEAF (1948)	35	35	30	27
9PB	9 / 18	PLAY BALL, BOWMAN (1951-52), DOUBLE PLAY, TOPPS MINIS, ALL GUM, INC SPORT AND NON-SPORT	35	35	30	27
1C	1 / 2	TURKEY REDS (T3), PEPSI (1977), PRESS GUIDES, MOST WRAPPERS SPORT AND NON-SPORT	35	35	30	27
3	3 / 6	HOSTESS PANELS, HIRES, ZELLERS PANELS	30	25	25	20
6V	6 / 12	TOPPS (DOUBLE HEADERS, GREATEST MOMENTS, 1951 TEAM, CONNIE MACK, CURRENT STARS), 1965 FOOT BALL AND HOCKEY, BUCKS, 1969-70 BASKETBALL, DADS HOCKEY, DOUBLE FOLDERS, TRIPLE FOLDERS	35	35	30	27
6D	6 / 12	RED MAN (WITH OR WITHOUT TABS), DISC, KAHN'S (1955-67)	35	35	30	27
1Y	1	YEARBOOKS, PROGRAMS, MAGAZINES HOBBYPAPERS TABLOIDS POCKET SIZE 9"X12"	35	35	30	27
1S	1	SMALL PROGRAMS, MAGAZINE PAGES AND PHOTOS, CRACKER JACK SHEETS POCKET SIZE 8½" X 11"	30	30	25	20
10	10 / 10	MATCHBOOK COVERS, POCKET SIZE 1 3/4" X 4 3/4"	35	35	30	27
3E	3 / 3	FIRST DAY COVERS, BASEBALL COMMEMORATIVE ENVELOPES, STANDARD SIZED ENVELOPES	35	35	30	27
3L	3 / 6	SQUIRT, PEPSI (1963), FLEER (STAMPS IN STRIPS), TOPPS (1964 AND 1969 STAMPS IN STRIPS)	35	35	30	27
6P	6 / 12	POLICE OR SAFETY CARDS (ALL SPORTS)	25	.23	21	19

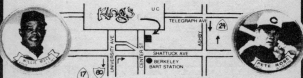

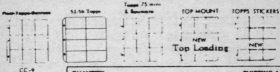

COLLECTORS WORLD
Buy – Sell – Trade

One of the largest selections of
NON – SPORTS, FOOTBALL & BASEBALL
GUM CARDS IN THE COUNTRY

Buying any vending packs, boxes, sport &
non-sport wrappers and wax packs of
baseball, football, basketball & non-sport

Buying complete non-sport collections
large or small

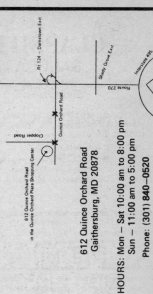

WRAPPERS

COMICS

MOVIE POSTERS

ROCK & ROLL RECORDS

612 Quince Orchard Road
in the Quince Orchard Plaza Shopping Center

Clopper Road

Quince Orchard Road

Rt 124 – Darnstown Exit

Shady Grove Exit

Route 270

Interstate 495

Washington, DC

612 Quince Orchard Road
Gaithersburg, MD 20878

HOURS: Mon – Sat 10:00 am to 8:00 pm
Sun – 11:00 am to 5:00 pm

Phone: (301) 840–0520

CLASSIFIED ADS

C.F.L.
FOOTBALL CARDS
by
JOGO Inc.
A MUST for all football collectotrs

FIRST BASE
SPORTS NOSTALGIA SHOP

231 Webb Chapel Village
Dallas, Texas 75229
(214) 243-5271

```
                                    N
                        I-35 (Stemmons)
                                    Webb Chapel
                        Hwy 635 (LBJ)
                        Forest Lane
                        First Base
                                    Hwy 75
                                    N. Central
                                    Expwy
```

OPEN: **TUESDAY THROUGH SATURDAY**
       11 A.M. to 7 P.M.

We are located on the Southeast corner of Webb Chapel and Forest just 15 minutes from the airport. Our large (1650 square foot showroom) store is convenient to all parts of Dallas being only one block south of the LBJ (635) Freeway at the Webb Chapel exit. Many collectors (and dealers) have told us that our store is the most complete they've ever seen. Just look on the opposite page for a few of our offers. We want you for a customer — please stop in and see for yourself.

FIRST
BASE

Sincerely,

Wayne Grove
Gervise Ford

P.S. We are always interested in buying your cards — let us know what you have.

SPECIAL OFFERS

#1: Type set: One card from each year of Topps baseball 1952 through 1986, our choice of cards 35 cards for $9.95.

#2: Baseball cigarette card from 1910, our choice $5.95.

#3: 500 assorted (mostly different) baseball cards from 1978 to 1984 in excellent condition for $16.95

#4: Dallas Cowboy Weekly: 20 different back issues, our choice, for $14.95. We also have most single issues from 1977 to date available from $1.00 to $2.00 each. Send your want list. Some older issues also available.

#5: Poster: Robert Redford as "The Natural" plus a free Bucky Dent "Best Little Shortstop in Texas" poster for $6.95 postpaid.

#6: 1978 Topps baseball cards 50 different in excellent to mint condition $2.50.

#7: 1979 Topps baseball cards 50 different in excellent to mint condition includes some stars $2.95.

#8: 1980 Topps baseball cards 50 different in excellent to mint condition includes some stars $2.95.

#9: 1981 Topps baseball cards 50 different in excellent to mint condition includes some stars $2.95.

#10: 89 different 1984-85 Topps hockey cards in excellent to mint condition includes some stars $2.50.

#11: 66 different 1981-82 Topps basketball cards in excellent to mint condition includes stars (Bird, Magic, Kareem, Dr. J, etc.) $3.50.

#12: 115 different 1983 Topps football cards in excellent to mint condition includes many stars $2.95.

#13: Donruss puzzle sets: Complete set of all seven puzzle card sets (Ruth, Cobb, Mantle, Williams, Snider, Gehrig, Aaron) for $9.95.

#14: 1985 Dallas Cowboy Media Guide (not issued to the public) $4.95; Cowboy Bluebook $12.95.

COMPLETE SETS

1985 Performance Rangers (28)	$4.95
1984 Jarvis Press Rangers (28)	$4.95
1983 Affiliated Foods Rangers (28)	$4.95
1984 Ralston-Purina Baseball (33)	$4.95
1983 Seven-Eleven 3-D Coins (12)	$12.95
1981 Topps 5x7 Dodgers/Angels (18)	$4.95
1978 Tucson Toros (Sample/Darwin) (24)	$3.50
1980 Tucson Toros (Heep/Knicely) (24)	$3.00
1983 Dallas Cowboy Police (28)	$9.95
1981 Dallas Cowboy Police (14)	$7.95
1980 Dallas Cowboy Police (14)	$9.95
1979 Dallas Cowboy Police (15)	$13.95
1981 Shell Dallas Cowboys Portraits (6)	$6.95
1981 Shell National Set Portraits (6)	$6.95
includes Walter Payton and Earl Campbell	

BASEBALL CARD LOTS

1958 Topps 25 diff (f-vg)	$4.95
1959 Topps 25 diff (f-vg)	$3.95
1960 Topps 25 diff (f-vg)	$3.50
1961 Topps 25 diff (f-vg)	$3.50
1962 Topps 25 diff (f-vg)	$3.50
1963 Topps 25 diff (f-vg)	$3.25
1964 Topps 25 diff (f-vg)	$3.25
1965 Topps 25 diff (f-vg)	$3.25
1966 Topps 25 diff (f-vg)	$2.95
1967 Topps 25 diff (f-vg)	$2.95
1968 Topps 25 diff (f-vg)	$2.95
1969 Topps 25 diff (f-vg)	$2.75
1970 Topps 25 diff (f-vg)	$1.95
1971 Topps 25 diff (f-vg)	$1.75
1972 Topps 25 diff (f-vg)	$1.75

FIRST BASE

— FOR SALE — MAIL ORDER —

First Base
231 Webb Chapel Village
Dallas, Texas 75229

BECKETT

BASEBALL CARD

MONTHLY

FLEER
ALL
STAR
TEAM

Mets
16

Dwight Gooden
METS • RIGHT HAND PITCHER

1986 Cards Here!

Current
Price Guide

Who's Hot
& Who's Not

Now! Get
BECKETT
BASEBALL
CARD
MONTHLY
for up to
½ OFF
the cover price!